The Philosophy of Sex

The Philosophy of Sex

Contemporary Readings

Sixth Edition

Edited by Nicholas Power,
Raja Halwani, and Alan Soble

ROWMAN & LITTLEFIELD PUBLISHERS, INC.
Lanham • Boulder • New York • Toronto • Plymouth, UK

Published by Rowman & Littlefield Publishers, Inc.
A wholly owned subsidiary of The Rowman & Littlefield Publishing Group, Inc.
4501 Forbes Boulevard, Suite 200, Lanham, Maryland 20706
www.rowman.com

10 Thornbury Road, Plymouth PL6 7PP, United Kingdom

British Library Cataloguing in Publication Information Available

Library of Congress Cataloging-in-Publication Data

The philosophy of sex : contemporary readings.—6th ed. / edited by Nicholas Power, Raja Halwani,
and Alan Soble.
    p. cm.
Includes bibliographical references (p.) and index.
ISBN 978-1-4422-1671-6 (pbk. : alk. paper)
1. Sex. 2. Sexual ethics. I. Power, Nicholas (Nicholas P.) II. Halwani, Raja. III. Soble, Alan.
HQ12.P47 2012
306.7—dc23
                                                                    2012020476

Printed in the United States of America

Nicholas Power
To my Father and the Memory of my Mother

Raja Halwani
*For my nephew, Fuad, and my nieces, Leen, Sarah, Aidan,
Lorena, and Serene*

Alan Soble
For my grand-nieces, Riley and Lily Marie, and my grand-nephew, Jacob

Contents

Preface

The second edition of *The Philosophy of Sex: Contemporary Readings* (1991) was an 80 percent revision of the first (published thirty-two years ago); the third (1997) was again 80 percent new; the fourth edition (2002) was roughly one-quarter a revision of the third, while the fifth (2008) doubled that rate. The edition you now hold is close to 40 percent new, with thirteen new essays (*viz.*, chapters 7, 8, 11–15, 19, 24–27, and 29) and, if measured in terms of word length, it's 45 percent new. What this indicates is that our collection of essays, meant to guide those interested in conceptual and ethical issues surrounding human sexuality, is more diverse, contemporary, and wide-ranging than any heretofore. (In the opinion of the only one of us whose opinion is authoritative in such matters, it is in fact "the best yet" of this long series.) The organization of *The Philosophy of Sex* is revamped, with a new section devoted to LGBT issues,[1] and new voices on the Kantian themes of objectification and rape. We leap into gendered spaces, leaving the relatively safe confines of sex *simpliciter*. Five years ago, Alan Soble and Nicholas Power weren't quite ready to make this move, in part because they were not yet impressed by the philosophical scholarship in some of these areas. But, fortunately, scholarly work has since then advanced as rapidly as the corresponding public debates.

How did this reorientation of *The Philosophy of Sex* come about? First and foremost, Raja Halwani accepted our invitation to coedit this version of the anthology, and he's responsible for more than a third of this effort. Second, we surveyed those who adopted the fifth edition and then we actually followed their advice (well, the advice of the half of the faculty who responded to our detailed survey). In accord with their wishes and preferences, we sought out the freshest voices in the field and joined them to the classic essays (which we continue to include) that serve as their stepping-off points. As a result, a number of authors in this sixth edition may well be new to you, while others, such as Nagel, Goldman, Mappes, and Nussbaum, already have a secure home in your lecture notes.

The field of philosophy of sex, like the discussion of sexuality in our society in general, has moved beyond traditional moral questions, for example, questions that were stubbornly or obsessively fixated on the morality of homosexuality. The field has become concerned about and interested in a much broader set of questions. Some are conceptual: Does "bisexuality" mean "pansexuality"? Must bisexual marriages be plural (that is, involve more than two people)? What is the idea of "sexual orientation," and is it still useful in understanding sexuality? Another part of the new focus is normative: Must casual and promiscuous sexual activity be objectifying? Can chatting sexually online be a form of cheating? Is marriage—whether it be opposite-sex or same-sex—a problematic institution, no longer obviously the best arrangement for personally rich adult lives and interpersonal relationships?

We also listened to faculty requests to make the collection and the field itself more accessible to students. To accomplish that, we have significantly lengthened the bibliography[2] and have overhauled many of the study questions that close each chapter. The study questions help readers, especially students, focus on the major arguments of the contributing author, while the bibliography, which is organized by subarea, allows them (as well as scholars) to explore their favorite topics in greater depth.

The sixth edition of *The Philosophy of Sex: Contemporary Readings* is organized into four parts, which are preceded by Soble's still critical and revised introduction to the field, the essay "The Analytical Categories of the Philosophy of Sex" (chapter 1). The four parts are entitled (I) "Analysis and Perversion," (II) "Queer Issues," (III) "Objectification and Consent—the Theory," and (IV) "Objectification and Consent—Applied Topics."

Part I, devoted to conceptual analysis, begins with Greta Christina's humorous attempt to comprehend her (long, varied, and adventuresome) sex life by defining "sex," the difficulty of which drives her to skepticism about an analytic project that is (obviously) central to the philosophy of sex. Many readers, teachers, and students will share the view that "sex" cannot be defined.[3] The enduring essay by Thomas Nagel complicates matters by possibly adding to the list of analysis-resistant concepts those of "natural sex" and "perverted sex." The four essays that follow, by Janice Moulton, Alan Goldman, Alan Soble, and Seiriol Morgan, all make direct reference to Nagel's existentialist-phenomenological account of sex, and even John Portmann's "penetration veneration," the last essay in part I, may be seen as a reply to the notion, found in both Nagel and Morgan, that sexual acts essentially involve "intentionality."[4]

Four of the seven essays that make up part II ("Queer Issues") revolve around the hot-button vicissitudes of same-sex marriage—namely, the ruminations of conservative commentator Stanley Kurtz, on the one side, and those of the liberal (or postliberal?) philosophers Cheshire Calhoun, Claudia Card, and Kayley Vernallis (whose provocative essay on bisexual foursomes could have been written to stretch Kurtz's "polyamory" to its breaking point). The essay by William Wilkerson raises basic questions about sexual orientation. Does it refer to perduring and universal traits? Or does it, less powerfully, stand only for a cultural or even a subjective, personal construct? Talia Bettcher's and Christine Overall's essays confront fundamental questions in philosophizing about transgendered persons. Are transsexuals really that much different from non-transsexuals in terms of the core issues of identity?

The continued centrality of the Kantian framework in contemporary sexual ethics and law sets the stage for each of the seven essays in part III. The essays by Thomas Mappes, his critic Howard Klepper, and Alan Soble deepen and amend Kant's view of sexual use, objectification, and exploitation and explore the relationship between sexual use and "free and informed" consent. Alan Wertheimer's essay examines the morally transformative power of consent and provides reasons why it is philosophically misleading to think that consent by itself can achieve as much as we would like it to. Ann Cahill attempts a feminist reframing of "objectification," drawing on the work of Simone de Beauvoir (among others), while Robin West, from another feminist perspective, rejects the consent standard as pallid. David Benatar also wonders whether consent could have the normative scope typically afforded it if it logically cannot be applied equally across impermissible pedophilic and permissible casual sexual interactions.

Part IV concerns itself with other serious sexual phenomena. Martha Nussbaum's unflinching comparison of sex work (prostitution, primarily) with other forms of work will astound many people who have cogitated about the selling of sexual activity. Similarly, many readers will be surprised by H. E. Baber's comparison of rape and ordinary labor. Rape is also discussed in the essays by the feminist philosophers Lois Pineau and Susan Brison. The latter's description of the sexual assault of which she was the victim is not easy to read, but the author nonetheless makes good philosophical use of the event. Raja Halwani's contribution may surprise many by concluding that "fucking around" (in the sexual sense, of course) can be morally treacherous given that it is rife with objectification. Joan Mason-Grant and Nicholas Power wrap up this edition by debating the harms of pornography.

The editors wish to thank Jonathan Sisk and Marissa Parks of Rowman and Littlefield for their support. We also thank the authors and publishers who granted permission to reprint their material and, especially, to those philosophers who wrote new essays for this edition. (They have undoubtedly discovered that working with a triumvirate of cranky editors is a challenge.) We also thank those "early adopters" who responded to our survey with thoughtful, useful advice. We hope that this new edition of *The Philosophy of Sex* continues to meet their needs. Please stay in touch![5]

NOTES

1. In yet another revision of his essay on masturbation, included here as chapter 6, Soble (perhaps insufferably and obstinately) proposes to expand this acronym to at least "LGBTM," where the "M" stands for people who have a strict preference for masturbation and behaviorally avoid, absolutely and on principle, all sexual contact with others—unlike Ls, Gs, Bs, and Ts, who, unless they are committed to celibacy, prefer sexual contact with another person of a certain anatomy or gender.

2. The section "Suggested Readings" in earlier editions has been appropriately renamed "A Bibliography of the Philosophy of Sex."

3. In several places in this book, it is proposed that it is wrong to assume that the analytic definitions (and the extensions) of "sex," "sexual activity," and "having sex" are the same. This issue is especially significant for understanding and evaluating the essays in this volume by Greta Christina and John Portmann.

4. In some courses that use our book, professors might have to explain this difficult philosophical concept, and to distinguish it from ordinary-language uses of "intention(al)."

5. The editors may be reached at npower@uwf.edu, rhalwa@saic.edu, and ags38@drexel.edu.

ONE

The Analytic Categories of the Philosophy of Sex

Alan Soble

In this introductory essay, **Alan Soble** *exhibits the range of topics that are studied—analytic, normative, and metaphysical—in the philosophy of sex. Analytic questions have to do with defining the central concepts in the field: sexual desire, sexual activity, and sexual pleasure. The goal of this analysis is to define each concept separately from each other (to avoid circularity) or, alternatively, to demonstrate that all the concepts can be defined in terms of just one of them, which would then be the basic concept in the philosophy of sex. Of particular interest is the analysis of the concept of sexual perversion and laying out the difference between the sexually natural and the unnatural. The analysis of sexual perversion requires that we be able to state what makes a desire, activity, or pleasure sexual to begin with, and then to identify the specific features of sexual desires, activities, or pleasures that make them sexually perverted. Other concepts that are important to analyze in the philosophy of sex, such as consent and coercion, are important in other areas of philosophy as well: applied ethics (e.g., medical ethics), social and political philosophy, and the philosophy of law.*

The fact that the philosophy of sex often discusses the natural and the unnatural and utilizes the concepts of consent and coercion means that normative issues make up a large part of the philosophy of sex. Natural Law ethics asserts that there are significant connections between the naturalness of a sexual desire or sexual act and its morality; this is denied by philosophies that emphasize, for moral judgments, the importance of the presence of consent and the absence of coercion. When we add the ethics of Immanuel Kant, which focuses on the wrongs of using people and treating them as objects, sexual ethics becomes complicated territory. Sexual behaviors and practices that are scrutinized morally

1

include the use of contraceptive devices, masturbation, adultery, casual sex, rape, sexual harassment, prostitution, and pornography.

Among the topics explored by the philosophy of sex are procreation, contraception, celibacy, marriage, adultery, casual sex, flirting, prostitution, homosexuality, masturbation, seduction, rape, sexual harassment, sadomasochism, pornography, bestiality, pedophilia, and sometimes birds.[1] What do all these activities or phenomena have in common? All are included in the vast domain of human sexuality, that is, they are related, on the one hand, to the human desires and activities that involve the search for and attainment of sexual pleasure and satisfaction and, on the other hand, to the human desires and activities that involve the creation of new human beings. It is a natural feature of humans that certain sorts of behaviors and certain bodily organs can be employed for pleasure or for reproduction, or for both, either at the same or different times.

The philosophy of sexuality explores these topics both conceptually and normatively. Conceptual analysis is carried out in the philosophy of sex in order to clarify fundamental notions, including *sexual desire* and *sexual activity*. Defining these concepts is no easy task. What are the distinctive features of an act (or desire) that make it a sexual act (desire) instead of some other kind of act (desire)? Conceptual analysis is also carried out to arrive at satisfactory definitions of specific sexual practices, such as adultery, rape, and prostitution. In what ways does seduction differ from rape? Is it conceptually plausible to say that women who are paid to engage in sexual activities in the making of hardcore pornographic films are prostitutes?

Normative philosophy of sexuality inquires about the value of sexual activity, sexual pleasure, and the various forms they take. It is concerned with the perennial questions of sexual morality and constitutes a large branch of applied ethics. Normative philosophy of sex inquires about the possible contribution made to the good or virtuous life by sexuality and tries to determine what moral duties we have to refrain from performing certain sexual acts and what moral permissions we have to engage in others. Moral issues surrounding same-sex sexual activity, abortion, date rape, sexual harassment, pornography, and prostitution, among other things, have been widely discussed by philosophers of sex.

SEXUAL METAPHYSICS

Our moral evaluations of sexual activity are often influenced by our views about, or our emotional reactions to, the nature of the sexual impulse or sexual desire. In this regard there is a deep divide between those philosophers that we might call the metaphysical sexual "optimists" and those we might call the metaphysical sexual "pessimists."

The pessimists in the philosophy of sexuality, such as St. Augustine, Immanuel Kant, and, sometimes, Sigmund Freud, perceive the sexual impulse and acting on it to be things that are nearly always, if not necessarily, unbefitting the dignity of the human person. They see the essence and the results of the sexual drive to be incompatible with more significant and lofty goals and aspirations of human existence. They fear that the power and demands of the sexual impulse make it a danger to harmonious civilized life. And they find in a person's sexuality a severe threat not only to his or her proper relations with, and moral treatment of, other persons but also a threat to his or her own dignity and humanity.

On the other side are the metaphysical sexual optimists (Plato, in some of his works; Bertrand Russell; Albert Ellis; and sometimes Sigmund Freud), who perceive nothing especially obnoxious in the sexual impulse. They frequently view human sexuality as merely another and mostly innocuous dimension of our existence as embodied or animal-like creatures (similar to the impulse to eat). They judge that our sexuality, which in substantial measure has been given to us by evolution, cannot but be conducive to our well-being. And they applaud rather than fear the power of an impulse that can lift us to high and exhilarating forms of happiness.

The particular metaphysics of sex a person holds, either for rational or emotional reasons, will influence his or her subsequent judgments about the value and role of sexuality in the virtuous or good life and about which sexual activities are morally wrong and which are morally permissible.

An extended version of metaphysical sexual pessimism might make the following claims: (1) Due to the nature of sexual desire, a person who sexually desires another person objectifies that other person, both before and during sexual activity. (Afterwards, too, if he or she immediately reaches for the clicker.) Sexual desire, says the German philosopher Immanuel Kant, "makes of the loved person an Object of appetite. . . . Taken by itself it is a degradation of human nature."[2] Our sexual desire for another person tends to make us view and treat him or her merely as a thing, as an object, as an instrument by which we attain our own goal of sexual pleasure. When one person sexually desires another, what is desired is the other person's body and the pleasure to be derived from it; this truncating attitude toward the other is demeaning.

(2) Furthermore, certain types of deception seem required prior to engaging in sex with another person (these are, I would argue, arranged by our social systems as well as by our evolutionary biology). We go out of our way to make ourselves look more physically attractive and more socially desirable to the other person than we think we really are, and we go to great lengths to conceal our physical, personality, and philosophical (or ideological) defects. Trying to make a good and hence misleading impression, we are never our true selves (or what we think our true selves are) on a first date. While it might be the case that men sexually objectify women more than women objectify men, it is undeniable that both men and women engage in deception in trying to elicit positive responses from other people.

(3) The sexual act itself is peculiar, with its uncontrollable arousal, involuntary jerkings, and its yearning to master and consume the other person's body. This is part of what Augustine had in mind when he wrote, "lust . . . is the more shameful in this, that the soul does neither rule itself . . . nor the body either."[3] During sexual activity, a person both loses control of himself or herself and loses regard for the humanity of the other person. Our sexuality threatens the other's personhood; but when we are in the grip of desire we also lose, or are on the verge of losing, our personhood.

(4) Moreover, a person who gives in to another's sexual desire makes an instrument of himself or herself. As Kant makes the point, "For the natural use that one sex makes of the other's sexual organs is *enjoyment*, for which one gives oneself up to the other. In this act a human being makes himself into a thing."[4] Those engaged in sexual activity make themselves into objects or tools for each other merely for the sake of sexual pleasure. Both persons are reduced to the level of an animal (or a fungus).

(5) Finally, once things get going it is often hard to stop them in their tracks, and as a result we often end up doing things sexually that we had never planned or wanted to do. Such is the "positive feedback" nature of the sexual impulse. Sexual desire is also powerfully inelastic, one of the passions most likely to challenge reason, compelling us to seek satisfaction even when doing so involves obvious physical, psychological, and social dangers (which extend, of course, into the inner chambers of the White House). The person who sexually desires another depends on the whims of that other person to gain satisfaction and thereby becomes susceptible to the demands of the other. People who are caught up in sexual desire and arousal can be easily exploited and manipulated. (From which it follows that the most effective strategy is to make the other think that he or she desires you more than you desire him or her.)

Given this pessimistic metaphysics of human sexuality, one might conclude that acting on the sexual impulse is always morally wrong, or that for purely prudential reasons one would do best by eschewing sexuality and embracing celibacy. That might be precisely the conclusion to draw, even if it implies the end of *Homo sapiens*. (This result, the extinction of humanity, is also implied by St. Paul's praising celibacy as the ideal state in 1 Cor 7.) More often, however, the pessimistic metaphysicians of sexuality conclude that sexual activity is morally permissible and prudentially wise only within lifelong, monogamous, heterosexual marriage. Some pessimists go further, insisting that sexual activity should be engaged in only or primarily for the purpose of procreation. Regarding bodily acts that are procreative and produce sexual pleasure, it is their procreative potential that is singularly significant and bestows value on these activities; seeking pleasure for its own sake, apart from procreation, is an impediment to morally virtuous sexuality and should not be undertaken deliberately. Sexual pleasure at most has instrumental value in inducing us to engage in an act that has procreation as its main purpose. Such views have been common among Christians. For example, here is Augustine again: "A man turns to good use the evil of concupiscence, and is not overcome by it, when he bridles and restrains its rage . . . and never relaxes his hold upon it except when intent on offspring, and then controls and applies it to the carnal generation of children . . . , not to the subjection of the spirit to the flesh in a sordid servitude."[5]

Metaphysical sexual optimists suppose that instead of dividing people through various processes of objectification, sexuality is a natural bonding mechanism that joins people together both sexually and nonsexually. Sexual activity involves pleasing the self and the other at the same time, and these joint efforts to exchange pleasure proceed from affection and generate gratitude and more affection, which in turn deepen human relationships, making them more satisfying and emotionally substantial. Furthermore, and this may be the most important point, sexual pleasure is, for a metaphysical optimist, a valuable thing in its own right, something to be cherished and promoted because it has intrinsic and not merely instrumental value. Hence the pursuit of sexual pleasure does not require any intricate or special justification. Nor must we make excuses for it; because sexual pleasure is an intrinsic good it surely need not be confined to marital sexual acts or acts that are directed at procreation. The good and virtuous life, while including much else, can also (logically, psychologically, and morally) include plentiful sexual relations.[6] Irving Singer is a contemporary philosopher who expresses metaphysical optimism:

> For though sexual interest resembles an appetite in some respects, it differs from hunger or thirst in being an *interpersonal* sensitivity, one that enables us to delight in the mind and character of other persons as

well as in their flesh. Though at times people may be used as sexual objects and cast aside once their utility has been exhausted, this is [not] . . . definitive of sexual desire. . . . By awakening us to the living presence of someone else, sexuality can enable us to treat this other being as just the person he or she happens to be. . . . There is nothing in the nature of sexuality as such that necessarily . . . reduces persons to things. On the contrary, sex may be seen as an instinctual agency by which persons respond to one another *through* their bodies.[7]

MORAL AND NONMORAL EVALUATIONS OF SEXUALITY

We often evaluate sexual activity *morally*: we inquire whether a sexual act—either a particular occurrence of a sexual act (the act we are doing or want to do right now) or a general type of sexual act (say, all instances of male-male fellatio)—is morally good or right or morally bad or wrong. More specifically, we evaluate or judge sexual acts to be morally obligatory, morally permissible, morally wrong, or even morally supererogatory. For example, a spouse might have a moral obligation to engage in sex with the other spouse; it might be morally permissible for married couples to employ contraception while engaging in pleasurable coitus; rape and prostitution are commonly thought to be morally wrong (or immoral); and one person's agreeing to have sexual relations with another person when the former has no sexual desire of his or her own but only wants to please the other might be supererogatory. "Morally supererogatory" sexual activity is a category that is infrequently discussed by sexual ethicists. Raymond Belliotti has this to say about it: "We cannot fully describe this type of sex, but we can say generally that it goes above and beyond the call of moral duty. It is sex that is not merely morally permissible, but morally exemplary. It would involve some extraordinary moral benefits to others not attainable in merely morally permissible sex."[8] I hope the nurse's aide who cares for me when I am ninety and terminally ill knows Belliotti.

Note that if a specific type of sexual act is immoral (say, homosexual fellatio), then every instance of that type of act is morally wrong. However, from the fact that the particular sexual act we are now doing or are contemplating doing is morally wrong, it does not follow that the specific type of act are performing is morally wrong in all cases; the sexual act that we are contemplating might be wrong for lots of reasons having nothing to do with the type of sexual act it is. For example, suppose a couple is engaging in heterosexual coitus, and that this particular sexual act is wrong because it is adulterous. The wrongfulness of this sexual activity does not imply that heterosexual coitus in general, as a type of sexual act, is morally wrong. In some cases, of course, a particular sexual act will be wrong for several reasons at once: not only is it wrong because it is an act of a specific type (say, it is an instance of male-female anal coitus), but it is wrong also because at least one of the participants is married to someone else (it is wrong also as adultery).

In addition to evaluating sexual acts morally, we can also evaluate sexual activity (again, either a particular occurrence of a sexual act or a specific type) *nonmorally*. Let us define "nonmorally good" sex as sexual activity that provides sexual pleasure to the participants or is physically or emotionally satisfying, while "nonmorally bad" sex is unexciting, tedious, boring, unenjoyable, or even unpleasant. (Be careful: "nonmoral" is not the same as "immoral," and "nonmorally bad sexual activity" does not mean "immoral sexual activity.") Two analogies will clarify the difference between morally evaluating something as good or bad and nonmorally evaluating it as good or bad. This radio on my desk is a good radio, in the nonmoral sense, because it does what I expect from a radio: it consistently provides clear tones. If, instead, the radio hissed and cackled most of the time, it would be a bad radio, nonmorally speaking, and it would be senseless for me to blame the radio for its faults and threaten it with a trip to hell if it did not improve its behavior. Another analogy involves the human activities surrounding eating. For some people, eating animal flesh (in the form of steaks or hamburger) provides a great deal of pleasure, and for that reason eating meat is nonmorally good. For other people, eating a burger results in nausea and vomiting. They cannot "stomach" this meat; the displeasure they experience means that, for them, the activity is nonmorally bad. The question of whether eating meat is nonmorally good or bad is distinct from the question of whether it is morally permissible or morally wrong. Someone who enjoys eating baby-back ribs might believe that doing so is, nevertheless, morally wrong (maybe because the factory farming of animals is cruel). Someone who dislikes eating meat can still claim, without contradiction, that doing so is morally permissible.

Similarly, sexual activity can be nonmorally good if it provides for us what we expect sexual activity to provide, which is usually sexual pleasure. But that sexual activity is or can be nonmorally good or bad does not necessarily generate any moral implications. For example, that a sexual activity is nonmorally good, by abundantly satisfying both persons, does not necessarily mean that the act is morally good: some adulterous sexual activity might be sexually pleasing to the participants yet be morally wrong. Furthermore, that a sexual activity is nonmorally bad—it does not produce sexual pleasure for the persons engaged in it—does not mean that the act is morally wrong. Unpleasant sexual activity might occur between persons who have little experience engaging in sexual activity (they do not yet know how to do sexual things or have not yet learned what their likes and dislikes are); their failure to provide pleasure for each other does not mean that they are performing morally wrongful acts.

So the moral evaluation of sexual activity is distinct from the nonmoral evaluation of sexual activity, even if there are sometimes important connections between them. For example, the fact that a sexual act provides pleasure to both participants, and is thereby nonmorally good, might be taken (especially by a metaphysical sexual optimist) as a strong, but only *prima facie* strong, reason for thinking that the act is morally good or has moral value. (A utilitarian moral philosopher, such as Jeremy Bentham, would say that in general the nonmoral goodness of sexual activity goes a long way by itself toward justifying it.) Another example: if one person never attempts to provide sexual pleasure for his or her partner but selfishly insists on experiencing only his or her own pleasure, that person is behaving in a morally suspicious way. That moral judgment might not rest simply on the fact that he or she did not provide pleasure for the other person, that is, on the fact that the sexual activity was for the other person nonmorally bad. The moral judgment might rest, more precisely, on his or her motives for not providing any pleasure, for not making the experience nonmorally good for the other person.

It is one thing to point out that as evaluative categories, moral goodness or badness is distinct from nonmoral goodness or badness. It is another thing to wonder, nonetheless, about the psychological connections between the moral quality of sexual activity and its nonmoral quality. Perhaps morally good sexual activity tends also to be the most satisfying sexual activity in the nonmoral sense. Whether that is true likely depends on what we mean by morally good sexual acts and on certain features of human moral psychology. What would our lives be like if there were always a neat correspondence between the moral quality of a sexual act and its nonmoral quality? Examples that violate such a neat correspondence are easy to come by. A sexual act might be morally good and nonmorally bad: consider the routine, bland sexual acts of a couple married for ten years ("bedroom death"). Furthermore, a sexual act might be morally bad yet nonmorally good: one spouse in that couple, married for ten years, commits adultery with another married person and finds the sexual activity to be extraordinarily satisfying. A world in which there was little or no discrepancy between the moral quality and the nonmoral quality of sexual activity might be a better world than ours, or it might be a worse world. I would refrain from making such a judgment unless I were pretty sure what the moral goodness and badness of sexual activity amounted to in the first place and until I knew a lot more than I now do about human psychology. Sometimes that a sexual activity is acknowledged to be morally wrong by its participants actually contributes to its being, for them, nonmorally good, that is, sexually exciting. In this sense, the metaphysical sexual pessimists, by issuing moral prohibitions against all sorts of sexual activities, might, ironically, be keeping our sexual lives satisfying.

DANGEROUS SEX

Whether a particular sexual act, or type of sexual act, provides pleasure is not the only factor in judging its nonmoral quality: pragmatic considerations also figure into whether a sexual act, all things considered, has a preponderance of nonmoral goodness or badness. Many sexual activities can be physically or psychologically harmful, risky, or dangerous. Anal coitus, for example, whether carried out by a heterosexual couple or by two gay males, can damage tissues and is a mechanism for the potential transmission of pathogens. The same can of course be said about ordinary heterosexual genital intercourse. Thus, in evaluating whether a sexual act is overall nonmorally good or bad, we must take into account not only its anticipated pleasure but all sorts of negative or undesired side effects: whether the sexual act is likely to damage the body, as in some sadomasochistic acts; or transmit a venereal disease; or result in an unwanted pregnancy; or even whether one might feel regret, anger, or guilt afterwards. Note that when we condemn a sexual act morally, we impugn a person's moral character; when we condemn a sexual act on pragmatic grounds, we impugn a person's intelligence or self-control. Is it recklessness or stupidity that leads politicians into sexual liaisons that they cannot really hope to keep secret? All these prudential factors may also figure into the moral evaluation of sexual activity: intentionally causing unwanted pain or discomfort to one's partner, or not taking adequate precautions against the possibility of pregnancy, or not informing one's partner of a suspected case of genital infection, might very well be morally wrong.[9] The metaphysical sexual pessimist will emphasize these problems: we must always be vigilant about the sexual urge and keep it on a short leash on account of its power to lead us into disaster. It may not be recklessness or stupidity alone that leads any of us into prudentially dangerous sexual activity. When we experience sexual desire and become sexually aroused, our "brains go out the window," as a Yiddish joke puts it.

SEXUAL PERVERSION

In addition to inquiring about the moral and nonmoral quality of sexual acts, we can also ask whether the act or type is natural or unnatural ("perverted"). Natural sexual acts—to provide a broad definition—are acts that either flow naturally from human sexual nature or do not frustrate, counteract, or interfere with sexual tendencies that flow naturally from human sexual desire. An account of what is natural in human sexuality is part of a philosophical account of human nature in general (or philosophical anthropology), which is a large undertaking.

Evaluating a particular sexual act or type of sexual activity as being natural or unnatural is often distinct from evaluating the act or type either as being morally good or bad or as being nonmorally good or bad. Suppose we assume, for the sake of discussion only, that heterosexual coitus is a natural human sexual activity and that male-male fellatio is not. Even so, it does not follow from the judgment that heterosexual coitus is natural that it is also morally good or right. (Some natural sexual acts might be adulterous or rape.) Nor does it follow that all male-male fellatio is morally bad or wrong (e.g., if engaged in by consenting adults, it might be morally permissible even if, *ex hypothesi* only, it is unnatural). Furthermore, from the judgment that heterosexual coitus is natural, it does not follow that acts of heterosexual coitus are nonmorally good (sexually pleasurable), nor does it follow from the judgment that male-male fellatio is unnatural that it is incapable of producing sexual pleasure for those who engage in it. Of course, both natural and unnatural sexual acts can be medically, psychologically, or socially risky or dangerous. It is nonsense to assume that natural sexual acts are in general less dangerous or risky than unnatural sexual acts. Unprotected heterosexual intercourse (*sans* condom) is dangerous in ways in which mutual male-male masturbation is not.

Because there are no necessary links between the naturalness of sexuality and its moral and nonmoral quality, why should we wonder about and investigate the sexually unnatural? Many philosophers suggest that we abandon the term *perversion* and hence the concept of the unnatural in talking about sexuality.[10] One reason for continuing to discuss the natural/unnatural distinction is that understanding what is sexually natural may help complete our picture of human nature in general and allows us to understand our species more fully. With such deliberations, human self-reflection (the heart of philosophy) about the human condition becomes more thorough. A second reason is that an account of the sexually natural/unnatural distinction might be useful for the discipline of psychology, if a desire or tendency to engage in unnatural sexual activities is a symptom of underlying mental pathology. (The American Psychiatric Association no longer considers a preference for same-sex sexual activity to be a mental disorder.)[11] A third reason: even though (un)natural sexual activity is not on that score *alone* morally good or bad, it is still possible to argue that whether a sexual act is (un)natural does contribute, to a greater or lesser extent, to the moral goodness or badness of the act, just as whether a sex act is nonmorally good or bad may be a factor, sometimes an important one, in the morality of the act (although it may also have little or no moral impact at all). Roman Catholic sexual ethics might be unique in claiming that the unnaturalness of a sexual act certainly makes it immoral and does so without our having to appeal to any other considerations.

NATURAL LAW

A comparison of the sexual philosophy of the medieval Catholic theologian St. Thomas Aquinas (ca. 1225–1275) with that of the contemporary secular philosophy of Thomas Nagel is in this matter instructive. Both Aquinas and Nagel make the innocuous assumptions that what is sexually unnatural is perverted and that what is unnatural in human sexuality is that which does not conform with or is inconsistent with natural human sexuality. But beyond these trivial areas of agreement, there are deep differences between Aquinas and Nagel.

Based partly on a comparison of the sexualities of humans and lower animals (birds and dogs, for example),[12] Aquinas concludes that what is natural in human sexuality is the impulse toward heterosexual coitus, which is the mechanism designed by God to ensure the preservation of animal species, including the human species. Hence engaging in this activity is the primary natural expression of human sexuality. Furthermore, God designed each of the parts of the human body to carry out specific functions and, on Aquinas's view, God designed the male penis to implant or inject sperm into the female's vagina to effect procreation. It follows, for Aquinas, that ejaculation elsewhere than inside a human female's vagina is unnatural: it is a violation of God's sagacious design. For this reason alone, on Aquinas's view, such activities are immoral, a grave offense to the Almighty. Seeking sexual pleasure is permissible, for Aquinas, but only during sexual activities that involve the proper use of the sexual pleasure organs.

Sexual intercourse with lower animals (bestiality), sexual activity with members of one's own sex (homosexuality), and masturbation, for Aquinas, are unnatural sexual acts. They are also immoral (if committed intentionally) exactly because they are unnatural; they disrupt the natural order of the world as created by God and which He commanded to be respected.[13] In none of these activities is there any possibility of procreation, and the sexual organs are used (misused) for purposes other than those for which they were designed. Although Aquinas does not say so explicitly but only hints in this direction, it follows from his philosophy that fellatio, even when engaged in by a married heterosexual couple, can be unnatural and so morally wrong. At least in those cases in which male orgasm occurs by means of this act, the sperm is not being placed where it should be placed, and procreation is therefore not possible.[14] If the penis entering the vagina is the paradigmatic natural act, any other combination of anatomical connections will be unnatural and hence immoral—for example, the penis or a finger entering the anus. Aquinas's criterion of a sexually natural act, that it must be procreative in form or potential, makes no mention of human psychology. His line of thought yields an anatomical or physiological criterion of natural and perverted sexuality that refers only to bodily organs, to where they are or are not put in relation to each other, and what they might accomplish as a result.

The contemporary philosopher Nagel denies Aquinas's presupposition that in order to discover what is natural in human sexuality we should emphasize what is *common* sexually between humans and lower animals.[15] Applying this formula, Aquinas concludes that the purpose of sexual activity and the sexual organs in humans is procreation. Everything else in Aquinas's sexual philosophy follows more or less logically from this. Nagel, by contrast, argues that to discover what is distinctive about natural human sexuality, and hence what is unnatural or perverted, we should focus, instead, on what humans and lower animals do *not* have in common. We should emphasize the ways in which humans are different from animals, the ways in which humans and their sexuality are special. As a result, Nagel argues that human sexual perversion should be understood as a psychological phenomenon rather than, as in Aquinas, an anatomical or physiological phenomenon. For it is human psychology that makes us different from other animals; an account of natural human sexuality must acknowledge the role of human psychology in sexuality.

Nagel proposes that sexual interactions in which each person responds with sexual arousal to noticing the sexual arousal of the other person exhibit the psychology that is natural to human sexuality. In such an encounter, each person becomes aware of himself or herself and the other person as both the subject and the object of their joint sexual experience. I am sexually aroused not only by your physical attractiveness or your touch but also by the fact that you are aroused by me and my touches; we become sexually aroused by recognizing that we are aroused. Nothing as complex as this occurs among the lower animals. Perverted sexual encounters are, on Nagel's view, those in which this mutual recognition of arousal is absent and in which a person remains fully a subject or fully an object of the sexual interaction. Sexual perversion, then, is a departure from or a truncation of a psychologically "complete" pattern of arousal.[16] (On Nagel's view, a person is sexually perverted only if he or she prefers to perform sexually perverted acts.) Nothing in Nagel's psychological account of the natural and perverted refers to bodily organs or physiological processes. For a sexual encounter to be natural, it need not be procreative in form as long as the requisite psychology of mutual recognition is present. Whether a sexual activity is natural or perverted does not depend, on Nagel's view, on what organs are used or where they are put but only on the character of its psychology. Thus Nagel disagrees with Aquinas that same-sex sexual activity is unnatural, for homosexual fellatio and anal intercourse can be accompanied by the mutual recognition of and response to the other person's sexual arousal.

Note that Aquinas and Nagel agree about other things—for example, that fetishism is unnatural. But they disagree about the grounds of that evaluation. For Aquinas, masturbating while fondling shoes or undergarments is unnatural because the sperm is not deposited where it should be; the act has no procreative potential. For Nagel, masturbatory fetishism is perverted for a different reason: there is no possibility of a person noticing and being aroused by the arousal of another person. In this example, there is one more difference between these two philosophers: Aquinas would judge the sexual activity of the fetishist to be immoral precisely because it is unnatural, while Nagel would not conclude that it is morally wrong (even though it is unnatural). After all, a fetishistic sexual act can be carried out without harming anyone. The move from a Thomistic moralistic account of sexual perversion to a morality-free psychological account such as Nagel's is one aspect of a more widespread phenomenon: the gradual replacement of religious or moral judgments, about all sorts of deviant behavior, by medical, psychiatric, or psychological judgments and interventions.[17]

A different kind of disagreement with Aquinas is registered by Christine Gudorf, a Christian theologian who otherwise has much in common with Aquinas. Gudorf agrees with Aquinas that the study of anatomy and physiology yields insights into God's design and that human sexual behavior should conform with God's creative intentions. Gudorf's philosophy is squarely within the Thomist or Natural Law tradition. But Gudorf argues that if we take a more careful look at the anatomy and physiology of the female sexual organs, especially the clitoris, instead of focusing exclusively on the sexual role of the male's penis and ejaculate (which is what Aquinas did), we arrive at very different conclusions about God's design. As a result, Christian sexual ethics turns out to be less restrictive. In particular, Gudorf claims that the clitoris is a tissue or organ whose only purpose is to yield sexual pleasure. Unlike the penis, which has three functions (elimination of urine, production of sexual pleasure, insertion of the seed into the vagina), the clitoris has no connection with procreation. Gudorf concludes that the existence of the clitoris in the female body suggests that God intended that the purpose of sexual activity was as much for sexual pleasure *for its own sake* as it was for procreation. Hence, according to Gudorf, pleasurable sexual activity apart from procreation does not violate God's design, is not unnatural, and is not morally wrong as long as it occurs within a monogamous marriage (even a same-sex monogamous marriage).[18] Gudorf, it seems, is advancing a Christian semi-optimistic sexual metaphysics. Today we are not as confident as Aquinas was that God's design can be discovered by a straightforward examination of human and animal bodies. However, this healthy skepticism about our ability to discern God's intentions and design from the facts of the natural world applies to Gudorf's proposal as well. That the clitoris, through its ability to provide sexual pleasure, plays a role in leading to procreative heterosexual sexual activity is not obviously false.

DEBATES IN SEXUAL ETHICS

The ethics of sexual behavior, as a branch of applied ethics, is no more and no less contentious than the ethics of anything else. Think of the notorious debates over euthanasia, welfare entitlement, capital punishment, abortion, environmental pollution, and our treatment of animals for food, clothing, entertainment, and scientific research. It should come as no surprise that even though a discussion of sexual ethics might remove some confusions and clarify some of the issues, few final or absolute answers to questions about the morality of sexual activity are likely to be forthcoming from studying the philosophy of sex. Of course, everyone, except the Marquis de Sade, agrees that rape is seriously morally wrong. Yet debates remain even here: What, exactly, is a case of rape? How can its occurrence be reliably identified? And *why* is it wrong? Some ethical systems assert that adultery is morally wrong. But, again, what counts as adultery? Is it merely having lustful thoughts, as claimed by Jesus in Matthew 5:28?

There are several important topics that have received much attention from philosophers of sex. We have already encountered one of them: the dispute between a Natural Law approach to sexual morality and a liberal-secular outlook that denies a connection between what is unnatural and what is immoral. Secular liberal philosophers emphasize the values of autonomous choice and self-determination in arriving at moral judgments about sexual behavior, in contrast to the Thomist tradition that justifies a more restrictive sexual ethics by invoking a divinely imposed scheme to which human action must conform. For a secular-liberal philosopher of sex, rape is the paradigmatically morally wrong sexual act: one person forces himself or herself on another or uses threats to coerce another to engage in sexual activity. By contrast, for the liberal, anything done voluntarily or consensually between two or more people is generally morally permissible. Thus a sexual act is morally wrong only if it is coercive, dishonest, or manipulative. Natural Law theory agrees that the use of coercion (and so forth) makes sexual activity morally wrong. It adds, however, that a sexual act's being unnatural is another, independent reason for condemning it morally, as in masturbation and same-sex sexual activity.[19] The sexual liberal finds nothing morally wrong with either masturbation or same-sex sexual activity. These activities might be unnatural, and perhaps sometimes prudentially unwise, but they can be carried out without harm being done either to anyone else or to the participants. Despite the current popularity of secular-liberal sexual ethics, Natural Law is still alive and well among some philosophers of sex, even if the details do not precisely match Aquinas's original version.[20]

CONSENT

When no harm is done to third parties (nonparticipants), is the free and informed consent of the people who together engage in sexual activity necessary and sufficient for making their interaction morally permissible? The Natural Law tradition denies that consent is sufficient; to willingly, voluntarily engage in unnatural sexual acts is (still) morally wrong. Natural Law is not alone in reducing the moral significance of consent. Sexual activity between two persons might be harmful to one or both participants, as in some sadomasochism, and a moral paternalist or perfectionist might claim that it is wrong for one person to harm another, or for the latter to allow the former to engage in harmful behavior, even when both persons provide free and informed consent to their joint activity. Consent, on this view, is not sufficient, even if the participants in, say, sadomasochism, deny that they are really being harmed or causing harm. Philosophers who claim that only in a committed relationship or marriage is sexual activity between two people morally permissible also deny that free and informed consent is sufficient. The consent of both parties may be a necessary condition for the moral goodness of their sexual activity, but in the absence of some other magical ingredient (love, marriage, devotion, and the like), their sexual activity remains mere mutual use or objectification and hence is morally objectionable.

About casual sex, for example, it might be said that two people are merely using each other for their own separate sexual pleasure; even when genuinely consensual, these mutual sexual uses do not yield a virtuous sexual act.[21] Kant and Karol Wojtyla (Pope John Paul II) take this position: willingly allowing oneself to be used sexually by another person makes an object of oneself. Hence mutual consent is not sufficient for the moral rightness of sexual acts. For Kant, sexual activity avoids treating a person merely as a means only in marriage because in such a state both persons have surrendered their bodies and souls to each other.[22] For Wojtyla, "only love can preclude the use of one person by another," because love is a unification of persons resulting from a mutual gift of their selves.[23] Note, however, that the thought that a unifying love is the ingredient that justifies (beyond consent) sexual activity has an interesting implication: gay and lesbian sexual relations would be permissible if they occur within homosexual marriages that are loving, committed, and monogamous. At this point, defenders of the view that sexual activity is justifiable only in marriage commonly appeal to Natural Law to rule out same-sex marriage. "God made Adam and Eve, not Adam and Steve," goes the slogan.

On another view of these matters, if sexual activity is carried out voluntarily by all persons involved (assuming no harm to third parties), the sexual activity is morally permissible. In defending the sufficiency of free and informed consent for the moral goodness of sexual activity, Thomas Mappes writes that "respect for persons entails that each of us recognize the rightful authority of other persons (as rational beings) to conduct their individual lives as they see fit."[24] Allowing the other person's consent to control when the other engages in sexual activity with me is to respect that person by taking seriously his or her autonomy, his or her ability to reason and make choices, while not to allow the other to make the decision about when to engage in sexual activity with me is disrespectful. According to such a view of the power of consent, there can be no moral objection in principle to casual sexual activity, to sexual activity with strangers, to promiscuous sexual behavior, or to sexual activity involving "monstrous techniques" or unusual organs and apertures as long as the participants genuinely agree to engage in their chosen sexual acts.

Even if Mappes's consent criterion is correct, difficult questions remain. How *specific* must consent be? When one person agrees vaguely, and in the heat of the sexual moment, with another person, "yes, let's have sex," has the speaker consented to every type of sexual caress or coital position the other person has in mind? How *explicit* must consent be? Can consent be reliably implied by involuntarily behavior (moans, for example), and do nonverbal cues (erection, lubrication, insistent tongue-kissing) decisively show that another person has consented to sex? Some insist that consent must be exceedingly specific as to the sexual acts to be carried out, and some would permit only explicit verbal consent, denying that body language can do an adequate job of expressing desires and intentions.[25]

Another debate concerns the meaning of "free" (or "voluntary") in the expression "free and informed consent." Whether consent is only necessary for the moral goodness of sexual activity, or also sufficient, any principle that relies on consent to make moral judgments assumes a clear understanding of the voluntary nature of consent. Participation in sexual activity ought not to be physically forced on one person by another. But this obvious and imprecise truth leaves matters wide open. The philosopher Onora O'Neill, for example, believes that much casual sex is morally wrong because the consent it involves is not likely to be sufficiently voluntary in light of subtle pressures people commonly put on each other to engage in sexual activity. On her view, these people who engage in casual sex are merely using each other, not treating each other with respect as persons in a Kantian sense.[26] We might want to go further than O'Neill and claim that if she is right that in casual sex the genuineness of consent is doubtful, then this casual sex is (acquaintance) rape.[27]

One moral ideal is that genuinely voluntary participation in sexual activity requires not a hint of coercion or pressure of any sort.[28] Because engaging in sexual activity can be risky or dangerous in many ways (physically, psychologically, or socially), we would like to be sure, according to this moral ideal, that anyone who engages in sexual activity does so with perfectly voluntarily and informed consent. Some philosophers have argued that this ideal can be realized only when there is substantial economic and social equality between the persons involved in a given sexual encounter. For example, a society that exhibits disparities in income or wealth is one in which some people will be exposed to economic coercion. If some groups of people (women and members of ethnic minorities, in particular) have less economic and social power than others, members of these groups will be exposed to sexual coercion, among other kinds.

One immediate application of this thought is that prostitution, which to many sexual liberals is a business bargain made by a provider of sexual services and a client and is largely characterized by adequately free and informed consent, may be morally wrong if the economic situation of the prostitute acts as a kind of pressure that negates the voluntary nature of his or her participation in the transaction. Furthermore, women who have children and who are dependent economically on their husbands may find themselves in the position of having to engage in sexual activity whether they want to or not for fear of being abandoned; these women, too, may not be engaging in sexual activity fully voluntarily. The woman who allows herself to be nagged into sex by her husband worries that if she says "no" too often, she will suffer economically, if not also physically and psychologically.[29]

The view that the presence of any kind of pressure is coercive and negates the voluntary nature of participation in sexual activity, and hence is morally objectionable, has been expressed by, among others, Charlene Muehlenhard and Jennifer Schrag.[30] They list—to provide only two of their examples—"status coercion" (women are coerced into sexual activity or marriage by a man's occupation) and "discrimination against lesbians" (which compels women into having sexual relationships only with men) as forms of coercion that undermine the voluntary nature of participation by women in sexual activity with men. But depending on the kind of case we have in mind, it might be more accurate to say either that some pressures are not coercive and do not appreciably undermine voluntariness or that some pressures are coercive but are nevertheless not morally objectionable. Is it true that the presence of any kind of pressure put on one person by another amounts to coercion that negates the voluntary nature of consent, so that any subsequent sexual activity is morally wrong? I wonder whether a woman who says to her husband, "buy me that mink coat or you will sleep on the couch for a month," is engaging in any objectionable behavior.[31]

NOTES

1. The writers, philosophies, and topics mentioned or discussed in this essay are covered in Alan Soble, ed., *Sex from Plato to Paglia: A Philosophical Encyclopedia*, 2nd ed. (Westport, Conn.: Greenwood Press, 2006). See also Alan Soble, *The Philosophy of Sex and Love* (St. Paul, Minn.: Paragon House, 2008) and Raja Halwani, *Philosophy of Love, Sex, and Marriage* (New York: Routledge, 2010).

2. *Lectures on Ethics*, trans. Louis Infield (New York: Harper and Row, 1963), 163. Kant, I think, uses the phrase "loved person" euphemistically, the way we sometimes use "make love" euphemistically for "have sex."

3. *The City of God*, vol. 2, trans. John Healey (London: J. M. Dent, 1945), bk. 14, sec. 23.

4. *The Metaphysics of Morals*, trans. Mary Gregor (Cambridge: Cambridge University Press, 1996), 62.

5. *On Marriage and Concupiscence*, in *The Works of Aurelius Augustine, Bishop of Hippo*, vol. 12, ed. Marcus Dods (Edinburgh, Scot.: T. & T. Clark, 1874), bk. 1, chap. 9.

6. See Russell Vannoy's defense of the value of sexual activity for its own sake in *Sex without Love: A Philosophical Exploration* (Buffalo, N.Y.: Prometheus, 1980).

7. *The Nature of Love*, vol. 2: *Courtly and Romantic* (Chicago: University of Chicago Press, 1984), 382. As we leave the metaphysics of sexuality, I must acknowledge my debt to Murray Davis, *Smut: Erotic Reality/Obscene Ideology* (Chicago: University of Chicago Press, 1983). I recommend the book for those who wish to learn more (and better) about the metaphysics of sex.

8. *Good Sex: Perspectives on Sexual Ethics* (Lawrence, Kan.: University Press of Kansas, 1993), 210. For a brief review of *Good Sex*, see Alan Soble, "Book Note," *Ethics* 105:2 (1995): 447–48.

9. The philosopher David Mayo argues that we do not necessarily have a moral obligation to reveal our HIV status to potential sexual partners. See his provocative essay "An Obligation to Warn of HIV Infection?" in Alan Soble, ed., *Sex, Love and Friendship* (Amsterdam: Rodopi, 1997), 447–53.

10. Michael Slote argues that "sexual perversion" is an "inapplicable concept" ("Inapplicable Concepts and Sexual Perversion," in *Philosophy and Sex*, 1st ed., ed. Robert Baker and Frederick Elliston [Buffalo, N.Y.: Prometheus, 1975], 261–67, at 266); Graham Priest also calls it "inapplicable" and adds that "the notion of sexual perversion makes no sense" any longer ("Sexual Perversion," *Australasian Journal of Philosophy* 75:3 [1997]: 360–72, at 370–71); Igor Primoratz thinks that "sexual perversion" is "a concept best discarded" (*Ethics and Sex* [London: Routledge, 1999], 63–66); Linda LeMoncheck wants to replace "sexual perversion" with "sexual difference" (*Loose Women, Lecherous Men: A Feminist Philosophy of Sex* [New York: Oxford University Press, 1997], 72, 80, 82–83); and Robert Gray submits that "sexual perversion" should "be dropped from our sexual vocabulary altogether" ("Sex and Sexual Perversion," *Journal of Philosophy* 75:4 [1978]: 189–99, at 199).

11. See the *Diagnostic and Statistical Manual of Mental Disorders* (*DSM*), 4th ed. (Washington, D.C.: American Psychiatric Association, 1994), 493–538. For discussion of how "sexual disorder" is handled in the *DSM*, see Alan Soble, "Paraphilia and Distress in *DSM-IV*," in Jennifer Radden, ed., *The Philosophy of Psychiatry: A Companion* (New York: Oxford University Press), 54–63.

12. Aquinas found the analogy between birds and humans with respect to monogamy to be illuminating. See his *Summa contra gentiles*, III/2: 122.8, 123.2; and *Summa theologiae*, IIa–IIae: 154.2. By the way, the Hebrew view of sexual perversion is not far from Aquinas's. See Louis M. Epstein, *Sex Laws and Customs in Judaism* (New York: Ktav, 1948), chap. 5.

13. *Summa theologiae*, IIa–IIae: 153–154.

14. Aquinas condemns heterosexual sexual acts in which "the natural style of intercourse is not observed, as regards the proper organ or according to rather beastly and monstrous techniques" (IIa–IIae: 154.11). I believe that he is referring to heterosexual

oral-genital, genital-anal, and oral-anal sexual acts. Depending on the theological leanings of your corner clergyman, these acts may be prohibited, or they may be forgiven or even allowed as foreplay, that is, as acts (just like kissing and caressing) that lead to and culminate in heterosexual coitus. For example, St. Paul's idea in 1 Cor 7:4, that the central, even only, purpose of marital sexual activity is as a "remedy against sin," that is, to provide sexual satisfaction so that neither spouse has any motive or inclination to commit adultery, might be interpreted as blessing the unnatural heterosexual acts that Aquinas condemns. Maximizing the sexual satisfaction of the spouses might require, say, oral-genital sexual activity, and thus these acts serve well as a remedy against sin. See Alan Soble, *Sexual Investigations* (New York: New York University Press, 1996), 8. One student of mine replied to this "theory of acceptable unnatural acts" by quipping: A married Catholic couple may engage in anal intercourse as long as it is followed by ejaculatory vaginal intercourse (and the penis is washed in between).

15. On the advantages and pitfalls of employing an animal model to understand human sexuality, see Jeffrey Hershfield, "Animal Sexuality," in Soble, *Sex from Plato to Paglia*, 45–50.

16. See Thomas Nagel's "Sexual Perversion," in this volume, and Soble, *The Philosophy of Sex and Love*, 78–82.

17. See Soble, *Sexual Investigations*, chap. 4; and Peter Conrad and Joseph W. Schneider, *Deviance and Medicalization: From Badness to Sickness* (St. Louis, Mo.: C. V. Mosby, 1980), especially "Homosexuality: From Sin to Sickness to Life-Style," 172–214.

18. *Sex, Body, and Pleasure: Reconstructing Christian Sexual Ethics* (Cleveland, Ohio: Pilgrim Press, 1994), 65. For another Christian defense of same-sex marriage, see Patricia Jung and Ralph Smith, *Heterosexism: An Ethical Challenge* (Albany, N.Y.: State University of New York Press, 1993).

19. Kant also held that masturbation "is abuse of the sexual faculty. . . . By it man sets aside his person and degrades himself below the level of animals. . . . Intercourse between *sexus homogenii* . . . too is contrary to the ends of humanity" (*Lectures on Ethics*, 170).

20. See, for example, John Finnis, "Law, Morality, and 'Sexual Orientation,'" *Notre Dame Law Review* 69:5 (1994): 1049–76.

21. On the morality of casual sex, in particular, see Raja Halwani's essay "On Fucking Around" in this volume. See also, in this volume, the essays by Alan Goldman, Thomas Mappes, and Howard Klepper.

22. For the details, see Alan Soble, "Sexual Use," in this volume.

23. *Love and Responsibility* (New York: Farrar, Straus and Giroux, 1981), 30.

24. "Sexual Morality and the Concept of Using Another Person," in this volume. Also defending the sufficiency of consent is Bernard Baumrin's "Sexual Immorality Delineated," in *Philosophy and Sex*, 2nd ed., ed. Robert Baker and Frederick Elliston (Buffalo, N.Y.: Prometheus, 1984), 300–311; and Igor Primoratz, "Sexual Morality: Is Consent Enough?" *Ethical Theory and Moral Practice* 4:3 (2001): 201–18. An important essay arguing against the sufficiency of consent is Seiriol Morgan's "Dark Desires," *Ethical Theory and Moral Practice* 6:4 (2003): 377–410. See also Morgan's discussion of Alan Goldman in "Sex in the Head" in this volume.

25. See Alan Soble, "Antioch's 'Sexual Offense Policy': A Philosophical Exploration," *Journal of Social Philosophy* 28:1 (1997): 22–36, reprinted, revised, in Alan Soble, ed., *Philosophy of Sex*, 4th ed. (323–40), and Soble and Powers, eds., *Philosophy of Sex*, 5th ed. (459–77). For criticisms, see Eva Feder Kittay, "Ah! My Foolish Heart," in Soble and Powers, eds., *Philosophy of Sex*, 5th ed. (479–87).

26. "Between Consenting Adults," in her *Constructions of Reason: Explorations of Kant's Practical Philosophy* (Cambridge: Cambridge University Press, 1989), 105–25.

27. On date rape, see Lois Pineau's essay in this volume.

28. See Alan Soble, "Ethics, Sexual," in *Sex From Plato to Paglia*, 273–79.

29. See also the points made by Robin West, "The Harms of Consensual Sex," in this volume.

30. "Nonviolent Sexual Coercion," in *Acquaintance Rape: The Hidden Crime*, ed. Andrea Parrot and Laurie Bechhofer (New York: John Wiley, 1991), 115–28. In this context, read Alan Wertheimer, "Consent and Sexual Relations," in this volume.

31. For additional introductory material on the topics of this essay, see my "Philosophy of Sexuality," *Internet Encyclopedia of Philosophy*, ed. James Fieser (www.utm.edu/research/iep); "Sexuality and Sexual Ethics," *Encyclopedia of Ethics*, 2nd ed. (New York: Routledge, 2001), 1570–77; "Sexuality, Philosophy of," *Routledge Encyclopedia of Philosophy*, ed. Edward Craig (London: Routledge, 1998), vol. 8, 717–30; and "Philosophy of Sex," *Encyclopedia of Philosophy*, 2nd ed., ed. Donald Borchert (New York: Macmillan/Thomson, 2006), vol. 7, 521–32.

STUDY QUESTIONS

1. What are some of the thematic differences between metaphysical sexual optimism and metaphysical sexual pessimism? Which position do you think is right or more accurate? Can you provide convincing reasons for your choice?

2. How could it be decided whether specific sexual desires and sexual acts are natural or unnatural? If a sexual desire or a sexual act is unnatural (i.e., contravenes human sexual nature), is that fact always, often, not often, or never an important consideration in judging whether the desire or the act is morally wrong? See how deeply you can go in defending your answer.

3. How could we decide whether a particular sexual act has been performed with the full consent of both (or all) parties or has, instead, occurred because one party has been coerced? Is this, however, a false dilemma? That is, does the presence of coercion always mean that the act was not performed with consent, and does the absence of coercion always mean that the act was done consensually? Try to think of situations (analogous to the sexual) in which we coerce or put pressure on people to do things they prefer not to do and yet our exerting pressure is not morally wrong.

4. Discuss to what extent and in what ways the nonmoral and pragmatic evaluations of sexual acts make a difference in evaluating them morally. If these evaluations do make a difference, and do so frequently, what might this mean about the difficulty of arriving at sound judgments in sexual ethics? Should we conclude that to be morally safe we should never engage in sexual activity unless every single moral and nonmoral consideration points in its favor?

5. Does the marital status, age, gender, species, race, or ethnicity of one's sexual partner (or of oneself) make a difference to the morality of sexual acts carried out with that partner? Why or why not? What other features of potential partners might be added to this list? Their physical attractiveness? Their income? Certain features of their biography?

6. In a legal case decided by the U.S. Supreme Court (*Rose v. Locke*, 423 U.S. 48 [1975]), the defendant was accused of forcing a woman, at knife point, "to submit to his twice performing cunnilingus upon her." What are the analytic criteria for individuating and counting sexual acts, such that it is possible and makes sense to say that X performed cunnilingus once, twice, or N times on another person? Similarly, suppose that a man ties up a woman and proceeds to rape her, that is, has penis-vagina intercourse with her without her consent and against her will. He stops for a while, going to the bathroom and then the kitchen, and afterwards again has penis-vagina intercourse with her. Has the woman been raped once or twice? In the *Rose* case, the defendant was not charged with rape but only of violating a Tennessee "crimes against nature" statute (by now, almost forty years later, abandoned). Did he commit an unnatural act? Should unnatural acts be illegal? Can you surmise why he was not charged with rape?

7. What do you believe about same-sex sexual activity? Is it natural or unnatural? Or, when is it natural and when is it unnatural? Is it ever morally wrong *per se*? (It might be morally wrong, but not *qua* same-sex sexual activity, if the act is also a case of adultery and if adultery is immoral.) Is it ever antiprudential? Provide reasons for your answers, and then ask the same questions about fetishism, sadomasochism, exhibitionism, and voyeurism.

8. What do you think of the author's analogy between eating food and engaging in sexual activity? In what ways are hunger and sexual desire, or eating and having sex, similar? In what ways are they not similar to each other? Try to understand your answers in terms of the difference between pessimistic and optimistic metaphysical philosophies of sex.

I

Analysis and Perversion

TWO

Are We Having Sex Now or What?

Greta Christina

Though sex, and the philosophy of sex, are often serious if not solemn affairs, it pays to approach them with a sense of humor, as **Greta Christina** *demonstrates. The philosophical topic at hand—what are the necessary and sufficient conditions for an act or encounter to be sexual—is addressed by the essays in part I of this book. Views about how to define "sex" properly are implicated in many issues, for example, in defining "rape" and "sexual harassment." While laying out commonsensical definitions of "sexual activity" (say, that it must include penis-in-vagina coitus; that it requires that the participants be naked; that it involves sexual pleasure for all concerned), Christina reveals counterexamples, often from her own experience. This reflective exercise might lead us to be, as Christina is, skeptical about ever finding a final definition of "sexual activity." Her essay has the virtue of forcing us to ask the analytic question and to realize that everyday understandings of "sex" are not very satisfying. Christina's essay was reprinted by the magazine* Ms. *in its 1995 "Feminism and Sex" issue (November/December, 60–62). The essay's last two paragraphs are missing from that version, and there is no editorial warning that the essay was abridged. Those paragraphs, included here, are perhaps the most provocative in Christina's essay: she admits to finding some sadomasochism "tremendously erotic," and she relates that when working as a nude dancer inside a peep show booth she had a "fabulous time" with one of her quarter-laden customers. These examples of "sex" are valuable to think about, both conceptually and normatively.*

Greta Christina is the author of *Bending*, an erotic novella published as part of a three-novella collection, *Three Kinds of Asking for It* (edited by Susie Bright; Simon & Schuster, 2005), and has edited *Paying for It: A Guide by Sex Workers for Their Clients* (Greenery Press, 2004). Her writing has appeared in magazines and newspapers, including *Ms.*, *Penthouse*, *Chicago Sun-Times*, *On Our Backs*, and *Skeptical Inquirer*, and numerous anthologies, including *Everything You Know About God Is Wrong* and three volumes of *Best*

American Erotica. The editor of *Best Erotic Comics*, an annual anthology series published by Last Gasp, she blogs in the Freethought Blogs network at http://freethoughtblogs.com/greta. Her web site is http://gretach-ristina.com. This essay originally appeared in David Steinberg's anthology, *The Erotic Impulse: Honoring the Sensual Self* (New York: Tarcher/Penguin, 1992), pp. 24–29. Reprinted here by the permission of Greta Christina.

When I first started having sex with other people, I used to like to count them. I wanted to keep track of how many there had been. It was a source of some kind of pride, or identity anyway, to know how many people I'd had sex with in my lifetime. So, in my mind, Len was number one, Chris was number two, that slimy awful little heavy metal barbiturate addict whose name I can't remember was number three, Alan was number four, and so on. It got to the point where, when I'd start having sex with a new person for the first time, when he first entered my body (I was only having sex with men at the time), what would flash through my head wouldn't be "Oh, baby, baby you feel so good inside me," or "What the hell am I doing with this creep," or "This is boring, I wonder what's on TV." What flashed through my head was "Seven!"

Doing this had some interesting results. I'd look for patterns in the numbers. I had a theory for a while that every fourth lover turned out to be really great in bed, and would ponder what the cosmic significance of the phenomenon might be. Sometimes I'd try to determine what kind of person I was by how many people I'd had sex with. At eighteen, I'd had sex with ten different people. Did that make me normal, repressed, a total slut, a free-spirited bohemian, or what? Not that I compared my numbers with anyone else's—I didn't. It was my own exclusive structure, a game I played in the privacy of my own head.

Then the numbers started getting a little larger, as numbers tend to do, and keeping track became more difficult. I'd remember that the last one was *seventeen* and so this one must be *eighteen*, and then I'd start having doubts about whether I'd been keeping score accurately or not. I'd lie awake at night thinking to myself, well, there was Brad, and there was that guy on my birthday, and there was David and . . . no, wait, I forgot that guy I got drunk with at the social my first week at college . . . so that's seven, eight, nine . . . and by two in the morning I'd finally have it figured out. But there was always a nagging suspicion that maybe I'd missed someone, some dreadful tacky little scumball that I was trying to forget about having invited inside my body. And as much as I maybe wanted to forget about the sleazy little scumball, I wanted more to get that number right.

It kept getting harder, though. I began to question what counted as sex and what didn't. There was that time with Gene, for instance. I was pissed off at my boyfriend, David, for cheating on me. It was a major crisis, and Gene and I were friends and he'd been trying to get at me for weeks and I hadn't exactly been discouraging him. I went to see him that night to gripe about David. He was very sympathetic of course, and he gave me a backrub, and we talked and touched and confided and hugged, and then we started kissing, and then we snuggled up a little closer, and then we started fondling each other, you know, and then all heck broke loose, and we rolled around on the bed groping and rubbing and grabbing and smooching and pushing and pressing and squeezing. He never did actually get it in. He wanted to, and I wanted to too, but I had this thing about being faithful to my boyfriend, so I kept saying, "No, you can't do that, Yes, that feels so good, No, wait that's too much, Yes, yes, don't stop, No, stop that's enough." We never even got our clothes off. Jesus Christ, though, it was some night. One of the best, really. But for a long time I didn't count it as one of the times I'd had sex. He never got inside, so it didn't count.

Later, months and years later, when I lay awake putting my list together, I'd start to wonder: Why doesn't Gene count? Does he not count because he never got inside? Or does he not count because I had to preserve my moral edge over David, my status as the patient, ever-faithful, cheated-on, martyred girlfriend, and if what I did with Gene counts then I don't get to feel wounded and superior?

Years later, I did end up fucking Gene and I felt a profound relief because, at last, he definitely had a number, and I knew for sure that he did in fact count.

Then I started having sex with women, and, boy, howdy, did *that* ever shoot holes in the system. I'd always made my list of sex partners by defining sex as penile-vaginal intercourse—you know, screwing. It's a pretty simple distinction, a straightforward binary system. Did it go in or didn't it? Yes or no? One or zero? On or off? Granted, it's a pretty arbitrary definition, but it's the customary one, with an ancient and respected tradition behind it, and when I was just screwing men, there was no compelling reason to question it.

But with women, well, first of all there's no penis, so right from the start the tracking system is defective. And then, there are so many ways women can have sex with each other, touching and licking and grinding and fingering and fisting—with dildoes or vibrators or vegetables or whatever happens to be lying around the house, or with nothing at all except human bodies. Of course, that's true for sex between women and men as well. But between women, no one method has a centuries-old tradition of being the one that counts. Even when we do fuck each other there's no dick, so you don't get that feeling of This Is What's Important, We Are Now Having Sex, objectively speaking, and all that other stuff is just foreplay or afterplay. So when I started having sex with women the binary system had to go, in favor of a more inclusive definition.

Which meant, of course, that my list of how many people I'd had sex with was completely trashed. In order to maintain it I would have had to go back and reconstruct the whole thing and include all those people I'd necked with and gone down on and dry-humped and played touchy-feely games with. Even the question of who filled the all-important Number One slot, something I'd never had any doubts about before, would have to be re-evaluated.

By this time I'd kind of lost interest in the list anyway. Reconstructing it would be more trouble than it was worth. But the crucial question remained: What counts as having sex with someone?

It was important for me to know. You have to know what qualifies as sex because when you have sex with someone your relationship changes. Right? *Right?* It's not that sex itself has to change things all that much. But knowing you've had sex, being conscious of a sexual connection, standing around making polite conversation with someone while thinking to yourself, "I've had sex with this person," that's what changes things. Or so I believed. And if having sex with a friend can confuse or change the friendship, think how bizarre things can get when you're not sure whether you've had sex with them or not.

The problem was, as I kept doing more kinds of sexual things, the line between *sex* and *not-sex* kept getting more hazy and indistinct. As I brought more into my sexual experience, things were showing up on the dividing line demanding my attention. It wasn't just that the territory I labeled sex was expanding. The line itself had swollen, dilated, been transformed into a vast gray region. It had become less like a border and more like a demilitarized zone.

Which is a strange place to live. Not a bad place, just strange. It's like juggling, or watchmaking, or playing the piano—anything that demands complete concentrated awareness and attention. It feels like cognitive dissonance, only pleasant. It feels like waking up from a compelling and realistic bad dream. It feels like the way you feel when you realize that everything you know is wrong, and a bloody good thing too, because it was painful and stupid and it really screwed you up.

But, for me, living in a question naturally leads to searching for an answer. I can't simply shrug, throw up my hands, and say, "Damned if I know." I have to explore the unknown frontiers, even if I don't bring back any secret treasure. So even if it's incomplete or provisional, I do want to find some sort of definition of what is and isn't sex.

I know when I'm *feeling* sexual. I'm feeling sexual if my pussy's wet, my nipples are hard, my palms are clammy, my brain is fogged, my skin is tingly and super-sensitive, my butt muscles clench, my heartbeat speeds up, I have an orgasm (that's the real giveaway), and so on. But feeling sexual with someone isn't the same as having sex with them. Good Lord, if I called it sex every time I was attracted to someone who returned the favor I'd be even more bewildered than I am now. Even *being* sexual with someone isn't the same as *having* sex with them. I've danced and flirted with too many people, given and received too many sexy, would-be-seductive backrubs, to believe otherwise.

I have friends who say, if you thought of it as sex when you were doing it, then it was. That's an interesting idea. It's certainly helped me construct a coherent sexual history without being a revisionist swine: redefining my past according to current definitions. But it really just begs the question. It's fine to say that sex is whatever I think it is; but then what do I think it *is*? What if, when I was doing it, I was *wondering* whether it counted?

Perhaps having sex with someone is the conscious, consenting, mutually acknowledged pursuit of shared sexual pleasure. Not a bad definition. If you are turning each other on and you say so and you keep doing it, then it's sex. It's broad enough to encompass a lot of sexual behavior beyond genital contact/orgasm; it's distinct enough not to include every instance of sexual awareness or arousal; and it contains the elements I feel are vital—acknowledgment, consent, reciprocity, and the pursuit of pleasure. But what about the situation where one person consents to sex without really enjoying it? Lots of people (myself included) have had sexual interactions that we didn't find satisfying or didn't really want and, unless they were actually forced on us against our will, I think most of us would still classify them as sex.

Maybe if *both* of you (or all of you) think of it as sex, then it's sex whether you're having fun or not. That clears up the problem of sex that's consented to but not wished-for or enjoyed. Unfortunately, it begs the question again, only worse: now you have to mesh different people's vague and inarticulate notions of what is and isn't sex and find the place where they overlap. Too messy.

How about sex as the conscious, consenting, mutually acknowledged pursuit of sexual pleasure of *at least one* of the people involved? That's better. It has all the key components, and it includes the situation where one person is doing it for a reason other than sexual pleasure—status, reassurance, money, the satisfaction and pleasure of someone they love, etc. But what if *neither* of you is enjoying it, if you're both doing it because you think the other one wants to? Ugh.

I'm having trouble here. Even the conventional standby—sex equals intercourse—has a serious flaw: it includes rape, which is something I emphatically refuse to accept. As far as I'm concerned, if there's no consent, it ain't sex. But I feel that's about the only place in this whole quagmire where I have a grip. The longer I think about the subject, the more questions I come up with. At what point in an encounter does it *become* sexual? If an interaction that begins nonsexually turns into sex, was it sex all along? What about sex with someone who's asleep? Can you have a situation where one person is having sex and the other isn't? It seems that no matter what definition I come up with, I can think of some real-life experience that calls it into question.

For instance, a couple of years ago I attended (well, hosted) an all-girl sex party. Out of the twelve other women there, there were only a few with whom I got seriously physically nasty. The rest I kissed or hugged or talked dirty with or just smiled at, or watched while they did seriously physically nasty things with each other. If we'd been alone, I'd probably say that what I'd done with most of the women there didn't count as having sex. But the experience, which was hot and sweet and silly and very, very special, had been created by all of us, and although I only really got down with a few, I felt that I'd been sexual with all of the women there. Now, when I meet one of the women from that party, I always ask myself: Have we had sex?

For instance, when I was first experimenting with sadomasochism, I got together with a really hot woman. We were negotiating about what we were going to do, what would and wouldn't be ok, and she said she wasn't sure she wanted to have sex. Now we'd been explicitly planning all kinds of fun and games—spanking, bondage, obedience—which I strongly identified as sexual activity. In her mind, though, *sex* meant direct genital contact, and she didn't necessarily want to do that with me. Playing with her turned out to be a tremendously erotic experience, arousing and stimulating and almost unbearably satisfying. But we spent the whole evening without even touching each other's genitals. And the fact that our definitions were so different made me wonder: Was it sex?

For instance, I worked for a few months as a nude dancer at a peep show. In case you've never been to a peep show, it works like this: the customer goes into a tiny, dingy black box, kind of like a phone booth, puts in quarters, and a metal plate goes up; the customer looks through a window at a little room/stage where naked women are dancing. One time, a guy came into one of the booths and started watching me and masturbating. I came over and squatted in front of him and started masturbating too, and we grinned at each other and watched each other and masturbated, and we both had a fabulous time. (I couldn't believe I was being paid to masturbate—tough job, but somebody has to do it. . . .) After he left I thought to myself: Did we just have sex? I mean, if it had been someone I knew, and if there had been no glass and no quarters, there'd be no question in my mind. Sitting two feet apart from someone, watching each other masturbate? Yup, I'd call that sex all right. But this was different, because it was a stranger, and because of the glass and the quarters. Was it sex?

I still don't have an answer.

STUDY QUESTIONS

1. Christina rejects her friends' "subjectivist" definition of "sex"—"if you thought of it as sex, then it was" sex—as being, in part, "revisionist." We seem to have objective, solid definitions of such things as chairs, dogs, asparagus. Why should defining "sex" be any dif-

ferent? Further, in conceding that her own experiences with women led her to redefine sex, for herself at least, is Christina embracing or practicing the subjectivist's definition? Why or why not?

2. Are there any differences between "having sex," "engaging in a sexual act," and "sex"? Would being more careful about these three expressions help Christina solve or overcome some of her worries about finding a definition? Genital kisses might not be, on some plausible definition, "having sex," yet it is still a "sexual act," and if your spouse committed only oral sex with a stranger, would you not be upset at his or her *sexual* infidelity? If not, why not?

3. Many of Christina's examples are sexual acts that cannot be procreative. What makes nonprocreative acts sexual—*if* they are sexual? That is, can you find one single feature that is shared by all sexual acts? Note that there is a difference in the way that contracepted heterosexual intercourse is not procreative and the way in which sadomasochist sexuality is not.

4. Would you count as "sex," as "having sex," or as a "sexual activity" (or none of these) the masturbatory encounter described by Christina at the end of her essay? (What *kind* of masturbation did the event involve? See Soble, "Jacking Off, Yet Again," in this volume.) What judgment would you make about the morality of this sexual encounter? Why?

5. What are some possible explanations for the abridgement of Christina's essay by the editors of *Ms.*? Was it merely a pragmatic matter of constraints on space, which often plagues editors, or might there have been political reasons for the exclusion of touchy material?

THREE

Sexual Perversion

Thomas Nagel

The contribution of **Thomas Nagel** *to the philosophy of sex cannot be overestimated. From his opening claim — "there is something to be learned about sex from the fact that we have a concept of sexual perversion" — to his final conclusion — that bad sex is preferable to no sex at all — the essay is full of controversial claims bravely asserted and defended. The essay brought rigorous analytic philosophy into the bedroom, invited existentialism along to help, and deepened our understanding of the distinction between the natural and the perverted that is central to the subsequent development of the philosophy of sex. Nagel offers a psychological account of unnatural sex, or sexual perversion, which many see as a refreshing departure from theological and biological approaches. Moving away from moralistic accounts of sexual perversion, Nagel focuses on its phenomenology — on what "it is like to have a perverted sexual desire-arousal system." For Nagel, a natural (psychologically "complete") sexual encounter for humans results in the increasing mutual embodiment of both persons through a reciprocal awareness of their emotional responses. "Truncated" versions of this pattern constitute sexual perversion, as in sex with inanimate objects, animals, and young children. Using this formula, Nagel argues that homosexual sexual acts are not perverted, because they can be as psychologically complete as heterosexual acts. Consistently with contemporary psychiatry, Nagel insists that perversion lies not in the nature of the act performed, but in the psychology of the person who performs it, and that a necessary part of sexual perversion resides in his* preferring *certain psychologically truncated sexual acts.*

Thomas Nagel is professor of philosophy and law at New York University and the author of *The Possibility of Altruism* (Oxford University Press, 1970), *Mortal Questions* (Cambridge University Press, 1979), *The View from Nowhere* (Oxford University Press, 1986), and *Concealment and Exposure and Other Essays* (Oxford University Press, 2002). © Cambridge University Press, 1979. This essay is reprinted, with the permission of Thomas

Nagel and Cambridge University Press, from Thomas Nagel, *Mortal Questions*, pp. 39–52. This chapter is a revised version of the article that appeared in *Journal of Philosophy* 66:1 (1969), pp. 5–17.

There is something to be learned about sex from the fact that we possess a concept of sexual perversion. I wish to examine the idea, defending it against the charge of unintelligibility and trying to say exactly what about human sexuality qualifies it to admit of perversions. Let me begin with some general conditions that the concept must meet if it is to be viable at all. These can be accepted without assuming any particular analysis.

First, if there are any sexual perversions, they will have to be sexual desires or practices that are in some sense unnatural, though the explanation of this natural/unnatural distinction is of course the main problem. Second, certain practices will be perversions if anything is, such as shoe fetishism, bestiality, and sadism; other practices, such as unadorned sexual intercourse, will not be; about still others there is controversy. Third, if there are perversions, they will be unnatural sexual *inclinations* rather than just unnatural practices adopted not from inclination but for other reasons. Thus contraception, even if it is thought to be a deliberate perversion of the sexual and reproductive functions, cannot be significantly described as a *sexual* perversion. A sexual perversion must reveal itself in conduct that expresses an unnatural *sexual* preference. And although there might be a form of fetishism focused on the employment of contraceptive devices, that is not the usual explanation for their use.

The connection between sex and reproduction has no bearing on sexual perversion. The latter is a concept of psychological, not physiological, interest, and it is a concept that we do not apply to the lower animals, let alone to plants, all of which have reproductive functions that can go astray in various ways. (Think of seedless oranges.) Insofar as we are prepared to regard higher animals as perverted, it is because of their psychological, not their anatomical, similarity to humans. Furthermore, we do not regard as a perversion every deviation from the reproductive function of sex in humans: sterility, miscarriage, contraception, abortion.

Nor can the concept of sexual perversion be defined in terms of social disapprobation or custom. Consider all the societies that have frowned upon adultery and fornication. These have not been regarded as unnatural practices, but have been thought objectionable in other ways. What is regarded as unnatural admittedly varies from culture to culture, but the classification is not a pure expression of disapproval or distaste. In fact, it is often regarded as a *ground* for disapproval, and that suggests that the classification has independent content.

I shall offer a psychological account of sexual perversion that depends on a theory of sexual desire and human sexual interactions. To approach this solution I shall first consider a contrary position that would justify skepticism about the existence of any sexual perversions at all, and perhaps even about the significance of the term. The skeptical argument runs as follows:

"Sexual desire is simply one of the appetites, like hunger and thirst. As such it may have various objects, some more common than others perhaps, but none in any sense 'natural.' An appetite is identified as sexual by means of the organs and erogenous zones in which its satisfaction can be to some extent localized, and the special sensory pleasures which form the core of that satisfaction. This enables us to recognize widely divergent goals, activities, and desires as sexual, since it is conceivable in principle that anything should produce sexual pleasure and that a nondeliberate, sexually charged desire for it should arise (as a result of conditioning, if nothing else). We may fail to empathize with some of these desires, and some of them, like sadism, may be objectionable on extraneous grounds, but once we have observed that they meet the criteria for being sexual, there is nothing more to be said on *that* score. Either they are sexual or they are not: sexuality does not admit of imperfection, or perversion, or any other such qualification—it is not that sort of affection."

This is probably the received radical position. It suggests that the cost of defending a psychological account may be to deny that sexual desire is an appetite. But insofar as that line of defense is plausible, it should make us suspicious of the simple picture of appetites on which the skepticism depends. Perhaps the standard appetites, like hunger, cannot be classed as pure appetites in that sense either, at least in their human versions.

Can we imagine anything that would qualify as a gastronomical perversion? Hunger and eating, like sex, serve a biological function and also play a significant role in our inner lives. Note that there is little temptation to describe as perverted an appetite for substances that are not nourishing: we should probably not consider someone's appetite *perverted* if he liked to eat paper, sand, wood, or cotton. Those are merely rather odd and very unhealthy tastes: they lack the psychological complexity that we expect of perversions. (Coprophilia, being already a sexual perversion, may be disregarded.) If on the other hand someone liked to eat cookbooks, or magazines with pictures of food in them, and preferred these to ordinary food—or if when hungry he sought satisfaction by fondling a napkin or ashtray from his favorite restaurant—then the concept of perversion might seem appropriate (it would be natural to call it gastronomical fetishism). It would be natural to describe as gastronomically perverted someone who could eat only by having food forced down his throat through a funnel, or only if the meal were a living animal. What helps is the peculiarity of the desire itself, rather than the inappropriateness of its object to the biological function that the desire serves. Even an appetite can have perversions if in addition to its biological function it has a significant psychological structure.

In the case of hunger, psychological complexity is provided by the activities that give it expression. Hunger is not merely a disturbing sensation that can be quelled by eating; it is an attitude toward edible portions of the external world, a desire to treat them in rather special ways. The method of ingestion: chewing, savoring, swallowing, appreciating the texture and smell, all are important components of the relation, as is the passivity and controllability of the food (the only animals we eat live are helpless mollusks). Our relation to food depends also on our size: we do not live upon it or burrow into it like aphids or worms. Some of these features are more central than others, but an adequate phenomenology of eating would have to treat it as a relation to the external world and a way of appropriating bits of that world, with characteristic affection. Displacements or serious restrictions of the desire to eat could then be described as perversions, if they undermined that direct relation between man and food which is the natural expression of hunger. This explains why it is easy to imagine gastronomical fetishism, voyeurism, exhibitionism, or even gastronomical sadism and masochism. Some of these perversions are fairly common.

If we can imagine perversions of an appetite like hunger, it should be possible to make sense of the concept of sexual perversion. I do not wish to imply that sexual desire is an appetite—only that being an appetite is no bar to admitting of perversions. Like hunger, sexual desire has as its characteristic object a certain relation with something in the external world; only in this case it is usually a person rather than an omelet, and the relation is considerably more complicated. This added complication allows scope for correspondingly complicated perversions.

The fact that sexual desire is a feeling about other persons may encourage a pious view of its psychological content—that it is properly the expression of some other attitude, like love, and that when it occurs by itself it is incomplete or subhuman. (The extreme Platonic version of such a view is that sexual practices are all vain attempts to express something they cannot in principle achieve: this makes them all perversions, in a sense.) But sexual desire is complicated enough without having to be linked to anything else as a condition for phenomenological analysis. Sex may serve various functions—economic, social, altruistic—but it also has its own content as a relation between persons.

The object of sexual attraction is a particular individual, who transcends the properties that make him attractive. When different persons are attracted to a single person for different reasons—eyes, hair, figure, laugh, intelligence—we nevertheless feel that the object of their desire is the same. There is even an inclination to feel that this is so if the lovers have different sexual aims, if they include both men and women, for example. Different specific attractive characteristics seem to provide enabling conditions for the operation of a single basic feeling, and the different aims all provide expressions of it. We approach the sexual attitude toward the person through the features that we find attractive, but these features are not the objects of that attitude.

This is very different from the case of an omelet. Various people may desire it for different reasons, one for its fluffiness, another for its mushrooms, another for its unique combination of aroma and visual aspect; yet we do not enshrine the transcendental omelet as the true common object of their affections. Instead we might say that several desires have accidentally converged on the same object: any omelet with the crucial characteristics would do as well. It is not similar¹ true that any person with the same flesh distribution and way of smoking can be substituted as object for a particular sexual desire that has been elicited by those characteristics. It may be that they recur, but it will be a new sexual attraction with a new particular object, not merely a transfer of the old desire to someone else. (This is true even in cases where the new object is unconsciously identified with a former one.)

The importance of this point will emerge when we see how complex a psychological interchange constitutes the natural development of sexual attraction. This would be incomprehensible if its object were not a particular person, but rather a person of a certain *kind*. Attraction is only the beginning, and fulfillment does not consist merely of behavior and contact expressing this attraction, but involves much more.

The best discussion of these matters that I have seen appears in part III of Sartre's *Being and Nothingness*.¹ Sartre's treatment of sexual desire and of love, hate, sadism, masochism, and further attitudes toward others depends on a general theory of consciousness and the body which we can neither expound nor assume here. He does not discuss perversion, and this is partly because he regards sexual desire as one form of the perpetual attempt of an embodied consciousness to come to terms with the existence of others, an attempt that is as doomed to fail in this form as it is in any of the others, which include sadism and masochism (if not certain of the more impersonal deviations) as well as several nonsexual attitudes. According to Sartre, all attempts to incorporate the other into my world as another subject, i.e. to apprehend him at once as an object for me and as a subject for whom I am an object, are unstable and doomed to collapse into one or other of the two aspects. Either I reduce him entirely to an object, in which case his subjectivity escapes the possession or appropriation I can extend to that object; or I become merely an object for him, in which case I am no longer in a position to appropriate his subjectivity. Moreover, neither of these aspects is stable; each is continually in danger of giving way to the other. This has the consequence that there can be no such thing as a *successful* sexual relation, since the deep aim of sexual desire cannot in principle be accomplished. It seems likely, therefore, that the view will not permit a basic distinction between successful or complete and unsuccessful or incomplete sex, and therefore cannot admit the concept of perversion.

I do not adopt this aspect of the theory, nor many of its metaphysical underpinnings. What interests me is Sartre's picture of the attempt. He says that the type of possession that is the object of sexual desire is carried out by "a double reciprocal incarnation" and that this is accomplished, typically in the form of a caress, in the following way: "I make myself flesh in order to impel the Other to realize *for herself* and *for me* her own flesh, and my caresses cause my flesh to be born for me insofar as it is for the Other *flesh causing her to be born as flesh*" (*Being and Nothingness*, p. 391; Sartre's italics) This incarnation in question is described variously as a clogging or troubling of consciousness, which is inundated by the flesh in which it is embodied.

The view I am going to suggest, I hope in less obscure language, is related to this one, but it differs from Sartre's in allowing sexuality to achieve its goal on occasion and thus in providing the concept of perversion with a foothold.

Sexual desire involves a kind of perception, but not merely a single perception of its object, for in the paradigm case of mutual desire there is a complex system of superimposed mutual perceptions—not only perceptions of the sexual object, but perceptions of oneself. Moreover, sexual awareness of another involves considerable self-awareness to begin with—more than is involved in ordinary sensory perception. The experience is felt as an assault on oneself by the view (or touch, or whatever) of the sexual object.

Let us consider a case in which the elements can be separated. For clarity we will restrict ourselves initially to the somewhat artificial case of desire at a distance. Suppose a man and a woman, whom we may call Romeo and Juliet, are at opposite ends of a cocktail lounge, with many mirrors on the walls which permit unobserved observation, and even mutual unobserved observation. Each of them is sipping a martini and studying other people in the mirrors. At some point Romeo notices Juliet. He is moved, somehow, by the softness of her hair and the diffidence with which she sips her martini, and this arouses him sexually. Let us say that X *senses* Y whenever X regards Y with sexual desire. (Y need not be a person, and X's apprehension of Y can be visual, tactile, olfactory, etc., or purely imaginary; in the present example we shall concentrate on vision.) So Romeo senses Juliet, rather than merely noticing her. At this stage he is aroused by an unaroused object, so he is more in the sexual grip of his body than she of hers.

Let us suppose, however, that Juliet now senses Romeo in another mirror on the opposite wall, though neither of them yet knows that he is seen by the other (the mirror angles provide three-quarter views). Romeo then begins to notice in Juliet the subtle signs of sexual arousal, heavy-lidded stare, dilating pupils, faint flush, etc. This of course intensifies her bodily presence, and he not only notices but senses this as well. His arousal is nevertheless still solitary. But now, cleverly calculating the line of her stare without actually looking her in the eyes, he realizes that it is directed at him through the mirror on the opposite wall. That is, he notices, and moreover senses, Juliet sensing him. This is definitely a new development, for it gives him a sense of embodiment not only through his own reactions but through the eyes and reactions of another. Moreover, it is separable from the initial sensing of Juliet; for sexual arousal might begin with a person's sensing that he is sensed and being assailed by the perception of the other person's desire rather than merely by the perception of the person.

But there is a further step. Let us suppose that Juliet, who is a little slower than Romeo, now senses that he senses her. This puts Romeo in a position to notice, and be aroused by, her arousal at being sensed by him. He senses that she senses that he senses her. This is still another level of arousal, for he becomes conscious of his sexuality through his awareness of its effect on her and of her awareness that this effect is due to him. Once she takes the same step and senses that he senses her sensing him, it becomes difficult to state, let alone imagine, further iterations, though they may be logically distinct. If both are alone, they will presumably turn to look at each other directly, and the proceedings will continue on another plane. Physical contact and intercourse are natural extensions of this complicated visual exchange, and mutual touch can involve all the complexities of awareness present in the visual case, but with a far greater range of subtlety and acuteness.

Ordinarily, of course, things happen in a less orderly fashion—sometimes in a great rush—but I believe that some version of this overlapping system of distinct sexual perceptions and interactions is the basic framework of any full-fledged sexual relation and that relations involving only part of the complex are significantly incomplete. The account is only schematic, as it must be to achieve generality. Every real sexual act will be psychologically far more specific and detailed, in ways that depend not only on the physical techniques employed and on anatomical details, but also on countless features of the participants' conceptions of themselves and of each other, which become embodied in the act. (It is a familiar enough fact, for example, that people often take their social roles and the social roles of their partners to bed with them.)

The general schema is important, however, and the proliferation of levels of mutual awareness it involves is an example of a type of complexity that typifies human interactions. Consider aggression, for example. If I am angry with someone, I want to make him feel it, either to produce self-reproach by getting him to see himself through the eyes of my anger, and to dislike what he sees—or else to produce reciprocal anger or fear, by getting him to perceive my anger as a threat or attack. What I want will depend on the details of my anger, but in either case it will involve a desire that the object of that anger be aroused. This accomplishment constitutes the fulfillment of my emotion, through domination of the object's feelings.

Another example of such reflexive mutual recognition is to be found in the phenomenon of meaning, which appears to involve an intention to produce a belief or other effect in another by bringing about his recognition of one's intention to produce that effect. (That result is due to H. P. Grice,[2] whose position I shall not attempt to reproduce in detail.) Sex has a related structure: it involves a desire that one's partner be aroused by the recognition of one's desire that he or she be aroused.

It is not easy to define the basic types of awareness and arousal of which these complexes are composed, and that remains a lacuna in this discussion. In a sense, the object of awareness is the same in one's own case as it is in one's sexual awareness of another, although the two awarenesses will not be the same, the difference being as great as that between feeling angry and experiencing the anger of another. All stages of sexual perception are varieties of identification of a person with his body. What is perceived is one's own or another's *subjection* to or *immersion* in his body, a phenomenon which has been recognized with loathing by St. Paul and St. Augustine, both of whom regarded "the law of sin which is in my members" as a grave threat to the dominion of the holy will.[3] In sexual desire and its expression the blending of involuntary response with deliberate control is extremely important. For Augustine, the revolution launched against him by his body is symbolized by erection and the other involuntary physical components of arousal. Sartre too stresses the fact that the penis is not a prehensile organ. But mere involuntariness characterizes other bodily processes as well. In sexual desire the involuntary responses are combined with submission to spontaneous impulses: not only one's pulse and secretions but one's actions are taken over by the body; ideally, deliberate control is needed only to guide the expression of those impulses. This is to some extent also true of an appetite like hunger, but the takeover there is more localized, less pervasive, less extreme. One's whole body does not become saturated with hunger as it can with desire. But the most characteristic feature of a specifically sexual immersion in the body is its ability to fit into the complex of mutual perceptions that we have described. Hunger leads to spontaneous interactions with food; sexual desire leads to spontaneous interactions with other persons, whose bodies are asserting their sovereignty in the same way, producing involuntary reactions and spontaneous impulses in *them*. These reactions are perceived, and the perception of them is perceived, and that perception is in turn perceived; at each step the domination of the person by his body is reinforced, and the sexual partner becomes more possessible by physical contact, penetration, and envelopment.

Desire is therefore not merely the perception of a pre-existing embodiment of the other, but ideally a contribution to his further embodiment which in turn enhances the original subject's sense of himself. This explains why it is important that the partner be aroused, and not merely aroused, but aroused by the awareness of one's desire. It also explains the sense in which desire has unity and possession as its object: physical possession must eventuate in creation of the sexual object in the image of one's desire, and not merely in the object's recognition of that desire, or in his or her own private arousal.

Even if this is a correct model of the adult sexual capacity, it is not plausible to describe as perverted every deviation from it. For example, if the partners in heterosexual intercourse indulge in private heterosexual fantasies, thus avoiding recognition of the real partner, that would, on this model, constitute a defective sexual relation. It is not, however, generally regarded as a perversion. Such examples suggest that a simple dichotomy between perverted and unperverted sex is too crude to organize the phenomena adequately.

Still, various familiar deviations constitute truncated or incomplete versions of the complete configuration, and may be regarded as perversions of the central impulse. If sexual desire is prevented from taking its full interpersonal form, it is likely to find a different one. The concept of perversion implies that a normal sexual development has been turned aside by distorting influences. I have little to say about this causal condition. But if perversions are in some sense unnatural, they must result from interference with the development of a capacity that is there potentially.

It is difficult to apply this condition, because environmental factors play a role in determining the precise form of anyone's sexual impulse. Early experiences in particular seem to determine the choice of a sexual object. To describe some causal influences as distorting and others as merely formative is to imply that certain general aspects of human sexuality realize a definite potential whereas many of the details in which people differ realize an indeterminate potential, so that they cannot be called more or less natural. What is included in the definite potential is therefore very important, although the distinction between definite and indeterminate potential is obscure. Obviously a creature incapable of developing the levels of interpersonal sexual awareness I have described could not be deviant in virtue of the failure to do so. (Though even a chicken might be called perverted in an extended sense if it had been conditioned to develop a fetishistic attachment to a telephone.) But if humans will tend to develop some version of reciprocal interpersonal sexual awareness unless prevented, then cases of blockage can be called unnatural or perverted.

Some familiar deviations can be described in this way. Narcissistic practices and intercourse with animals, infants, and inanimate objects seem to be stuck at some primitive version of the first stage of sexual feeling. If the object is not alive, the experience is reduced entirely to an awareness of one's own sexual embodiment. Small children and animals permit awareness of the embodiment of the other, but present obstacles to reciprocity, to the recognition by the sexual object of the subject's desire as the source of his (the object's) sexual self-awareness. Voyeurism and exhibitionism are also incomplete relations. The exhibitionist wishes to display his desire without needing to be desired in return; he may even fear the sexual attention of others. A voyeur, on the other hand, need not require any recognition by his object at all: certainly not a recognition of the voyeur's arousal.

On the other hand, if we apply our model to the various forms that may be taken by two-party heterosexual intercourse, none of them seem clearly to qualify as perversions. Hardly anyone can be found these days to inveigh against oral-genital contact, and the merits of buggery are urged by such respectable figures as D. H. Lawrence and Norman Mailer. In general, it would appear that any bodily contact between a man and a woman that gives them sexual pleasure is a possible vehicle for the system of multilevel interpersonal awareness that I have claimed is the basic psychological content of sexual interaction. Thus a liberal platitude about sex is upheld.

The really difficult cases are sadism, masochism, and homosexuality. The first two are widely regarded as perversions and the last is controversial. In all three cases the issue depends partly on causal factors: do these dispositions result only when normal development has been prevented? Even the form in which this question has been posed is circular, because of the word "normal." We appear to need an independent criterion for a distorting influence, and we do not have one.

It may be possible to class sadism and masochism as perversions because they fall short of interpersonal reciprocity. Sadism concentrates on the evocation of passive self-awareness in others, but the sadist's engagement is itself active and requires a retention of deliberate control which may impede awareness of himself as a bodily subject of passion in the required sense. De Sade claimed that the object of sexual desire was to evoke involuntary responses from one's partner, especially audible ones. The infliction of pain is no doubt the most efficient way to accomplish this, but it requires a certain abrogation of one's own exposed spontaneity. A masochist on the other hand imposes the same disability on his partner as the sadist imposes on himself. The masochist cannot find a satisfactory embodiment as the object of another's sexual desire, but only as the object of his control. He is passive not in relation to his partner's passion but in relation to his nonpassive agency. In addition, the subjection to one's body characteristic of pain and physical restraint is of a very different kind from that of sexual excitement: pain causes people to contract rather than dissolve. These descriptions may not be generally accurate. But to the extent that they are, sadism and masochism would be disorders of the second stage of awareness—the awareness of oneself as an object of desire.

Homosexuality cannot similarly be classed as a perversion on phenomenological grounds. Nothing rules out the full range of interpersonal perceptions between persons of the same sex. The issue then depends on whether homosexuality is produced by distorting influences that block or displace a natural tendency to heterosexual development. And the influences must be more distorting than those which lead to a taste for large breasts or fair hair or dark eyes. These also are contingencies of sexual preference in which people differ, without being perverted.

The question is whether heterosexuality is the natural expression of male and female sexual dispositions that have not been distorted. It is an unclear question, and I do not know how to approach it. There is much support for an aggressive-passive distinction between male and female sexuality. In our culture the male's arousal tends to initiate the perceptual exchange, he usually makes the sexual approach, largely controls the course of the act, and of course penetrates whereas the woman receives. When two men or two women engage in intercourse they cannot both adhere to these sexual roles. But a good deal of deviation from them occurs in heterosexual intercourse. Women can be sexually aggressive and men passive, and temporary reversals of role are not uncommon in heterosexual exchanges of reasonable length. For these reasons it seems to be doubtful that homosexuality must be a perversion, though like heterosexuality it has perverted forms.

Let me close with some remarks about the relation of perversion to good, bad, and morality. The concept of perversion can hardly fail to be evaluative in some sense, for it appears to involve the notion of an ideal or at least adequate sexuality which the perversions in some way fail to achieve. So, if the concept is viable, the judgment that a person or practice or desire is perverted will constitute a sexual evaluation, implying that better sex, or a better specimen of sex, is possible. This in itself is a very weak claim, since the evaluation might be in a dimension that is of little interest to us. (Though, if my account is correct, that will not be true.)

Whether it is a moral evaluation, however, is another question entirely—one whose answer would require more understanding of both morality and perversion than can be deployed here. Moral evaluation of acts and of persons is a rather special and very complicated matter, and by no means all our evaluations of persons and their activities are moral evaluations. We make judgments about people's beauty or health or intelligence which are evaluative without being moral. Assessments of their sexuality may be similar in that respect.

Furthermore, moral issues aside, it is not clear that unperverted sex is necessarily *preferable* to the perversions. It may be that sex which receives the highest marks for perfection *as sex* is less enjoyable than certain perversions; and if enjoyment is considered very important, that might outweigh considerations of sexual perfection in determining rational preference.

That raises the question of the relation between the evaluative content of judgments of perversion and the rather common *general* distinction between good and bad sex. The latter distinction is usually confined to sexual acts, and it would seem, within limits, to cut across the other: even someone who believed, for example, that homosexuality was a perversion could admit a distinction between better and worse homosexual sex, and might even allow that good homosexual sex could be better sex than not very good unperverted sex. If this is correct, it supports the position that, if judgments of perversion are viable at all, they represent only one aspect of the possible evaluation of sex, even *qua* sex. Moreover it is not the only important aspect: sexual deficiencies that evidently do not constitute perversions can be the object of great concern.

Finally, even if perverted sex is to that extent not so good as it might be, bad sex is generally better than none at all. This should not be controversial: it seems to hold for other important matters, like food, music, literature, and society. In the end, one must choose from among the available alternatives, whether their availability depends on the environment or on one's own constitution. And the alternatives have to be fairly grim before it becomes rational to opt for nothing.

NOTES

1. Jean-Paul Sartre, *L'Etre et le Néant* (Paris: Gallimand, 1943), translated by Hazel E. Barnes (New York: Philosophical Library, 1956).
2. H. P. Grice, "Meaning," *Philosophical Review* lxvi: 3 (July 1957), 377–88.
3. See Romans 7:23; and *Confessions*, bk. viii, pt. v.

STUDY QUESTIONS

1. Try to provide examples of sexual acts that would be judged perverted on Nagel's model yet are not usually considered perverted, and of psychologically complete sexual events that may, nonetheless, be considered perverted by many people. If you can find such examples, what would this mean about the accuracy of Nagel's theory?
2. On what grounds does Nagel argue against sexual desire's being an appetite, such as hunger (or the desire to eat food)? How does sexual desire differ from, and how is it similar to, the desire for pizza? How do these comparisons or contrasts affect Nagel's argument? We can stay alive without eating pizza; we cannot stay alive if we do not eat at all. Can we stay alive without engaging in some sexual activities? Can we stay alive *well*, i.e., flourish, if we are totally abstinent?

3. Nagel writes, "Let us say that X *senses* Y whenever X regards Y with sexual desire. (Y need not be a person, and X's apprehension of Y can be visual, tactile, olfactory, etc., or purely imaginary; in the present example we shall concentrate on vision.)" So Nagel claims that a person could become sexually aroused by someone who is "purely imaginary" (or fantasized). Might he be referring to fantasizing during solitary masturbation, which seems not to be complete sexuality? Indeed, consider also both "deviant" Nagelian patterns (a person is sexually aroused not by the sexual arousal of the other person, but by the other's fear or disgust), and "degenerate" Nagelian patterns (in which one person is aroused not by the genuine arousal of the other person, but by the other person's feigned or pretended arousal).

4. Why does Nagel claim that "bad" sex may be better than none at all? Granted, he does not seem to mean that "morally bad" sex may be better than none. Still, does he claim that perverted sex (a kind of nonideal sex) may be better—more arousing? more satisfying?— than either having no sex at all, or at least better than nonperverted, psychologically complete sex?

5. Nagel proposes that we need an account of the "distorting influences" that cause some people to have unusual sexual preferences. He also admits that this theoretical requirement has the potential of leading any model of sexual perversion into failure. Explain. What are the implications of this problem for a science of sexual perversion, or a medical/psychiatric account of sexual mental health and illness?

6. Nagel is careful to assert that a person who performs a perverted sexual act is not necessarily a perverted person or a pervert. (Someone who performs same-sex sexual acts is, likewise, not necessarily "homosexual" in orientation.) A sexual act rises to the level of a sexual perversion, or a person rises to the level of a pervert, only if psychologically incomplete (or truncated) sexual acts are the preferred route to sexual satisfaction. If so, how can we make sense of Nagel's parenthetical remark that "a chicken might be called perverted in an extended sense if it had been conditioned to develop a fetishistic attachment to a telephone"? Part of the issue is whether it makes sense to talk about a chicken's conditioned response as a preference. Further, should we understand the "distorting influences" and "contingencies of sexual preference" mentioned by Nagel in terms of "conditioning"?

FOUR

Sexual Behavior: Another Position

Janice Moulton

In this essay, **Janice Moulton** *criticizes, among other philosophies of sex, Thomas Nagel's model of natural and unnatural human sexuality (see his "Sexual Perversion," in this volume.) Against Nagel, she argues that although the reciprocal awareness of increasing levels of mutual arousal and embodiment may characterize flirtation, seduction, and the anticipation present in novel sexual encounters, it does not accurately characterize everyday or more ordinary sexual relations or those between partners in longstanding relationships. As a result, "completeness" and "incompleteness" fall short as general accounts of natural human sexual psychology and of human sexual perversion. Moulton professes a skeptical view of the conceptual enterprise in which Nagel and other philosophers engage, and proposes instead the psychological or sociological thesis that people (or we) label as perverted whatever sexual acts strike them (or us) as bizarre.*

Janice Moulton is professor of philosophy at Smith College and coauthor, with George M. Robinson, of *The Organization of Language* (Cambridge University Press, 1981), *Ethical Problems in Higher Education* (Prentice-Hall, 1985), and *Scaling the Dragon* (Cross Cultural Publications, 1994), a whimsical story of her adventures while teaching in the People's Republic of China. This essay is reprinted, with the permission of Janice Moulton and the *Journal of Philosophy*, from *Journal of Philosophy* 73:16 (1976): 537–46.

We can often distinguish behavior that is sexual from behavior that is not. Sexual intercourse may be one clear example of the former, but other sexual behaviors are not so clearly defined. Some kissing is sexual; some is not. Sometimes looking is sexual; sometimes *not* looking is sexual. Is it possible, then, to *characterize* sexual behavior?

Thomas Nagel in "Sexual Perversion"[1] and Robert Solomon in "Sexual Paradigms"[2] each offer an answer to this question. Nagel analyzes sexual desire as a "complex system of superimposed mutual perceptions." He claims that sexual relations that do not fit his account are incomplete and, consequently, perversions. Solomon claims that sexual behavior should be analyzed in terms of goals rather than feelings. He maintains that "the end of this desire is interpersonal communication" and not enjoyment. According to Solomon, the sexual relations between regular partners will be inferior to novel encounters because there is less remaining to communicate sexually.

I believe that sexual behavior will not fit any single characterization; that there are at least two sorts of sexual behavior to characterize. Both Nagel and Solomon have interesting things to say about one sort of sexual behavior. However, both have assumed that a model of flirtation and seduction constitutes an adequate model of sexual behavior in general. Although a characterization of flirtation and seduction can continue to apply to a relationship that is secret, forbidden, or in which there is some reason to remain unsure of one's sexual acceptability, I shall argue that most sexual behavior does not involve flirtation and seduction, and that what characterizes flirtation and seduction is not what characterizes the sexual behavior of regular partners. Nagel takes the development of what I shall call "sexual anticipation" to be characteristic of all sexual behavior and gives no account of sexual satisfaction.[3] Solomon believes that flirtation and seduction are different from regular sexual relationships. However, he too considers only characteristics of sexual anticipation in his analysis and concludes that regular sexual relationships are inferior to novel ones because they lack some of those characteristics.

Flirtation, seduction, and traditional courtship involve sexual feelings that are quite independent of physical contact. These feelings are increased by anticipation of success, winning, or conquest. Because what is anticipated is the opportunity for sexual intimacy and satisfaction, the feelings of sexual satisfaction are usually not distinguished from those of sexual anticipation. Sexual satisfaction involves sexual feelings which are increased by the other person's knowledge of one's preferences and sensitivities, the familiarity of their touch or smell or way of moving, and not by the novelty of their sexual interest.

It is easy to think that the more excitement and enthusiasm involved in the anticipation of an event, the more enjoyable and exciting the event itself is likely to be. However, anticipation and satisfaction are often divorced. Many experiences with no associated build-up of anticipation are very satisfying, and others, awaited and begun with great eagerness, produce no feelings of satisfaction at all. In sexual activity this dissociation is likely to be frequent. A strong feeling of sexual anticipation is produced by the uncertainty, challenge, or secrecy of novel sexual experiences, but the tension and excitement that increase anticipation often interfere with sexual satisfaction. The comfort and trust and experience with familiar partners may increase sexual satisfaction, but decrease the uncertainty and challenge that heighten sexual anticipation. Given the distinction between anticipation and satisfaction, there is no reason to believe that an increase of trust and love ought to increase feelings of sexual anticipation or that sexual anticipation should be a prerequisite for any long-term sexual relationship.

For some people the processes that create sexual anticipation, the exchange of indirect signals, the awareness of the other person's sexual interest, and the accompanying sexual anticipation may be *all* that is valued in sexual behavior. Satisfaction is equated with release, the end of a good time, and is not considered a process in its own right. But although flirtation and seduction are the main objects of sexual fantasy and fiction, most people, even those whose sexual relations are frequently casual, seek to continue some sexual relationships after the flirtation and seduction are over, when the uncertainty and challenge are gone. And the motives, goals, and feelings of sexual satisfaction that characterize these continued sexual relations are not the same as the motives, goals, and feelings of sexual anticipation that characterize the novel sexual relations Nagel and Solomon have tried to analyze. Let us consider their accounts.

Nagel's account is illustrated by a tale of a Romeo and a Juliet who are sexually aroused by each other, notice each other's arousal and become further aroused by that:

> He senses that she senses that he senses her. This is still another level of arousal, for he becomes conscious of his sexuality through his awareness of its effect on her and of her awareness that this effect is due to him. Once she takes the same step and senses that he senses her sensing him, it becomes difficult to state, let alone imagine, further iterations, though they may be logically distinct. If both are alone, they will presumably turn to look at each other directly, and the proceedings will continue on another plane. Physical contact and intercourse are natural extensions of this complicated visual exchange, and mutual touch can involve all the complexities of awareness present in the visual case, but with a far greater range of subtlety and acuteness.
>
> Ordinarily, of course, things happen in a less orderly fashion— sometimes in a great rush—but I believe that some version of this overlapping system of distinct sexual perceptions and interactions is the basic framework of any full-fledged sexual relation and that relations involving only part of the complex are significantly incomplete.

Nagel then characterizes sexual perversion as a "truncated or incomplete version" of sexual *arousal*, rather than as some deviation from a standard of subsequent physical interaction.

Nagel's account applies only to the development of sexual anticipation. He says that "the proliferation of levels of mutual awareness . . . is . . . a type of complexity that typifies human interactions," so he might argue that his account will cover Romeo and Juliet's later relationship as well. Granted that levels of mutual awareness exist in any close human relationship. But it does not follow that the development of levels of awareness *characterize* all human relationships, particularly sexual relationships between familiar partners. In particular, the sort of awareness Nagel emphasizes—"a desire that one's partner be aroused by the recognition of one's desire that he or she be aroused"—does not seem essential to regular sexual relationships. If we accept Nagel's account for sexual behavior in general, then we must classify as a perversion the behavior of an intimate and satisfying sexual relation begun without any preliminary exchange of multilevel arousals. [4]

Sexual desire can be generated by many different things—a smell, a phrase in a book, a familiar voice. The sexual interest of another person is only on occasion novel enough to be the main cause or focus of sexual arousal. A characterization of sexual behavior on other occasions should describe the development and sharing of sexual pleasure—the creation of sexual satisfaction. Nagel's contribution lies in directing our attention to the analysis of sexual behavior in terms of its perceptions and feelings. However, he characterizes only a limited sort of sexual behavior, flirtation and seduction.

Solomon characterizes sexual behavior by analogy with linguistic behavior, emphasizing that the goals are the same. He says:

> Sexual activity consists in speaking what we might call "body language." It has it own grammar, delineated by the body, and its own phonetics of touch and movement. Its unit of meaningfulness, the bodily equivalent of a sentence, is the *gesture*. . . . [B]ody language is essentially expressive, and its content is limited to interpersonal attitudes and feelings.

The analogy with language can be valuable for understanding sexual behavior. However, Solomon construes the goals of both activities too narrowly and hence draws the wrong conclusions. He argues that the aim of sexual behavior is to communicate one's attitudes and feelings, to express oneself, and further, that such self-expression is made less effective by aiming at enjoyment:

> That is why the liberal mythology has been so disastrous, for it has rendered unconscious the expressive functions of sex in its stress on enjoyment. . . . It is thus understandable why sex is so utterly important in our lives, and why it is typically so unsatisfactory.

Does stress on enjoyment hinder self-expression? Trying to do one thing, X, may interfere with trying to do another, Y, for some Xs and Ys. For example, trying to eat peanut butter or swim under water may interfere with vocal self-expression. But enjoyment is a different sort of goal. One isn't trying to do both Y and something else when aiming at Y and enjoyment, but to do one sort of thing, Y, a certain way. Far from interfering, one is more likely to be successful at a venture if one can manage to enjoy oneself during the process.

Solomon claims to refute that enjoyment is the essential aim of sexual activity, but he erroneously identifies enjoyment with orgasm:[5]

> No one would deny that sex is enjoyable, but it does not follow that sexuality is the activity of "pure enjoyment" and that "gratification," or "pure physical pleasure," that is, orgasm, is its end.

Consequently he shows merely that orgasm is not the only aim of sexual activity. His main argument is:

> If sex is pure physical enjoyment, why is sexual activity between persons far more satisfying than masturbation, where, if we accept recent physiological studies, orgasm is at its highest intensity and the post-coital period is cleansed of its interpersonal hassles and arguments?

One obvious answer is that, even for people who have hassles and arguments, interpersonal sexual activity is more enjoyable, even in the "pure physical" sense.[6] Solomon's argument does not show that enjoyment is not the appropriate aim of sexual activity, only that maximum-intensity orgasm is not. As those recent physiological studies pointed out, participants report interpersonal sexual activity as more enjoyable and satisfying even though their orgasms are less intense.[7] Only someone who mistakenly equated enjoyment with orgasm would find this paradoxical.

One need not claim that orgasm is always desired or desirable in sexual activity. That might be like supposing that in all conversations the participants do, or should, express their deepest thoughts. In sexual, as in linguistic, behavior, there is great variety and subtlety of purpose. But this is not to say that the desire for orgasm should be ignored. The disappointment and physical discomfort of expected but unachieved orgasm is only faintly parallel to the frustration of not being able to "get a word in edgewise" after being moved to express an important thought. It is usually rude or boorish to use language with indifference to the interests and cares of one's listeners. Sexual behavior with such indifference can be no better.

Solomon does not need these arguments to claim that enjoyment is not the only or the essential goal of sexual behavior. His comparison of sexual behavior with linguistic (or other social) behavior could have been used to do the job. The same social and moral distinctions and evaluations can be applied to both behaviors: hurting and humiliating people is bad; making people happy is good; loyalty, kindness, intelligence, and wit are valued; stupidity, clumsiness, and insincerity are not. The purpose of contact, sexual or otherwise, with other people is not just to produce or receive enjoyment—there are times of sadness, solace, and anguish that are important and meaningful to share, but not enjoyable.

Is self-expression, then, the essential goal of sexual behavior? Solomon lists a number of feelings and attitudes that can be expressed sexually:

- *love, tenderness and trust, "being-with," mutual recognition*
- hatred, indifference, jealousy, conflict
- shyness, fear, lack of confidence, embarrassment, shame
- domination, submissiveness, dependence, possessiveness, passivity

He claims "some attitudes, e.g., tenderness and trust, domination and passivity, are best expressed sexually," and says his account makes it evident why Nagel chose as his example a couple of strangers; one has far more to say, for one can freely express one's fantasies as well as the truth, to a stranger. A husband and wife of seven years have probably been repeating the same messages for years, and their sexual activity now is probably no more than an abbreviated ritual incantation of the lengthy conversations they had years before.

A glance at the list of feelings and attitudes above will show that its items are not independent. Shame, for example, may include components of embarrassment, lack of confidence, fear, and probably mutual recognition and submissiveness. To the extent that they can be conveyed by sexual body language,[8] a mere grunt or whimper would be able to express the whole range of the attitudes and feelings as well, if not better, than sexual gestures. Moreover, it is not clear that some attitudes are best expressed sexually. Tenderness and trust are often expressed between people who are not sexual partners. The tenderness and trust that may exist between an adult and a child are not best expressed sexually. Even if we take Solomon's claim to apply only to sexual partners, a joint checking account may be a better expression of trust than sexual activity. And domination, which in sadomasochistic sexual activity is expressed most elaborately with the cooperation of the partner, is an attitude much better expressed by nonsexual activities[9] such as beating an opponent, firing an employee, or mugging a passerby, where the domination is real, and does not require the cooperation of the other person. Even if some attitudes and feelings (for example, prurience, wantonness, lust) are best expressed sexually, it would be questionable whether the primary aim of sexual activity should be to express them.

The usual conversation of strangers is "small talk": cautious, shallow, and predictable because there has not been time for the participants to assess the extent and nature of common interests they share. So too with sexual behavior; first sexual encounters may be charged with novelty and anticipation, but are usually characterized by stereotypic physical interactions. If the physical interaction is seen as "body language," the analogy with linguistic behavior suggests that first encounters are likely to consist of sexual small talk.

Solomon's comparison of sexual behavior with linguistic behavior is handicapped by the limited view he has about their purposes. Language has more purposes than transmitting information. If all there were to sexual behavior was the development of the sexual anticipation prominent in flirtation and seduction, then Solomon's conclusions might be correct. The fact that people will continue sexual relations with the same partners even after the appropriate attitudes and feelings from Solomon's list have been expressed indicates that sexual behavior, like linguistic behavior, has other functions that are important. Solomon's analogy with linguistic behavior is valuable not because communication is the main goal of sexual behavior but because he directs attention to the social nature of sexual behavior. Solomon's analogy can be made to take on new importance by considering that sexual behavior not only transmits information about feelings and attitudes—something any activity can do—but also, like language, it has a *phatic* function to evoke feelings and attitudes.

Language is often used to produce a shared experience, a feeling of togetherness or unity. Duets, greetings, and many religious services use language with little information content to establish or reaffirm a relation among the participants. Long-term sexual relationships, like regular musical ensembles, may be valued more for the feelings produced than the feelings communicated. With both sexual and linguistic behavior, an interaction with a stranger might be an enjoyable novelty, but the pleasures of linguistic and sexual activity with good friends are probably much more frequent and more reliable. Solomon's conclusion that sexually one should have more to "say" to a stranger and will find oneself "repeating the same messages for years" to old acquaintances,[10] violates the analogy. With natural language, one usually has more to say to old friends than to strangers.

Both Nagel and Solomon give incomplete accounts because they assume that a characterization of flirtation and seduction should apply to sexual behavior in general. I have argued that this is not so. Whether we analyze sexual behavior in terms of characteristic perceptions and feelings, as Nagel does, or by a comparison with other complex social behavior, as Solomon does, the characteristics of novel sexual encounters differ from those of sexual relationships between familiar and recognized partners.

What about the philosophical enterprise of characterizing sexual behavior? A characterization of something will tell us what is unique about it and how to identify a standard or paradigm case of it. Criteria for a standard or paradigm case of sexual behavior unavoidably have normative implications. It is my position that normative judgments about sexual behavior should not be unrelated to the social and moral standards that apply to other social behavior. Many people, in reaction to old standards, avoid disapproving of sexual behavior that involves deceit or humiliation to another, but will condemn or ridicule sexual behavior that hurts no one yet fails to conform to a sexual standard. Both Nagel and

Solomon classify sexual behavior that does not fit their characterizations as perversion, extending this strong negative judgment to behavior that is neither morally nor socially condemned (i.e., sex without multilevel awareness of arousal; sex without communication of attitudes and feelings). Yet perversion can be more accurately accounted for as whatever makes people frightened or uncomfortable by its bizarreness.[11]

Sexual behavior differs from other behavior by virtue of its unique feelings and emotions and its unique ability to create shared intimacy. These unique features of sexual behavior may influence particular normative judgments, but they do not justify applying *different* normative principles to sexual behavior.[12]

NOTES

1. *Journal of Philosophy* 66: 1 (1969): 5–17 [in this volume].

2. *Journal of Philosophy* 71: 11 (1974): 336–45. (Reprinted in Alan Soble, ed., *The Philosophy of Sex*, 3rd edition [Lanham, Md.: Rowman and Littlefield, 2002], 21–29.)

3. Satisfaction includes the good feelings of intimacy, warm friendship, the pleasure of being appreciated and of giving pleasure. "Satisfaction" is not intended as a euphemism for orgasm, although the physical and social discomforts of the absence of orgasm often make a feeling of satisfaction impossible.

4. This was first pointed out to me by Sara Ketchum.

5. Solomon also claims that aiming at *orgasm* "overwhelms or distorts whatever else is being said sexually." In this case there might be interference. However, if one is trying to express feelings and attitudes through the giving or having of an orgasm, then "aiming at self-expression" and "aiming at orgasm" will describe the same activity and there will be no interference. It should be pointed out that whatever else is being said sexually should have been said before orgasm is imminent or should be postponed because one will not do a very good job of transmitting or receiving any other communication during orgasm. Instead of an objection to aiming at orgasm, the potential interference raises an objection to aiming at self-expression during the time that orgasm is the goal.

6. Several theories of motivation in psychology (e.g., [David] McClelland's) easily incorporate this fact: Creatures find moderate discrepancies from predicted sensation more pleasurable than sensations that are completely expected. Sensations produced by a sexual partner are not as adequately predicted as autoerotic stimulation.

7. William Masters and Virginia Johnson, *Human Sexual Response* (Boston: Little, Brown, 1966), 113.

8. More than gestures must be employed to communicate such feelings as love, trust, hatred, shame, dependence, and possessiveness. I doubt that jealousy or a distinction between "one's fantasies [and] the truth" (Solomon) can be communicated by sexual body language at all.

9. In her comments on a version of this paper at the 1976 Pacific Division American Philosophical Association meetings, Sara Ketchum pointed out that I have completely overlooked one sort of sexual activity in which the domination is real and the cooperation of the other person is not required: rape.

10. Repeated messages about one's feelings are not merely redundant; they convey new information: the continuation, renewal, or salience of those feelings.

11. See Mary Douglas, *Purity and Danger* (London: Routledge & Kegan Paul, 1966).

12. This paper has been greatly improved by the discussions and careful criticisms of G. M. Robinson and Helen Heise, the suggestions of Tim Binkley and Jay Rosenberg that it be expanded, and the comments from audiences of The Society for Women in Philosophy and the American Philosophical Association.

STUDY QUESTIONS

1. Even if we agree with Moulton that the psychologies of flirtation, seduction, and anticipation differ in important ways from the psychology of more routine sexual events, does this entail that Nagel is wrong to think that the reciprocal awareness of embodiment that deepens arousal is significantly absent from more routine sexual events? Similarly, is it possible that much routine sex also involves, even if in a brief or rudimentary way, some of the elements of flirtation, seduction, or anticipation?

2. How does Moulton account for the fact that we (apparently) prefer engaging in sexual activity with other people as opposed to solitary masturbation, even at the cost of a less intense orgasm? Explore the implications of her explanation. What might be more important in producing sexual satisfaction, the novelty or newness of a touch or partner's body, or his or her familiarity? Does sex/gender matter here?

3. Philosophers have been trying to understand the nature of sexuality, and to provide convincing analyses of concepts such as "sexual activity," "sexual desire," and so forth. Moulton's contribution to this ongoing discussion might be summarized in her claim, "sexual behavior differs from other behavior by virtue of its unique feelings and emotions and its unique ability to create shared intimacy." Are you able to state clearly the several sorts of uniqueness that Moulton attributes to sexuality? Is she correct to find unique "feelings and emotions" in sexual behavior?

4. Identify some advantages and disadvantages of Moulton's account of sexual perversion in terms of what people find "bizarre." Think over this question again after reading Alan Goldman's claims about sexual perversion (see his "Plain Sex," in this volume).

5. Moulton is a woman; Nagel is a man. Might it be argued plausibly that sex/gender has influenced their differing views not only about sexuality but also in their philosophies of sexuality? Provide specific examples from each essay that might support (or refute) the idea that their ideas are sex/gender-related.

FIVE

Plain Sex

Alan Goldman

Whereas many accounts of human sexuality connect, in some way or another, sexual activity to love, marriage, or progeny, **Alan Goldman** *believes that it is a mistake to focus on these contingent ends or purposes of sexual desire and activity as either conceptually or morally central for understanding sexuality. His title, "Plain Sex," is meant to alert us that if we want to capture the lowest common denominator of all sexuality, and if we want to expose what is analytically central to sexuality per se, we had better ignore these variable concomitants of sexuality. His proposal is that sexual desire is simply the desire for certain pleasures that are produced by bodily contact and that sexual activity is activity that "tends to fulfill" this desire for pleasurable contact. Goldman provides arguments that his account of sexual desire is neither overly broad (i.e., does not judge to be sexual, desires that are not sexual) nor too narrow (i.e., does not fail to judge as sexual, desires that are sexual). Assuming that his analyses of "plain" sexual desire and activity are correct, Goldman then explores the morality of sexual behavior and the notion of sexual perversion. In particular, he advances an interesting interpretation of Immanuel Kant's ethics (the Formula of Humanity) as applied to sexual behavior, which the student should keep in mind when reading the essays in part III and part IV of this volume.*

Alan Goldman is the Kenan Professor of Humanities at the College of William and Mary. He is the author of *Justice and Reverse Discrimination* (Princeton, 1979); *The Moral Foundations of Professional Ethics* (Rowman & Littlefield, 1980); *Empirical Knowledge* (California, 1988); *Moral Knowledge* (Routledge, 1988); *Aesthetic Value* (Westview, 1995); *Practical Rules: When We Need Them and When We Don't* (Cambridge, 2002); and *Reasons from Within: Desires and Values* (Oxford, 2010). This essay is Alan Goldman, "Plain Sex," *Philosophy and Public Affairs* 6:3 (1977): 267–87. © 1977, Princeton University Press. It is reprinted by permission of the publisher, Blackwell, Oxford, U.K.

I

Several recent articles on sex herald its acceptance as a legitimate topic for analytic philosophers (although it has been a topic in philosophy since Plato). One might have thought conceptual analysis unnecessary in this area; despite the notorious struggles of judges and legislators to define pornography suitably, we all might be expected to know what sex is and to be able to identify at least paradigm sexual desires and activities without much difficulty.

Philosophy is nevertheless of relevance here if for no other reason than that the concept of sex remains at the center of moral and social consciousness in our, and perhaps any, society. Before we can get a sensible view of the relation of sex to morality, perversion, social regulation, and marriage, we require a sensible analysis of the concept itself; one which neither understates its animal pleasure nor overstates its importance within a theory or system of value. I say "before," but the order is not quite so clear, for questions in this area, as elsewhere in moral philosophy, are both conceptual and normative at the same time. Our concept of sex will partially determine our moral view of it, but as philosophers we should formulate a concept that will accord with its proper moral status. What we require here, as elsewhere, is "reflective equilibrium," a goal not achieved by traditional and recent analyses together with their moral implications. Because sexual activity, like other natural functions such as eating or exercising, has become embedded in layers of cultural, moral, and superstitious superstructure, it is hard to conceive it in its simplest terms. But partially for this reason, it is only by thinking about plain sex that we can begin to achieve this conceptual equilibrium.

I shall suggest here that sex continues to be misrepresented in recent writings, at least in philosophical writings, and I shall criticize the predominant form of analysis which I term "means–end analysis." Such conceptions attribute a necessary external goal or purpose to sexual activity, whether it be reproduction, the expression of love, simple communication, or interpersonal awareness. They analyze sexual activity as a means to one of these ends, implying that sexual desire is a desire to reproduce, to love or be loved, or to communicate with others. All definitions of this type suggest false views of the relation of sex to perversion and morality by implying that sex which does not fit one of these models or fulfill one of these functions is in some way deviant or incomplete.

The alternative, simpler analysis with which I will begin is that sexual desire is desire for contact with another person's body and for the pleasure which such contact produces; sexual activity is activity which tends to fulfill such desire of the agent. Whereas Aristotle and Butler were correct in holding that pleasure is normally a byproduct rather than a goal of purposeful action, in the case of sex this is not so clear. The desire for another's body is, principally among other things, the desire for the pleasure that physical contact brings. On the other hand, it is not a desire for a particular sensation detachable from its causal context, a sensation which can be derived in other ways. This definition in terms of the general goal of sexual desire appears preferable to an attempt to more explicitly list or define specific sexual activities, for many activities such as kissing, embracing, massaging, or holding hands may or may not be sexual, depending upon the context and more specifically upon the purposes, needs, or desires into which such activities fit. The generality of the definition also represents a refusal (common in recent psychological texts) to overemphasize orgasm as the goal of sexual desire or genital sex as the only norm of sexual activity (this will be hedged slightly in the discussion of perversion below).

Central to the definition is the fact that the goal of sexual desire and activity is the physical contact itself, rather than something else which this contact might express. By contrast, what I term "means–end analyses" posit ends which I take to be extraneous to plain sex, and they view sex as a means to these ends. Their fault lies not in defining sex in terms of its general goal, but in seeing plain sex as merely a means to other separable ends. I term these "means–end analyses" for convenience, although "means–separable–end analysis," while too cumbersome, might be more fully explanatory. The desire for physical contact with another person is a minimal criterion for (normal) sexual desire, but is both necessary and sufficient to qualify normal desire as sexual. Of course, we may want to express other feelings through sexual acts in various contexts; but without the desire for the physical contact in and for itself, or when it is sought for other reasons, activities in which contact is involved are not predominantly sexual. Furthermore, the desire for physical contact in itself, without the wish to express affection or other feelings through it, is sufficient to render sexual the activity of the agent which fulfills it. Various activities with this goal alone, such as kissing and caressing in certain contexts, qualify as sexual even without the presence of genital symptoms of sexual excitement. The latter are not therefore necessary criteria for sexual activity.

This initial analysis may seem to some either over- or underinclusive. It might seem too broad in leading us to interpret physical contact as sexual desire in activities such as football and other contact sports. In these cases, however, the desire is not for contact with another body per se, it is not directed toward a particular person for that purpose, and it is not the goal of the activity—the goal is winning or exercising or knocking someone down or displaying one's prowess. If the desire is purely for contact with another specific person's body, then to interpret it as sexual does not seem an exaggeration. A slightly more difficult case is that of a baby's desire to be cuddled and our natural response in wanting to cuddle it. In the case of the baby, the desire may be simply for the physical contact, for the pleasure of the caresses. If so, we may characterize this desire, especially in keeping with Freudian theory, as sexual or protosexual. It will differ nevertheless from full-fledged sexual desire in being more amorphous, not directed outward toward another specific person's body. It may also be that what the infant unconsciously desires is not physical contact per se but signs of affection, tenderness, or security, in which case we have further reason for hesitating to characterize its wants as clearly sexual. The intent of our response to the baby is often the showing of affection, not the pure physical contact, so that our definition in terms of action which fulfills sexual desire *on the part of the agent* does not capture such actions, whatever we say of the baby. (If it is intuitive to characterize our responses as sexual as well, there is clearly no problem here for my analysis.) The same can be said of signs of affection (or in some cultures polite greeting) among men or women: these certainly need not be homosexual when the intent is only to show friendship, something extrinsic to plain sex although valuable when added to it.

Our definition of sex in terms of the desire for physical contact may appear too narrow in that a person's personality, not merely her or his body, may be sexually attractive to another, and in that looking or conversing in a certain way can be sexual in a given context without bodily contact. Nevertheless, it is not the contents of one's thoughts per se that are sexually appealing, but one's personality as embodied in certain manners of behavior. Furthermore, if a person is sexually attracted by another's personality, he or she will desire not just further conversation, but actual sexual contact. While looking at or conversing with someone can be interpreted as sexual in given contexts it is so when intended as preliminary to, and hence parasitic upon, elemental sexual interest. Voyeurism or viewing a pornographic movie qualifies as a sexual activity, but only as an imaginative substitute for the real thing (otherwise a deviation from the norm as expressed in our definition). The same is true of masturbation as a sexual activity without a partner.

That the initial definition indicates at least an ingredient of sexual desire and activity is too obvious to argue. We all know what sex is, at least in obvious cases, and do not need philosophers to tell us. My preliminary analysis is meant to serve as a contrast to what sex is not, at least not necessarily. I concentrate upon the physically manifested desire for another's body, and I take as central the immersion in the physical aspect of one's own existence and attention to the physical embodiment of the other. One may derive pleasure in a sex act from expressing certain feelings to one's partner or from awareness of the attitude of one's partner, but sexual desire is essentially desire for physical contact itself. It is a bodily desire for the body of another that dominates our mental life for more or less brief periods. Traditional writings were correct to emphasize the purely physical or animal aspect of sex; they were wrong only in condemning it. This characterization of sex as an intensely pleasurable physical activity and acute physical desire may seem to some to capture only its barest level. But it is worth distinguishing and focusing upon this least common denominator in order to avoid the false views of sexual morality and perversion which emerge from thinking that sex is essentially something else.

II

We may turn then to what sex is not, to the arguments regarding supposed conceptual connections between sex and other activities which it is necessary to conceptually distinguish. The most comprehensible attempt to build an extraneous purpose into the sex act identifies that purpose as reproduction, its primary biological function. While this may be "nature's" purpose, it certainly need not be ours (the analogy with eating, while sometimes overworked, is pertinent here). While this identification may once have had a rational basis which also grounded the identification of the value and morality of sex with that applicable to reproduction and childrearing, the development of contraception rendered the connection weak. Methods of contraception are by now so familiar and so widely used that it is not necessary to dwell upon the changes wrought by these developments in the concept of sex itself and in a rational sexual ethic dependent upon that concept. In the past, the ever-present possibility of children rendered the concepts of sex and sexual morality different from those required at present. There may be good reasons, if the presence and care of both mother and father are beneficial to children, for restricting reproduction to marriage. Insofar as society has a legitimate role in protecting children's interests, it may be justified in giving marriage a legal status, although this question is complicated by the fact (among others) that children born to single mothers deserve no penalties. In any case, the point here is simply that these questions are irrelevant at the present time to those regarding the morality of sex and its potential social regulation. (Further connections with marriage will be discussed below.)

It is obvious that the desire for sex is not necessarily a desire to reproduce, that the psychological manifestation has become, if it were not always, distinct from its biological roots. There are many parallels, as previously mentioned, with other natural functions. The pleasures of eating and exercising are to a large extent independent of their roles in nourishment or health (as the junk-food industry discovered with a vengeance). Despite the obvious parallel with sex, there is still a tendency for many to think that sex acts which can be reproductive are, if not more moral or less immoral, at least more natural. These categories of morality and "naturalness," or normality, are not to be identified with each other, as will be argued below, and neither is applicable to sex by virtue of its connection to reproduction. The tendency to identify reproduction as the conceptually connected end of sex is most prevalent now in the pronouncements of the Catholic Church. There the assumed analysis is clearly tied to a restrictive sexual morality according to which acts become immoral and unnatural when they are not oriented toward reproduction, a morality which has independent roots in the Christian sexual ethic as it derives from Paul. However, the means–end analysis fails to generate a consistent sexual ethic: homosexual and oral-genital sex is condemned while kissing or caressing, acts equally unlikely to lead in themselves to fertilization, even when properly characterized as sexual according to our definition, are not.

III

Before discussing further relations of means–end analyses to false or inconsistent sexual ethics and concepts of perversion, I turn to other examples of these analyses. One common position views sex as essentially an expression of love or affection between the partners. It is generally recognized that there are other types of love besides sexual, but sex itself is taken as an expression of one type, sometimes termed "romantic" love.[1] Various factors again ought to weaken this identification. First, there are other types of love besides that which it is appropriate to express sexually, and "romantic" love itself can be expressed in many other ways. I am not denying that sex can take on heightened value and meaning when it becomes a vehicle for the expression of feelings of love or tenderness, but so can many other usually mundane activities such as getting up early to make breakfast on Sunday, cleaning the house, and so on. Second, sex itself can be used to communicate many other emotions besides love, and, as I will argue below, can communicate nothing in particular and still be good sex.

On a deeper level, an internal tension is bound to result from an identification of sex, which I have described as a physical-psychological desire, with love as a long-term, deep emotional relationship between two individuals. As this type of relationship, love is permanent, at least in intent, and more or less exclusive. A normal person cannot deeply love more than a few individuals even in a lifetime. We may be suspicious that those who attempt or claim to love many love them weakly if at all. Yet, fleeting sexual desire can arise in relation to a variety of other individuals one finds sexually attractive. It may even be, as some have claimed, that sexual desire in humans naturally seeks variety, while this is obviously false of love. For this reason, monogamous sex, even if justified, almost always represents a sacrifice or the exercise of self-control on the part of the spouses, while monogamous love generally does not. There is no such thing as casual love in the sense in which I intend the term "love." It may occasionally happen that a spouse falls deeply in love with someone else (especially when sex is conceived in terms of love), but this is relatively rare in comparison to passing sexual desires for others; and while the former often indicates a weakness or fault in the marriage relation, the latter does not.

If love is indeed more exclusive in its objects than is sexual desire, this explains why those who view sex as essentially an expression of love would again tend to hold a repressive or restrictive sexual ethic. As in the case of reproduction, there may be good reasons for reserving the total commitment of deep love to the context of marriage and family—the normal personality may not withstand additional divisions of ultimate commitment and allegiance. There is no question that marriage itself is best sustained by a deep relation of love and affection; and even if love is not naturally monogamous, the benefits of family units to children provide additional reason to avoid serious commitments elsewhere which weaken family ties. It can be argued similarly that monogamous sex strengthens families by restricting and at the same time guaranteeing an outlet for sexual desire in marriage. But there is more force to the argument that recognition of a clear distinction between sex and love in society would help avoid disastrous marriages which result from adolescent confusion of the two when sexual desire is mistaken for permanent love, and would weaken damaging jealousies which arise in marriages in relation to passing sexual desires. The love and affection of a sound marriage certainly differ from the adolescent romantic variety, which is often a mere substitute for sex in the context of a repressive sexual ethic.

In fact, the restrictive sexual ethic tied to the means–end analysis in terms of love again has failed to be consistent. At least, it has not been applied consistently, but forms part of the double standard which has curtailed the freedom of women. It is predictable in light of this history that some women would now advocate using sex as another kind of means, as a political weapon or as a way to increase unjustly denied power and freedom. The inconsistency in the sexual ethic typically attached to the sex-love analysis, according to which it has generally been taken with a grain of salt when applied to men, is simply another example of the impossibility of tailoring a plausible moral theory in this area to a conception of sex which builds in conceptually extraneous factors.

I am not suggesting here that sex ought never to be connected with love or that it is not a more significant and valuable activity when it is. Nor am I denying that individuals need love as much as sex and perhaps emotionally need at least one complete relationship which encompasses both. Just as sex can express love and take on heightened significance when it does, so love is often naturally accompanied by an intermittent desire for sex. But again love is accompanied appropriately by desires for other shared activities as well. What makes the desire for sex seem more intimately connected with love is the intimacy which is seen to be a natural feature of mutual sex acts. Like love, sex is held to lay one bare psychologically as well as physically. Sex is unquestionably intimate, but beyond that the psychological toll often attached may be a function of the restrictive sexual ethic itself, rather than a legitimate apology for it. The intimacy involved in love is psychologically consuming in a generally healthy way, while the psychological tolls of sexual relations, often including embarrassment as a correlate of intimacy, are too often the result of artificial sexual ethics and taboos. The intimacy involved in both love and sex is insufficient in any case in light of previous points to render a means–end analysis in these terms appropriate.

IV

In recent articles, Thomas Nagel and Robert Solomon, who recognize that sex is not merely a means to communicate love, nevertheless retain the form of this analysis while broadening it. For Solomon, sex remains a means of communicating (he explicitly uses the metaphor of body language), although the feelings that can be communicated now include, in addition to love and tenderness, domination, dependence, anger, trust, and so on.[2] Nagel does not refer explicitly to communication, but his analysis is similar in that he views sex as a complex form of interpersonal awareness in which desire itself is consciously communicated on several different levels. In sex, according to his analysis, two people are aroused by each other, aware of the other's arousal, and further aroused by this awareness.[3] Such multileveled conscious awareness of one's own and the other's desire is taken as the norm of a sexual relation, and this model is therefore close to that which views sex as a means of interpersonal communication.

Solomon's analysis is beset by the same difficulties as those pointed out in relation to the narrower sex-love concept. Just as love can be communicated by many activities other than sex, which do not therefore become properly analyzed as essentially vehicles of communication (making breakfast, cleaning the house, and so on), the same is true of the other feelings mentioned by Solomon. Domination can be communicated through economic manipulation, trust by a joint savings account. Driving a car can be simultaneously expressing anger, pride, joy, and so on. We may, in fact, communicate or express feelings in anything we do, but this does not make everything we do into language. Driving a car is not to be defined as an automotive means of communication, although with a little ingenuity we might work out an automotive vocabulary (tailgating as an expression of aggression or impatience; beating another car away from a stoplight as expressing domination) to match the vocabulary of "body language." That one can communicate various feelings during sex acts does not make these acts merely or primarily a means of communicating.

More importantly, to analyze sex as a means of communication is to overlook the intrinsic nature and value of the act itself. Sex is not a gesture or series of gestures, in fact not necessarily a means to any other end, but a physical activity intensely pleasurable in itself. When a language is used, the symbols normally have no importance in themselves; they function merely as vehicles for what can be communicated by them. Furthermore, skill in the use of language is a technical achievement that must be carefully learned; if better sex is more successful communication by means of a more skillful use of body language, then we had all better be well schooled in the vocabulary and grammar. Solomon's analysis, which uses the language metaphor, suggests the appropriateness of a sex-manual approach, the substitution of a bit of technological prowess for the natural pleasure of the unforced surrender to feeling and desire.

It may be that Solomon's position could be improved by using the analogy of music rather than that of language, as an aesthetic form of communication. Music might be thought of as a form of aesthetic communicating, in which the experience of the "phonemes" themselves is generally pleasing. And listening to music is perhaps more of a sexual experience than having someone talk to you. Yet, it seems to me that insofar as music is aesthetic and pleasing in itself, it is not best conceived as primarily a means for communicating specific feelings. Such an analysis does injustice to aesthetic experience in much the same way as the sex-communication analysis debases sexual experience itself.[4]

For Solomon, sex that is not a totally self-conscious communicative act tends toward vulgarity,[5] whereas I would have thought it the other way around. This is another illustration of the tendency of means–end analyses to condemn what appears perfectly natural or normal sex on my account. Both Solomon and Nagel use their definitions, however, not primarily to stipulate moral norms for sex, as we saw in earlier analyses, but to define norms against which to measure perversion. Once again, neither is capable of generating consistency or reflective equilibrium with our firm intuitions as to what counts as subnormal sex, the problem being that both build factors into their norms which are extraneous to an unromanticized view of normal sexual desire and activity. If perversion represents a breakdown in communication, as Solomon maintains, then any unsuccessful or misunderstood advance should count as perverted. Furthermore, sex between husband and wife married for several years, or between any partners already familiar with each other, would be, if not perverted, nevertheless subnormal or trite and dull, in that the communicative content would be minimal in lacking all novelty. In fact, the pleasures of sex need not wear off with familiarity, as they would if dependent upon the communicative content of the feelings. Finally, rather than a release or relief from physical desire through a substitute imaginative outlet, masturbation would become a way of practicing or rehearsing one's technique or vocabulary on oneself, or simply a way of talking to oneself, as Solomon himself says. [6]

Nagel fares no better in the implications of his overintellectualized norm. Spontaneous and heated sex between two familiar partners may well lack the complex conscious multileveled interpersonal awareness of which he speaks without being in the least perverted. The egotistical desire that one's partner be aroused by one's own desire does not seem a primary element of the sexual urge, and during sex acts one may like one's partner to be sometimes active and aroused, sometimes more passive. Just as sex can be more significant when love is communicated, so it can sometimes be heightened by an awareness of the other's desire. But at other times this awareness of an avid desire of one's partner can be merely distracting. The conscious awareness to which Nagel refers may actually impede the immersion in the physical of which I spoke above, just as may concentration upon one's "vocabulary" or technique. Sex is a way of relating to another, but primarily a physical rather than intellectual way. For Nagel, the ultimate in degeneration or perversion would have to be what he calls "mutual epidermal stimulation"[7] without mutual awareness of each other's state of mind. But this sounds like normal, if not ideal, sex to me (perhaps only a minimal description of it). His model certainly seems more appropriate to a sophisticated seduction scene than to the sex act itself,[8] which according to the model would often have to count as a subnormal anticlimax to the intellectual foreplay. While Nagel's account resembles Solomon's means–end analysis of sex, here the sex act itself does not even qualify as a preferred or central means to the end of interpersonal communication.

V

I have now criticized various types of analysis sharing or suggesting a common means–end form. I have suggested that analyses of this form relate to attempts to limit moral or natural sex to that which fulfills some purpose or function extraneous to basic sexual desire. The attempts to brand forms of sex outside the idealized models as immoral or perverted fail to achieve consistency with intuitions that they themselves do not directly question. The reproductive model brands oral-genital sex a deviation, but cannot account for kissing or holding hands; the communication account holds voyeurism to be perverted but cannot accommodate sex acts without much conscious thought or seductive nonphysical foreplay; the sex-love model makes most sexual desire seem degrading or base. The first and last condemn extramarital sex on the sound but irrelevant grounds that reproduction and deep commitment are best confined to family contexts. The romanticization of sex and the confusion of sexual desire with love operate in both directions: sex outside the context of romantic love is repressed; once it is repressed, partners become more difficult to find and sex becomes romanticized further, out of proportion to its real value for the individual.

What all these analyses share in addition to a common form is accordance with and perhaps derivation from the Platonic-Christian moral tradition, according to which the animal or purely physical element of humans is the source of immorality, and plain sex in the sense I defined it is an expression of this element, hence in itself to be condemned. All the analyses examined seem to seek a distance from sexual desire itself in attempting to extend it conceptually beyond the physical. The love and communication analyses seek refinement or intellectualization of the desire; plain physical sex becomes vulgar, and too straightforward sexual encounters without an aura of respectable cerebral communicative content are to be avoided. Solomon explicitly argues that sex cannot be a "mere" appetite, his argument being that if it were, subway exhibitionism and other vulgar forms would be pleasing.[9] This fails to recognize that sexual desire can be focused or selective at the same time as being physical. Lower animals are not attracted by every other member of their species, either. Rancid food forced down one's throat is not pleasing, but that certainly fails to show that hunger is not a physical appetite. Sexual desire lets us know that we are physical beings and, indeed, animals; this is why traditional Platonic morality is so thorough in its condemnation. Means–end analyses continue to reflect this tradition, sometimes unwittingly. They show that in conceptualizing sex it is still difficult, despite years of so-called revolution in this area, to free ourselves from the lingering suspicion that plain sex as physical desire is an expression of our "lower selves," that yielding to our animal natures is subhuman or vulgar.

VI

Having criticized these analyses for the sexual ethics and concepts of perversion they imply, it remains to contrast my account along these lines. To the question of what morality might be implied by my analysis, the answer is that there are no moral implications whatever. Any analysis of sex which imputes a moral character to sex acts in themselves is wrong for that reason. There is no morality intrinsic to sex, although general moral rules apply to the treatment of others in sex acts as they apply to all human relations. We can speak of a sexual ethic as we can speak of a business ethic, without implying that business in itself is either moral or immoral or that special rules are required to judge business practices which are not derived from rules that apply elsewhere as well. Sex is not in itself a moral category, although like business it invariably places us into relations with others in which moral rules apply. It gives us opportunity to do what is otherwise recognized as wrong, to harm others, deceive them, or manipulate them against their wills. Just as the fact that an act is sexual in itself never renders it wrong or adds to its wrongness if it is wrong on other grounds (sexual acts toward minors are wrong on other grounds, as will be argued below), so no wrong act is to be excused because done from a sexual motive. If a "crime of passion" is to be excused, it would have to be on grounds of temporary insanity rather than sexual context (whether insanity does constitute a legitimate excuse for certain actions is too big a topic to argue here). Sexual motives are among others which may become deranged, and the fact that they are sexual has no bearing in itself on the moral character, whether negative or exculpatory, of the actions deriving from them. Whatever might be true of war, it is certainly not the case that all's fair in love or sex.

Our first conclusion regarding morality and sex is therefore that no conduct otherwise immoral should be excused because it is sexual conduct, and nothing in sex is immoral unless condemned by rules which apply elsewhere as well. The last clause requires further clarification. Sexual conduct can be governed by particular rules relating only to sex itself. But these precepts must be implied by general moral rules when these are applied to specific sexual relations or types of conduct. The same is true of rules of fair business, ethical medicine, or courtesy in driving a car. In the latter case, particular acts on the road may be reprehensible, such as tailgating or passing on the right, which seem to bear no resemblance as actions to any outside the context of highway safety. Nevertheless, their immorality derives from the fact that they place others in danger, a circumstance which, when avoidable, is to be condemned in any context. This structure of general and specifically applicable rules describes a reasonable sexual ethic as well. To take an extreme case, rape is always a sexual act and it is always immoral. A rule against rape can therefore be considered an obvious part of sexual morality which has no bearing on nonsexual conduct. But the immorality of rape derives from its being an extreme violation of a person's body, of the right not to be humiliated, and of the general moral prohibition against using other persons against their wills, not from the fact that it is a sexual act.

The application elsewhere of general moral rules to sexual conduct is further complicated by the fact that it will be relative to the particular desires and preferences of one's partner (these may be influenced by and hence in some sense include misguided beliefs about sexual morality itself). This means that there will be fewer specific rules in the area of sexual ethics than in other areas of conduct, such as driving cars, where the relativity of preference is irrelevant to the prohibition of objectively dangerous conduct. More reliance will have to be placed upon the general moral rule, which in this area holds simply that the preferences, desires, and interests of one's partner or potential partner ought to be taken into account. This rule is certainly not specifically formulated to govern sexual relations; it is a form of the central principle of morality itself. But when applied to sex, it prohibits certain actions, such as molestation of children, which cannot be categorized as violations of the rule without at the same time being classified as sexual. I believe this last case is the closest we can come to an action which is wrong *because* it is sexual, but even here its wrongness is better characterized as deriving from the detrimental effects such behavior can have on the future emotional and sexual life of the naive victims, and from the fact that such behavior therefore involves manipulation of innocent persons without regard for their interests. Hence, this case also involves violation of a general moral rule which applies elsewhere as well.

Aside from faulty conceptual analyses of sex and the influence of the Platonic moral tradition, there are two more plausible reasons for thinking that there are moral dimensions intrinsic to sex acts per se. The first is that such acts are normally intensely pleasurable. According to a hedonistic, utilitarian moral theory they therefore should be at least prima facie morally right, rather than morally neutral in themselves. To me this seems incorrect and reflects unfavorably on the ethical theory in question. The pleasure intrinsic to sex acts is a good, but not, it seems to me, a good with much positive moral significance. Certainly I can have no duty to pursue such pleasure myself, and while it may be nice to give pleasure of any form to others, there is no ethical requirement to do so, given my right over my own body. The exception relates to the context of sex acts themselves, when one partner derives pleasure from the other and ought to return the favor. This duty to reciprocate takes us out of the domain of hedonistic utilitarianism, however, and into a Kantian moral framework, the central principles of which call for such reciprocity in human relations. Since independent moral judgments regarding sexual activities constitute one area in which ethical theories are to be tested, these observations indicate here, as I believe others indicate elsewhere, the fertility of the Kantian, as opposed to the utilitarian, principle in reconstructing reasoned moral consciousness.

It may appear from this alternative Kantian viewpoint that sexual acts must be at least prima facie wrong in themselves. This is because they invariably involve at different stages the manipulation of one's partner for one's own pleasure, which might appear to be prohibited on the formulation of Kant's principle which holds that one ought not to treat another as a means to such private ends. A more realistic rendering of this formulation, however, one which recognizes its intended equivalence to the first universalizability principle, admits no such absolute prohibition. Many human relations, most economic transactions for example, involve using other individuals for personal benefit. These relations are immoral only when they are one-sided, when the benefits are not mutual, or when the transactions are not freely and rationally endorsed by all parties. The same holds true of sexual acts. The central principle governing them is the Kantian demand for reciprocity in sexual relations. In order to comply with the second formulation of the categorical imperative, one must recognize the subjectivity of one's partner (not merely by being aroused by her or his desire, as Nagel describes). Even in an act which by its nature "objectifies" the other, one recognizes a partner as a subject with demands and desires by yielding to those desires, by allowing oneself to be a sexual object as well, by giving pleasure or ensuring that the pleasures of the acts are mutual. It is this kind of reciprocity which forms the basis for morality in sex, which distinguishes right acts from wrong in this area as in others. (Of course, prior to sex acts one must gauge their effects upon potential partners and take these longer-range interests into account.)

VII

I suggested earlier that in addition to generating confusion regarding the rightness or wrongness of sex acts, false conceptual analyses of the means–end form cause confusion about the value of sex to the individual. My account recognizes the satisfaction of desire and the pleasure this brings as the central psychological function of the sex act for the individual. Sex affords us a paradigm of pleasure, but not a cornerstone of value. For most of us it is not only a needed outlet for desire but also the most enjoyable form of recreation we know. Its value is nevertheless easily mistaken by being confused with that of love, when it is taken as essentially an expression of that emotion. Although intense, the pleasures of sex are brief and repetitive rather than cumulative. They give value to the specific acts which generate them, but not the lasting kind of value which enhances one's whole life. The briefness of the pleasures contributes to their intensity (or perhaps their intensity makes them necessarily brief), but it also relegates them to the periphery of most rational plans for the good life.

By contrast, love typically develops over a long-term relation; while its pleasures may be less intense and physical, they are of more cumulative value. The importance of love to the individual may well be central in a rational system of value. And it has perhaps an even deeper moral significance relating to the identification with the interests of another person, which broadens one's possible relationships with others as well. Marriage is again important in preserving this relation between adults and children, which seems as important to the adults as it is to the children in broadening concerns which have a tendency to become selfish. Sexual desire, by contrast, is desire for another which is nevertheless essentially self-regarding. Sexual pleasure is certainly a good for the individual, and for many it may be necessary in order for them to function in a reasonably cheerful way. But it bears little relation to those other values just discussed, to which some analyses falsely suggest a conceptual connection.

VIII

While my initial analysis lacks moral implications in itself, as it should, it does suggest by contrast a concept of sexual perversion. Since the concept of perversion is itself a sexual concept, it will always be defined relative to some definition of normal sex; and any conception of the norm will imply a contrary notion of perverse forms. The concept suggested by my account again differs sharply from those implied by the means–end analyses examined above. Perversion does not represent a deviation from the reproductive function (or kissing would be perverted), from a loving relationship (or most sexual desire and many heterosexual acts would be perverted), or from efficiency in communicating (or unsuccessful seduction attempts would be perverted). It is a deviation from a norm, but the norm in question is merely statistical. Of course, not all sexual acts that are statistically unusual are perverted—a three-hour continuous sexual act would be unusual but not necessarily abnormal in the requisite sense. The abnormality in question must relate to the *form of the desire* itself in order to constitute sexual perversion; for example, desire, not for contact with another, but for merely looking, for harming or being harmed, for contact with items of clothing. The concept of sexual abnormality is that suggested by my definition of normal sex in terms of its typical desire. However, not all unusual desires qualify either, only those with the typical physical sexual effects upon the individual who satisfies them. These effects, such as erection in males, were not built into the original definition of sex in terms of sexual desire, for they do not always occur in activities that are properly characterized as sexual, say, kissing for the pleasure of it. But they do seem to bear a closer relation to the definition of activities as perverted. (For those who consider only genital sex sexual, we could build such symptoms into a narrower definition, then speaking of sex in a broad sense as well as "proper" sex.)

Solomon and Nagel disagree with this statistical notion of perversion. For them the concept is evaluative rather than statistical. I do not deny that the term "perverted" is often used evaluatively (and purely emotively for that matter), or that it has a negative connotation for the average speaker. I do deny that we can find a norm, other than that of statistically usual desire, against which all and only activities that properly count as sexual perversions can be contrasted. Perverted sex is simply abnormal sex, and if the norm is not to be an idealized or romanticized extraneous end or purpose, it must express the way human sexual desires usually manifest themselves. Of course not all norms in other areas of discourse need be statistical in this way. Physical health is an example of a relatively clear norm which does not seem to depend upon the numbers of healthy people. But the concept in this case achieves its clarity through the connection of physical health with other clearly desirable physical functions and characteristics, for example, living longer. In the case of sex, that which is statistically abnormal is not necessarily incapacitating in other ways, and yet these abnormal desires with sexual effects upon their subject do count as perverted to the degree to which their objects deviate from usual ones. The connotations of the concept of perversion beyond those connected with abnormality or statistical deviation derive more from the attitudes of those likely to call certain acts perverted than from specifiable features of the acts themselves. These connotations add to the concept of abnormality that of *sub*normality, but there is no norm against which the latter can be measured intelligibly in accord with all and only acts intuitively called perverted.

The only proper evaluative norms relating to sex involve degrees of pleasure in the acts and moral norms, but neither of these scales coincides with statistical degrees of abnormality, according to which perversion is to be measured. The three parameters operate independently (this was implied for the first two when it was held above that the pleasure of sex is a good, but not necessarily a moral good). Perverted sex may be more or less enjoyable to particular individuals than normal sex, and more or less moral, depending upon the particular relations involved. Raping a sheep may be more perverted than raping a woman, but certainly not more condemnable morally.[10] It is nevertheless true that the evaluative connotations attaching to the term "perverted" derive partly from the fact that most people consider perverted sex highly immoral. Many such acts are forbidden by long-standing taboos, and it is sometimes difficult to distinguish what is forbidden from what is immoral. Others, such as sadistic acts, are genuinely immoral, but again not at all because of their connection with sex or abnormality. The principles which condemn these acts would condemn them equally if they were common and nonsexual. It is not true that we properly could continue to consider acts perverted which were found to be very common practice across societies. Such acts, if harmful, might continue to be condemned properly as immoral, but it was just shown that the immorality of an act does not vary with its degree of perversion. If not harmful, common acts previously considered abnormal might continue to be called perverted for a time by the moralistic minority; but the term when applied to such cases would retain only its emotive negative connotation without consistent logical criteria for application. It would represent merely prejudiced moral judgments.

To adequately explain why there is a tendency to so deeply condemn perverted acts would require a treatise in psychology beyond the scope of this paper. Part of the reason undoubtedly relates to the tradition of repressive sexual ethics and false conceptions of sex; another part to the fact that all abnormality seems to disturb and fascinate us at the same time. The former explains why sexual perversion is more abhorrent to many than other forms of abnormality; the latter indicates why we tend to have an emotive and evaluative reaction to perversion in the first place. It may be, as has been suggested according to a Freudian line,[11] that our uneasiness derives from latent desires we are loath to admit, but this thesis takes us into psychological issues I am not competent to judge. Whatever the psychological explanation, it suffices to point out here that the conceptual connection between perversion and genuine or consistent moral evaluation is spurious and again suggested by misleading means–end idealizations of the concept of sex.

The position I have taken in this paper against those concepts is not totally new. Something similar to it is found in Freud's view of sex, which of course was genuinely revolutionary, and in the body of writings deriving from Freud to the present time. But in his revolt against romanticized and repressive conceptions, Freud went too far—from a refusal to view sex as merely a means to a view of it as the end of all human behavior, although sometimes an elaborately disguised end. This pansexualism led to the thesis (among others) that repression was indeed an inevitable and necessary part of social regulation of any form, a strange consequence of a position that began by opposing the repressive aspects of the means–end view. Perhaps the time finally has arrived when we can achieve a reasonable middle ground in this area, at least in philosophy if not in society.

NOTES

1. Even Bertrand Russell, whose writing in this area was a model of rationality, at least for its period, tends to make this identification and to condemn plain sex in the absence of love: "sexual intercourse apart from love has little value, and is to be regarded primarily as experimentation with a view to love." *Marriage and Morals* (New York: Bantam, 1959), 87.

2. Robert Solomon, "Sex and Perversion," in Robert Baker and Frederick Elliston, eds., *Philosophy and Sex*, 1st ed. (Buffalo, N.Y.: Prometheus, 1975), 268–87.

3. Thomas Nagel, "Sexual Perversion," *Journal of Philosophy* 66:1 (1960): 5–17. [The slightly revised version from *Mortal Questions* is reprinted in this volume—eds.]

4. Sex might be considered (at least partially) as communication in a very broad sense in the same way as performing ensemble music, in the sense that there is in both ideally a communion or perfectly shared experience with another. This is, however, one possible ideal view whose central feature is not necessary to sexual acts or desire per se. And in emphasizing the communication of specific feelings by means of body language, the analysis under consideration narrows the end to one clearly extrinsic to plain and even good sex.

5. Solomon, "Sex and Perversion," 284–85.

6. *Ibid.*, 283. One is reminded of Woody Allen's rejoinder to praise of his technique: "I practice a lot when I'm alone."

7. Nagel, "Sex and Perversion," 15 [original page number in *Journal of Philosophy*; this passage is omitted from the later version of Nagel's essay that is reprinted in this volume—eds.].

8. Janice Moulton made the same point in a paper at the Pacific [American Philosophical Association] meeting, March 1976. [See Janice Moulton's "Sexual Behavior: Another Position," in this volume.—eds.]

9. Solomon, "Sex and Perversion," 285.

10. The example is like one from Sara Ruddick, "Better Sex," in *Philosophy and Sex,* ed. Baker and Elliston, 96.

11. See Michael Slote, "Inapplicable Concepts and Sexual Perversion," in *Philosophy and Sex,* ed. Baker and Elliston, 261–67.

STUDY QUESTIONS

1. Goldman defines "sexual activity" as acts that "tend to fulfill" sexual desire. Devise counterexamples to this definition that turn either on (a) the vagueness of "tends to fulfill" or, instead, (b) the purported link between activity and desire. Do these counterexamples deal a decisive blow to Goldman's conceptual analysis?

2. Suppose that the ancient Greek philosopher Aristotle was right that "every art and inquiry" has an aim. Does Goldman run afoul of Aristotle's insight by understanding sexual desire as, at root, the desire for the pleasure of physical contact and not in terms of other goals, such as the expression of love or procreation? Review what Goldman says about the appropriateness of his "means–ends" terminology.

3. Though disagreeing with Thomas Nagel's essay "Sexual Perversion" on several counts, Goldman identifies, as Nagel does, another person (or person's body) as the locus, object, or source of sexual pleasure. What are the drawbacks, if any, to the conceptual requirement that sexuality is, ontologically, a relation between two people? Or does this requirement make all the sense in the world to you? If so, how do you understand solitary masturbation? (See, in this volume, Alan Soble's "Jacking Off, Yet Again.")

4. Goldman admits that if sexual desire is the desire for the pleasure of contact with another person's body, then sexual desire and its generated sexual activity at least *prima facie* involve treating the other person, in a negative moral sense, as an object or instrument. As Goldman concedes, sexual desire and activity seem to violate the ethics of Immanuel Kant, according to which it is morally wrong to treat other people merely as means or tools. Goldman tries to avoid this conclusion. Explain how he does so and evaluate the sexual morality that he espouses. (After trying to answer this question on your own, see Alan Soble's "Sexual Use," in this volume.)

5. There may be some tension between Goldman's analysis of sexual desire and his account of sexual perversion as "statistically abnormal desire." Consider voyeurism, for example. On Goldman's

view, is voyeurism a sexual perversion, because it involves an unusual sexual desire (to watch from a distance), or is it not even sexual to begin with, because it does not involve the desire for physical contact? What other desires and activities might give us reason to raise similar questions? On Goldman's view, is there room to argue that homosexual desire and activity do not have the right "form"?

SIX

On Jacking Off, Yet Again

Alan Soble

*In this essay, **Alan Soble** discusses conceptual and normative issues about masturbation. The conceptual analysis of "masturbation" recognizes three types: solitary, dual, and mutual masturbation. It unsurprisingly turns out that defining "masturbation" simpliciter is difficult. Some analytic problems might be avoided by acknowledging that "mutual masturbation" is a misnomer, not "really" being a case of masturbation at all. Moral questions about masturbation are suggested by the claim of Roman Catholic and Natural Law sexual ethics that for sexual acts to be morally permissible, they must bear a significantly direct relation to procreation. On this standard, both masturbation and same-sex sexual acts fail. Immanuel Kant's sexual ethics have, by his own application, similarly negative implications. As the essay demonstrates, not even purportedly liberal philosophy of sex has been hospitable to masturbation, either ontologically or normatively. It is an intriguing question why a harmless act that brings pleasure, and is engaged in by most humans at some time or another, continually requires defense. A related question is why Joycelyn Elders, surgeon general of the United States, was fired by President Bill Clinton in 1994 in part for defending masturbation as safe sex. (Note the irony, given the political and medical dangers of White House fellatio.) As the author claims, "Masturbation is queer"—and queer enough, on his view, that the letter "M" deserves a place in an expanded LGBT acronym (see Study Question 6).*

This vice . . . has a particular attraction for lively imaginations. It allows them to dispose, so to speak, of the whole female sex at their will, and to make any beauty who tempts them serve their pleasure without the need of first obtaining her consent.

—Jean-Jacques Rousseau

If your right hand causes you to sin, cut it off and throw it away.

—Jesus [Matthew 5:30]

[They were copulating in a grass field, the woman on top, as an unknown person drew near.] "Please don't move, please," Simone begged. The steps halted, but it was impossible to see who was approaching. Our breathing had stopped together. Simone's arse, raised aloft, did strike me as an all-powerful entreaty, perfect as it was; with its two narrow, delicate buttocks and its deep crevice; and I never doubted for an instant that the unknown man or woman would soon give in and feel compelled to masturbate endlessly while watching that behind.

—Georges Bataille[2]

Masturbation is queer. It is similar to sexual activity that I've had with admired and intimate lovers, in the sense that it is sex with someone I care about, whose satisfaction and welfare are important to me. It is incestuous, because I am a blood-member of my own family. When I was married, it was adulterous because I was enjoying sexual activity apart from, and with someone who was not, my spouse. It is gay or lesbian; a man, say, sexually pleases a man and enjoys touching a penis. Youthful masturbation, before the age of sixteen, is pederastic or ephebophilic. I might fall into masturbation inadvertently ("if you shake it more than twice, you're playing with it"); at those times I do not fully consent to it, but it is also not against my will. When I masturbate while fantasizing, it is (see Rousseau) the promiscuous rape of every man, woman, or beast to which I take a fancy.

Sexual activity that is loving, adulterous, incestuous, same-sex, pederastic, involuntary, and rape-ish must be queer. As a result, it makes sense that we advertise our marriages and brag about our affairs but keep silent about our masturbatory acts. The sexual revolution (is it over, already? did it really happen?) made sexual activity outside matrimony socially acceptable; it encouraged the toleration if not the celebration of homosexual lifestyles; it breathed respectable life into the colorful practices of the philosophical children of the Marquis de Sade.[3] But to call a man a "jerk off" is still, in the twenty-first century, derogatory and an accusation that masturbating women, throughout history, have avoided. Male masturbation is the black sheep of the universe of sex. Women, having no seed to waste, may and can masturbate again and again and again. Is this advantage worth not being able to pee effectively while standing?

THE CONCEPT

How to define "masturbation" or get at its essence? A paradigm case gives us something to start with: a person in a private place manually rubs the penis or clitoris and eventually reaches orgasm (perhaps aided by fantasy or pornography). But one could masturbate in public, on a bus, although that will get you into legal trouble. Your hands do not have to be used, if the sexually sensitive areas of the body can be pressed against the back of a horse, the seat of a bicycle or motorcycle, or rugs or pillows. Further, orgasm need not be attained, nor need it be the goal. Prolonged sexual pleasure itself is often the point of masturbation, which might be curtailed by orgasm. (Masturbation conforms to a Tantric principle of *reservatus*.) The clitoris and the penis need not receive the most attention; the anus and nipples can be the target body parts. What remains of the paradigm case? Perhaps only this: the person who, by touching sexually sensitive areas of the body, causally produces the sensations is the same person who experiences the sensations. The rubber is the rubbed and *vice versa*. Masturbation: the "solitary vice" of "self-abuse." (Is it a vice? True, it is neither abstinence nor chastity, but it is virginal and celibate.)

Mutual masturbation would be conceptually impossible if masturbation were logically solitary, yet we have a paradigm case of mutual masturbation: two people rubbing each other between the legs. Now, if it is conceptually possible for two persons X and Y to masturbate each other, it must also be conceptually possible for X to masturbate Y, while Y simply relaxes and receives this attention, not doing anything to or for X. To give to another person, or to receive from another person, what is sometimes called a "hand job" is to engage in half of a mutual masturbation. "To masturbate," then, is both transitive and intransitive. Similarly, I can both respect or deceive myself and respect or deceive others. Reflexivity, then, may be sufficient, but it does not seem to be necessary, for a sexual act to be masturbatory.

Why, then, is mutual masturbation masturbation? *Dual* masturbation, in which X rubs X and Y rubs Y in each other's presence or while talking on the telephone does not present this problem. Saying (Attempt One) that the paradigm case of mutual masturbation is masturbatory because it involves the hands and genitals is awkward. It allows that solitary sex acts, even those that do not involve the hands and genitals, are masturbatory but entails that paired sexual acts are masturbatory exactly when they do involve the hands and the genitals. So X's tweaking her own nipples when she is alone would be masturbatory, Y's doing it to X when they are together is *not* masturbatory, yet Y's manually tweaking X's clitoris *is* masturbatory. These implications of Attempt One are chaotic.

There must be a better way to distinguish paired masturbatory from paired nonmasturbatory sexual acts.

Another way (Attempt Two) to distinguish paired nonmasturbatory sexual acts from mutual masturbation is to contrast sexual acts that involve insertion and those that do not. The idea is that without the bodily insertion of something, somewhere, no mixing of two fleshes occurs and the participants remain to that extent physically isolated (as the solitary masturbator is physically isolated). On this view, the paradigm case of mutual masturbation, in which the persons rub each other between the legs, and the hand job are both masturbatory because no insertion occurs. Male-female coitus and male-male anal coitus are not masturbatory because insertion occurs. Further, X's fellating Y is not masturbatory (which seems correct), and the view plausibly implies that insertion-coitus between a human male and a female sheep, or between a human female and a male dog, is not masturbatory, assuming that a person is not engaged in a *solitary* act if an animal is involved. The view also implies that frottage in a crowded subway car is masturbatory, even though it requires the presence of another person, the unknowing or unwilling victim, and that tribadism is mutually masturbatory. But relying on insertion as the criterion is inadequate. In mutual masturbation, insertion of one person's fingers into the other's vagina might occur; that some insertion takes place should not imply that the act is not mutually masturbatory. Further, to claim that cunnilingus is masturbatory exactly when it does not involve the insertion of the tongue into the vagina implies that one continuous act of cunnilingus changes from not masturbatory to masturbatory and back again often within a few minutes. What about a male who punctures a hole in a watermelon to make room for his penis, or a female who reaches for her G-spot with a zucchini? These acts are masturbatory yet involve insertion. So Attempt Two also has chaotic and counterintuitive implications.

Some of these problems can be avoided by narrowing what counts as "insertion" (Attempt Three). Masturbation might be characterized as sexual activity not involving the insertion of a real penis into a hole of a living being. Then the watermelon and zucchini cases are solved. But it seems to follow that paired lesbian sexuality, which does not involve a penis, is masturbatory,[4] while paired sexual acts (fellatio and anal intercourse) engaged in by male homosexuals are not masturbatory. This conclusion doesn't make any sense at all.

Were we to decide that a male having intercourse with a sheep is, after all, engaging in a masturbatory act, that is, if no difference exists between this bestiality and his rubbing his penis on a rug or woman's panties (here "solitary" means being apart from other *people*), we could define masturbation even more specifically (Attempt Four) as activity not involving the insertion of a real penis into a hole of a human. This scholastic account of masturbation is phallocentric in characterizing sexual acts with reference to the male organ. As a result, the analysis implies an implausible *conceptual* double standard: fellatio done on a male (whether by a male or female) is not masturbatory, but cunnilingus done on a female (by a male or female) is always masturbatory. Fellatio is "real sex"; cunnilingus is a masturbatory fraud. This refined view is sexist but not heterosexist; its point does not depend on the sex or gender of the fellator. It is similar to the claim, which is heterosexist but not necessarily sexist, that the paradigm case of a natural, normal, or proper sexual act is male-female coitus. What is conceptually and normatively emphasized in another view (Attempt Five), the most specific we can get about "insertion," is the insertion of a real penis into a particular hole of a human woman, the vagina. This view suggests that masturbation be understood as any sexual act that is not procreative in its form or potential, whether solitary or paired. "Useless" sexual acts, those that have no potential to perpetuate the species and whose purpose is to yield pleasure for the participant(s), are masturbatory. If so, our sexual lives contain a *lot* more masturbation than we had thought. Maybe this is the right conclusion, that most of our paired sexual acts (plus our solitary acts) are masturbatory, but we would like convincing grounds for it. Maybe, though, we should abandon trying to distinguish paired masturbatory from paired nonmasturbatory acts, and jettison the notion of "mutual masturbation" from our sexual discourse as being a misleading misnomer. For now, let us stubbornly press forward.

Under certain physical descriptions of paired sexual activity, no difference exists between paired sex and solitary masturbation. The young, precocious, helpful Alexander Portnoy offered his cheating father an exculpating (re)description of adultery:

> What after all does it consist of? You put your dick some place and moved it back and forth and stuff came out the front. So, Jake, what's the big deal?[5]

Adulterous coitus is described as solitary masturbation: you put your penis someplace (a fist or vagina) and move it back and forth until it ejaculates. Alex's sarcasm has wider implications: there is no difference between mutual masturbation and heterosexual genital-anal or homosexual anal intercourse. *Every* paired sexual act is masturbatory because the rubbing of sensitive areas, the friction of skin against skin, that occurs during mutual masturbation is, physically, the same as the rubbing of skin that occurs during intercourse. The bare difference is that different patches of skin are involved, but no patch of skin has any sexual ontological privilege over any other. Further, there is only one difference between solitary masturbation and paired masturbation or paired sexual activity: the number of people who accomplish these physical rubbings. We have reason for concluding that *all* sex is masturbatory.

Further, suppose X engages in a sexual activity with another person Y, and X's arousal is sustained during this physical interaction by X's private fantasies. This sex act is solitary and hence masturbatory in the sense that Y is absent from X's sexual consciousness. It is as if X were alone. That which would be arousing X during solitary masturbation (X's fantasies) is doing the same thing for X while X rubs his penis or clitoris on or with Y's body instead of with X's hand. Paired sex, then, even heterosexual genital intercourse, can be seen as masturbation, depending on certain mental components of the sexual act. Perhaps, then, mental aspects of sexual activity are that which distinguishes masturbation from non-masturbatory sex, even though the acts are physically the same.

Quite ordinary interpersonal considerations are helpful here. We might say (Attempt Six) that a sexual act between two people who are concerned not only (or not at all) with their own pleasure but also (or only) with the sexual pleasure of the other person is not masturbatory (no matter what physical acts they engage in), while sexual acts in which a person is concerned solely with her or his own pleasure are masturbatory. So rapists and inconsiderate husbands are the authors of masturbatory acts. Also, mutual masturbation is not masturbatory as long as the touches are meant to produce sexual pleasure not only for the toucher but also for the touched. Attempt Six is plausible if what lies at the heart of solitary masturbation is the person's effort to cause sexual pleasure for the self. However, it is not exactly true that solitary masturbation is reflexive, for the attempt to produce sexual pleasure for the self can causally involve other people, animals, or the whole universe. Or we might say that acting on and for oneself does not exclude acting on and for oneself, ultimately, by acting on others. To be sure, in light of the kind of physical creatures we are, attempting to please the self by acting on oneself is easy. Our own bodies are handy, more accessible than the bodies of others. As a result, though, we are misled into associating masturbation with only one form of it, the case in which X touches X. Producing one's own pleasure can involve others. Solitary and paired sexual acts are masturbatory, then, insofar as the actor produces pleasure for the actor; paired sexual activity is not masturbatory when one person tries to produce pleasure for the other. (Yes, a single paired sexual act can be masturbatory for one person and not for the other.)

This notion of masturbation is conceptual, not normative. By itself, it neither praises nor condemns masturbation. That is because we have defined masturbation as sexual activity in which a person is out to provide his or her own sexual pleasure without adding that such behavior is immoral. We could embrace or reject that moral judgment. It would be an addition to the conceptual analysis, not a logical implication of it.

FULFILLING DESIRE

Contemporary philosophical accounts of sexuality, proffered by thinkers within a sexually liberal tradition, yield the conclusions that solitary masturbation is not a sexual activity at all (Alan Goldman), is perverted sexuality (Thomas Nagel), or is "empty" sex (Robert Solomon). These conclusions are surprising, given the pedigree of these philosophers.[6] Let's begin with Alan Goldman's[7] definitions of "sexual desire" and "sexual activity":

> Sexual desire is desire for contact with another person's body and for the pleasure which such contact produces; sexual activity is activity which tends to fulfill such desire of the agent.

On Goldman's view, sexual desire is the desire for the pleasure of physical contact itself, nothing else; it does not include a component desire for, say, love, communication, emotional expression, or progeny. Goldman takes himself to be offering a liberating analysis of sexuality that does not tether sex normatively or conceptually to these other things. But while advocating the superiority of his notion of "plain sex," Goldman apparently forgot that masturbation needed protection from the same (conservative) philosophy that requires sexual activity to occur within a loving marriage or to be procreative for it to be morally acceptable. On Goldman's analysis, solitary masturbation is not a sexual activity to begin with, for it does not "tend to fulfill" sexual desire, that is, the desire for contact with another person's body. Solitary masturbation, on this view, is different from mutual masturbation, which does tend to fulfill the desire for contact because it involves that contact. Goldman seems not to be troubled that on his view solitary masturbation is not a sexual act. But it is funny that masturbation is, for Goldman, not sexual, for the conservative philosophy that he rejects could reply to his account like this: by *reducing* sexuality entirely to meaningless desires for the pleasure of physical contact ("meaningless" because divorced from love, marriage, and procreation), what Goldman has analyzed as *being* sexual is merely a form of masturbation, even if it occurs between two people.

"Tends to fulfill" in Goldman's analysis of sexual activity presents problems. Goldman intended, I think, a narrow causal reading of this phrase: actually touching another person's body is a sexual act because by the operation of a simple mechanism the act fulfills the desire for that contact and its pleasure. The qualification "tends to" functions to allow bungled kisses to count as sexual acts, even though they did not do what they were intended to do. Kisses "tend to fulfill" desire in the sense that they normally produce pleasure, prevented from doing so only by the odd infelicity (the hurrying lips land on the chin). The qualification also allows disappointing sex, which does not bring what anticipation promised, to count as sexual activity. In this sense of "tends to fulfill," solitary masturbation is not a sexual act. Suppose that X sexually desires Y but Y declines X's invitations, and so X masturbates thinking about Y. Goldman's view is not that X's masturbation satisfies X's desire for contact with Y at least a little bit and hence is a sexual act, even if an inefficient one. X's solitary masturbation is not a sexual act at all, despite the sexual pleasure it yields, unlike the not pleasurable but still sexual bungled kiss that does involve the desired contact.

Let's read "tends to fulfill" in a causally broader way. Giving money to a prostitute—the act of taking bills out of a wallet and handing them to her—might be a sexual act, even if no sexual arousal accompanies the act, because doing so allows the client to (tend to) fulfill his desire for contact with her body. (Handing over $100 would be a *more efficient* sexual act than handing over $10.) On this broader reading, however, solitary masturbation is still not a sexual activity; despite the causal generosity, masturbation is still precluded from fulfilling sexual desire in Goldman's sense. For similar reasons, masturbating while looking at erotic photographs is not a sexual act. Indeed, solitary masturbation would be a *contrasexual* act if the more X masturbates, the less time, energy, or interest X has for fulfilling the desire for contact with someone's body.

Goldman proposes one way in which solitary masturbation is a sexual activity:

> Voyeurism or viewing a pornographic movie qualifies as a sexual activity, but only as an imaginative substitute for the real thing. . . . The same is true of masturbation as a sexual activity without a partner.

Goldman is claiming that masturbation done for its own sake, done only for the specific pleasure it yields, is *not* sexual because it is not connected with a desire for contact with another's body. (Nor would it be a sexual act were it done to produce a sperm sample.) Masturbation is a sexual act only when performed as a substitute for the not available "real thing," that is, when it serves as a substitute for genuine sexual contact. On what grounds can it be claimed that masturbation's being an "imaginative substitute" for a sexual act makes it a sexual act? Being a *substitute* for a kind of act does not generally make it an act of that kind: to eat soyburger as a beef substitute is not to eat hamburger, even if the soyburger tastes exactly like hamburger. Eating hamburger as a substitute for the sexual activity I want but cannot have does not make my going to Burger King a sexual event. At best it is *compensation*. (So, no sexual transubstantiation exists.)

Given Goldman's analyses of sexual desire and activity, the claim that masturbation done for its own sake is not sexual makes sense. If the solitary masturbator desires physical contact and the pleasure of contact and masturbates valiantly trying—albeit in vain—to get that pleasure, the act, by a stretch, is sexual because it involves sexual desire. By contrast, if the masturbator wants to experience only pleasurable genital sensations, the masturbator does not have sexual desire in Goldman's sense, and activity engaged in to fulfill this nonsexual desire is not sexual activity. Now we have a different problem: What are we to call the act of this masturbator? In what conceptual category does it belong if not the sexual? Goldman argues, along the same lines, that if a parent's desire to cuddle a baby, to have physical contact with it, is a desire only to show affection and not a desire for the pleasure of physical contact, then the parent's act is not sexual. Goldman assumes that if the *desire* that accompanies an act is not sexual, then neither is the *act* sexual. If so, a woman who performs fellatio on a man exactly for the money she earns from doing so is not performing a sexual act. It does not fulfill the sexual desire "of the agent," for, like the baby-cuddling parent, she has no sexual desire to begin with. The prostitute's fellatio must be called, instead, a "rent-paying" or "food-gathering" act because it tends to fulfill her desires to have shelter and eat. That we should classify an act in part by its motive and not only in terms of its physical characteristics is an interesting idea. Still, what Goldman's account implies about a prostitute's participation in fellatio, that it is for her not sexual because it does not proceed from the appropriate desire, is counterintuitive. It flies in the face of the usual definition of prostitution as engaging in sexual activity in exchange for money. We are better off saying that what the prostitute does is to pay the rent *by* engaging in sex.

COMPLETENESS

Nagel designed a theory of sexuality to distinguish between the humanly natural and unnatural (or the perverted).[8] Human sexuality differs from animal sexuality in the role played by a spiral phenomenon that depends on our consciousness. Suppose (1) X looks at Y or hears Y's voice or smells Y's hair (that is, X "senses" Y) and as a result becomes sexually aroused. Also suppose (2) Y senses X, too, and as a result becomes aroused. X and Y are at the earliest or lowest stage of human sexual interaction: the animal level of awareness and arousal. But if (3) X becomes aroused further by noticing ("sensing") that Y is aroused by sensing X, and (4) Y becomes further aroused by noticing that X is aroused by sensing Y, then X and Y have reached a level of distinctively natural psychological human sexuality. Higher iterations of the pattern are also characteristic of human sexuality: (5) X is aroused even further by noticing (4), namely, that Y has become further aroused by noticing that X has been aroused by sensing Y. We might express Nagel's view of human sexuality this way: when X senses Y at the purely animal stage of sexual interaction, X is in X's own consciousness only a subject of a sexual experience, while Y is for X at this stage only an object of sexual attention. When X advances to the distinctively human level of sexuality by noticing that Y is aroused by sensing X, X then becomes in X's own consciousness also an object (X sees him- or herself through the eyes, or through the desire and arousal, of Y), and so at this level X experiences X as both subject and object. If Y, too, progresses up the spiral, Y also recognizes Y as both subject and object. For Nagel, consciousness of oneself as both subject and object during sexual activity marks it as psychologically natural, as "complete."

Nagel's theory, because it is about natural sexuality and not about the essence of the sexual, does not entail that masturbation is not sexual. However, the judgment that solitary masturbation is unnatural *seems* to follow. Mutual masturbation can, but solitary masturbation cannot, exhibit the completeness of natural sexuality; it lacks the combination of an awareness of the embodiment of another person and an awareness of being sensed as embodied, in turn, by that person. This explains, apparently, why Nagel claims that "narcissistic practices"—which for him seem to include solitary masturbation—are "stuck at some primitive version of the first stage" of the spiral of arousal; "narcissistic practices" are perverted because they are "truncated or incomplete versions of the complete configuration." However, there is a world of difference between narcissism in some technical (perhaps Freudian) sense and solitary masturbation, so even if looking on one's own body in a mirror with delight is a sexual perversion, a theorist of sex should not feel compelled for that reason to judge perverted the prosaic practice of solitary masturbation. Nagel also claims that shoe fetishism is perverted: "intercourse with . . . inanimate objects" is incomplete. But just because shoe fetishism might be a sexual perversion that involves masturbation, a theory of sex need not conclude that shoeless masturbation is perverted.[9]

A case can be made that sexual fantasy allows masturbation to be complete enough to be natural in Nagel's sense. Consider someone who is masturbating while looking at erotic images. This sexual act avoids incompleteness insofar as the person is aroused not only by sensing the model's body (the animal level) but by being aware of the model's intention to arouse the viewer or by sensing his or her real or feigned arousal (the human level) as much as these things are captured by the camera (or read into the image by the masturbator). Completeness seems not to require that X's arousal as a result of X's awareness of Y's arousal occur at the same time as Y's arousal. Nor does completeness require that X and Y be in the same place: X and Y can cause each other pleasure by talking over the telephone, ascending without any trouble into the spiral of arousal. Further, if X masturbates while fantasizing, *sans* photograph, about another person, X might be aroused by the intentions expressed or arousal experienced by the imagined partner. (Nagel does say that X might become aroused in response to a "purely imaginary" Y but does not explain this observation or explore its implications.) A masturbator can imagine, conjure up, these details and experience heightened arousal and pleasure as a result. If the masturbator is aroused not only by sensing, in imagination, the other's body but is aroused also by noticing (having created the appropriate fantasy) that the other is aroused by sensing X, then X can be conscious of X as both subject and object, which is the mark of complete, natural sexuality.

This argument that masturbation can be psychologically complete exposes a complication in Nagel's account. Consider a sexual encounter between a man and a female prostitute. The woman, in order to spend as little time as possible engaging in coitus with her client (she is a businessperson for whom time is money; besides, she might be repulsed by him), would like the client to achieve his orgasm quickly so she can be done with him. She knows, by intuition or experience, that her feigning arousal both at the animal level and at Nagel's human level will greatly increase the sexual arousal of her client and thereby instigate his orgasm. She knows, equivalently, that failing to express arousal, lying mute and motionless on the bed, will impede his becoming aroused and delay or prevent his orgasm. The smart prostitute pretends, first, to be aroused at the animal level and then pretends to enter the spiral of arousal, while her client really does enter the spiral of arousal. The client is not responding with arousal to her being aroused but to his false belief that she is aroused. (She must fake it credibly, without histrionics.) He experiences himself as both subject and object of the sexual encounter, even though the prostitute remains altogether a sexual object. Thus, in order for one person X to ascend in the spiral of arousal, it need not be the case that the other person ascend as well; X need only *believe* that the other person is ascending. Whether this phenomenon (which is not confined to prostitution; it occurs as well in marital sex) confirms Nagel's account of human sexual psychology or shows that his notion of psychological completeness is inadequate is unclear.

COMMUNICATION

Solomon, as does Nagel, thinks it crucial to distinguish between animal and human sexuality.[10] On Solomon's view, human sexuality is differentiated by its being "primarily a means of communicating with other people" (*SAP*, 279). Sensual pleasure is important in sexual activity, but pleasure is not the main point of sexual interaction or its defining feature (*SAP*, 277–79). Sexuality is, instead, "first of all language" (*SAP*, 281). As "a means of communication, it is . . . *essentially* an activity performed with other people" (*SAP*, 279). Could such a view of human sexuality be kind to solitary masturbation? Apparently not:

> If sexuality is essentially a language, it follows that masturbation, while not a perversion, is a deviation. . . . Masturbation is not "self-abuse" . . .

> but it is . . . self-denial. It represents an inability or a refusal to say what one wants to say. . . . Masturbation is . . . essential as an ultimate retreat, but empty and without content. Masturbation is the sexual equivalent of a Cartesian soliloquy. (*SAP*, 283)

If sexuality is communicative, as Solomon claims, solitary masturbation can *be* a sexual activity, for conversing with oneself is not impossible, even if not the paradigm case of communication. The distinctive flaw of masturbation, for Solomon, is that communicative intent, success, or content is missing from masturbation. Hence solitary masturbation is "empty" and a "deviation," a conclusion that seems to follow naturally from the proposition that sexuality is "essentially" a way persons communicate *with each other*.

Solomon's denouncing masturbation as a "refusal to say what one wants to say," however, slights the fact that a person might not have, at a given time, something to say to someone else (without thereby being dull); or that there might be nothing worthy of being said, and so silence toward another person is appropriate. Solomon's communication model of sexuality seems to force people to have sexual activity with each other, to talk with each other, in order to avoid the "deviation" of masturbation, even when they have nothing special to say. (*That* looks like "empty" sex.) Further, even if the masturbator is merely babbling to himself or herself, he or she still enjoys this harmless pastime as much as does the baby who, for the pure joy if it, makes noises having no communicative intent or meaning. This is not to say that the masturbator is an infant in a derogatory sense. The point is that as the baby who babbles confirms and celebrates its own existence, the person who masturbates can accomplish the same valuable thing at the same time that he or she experiences the sheer physical pleasure of the act. Thus for Solomon to call masturbation "self-denial" is wrong. (It would be self-denial only if the masturbator wanted to say something to another person and fled the opportunity to do so.) At least the accusation is a change from the popular conservative criticism of masturbation as being a *failure* of self-denial, a succumbing to distracting temptations, an immersing of the self in the hedonistic excess of self-gratification.[11]

There is little warrant to conclude, within a communicative model of sexuality, that masturbation is inferior.[12] Solomon meant his analogy between masturbation and a "Cartesian soliloquy" to reveal the shallowness of solitary sex. But Rene Descartes' philosophical soliloquies are hardly uninteresting. Even if we reject the foundationalism of Cartesian epistemology, we must admit the huge significance of Descartes' project. I suspect that many people would be proud to masturbate as well as the *Meditations* does philosophy. Diaries, also analogous to masturbation, are often not masterpieces of literature, but that does not make them "empty" or unimportant. Indeed, some of the most fruitful discussions one can have are precisely with oneself, not as a substitute for dialogue with another person, and not as compensation for lacking conversation with another person, but exactly to explore one's mind, to get one's thoughts straight. This is the stuff from which intellectual integrity emerges and is not necessarily merely a preparation for polished public utterances. Woody Allen's answer to the question, "Why are you so good in bed?" ("I practice a lot when I am alone") further diffuses the communicative critique of masturbation.

Solomon acknowledges that not only "children, lunatics, and hermits" talk to themselves, "poets and philosophers" do so, too (*SAP*, 283). This misleading concession has obvious derogatory implications for solitary masturbation. It plays on the silly notion that philosophers and poets are a type of lunatic. Where are the bus drivers, the cooks, and the accountants? Solomon's abuse of solitary masturbation trades unfairly on the fact that talking to oneself has always received undeservedly bad publicity—unfair because we all do it, lips moving and heads bouncing, without thereby damning ourselves.

Solomon admits, given that philosophers talk to themselves (which is a counterexample to his argument that "sexuality is a language . . . and primarily communicative" and, hence, masturbation is deviant) that "masturbation might, *in different contexts*, count as wholly different extensions of language" (*SAP*, 283; italics added). This crucial qualification implies that Solomon's negative judgment of masturbation is, after all, unjustified. Sometimes we want to converse with another person; sometimes we want to have that conversation sexually. In other contexts—in other moods, with other people, in different settings—we want only the pleasure of touching the other's body or of being touched without communicating serious messages. To turn around one of Solomon's points: sometimes pleasure alone *is* the goal of sexual activity, and even though communication might occur at the same time it is not the desired or intended result but an unremarkable side effect. In still other contexts or moods, we will not want to talk with anyone at all but to spend time alone. We might want to avoid intercourse of all types with human beings, those hordes from whose noisy prattle we try to escape by running off to Montana—not an "ultimate retreat" but a blessed haven, a sanctuary.

MEN'S LIBERATION

One curiosity of the late twentieth century and early twenty-first century is that deciding who is liberal and who is conservative is no longer easy. Consider, for example, the views of John Stoltenberg, a student of the feminist writers Catharine MacKinnon and Andrea Dworkin. Stoltenberg rightly complains about our "cultural imperative" that asserts that men

in our society must "fuck" in order to *be* men, and he rightly calls "balo-
ney" the idea that "if two people don't have intercourse, they have not
had real sex."[13] Stoltenberg also observes that "sometimes men have coital sex . . . not because they particularly feel like it but because they feel
they *should* feel like it." This is a reasonable philosophy of men's liberation and men's feminism. But from these observations Stoltenberg fails to
draw the almost obvious conclusion about the value of men's masturbation. Indeed, it is jolting to find him, in a passage reminiscent of Catholic
objections to contraception (it makes women into sexual objects), laying a
guilt trip on men who masturbate with the aid of pornography:

> Pay your money and imagine. Pay your money and get real turned on.
> Pay your money and jerk off. That kind of sex helps . . . support an
> industry committed to making people with penises believe that people
> without are sluts who just want to be ravished and reviled—an indus-
> try dedicated to maintaining a sex-class system in which men believe
> themselves sex machines and men believe women are mindless fuck
> tubes. (35–36)

In light of Stoltenberg's criticism of the social imperative that men must
fuck women to be men, surely *something* should be said on behalf of
men's solitary masturbation. The men's movement attack on oppressive
cultural definitions of masculinity, in hand with feminist worries about
the integrity of sexual activity between unequally empowered men and
women, suggests that men's masturbation is at least a partial solution to a
handful of problems. A man pleasing himself by masturbating is not
taking advantage of economically and socially less powerful women; he
is not refurbishing the infrastructure of his fragile ego at the expense of
womankind. He is, instead, flouting cultural standards of masculinity
that instruct him that he must perform sexually with women, and not jerk
off, in order to be a man.

Yet, for Stoltenberg, fantasizing and the heightened sexual pleasure
that the imagination makes possible (44), the things I mentioned while
arguing that masturbation is psychologically complete in Nagel's sense,
constitute wrongful sexual objectification. Stoltenberg does not merely
condemn masturbating with pornography (35–36, 42–43, 49–50). Fantasy
per se is at fault: Stoltenberg condemns men's masturbating with memo-
ries and passing thoughts about women, even when these fantasies are
not violent (41–44). A man's conjuring up a mental image of a woman,
her body, or its various parts is to view the woman as an object, as a
thing. Stoltenberg thus takes Jesus and Rousseau *very* seriously. In response to Robert Nozick's deconstructive, sarcastic questions—"In getting pleasure from seeing an attractive person go by, does one use the
other solely as a means? Does someone so use an object of sexual fantasies?"—Stoltenberg answers "yes."[14]

The mental sexual objectification involved in sexual fantasy is both a cause and a result of "male supremacy," according to Stoltenberg (51, 53–54). Further, mental sexual objectification makes its own contribution to violence against women (54–55). Stoltenberg's reason for thinking this is flimsy. He supposes that when a man fantasizes sexually about women, he reduces them from persons to objects. Further, when a man thinks of women as things, he has given himself *carte blanche* in his behavior toward them, including violence: regarding an object, "you can do anything to it you want" (55). The last claim is obviously false. There are innumerable lifeless objects to which I would never lay a hand because other people value them and I value these people, or because I myself dearly value the objects. Therefore, reducing a woman to a thing (or, to describe it more faithfully to men's experiences than Stoltenberg is willing to do: emphasizing for a while the beauty of one aspect of a person's existence) does not mean that she can or will be tossed around the way a young girl slings her Barbie and Ken.

Stoltenberg underestimates the nuances of men's fantasies about women. His account of what occurs in the minds of fantasizing men, the purported reduction of persons to things, is crude. Her smile, the way she moves down the stairs, the bounce of her tush, the sexy thoughts in her own mind, her lusty yearning for me—these are, I admit, mere parts of her. But imagining them while masturbating, or driving my car, or having coffee, need not amount to—indeed is *the opposite of*—my reducing her to plastic. These are fantasies about people, not things, and they remain people during the fantasy. My fantasy of her (having a) fantasy of me (or of her having a fantasy of my [having a] fantasy of her) is structurally too sophisticated to be objectification. The fantasizer makes himself in his consciousness both subject and object and imagines his partner as both subject and object. Recognizing the imagined person ontologically as a person is hardly a superfluous component of men's or women's fantasies. That Stoltenberg overlooks the complex structure of men's fantasies about women is not surprising. The primitive idea that men vulgarly reduce women to objects in their fantasies is precisely the idea that would occur to someone (Stoltenberg) who has already objectified men, who has reduced men from full persons having intricate psychologies to robots with penises.

CONJUGAL UNION

The New Natural Law philosopher and legal scholar John Finnis claims, plausibly, that there are morally worthless sexual acts in which "one's body is treated as instrumental for the securing of the experiential satisfaction of the conscious self."[15] Out of context, this claim seems to be condemning rape, the use of a person's body by another person for mere "experiential satisfaction." Rape is the furthest thing from Finnis's mind; he is talking not about coerced sex, but that which is voluntary. When is sex instrumental and worthless even though consensual? Finnis immediately mentions, implying that these sexual act are his primary targets, that "in masturbating, as in being . . . sodomized," the body is merely a tool of satisfaction. As a result of one's body being used, a person undergoes "disintegration": in masturbation and homosexual anal intercourse "one's choosing self [becomes] the quasi-slave of the experiencing self which is demanding gratification." We should ask (because Finnis sounds remarkably like the Kant who claims that sex by its nature is instrumental and objectifying)[16] how acts other than masturbation and sodomy avoid this problem. Finnis's answer is the surprising "they don't": the worthlessness and disintegration of masturbation and sodomy attach to "all extramarital sexual gratification." The physical nature of the act, after all, is not the decisive factor; the division between the sexually wholesome and the worthless is between potentially procreative "conjugal activity" and everything else. Finnis's notion of masturbation is broad, which explains why he mentions this practice as his first example of a worthless, disintegrating sexual act. For Finnis, a married couple that performs anal intercourse or fellatio (nonprocreative sexual acts) engages in *masturbatory* sex.[17]

The question arises: what is so special about the conjugal bed that allows marital sex to avoid promoting disintegration? Finnis replies that worthlessness and disintegration attach to masturbation and sodomy in virtue of the fact that in these activities "one's conduct is not the actualizing and experiencing of a real common good." Marriage, on the other hand,

> with its double blessing—procreation and friendship—is a real common good . . . that can be both actualized and experienced in the orgasmic union of the reproductive organs of a man and a woman united in commitment to that good.

Being married is, we can grant, often conducive to the value of sexual activity. But what is objectionable about sexual activity between two single consenting adults who care about and enjoy pleasing each other? Does not this mutual pleasing avoid worthlessness? No: the friends might be seeking only pleasure for its own sake, as often occurs in sodomy and masturbation. And although Finnis thinks that "pleasure is indeed a good," he qualifies that concession with "when it is the experienced aspect of one's participation in some intelligible good." For Finnis's argument to work, however, he must claim that pleasure is a good *only when* it is an aspect of the pursuit or achievement of some other good. This is not what Finnis says. Perhaps he does not say it because he fears his readers will reject such an extreme reservation about the value of pleasure. Or, perhaps, he doesn't say it because he realizes that it is false: the pleasure of tasting food is good in itself regardless of whether eating is part of the good of securing nutrition.

What if the friends say that they do have a common good, their friend-ship, the same way a married couple has the common good that is their marriage? If "their friendship is not marital . . . activation of their repro-ductive organs cannot be, in reality, an . . . actualization of their friend-ship's common good," replies Finnis. The claim is obscure. Finnis tries to explain, and in doing so reveals the crux of his sexual philosophy:

> the common good of friends who are not and cannot be married (man and man, man and boy, woman and woman) has nothing to do with their having children by each other, and their reproductive organs can-not make them a biological (and therefore a personal) unit.

Finnis began with the Kantian intuition that sexual activity involves treating the body instrumentally, and he concludes with the Kantish in-tuition that sex in marriage avoids disintegrity because the couple is a biological "unit," or insofar as "the orgasmic union of the reproductive organs of husband and wife really unites them biologically." In order for persons to be part of a genuine union, their sexual activity must be both marital and procreative. The psychic falling apart each person would undergo in nonmarital sex is prevented in marital sex by their joining into one; this bolstering of the self against a metaphysical hurricane is gained by the tempestuous potentially procreative orgasm (of all things). At the heart of Finnis's philosophy is a scientific absurdity, if not also an absurdity according to common sense, and further conversation with him becomes difficult.

TRANSCENDENTAL ILLUSIONS

For Finnis, the self is so fragile metaphysically that engaging in sexual activity for the sheer pleasure of it threatens to burst it apart. For Roger Scruton, another conservative who condemns masturbation, the ephem-eral self is in continual danger of being exposed as a fraud: "In my [sexu-al] desire [for you] I am gripped by the illusion of a transcendental unity behind the opacity of [your] flesh."[18] We are not transcendental selves but fully material beings, which is why "excretion is the final 'no' to all our transcendental illusions" (151). We are redeemed only through "a metaphysical illusion residing in the heart of sexual desire" (95). Our passions make it *appear* that we are ontologically more than we really are. Sexuality must be treated with kid gloves, then, lest we lose the spiritual-ly uplifting and socially useful reassurance that we humans are the onto-logical pride of the universe, the crown of creation.

The requirement that human sexuality be approached somberly trans-lates, for Scruton, not only into the ordinary claim that the sexual impulse must be educated or tamed to be the partner of heterosexual love but also into a number of silly judgments. While discussing the "obscenity" of masturbation, Scruton offers this example:

> Consider the woman who plays with her clitoris during the act of coition. Such a person affronts her lover with the obscene display of her body, and, in perceiving her thus, the lover perceives his own irrelevance. She becomes disgusting to him, and his desire may be extinguished. The woman's desire is satisfied at the expense of her lover's, and no real union can be achieved between them. (319)

The obvious reply is to say that without the woman's masturbation, *her* desire might be extinguished and *his* desire satisfied at the expense of hers, and still no union is achieved. Further, her masturbating can help the couple attain the union Scruton hopes for as the way to sustain the metaphysical illusion, by letting them experience and recognize the mutual pleasure, perhaps the mutual orgasm, that results. Scruton's claim is false, I think, that most men would perceive a woman's masturbating during coitus as "disgusting." But even if there is some truth in this, we could, instead of blessing this disgust, offer the pastoral advice to the man who "perceives his own irrelevance" that he become more involved in his partner's pleasure by helping her massage her clitoral region or doing the rubbing for her. When they are linked together coitally, he will find the arms long and the body flexible.

Why does Scruton judge the woman's masturbation an "obscene display"? Here is one part of his thought. When masturbation is done in public (a bus station), it is obscene; it "cannot be witnessed without a sense of obscenity." Scruton then draws the astounding conclusion that *all* masturbation is obscene, even when done privately, on the grounds that "that which cannot be witnessed without obscene perception is itself obscene" (319). Scruton's argument proves too much: it implies that coitus engaged in by a loving, heterosexual, married couple in private is also obscene because (to use his language) this act cannot be witnessed in public without obscene perception. The fault lies in the major premise of Scruton's syllogism. Whether an act is obscene might turn exactly on whether it is done publicly or privately. Scruton fails to acknowledge the difference between exposing oneself to anonymous spectators and opening oneself to the gaze of a lover.

All masturbation is obscene, for Scruton, also because the act "involves a concentration on the body and its curious pleasures" (319). Obscenity is an "obsession . . . with the organs themselves and with the pleasures of sensation" (154), and even if the sexual acts that focus on the body and its pleasures are paired sexual acts, they are nonetheless "masturbatory." (Recall how the religious conservative criticized Goldman's "plain sex.") "In obscenity, attention is taken away from embodiment towards the body" (32), and there is "a 'depersonalized' perception of human sexuality, in which the body and its sexual function are uppermost in our thoughts" (138). A woman's masturbation during coitus is obscene because it leads the couple to focus too sharply on their physicality. She is a depersonalized body instead of a person-in-a-body. Thus, for Scruton, this obscene masturbation threatens the couple's metaphysical illusion. But if her masturbating during coitus is greeted with delight by her male partner rather than with disgust, and increases the pleasure they realize and recognize in the act together, then, contrary to Scruton, either not all masturbation is obscene (the parties have not been reduced altogether to flesh) or obscenity, all things considered, is not a sexual, normative, or metaphysical disaster.

NOTHING MUCH EVER CHANGES

I once quipped, at the beginning of a lecture I gave at Bloomsburg University (in October 2005), concerning Thomas Hobbes's view of human sexuality, that reciting his famous slogan in *Leviathan* would sum up his sexual philosophy. Sexual interactions, for Hobbes, would be *nasty, brutish,* and *short*—and they would certainly be *solitary* if the sexual agent were *poor.* The joke expresses, as do many jokes, a germ of truth: heterosexual men's access to sexual activity with women has long depended, and still in part depends, on the male's ability to provide resources to women that are necessary for their lives and the lives of children. For the ancient Hebrews, the number of wives a man had (if any!) was a function of his wealth and the length of his beard. A young man today will not get far with the babes if he doesn't have his own ride and crib. But the phenomenon was also at work in ancient Greece. A scholar of the first rank, K. J. Dover, informs us that there was "a certain tendency in [Attic] comedy to treat masturbation as behaviour characteristic of slaves, who could not expect sexual outlets comparable in number or quality with those of free men,"[19] those aristocrats who had at their disposal teenage girls as wives, courtesans with whom they could enjoy both intercourse and discourse, and beautiful boys (*eromenos*) who offered their bodies in exchange for the education made possible by their older lover's (*erastes*) wisdom. But not much has changed in another sense: even with all those outlets for his sexual urges, I submit, the ancient Greek free, propertied, erudite male would, as a slave to his own desires, occasionally give in and jack off.[20]

NOTES

1. The first essay I wrote on masturbation, "Sexual Desire and Sexual Objects," was presented at the Pacific Division meetings of the American Philosophical Associa-

tion (San Francisco, March 1978). I then published "Masturbation" in *Pacific Philosophical Quarterly* 61:3 (1980): 233–44. That essay was reprinted, unchanged, in Igor Primoratz, ed., *Human Sexuality* (Dartmouth, 1997), 139–50. Part of my introduction to *The Philosophy of Sex*, 1st ed. (1980), was devoted to masturbation and was developed into another version of the essay, "Masturbation and Sexual Philosophy," which was included in my *The Philosophy of Sex*, 2nd ed. (1991), 133–57. I continued to read and think about masturbation, and the results of my additional research emerged as chapter 2 of my *Sexual Investigations* (New York University Press, 1996). Part of that chapter became "Masturbation" in my *The Philosophy of Sex*, 3rd ed. (1997), 67–85. That version was reprinted in David Benatar, ed., *Ethics for Everyday* (McGraw-Hill, 2002), 180–96; it was further modified to become "Philosophies of Masturbation" in Martha Cornog, ed., *The Big Book of Masturbation: From Angst to Zeal* (San Francisco: Down There Press, 2003), 149–66. The essay printed here is also partly derived from my entry "Masturbation" in Alan Soble, ed., *Sex from Plato to Paglia: A Philosophical Encyclopedia* (2006).

In most of the versions of my various essays on masturbation (although not the version printed in this volume), I made a distinction between "binary" and "unitary" theories of sexuality: those that assume that sexuality is ontologically or analytically a two-person affair and those that do not make this assumption, and I expanded the arguments for considering the unitary theory to be superior (in, for example, empirical research on human sexuality). The first places I made this distinction were the 1980 *Pacific Philosophical Quarterly* essay and the "Introduction" to the first edition of *Philosophy of Sex* in 1980:

> The problem that arises here appears clearly if we examine an account of sexuality that has much in common with Goldman's but which attempts to overcome the main drawback of his theory—the fact that masturbation was excluded from the domain of sexual activity. This account would say that Goldman has not really exposed the bare level or core of sexuality, that there is a sexuality that is "plainer" than his plain sex. Sexual desire, on this view, is the desire for certain pleasurable sensations (*period*; no mention of contact with another body).

Please note my use here of both "plainer" and "period" ("Introduction," p. 18; see also pp. 48n9 and 49n10) well before other scholars in the philosophy of sex picked up these terms for their own use (e.g., Igor Primoratz, *Ethics and Sex* [London: Routledge], 1999).

2. Rousseau, *The Confessions* (New York: Penguin, 1979), bk. 3, 109; Georges Bataille, *Story of the Eye* (New York: Urizen Books, 1977), 8.

3. The mainstreaming of sadomasochism is illustrated by Daphne Merkin's spanking confessional, "Unlikely Obsession: Confronting a Taboo," *New Yorker* (February 26 and March 4, 1996), 98–115. (See an update in *Slate*: www.slate.com/articles/arts/the_book_club/features/2006/the_female_thing/bratty_beauties_and_babyish_boys.html; accessed March 9, 2012.) For explorations and defenses of more intense sadomasochism, see Samois, ed., *Coming to Power*, 2nd ed. (Boston: Alyson Publications, 1982), and especially the writings of Pat Califia: *Macho Sluts* (Los Angeles: Alyson Books, 1988) and *Public Sex: The Culture of Radical Sex* (Pittsburgh, Penn.: Cleis Press, 1994).

4. About problems in defining "sexual activity" for lesbians, see the wonderful essay by Marilyn Frye, "Lesbian 'Sex,'" in her *Willful Virgin: Essays in Feminism 1976–1992* (Freedom, Calif.: Crossing Press, 1992), 109–19.

5. Philip Roth, *Portnoy's Complaint* (New York: Random House, 1969), 88.

6. A notable contrast is Russell Vannoy's humanist-liberal treatment of masturbation in *Sex without Love: A Philosophical Exploration* (Buffalo, N.Y.: Prometheus, 1980), 111–17. I have already discussed the "old-fashioned" medieval Natural Law philosophy of sex as found in the writings of Thomas Aquinas. It condemns masturbation because it is nonprocreative sex carried out only for sexual pleasure. See the section "Natural Law" in my "The Analytic Categories of the Philosophy of Sex" (chapter 1 in this volume).

7. "Plain Sex," *Philosophy and Public Affairs* 6 (1977): 267–87, reprinted in this volume.

8. "Sexual Perversion," *Journal of Philosophy* 66 (1969): 5–17, reprinted in this volume.

9. A sexual act is perverted, for Nagel, if it is "incomplete." Persons performing these acts are perverted only if they prefer perverted acts to psychologically natural acts. Some people (e.g., prostitutes) are not perverts despite performing perverted acts; they perform them for reasons unrelated to sexual pleasure.

10. "Sex and Perversion" (*SAP*), in Robert Baker and Frederick Elliston, eds., *Philosophy and Sex*, 1st edition (Buffalo, N.Y.: Prometheus, 1975), 268–87. See also his "Sexual Paradigms," *Journal of Philosophy* 71 (1974): 336–45.

11. See Thomas Laqueur, *Solitary Sex: A Cultural History of Masturbation* (New York: Zone Books, 2003).

12. See Hugh Wilder, "The Language of Sex and the Sex of Language," in Alan Soble, ed., *Sex, Love, and Friendship* (Amsterdam: Rodopi, 1997), 23–31.

13. *Refusing to Be a Man* (Portland, Ore.: Breitenbush Books, 1989), 39.

14. Nozick, *Anarchy, State, and Utopia* (New York: Basic Books, 1974), 32.

15. John Finnis, "The Wrong of Homosexuality," *New Republic* (November 15, 1993), 12–13.

16. On Kant, see Alan Soble, "Sexual Use," in this volume.

17. Finnis, "Law, Morality, and 'Sexual Orientation'," *Notre Dame Law Review* 69:5 (1994): 1049–76, at 1068.

18. *Sexual Desire: A Moral Philosophy of the Erotic* (New York: Free Press, 1986), 130.

19. *Greek Homosexuality*, updated ed. (Cambridge, Mass.: Harvard University Press, 1989), 97.

20. For a typology of masturbators in relation to virtue theory see my "Concealment and Exposure," in *Sex and Ethics: Essays on Sexuality, Virtue, and the Good Life*, ed. Raja Halwani (New York: Palgrave Macmillan, 2007), 229–52, at 240–41.

STUDY QUESTIONS

1. Define "solitary masturbation," "dual masturbation," and "mutual masturbation." In what situations might it be difficult to decide whether a sexual act falls into one category instead of another or into none of them at all? Does it matter?

2. Is solitary masturbation a *sexual* act? If it is a sexual act, what feature of the act makes it a sexual act? If it is not a sexual act, why not? What would it lack that sexual acts possess? And if it is not a sexual act, what *kind* of act is it? Does a male's rubbing his penis to produce a sperm sample for donation or medical analysis count as masturbation? Only if the room supplied by the physician or donor bank contains a table full of a mixture of *Playboys* and *Playgirls*?

3. Employ the conceptual framework from "The Analytic Categories of the Philosophy of Sex" (chapter 1 in this volume) to discuss masturbation. Is it, or when is it, moral or immoral, nonmorally good or nonmorally bad, pragmatically useful or counterproductive, and natural or perverted? Given your answers, what is your overall assessment of masturbation?

4. What are the various roles of fantasy in solitary masturbation? What do they imply about the morality or naturalness of solitary masturbation? What *is* a sexual fantasy—a fantasy that has sexual content, or a fantasy, regardless of its content, that produces sexual arousal or pleasure? What would fantasy-less masturbation be like? A quickie in the last stall in the john between classes? Sperm donation? A circle jerk?

5. If Roman Catholic sexual ethics were altered such that the use of contraception by a married heterosexual couple to avoid procreation was morally licit in some circumstances, would Roman Catholic sexual ethics also have to abandon its claim that solitary masturbation and same-sex sexual acts are sinful? Why or why not?

6. What might the reasons be for and against including masturbation as the behavioral manifestation of a distinct sexual orientation? What might the reasons be for and against expanding "LGBT" (lesbian, gay, bisexual, and transgender) to include "M"? Do not forget that masturbation offends and is rejected by the same ethical and social consciousness that rejects all the other orientations in the acronym, and for similar and familiar reasons. So, are there significant differences between confirmed lesbians, confirmed gays, and confirmed bisexuals (who might occasionally masturbate), on the one hand and, on the other, behaviorally *confirmed* masturbators? All of "L," "G," "B," and "T," to the extent that behavior type figures into the definition of a sexual orientation, are *binary* orientations. "M" is a distinct sexual orientation, then, because it is behaviorally *unitary* and because its preference component is *not* for binary sexual encounters. Furthermore, after "LGBT" has already, with good reasons, been bloated into "LGBTQQIAP," there could not be any cogent reason to exclude "M." One conclusion to draw after adding "Q" (queer), "Q" (questioning), "I" (intersexed), "A" (allies, some of which are "H"–heterosexuals), "P" (Pansexual), and "M" is that the concept of sexual orientation, in this democratized sense, is no longer an interesting or significant concept. (In the same way, the democratization of the bagel—blueberry raisin [?!] and the "everything bagel" [or the Rainbow Coalition bagel]—trivialized the bagel as an ethnic icon.) Those gay men, for example, who think of themselves primarily as attorneys, decent golfers, and household handymen and as "gay" only in a lower-case "g" (vs. "G"), that is, whose self-concept is not determined by sexual orientation, also believe that sexual orientation, although it was once (not long ago) sexually and politically useful, is now passé.

7. Try to defend, against the criticisms of the author, the positions on masturbation offered by Goldman, Nagel, Solomon, Stoltenberg, Finnis, and Scruton. On your view, is there an author who comes

out as successful (or most successful) in his criticism of masturbation?

8. Can you find anything unusual or provocative in the article's epigraph written by Bataille? (This might be a good question for class discussion.)

SEVEN

Sex in the Head

Seiriol Morgan

Seiriol Morgan *argues that the apparent plausibility of understanding sexual desire as aiming essentially at bodily pleasure (as Alan Goldman understands it; see "Plain Sex" in this volume) rests on the flawed assumption that sexual pleasure has the same uniform bodily character in all sexual encounters, which in turn rests on flawed assumptions in the philosophy of mind. Conceiving of persons as embodied minds, Morgan outlines an alternative account of sexual desire. In his view, the nature of the sexual pleasure we take in the body of another can be transformed by the significance the person or situation has for us. In general, sexual desire and the pleasure resulting from it involve "intentionality"—our beliefs about the object of our desire and the acts in which we are engaging influence the amount and even the quality of the pleasure we experience. This account of sexual desire, for Morgan, can accommodate the entire range of sexual phenomena. He ends with some suggestions about why universal participant consent might not be sufficient for sexual activity to be morally permissible or unproblematic, a theme he develops in "Dark Desires"* (Ethical Theory and Moral Practice 6:4 [2003]: 377–410).

Seiriol Morgan is senior lecturer in philosophy at the University of Bristol. He works mainly on moral philosophy and the history of philosophy, particularly on Kant. This essay is reprinted with the permission of Seiriol Morgan, the *Journal of Applied Philosophy* (Blackwell Publishing Ltd.), and John Wiley and Sons.

§1

My aim in this paper is to advance a number of arguments against an influential philosophical account of sexual desire, an account which has

101

become known as the "plain sex" view, after Alan Goldman's paper of
the same name.[1] This view takes as its central observation the manifest
fact that human beings experience through sexual activity intense physical sensations which are extremely pleasurable, and endorses our com-
monsense view that it is just these pleasurable physical sensations which
are the object of sexual desire. When one human being desires to have
sexual intercourse with another, what she primarily desires is to experience the physical pleasure that contact with his body and their mutual
dynamic bodily interaction will bring. Sexual desire is "desire for contact
with another person's body and for the pleasure that such contact produces."[2] Sexual desire is satisfied when that pleasure is experienced and
frustrated when it is not, and is most effectively satisfied when pleasure
reaches its maximum intensity, usually in orgasm. Sex is good as sex on
those occasions and with those partners that provide us with the most
pleasure, best when that pleasure is maximized. For this reason it is also
known as the "hedonistic" account of sexual desire.[3]

This is not to say that other things may not be going on during sex,
some of which may be pleasurable in non-sexual ways. For instance, the
sexual partners might be in love with one another, and taking pleasure in
the mutually shared intimacy that the sexual encounter brings them. But
this pleasure, although perhaps very important to the experience overall,
will not be sexual pleasure, but concurrently experienced emotional
pleasure. Sexual pleasure is physical pleasure, and sexual desire *per se* is
desire for that physical pleasure.[4] This is borne out by the observation
that it is perfectly possible to experience really intense sexual pleasure
through intercourse with someone one is not in love with, and to be in
love with someone one does not desire to have sex with. Admittedly, on
occasion this other factor might be a person's prime motive for engaging
in sexual activity. But this just goes to show that people can have varied
motives for engaging in sexual activity, and does not impugn the plain
sex view as an account of sexual desire.

For reasons which will become clear, I will call this the "reductionist"
account.[5] The view is widely held amongst the public in general, and has
recently been defended by Igor Primoratz as part of a book length study
of sexual morality.[6] Nevertheless, as it is stated by its contemporary defenders, the view is mistaken. This is because it rests on an inadequate
philosophy of mind, which misrepresents the relationship between our
consciousness and our embodiment. At any rate, so I shall argue. The
issue is important because the reductionist view of sexual desire has been
taken by Primoratz and others to provide important support for an influential view of sexual morality, that (genuine) universal participant
consent is sufficient for a sexual act to be morally unproblematic.[7] In my
view, because Primoratz misunderstands the nature of sexual desire, he
fails to see that some of it is pretty dark in character, and consequently
that we can sometimes have good reason not to indulge it, even if every-

one involved were to consent to its gratification. I will touch on the moral implications of my views on sexual desire at the end of the paper, but I will have to leave a fuller treatment of the issue to another occasion.

Apart from theological views emphasizing procreation, the main competitors of the plain sex view are a cluster of views which argue that understanding the interpersonal intentionality that occurs during sexual intercourse is essential for understanding sexual desire. I'll call these "intentionalist" accounts.[8] These views also take physical arousal to be central, but root that arousal not merely in a physical pleasure at contact with the body of another, but through the mutual inter-relation of the experiences of the partners. All these accounts claim that bodily arousal or "incarnation" is, at least in normal cases, necessarily connected through mutual perception and interaction with the experiences of one's sexual partner. Normal physical arousal is thus "double reciprocal," depending on and responding to the arousal of one's partner.[9] According to the intentionalists, then, sexual desire as humans experience it is not an "appetite," and its complex object precludes it being possessed except by creatures able to appreciate the significance of and respond to the mental states of others, something only persons can do.

Different intentionalist views disagree about the typical depth and focus of this mutual reciprocal intentionality. Roger Scruton for instance takes a primary focus on the particular individuality of a sexual partner to be of crucial importance for healthy arousal.[10] And Robert Solomon, whilst playing down individuality, thinks that other intentionalist accounts have failed to appreciate the complexity of sexual intentionality. In his view we are aroused not by the mere arousal of a partner, but by the complex interpersonal attitudes she aims to communicate and her arousal at the messages one oneself communicates, this communication taking place through a universally understood language of the body.[11] They also differ in whether they take the claim to be solely descriptive or both descriptive and normative, and in the frequency and degree to which they think actual sex acts display intentionality. Thomas Nagel for example seems to take mutual reciprocal incarnation to take place in all normal human sexual encounters, whereas Scruton thinks that a lot of casual sex does not have the fully individualizing intentional structure that we are normatively required to aim at.[12] Nevertheless, despite these differences the views share enough in their essentials to be grouped together in opposition to the anti-intentionalist "plain sex" view, which takes sexual desire to be for a non-intentional bodily pleasure.

It seems to be generally agreed by the advocates of the competing views that a central test of the adequacy of any and all of them is their ability to give convincing accounts of the many and varied phenomena of human sexuality. There are a great many ways in which people behave which are obviously aimed at gratifying sexual desire. They range from penetrative vaginal intercourse between a fertile married couple to some of the more bizarre of the activities traditionally labelled perversions.[13] Each of the phenomena must be accounted for, as sexual, either completely by the account of sexual desire itself or by that account combined with a claim about factors external to sexual desire. Upon examination, they can be grouped, since some seem more amenable to construal in terms of purely physical pleasure, and others in terms of interpersonal intentional arousal. Positions emphasizing intentionality tend to point to those cases where an individual's pleasure appears to depend on the individuality of a partner or the nature of her attitudes, such as the personal exclusivity of some individuals' desires, the way arousal can be "mutually reciprocal," or the way pleasure can quickly turn to disgust if our beliefs about the identity or attitudes of the person who has aroused us change. Their proponents argue that only accounts which place intentionality at the heart of desire can account for these phenomena. On the other hand, the advocates of the "plain sex" view point to a number of prevalent phenomena in which the object of desire most plausibly appears to be a purely physical pleasure. The participants in casual sexual encounters quickly initiated and lasting but a short time seem to be entirely unconcerned about the particular identity and sometimes even the thoughts of their sexual partners. So do most men who use the services of prostitutes. And solo masturbation is clearly sexual but cannot involve interpersonal intentionality for obvious reasons. Such phenomena are highly problematic for accounts of sexual desire in which such intentionality is central.

This seeming inability of intentionalist accounts to capture the obviously sexual nature of these phenomena is a central plank in the reductionists' case against them. In their view it is obvious that human beings frequently engage in sexual activity which can only be seen as motivated by a desire for physical pleasure, unconnected with love or communication or reproduction or anything else. So accounts which locate the essence of sexual desire in something beyond simple bodily pleasure must be mistaken.[14] By contrast, they observe, the participants in sexual encounters where the individuality of the partners or the beliefs of the participants about each others' experiences seem important still experience bodily pleasure, and still seem to aim at it. They therefore take themselves to have identified the common denominator in all these cases of sexual desire, and accordingly conclude that the essence of sexual desire is a desire for the peculiar bodily pleasure that sexual activity brings. Some concede that intentionalist accounts have made important and interesting observations. Participants in a sexual act may indeed communicate attitudes to one another, or experience sex as strengthening their loving bond. But reductionists take these to be observations about additional things that take place during sexual encounters, which are extraneous to the gratification of sexual desire itself.[15]

Of course, the hedonistic view of sexual desire as aiming at bodily pleasure does not of itself entail the liberal sexual morality that Primoratz and Goldman advocate. After all, this is exactly how traditional anti-eroticists like Plato and Augustine are supposed to have thought of sexual desire. As far as they were concerned this is exactly what is wrong with it—it focuses our attention on fleeting bodily pleasures and distracts us from what is truly important, God or the Good. But the hedonistic view does entail the liberal morality in conjunction with various claims that have been thought in the modern period to be highly plausible, for example the view that pleasure is intrinsically good. And indeed Goldman in particular suspects that the spectre of pre-modern anti-eroticism lingers within intentionalism.[16] In his view all these accounts share an inability to acknowledge the animality of our sexual nature. This is due to an unwillingness to accept that the essence of human sexuality lies in the sensual embodiment we share with the animals, because of the unacknowledged hangover from a pre-modern Christian-Platonic mind/body dualism, which denigrates the "merely" bodily in favour of the mental. On this view Augustine, for example, accepted the evaluative contrast between mind and body, placed sex firmly on the bodily side of the divide and accordingly denigrated sexuality.[17] Goldman's charge is that intentionalists secretly accept the evaluative contrast, but, unwilling to denigrate sex, attempt to give an account of our sexual desire which locates its essence in the higher human faculties, so assimilating sex to the privileged mental side of the dualism. In so doing they misrepresent its nature. But there is no need to so assimilate it in order to avoid denigrating it. All that needs to be done is to reject the negative evaluative connotations that have traditionally been associated with the body and its pleasures.[18]

§2

These arguments rest upon a crucial but flawed assumption, however. The assumption is one about the uniformity of the phenomenon of sexual pleasure. The reductionists observe that there are obviously types of human sexual behaviour which express a sexual desire which appears at best marginally connected with intentionality. In such cases the participants are clearly best interpreted as aiming at uncomplicated bodily pleasure. They then conclude from this observation that the essence of sexual desire is a desire for bodily pleasure, taking the pleasure aimed at in these encounters as paradigmatic of sexual pleasure as such. But this is a mistake, because it assumes without argument that sexual pleasure is a simple phenomenon which manifests a uniform essentially physical character in all its instances. As I will soon show, sexual pleasure is in fact often much more complicated than this. As it turns out, in accepting the account Primoratz makes just the same kind of mistake as he detects in the accounts of all his rivals. As far as he is concerned, each of his rivals successfully identifies a genuine phenomenon of human sexuality. Unfortunately, however, they then all obsessively focus on the particular chosen phenomenon, and attempt to build accounts of sexual desire based on their implausible generalization to all cases. His own account avoids this, he thinks, because the element of sexual encounters upon which he focuses is sufficiently simple and general to be present both in the kind of highly personalized encounters that impress the intentionalists, and in the very impersonal encounters their accounts have difficulty with. And his mistake is indeed much harder to see, because sexual pleasure as an aim does seem to be common to all these cases. But he is in fact doing the same thing, by generalizing the *nature* of the pleasure which is the aim of impersonal sex across the entire field of sexual desire. This is why it is a reductionist account.

To see this, consider Aristotle's account of desire and action.[19] All animal action for Aristotle is rooted in desire (*orexis*, literally a "reaching out for"), including that of ourselves, the special animals possessing language and rationality (*logos*). Non-human action is prompted by a combination of appetite (*epithumia*) and immediate perception (*aisthesis*). The animal feels a desire, sees how the desire can be satisfied and automatically acts to do so. Much human action is very similar. Human beings are cleverer, of course, so we can use effective means-end calculation (*deinotes*) in order to more efficiently gratify our appetites, and gratify more complex appetites. But in Aristotle's view a being possessing *logos* can do more than this. For us *epithumia* does not exhaust the category of *orexis*. A human being can reflect upon his appetites, asking which ones it is appropriate to gratify. He can also over time transform his desires from mere animalistic appetites to desires which are in accord with these deliverances of reason (*boulesis*). For example, the natural human appetite is for food that is bad for one, in quantities which are bad for one. But a person possessing the virtue of temperance (*sophrosune*) has transformed her desires under the influence of proper habituation and right reason, and now desires only that food that it is good for her to desire. She could not have the desires she now has without bodily urges "reaching out" towards food. But nonetheless under the influence of reason the object of her desire (*orekton*) will be subtly different, as will the pleasure she takes in its gratification.

Similar accounts of the transformation of desire and pleasure under the influence of self-consciousness are provided by a number of major philosophers.[20] I argue that sexual desire must be understood in a similar way, and the failure of the reductionist account lies in its failure to do so. To borrow Aristotle's very useful term, the plain sex account insists on modeling all sexual desire upon *epithumia*, simply because some sexual desire must be understood as *epithumia*. To do this is to assume without argument that the phenomenon is simple and uniform, and not subject to transformation as it interacts with the faculties of a self-conscious being. This is not to say that there aren't very significant differences between *boulesis* and sexual desire, of course. In particular, sexual desire in any of its forms is a notoriously arational force, often opaque to our understanding and sometimes running counter to values we generally endorse. And whereas *logos* is universal, sexual desire is frequently highly personal and idiosyncratic. The similarity is that neither Aristotle's moral psychology nor an adequate account of sexual desire can be understood without properly grasping how the "bodily" and the "mental" mutually interact.

It is precisely this that the intentionalist accounts are variously trying to capture, of course. Their proponents see clearly that there are numerous sexual phenomena which are quite unintelligible unless the nature of our bodily experiences is bound up with our mental lives. Much of our sexual desire is individualizing in just the way Scruton describes, for example. The person whose desire is for one particular person desires sexual bodily experiences, but these experiences are desired in a particular way, which make them subtly different from the experiences desired by the sensualist. The sensualist wants the pleasure of sexual contact with another, the devoted lover wants the pleasure of contact with *her* body, which he experiences as *pleasure at contact with her body*. Bodily pleasure as such is not what he wants—this kind of lover would find a sexual experience with another unsatisfying or even downright unpleasant. Because of her significance for him, the physical experiences he has with her have a particular nature for him—it is these he wants, and he can have them with no other.

The reductionist view has little to say about such phenomena. All it can say about these cases is that the sexual desire of the participants is a desire for physical pleasure. As far as it goes, this is right, in the sense that in a large majority of cases the participants would not engage in the sexual activity if they did not anticipate physical pleasure from it, and would cease to desire the activity if that pleasure were not forthcoming for whatever reason. But the complex nature of that pleasure is invisible from the plain sex perspective. At best it can simply stipulate that for a particular person it is a contingent fact that bodily pleasure can only be achieved with a particular person or in particular circumstances. It must be silent about the nature of that contingency. And because it underdescribes the phenomena, it misunderstands the phenomena. Sexual pleasure in a great many encounters does not have the uncomplicated physical nature that the reductionists ascribe to it. Their account achieves the generality they see the other accounts as failing to achieve, but only at the price of inarticulacy and distortion, because the fact is that sexual relations can be and frequently are *meaningful* for their participants, and this significance feeds into and shapes the nature of the pleasure taken in them, both in quality and in intensity. So in order to understand sexual desire and sexual pleasure we need to appreciate that it is essentially open to meaning, in that it can be bound up with issues of significance. Precisely who or what has significance for a person, and the extent to which any individual's sexual pleasure is so bound up, is a variable and idiosyncratic matter.

It turns out then, ironically, that the problems the reductionists have in accounting for such phenomena stem from their implicit acceptance of just that pre-modern mind/body dualism which they accused the intentionalists of having failed to overcome. But it is they who have more signally failed to overcome it, since they take themselves to have done so merely by rejecting the normative connotations the tradition attached to the bodily side of the dualism. This is not enough. To properly overcome it we need to reject it altogether, since, as the Aristotelian and phenomenological traditions have long understood, what we are is not a dualist fusion of the mental and the physical but *essentially embodied minds*. It is not possible to understand many of the "bodily" elements of our nature in abstraction from our mentality, nor many of our "mental" elements in abstraction from our embodiment. We need to give up the old mind/body dualist habit of classifying experience into the mutually exclusive categories of "mental" and "physical," and replace it with the idea that many of the phenomena of our experience form continua, in which both our embodiment and our self-consciousness can be implicated to greater or lesser degrees. For some instances of each phenomenon the mental element is minimal, for others it is central. Sexual desire forms just such a continuum. We can explain some sexual activity simply in terms of the body and its capacity to experience pleasurable physical sensations. A little further along the continuum we find we need to make reference to a minimal level of intentional awareness of the mental states of others. But as we proceed further, we discover that some sexual desire is an extremely complex affair, which we cannot understand without making essential reference to complex cognitive capacities and intentional awareness, which often reach out to cultural and personal meanings associated with individuals, objects and situations.

§3

As I mentioned earlier, the accepted test of adequacy for any account of sexual desire is its ability to deal with the multitude of sexual phenomena. I claim that my account does this better than any of the accounts I have been discussing, and it is precisely my observation that the content of sexual desire is not unitary but forms a continuum that underlies this. First, my account plausibly explains the motivations of people pursuing the gratification of sexual desire through casual sex and the like. Because my account does not claim that sexual desire is essentially intentional or essentially individualizing or essentially meaningful, but rather that it is essentially *open* to significance, I can acknowledge that a great deal of sexual desire is desire for a kind of raw bodily pleasure unmediated by complex considerations about individuality and the experiences of one's partner, analogous to Aristotle's *epithumia*. And I can give just the same description of the motivations behind such behaviour as the reductionists. So I am not forced into implausibly attempting to attribute greater complexity to these people's motives than they in fact possess.[21]

My account is also able to deal with the phenomena which underpin the views of the reductionists' intentionalist opponents. My claim is that sexual desire is essentially open to being caught up in intentional significance, and that its nature is partially transformed when this happens. But amongst the things that human beings tend to find most significant in their lives is their relationships with others, how they feel about others and how those others feel about them. It should be no surprise, then, that facts about the identity and mental states of our partners can be central to our experience of sexual desire. It is also no surprise that this is sufficiently common that various intentionalist writers on sexual desire have come to see it as the essence of sex. We can explain exclusive desire for sex with a particular person, the way pleasure can deepen and become more intense with the perception of one's partner's pleasure and the disgust people feel upon discovering that a touch initially felt as pleasurable originated from an unwelcome source by citing a person's desire for an intentionalized pleasure—pleasure at contact with *him*, or in *her excitement*.

The account really comes into its own when we consider the more complex phenomena, however. Here are two interesting anecdotal examples illustrating how personal significance can be central to human sexual experience:

(i) *"Fucking the Police."* When I was a young man I had a friend who for obvious reasons was popularly known as "Johnny Drugs." One summer, to everyone's astonishment, Johnny had a brief sexual relationship with a female police officer. He cheerfully told me that his attraction to her was dramatically enhanced by the fact that she was in the police force, to the extent that he found himself repeating the inner mantra "I'm fucking the Police! I'm fucking the Police!" as he was penetrating her. This activity, I was informed, had the effect of dramatically increasing the intensity of his physical pleasure, in particular his eventual orgasm. ("Fucking the Police" was clearly an idea that very much appealed to Johnny.)[22]

(ii) *Victory.* I was once told the story of a rather messy love triangle, in which my interlocutor had left one woman for another, before subsequently returning to the first. At the culmination of the episode he made love to the first woman in the bed in which he'd had the majority of his encounters with the second, the significance of which was initially lost on

him. (Indeed, it hadn't occurred to him when they commenced intercourse.) Their recent intercourse had been pretty strained and unsatisfactory, as one might expect when partners get back together after infidelity.
To his surprise, their lovemaking on this occasion was the most intense it
had ever been, and his partner's orgasms the most violent. Astonished,
he was forcefully presented with the impression that the reason the experience was so intense for her was that it was replete with significance.
That she was making love to *him, now, in this bed*, signified her personal
and sexual defeat of the other woman, a victory which struck her with
incredible emotional force, and which immensely intensified her physical
experiences.

I could have taken examples from philosophy and literature to illustrate the point, since they are present in the work of a number of writers
who have a profound understanding of the complexity of sexual desire,
or at least some of its manifestations—Laclos, de Sade, Sacher-Masoch,
Nin, Sartre, Kundera and others. But I think the above examples are
particularly striking, and they clearly show the very personal and idiosyncratic nature of the sources of certain individuals' arousal.[23] These
examples show that we find social and personal facts about our partners
sexually attractive and arousing, and that these facts affect both the intensity and the quality of our sexual pleasure. We can desire someone because of *who* they are, "who" being cashed out under various possible
increasingly individualizing descriptions. Sometimes a fact about someone is very widely taken to have sexual significance. Someone can be
desired because they are socially powerful or famous or widely desired
("I'm fucking the best-looking girl in town! I'm fucking the best-looking
girl in town!"). Other facts about a person may be of great significance,
but to a smaller number of people or just to particular individuals. The
specific nature of Johnny Drugs' arousal is very personal to who he is.
Although many men would no doubt experience some kind of frisson
having sex with a policewoman, it is Johnny's history and self-image that
give the sexual situation he finds himself in its extreme erotic significance
for him. Very frequently, the significance structuring an individual's desire and experience is the individuality of her partner, of course. In "Victory" the personal identity and recent history of the individuals involved
is obviously absolutely central to understanding the woman's arousal.
But this is not always the case. The individuality of Johnny's partner is
not particularly prominent, for example. Any woman of the right kind of
age and general attractiveness with the property of being a policewoman
would likely have had much the same effect on him.

Interestingly, some of the phenomena which at first glance seem to be
most easily accounted for by the plain sex account turn out to be much
better construed on an intentionalist model, once we have broadened our
understanding of sexual intentionality. Consider the highly impersonal
and anonymous sex engaged in by some gay men, for example. They

certainly don't care about the particular individuality of their partners, nor do they seem to be interested in communicating complex interpersonal attitudes. It looks as though they are pursuing plain sexual pleasure, then. But in some cases their behaviour is such that it can only be adequately understood if we see their sexual pleasure as mediated by their arousal at the sheer anonymity of their sexual partners, an essentially intentional arousal. Apparently, for instance, in certain of the gay bathhouses that flourished in San Francisco in the '70s and early '80s, men could be found lying face down on benches in side rooms with their heads covered by towels. Other men would enter, mount and penetrate a prone man, in due course ejaculate, withdraw and leave, and at no time during an encounter would either of the participants see the face of the other.[24]

How should we construe this phenomenon? The reductionist account will have to point to the physical pleasure that the participants will experience as motivating their behaviour. But once again the account underdescribes the situation. Clearly they will experience sexual pleasure, but if what they desire is merely an essentially bodily satisfaction what is the point of going through this bizarre ritual? The only explanation of the rationale behind the ritual is that for these men the very anonymity of the encounter is part of what is *sexually* enjoyable about it. The prone man will not experience himself as feeling the physical sensation of a moving penis penetrating his anus, he will experience the sensation of the moving penis *of a stranger* penetrating his anus. The significance of the situation feeds into the physical, transforming and enhancing the experience for him. The reductionist account has no resources to articulate this. It is only with essential reference to the participants' intentional understanding that we can give an account of their behaviour which doesn't leave its motivation entirely opaque.[25]

§4

On reflection, the fact that the transformation of a bodily urge through mentality is implicated in all manner of desires should be obvious in both the social and the sexual spheres.[26] A vast number of the desires of twenty-first-century human beings are for the contingent products of human culture, things that no one could possibly have wanted outside of the cultural milieu in which they became possible and were given meaning. Many such desires and meanings are incorporated into people's sexual fantasies, producing desires that are only possible for highly intelligent imperfectly rational beings existing in a social context saturated with significance. One clearly cannot have a brute animal urge to be beaten with a horse crop by a woman clad only in a fur coat standing on one's chest in stilettos, both because such a fantasy involves essential reference to the contingent products of culture and the contingent significances they have come to possess, and because of the obvious roots of such desires in the idiosyncratic psychological histories of those who possess them.[27] Numerous phenomena of human sexuality illustrate this—sadomasochism, people's attraction to celebrities, people dressing up in various ways, and all the other weird and wonderful (and perfectly ordinary) highly individual sexual fantasies that people have.

The immense variability of the phenomena shows us the futility of attempting to give a unitary account of the nature of sexual desire, as virtually everyone contributing to the debate so far seems to have done. All the intentionalist accounts in play go wrong somewhere, either by making too narrow a claim about the normative parameters of sex, or by crediting all sexual desire with complicated interpersonal intentionality, since much of what humans find attractive about one another can be located in essentially physical factors, and these physical factors are sometimes the main or only thing that we find attractive about each other.[28] They also all fail to capture the range of complicated intentionality itself. *Pace* Nagel, what a person finds significant need not be the mutual reciprocal arousal of his partner. It might be something entirely unrelated to his partner's experiences, or perhaps the experiences of his partner he finds arousing might not themselves be ones of arousal. *Pace* Scruton, the significance underlying a person's arousal need not be individually intentionalizing. And *pace* Solomon, it need not lie in anything communicated from either partner to the other.[29] But each of these accounts gets something right and identifies a genuine facet of sexual desire, since all of these things can play the meaningful role that transforms *epithumia* into something more complicated.

One interesting question is why the reductionists miss the importance of intentionality in an adequate characterization of sexual desire, since the phenomena which intentionalists see as calling for an intentionalist construal are so prevalent. And of course, they are not unaware of them. All reductionists agree that things are aimed at and things are expressed during sexual activity which are not raw physical pleasure. How they characterize these phenomena varies, and it seems to me that characterizations vary within individual accounts. Sometimes they are characterized as occurrences parallel to the main aim of gratifying physical sexual desire.[30] Sometimes they can be read as implying that love or communication or mutual reciprocity can enhance *sexual* pleasure.[31] The latter move would seem to me like an attempt to have things both ways. But at root reductionists are committed to the view that the person's desires are for independently specifiable sexual pleasure and (say) emotional communion, so that the reason the individual's desire is exclusive is that they aim through sleeping with the other person to satisfy a non-sexual desire as well as sexual desire, a non-sexual desire which can only be satisfied by that particular person.

I want to be clear that this description of the phenomenon of exclusive sexual desire fails to capture crucial elements of it. Consider the idiosyncratic tastes and smells of one's partners. In certain situations these can be extremely erotic—for example, if one sleeps with a former lover after a lengthy period of separation, perhaps someone one still feels great fondness for, coupled with nostalgia for the former relationship. In such a situation the particular smell and taste of that person can be intensely present to one's consciousness, and intensely sexually exciting. On the face of it, a taste or a smell is just a raw non-intentional sensation. But it would be totally wrong to describe this kind of experience as finding a raw non-intentional sensation pleasurable. Indeed, this would be to get things entirely the wrong way around. The person doesn't want to have sex with someone who smells and tastes like that, he finds the sensation pleasurable because it is the scent of that particular person. If there were someone else who happened to smell exactly the same, the effect would not be the same at all.[32] Nor is the sensation *as sensation* in itself particularly interesting—it is not a precondition of this phenomenon that one was struck by it on sleeping with the person for the first time, for instance. This is a very clear example of how experiences can be "psychosomatic," straddling the boundary of sensation and thought, for it is clear that one could experience this sensation non-intentionally, if one were to encounter it in a situation in which it held no significance. Saturated with significance as it is, it is experienced very differently, though it is still *that sensation* that is being experienced.[33]

What the reductionist account does get right is the essential role of the body and its capacity to experience pleasurable sensations in sexual desire. As Primoratz rightly points out, in focusing too exclusively on the mental some intentionalist accounts can seem to lose the sexual element of desire altogether. Solomon's excessive emphasis on communication, for example, leaves it mysterious why we would bother with bodily communion, since many of the attitudes he claims it is the primary aim of sexual activity to communicate seem perfectly easily and often more effectively communicated in other ways. His claim that sex communicates them best is hardly convincing. He also has considerable trouble in explaining why much of our body language, including that involving bodily contact, is obviously non-sexual.[34] The reductionists are quite right that what we desire has an essentially bodily element, and it is that which gives sex its peculiar intensity and sexual desire its strength. The person who wants sex with a particular person and to express and share a communicated intimacy with him wants *sexual* intimacy, not intimacy as such. And of course, if we were not the kinds of creatures capable of experiencing the kind of essentially pleasurable physical experiences the reductionists focus on, there would be no phenomenon anything like sexuality in our lives. This is the other side of the dualist coin. Just as we can't properly understand the physical element of some sexual desire without paying attention to the mental, so we misunderstand its mental element if we try to abstract it from the physical in which it is manifested.[35]

§5

I want to conclude by making some brief remarks about the implications of my account for sexual morality. We can begin to see now how the complexity of human sexual desire might introduce specifically sexual moral considerations. What worries me is the fact that human beings can find significance in some very dark things indeed. My worry is therefore quite different from that of some other intentionalists, for instance Scruton, who is worried by the gratification of sexual desire which expresses itself as *epithumia*. I don't find this morally problematic at all, assuming it is circumscribed by a minimal level of intentional awareness and concern (which nevertheless leaves its bodily character untransformed). In this I entirely agree with Goldman and Primoratz, who see nothing whatever wrong with the pursuit of purely physical pleasure.[36] What I find much more worrying are complex intentional desires loaded with the wrong kind of significance. As we saw, it should be no surprise to find intentionalists trying to provide accounts of sexual desire which essentially connect it to love, the individuality of our partners and our partners' mental states, since our relationships with and concern for other people are amongst the most significant things in our lives. But human beings also take victories, vengeances, envies, hatreds and their desires that others should suffer as being of great significance, and such things can be eroticized in just the same kind of way as "morally wholesome" things like love.

An element of unease might introduce itself with the examples I gave above. They might be thought to be "borderline cases," although I actually think the desire of neither Johnny Drugs nor the woman in "Victory" was such that it should not have been indulged. I must admit that I have always found the "Fucking the Police" story amusing, although I wouldn't have found it amusing if the woman involved were not clearly fully self-possessed, in control and, so it seemed to me, using him in just the same kind of way he was using her (a "bit of rough"). Similarly with "Victory." Granted what the woman had been through, I think it would be a very harsh person who took her reaction to the situation as evidence of a bad character. We have no reason to think that her experience of her victory was along the lines of a malicious delight at her rival's misfortune, rather than, say, joy that it was to be her who would have him. And in neither case does it seem that the significance in question was the central psychological focus of the individual, because the pleasure in the significance was taken in the course of a sexual encounter which had already been embarked on for other reasons. But one can well imagine both individuals who have eroticized much darker significances than these, so that what they take pleasure in is entirely unwholesome, and individuals for whom this is the central psychological focus of their sexual desire. At the extreme, we know perfectly well that there are individuals who are aroused (and only really aroused) by domination, violence, even murder.

Of course, reductionists who deny that anything other than universal participant consent is required for a sex act to be morally unproblematic will not have a problem with accounting for the wrongness of much of this kind of thing. The desires of those who eroticize domination or violence or injury will be such that they cannot be satisfied without violating the autonomy and bodily integrity of other people. Genuine consent to such behaviour will clearly not be forthcoming, and so it is easy to see why acting on such desires is wrong on any plausible general moral view. But it seems to me that it is quite possible for individuals to take pleasure in dark significances which are less extreme than this and do not need to be satisfied through coercion. Some people clearly eroticize contempt, for example, and take pleasure in the thought that they are doing something to someone which degrades them, or somebody else.[37] Various common misogynist attitudes spring to mind. Or one might take a kind of narcissistic contemptuous delight in seducing someone, reveling in one's success, entirely unconcerned with their pleasure and happiness except as testament to one's own desirability. Such pleasure need not involve violating the autonomy and consent of the other person, since it is quite possible to consent to something that is bad for one, or for which one's partner holds one in contempt. These possibilities raise moral issues, moral issues which are perhaps best exhibited not through the broadly deontological ethical framework which Primoratz endorses, but through a virtue ethics framework focusing on character and human flourishing. However I will have to attempt a fuller investigation of this issue elsewhere.[38]

NOTES

1. Alan Goldman, "Plain Sex," *Philosophy and Public Affairs* 6:3 (1977): 267–87; reprinted in *The Philosophy of Sex: Contemporary Readings*, 3rd edition, edited by Alan Soble (Lanham, Md.: Rowman and Littlefield, 1997), pp. 39–55. All page references are to this reprint. [We have inserted the pages numbers in this volume—eds.]

2. Goldman, 40 (58 in this volume).

3. Goldman describes sex as "a physical activity intensley pleasurable in itself" (46; 65 in this volume), emphasizes that "central to the definition is the fact that the goal of sexual desire is bodily contact itself" (40; 59 in this volume), and criticizes the "means–end" accounts of sexual desire he opposes for "attempting to extend it conceptually beyond the physical" (48; 67 in this volume).

4. "One may derive pleasure in a sex act from expressing certain feelings, . . . but sexual desire is essentially the desire for physical contact itself: it is bodily desire for the body of another that dominates our mental life for more or less brief periods" (Goldman, 42; 60 in this volume).

5. The term is borrowed from Alan Soble, "An Introduction to the Philosophy of Sex," in *The Philosophy of Sex: Contemporary Readings*, 1st edition, edited by Alan Soble (Totowa, N.J.: Rowman and Littlefield, 1980), 12.

6. Igor Primoratz, *Ethics and Sex* (Routledge: London, 1999). Primoratz describes sex as "simply a bodily activity intensely pleasurable in itself" (42), describes his notion of sexuality as "essentially physical . . . reducing sex to bodily activity" (42), claims that sexual desire is "sufficiently defined as the desire for certain bodily pleasures, period" (46), and describes sexual pleasure as "*a* distinctive type of pleasure" (41, my emphasis), "basically physical" (43), [and] "the sort of bodily pleasure experienced in the sexual parts of the body" (46). He also agrees with Goldman that we can aim at more than bodily pleasure in sexual acts—e.g. procreation, the expression of love—but that such aims "are possible uses of sex, or additions to it, not something that belongs to its intrinsic nature" (43).

7. Primoratz, "Sexual Morality: Is Consent Enough?" *Ethical Theory and Moral Practice* 4:3 (2001): 201–18.

8. A mental state is an intentional one if it has the quality it has because it is in some way "about" the world. The difference between intentional and non-intentional mental states can be usefully illustrated by contrasting itches and shame. Both these states are unpleasant, but the nature of the unpleasantness is significantly different. Itches are non-intentional. They are not about anything, they just are. By contrast, one cannot "just feel shame." One feels shame *about* something one has done or failed to do. It is therefore dependent both upon one's beliefs about how the world is, and on what one values. So whereas no change in my beliefs will cause an itch to disappear, a change in my beliefs (e.g., it wasn't me after all who offended the duchess) can eliminate shame. See, e.g., Ludwig Wittgenstein, *Philosophical Investigations*, trans. G. E. M. Anscombe (Oxford, U.K.: Blackwell, 1963), 174: "'For a second he felt violent pain.' Why does it sound queer to say 'For a second he felt deep grief'? Only because it so seldom happens?"

9. Thomas Nagel, "Sexual Perversion" *Journal of Philosophy* 66:1 (1969): 5–17; reprinted in *The Philosophy of Sex and Love*, 3rd edition, edited by Alan Soble (Lanham, Md.: Rowman and Littlefield, 1997), 9–20, at 13 [38 in this volume]. All page references are to this reprint. [We have added the pages in this volume—eds.]

10. Roger Scruton, *Sexual Desire* (London: Weidenfeld and Nicolson, 1986).

11. Robert Solomon, "Sexual Paradigms" *Journal of Philosophy* 71:11 (1974): 336–45; reprinted in *The Philosophy of Sex and Love*, 3rd edition, edited by Alan Soble (Lanham, Md.: Rowman and Littlefield, 1997), 21–29. All page references are to this reprint.

12. Nagel, 15 (39 in this volume). Scruton, e.g., 344.

13. Thus the sexual phenomena include the following: some people are highly promiscuous for at least some periods of their lives, and clearly aim to have sex with as many different people as possible. A very large number of people masturbate. Some people are only interested in having sex with one particular person. Sometimes this is requited, sometimes not. Human beings have been known to copulate with animals and corpses. We can be intensely aroused if a sexual partner wears a certain kind of attire, or if intercourse occurs in a particular place. ["In a particular place" is amphibolous—eds.] Some people enjoy sexual activity involving more than two partners, others are repelled by this. Certain bodily gestures are "eloquent"; for instance, a kiss can convey anything from love to indifference and irritation. Some people are sexually aroused by receiving or inflicting pain, or by playing dominant or submissive sexual roles. People are frequently intensely jealous of their sexual partners. And so on.

14. Goldman (rather confusingly) calls these "means-end" accounts of desire (40; 58 in this volume).

15. Primoratz, *Ethics and Sex*, 41, 43.

16. Goldman, 48–49 (67 in this volume).

17. See, for example, *Marriage and Desire* 4.5, trans. R. J. Teske, in *Answer to the Pelagians II*, edited by John Rotelle (New York: New City Press, 1998), where the pursuit of sexual pleasure is explicitly described as "animal," and *The City of God* 14.16, trans. Henry Bettenson (London: Penguin, 1972), where he describes the "almost total extinction of mental alertness" in orgasm. In actual fact, although Augustine constantly emphasizes the bodily focus of sexual desire (referring throughout *Marriage and Desire* to the "concupiscence of the flesh," for example), he is a subtle observer of the phenomenology of sexuality, and many of his observations anticipate those of modern intentionalists, in particular about the crucial connections between arousal and passivity (*The City of God* 14.26) and its possible emotional intensification (14.16).

18. Goldman: "Traditional writings were correct to emphasize the purely physical or animal aspect of sex; they were wrong only in condemning it" (42; 60 in this volume).

19. See, especially, *Nicomachean Ethics*, books 2 and 3; *De Motu Animalium* 6 and 7; and *De Anima* III 9-11. For discussion, see Martha Nussbaum, *The Fragility of Goodness* (Cambridge, Mass.: Cambridge University Press, 1986), chapter 9.

20. Most notably by Immanuel Kant, who describes in his later work the way that a free being is able to reflect upon its inclinations as presented to it by the faculty of sensibility, extending and transforming them by exercise of the imagination. For Kant our animality is a prerequisite for each and every one of our inclinations, but the inclinations we actually have are not determined by our animality, but rather our animality as mediated by our mentality. And as he clearly sees, our mentality can transform our sensibility in dramatic ways, producing inclinations very different from the animal urges with which they began:

> But reason soon began to stir, and sought, by means of comparing food with what some sense other than those to which instinct was tied—the sense of sight perhaps—presented to it as similar to those foods, so as to extend the knowledge of the sources of nourishment beyond the limits of instinct. If only this attempt had not contradicted nature it could, with luck, have turned out well enough, even though instinct did not advise it. However, it is a characteristic of reason that it will with the aid of the imagination cook up desires for things for which there is no natural urge, but even an urge to avoid.

From Kant's *Speculative Beginning of Human History* 8:111, trans. Ted Humphrey (Indianapolis, Ind.: Hackett, 1983).

21. I actually think that intentionality is in fact central to sexual pleasure in the vast majority of sexual encounters. Perhaps the reason Primoratz misses this is that both his main intentionalist targets overstate its standard complexity, insisting that sexual intentionality as such displays the characteristics it displays only on certain occasions. On Scruton's understanding of it, for instance, intentionality is essentially individualizing, in the sense that it focuses on the individuality of a sexual partner as the very particular person she is. And clearly there are people for whom the individuality of their partner is so central that they are incapable of becoming aroused by anyone else. But Primoratz rightly notes that there are many sexual encounters in which the partner's personal individuality has little importance. The person looking for casual sex, for example, aims to find a partner possessing characteristics of an entirely general nature. An unwillingness to accept this natural description leads Scruton into absurdities like his claim that such a person "desires to desire" to have sex, rather than desires sex (*Sexual Desire*, 90). Similarly, Solomon's account of sexual desire as aiming at the communication of complex interpersonal attitudes appropriately describes some "eloquent" lovemaking, but seems quite implausible as a description of much impersonal or routine sex. So Primoratz rejects intentionalist accounts. But sexual pleasure in fact depends on intentionalist considerations, albeit much less specific and complicated ones, in a vastly greater number of cases. Uncomplicated bodily pleasure

may be what the participants are pursuing in casual or routine encounters, but that pursuit is circumscribed in normal people by a number of minimal beliefs about their partner's mental states. Most minimally, most people's sexual pleasure is dependent on their belief that their partner consents to the activity. Slightly less minimally, an individual's own sexual pleasure is by and large dependent on the belief that his or her partner is finding the experience pleasurable. It is also dependent on the absence of any number of beliefs, for example that one is held in contempt by one's partner. So whilst Goldman may be right to point out that in some particularly satisfying sexual encounters complicated intentionality would just get in the way (47; 66 in this volume), minimal intentionality is necessary for the kind of bodily immersion which he describes. If a normal person were to come to believe that his partner was not finding an encounter or some activity within it enjoyable, his pleasure would be quickly "deflated." *Epithumia* remains *epithumia* (or something not very far removed from it) in these sexual encounters, but certain intentional conditions need to be satisfied for *epithumia* to be satisfied.

22. Names have been changed to protect the guilty. "Fuck the Police" is the title of a controversial track on the album "Straight Outta Compton," released by the rap group NWA (Priority Records, 1988).

23. A literary parallel for the first case can be found in De Sade's *Philosophy in the Bedroom* (trans. Richard Seaver and Austryn Wainhouse [London: Arrow Books, 1965], 250–51), where the character Dolmancé describes how blaspheming and desecrating religious icons during sexual acts brings a peculiarly "sweet" and intense pleasure which "actively affects my imagination." This seems to be straightforward autobiography on Sade's part. See the prostitute Jeanne Testard's testimony regarding Sade's "first outrage" of 1763, discussed in Francine du Plessix Gray, *At Home with the Marquis de Sade* (London: Pimlico, 2000), 64–66. See also George Bataille, *Story of the Eye* (London: Penguin, 1979). A literary parallel to the second example is the subject matter of Milan Kundera's *The Joke* (London: Penguin, 1970), although the case is slightly different, because the entire *raison d'être* of the main character's seduction of a particular woman is to revenge himself upon a third party. He has no interest in the woman herself; indeed, in herself she disgusts him. Kundera is a writer acutely aware of the connection between sexuality and contingent meaning. See especially *The Unbearable Lightness of Being* (London: Faber and Faber, 1984), part 3, section 2. Another reason I prefer to discuss my examples is to show that complex idiosyncratic significance can be central to the arousal of perfectly ordinary people, and not just moral and sexual monsters like de Sade and Bataille's Simone.

24. I've unfortunately been unable to locate the source in which I read about this, but it is not at all unbelievable. Indeed it seems that in some establishments this behaviour would be somewhat on the tame side. See, for example, Edmund White, *States of Desire: Travels in Gay America* (London: Picador, 1986), in particular his description of "The Mine Shaft" (282–85). There are a number of literary and autobiographical accounts detailing the particular excitement that can accompany anonymous sexual encounters. See for instance Joe Orton's diary entry for Saturday, March 4, 1967 in *The Orton Diaries* (edited by John Lahr [London: Methuen, 1986]).

25. Obviously there's an important sense in which the account I am outlining leaves matters opaque, since it provides no explanation of the natural history of desires of this nature. I don't pretend to be able to offer an explanation of why some people eroticize anonymity or pain or domination or stiletto heels or anything else. Perhaps we must turn to psychology for this. For instance, see the interesting speculative account of the origins of sadomasochism in J. Roger Lee, "Sadomasochism: An Ethical Analysis," in *Philosophical Perspectives on Sex and Love*, edited by Robert Stewart (Oxford, U.K.: Oxford University Press, 1995), 125–37. But unlike the reductionist account, my account accurately characterizes the nature of the desire, which explains the activity. The prone man does not want bodily pleasure caused by a penis in his anus; he wants to be buggered by a stranger, which he anticipates will provide him with a very particular pleasure of great physical intensity.

26. An interesting example of the effect of significance on a non-sexual appetite is Alex de Jonge's story of the henchman of Stalin who described how his steak tasted that much more delicious when he recalled that others didn't have any (*Stalin* [London: Collins, 1986], 513).

27. See Leopold von Sacher-Masoch's "The Origins of Masochism," a fascinating account of the development of his own sexual obsessions; reprinted in *Sexuality: A Reader*, edited by Robert Nye (Oxford, U.K.: Oxford University Press, 1999), 166–67.

28. This is clear from a number of phenomena. We find individuals attractive or unattractive simply by looking at photographs of their faces or bodies, whilst knowing nothing about their personalities or social standing. Individuals have particular preferences about physical types, going out with a string of slim brunettes, for example. Some individuals are seen as attractive by large numbers of other individuals, who vary dramatically in their values and preferences regarding personality traits. And so on.

29. Solomon's account ("Sexual Paradigms") seems to come closest to capturing some of the more complex phenomena. See the list of highly complex interpersonal attitudes that Solomon believes are sexually communicable (28), and also his attack on Nagel for assuming that we should take a very particular (and basic) sexual scenario as our "sexual paradigm" (22). But he is wrong that these significances need to be communicated. The woman in "Victory" was not communicating her triumph but reveling privately in it, though the intensity of its physical manifestation alerted her partner. Johnny Drugs hardly wants to communicate the significance to him of his partner's job, since that significance at least in part lies precisely in the fact that she does not know he is "on the other side of the law." Besides, there was presumably a good chance she wouldn't have been impressed if he had.

30. For example Goldman, "Plain Sex," 46 (64 in this volume); Primoratz, *Ethics and Sex*, 43.

31. For example, Goldman: "sex can express love and take on heightened significance when it does . . ." (45; 63 in this volume); Primoratz: "The fact that one's sexual touch expresses certain feelings for the other may well add to the other's pleasure" (*Ethics and Sex*, 39). Note, however, that Primoratz does not clearly state that it is the other's sexual pleasure which is enhanced, and that Goldman is not at all explicit about the relationship between sexual pleasure and significance.

32. Indeed, it might be quite the opposite. One can find it unpleasant if someone wears the same perfume as a former partner, for example, since this can be intrusive and distracting, bringing quite unwanted thoughts of the other person into one's head at an entirely inopportune moment.

33. The fact that someone's idiosyncratic taste is not in itself pleasurable makes this an especially good example. One can easily miss the way a tactile sexual sensation is eroticized through sexual significance, by insisting on focusing on its intrinsic pleasurableness. But it is hard to believe that the taste of a mixture of whisky, cigarettes, and a particular flavour of saliva could be in itself intrinsically pleasant, let alone erotic. It is so because that is how *she* always used to taste, all that time ago.

34. Primoratz, *Ethics and Sex*, 39–40.

35. It would, I think, be unfair to accuse the intentionalists I have been discussing of missing this. Nagel and Scruton are quite clear that we seek mutual reciprocal *arousal*, for instance. The impression that reductionists seem to have, that intentionalism loses the bodily element of sex, lies in the refusal of some of them to see that a great deal of normal sexual pleasure has minimal intentionality associated with it, and in the impression their writings can convey that everything is going on at some rarified mental level. (Solomon is the worst offender here.) So even though I have been claiming that my account incorporates the insights of all the positions, it is clearly much closer to the accounts of Scruton, Solomon, and Nagel than to those of Goldman and Primoratz. Since I think that we cannot understand the phenomenon of sexual desire without grasping its potential intentionality, mine is clearly an intentionalist account. I take

mine to be an advance on the others because it incorporates a much greater range of relevant intentional factors than theirs.

36. Indeed, one gets the feeling from their writing that it is their conviction that there is nothing wrong with this that drives their view that "means-end" accounts of desire must be mistaken, rather than the other way around. See, for example, Goldman: "Any analysis of sex which imputes a moral character to sex acts in themselves is wrong for that reason" (49; 67 in this volume).

37. Here's an interesting example: I was once told by a married woman who frequently indulged in extra-marital affairs that she'd had to ditch one particular lover because he was obviously turned on by the fact that she was married, paying attention to her wedding ring and mentioning her husband during lovemaking and the like. (This quite turned her off, presumably because he was excited by a very impersonal fact about her, and in any case, it reminded her she was cheating on her husband. [For a relationship in which being married to others played an erotic role in their adultery, see Mickey and Drenka in Philip Roth's *Sabbath's Theater* (New York: Houghton Mifflin, 1995), e.g., 32—eds.])

38. Thanks to Matthew Kieran, Mark Nelson, and Bryan Frances for helpful comments. Bryan in particular was a very stern critic, and he is unlikely to think I have made any great effort to address his concerns.

STUDY QUESTIONS

1. Explain how Morgan characterizes the "reductionist" and "nonreductionist" views of sexual desire. Assemble a list of the crucial differences between the two views, according to Morgan. Compare your results with what you gleaned from reading the essay by Alan Goldman.

2. One of Morgan's important arguments for his "intentionalist" reading of sexual desire invokes an example: "In . . . gay bathhouses that flourished in San Francisco in the '70s and early '80s, men could be found lying face down on benches . . . with their heads covered by towels. Other men would . . . mount and penetrate a prone man, in due course ejaculate, withdraw and leave, and at no time during an encounter would either of the participants see the face of the other. . . . The reductionist account will have to point to the physical pleasure that the participants will experience as motivating their behaviour. But . . . the account under-describes the situation. . . . The *only explanation* [emphasis added—eds.] of the rationale behind the ritual is that for these men the very anonymity of the encounter is part of what is *sexually* enjoyable about it. The prone man will not experience himself as feeling the physical sensation of a moving penis penetrating his anus, he will experience the sensation of the moving penis *of a stranger* penetrating his anus . . . (which he anticipates will provide him with a very particular pleasure of great physical intensity)."

   How plausible do you find the following reply to Morgan? We can imagine that in this scenario it is exactly the pleasure of a penis moving in and out of his bottom that the prone man desires; the towel covering his face may be there to protect his identity as a local attorney, and he is not "intentionalizing" his desire and pleasure by the *thought* that *a stranger* is doing the job. He may look forward to many penises doing the job in succession, but not because they are the penises of strangers. Would it help if we were we able to ask these prone men if the intentionalizing thought was sexually important to them? If so, are we dealing with an empirical psychological matter and not a philosophical conceptual matter?

If Morgan's claim that he is supplying the "only" explanation is false, if his example does not succeed in accomplishing what he was trying to do with it, that is, to provide an example that *cannot* be adequately handled by the "reductionists," what follows about his intentionality thesis? Should we say that the reductionists are right, that sexual desire aims directly at pleasurable sensations, because there are clearly some sexual experiences that conform with this pattern? Or should we say that the intentionalists are right because there are some sexual phenomena that make "better" sense to us if looked at as intentionalist experiences?

3. In his essay, Alan Goldman writes, "sexual desire is essentially desire for physical contact itself. It is a bodily desire for the body of another that dominates our mental life for more or less brief periods" ("Plain Sex," in this volume, 60). In this sentence, the word "another" seems to have a broad scope, as referring *de dicto* to anyone at all. But in this sentence—"it is not a desire for a particular sensation detachable from its causal context, a sensation which can be derived in other ways" (59)—he may be read as asserting that sexual desire is *de re*, that is, is focused on the particular person that causally arouses it and toward which it is directed. Is that a fair reading? (It exposes a Scrutonish Goldman.) If yes, has Goldman already admitted what Morgan argues, that any account of sexual desire will be at least minimally intentionalist?

4. Morgan asserts that "it is quite possible to consent to something that is bad for one, or for which one's partner holds one in contempt." In such cases, according to Morgan, consent is not sufficient to make the sexual act morally "wholesome" or avoid being in some way problematic. Provide an example of such a case and an argument as to why, despite the presence of genuine consent, the act is still morally questionable. (Before answering, try to get clear about what Morgan means by morally "problematic" sexual activity.)

5. Ann Cahill ("Why 'Derivatization' Is Better Than 'Objectification,'" in this volume) tries to restore, protect, or save a sort of "carnal" sexual desire from those feminist accounts of sexuality according to which objectification is branded as inherently illicit. Might Ca-

hill's notion of "derivatization" be understood as a moralized version of the metaphysical account of sexual desire offered by Morgan? Basing your estimates on her examples of derivatizing and non-derivatizing sexual interactions, try to locate various kinds and degrees of derivatization on Morgan's continuum between "reductionist" and "intentionalist" accounts of sex. More generally, which approach to sexual desire, Morgan's or reductionism, is more feminism(s)-friendly?

EIGHT

Chatting Is Not Cheating

John Portmann

John Portmann *argues that our interacting verbally through erotically desig-*
nated chat rooms available on the Internet does not count as our "having sex," or
as "sex," because no skin-against-skin physical contact occurs. Erotic keyboard
chatting with another person, which is akin to "dirty talk," is no more "having
sex" with that person than is flirting visually with another person (but only a
prelude to "sex"). By using the expression "chatting is not cheating," Portmann
means to deny that erotic chatting is adultery. Not only does erotic chatting
(whether done through the Internet or over the telephone) not involve any "pene-
tration" (an old, suspicious, but possibly unavoidable criterion of "adultery"),
but it also fails to be adultery because it is not "having sex" to begin with, on
Portmann's criterion. Chatting allows us to satisfy sexual desires by relying on
our imaginations while also not violating the rules of marriage or monogamy,
much like viewing pornography provides sexual satisfaction while not involving
any real, physical sexual interaction with another person (and hence is not
cheating).

John Portmann studied philosophy at Yale and Cambridge and teaches religious studies at the University of
Virginia. This essay is from John Portmann, ed., *In Defense of Sin*, pp. 223–41, published in 2001, reproduced here with the permission of Palgrave Macmillan. (Scholars are hereby advised that in the process of
preparing chapter 8, a number of changes were made to the original text.) "Chatting Is Not Cheating" and its
author received national media attention in the summer of 2011, in the wake of the Anthony Wiener scandal.
Wiener, a Democratic member of the U.S. House of Representatives from New York, was forced to step down
after sexting a woman who wasn't his wife.

> Do you know what it is as you pass to be
> loved by strangers?
> Do you know the talk of those
> turning eye-balls?
> —Walt Whitman, "Song of the Open Road" (1856)

A triumph of human imagination, the Internet has expanded and facilitated communication. Lust, an age-old focus of human imagination, now enjoys a new stage on which to triumph.

The Internet simplifies life in ways many people have noticed. It complicates life as well, though, particularly with regard to sexual morality. Anonymous dirty talk over the Internet presents what may seem to be a new moral puzzle: Is it sex? Does it amount to betrayal if your boyfriend, girlfriend, husband, or wife logs on to an erotic chat room? Your mother or father? Your son or daughter? A priest, nun, rabbi, or minister? No. The Internet has not given us a new way to *have* sex but rather an absorbing new way to *talk about* sex. Distinguishing between flirting and fidelity will show that talking dirty, whether on the Internet or over the phone, does not amount to having sex.

I make a case for the moral acceptability of anonymous dirty talk, which is no better or worse than viewing pornography. Along the way, I suggest that reflection on the erotics of the Internet usefully exposes the largely intuitive and pre-articulate anxiety with which most of us approach the topic of sex.

WAYS OF FLIRTING

Probably as long as *Homo sapiens* have been around they have been having dirty thoughts. Like some Greeks before them, many ancient Jews (Genesis 20:2 and Leviticus 18) and Christians suffered through lust as if it were a curse. Famously, Jesus taught that the man who lusted after a woman in his heart had already committed adultery (Matthew 5:28). When, some two thousand years later, Jimmy Carter confessed in a *Playboy* interview to having lusted after women other than his wife, Americans took the news badly. Carter lost the 1980 presidential election.

What's so bad about lust? Certainly it can lead to bad consequences, but so can love, charity, mercy, and a host of other decidedly laudable motivations. We might place the blame on how lust affects our relations to others, but Plato objects to how lust affects our relation to *ourselves*. The true philosopher doesn't concern himself with sexual pleasure, according to Plato, who refers to sexual desire as a disease of the personality. Plato counsels us to sublimate sexual energy in intellectual pursuits.[1]

Many Jewish and Christian thinkers have endorsed Plato's denunciation. In 1 Cor. 7, a text that shaped Christian thinking about sexuality for many centuries, Paul warns married couples which refrain from sexual relations to resume intercourse, "lest Satan tempt you through lack of self-control." Augustine, perhaps the greatest Christian theologian of all," implored God to free him from the lust that controlled him: "Oh Lord, you will increase your gifts in me, so that my soul may follow me to you, freed from the concupiscence [that is, lust] which binds it, and rebel no more against itself."[2] Luther, among other theologians, regarded lust as a consequence of self-love or pride, an obstacle to be overcome.[3] Thomas More accused Luther, a common lecher, of having begun the Reformation simply because he could not control his own lust.

Lust prevents us from being who we really are, Augustine says. He cultivates an athletic ideal, one in which we become strong enough to surmount lust as a champion hurdler mechanically leaps over obstacles in his path. Augustine's reflections leave us to wonder whether he understood the harmful effects of repressing sexual desire. (Freud made a career out of detailing these effects.) Missing from Augustine is the idea that lust completes us (however temporarily), fills us with a vivid sense of being alive, propels us along the way to self-fulfillment. (The zeal with which religious figures such as St. Teresa of Avila, St. John of the Cross, or St. Jerome have sought God approximates lust, it may sometimes seem.) Lust, like the playfulness of children or the treasures of the Louvre, lights up a rainy day.

Not surprisingly, dirty thoughts can terrorize those who condemn lust. Hemingway's short story "God Rest You Merry, Gentlemen" introduces a sixteen-year-old boy whose fear of lust drives him to castrate himself. Some parents subject their daughters to female genital mutilation in order to prevent lustful desires or, worse, succumbing to passion. An official document from the World Health Organization estimated in February, 2012, that over 92 million African girls and women had been subjected to the procedure.[4]

At the dawn of a new century, there is considerably less public fear of dirty thoughts than there used to be. In the 1990s the American press trumpeted the singer Madonna's confessing to fantasies of having sex in a Catholic church (her 1989 video "Like a Prayer," set in a church, stirred controversy upon its release).[5] And in that same decade, Americans largely forgave President Bill Clinton his now-famous marital misdeeds.

Even now, though, some conservative religious people will still insist that sex ought to be procreative, not merely recreational (as in adultery). As late as 1972, one of the better-known philosophers in the West insisted that this view is a necessary step if one is morally to oppose petting, prostitution, sodomy, and "homosexual intercourse."[6] People who morally object to dirty thoughts will naturally (and reasonably) object to talking dirty (in person) and chatting dirty (over the phone or on the Internet). My thoughts will do nothing to dissuade them. Here I address what must be the overwhelming majority of people who see some moral leeway in dirty thoughts and indeed dirty talk.

‿

On the Internet, dirty talk passes as "chatting" (which is not to say that all chat rooms are erotically oriented). As if chatting were not already ambiguous enough, some people have taken to referring to it as "phone sex." What is phone sex? Do you need a phone for it? Will a chat room do? Is phone sex any different from what we call "talking dirty"?

For at least a decade before the advent of the Internet, pornographic magazines and subway advertisements (ubiquitous in Paris) offered the telephone numbers of professionals (in the sense that they got paid) available to explore sexual fantasies. A business transaction, this call entailed a fee, charged to your phone bill, based on time spent talking. You paid, and the pro profited.

By "phone sex," people seem to mean talking dirty on the phone. You may have a private phone conversation with an amateur you have "met" in a chat room, or you may call a "pro" and pay for his or her services, as advertised on the Internet or elsewhere. In any event, you do not meet, although you may have seen a photograph of him or her (or think you have—you may have exchanged pictures on the Internet, but he or she may have submitted a photo of someone else). "Phone sex" involves another person in a way that solitary sprints through pornographic magazines do not.

Is this talk a way of having sex? The idea that words can seduce others, or might serve as a kind of foreplay, has been around for centuries. Poets from around the world have left us some shining examples. With Freud came the idea that talking might be equivalent to sex itself. Certainly talking dirty falls within the realm of sexual harassment—it is not something a manager can do at work to subordinates, for example (although technically, the dirty talk must be unwelcome, severe, and protracted in order to win a lawsuit against an employer). The idea that "phone sex" is a "gateway drug" that will escalate to something much bigger and more dangerous does not seem obvious, though. Chat rooms are journeys that needn't lead to physical contact with another. Of course, they sometimes do.

What people call "phone sex" isn't really sex at all. Of crucial importance is the lack of touching (despite AT&T's commercial invitations to "reach out and touch someone"). Thinking of dirty talk over the phone as sex confuses moral evaluation. The verbal innovation "phone sex," clever as it may sound, ought to be abandoned. We already have a perfectly apt way of describing this activity: talking dirty. Anyone wishing to emphasize the phone's role in dirty talk would do better to speak of phone flirting. Flirting may or may not lead to sexual contact, but flirting itself is not sex.

Neither is voyeurism sex. Ogling pornographic images, either in an old-fashioned magazine or on the Internet, is a kind of voyeurism. It is not sex. Most of us are soft-core voyeurs to some extent (not just the prosaic husband with "a wandering eye"). Depending on the configuration of the shower room, lesbian, gay, and bisexual people can hardly avoid becoming voyeurs each time they wash off at the gym. Looking into other people's windows, what a peeping Tom does, is hardcore voyeurism. Although a peeping Tom can get into trouble with the law, what he or she does is not sex. People who talk dirty in Internet chat rooms are a new kind of peeping Tom—typing Toms we might call them. They are not having sex.

Whatever else flirting may be, it is not sex. Patting someone on the bottom or giving a hug may sometimes arouse us; neither amounts to sex, though. And what about dancing? Is that sex? Indeed, there is such a thing as "dirty dancing"—even a movie by that title. Flirting and dancing have long troubled religious leaders because of the confusing dynamic that these activities inaugurate. We want to insist that waltzing with the boss's husband or the boss's wife can be morally innocent, despite the close physical contact involved. Dancing, like flirting, is not sex.

It might be thought that flirting is intentional, that is to say that we flirt only if we intend to do so. But this view misses the ease with which we can hide behind our roles as sales clerks, waiters, and entertainers. We can flirt even when we pretend we are just doing what's expected of us. We can deceive others, even ourselves, about what we intend.

Waiters and sales clerks routinely report that flirting with customers is good for business. It is hard to deny that flirting becomes us. The stodgy butler from Ishiguro's novel *The Remains of the Day* ruminates on his refusal to flirt and the colorless, lonely existence to which it has led: "Perhaps it is indeed time I began to look at this whole matter of bantering more enthusiastically. After all, when one thinks about it, it is not such a foolish thing to indulge in—particularly if it is the case that in bantering lies the key to human warmth."[7] Flirting can build rapport with others. We understand what it means, for example, to dress for success in the workplace or to keep up with fashion trends when going to parties. We may find ourselves flirting by wearing clothing that fits our bodies closely or exposes a certain amount of leg, chest, or arm. We might wonder, What is the difference between the sight of a woman's cleavage emerging from an expensive French gown and the chat room journey of someone who never intends to have sex with anyone he meets in cyberspace? It may well be that flirting amounts to self-centered bragging or exhibitionism: "Look how beautiful I am," fashionably dressed people may be saying. Flirting may sometimes ask nothing more of others than admiration.

In contrast to flirting, it is possible to engage in another suspect kind of activity all by yourself: masturbation. Involving no mutuality, masturbation is known as a distinctly inferior form of sexual activity. In his early writings, Karl Marx derided what he took to be Hegel's extravagantly theoretical books through a mean analogy: Hegel is to "real" philosophy what masturbation is to "real" sex. Those who view anonymous cyberchatting as a new way of having sex would presumably conclude that chatting is a disappointing and even embarrassing substitute for a higher pleasure.

Long-standing opposition to pornography is rooted in an ancient fear of (male) masturbation. (Most moral thinking about masturbation has ignored female masturbation.) Chatting will likely (and reasonably) offend anyone who objects to pornography, in part because of the alleged link between pornography and masturbation.

Vilification of masturbation, or, onanism, stretches back over two thousand years. Modern people often find the received reasons for condemning masturbation hilarious. Ancient Greeks and Romans, for example, thought of semen as costly horsepower. Ejaculation robbed a man of a vital fluid without which he could not roar or soar. As recently as a hundred years ago, some religious thinkers in the United States insisted that unused semen was reabsorbed by the body and then harnessed as energy. Proper religious devotion was impossible without the tremendous energy supplied by conserved semen. Frequent intercourse in a marriage was therefore discouraged and masturbation vilified (soldiers in the ancient world were cautioned against any ejaculations at all). Rabbinical Judaism and Roman Catholicism have long condemned the sin of Onan. The film *Monty Python's The Meaning of Life* even includes a musical send-up of Catholic reverence for semen called "Every Sperm Is Sacred."[8] To the extent that chatting, like pornography, induces masturbation, it is not surprising that a cultural tide of objection rises up to greet this cyber-innovation.

⌒

Men fantasize about sex roughly twice as frequently as women, according to studies in Japan, the United Kingdom, and the United States. Men are more likely to fantasize about strangers as well, which means that chatting might tempt men more than women.

But if Oscar Wilde is correct that women fall in love with their ears and men with their eyes, then the textual, nonpictorial world of chat rooms might appeal more to women than men. Some recent fiction (such as Sylvia Brownrigg's *The Metaphysical Touch*, Jeanette Winterson's *The Powerbook*, and Alan Lightman's *The Diagnosis*) prominently features women chatting. We are sure to see a steady stream of novels involving chatting in the near future, and these works may challenge the very idea that chatting appeals more to one gender than the other.

Women may risk more in chatting or flirting. Culture and law have long been men's domains. It is hardly surprising that religious and secular cultures both reflect a masculine bias. To be sure, there are words for men who "get around": We call them a Don Juan, a Casanova, a Lothario. We call women other names, names that should not be repeated in polite society. For millennia, fathers and husbands have made it difficult for their daughters and wives to flirt. The Internet makes it easier for anyone with access to cyberspace to flirt. As long as women remain economically dependent on men, though, they will risk more in chatting (assuming, of course, that those on whom they depend consider chatting cheating).

Flirting requires a certain comfort level with uncertainty. As the popular saying "flirting with disaster" indicates, we are on our way somewhere when we flirt. We have not arrived, nor will we necessarily. Augustine, who cast greater aspersion on sex than perhaps any other Western thinker, started out as an adventurous young man. His famous plea to God "Give me chastity and continence—but not yet" plays off of flirting. Augustine had not yet embraced the ideal moral life and so, his reasoning goes, did not deserve any credit for the desire. By the same reasoning, we do not deserve blame for flirting with attractive people.

We sustain our notion of fidelity by banishing uncertainty and policing its attendant complications, such as devouring porn magazines, a night at Chippendale's or a topless bar, and everyday flirting. We may understandably fear ambivalence once we have made a romantic commitment. Nonetheless, the idea that better or deeper erotic fulfillment lies elsewhere may nag at us. Through flirting, we enjoy uncertainty. Our comfort level with uncertainty (and love is notoriously unstable) drives our moral evaluation of online dalliances.

WAYS OF CHEATING

Strangers in the Net, exchanging glances, strangers in the Net, what are the chances? They'll be sharing love, before the night is through? The chances of falling in love on-line may not be any worse than in the street. Yet, as always, a person intent on remaining faithful to a spouse or partner must be careful to avoid crossing a certain line. Whatever else a monogamous commitment may entail, it forbids sex outside the couple.

As I have acknowledged, some people certainly do believe that talking dirty is a form of having sex.[9] In some arenas (such as the office), talking dirty qualifies as sexual harassment, but, as I have said, I don't think it makes sense to call this sex. I hold on to the notion, admittedly old-fashioned, that sex entails skin-to-skin contact. Peeping Toms may get into real legal trouble, but it doesn't make sense to say that voyeurism amounts to having sex. Like sexual harassment, voyeurism implicates the active party but not necessarily the passive one.

Ranking sexual misdeeds requires talent and time. Our legal system can help. "Adultery" signifies penal-vaginal penetration and applies to the illicit sexual activity of two or more people, at least one of whom is married. Only married people can be guilty of adultery: if an unmarried woman engages in vaginal intercourse with a married man, he is guilty of adultery, whereas she is guilty of fornication. "Fornication" is to unmarried people what "adultery" is to the married, which is not to say that married people can't fornicate. "Sodomy" applies to both the married and the unmarried and involves anal and/or oral sex. Because they cannot legally marry, gay and lesbian couples can in principle never be guilty of adultery, only of fornication or sodomy. In the highly publicized Monica Lewinsky case, President Clinton (a married man) was guilty of fornication and Lewinsky was guilty of sodomy.

Moral distinctions loom behind such legal ones. There is nothing legally wrong with serial monogamy, for instance. Lots of people in their late teens and twenties devote themselves in earnest to a sexual relationship that they claim has long-term potential. After the break-up, another relationship begins and then ends. The cycle continues. Morally speaking, such serial monogamy may not seem very different from fornication. And yet most of us will feel there has to be some difference between promiscuity and failing to carry through on good intentions.

It is important to recognize these distinctions as culturally conditioned. Not everyone agrees with American mores (not even in America). Throughout much of Asia, for example, married men have openly taken concubines with apparent impunity:

> A traditional Chinese or Japanese man could be branded as adulterous only if he slept with the wife of another man. This was taboo. Illicit sex with a married woman was a violation against the woman's husband and his entire ancestry. In China these lawbreakers were burned to death. If a man seduced the wife of his guru in India, he might be made to sit on an iron plate that was glowing hot, then chop off his own penis. A Japanese man's only honorable course was suicide. In traditional Asian agricultural societies, only geishas, prostitutes, slaves, and concubines were fair game. Sex with them was simply not considered adultery.[10]

Not surprisingly, extramarital sex in traditional East Asian cultures was strictly off limits to women, always. What is nonetheless interesting here is the notion that morality (like immorality) has a limit. Adultery doesn't signify *all* sex with someone other than your spouse, just some. This is roughly analogous to the idea that on the third Friday of every month, husbands and wives may morally have sex with anyone they like. If the analogy seems arbitrary, it is because so little of cultural practice is transparent to people who live beyond it.

And so the identity of the person one courted or bedded has figured into the ways other cultures have defined adultery. That identity counts for little in America, where *all* sex with someone other than your spouse qualifies as adultery. Where does cyberflirting fit into this schema? Legally, Internet flirting (what typing Toms do) does not fall into any of our three categories (adultery, fornication, or sodomy). And yet many people will maintain that chatting threatens, or could threaten, monogamous unions. If chatting did represent a kind of cheating, then it would have to be acknowledged as a genuinely new one. I do not think there is anything new under the sun.

Despite the criticism heaped upon Bill Clinton in the wake of his "rationalizations" of sexual adventures (or nonadventures, as he insisted) in the white House, still it remains that most of us agree there is a difference between all-out adultery, hanky-panky, and just talking about one or the other. I am not claiming that we should think of the ethics of virtual flirting on a case-by-case basis but that we should think of chat rooms as morally ambiguous—neither wholly bad nor wholly good.

Another way of thinking about online fidelity is to ask whether a virgin is still a virgin after chatting. In strict religious terms, certainly not.[11] He or she has affronted modesty—"sinned against purity," as Catholic theologians say. Nowadays it is hard to imagine such a view commanding much agreement, even among Catholics. It is still important to remember that rules in a given religion or society go far toward shaping cultural attitudes, though. We can tell something important about Catholicism, for example, from the fact that its greatest moral theologian of the past century maintained that fantasizing about someone else during sex (with your spouse) was a grave moral sin.[12]

Even virgins may burn with lust. The people whom chatting helps most are those committed to celibacy or monogamous relationships. We should expect these people to become the most ardent defenders of imaginative possibilities wrought by the Internet. An obvious advantage to chat rooms is that they keep people out of bars and clubs: away from actual (as opposed to virtual) adulterous possibilities, and away from sexually transmitted diseases as well. This is hardly a moral defense, admittedly.

A good way of defending chatting in the context of committed relationships (whether straight, gay, or religiously committed) is as a temporary "fix"—not unlike a sleeping pill or an antidepressant. Chatting can help you through the inevitable tough times in a relationship aiming at permanency.

Chatting is dangerous to the extent that it absorbs some of the energy required to make a couple a success. A double life carried out in veiled Internet spaces resembles the closet against which most gay and lesbian people develop a sense of self-identity. Chat rooms can become a new closet of sorts (at base, any deep secret can). Double lives can exhaust us, and the Internet can become a demanding mistress indeed, even an addiction. Until chat room adventures start taking up more time than the relationship from which they are a distraction, this danger has nothing to do with the moral acceptability of courting strangers in cyberspace.

While perhaps not the moral ideal, chat room adventures should not be considered adultery or infidelity. The possibility of deceit lurks here, as it does in so many other places. We may pretend to our spouses or spouse equivalents that we would not, could not, even look at another man or woman. There is no question that Romeos and Juliets would be guilty of deceiving their partners if they entered a chat room after having declared they couldn't conceive of doing so. How many among us pretend never to notice attractive strangers? How many of us feel threatened when our partners do notice attractive strangers (or familiars, for that matter)? Chiding chatters may reveal more personal insecurity than moral concern. In any event, it seems the only durable moral objection to chatting is deceit. There might be a good practical objection as well: that chatting will inure us to erotic pleasure with our spouses. If the mind could be so easily dulled by the computer screen, then chatting might in fact threaten a sexual tie to a spouse or spouse equivalent.

Some people are better at flirting than others, and some people are better at fidelity than others. Those who excel at flirting may strike us as cruel if they insist on pointing out our inferior charms and relative unattractiveness. And those who excel at fidelity might strike us as cruel if they were to demand perennial center stage in the thoughts of their spouses or spouse equivalents.

PENETRATION VENERATION

Why should penetration serve as the pivotal criterion for infidelity? Precision is a ready answer. It may seem impossibly difficult to ascertain what someone wants from flirting. She bats her eyelashes and he thinks he has a chance. Then she declines his invitation for a drink, and he furiously demands an explanation. She maintains that he misunderstood her attempt at civil conversation. Or another scenario: Eager to show her interest, she requests help repairing her car. He agrees to try. She cries when he leaves without having asked to see her again. Intentions and desires may sometimes drive our behavior, but others may quite understandably fail to see our motives.

Penetration is another story. A penis in a vagina or someone else's tongue in your mouth can be readily felt or observed. Even if we are under the influence of drugs or alcohol, we will almost certainly realize that penetration is taking place. Act and motive overlap, and so penetration lends itself to the certainty lacking in flirting.

Both formally in the law and informally in the streets, we have long venerated penetration as a reliable threshold for whether sexual intercourse is taking place. Two thousand years ago, for instance, the poet Ovid lamented his impotence. In a poem included in the "Amores" series, he wrote: "Although I wanted to do it, and she was more than willing, / I couldn't get my pleasure part to work. / She tried everything and then some. . . ." [13]

Ovid piques our curiosity through the terseness of this last line. Despite the diligence of his partner, Ovid tells us that: "She left me, pure as any Vestal virgin / polite as any sister to her brother." [14] He leaves us to wonder how seriously Vestal virgins took their profession and also how well he knew his sister. Ovid's coquettishness aside, we should take him at his word here. He apparently believed that he had not had sex with this woman, who so exerted herself and with whom he tried "everything and then some." Anne Fausto-Sterling has woven this notion into a description of male identity. "Of course, we know already that for men the true mark of heterosexuality involves vaginal penetration with the penis. Other activities, even if they are with a woman, do not really count." [15] Other writers have used penetration as a dramatic psychological threshold. Entering another person may excite fear, a fear that even marriage may not dislodge:

> Among couples who come to a sex-therapy clinic, the prevalence of the madonna/whore or saint/sinner phenomenon is astonishingly high. It wears a proverbial coat of many colors and designs, and so has many disguises. A classic example is that in which the period of romance and courtship was intensely positive for both partners. They engage in much above-the-belt activity and some heavy petting of the genitals to the point of climax, but no genital union itself. They don't actually say that they are saving the dirty part of sex until after they are legally married. Their own explanation is that they are applying their own moral standards by postponing actual penovaginal penetration.
>
> Once they are legally married, they gradually reach the discovery that they can't have ordinary sexual intercourse. He blames himself for ejaculating too soon and for not being able to arouse her to have much active desire or enthusiasm for his penis. She goes along with his self-blame and keeps both of them blinded to the fact that she has a paralyzing fear of having anything actually penetrate into the cavity of her vagina. For her that would be as degrading as being a whore. [16]

Johns Hopkins psychologist John Money draws our attention to a primitive fear of one of the most sensitive boundaries of all—that between our bodies and the outside world. Religious anxiety blossoms on this boundary. This is how sex writer Lisa Palac recounts her furtive sexual debut while a Catholic high school girl in 1970s Chicago:

> Just before the big moment, I admitted that I didn't *exactly* know what
> to do. "Just open your legs and rock," he told me, which sounded
> remarkably like a Foghat song. It was over in minutes. Afterwards, I
> was extremely disappointed and felt sick with guilt. I kept torturing
> myself with the mantra "I am not a virgin I am not a virgin," which
> was stupid because I'd done practically everything else—as many oth-
> er girls in my class had done—yet none of that constituted sex. It
> wasn't sex until he put it in.[17]

Penetration veneration finds itself covertly transmitted through the celebration of modesty in this confession. Later recounting one of her first
online erotic encounters, Palac tells us of the terrible guilt she felt after
the fact. She warned her chat man: "If you tell anyone what we just did,
I'll never speak to you again!" She added, "I felt so uncontrollably Catholic. I shouldn't have had cybersex on the first date. Big sin. I should have
waited. It would have meant more to me if I'd waited."[18]

Ironic chuckles aside, Palac contradicts herself. Her dirty talk, which
in this case eventually progressed from the Internet to the telephone, was
not sex, even on her own terms. But vestiges of Catholic school modesty
surfaced and prompted guilty feelings.

Carnal contact cannot by itself distinguish flirting from cheating. Unlike exhibitionism or rape, flirting plays off of negotiation. We do not
force ourselves on others in flirting; we toy with the exploration of another's opinion of us. It would be too simplistic to reduce flirting to
sexual playfulness, though. The ancient Greeks and Romans were notoriously playful sexually. Ascetic Jews and then Christians challenged this
playfulness and replaced it with *gravitas*, a high moral seriousness. It is
difficult to ally flirtatiousness with either side of this divide. For the
sexually playful will pursue flirting until sex, which is to say that the
flirting is actually foreplay. The morally serious will swear off flirting
generally but smile on a scripted version of chaste romance. Who, then,
flirts?

Technically speaking, gregarious people who do not really intend to
have sex are just flirting (using penetration as the criterion here). Of
course, it is often difficult to predict whether any spirited conversation or
eye exchange will lead to full-fledged physical contact. But people who
know what they want will see the sense of setting foreplay off from
flirting. Seduction can be a game that consciously starts with words and
glances. Flirting is an end unto itself—a way of showing someone else
that we know "how to play the game" or, perhaps, a test in which we
prove to ourselves that we are still attractive. Happily (or even not so
happily) married people flirt with colleagues and cocktail party strangers, and it is perfectly acceptable for them to do so. Chatting is the technological celebration of flirting. Adulterous impulses lurking in protected
cyberspace will likely lead to penetration; curiosity, playfulness, or bore-
dom, however, will just end in chatting.

The problem with penetration veneration, to which I myself fall victim, is that we end up saying that a man who receives anonymous fellatio has had sex, whereas two close friends who spend a night cuddling naked in bed have not. Even this position is easier to accept than the idea that typing amounts to having sex, though. In the second scenario, we might applaud whatever moral motivation prevented the two friends from consummating their passion. The first scenario, meaningless as it might have been, lacks this moral motivation.

Penetration veneration molds the mind of many a Westerner, sometimes to quite surprising effect. In *Been There, Haven't Done That*, recent Harvard graduate Tara McCarthy, also Catholic, tells us that she is a virgin, despite having been "touched, kissed, poked, prodded, rubbed, caressed, sucked, licked, bitten—you name it."[19] Reflection on this so-called virgin's way of seeing the world should remind us that sex, despite all the advertising it gets, is neither transparently obvious nor wholly intuitive. If it accomplished nothing else, the media coverage of the Monica Lewinsky scandal made clear the extent to which people can differ over the question of when sex begins and flirting ends.

In a sea of ambiguity, penetration emerges as the best single criterion of cheating we may expect to find.

INFIDELITY ONLINE?

Nothing prompts divorce so often as infidelity. We can't stand it when our partners go astray—"go astray" may mean sex, lying about having had sex, or both. Many of our most engaging plays and novels have relied on infidelity as a plot device.

Who cares about the ethics of cyberchatting? Many if not most couples naturally do, as well as those who worry about the moral health of the communities they inhabit. The sex lives of strangers have something to do with us, after all. Our children may someday attend school or play soccer with their children, and we want those meetings to be as constructive as possible. Our fear of lust affects our children, our neighbors, and our laws.

Moral evaluation of chatting colors the ways couples interact with one another as well as what we think of our teachers, colleagues, priests, and rabbis. It should go without saying that in order to care about the ethics of chatting, you first have to care about something else: fidelity, "sins against purity," or trust. I consider fidelity a moral ideal, one I certainly endorse.

We can remain agnostic as to whether or how often chatting will lead to a face-to-face encounter. My goal here is to isolate chatting from attendant activities and ask whether there is something intrinsic to chatting itself that qualifies as betrayal (of a promise to a lover or to God), as opposed to an exercise of the imagination (whether we can betray others through the free use of our imagination is a question I do not take up here). I have presented penetration as the decisive test of whether someone has cheated, while indicating the unsettling underside of flirting. I concede that a whole-hearted person, a saint of heroic integrity, would consistently avoid flirting of any sort.

Is cyberchatting the moral equivalent of talking to someone in a bar, then? Anonymous chatting is morally superior to the extent that it is less likely to lead to physical contact. Is Net naughtiness, even when it becomes a habit, morally worse than an actual (and physical) one-night stand? No. Net naughtiness enhances the sexual imagination. It teaches as it titillates. Giving into lust and allowing ourselves to chat may provide the illusion of flying over personal limitations that reduce our attractiveness to others. So much of human industry (for example, cosmetics, fitness, fashion, and real estate) comes down to this goal that we really should look sympathetically on chatting. Moreover, we may deepen our sense of who we are and what we want from anonymous chatting. Net naughtiness challenges the sexual uniformity many take monogamy to impose. It shows us that something like sexual diversity is possible without shattering monogamous bonds.

Net naughtiness strains traditional ideas about what a person is. Are the faceless strangers we meet online real people? Can we hurt their feelings? Can they have us arrested? They understand that we do not know who they are; presumably they cannot be slighted by us over the Internet in the way they can in person. Given the way the Internet depersonalizes human contact (even as it increases the opportunities for locating other people), it is hard to say whether chatting involves another human being in the way that even a one-night stand does. How thinly can we stretch our notion of a person? Very thin indeed, chatting shows us. Those we chat with may seem no more human than the characters who populate the fiction we read.

In the course of defending it, I have recognized the danger of chatting. If it is true that "women are more forgiving and less upset if no emotional involvement accompanies their husband's affair,"[20] then extensive chatting might seem more threatening than a one-night stand. Pen pals or Net pals might seem to develop an emotional attachment to one another over time, an attachment unlikely to begin in a one-night stand. Time, or duration, has a lot to do with both the psychological and moral evaluation of chatting. A night of passion is for many fuming spouses easier to forgive than a cultivated attachment. Chatting certainly can fray our commitments to others, no less than our quest for self-fulfillment.

In sum, the Internet has given lust a new outlet. Fantasy life has always been possible, and pornography already abounded in ancient Greece and Rome (despite Plato's disapproval). Being human just got more exciting—and more complicated. The Internet and the phone may threaten fidelity, chastity, even integrity—but no more so than old-fashioned pornography. Chat rooms may in the long run facilitate fidelity, insofar as they can in themselves satisfy an active imagination.

A pleasure both simple and complex, chatting captures nicely the undying tension between trust and lust. Making room for chatting in a monogamous relationship honors both the promise of sexual exclusivity and the titanic power of the imagination.[21]

NOTES

1. Edith Hamilton and Huntington Cairns, eds., *The Collected Dialogues of Plato*. Translated by Lane Cooper et al. (Princeton, N.J.: Princeton University Press, 1961), 64, 82 (the *Phaedo*, 485–88), (the *Phaedrus*, lines 237–42).

2. Augustine, *Confessions*. Translated by R. S. Pine-Coffin (Baltimore, Md.: Penguin Books, 1961), 234.

3. See Richard Marius, *Martin Luther: The Christian between God and Death* (Cambridge, Mass.: Harvard University Press, 2000): "Our bodies, he said, are ordered for honorable marriage or still more honorable chastity, and the cure for lust is prayer" (109).

4. http://www.who.int/mediacentre/factsheets/fs241/en/index.html (accessed April 2, 2012).

5. This, despite the allowance of the highly influential eighteenth-century Roman Catholic theologian St. Alphonsus Liguori that having sex in a church or a public place might be allowed in a case of "necessity." See Peter Gardella, *Innocent Ecstasy: How Christianity Gave America an Ethic of Sexual Pleasure* (New York: Oxford University Press, 1985), 18.

6. G. E. M. Anscombe, "Contraception and Chastity," *The Human World*, No. 7 (1972), 22.

7. Kazuo Ishiguro, *The Remains of the Day* (New York: Vintage, 1990), 245.

8. *Monty Python's The Meaning of Life* (Celandine Films, 1983), starring Graham Chapman, John Cleese, Terry Giliam, Eric Idle, Terry Jones, Michael Palin, Sydney Arnold, and Guy Bertrand. Kasy Moon provided the correct reference here.

9. "You can meet someone on-line. You can fall in love on-line. You can even consummate that love on-line." Paco Underhill, *Why We Buy: The Science of Shopping* (New York: Simon & Schuster, 1999), 212.

10. Helen Fisher, *Anatomy of Love* (New York: W. W. Norton, 1992), 79–80.

11. Bernard Häring, *The Law of Christ*. Translated by Edwin G. Kaiser (Westminster, Md.: Newman Press, 1966), vol. III, 306.

12. *Ibid.*, 375–76.

13. Quoted in Elizabeth Abbott, *A History of Celibacy* (New York: Scribners, 2000), 354.

14. *Ibid.*

15. Anne Fausto-Sterling, "How to Build a Man," in Vernon A. Rosario, ed., *Science and Homosexualities* (New York: Routledge, 1997), 219-25. Quoted in Robert A. Nye, ed., *Sexuality* (New York: Oxford University Press, 1999), 238.

16. John Money, *The Destroying Angel* (Buffalo, NY: Prometheus Books, 1985), 127.

17. Lisa Palac, *The Edge of the Bed: How Dirty Pictures Changed My Life* (Boston: Little, Brown, 1998), 20.

18. *Ibid.*, 106.

19. Tara McCarthy, *Been There, Haven't Done That: A Virgin's Memoir* (New York: Warner Books, 1997), 3.

20. David M. Buss, *The Evolution of Desire: Strategies of Human Mating* (New York: Basic Books, 1994), 155.

21. Pamela Karlan, Jerome Neu, and Anthony Ellis graciously provided comments on this essay, which Daniel Ortiz especially enriched.

STUDY QUESTIONS

1. Is Portmann's view of sexual desire and arousal—"lust completes us [however temporarily], fills us with a vivid sense of being alive, propels us along the way to self-fulfillment"—either naively idealistic or implausibly optimistic? Compare his view to what the metaphysical pessimists might say about lust (as outlined by Alan Soble, "The Analytic Categories of the Philosophy of Sex," in this volume), and for which they use the term, often meant to be derogatory, "concupiscence."

2. Explicate the details of Portmann's major arguments, making sure to explain the role that concepts such as "adultery," "fornication," "serial monogamy," and "virginity" play in them. Ask, while reconstructing his arguments, whether his conclusion is that erotic chatting is not "sex," or that it is "sex" but a morally acceptable type.

3. Is physical touching, skin-to-skin, necessary for "sex" or for people to be "having sex," as Portmann believes? Consider the dual masturbation spoken of by Alan Soble (in "On Jacking Off, Yet Again," in this volume): two people masturbate, in the sense of "self-stimulation," in front of each other, without touching but aroused by the sight of each other. Is this "sex"? Is it "having sex"? Why or why not? Does the presence or absence of orgasm make a difference?

4. Evaluate Portmann's "penetration" criterion for "sex" (about which he does have some doubts, as does Greta Christina, "Are We Having Sex Now or What?" in this volume). Given that criterion, would lesbian couples not "have sex" unless they used objects with which to penetrate each other? Would penetration by tongues, fingers, or fists, rather than by dildoes or vegetables, be the right amount or kind of penetration to make their acts "sex"? (On this topic see Marilyn Frye, "Lesbian 'Sex'," in *Willful Virgin: Essays in Feminism 1976-1992* [Freedom, Calif.: Crossing Press, 1992], 109-19.)

5. Even if cyberchatting is not sexual cheating, might it still not be a form of non-sexual (e.g., emotional) cheating or unfaithfulness? Following the words of Jesus (Matthew 5:28), might there be a metaphorical adultery *of* the heart, in terms of a person's character, their virtues, or even spiritually? Imagine a woman coming home to find her boyfriend or husband masturbating furiously with one

hand while typing furiously with the other. Will she be much mollified by Portmann's philosophy? (Maybe, if she gave the guy permission.)

6. Note that Portmann uses the term "sexual activity" only twice in his essay, preferring to talk, instead, about whether a behavior is "sex" or "having sex." Is it possible that his language involves an equivocation or makes defending his theses too easy? It is one thing to say that to chat erotically is not "sex" or "having sex," and another (perhaps quite different) thing to say that to chat erotically is not (even) a "sexual activity." The former seems trivial; the latter seems to be an important substantive thesis. Which one is Portmann's? Consider a similar linguistic problem that arises about Greta Christina's essay "Are We Having Sex Now or What?" in this volume.

II

Queer Issues

NINE

Beyond Gay Marriage: The Road to Polyamory

Stanley Kurtz

Though the U.S. Census Bureau reports difficulties in identifying "married" couples, there can be little doubt that the profile of marriage has been changing: same-sex/gender households now make up about one-sixth of all households that are composed of unmarried partners. Gay and lesbian couples are still a small minority of the nontraditional alternatives to marriage found in America today, yet **Stanley Kurtz** *perceives a gay-lesbian tail wagging this pluralistic dog. On his view, at the forefront of many recent debates in family law is the gay and lesbian agenda, the key item of which may well be the eventual abolition of marriage as an institution. In this socially conservative essay, Kurtz provides a sustained, detailed account of why contemporary American society should resist same-sex marriage. One of his concerns is revealed in his polemical slippery-slope argument: same-sex marriage will lead to polygamy and its latest incarnation, polyamory ("having many lovers"). Whereas other theorists might see the increasing legal frameworks for alternatives to marriage as a good thing because, for one thing, they add to people's options, Kurtz weighs in on the negative side, forecasting only doom.*

Stanley Kurtz was formerly a research fellow at the Hoover Institution of Stanford University. In addition to being a contributing editor to *National Review*, he is a senior fellow at the Ethics and Public Policy Center, Washington, D.C. This essay is reprinted from *Weekly Standard* 8:45 (August 4–11, 2003). © Copyright 2006, News Corporation, *Weekly Standard*.

After gay marriage, what will become of marriage itself? Will same-sex matrimony extend marriage's stabilizing effects to homosexuals? Will gay marriage undermine family life? A lot is riding on the answers to these questions. But the media's reflexive labeling of doubts about gay marriage as homophobia has made it almost impossible to debate the social effects of this reform. Now with the Supreme Court's ringing affirmation of sexual liberty in *Lawrence v. Texas*, that debate is unavoidable.

Among the likeliest effects of gay marriage is to take us down a slippery slope to legalized polygamy and "polyamory" (group marriage). Marriage will be transformed into a variety of relationship contracts, linking two, three, or more individuals (however weakly and temporarily) in every conceivable combination of male and female. A scare scenario? Hardly. The bottom of this slope is visible from where we stand. Advocacy of legalized polygamy is growing. A network of grass-roots organizations seeking legal recognition for group marriage already exists. The cause of legalized group marriage is championed by a powerful faction of family law specialists. Influential legal bodies in both the United States and Canada have presented radical programs of marital reform. Some of these quasi-governmental proposals go so far as to suggest the abolition of marriage. The ideas behind this movement have already achieved surprising influence with a prominent American politician.

None of this is well known. Both the media and public spokesmen for the gay marriage movement treat the issue as an unproblematic advance for civil rights. True, a small number of relatively conservative gay spokesmen do consider the social effects of gay matrimony, insisting that they will be beneficent, that homosexual unions will become more stable. Yet another faction of gay rights advocates actually favors gay marriage as a step toward the abolition of marriage itself. This group agrees that there is a slippery slope, and wants to hasten the slide down.

To consider what comes after gay marriage is not to say that gay marriage itself poses no danger to the institution of marriage. Quite apart from the likelihood that it will usher in legalized polygamy and polyamory, gay marriage will almost certainly weaken the belief that monogamy lies at the heart of marriage. But to see why this is so, we will first need to reconnoiter the slippery slope.

PROMOTING POLYGAMY

During the 1996 congressional debate on the *Defense of Marriage Act*, which affirmed the ability of the states and the federal government to withhold recognition from same-sex marriages, gay marriage advocates were put on the defensive by the polygamy question. If gays had a right to marry, why not polygamists? Andrew Sullivan, one of gay marriage's most intelligent defenders, labeled the question fear-mongering—akin to the discredited belief that interracial marriage would lead to birth defects. "To the best of my knowledge," said Sullivan, "there is no polygamists' rights organization poised to exploit same-sex marriage and return the republic to polygamous abandon." Actually, there are now many such organizations. And their strategy—even their existence—owes much to the movement for gay marriage.

Scoffing at the polygamy prospect as ludicrous has been the strategy of choice for gay marriage advocates. In 2000, following Vermont's enactment of civil unions, Matt Coles, director of the American Civil Liberties Union's Lesbian and Gay Rights Project, said, "I think the idea that there is some kind of slippery slope [to polygamy or group marriage] is silly." As proof, Coles said that America had legalized interracial marriage, while also forcing Utah to ban polygamy before admission to the union. That dichotomy, said Coles, shows that Americans are capable of distinguishing between better and worse proposals for reforming marriage.

Are we? When Tom Green was put on trial in Utah for polygamy in 2001, it played like a dress rehearsal for the coming movement to legalize polygamy. True, Green was convicted for violating what he called Utah's "don't ask, don't tell" policy on polygamy. Pointedly refusing to "hide in the closet," he touted polygamy on the Sally Jessy Raphael, Queen Latifah, Geraldo Rivera, and Jerry Springer shows, and on "Dateline NBC" and "48 Hours." But the Green trial was not just a cable spectacle. It brought out a surprising number of mainstream defenses of polygamy. And most of the defenders went to bat for polygamy by drawing direct comparisons to gay marriage.

Writing in the *Village Voice*, gay leftist Richard Goldstein equated the drive for state-sanctioned polygamy with the movement for gay marriage. The political reluctance of gays to embrace polygamists was understandable, said Goldstein, "but our fates are entwined in fundamental ways." Libertarian Jacob Sullum defended polygamy, along with all other consensual domestic arrangements, in the *Washington Times*. Syndicated liberal columnist Ellen Goodman took up the cause of polygamy with a direct comparison to gay marriage. Steve Chapman, a member of the *Chicago Tribune* editorial board, defended polygamy in the *Tribune* and in *Slate*. The *New York Times* published a "Week in Review" article juxtaposing photos of Tom Green's family with sociobiological arguments about the naturalness of polygamy and promiscuity.

The ACLU's Matt Coles may have derided the idea of a slippery slope from gay marriage to polygamy, but the ACLU itself stepped in to help Tom Green during his trial and declared its support for the repeal of all "laws prohibiting or penalizing the practice of plural marriage." There is of course a difference between repealing such laws and formal state recognition of polygamous marriages. Neither the ACLU nor, say, Ellen Goodman has directly advocated formal state recognition. Yet they give us no reason to suppose that, when the time is ripe, they will not do so. Stephen Clark, the legal director of the Utah ACLU, has said, "Talking to Utah's polygamists is like talking to gays and lesbians who really want the right to live their lives."

All this was in 2001, well before the prospect that legal gay marriage might create the cultural conditions for state-sanctioned polygamy. Can anyone doubt that greater public support will be forthcoming once gay marriage has become a reality? Surely the ACLU will lead the charge.

Why is state-sanctioned polygamy a problem? The deep reason is that it erodes the ethos of monogamous marriage. Despite the divorce revolution, Americans still take it for granted that marriage means monogamy. The ideal of fidelity may be breached in practice, yet adultery is clearly understood as a transgression against marriage. Legal polygamy would jeopardize that understanding, and that is why polygamy has historically been treated in the West as an offense against society itself.

In most non-Western cultures, marriage is not a union of freely choosing individuals, but an alliance of family groups. The emotional relationship between husband and wife is attenuated and subordinated to the economic and political interests of extended kin. But in our world of freely choosing individuals, extended families fall away, and love and companionship are the only surviving principles on which families can be built. From Thomas Aquinas through Richard Posner, almost every serious observer has granted the incompatibility between polygamy and Western companionate marriage.

Where polygamy works, it does so because the husband and his wives are emotionally distant. Even then, jealousy is a constant danger, averted only by strict rules of seniority or parity in the husband's economic support of his wives. Polygamy is more about those resources than about sex.

Yet in many polygamous societies, even though only 10 or 15 percent of men may actually have multiple wives, there is a widely held belief that men need multiple women. The result is that polygamists are often promiscuous—just not with their own wives. Anthropologist Philip Kilbride reports a Nigerian survey in which, among urban male polygamists, 44 percent said their most recent sexual partners were women other than their wives. For monogamous, married Nigerian men in urban areas, that figure rose to 67 percent. Even though polygamous marriage is less about sex than security, societies that permit polygamy tend to reject the idea of marital fidelity—for everyone, polygamists included.

Mormon polygamy has always been a complicated and evolving combination of Western mores and classic polygamous patterns. Like Western companionate marriage, Mormon polygamy condemns extramarital sex. Yet historically, like its non-Western counterparts, it de-emphasized romantic love. Even so, jealousy was always a problem. One study puts the rate of nineteenth-century polygamous divorce at triple the rate for monogamous families. Unlike their forebears, contemporary Mormon polygamists try to combine polygamy with companionate marriage—and have a very tough time of it. We have no definitive figures, but divorce is frequent. Irwin Altman and Joseph Ginat, who've written the most detailed account of today's breakaway Mormon polygamist sects, highlight the special stresses put on families trying to combine modern notions of romantic love with polygamy. Strict religious rules of parity among wives make the effort to create a hybrid traditionalist/modern version of Mormon polygamy at least plausible, if very stressful. But polygamy let loose in modern secular America would destroy our understanding of marital fidelity, while putting nothing viable in its place. And postmodern polygamy is a lot closer than you think.

POLYAMORY

America's new, souped-up version of polygamy is called "polyamory." Polyamorists trace their descent from the anti-monogamy movements of the sixties and seventies—everything from hippie communes, to the support groups that grew up around Robert Rimmer's 1966 novel *The Harrad Experiment*, to the cult of Bhagwan Shree Rajneesh. Polyamorists proselytize for "responsible non-monogamy"—open, loving, and stable sexual relationships among more than two people. The modern polyamory movement took off in the mid-nineties—partly because of the growth of the Internet (with its confidentiality), but also in parallel to, and inspired by, the rising gay marriage movement.

Unlike classic polygamy, which features one man and several women, polyamory comprises a bewildering variety of sexual combinations. There are triads of one woman and two men; heterosexual group marriages; groups in which some or all members are bisexual; lesbian groups, and so forth. (For details, see Deborah Anapol's *Polyamory: The New Love without Limits*, one of the movement's authoritative guides, or Google "polyamory.")

Supposedly, polyamory is not a synonym for promiscuity. In practice, though, there is a continuum between polyamory and "swinging." Swinging couples dally with multiple sexual partners while intentionally avoiding emotional entanglements. Polyamorists, in contrast, try to establish stable emotional ties among a sexually connected group. Although the subcultures of swinging and polyamory are recognizably different, many individuals move freely between them. And since polyamorous group marriages can be sexually closed or open, it's often tough to draw a line between polyamory and swinging. Here, then, is the modern American version of Nigeria's extramarital polygamous promiscuity. Once the principles of monogamous companionate marriage are breached, even for supposedly stable and committed sexual groups, the slide toward full-fledged promiscuity is difficult to halt.

Polyamorists are enthusiastic proponents of same-sex marriage. Obviously, any attempt to restrict marriage to a single man and woman would prevent the legalization of polyamory. After passage of the Defense of

Marriage Act in 1996, an article appeared in *Loving More*, the flagship magazine of the polyamory movement, calling for the creation of a polyamorist rights movement modeled on the movement for gay rights. The piece was published under the pen name Joy Singer, identified as the graduate of a "top ten law school" and a political organizer and public official in California for the previous two decades.

Taking a leaf from the gay marriage movement, Singer suggested starting small. A campaign for hospital visitation rights for polyamorous spouses would be the way to begin. Full marriage and adoption rights would come later. Again using the gay marriage movement as a model, Singer called for careful selection of acceptable public spokesmen (i.e., people from longstanding poly families with children). Singer even published a speech by Iowa state legislator Ed Fallon on behalf of gay marriage, arguing that the goal would be to get a congressman to give exactly the same speech as Fallon, but substituting the word "poly" for "gay" throughout. Try telling polyamorists that the link between gay marriage and group marriage is a mirage.

The flexible, egalitarian, and altogether postmodern polyamorists are more likely to influence the larger society than Mormon polygamists. The polyamorists go after monogamy in a way that resonates with America's secular, post-sixties culture. Yet the fundamental drawback is the same for Mormons and polyamorists alike. Polyamory websites are filled with chatter about jealousy, the problem that will not go away. Inevitably, group marriages based on modern principles of companionate love, without religious rules and restraints, are unstable. Like the short-lived hippie communes, group marriages will be broken on the contradiction between companionate love and group solidarity. And children will pay the price. The harms of state-sanctioned polyamorous marriage would extend well beyond the polyamorists themselves. Once monogamy is defined out of marriage, it will be next to impossible to educate a new generation in what it takes to keep companionate marriage intact. State-sanctioned polyamory would spell the effective end of marriage. And that is precisely what polyamory's new—and surprisingly influential—defenders are aiming for.

THE FAMILY LAW RADICALS

State-sanctioned polyamory is now the cutting-edge issue among scholars of family law. The preeminent school of thought in academic family law has its origins in the arguments of radical gay activists who once *opposed* same-sex marriage. In the early nineties, radicals like longtime National Gay and Lesbian Task Force policy director Paula Ettelbrick spoke out against making legal marriage a priority for the gay rights movement. Marriage, Ettelbrick reminded her fellow activists, "has long been the focus of radical feminist revulsion." Encouraging gays to marry, said Ettelbrick, would only force gay "assimilation" to American norms, when the real object of the gay rights movement ought to be getting Americans to accept gay difference. "Being queer," said Ettelbrick, "means pushing the parameters of sex and family, and in the process transforming the very fabric of society."

Promoting polyamory is the ideal way to "radically reorder society's view of the family," and Ettelbrick, who has since formally signed on as a supporter of gay marriage (and is frequently quoted by the press), is now part of a movement that hopes to use gay marriage as an opening to press for state-sanctioned polyamory. Ettelbrick teaches law at the University of Michigan, New York University, Barnard, and Columbia. She has a lot of company.

Nancy Polikoff is a professor at American University's law school. In 1993, Polikoff published a powerful and radical critique of gay marriage. Polikoff stressed that during the height of the lesbian feminist movement of the seventies, even many heterosexual feminists refused to marry because they believed marriage to be an inherently patriarchal and oppressive institution. A movement for gay marriage, warned Polikoff, would surely promote marriage as a social good, trotting out monogamous couples as spokesmen in a way that would marginalize non-monogamous gays and would fail to challenge the legitimacy of marriage itself. Like Ettelbrick, Polikoff now supports the right of gays to marry. And like Ettelbrick, Polikoff is part of a movement whose larger goal is to use legal gay marriage to push for state-sanctioned polyamory—the ultimate subversion of marriage itself. Polikoff and Ettelbrick represent what is arguably now the dominant perspective within the discipline of family law.

Cornell University law professor Martha Fineman is another key figure in the field of family law. In her 1995 book *The Neutered Mother, the Sexual Family, and Other Twentieth Century Tragedies*, she argued for the abolition of marriage as a legal category. Fineman's book begins with her recollection of an experience from the late seventies in politically radical Madison, Wisconsin. To her frustration, she could not convince even the most progressive members of Madison's Equal Opportunities Commission to recognize "plural sexual groupings" as marriages. That failure helped energize Fineman's lifelong drive to abolish marriage.

But it is University of Utah law professor Martha Ertman who stands on the cutting edge of family law. Building on Fineman's proposals for the abolition of legal marriage, Ertman has offered a legal template for a sweeping relationship contract system modeled on corporate law. (See *Harvard Civil Rights and Civil Liberties Law Review*, Winter 2001.) Ertman wants state-sanctioned polyamory, legally organized on the model of limited liability companies.

In arguing for the replacement of marriage with a contract system that accommodates polyamory, Ertman notes that legal and social hostility to polygamy and polyamory are decreasing. She goes on astutely to imply that the increased openness of homosexual partnerships is slowly collapsing the taboo against polygamy and polyamory. And Ertman is frank about the purpose of her proposed reform—to render the distinction between traditional marriage and polyamory "morally neutral."

A sociologist rather than a professor of law, Judith Stacey, the Barbra Streisand Professor in Contemporary Gender Studies at USC, is another key member of this group. Stacey has long championed alternative family forms. Her current research is on gay families consisting of more than two adults, whose several members consider themselves either married or contractually bound.

In 1996, in the *Michigan Law Review*, David Chambers, a professor of law at the University of Michigan and another prominent member of this group, explained why radical opponents of marriage ought to support gay marriage. Rather than reinforcing a two-person definition of marriage, argued Chambers, gay marriage would make society more accepting of further legal changes. "By ceasing to conceive of marriage as a partnership composed of one person of each sex, the state may become more receptive to units of three or more."

Gradual transition from gay marriage to state-sanctioned polyamory, and the eventual abolition of marriage itself as a legal category, is now the most influential paradigm within academic family law. As Chambers put it, "All desirable changes in family law need not be made at once."

Finally, Martha Minow of Harvard Law School deserves mention. Minow has not advocated state-sanctioned polygamy or polyamory, but the principles she champions pave the way for both. Minow argues that families need to be radically redefined, putting blood ties and traditional legal arrangements aside and attending instead to the functional realities of new family configurations.

Ettelbrick, Polikoff, Fineman, Ertman, Stacey, Chambers, and Minow are among the most prominent family law theorists in the country. They have plenty of followers and hold much of the power and initiative within their field. There may be other approaches to academic family law, but none exceed the radicals in influence. In the last couple of years, there have been a number of conferences on family law dominated by the views of this school. The conferences have names like "Marriage Law: Obsolete or Cutting Edge?" and "Assimilation & Resistance: Emerging Issues in Law & Sexuality." The titles turn on the paradox of using marriage, seemingly a conservative path toward assimilation, as a tool of radical cultural "resistance."

One of the most important recent family law meetings was the March 2003 Hofstra conference on "Marriage, Democracy, and Families." The radicals were out in full force. On a panel entitled "Intimate Affiliation and Democracy: Beyond Marriage?" Fineman, Ertman, and Stacey held forth on polyamory, the legal abolition of marriage, and related issues.

Although there were more moderate scholars present, there was barely a challenge to the radicals' suggestion that it was time to move "beyond marriage." The few traditionalists in family law are relatively isolated. Many, maybe most, of the prominent figures in family law count themselves as advocates for lesbian and gay rights. Yet family law today is as influenced by the hostility to marriage of seventies feminism as it is by advocacy for gay rights. It is this confluence of radical feminism and gay rights that now shapes the field.

BEYOND CONJUGALITY

You might think the radicals who dominate the discipline of family law are just a bunch of eccentric and irrelevant academics. You would be wrong. For one thing, there is already a thriving non-profit organization, the Alternatives to Marriage Project, that advances the radicals' goals. When controversies over the family hit the news, experts provided by the Alternatives to Marriage Project are often quoted in mainstream media outlets. While the Alternatives to Marriage Project endorses gay marriage, its longer-term goal is to replace marriage with a system that recognizes "the full range" of family types.

That includes polyamorous families. The Alternatives to Marriage Project's statement of purpose—its "Affirmation of Family Diversity"—is signed not only by Ettelbrick, Polikoff, and Stacey but by several polyamorists as well. On a list of signatories that includes academic luminaries like Yale historian Nancy Cott, you can find Barry Northrup of *Loving More* magazine. The Alternatives to Marriage Project, along with Martha Ertman's pioneering legal proposals, has given polyamory a foothold on respectability.

The first real public triumph of the family law radicals has come in Canada. In 1997, the Canadian Parliament established the Law Commission of Canada to serve Parliament and the Justice Ministry as a kind of advisory board on legal reform. In December 2001, the commission submitted a report to Parliament called "Beyond Conjugality," which stops just short of recommending the abolition of marriage in Canada.

"Beyond Conjugality" contains three basic recommendations. First, judges are directed to concentrate on whether the individuals before them are "functionally interdependent," regardless of their actual marital status. On that theory, a household consisting of an adult child still living with his mother might be treated as the functional equivalent of a married couple. In so disregarding marital status, "Beyond Conjugality" is clearly drawing on the work of Minow, whose writings are listed in the bibliography.

The second key recommendation of "Beyond Conjugality" is that a legal structure be established allowing people to register their personal relationships with the government. Not only could heterosexual couples register as official partners, so could gay couples, adult children living with parents, and siblings or friends sharing a house. Although the authors of "Beyond Conjugality" are politic enough to relegate the point to footnotes, they state that they see no reason, in principle, to limit registered partnerships to two people.

The final recommendation of "Beyond Conjugality"—legalization of same-sex marriage—drew the most publicity when the report was released. Yet for the Law Commission of Canada, same-sex marriage is clearly just one part of the larger project of doing away with marriage itself. "Beyond Conjugality" stops short of recommending the abolition of legal marriage. The authors glumly note that, for the moment, the public is unlikely to accept such a step.

The text of "Beyond Conjugality," its bibliography, and the Law Commission of Canada's other publications unmistakably reveal the influence of the radical theorists who now dominate the discipline of family law. While Canada's parliament has postponed action on "Beyond Conjugality," the report has already begun to shape the culture. The decision by the Canadian government in June 2003 not to contest court rulings legalizing gay marriage is only the beginning of the changes that Canada's judges and legal bureaucrats have in mind. The simultaneity of the many reforms is striking. Gay marriage is being pressed, but in tandem with a registration system that will sanction polyamorous unions, and eventually replace marriage itself. Empirically, the radicals' hopes are being validated. Gay marriage is not strengthening marriage but has instead become part of a larger unraveling of traditional marriage laws.

Ah, but that's Canada, you say. Yet America has its rough equivalent of the Law Commission of Canada—the American Law Institute (ALI), an organization of legal scholars whose recommendations commonly shape important legal reforms. In 2000, ALI promulgated a report called "Principles of the Law of Family Dissolution" recommending that judges effectively disregard the distinction between married couples and long-time cohabitors. While the ALI principles do not go so far as to set up a system of partnership registration to replace marriage, the report's framework for recognizing a wide variety of cohabiting partnerships puts it on the same path as "Beyond Conjugality."

Collapsing the distinction between cohabitation and marriage is a proposal especially damaging to children, who are decidedly better off when born to married parents. (This aspect of the ALI report has been persuasively criticized by Kay Hymowitz, in the March 2003 issue of *Commentary*.) But a more disturbing aspect of the ALI report is its evasion of the polygamy and polyamory issues.

Prior to the publication of the ALI Principles, the report's authors were pressed (at the 2000 annual meeting of the American Law Institute) about the question of polygamy. The authors put off the controversy by defining legal cohabitors as couples. Yet the ALI report offers no principled way of excluding polyamorous or polygamous cohabitors from recognition. The report's reforms are said to be based on the need to recognize "statistically growing" patterns of relationship. By this standard, the growth of polyamorous cohabitation will soon require the legal recognition of polyamory.

Although America's ALI Principles do not follow Canada's "Beyond Conjugality" in proposing either state-sanctioned polyamory or the outright end of marriage, the University of Utah's Martha Ertman has suggested (in the Spring/Summer 2001 *Duke Journal of Gender Law and Policy*) that the American Law Institute is intentionally holding back on more radical proposals for pragmatic political reasons. Certainly, the ALI Principles' authors take Canadian law as the model for the report's most radical provisions.

Further confirmation, if any were needed, of the mainstream influence of the family law radicals came with Al and Tipper Gore's 2002 book *Joined at the Heart*, in which they define a family as those who are "joined at the heart" (rather than by blood or by law). The notion that a family is any group "joined at the heart" comes straight from Harvard's Martha Minow, who worked with the Gores. In fact, the Minow article from which the Gores take their definition of family is also the article in which Minow tentatively floats the idea of substituting domestic partnership registries for traditional marriage ("Redefining Families: Who's In and Who's Out?" *University of Colorado Law Review* 62: 2 [1991]). So one of the guiding spirits of Canada's "Beyond Conjugality" report almost had a friend in the White House.

TRIPLE PARENTING

Polygamy, polyamory, and the abolition of marriage are bad ideas. But what has that got to do with gay marriage? The reason these ideas are connected is that gay marriage is increasingly being treated as a civil rights issue. Once we say that gay couples have a right to have their commitments recognized by the state, it becomes next to impossible to deny that same right to polygamists, polyamorists, or even cohabiting relatives and friends. And once everyone's relationship is recognized, marriage is gone, and only a system of flexible relationship contracts is left. The only way to stop gay marriage from launching a slide down this slope is if there is a compelling state interest in blocking polygamy or polyamory that does not also apply to gay marriage. Many would agree that the state has a compelling interest in preventing polygamy and polyamory from undermining the ethos of monogamy at the core of marriage. The trouble is, gay marriage itself threatens the ethos of monogamy.

The "conservative" case for gay marriage holds that state-sanctioned marriage will reduce gay male promiscuity. But what if the effect works in reverse? What if, instead of marriage reducing gay promiscuity, sexually open gay couples help redefine marriage as a non-monogamous institution? There is evidence that this is exactly what will happen.

Consider sociologist Gretchen Stiers's 1998 study "From this Day Forward." (Stiers favors gay marriage, and calls herself a lesbian "queer theorist.") "From this Day Forward" reports that while exceedingly few of even the most committed gay and lesbian couples surveyed believe that marriage will strengthen and stabilize their personal relationships, nearly half of the surveyed couples who actually disdain traditional marriage (and even gay commitment ceremonies) will nonetheless get married. Why? For the financial and legal benefits of marriage. And Stiers's study suggests that many radical gays and lesbians who yearn to see marriage abolished (and multiple sexual unions legitimized) intend to marry, not only as a way of securing benefits but as part of a self-conscious attempt to subvert the institution of marriage. Stiers's study suggests that the "subversive" intentions of the radical legal theorists are shared by a significant portion of the gay community itself.

Stiers's study was focused on the most committed gay couples. Yet even in a sample with a disproportionate number of male couples who had gone through a commitment ceremony (and Stiers had to go out of her research protocol just to find enough male couples to balance the committed lesbian couples) nearly 20 percent of the men questioned did not practice monogamy. In a representative sample of gay male couples, that number would be vastly higher. More significantly, a mere 10 percent of even this skewed sample of gay men mentioned monogamy as an important aspect of commitment (meaning that even many of those men who had undergone "union ceremonies" failed to identify fidelity with commitment). And these, the very most committed gay male couples, are the ones who will be trailblazing marital norms for their peers, and exemplifying gay marriage for the nation. So concerns about the effects of gay marriage on the social ideal of marital monogamy seem justified.

A recent survey of gay couples in civil unions by University of Vermont psychologists Esther Rothblum and Sondra Solomon confirms what Stiers's study suggests—that married gay male couples will be far less likely than married heterosexual couples to identify marriage with monogamy. Rothblum and Solomon contacted all 2,300 couples who entered civil unions in Vermont between June 1, 2000, and June 30, 2001. More than 300 civil union couples residing in and out of the state responded. Rothblum and Solomon then compared the gay couples in civil unions with heterosexual couples and gay couples outside of civil unions. Among married heterosexual men, 79 percent felt that marriage demanded monogamy, 50 percent of men in gay civil unions insisted on monogamy, while only 34 percent of gay men outside of civil unions affirmed monogamy.

While gay men in civil unions were more likely to affirm monogamy than gays outside of civil unions, gay men in civil unions were far less supportive of monogamy than heterosexual married men. That discrepancy may well be significantly greater under gay marriage than under civil unions. That's because of the effect identified by Stiers—the likelihood that many gays who do not value the traditional monogamous ethos of marriage will marry anyway for the financial benefits that marriage can bring. (A full 86 percent of the civil unions couples who responded to the Rothblum-Solomon survey live outside Vermont, and therefore receive no financial benefits from their new legal status.) The Rothblum-Solomon study may also undercount heterosexual married male acceptance of monogamy, since one member of all the married heterosexual couples in the survey was the sibling of a gay man in a civil union, and thus more likely to be socially liberal than most heterosexuals.

Even moderate gay advocates of same-sex marriage grant that, at present, gay male relationships are far less monogamous than heterosexual relationships. And there is a persuasive literature on this subject: Gabriel Rotello's *Sexual Ecology*, for example, offers a documented and powerful account of the behavioral and ideological barriers to monogamy among gay men. The moderate advocates say marriage will change this reality. But they ignore, or downplay, the possibility that gay marriage will change marriage more than it changes the men who marry. Married gay couples will begin to redefine the meaning of marriage for the culture as a whole, in part by removing monogamy as an essential component of marriage. No doubt, the process will be pushed along by cutting-edge movies and TV shows that tout the new "open" marriages being pioneered by gay spouses. In fact, author and gay marriage advocate Richard Mohr has long expressed the hope and expectation that legal gay marriage will succeed in defining monogamy out of marriage.

Lesbians, for their part, do value monogamy. Over 82 percent of the women in the Rothblum-Solomon study, for example, insisted on monogamy, regardless of sexual orientation or marital status. Yet lesbian marriage will undermine the connection between marriage and monogamy in a different way. Lesbians who bear children with sperm donors sometimes set up de facto three-parent families. Typically, these families include a sexually bound lesbian couple, and a male biological father who is close to the couple but not sexually involved. Once lesbian couples can marry, there will be a powerful legal case for extending parental recognition to triumvirates. It will be difficult to question the parental credentials of a sperm donor, or of a married, lesbian non-birth mother spouse who helps to raise a child from birth. And just as the argument for gay marriage has been built upon the right to gay adoption, legally recognized triple parenting will eventually usher in state-sanctioned triple (and therefore group) marriage.

This year, there was a triple parenting case in Canada involving a lesbian couple and a sperm donor. The judge made it clear that he wanted to assign parental status to all three adults but held back because he said he lacked jurisdiction. On this issue, the United States is already in "advance" of Canada. Martha Ertman is now pointing to a 2000 Minnesota case (*La Chapelle v. Mitten*) in which a court did grant parental rights to lesbian partners and a sperm donor. Ertman argues that this case creates a legal precedent for state-sanctioned polyamory.

GAY MARRIAGES OF CONVENIENCE

Ironically, the form of gay matrimony that may pose the greatest threat to the institution of marriage involves heterosexuals. A Brigham Young University professor, Alan J. Hawkins, suggests an all-too-likely scenario in which two heterosexuals of the same sex might marry as a way of obtaining financial benefits. Consider the plight of an underemployed and uninsured single mother in her early thirties who sees little real prospect of marriage (to a man) in her future. Suppose she has a good friend, also female and heterosexual, who is single and childless but employed with good spousal benefits. Sooner or later, friends like this are going to start contracting same-sex marriages of convenience. The single mom will get medical and governmental benefits, will share her friend's paycheck, and will gain an additional caretaker for the kids besides. Her friend will gain companionship and a family life. The marriage would obviously be sexually open. And if lightning struck and the right man came along for one of the women, they could always divorce and marry heterosexually.

In a narrow sense, the women and children in this arrangement would be better off. Yet the larger effects of such unions on the institution of marriage would be devastating. At a stroke, marriage would be severed not only from the complementarity of the sexes but also from its connection to romance and sexual exclusivity—and even from the hope of permanence. In Hawkins's words, the proliferation of such arrangements "would turn marriage into the moral equivalent of a Social Security benefit." The effect would be to further diminish the sense that a woman ought to be married to the father of her children. In the aggregate, what we now call out-of-wedlock births would increase. And the connection between marriage and sexual fidelity would be nonexistent.

Hawkins thinks gay marriages of convenience would be contracted in significant numbers—certainly enough to draw the attention of a media eager to tout such unions as the hip, postmodern marriages of the moment. Hawkins also believes that these unions of convenience could begin to undermine marriage's institutional foundations fairly quickly. He may be right. The gay marriage movement took more than a decade to catch fire. A movement for state-sanctioned polygamy-polyamory could take as long. And the effects of sexually open gay marriages on the ethos of monogamy will similarly occur over time. But any degree of publicity for same-sex marriages of convenience could have dramatic effects. Without further legal ado, same-sex marriages of convenience will realize the radicals' fondest hopes. Marriage will have been severed from monogamy, from sexuality, and even from the dream of permanence. Which would bring us virtually to the bottom of the slippery slope.

We are far closer to that day than anyone realizes. Does the Supreme Court's defense of sexual liberty last month in the *Lawrence v. Texas* sodomy case mean that, short of a constitutional amendment, gay marriage is inevitable? Perhaps not. Justice Scalia was surely correct to warn in his dissent that *Lawrence* greatly weakens the legal barriers to gay marriage. Sodomy laws, although rarely enforced, did provide a public policy basis on which a state could refuse to recognize a gay marriage performed in another state. Now the grounds for that "public policy exception" have been eroded. And as Scalia warned, *Lawrence*'s sweeping guarantees of personal autonomy in matters of sex could easily be extended to the question of who a person might choose to marry.

So it is true that, given *Lawrence*, the legal barriers to gay marriage are now hanging by a thread. Nonetheless, in an important respect, Scalia underestimated the resources for a successful legal argument against gay marriage. True, *Lawrence* eliminates moral disapprobation as an acceptable, rational basis for public policy distinctions between homosexuality and heterosexuality. But that doesn't mean there is no rational basis for blocking either same-sex marriage or polygamy.

There is a rational basis for blocking both gay marriage and polygamy, and it does not depend upon a vague or religiously based disapproval of homosexuality or polygamy. Children need the stable family environment provided by marriage. In our individualist Western society, marriage must be companionate—and therefore monogamous. Monogamy will be undermined by gay marriage itself, and by gay marriage's ushering in of polygamy and polyamory.

This argument ought to be sufficient to pass the test of rational scrutiny set by the Supreme Court in *Lawrence v. Texas*. Certainly, the slippery-slope argument was at the center of the legislative debate on the federal Defense of Marriage Act, and so should protect that act from being voided on the same grounds as Texas's sodomy law. But of course, given the majority's sweeping declarations in *Lawrence*, and the hostility of the legal elite to traditional marriage, it may well be foolish to rely on the Supreme Court to uphold either state or federal Defense of Marriage Acts.

This is the case, in a nutshell, for something like the proposed Federal Marriage Amendment to the Constitution, which would define marriage as the union of a man and a woman. At a stroke, such an amendment would block gay marriage, polygamy, polyamory, and the replacement of marriage by a contract system. Whatever the courts might make of the slippery-slope argument, the broader public will take it seriously. Since *Lawrence*, we have already heard from Jon Carroll in the *San Francisco Chronicle* calling for legalized polygamy. Judith Levine in the *Village Voice* has made a plea for group marriage. And Michael Kinsley—no queer theorist but a completely mainstream journalist—has publicly called for the legal abolition of marriage. So the most radical proposal of all has now moved out of the law schools and legal commissions, and onto the front burner of public discussion.

Fair-minded people differ on the matter of homosexuality. I happen to think that sodomy laws should have been repealed (although legislatively). I also believe that our increased social tolerance for homosexuality is generally a good thing. But the core issue here is not homosexuality; it is marriage. Marriage is a critical social institution. Stable families depend on it. Society depends on stable families. Up to now, with all the changes in marriage, the one thing we've been sure of is that marriage means monogamy. Gay marriage will break that connection. It will do this by itself, and by leading to polygamy and polyamory. What lies beyond gay marriage is no marriage at all.

STUDY QUESTIONS

1. Kurtz points out, "From Thomas Aquinas through Richard Posner, almost every serious observer has granted the incompatibility between polygamy and Western companionate marriage." What are we warranted in believing on the basis that all these writers make the same observation? Is the agreement of "serious observers" a weighty consideration or a mere rhetorical device? Similarly, once we know that most ordinary Americans prefer heterosexual, monogamous marriage to other forms of marriage, is anyone else logically compelled to agree with them? Suppose at some future time that most ordinary Americans supported a pluralistic marriage structure. What would that mean?

2. Kurtz claims that gay and lesbian marriages will "almost certainly weaken the belief that monogamy lies at the heart of marriage." He concedes, however, that lesbians value monogamy in their relationships (and might be naturally suited to it?), and even that gay men within civil unions affirm the value of monogamy more than do gay men outside such unions. Is Kurtz's position in this respect consistent? (Of course, there's the joke: "What do a pair of lesbians

do on their second date?—They rent a U-Haul. What do two gay males do on their second date? —What second date?")

3. Consider a triumvirate of which Kurtz speaks: a lesbian couple and the male sperm donor who is their child's biological father. Is this a "polygamous" relationship? Do you find it objectionable or a viable option in the expanding realm of possibilities?

4. Kurtz, apparently, would have us all be straight, monogamous, and married (unless, as recommended by St. Paul in 1 Cor. 7, we committed ourselves to the celibate life). Which of these conditions (straight, monogamous, married) tops his wish list? Which of these conditions tops your wish list, and why?

5. Kurtz's views imply that the bisexual marriages favored by Kayley Vernallis (see "Bisexual Marriage," in this volume) are not marriages at all. In fact, Vernallis herself sometimes speaks of "marriage-like" arrangements. Is there a significant and cogent difference between "not a marriage at all" and "an improper or troublesome type of marriage" that should be acknowledged? Even if the variants are merely marriage-like, in some technical sense, is that by itself a reason to judge these arrangements improper or troublesome?

TEN

In Defense of Same-Sex Marriage

Cheshire Calhoun

Why would gays and lesbians (or other same-sex couples) want to participate in the institution of marriage, given the central role of traditional marriage in the social standards and practices of heteronormativity and compulsory pairing, and the fact that nearly half of all heterosexual marriages end in divorce? Why are many people intensely opposed to same-sex marriage, so that it has become a notoriously divisive issue in U.S. politics? The sophisticated approach to the topic of **Cheshire Calhoun** *begins to answer these questions. She argues that the right to marry must be at the center of gay and lesbian liberation, but not for the usual reasons circulated in the debate. Gays and lesbians should not press for same-sex marriage on the typical utilitarian grounds of extending a set of benefits (economic, legal, and social) to the partners; nor by claiming, on the grounds of equality, that marriage is a moral good that should be accessible to everyone; nor for the reason that same-sex marriage furthers, by rebuking sexist assumptions about male and female roles, the cause of breaking down gender conformity. During Calhoun's rejection of these arguments, we are led to (re)consider homophobia, the social construction of queerness, legal sexism, and the basis of the perceived threat that same-sex marriage represents. Her positive arguments in defense of same-sex marriage rest on the common meaning of "marriage" as used by all parties to this dispute and what is done by discriminatory marriage laws in the political subordination of homosexuals.*

Cheshire Calhoun teaches philosophy at Arizona State University. She is the author of *Feminism, the Family, and the Politics of the Closet* (Oxford University Press, 2000) and editor of *Setting the Moral Compass: Essays by Women Philosophers* (Oxford University Press, 2004). She has written essays in feminist ethics, moral psychology, normative ethics, and philosophy of emotion. This essay is reprinted, abridged, with the permission of Cheshire Calhoun and Oxford University Press, from *Feminism, the Family, and the Politics of the Closet* (Oxford University Press, 2000), chap. 5, pp. 107–31. © Cheshire Calhoun, 2000.

On September 21, 1996, President Clinton signed into law the Defense of Marriage Act (DOMA). That Act did two things. It amended the Full Faith and Credit Clause so that no state is required to honor same-sex marriages performed in another state. Second, it "defended" marriage by defining marriage for federal purposes as involving one man and one woman.

The immediate impetus behind the Defense of Marriage Act was the Hawaii Supreme Court's ruling in *Baehr v. Lewin* (74 Haw. 530, 852 P.2d 44 [1993]) that absent a compelling state interest, the same-sex marriage bar would be deemed an unconstitutional form of sex discrimination. Court suits for the right of gays and lesbians to marry, however, are not new. They date from the 1970s. Gay men and lesbians now divide over the issue of same-sex marriage rights. Proponents point to both the practical benefits of legal marriage—such as immigration preference and spousal health insurance—and to the importance of securing gays' and lesbians' equal treatment under the law. Opponents argue that distributing benefits such as health insurance through marriage is itself unjust. They also argue that, rather than endorsing a sexist and normalizing institution like marriage, gay men and lesbians would be better off creating new intimate and familial arrangements outside the scope of the law.

My aim in this essay is to try to forge some common ground. I side with proponents of marriage rights in thinking that the right to marry is critical to gay and lesbian equality. But I side with opponents in thinking that some prominent arguments for marriage rights are bad ones. And I mean politically bad. What matters politically is not just which rights we strive for, but also which arguments get culturally circulated in the process.

In what follows, I examine three different arguments for same-sex marriage. The first defends marriage rights by appealing to the value of long-term, monogamous, sexually faithful intimacy. The second argues that same-sex marriage rights would reduce sexism. The third claims that denying same-sex marriage rights currently enables heterosexuals to claim for themselves a privileged political status as sustainers of culture, society, and civilization. I will critique the first two arguments. I will defend a variant of the third argument.

MARRIAGE AS NORMATIVE IDEAL

For many, the legal institution of marriage rests on the moral ideal of an emotional and spiritual unity of two people. That unity is expressed in monogamy, long-term commitment, sexual fidelity, mutual economic support, procreation, and child-rearing. Marriage, in this sense, represents the normative ideal for how sexuality, companionship, affection, personal economics, and child-rearing should be organized. On this view, the fact that marriage is a moral ideal justifies state regulation of marriage. The state protects both the legal right to marry and marital privacy, provides unique benefits to marital couples, and regulates the dissolution of marriages because marriage is a basic personal and social good. Although state neutrality may require permitting other forms of intimate relationship, the state has a special obligation to promote valued ways of living. Thus the answer to the question, "Why should anyone have the right to marry?" is that committed, monogamous, sexually faithful relationships contribute to personal and social flourishing.

William Eskridge, Jr., author of *The Case for Same-Sex Marriage*, uses this argument to defend same-sex marriage rights. In his view, state promotion of long-term commitment in both heterosexual and same-sex couples is important because commitment both adds depth to a relationship and helps individuals maintain a stable sense of self within lives that are often fragmented by our occupying too many roles, by our geographical mobility, and often by our lack of stable employment.[1] Because a stable sense of self is such an important good to the individual, the law needs to protect both heterosexual and same-sex relationships from external intervention and internal dissolution.

Eskridge's argument dovetails with that of cultural conservatives.[2] Cultural conservatives often charge liberalism with overvaluing personal choice, self-expression, and lifestyle experimentation and undervaluing such personal and civic virtues as self-sacrifice, self-discipline, planning for the future, concern for others, responsible conduct, and loyalty.[3] What makes marriage important is precisely that it presupposes the value of these virtues. And because the virtues of loyalty, self-discipline, and self-sacrifice are good both for individuals and for society, the state should promote and to some extent coercively enforce long-term marriage. Eskridge himself points out that the costliness of dissolving a legal marriage is a prime benefit of legal marriage. People must enter *legal* marriage with a higher personal commitment than domestic partnerships require and, once married, have additional incentives to stay married. Such incentives, he hypothesizes, are especially important for sexually promiscuous gay men who have difficulty sustaining committed relationships.

Would it be a good thing to win same-sex marriage rights by using this argument? I do not think so. As I see it, the basic problem with this argument is that it is fundamentally anti-liberal. It assumes that it is the legitimate business of the state to promote one particular moral conception of marriage. It also elevates long-term commitment to such importance that the state is permitted to coercively enforce the continuance of marriages even though people may have very good reasons for not staying married. Of course, most states presently have no-fault divorce laws, and thus the coercive pressures exerted on couples to stay married are limited to the tax incentives and the costliness of divorce proceedings.

But Eskridge's argument clearly would justify toughening divorce laws. And many, who like Eskridge value long-term commitment, have recommended less modestly coercive measures, such as re-stigmatizing divorce, toughening divorce laws for couples with children, enacting punitive welfare policies for poor women who have children out of wedlock, and returning to some form of gender structured marriage.[4] What is especially worrisome about Eskridge's argument, then, is not his specific argument but its natural place within a larger cultural conversation about the benefits of returning to a particular normative ideal of marriage and parenting. Returning to that ideal means using the law to dissuade individuals from pursuing a plurality of conceptions of how intimate relationships ought to be organized.

Eskridge's argument also plays into queer theorists' and lesbian feminists' worst fears about what advocating same-sex marriage might mean. Queer theorists worry that gays and lesbians who seek to marry are seeking simply to assimilate to mainstream culture. Now, I think this worry about assimilation is often misplaced. To claim that same-sex marriage would necessarily assimilate gays and lesbians to mainstream culture ignores the fact that many heterosexuals (who of course do have the right to marry) have been anything but assimilationists. Indeed, marriage law has evolved because of heterosexuals' resistance to legal and social conceptions of marriage.

However, when same-sex marriage rights are tied to the policy goal of promoting *one* normative ideal for intimacy, queer theorists are right to worry. Marriage rights, so construed, ought not to have priority in a gay/lesbian political agenda. Because gays and lesbians have also developed alternative families composed of friends rather than biological kin, it is important to secure legal rights for those who function as family members even if these families diverge from the conventional picture. Securing such rights requires abandoning the culturally conservative idea that there is only one normative ideal for intimacy. In short, tying same-sex marriage rights to state promotion of one normative conception of marriage and family means not critically rethinking which rights and benefits should be distributed to whom given a plurality of family forms.

Eskridge's argument also plays into lesbian-feminists' worst fears. Lesbian feminists worry that same-sex marriage rights would simply endorse patriarchal gender-structured marriage. I think this worry is often misplaced too. It ignores the fact that many heterosexuals have themselves resisted the gender structuring of marriage, producing substantial changes in marriage law that have included eliminating separate husband-wife roles, fault-based divorce, long-term alimony, and a required shared domicile.[5]

However, when same-sex marriage rights are tied to the policy goal of promoting one normative ideal for intimacy, lesbian feminists are right to worry. What gets put into cultural circulation is a particular style of thinking about marriage. It is a style that resists any thoroughgoing departure from the most traditional normative ideal of marriage and family. It is a style that links marital-familial arrangements so tightly to the public good that state neutrality with respect to conceptions of the intimate good cannot go all the way down. And it is a style whose terms—pro-commitment, profamily, antipromiscuity—are easily invoked to support moral norms and social policies that constrain women's reproductive, sexual, and relational liberty.

One last objection. To my mind, the greatest defect of this culturally conservative argument for same-sex marriage rights is that it doesn't explain why same-sex marriage rights belong on a specifically *gay and lesbian* political agenda. For this, we would need a different sort of argument. In particular, we need a reason for thinking that the bar on same-sex marriage sustains heterosexual privilege. This is exactly what gender-based arguments claim to do.

GENDER-BASED ARGUMENTS

Gender-based arguments occur most commonly in legal literature and were central in the Hawaii case. In a nutshell, gender-based arguments claim that homophobia, including the bar on same-sex marriage, originates from a system of male domination over women. The bar on gay and lesbian marriage is thus really an instance of sex discrimination and should be eliminated for that reason.[6]

Gender-based arguments for same-sex marriage take two forms. Because one does a better job than the other of answering the question "Why should marriage rights be a political priority for gays and lesbians?" it is worth sorting them out.

The first view claims that there is cultural hostility to same-sex marriage because same-sex marriages are likely to be gender-free. A marriage between two women or two men cannot easily be organized around husband and wife roles. And were same-sex marriages held up as a possible model, heterosexual couples might be tempted to follow suit, modeling their own marriages on the already more egalitarian models adopted by lesbians and gay men. Thus legalizing same-sex marriage poses a threat to the gender system, because it would, in essence, declare that gendered husband and wife roles are inessential to any marriage, whether same-sex or opposite-sex.

On this view, the bar on same-sex marriage is like earlier anti-miscegenation laws. The premise of interracial marriage bars was that there are two distinct races whose differences must be preserved. So, too, the premise of same-sex marriage bars is that there are two distinct genders whose differences must be preserved.[7] This means that the same-sex marriage bar is simply a specific expression of a general intolerance to the

blurring of gender difference anywhere, by anyone, including by heterosexuals in heterosexual marriages. Thus the answer to the question,
"Why should gays and lesbians have the right to marry?" is that same-
sex marriage would make gender difference irrelevant within *all* marriages and would help bring about a gender-just society.

Would it be a good thing to win same-sex marriage rights by using
this argument? I do not think so. While it is always desirable to culturally
circulate arguments for gender justice, the central problem with this argument is that it gives *heterosexuals* a better reason to make same-sex
marriage a political priority than it does for gays and lesbians to do so.
After all, the primary beneficiaries on this view would be heterosexual
couples, particularly heterosexual women. The argument assumes that
lesbians and gay men *already* have gender-just relationships. Only heterosexuals persist in imagining that marriages require gendered husband
and wife roles.

Equally troubling, this argument loses sight of the special animus
visited upon lesbians and gay men. It does so because it assumes that
there are only two kinds of persons—men and women. The fact that a
lesbian is a *lesbian* turns out to be irrelevant. All that matters is that she is
a gender deviant *woman*. Gender deviant heterosexual women and gender deviant lesbians are, on this view, in exactly the same boat; whatever
hostility they may encounter is solely a result of their gender deviance,
not their sexual orientation. But this seems false. Hostility to legal same-
sex marriage runs high even though heterosexual marriages have already
been de-gendered under the law. For example, the law no longer compels
married women to adopt their husband's name, to share his domicile
wherever he chooses it to be, to provide domestic services, and to submit
to marital rape. Long-term alimony for wives was eliminated and alimony for needy ex-husbands was introduced when the law gave up the idea
that only husbands are economic providers. In addition, antidiscrimina-
tion laws forbidding formal and informal enforcement of gender differences in the workplace, education, access to housing, and loans have
helped de-gender the public sphere. These legal changes suggest that
hostility to unsettling gender categories is much less when heterosexual
women and men do the unsettling than when lesbians and gay men do it.
Thus, hostility to same-sex marriage cannot adequately be explained by
appeal to the fear that such marriages spell disaster for the gender structure of heterosexual marriages.

The second gender-based argument tries to explain the special animus
directed at lesbians and gay men by rejecting the idea that there are just
two kinds—men and women. Rather, the social construction of the
homosexual and the lesbian at the turn of the century pluralized sex-
gender categories beyond the original two. Both gay men and lesbians
were described as a third sex, as men-women, as inverts, as the unsexed,
the semi-women and semi-men, as men trapped in female bodies or

women trapped in male bodies, as people with a touch of the hermaphrodite. Gays and lesbians were not *just* gender deviant men and women. For them, gender deviance was a uniquely constitutive and unavoidable part of their nature.

Hostility to this third sex derives from the view that the only normal, natural, healthy kinds of people are real women and real men, who at least by nature have the *capacity* to conform to gender norms. Heterosexuals have this capacity to conform to gender norms, even if they sometimes choose to violate gender norms. By contrast, gays and lesbians constitute a category of persons who are naturally unfit for incorporation into a society governed by gender norms because gender deviance is built into their very nature.

Lesbians and gays are thus singled out for special mistreatment and legal regulation not visited upon gender deviant heterosexuals. Nevertheless, the special opprobrium felt toward lesbians and gay men is ultimately rooted in gender ideology. Same-sex marriage bars may not be, precisely, sex discrimination, since they are not aimed at controlling all women. They are, nevertheless, of a piece with policies that discriminate on the basis of sex.

There is a good deal to be said for this second argument. It accounts for the special animus motivating mistreatment of gays and lesbians. It thus explains why gays and lesbians have a special political interest in challenging legal regulations that target them. In addition, this argument also accounts for the intimate connection between gay and lesbian oppression and male dominance.

Even so, I think this is the wrong argument for same-sex marriage rights—or at least it is seriously incomplete. All gender-based arguments start from an assumption that merits questioning. The assumption is that the fundamental inequality at stake in all gay rights issues is the inequality between men and women. On these arguments, male dominance alone accounts for both the oppression of women and the oppression of gays and lesbians. As a result, the possibility is never entertained that heterosexual domination might be a separable axis of oppression; nor is the possibility entertained that in maintaining same-sex marriage bars, in maintaining the liberty to discriminate against lesbians and gays, and in limiting gay and lesbian access to children, what is at stake is preserving heterosexuals' privileged sociopolitical status.

In addition, both gender-based arguments under-describe the ideological construction of "gay" and "lesbian" as stigmatized social identities. It *is* true that cross-genderization was the defining feature of the third sex at the turn of the century. It is also true that hostility to gender blurring continues to sustain the stigma attached to being gay or lesbian.

However, gender deviance does not fully exhaust the content of what it culturally means to be gay or lesbian. Equally important to the cultural construction of gay and lesbian identities is the idea that both gays' and lesbians' sexuality is dangerously uncontrolled, predatory, insatiable, narcissistic, and self-indulgent. This aspect of gay and lesbian identity came to particular cultural prominence during the 1930s through the 1950s—the era of both the sex crime panics and the formal exclusion of so-called "sex perverts" from all governmental service.[8] Imagined to possess an excessive and unregulated sexuality, both gays and lesbians allegedly posed a threat to heterosexual adults and to children, who might be either molested or seduced. Because of their sexual insatiability, gays and lesbians were also presumed psychologically unable to maintain stable intimate relationships.

Linking both the images of the gender deviant and the sex pervert is the culturally elaborated view that gays and lesbians are multiply unfit for marriage and family: they are unfit for assuming gendered familial roles and producing properly gendered children; they are incapable of sustaining long-term stable relationships; they pose a sexual threat to their own and others' children; and they risk reproducing their own defects in a second generation.

In sum, gender-based arguments for same-sex marriage take up only one theme in a historically complex construction of lesbian and gay identity. As a result, they fail to explain why hostility to homosexuality and lesbianism crystallizes around marital and familial issues in the way that it does. They also fail to explain the content of contemporary anti-gay discourse. If gender-based arguments were correct, the House and Senate debates over the Defense of Marriage Act should have focused on gays' and lesbians' unsuitability for fulfilling husband and wife roles, the possibility of their producing gender deviant children, the unnaturalness of men marrying men or women marrying women, and the importance of traditional gender structured marriage. The DOMA debates, however, are strikingly *devoid* of any references to gender.

I turn now to the DOMA debates and what I think the moral argument for same-sex marriage should be.

DOMA'S DEFENSE OF HETEROSEXUAL STATUS

Let me begin with two observations. First, all anti-gay policies—including same-sex marriage bars, sodomy laws, bars to adoption or foster parenting, court denial of child custody, and the absence of anti-discrimination laws—are predicated on stereotypes about gays' and lesbians' difference from heterosexuals. Specifically they presuppose views about gays' and lesbians' gender deviance, lack of sexual control, and unfitness for family life. They thus assume that heterosexuals and nonheterosexuals are different kinds of people who can thus be treated differently under the law.

Second, anti-gay policies differ from racist or sexist policies. The aim of racist or sexist policies is to keep racial minorities and women *in their place*. Anti-gay policies, I think, have a different aim, namely, to displace gays and lesbians from civil society by refusing to recognize that lesbians and gay men belong in either the public or the private sphere.[9]

What I want to suggest is that same-sex marriage bars play an especially critical role in displacing gays and lesbians from civil society. And this is the reason why same-sex marriage rights belong at the center of a gay/lesbian political agenda.

The same-sex marriage bar works in a particularly powerful way to displace gays and lesbians because we, as a culture, assume that married couples play a unique role in sustaining civil society. Within both legal reasoning and broader cultural discourse, marriage and the family are typically taken to be the bedrock on which social and political life is built. Indeed, proponents of DOMA repeatedly emphasized the way marriages provide the foundation for civil society: "Marriage is the *foundation* of our society; families are built on it and values are passed through it."[10] Marriage is "the *keystone* in the arch of civilization."[11] "The time-honored and unique institution of marriage between one man and one woman is a *fundamental pillar* of our society and its values."[12] "[T]hroughout the annals of human experience, in dozens of civilizations and cultures of varying value systems, humanity has discovered that the permanent relationship between man and woman is a *keystone* to the stability, strength, and health of human society—a relationship worthy of legal recognition and judicial protection."[13] And "governments have recognized the traditional family as the *foundation* of prosperity and happiness, and in democratic societies, as the *foundation* of freedom."[14] (All italics mine.)

DOMA proponents clearly conceived of marriage as a prepolitical institution. Although states create the legal package of rights and benefits that attach to marriage and states set age, sex, biological relationship, and other restrictions on who may marry, the state does not create the institution of marriage itself. In addition, while a state might *choose* to legally recognize and protect a variety of voluntary relationships—for example, domestic partnerships—recognizing marriages is not a matter of choice. Since the very possibility of civil society depends on people entering marriages and forming families, the state *must* recognize marriages.

This conception of marriage as the prepolitical foundation of society has an important implication: It means that if a social group can lay claim to being inherently qualified or fit to enter into marriage and found a family, it can also claim a distinctive political status. Members of the group can claim that they play an essential role in sustaining the very foundation of civil society. Conversely, if a particular social group is deemed unfit to enter marriage and found a family, that group can then be denied this distinctive political status. Members of a group judged incapable of providing the necessary foundation for civil society become inessential citizens. Or at best, they are dependent citizens, because whatever social contribution they might make to civil society depends on the antecedent marital and familial labor of others.

For proponents of DOMA, the central question was "*Who* is entitled to the political status that comes with being deemed qualified for marriage and the family?"[15] The aim of proponents was to reaffirm, by constructing a federal definition of marriage, that only heterosexuals are entitled to this status.

Anxiety about what would happen to heterosexuals' status if same-sex marriages were legally recognized ran very close to the surface in these debates. Representative Smith, for example, asserted that "[s]ame-sex 'marriages' demean the fundamental institution of marriage. . . . And they trivialize marriage as a mere 'lifestyle choice.'"[16] Others echoed this sentiment: "[I]t is vital that we protect marriage against attempts to redefine it in a way that causes the family to lose its special meaning."[17] "Should the law express its neutrality between homosexual and heterosexual relationships? Should the law elevate homosexual unions to the same status as the heterosexual relationships on which the traditional family is based, a status which has been reserved from time immemorial for the union between a man and a woman?"[18] "Allowing for gay marriages would be the final straw, it would devalue the love between a man and a woman and weaken us as a Nation."[19]

But exactly why would same-sex marriages devalue heterosexual love, belittle marriage, and render it a mere lifestyle choice? The obvious answer is that homosexuality is immoral. To legally recognize same-sex marriages would place the sacred institution of marriage in the disreputable company of immoral, unnatural unions, thus cheapening its status. This was surely part of the thinking. But it is not the whole story. For if concern about giving the same state seal of approval to immoral same-sex unions as to honorable heterosexual marriages were the primary concern, then one would expect proponents of DOMA to also be adamantly opposed to any legal protection of same-sex unions. Yet Representative Lipinski, who thought that allowing gay marriages would be the final straw devaluing love between man and woman also observed that "gays can legally achieve the same ends as marriage through draft wills, medical powers of attorney, and contractual agreements in the event that the relationship should end."[20] Other proponents affirmed the importance of guaranteeing the right to privacy[21] and pointed out that the law protects a variety of unions outside of marriage law (which presumably might also include same-sex unions).[22] These sorts of remarks suggest that the immorality of homosexuality was not the only issue.

The central worry instead seemed to be that recognizing same-sex unions as marriages would *demote marriage from a naturally defined prepolitical institution to a state-defined contract*. Senators Gramm and Byrd clearly expressed this concern. According to Gramm, "[h]uman beings have always given traditional marriage a special sanction. Not that there cannot be contracts among individuals, but there is something unique about the traditional family in terms of what it does for our society and the foundation it provides."[23] Byrd articulated a similar distinction:

> Obviously, human beings enter into a variety of relationships. Business partnerships, friendships, alliances for mutual benefits, and team memberships all depend upon emotional unions of one degree or another. For that reason, a number of these relationships have found standing under the laws of innumerable nations. . . . However, in no case, has anyone suggested that these relationships deserve the special recognition or the designation commonly understood as "marriage."[24]

Reading between the lines, the underlying view seems to be this: Free, self-defining, sociable citizens may choose to enter a variety of voluntary relationships with each other. In deciding what legal protections might be in order for these relationships, a liberal political society that values freedom of association and the right to pursuit of happiness must adopt a position of neutrality. Rather than giving priority to some of these relationships on moral grounds, the state instead assumes that citizens may reasonably choose any of these relationships on the basis of their own conception of the good. Thus, such voluntary associations might reasonably be dubbed "lifestyle choices." To call them "lifestyle choices" is not to say that they are in fact morally equivalent. One might, for example, think that same-sex unions are immoral, but nevertheless think the state should adopt a neutral position, and it should offer legal protection for same-sex unions under domestic partnership laws. To say that a particular form of relationship is a "lifestyle choice," then, is simply to say that it falls within the category of relationships with respect to which *state* neutrality is appropriate.

What proponents of DOMA took pains to emphasize was that marriage falls in a different category. Marriage is not one among many voluntary associations that citizens might make a "lifestyle" choice to enter. Marriage constitutes the prepolitical foundation of society. In other words, societies depend for their functioning on marriages *and* the essential nature of marriage is fixed independently of liberal society—by God, or by human nature, or by the prerequisites for civilization. Consequently, state neutrality with respect to the definition of marriage involves a category mistake. State neutrality would involve treating a prepolitical institution as though it were a political institution, that is, as though it were an institution that must be compatible with multiple conceptions of the good. Since, on this view, marriage is not in fact a political institution, it is legitimate to insulate marriage against liberal revisions. This is what DOMA does.

In my view, then, what makes same-sex marriage rights so important is that marriage bars do not represent merely one among many ways that the state may discriminate against gays and lesbians by enacting laws based on stereotypes about lesbians' and gay men's gender deviance, undisciplined sexual desire, and unfitness for family life. Marriage bars specifically enact the view that *heterosexual* love, marriage, and family have a uniquely prepolitical, foundational status in civil society. Marriage bars assume that heterosexual relationships are not just morally superior, but that they have a uniquely privileged status beyond the reach of liberal political values. Marriage bars also enact the view that because only heterosexuals are fit to participate in this foundational marital institution, only heterosexuals are entitled to lay claim to a unique citizenship status: Heterosexuals are not just free, rational, self-defining persons. They are also naturally fit to participate in the one institution that all societies, liberal or otherwise, must presuppose. Thus they may lay claim to a citizenship status that exceeds what individuals are entitled to on the basis of being free, rational, self-defining persons. So, for example, in addition to the rights of free association, including intimate association, to which all citizens are entitled, heterosexuals may also lay claim to special state solitude for their private lives, a partial insulation of their legal privileges from liberal principles, and special entitlement to influence future generations.

CONCLUSION

So, what is my conclusion? What, given the backdrop of the DOMA debates, ought lesbians and gay men to want with respect to same-sex marriage rights? Here there are two options. On the one hand, one might agree, in part, with proponents of DOMA that marriage, even if not heterosexual marriage, is unlike other possible voluntary intimate arrangements—for example, it is unlike the families of choice described by Kath Weston—because some form of marriage is indeed a prepolitical, foundational institution meriting special legal treatment. One might then argue that heterosexuals are *not* the only ones qualified to enter this prepolitical institution. This option would, of course, take us back to some form of the argument based on a normative ideal for how persons should organize their intimate, affectional, personal economic, reproductive, sexual, and child-rearing lives. The legal task would then be to determine which forms of heterosexual and nonheterosexual intimacy would be dignified with the label "marriage" and the status of being regarded as foundational to civil society. Under this option, the bid for same-sex marriage rights would amount to a demand to be deemed fit to participate in the foundational social institution and thus to be deemed an essential citizen who is not dependent on the marital and familial work of others.

The second option is that one might reject the idea altogether that there are any prepolitical, foundational forms of intimacies. Civil societies depend only in the most general way on their citizens having the capacities for and interest in casting their personal lot with others, sharing, in voluntary private arrangements, sex, affection, reproduction, care for the young, the infirm, and the elderly, and economic support. But no one form or set of forms for doing so is foundational to civil society. Instead, one might envision a fully liberal society in which no private relationships are insulated from liberal principles and in which legal protection and support of the private sphere and the production of future generations is predicated on the assumption that persons might choose a plurality of intimate arrangements in accord with their own conceptions of the good. In this case, the bid for same-sex marriage rights would amount to a demand to be deemed equal citizens within a fully liberal society.

To many, the obviously correct option is the second one. Of course, the state should be neutral with respect to conceptions of the good. Of course, it is always a bad thing for the state to promote any normative ideal of intimate relations. While I agree, I also find the choice of option two more difficult to make. Defending same-sex marriage on grounds of state neutrality requires only that same-sex marriages be legally permitted *regardless* of how they are morally viewed. Genuine equality for gays and lesbians, however, requires more than merely coming to be tolerated. It requires that we, as a culture, give up the belief that gays and lesbians are unfit to participate in normatively ideal forms of marriage, parenting, and family. Only the first option permits us to put into cultural circulation arguments that directly challenge the ideology sustaining gays' and lesbians' social inequality.

NOTES

1. William Eskridge, *The Case for Same-Sex Marriage: From Sexual Liberty to Civilized Commitment* (New York: The Free Press, 1996), 72.

2. Karen Struening, "Feminist Challenges to the New Familialism: Lifestyle Experimentation and the Freedom of Association," *Hypatia* 11 (1996): 135–54.

3. Stephen Macedo, "Sexuality and Liberty: Making Room for Nature and Tradition?" in *Sex, Preference, and Family*, ed. David M. Estlund and Martha C. Nussbaum (New York: Oxford University Press, 1996), 86–101. Struening surveys the main themes of cultural conservatives with respect to the family, focusing particularly on William Galston.

4. Struening, "Feminist Challenges."

5. Of course, not all these changes have been salutary for women, since the beneficial consequences of eliminating the formal gender structure of marriage depends in large part on the *actual* de-gendering of marital practices as well as gender equity in the paid workforce.

6. See, for example, Sylvia Law, "Homosexuality and the Social Meaning of Gender," *Wisconsin Law Review* 1988 (1998): 187-235; Cass R. Sunstein, "Homosexuality

and the Constitution," in Estlund and Nussbaum, *Sex, Preference, and Family*, 208–26; Andrew Koppelman, "The Miscegenation Analogy: Sodomy Law as Sex Discrimination," *Yale Law Journal* 98 (1988): 145-64; Andrew Koppelman, "Why Discrimination Against Lesbians and Gay Men is Sex Discrimination," *NYU Law Review* 69 (1994): 197-287; Nan D. Hunter, "Marriage, Law, and Gender: A Feminist Inquiry," in Lisa Duggan and Nan D. Hunter, *Sex Wars: Sexual Dissent and Political Culture* (New York: Routledge, 1995), 107–22.

7. Sunstein, "Homosexuality."

8. I give a more detailed account of the multilayered construction of lesbians and gay men as unfit for family life in "Constructing Lesbians and Gay Men as Family's Outlaws," chapter 6 of my *Feminism, the Family, and the Politics of the Closet* (New York: Oxford University Press, 2000), 132–60.

9. Cheshire Calhoun, "Sexuality Injustice," *Notre Dame Journal of Law, Ethics, and Public Policy* 9 (1995): 241–74.

10. Representative Lipinski, *Congressional Record* 142: 103 (July 12, 1996), H7495.

11. William J. Bennett, "Not a Very Good Idea," quoted from the *Washington Post* (May 21, 1996) in *Congressional Record* 142: 103 (July 12, 1996), H7495.

12. Representative Ensign, *Congressional Record* 142: 103 (July 12, 1996), H7493.

13. Senator Byrd, *Congressional Record* 142: 123 (September 10, 1996), S10109.

14. Senator Gramm, *Congressional Record* 142: 123 (September 10, 1996), S10106.

15. Opponents clearly took the debate to be about something else, namely, about why, in practice, real families aren't doing very well. Completely bypassing proponents' point, opponents instead focused on the misbehavior of heterosexual family members as well as inadequate health, education, day care, unemployment, the absence of a livable minimum wage, inability to afford single-family homes, loss of pensions, and insufficient Medicare payments.

16. *Congressional Record* 123: 103 (July 12, 1996), H7494.

17. Representative Weldon, *ibid.*, H7493.

18. Representative Canady, *ibid.*, H7491.

19. Representative Lipinski, *ibid.*, H7495.

20. *Ibid.*, H7495.

21. Senator Burns, *Congressional Record* 142: 123 (September 10, 1996), S10117.

22. Senator Byrd, *ibid.*, S10109.

23. Senator Gramm, *ibid.*, S10106.

24. Senator Byrd, *ibid.*, S10109.

STUDY QUESTIONS

1. Explain the meaning and draw out the implications of Calhoun's mentioning that marriage is a "prepolitical institution." Do some library (or www?) research in order to explore a similar idea in the writings of such disparate political philosophers as John Rawls and Karl Marx.

2. Why, according to Calhoun, is a straightforward analogy to anti-miscegenation laws not a sufficient basis to oppose laws banning same-sex marriage? To help you think about different kinds of discrimination, read the 1967 U.S. Supreme Court decision *Loving v. Virginia* (388 U.S. 1), which ruled that state laws that prohibit interracial marriage are unconstitutional.

3. Evaluate the threat the supporters of the Defense of Marriage Act (DOMA) say that same-sex marriage holds for children. What are

some other perceived threats to children spoken of within the larger cultural debate over same-sex marriage? Do they have any merit? Think about how same-sex couples and their children are portrayed in television programs and Hollywood films.

4. Discuss the strengths and weaknesses of Calhoun's position in light of Stanley Kurtz's many arguments against same-sex marriage ("Beyond Gay Marriage: The Road to Polyamory," in this volume). Figure out how Calhoun might respond to this common sentiment: "But why must they demand the right to marry? Why can they not settle for domestic partnerships?" Also, how would she respond to another sentiment, that gays and lesbians should not even have recourse to civil unions? Finally, how might she defend her defense of marriage against the radically feminist sentiment that the institution of marriage is a disaster and should be done away with, not expanded? (See Claudia Card's "Gay Divorce: Thoughts on the Legal Regulation of Marriage," in this volume.)

5. What does the issue of same-sex marriage have to do with sexuality and sexual relations? Could there be same-sex marriages that do not include any sexual activity between the spouses? Are there heterosexual marriages that do not include much if any sexual activity between the partners? Is sex, or must sex be, one of the (main) points of marriage? If being married morally justifies the sexual activity of a heterosexual couple, does being married also morally justify homosexual sexual activity?

ELEVEN

Gay Divorce: Thoughts on the Legal Regulation of Marriage

Claudia Card

*Although **Claudia Card** agrees that achieving the legal right of same-sex couples to marry is an important symbolic and political victory, she argues that the state should not regulate intimate unions between freely consenting adults. Ideally, marriage should be abolished because it is an evil institution: it foreseeably facilitates culpable wrongdoing and intolerable harm, such as making it difficult for spouses to escape abusive relationships and denying health benefits to single individuals and non-married couples. However, marriage as a legal institution is not likely to disappear soon. For this reason, Card argues that lesbians and gays, instead of agitating for marriage rights, should put their political energies into worthier fights, such as improving environmental, health care, and foreign policies.*

Claudia Card is the Emma Goldman Professor of Philosophy at the University of Wisconsin–Madison with teaching affiliations in women's studies, Jewish studies, environmental studies, and LGBT studies. Among her books are *Confronting Evils: Terrorism, Torture, Genocide* (Cambridge, 2010); *Genocide's Aftermath: Responsibility and Repair*, edited with Armen Marsoobian (Blackwell, 2007); her edited volume *The Cambridge Companion to Simone de Beauvoir* (Cambridge, 2003); and *The Atrocity Paradigm: A Theory of Evil* (Oxford, 2002). In 2010–2011 Card was the president of the American Philosophical Association Central Division. © Claudia Card, 2012. This essay is printed here with her permission.

Advocates usually pose the issue of marriage for same-sex partners as one of *recognition*, as though such marriages were already here and the only issue is whether the law should recognize them. "Recognition" has a positive ring. Yet what is at stake is not just recognition but *regulation* by the state, including the power to determine what counts as a marriage. "Marriage" is systematically ambiguous between a committed personal relationship antecedent to legal definitions and a union legitimated by external authority, such as a religious or governmental body. Hopefully, the phrase "legal regulation of marriage" surmounts that ambiguity and makes clear the topic of this essay.

My position on the regulation of marriage has been, and remains, that the law should no more declare which durable intimate sexual unions between freely consenting adults are legitimate and which are not than it should declare which newborns are legitimate and which not. My objection is not to durable intimate unions as extra-legal relationships between consenting adults. The target of my criticism is the vague, open-ended, state-enforceable legal marriage contract, rarely entered into voluntarily by any who are adequately informed of its consequences.

Yet opposition to legal marriage does not settle what we should do here and now, given that marriage (a) is part of what John Rawls called "the basic structure of society" and (b) has had recently attached to it in the U.S. critical *auxiliary* benefits (such as health coverage) that should be available independently but are currently economically beyond the reach of many except through marriage.[1] We face a kind of situation that Rawls used to say (in class lectures) presents the most difficult questions of moral philosophy, namely, how to determine what to do when every option confronting us is riddled with injustice, thanks to prior wrongful deeds of others. In such situations the objective, as he saw it, should be to try to identify the path of least injustice. I try to be guided by that objective in what follows.

Briefly, here are some of the injustices. First, consider injustices in the option of *advocating* legal regulation of marriage for same-sex partners. Auxiliary benefits currently attached to marriage can make the difference between having a place to live and being rendered homeless or, in some cases, between life and death. This should not be so. Marriage should not make this kind of difference to the satisfaction of basic needs. Yet currently in the United States it does. Lack of access to adequate health coverage is suffered not only by many lesbian and gay partners (and dependents) who are not members of the professions but by the poor in general who for whatever reason are not married. This is not a problem in countries with universal health care. But the U.S. does not appear headed in that direction soon. Thus legal regulation of same-sex marriage in the U.S. at present supports a profoundly unjust distribution of benefits.

But it is important to appreciate also that even these benefits are insufficient to enable an abused spouse to exit a marriage and protect children, if need be, before any of them suffers intolerable harm. Abusive marriages easily become lethal. A major problem with marriage in many jurisdictions is its burden of proof requirement that to terminate it when one spouse does not consent, the other must justify before the law the request for a divorce. Abused partners are commonly unable to produce convincing objective evidence of abuse, for a variety of reasons. No-fault divorce in many states means only that spouses who *mutually agree* are no longer guilty of the crime of collusion (as they were when my parents divorced in 1969 in Wisconsin). Relief from that criminal charge is not sufficient, however, to allow a spouse to terminate a marriage unilaterally without showing grounds acceptable to the state (such as, in the state of New York, that one's spouse has been in prison for more than three years or that one has not lived with or slept with one's spouse in at least a year). As long as the state retains a divorce-granting power that prevents unilateral dissolution at will—historically, a major distinction between marriages and less formal unions—marriage is a trap for abused partners and their children. The abusive spouse is commonly unwilling to let go and is able to conceal abuse from third parties, often with forced collusion of the abused spouse. Linda Marciano, popularly known as Linda Lovelace, forced to star in the film *Deep Throat*, was compelled by her abuser to marry him so she could not be made to testify against him in court.[2] This is an oppressive trap.

Next, consider the injustices of *refusing* to support the legal recognition of marriage for same-sex partners. This option condones the arbitrary denial to lesbians and gays and their dependents of benefits made available to heterosexual couples that can make the difference between major hardship and a decent life, or at the extreme, between life and death. Further, the right to marry is currently enshrined in the *Universal Declaration of Human Rights* (1948)[3] in language that does not specify the genders of the partners. Denial of that right to any group of law-abiding rational adults is dangerous in that it may lead to denying lesbians and gays other human rights. Further, it makes lesbian and gay partners socially less visible, thereby facilitating the survival of oppressive stereotypes, which can have their own lethal consequences.

Thus, whether one supports extending legal regulation of marriage to same-sex partners or refuses to support its legal regulation at all, at the present time, people's lives are at stake. People will die, either way. They will be killed by a spouse, or they will not receive health care needed for survival. These worst case scenarios are common enough to take seriously. Consequences will often be less dire but still intolerable. It need not be the same people who face these alternatives. But, interestingly, it *can* be. Behind a Rawlsian "veil of ignorance," which screens out knowledge of particular facts that would enable one to distinguish oneself from others, one should take seriously the possibility of being in either position: that of a dangerously abused spouse or that of an unemployed (or underemployed) and seriously ill or injured dependent without access to decent health coverage.

Behind that "veil of ignorance," one is to choose principles on the assumption that once the principles are chosen and the veil removed, people will generally comply with the requirements of institutions in the basic structure of society, which, in turn, will, for the most part, satisfy those principles. This is why he calls "justice as fairness" a "strict compliance" theory and an "ideal theory."[4] *A Theory of Justice* does not address the reasoning of parties behind the veil for choosing principles to rectify widespread deep injustices. When we do confront such injustices, the path of sanity should at least include the long-range objective of creating a better set of options. But that aim leaves open the question of what our short-range objective should be, what to do here and now. The next two sections explore further the dilemma of what to do now and conclude that we should take marriage off our political agenda for the next few years, maybe longer, and put our energies, beginning now, into improving our options. But I begin with the ideal, which appears unattainable in the near future.

THE IDEAL: DEREGULATE, NOT FURTHER REGULATE

My ideal regarding marriage is not that the law regulating it become perfectly just, which I think is not possible. My ideal is that the law not define or in any other way regulate durable intimate unions between freely consenting adults. According to George Chauncey's retelling of the story of the evolution of marriage-as-we-know-it in his highly informative (and delightfully readable) short book *Why Marriage?*, the legal regulation of marriage in Europe is a relatively recent matter of the past few centuries.[5] For a long time, state and church battled over who was to be the regulator. Before that, and for most of human history, marriage was unregulated by either. It was left to individuals to work out among themselves. Such anarchy in the absence of legal regulation of much else was hardly a rosy situation. Spouses commonly did not choose each other. Women had little protection against being stolen to become brides (even if already married).[6] Many women were more economically dependent on men than they need be today. State regulation of marriage could offer them and their children some protection against being left destitute. The reality, however, was that many were (and continue to be) left destitute anyway. In the context of a legal system that offers some protection against kidnap and coercion and enables women to become relatively independent of families economically, motives to form durable intimate unions do not translate as readily into motives to turn those unions into legal contracts. What motivate many to turn their relationships into legal marriages are a variety of penalties, including social stigma, attached to not doing so in a context in which (legal) marriage has become part of the basic structure of society.

My ideal is for legally regulated marriage to be no longer part of that basic structure, much as legitimate birth is no longer part of it. In the United States, birth certificates of children born to women who are not married are no longer stamped "illegitimate." They are not, however, stamped "legitimate" instead. There is today rightly no stamp at all regarding legitimacy on birth certificates. Like all analogies, the analogy with birth certificates is imperfect. A case by case stamp of illegitimacy is not explicitly placed upon same-sex relationships, although the judgment is implicitly there, because the state does officially *legitimate* heterosexual ones case by case with first a license and then a certificate for all who marry. These procedures of licensing and certification should ideally go the way of the stamp of illegitimacy on birth certificates. (I set aside the interesting question of whether births should be certified at all.) In short, marital status, like legitimacy of birth, would ideally disappear as a legal status.

The slogan "every child is a legitimate child" really means only that no child is *il*legitimate. Likewise, if the state ceased to sanction marriages, it would not follow that all kinds of intimate unions, no matter how bizarre, would suddenly be legitimate, as slippery-slope arguers fear. Rather, the concept of legitimacy would cease to apply. Some such relationships might be deplorable, for a variety of moral reasons. But any that violated laws against assault, fraud, kidnap, and so on could and should be dealt with under existing laws addressing those crimes. Presumably, "doing it with dogs" could be dealt with under laws pertaining to cruelty to animals.

To those who regard marriage romantically as signifying to the world at large the eternal commitment of two people in love, I say, "Contemplate equally seriously the nightmare of legal divorce." A dash of realism needed in the debate over same-sex marriage might be to think of it as the gay divorce issue, for part of the baggage of marriage is the liability to being divorced and the requirement of getting a divorce in order to signify similarly one's eternal commitment to a new partner. "Divorced," like "married," is a matter of public record, available to anyone interested enough to inquire, whereas there is no public record of one's extra-legal intimate relationships. And roughly half of all marriages do end in divorce.

Contemplate the prospect of having to sue for divorce because your spouse does not agree to it (even if she or he is not generally abusive). Contemplate the likely legal battles over property, custody, and visitation rights that often underlie a spouse's unwillingness to agree. Marriage and divorce can be such nightmares that I have difficulty wrapping my mind around the evident fact that so many same-sex couples in the U.S. have demonstrated their desire to marry by participating in public ceremonies. (It would be interesting to know how many are not survivors of a contested legal divorce.) The influence of dire economic circumstances I do understand. But the romanticism of much of the rhetoric of marriage, when what is at issue is a *legal* status, is misplaced. The really "good marriages" I know are good in spite of the law, not because of it. For every story of those who live happily together for twenty-five years or more, it is possible to produce other stories of those irreversibly injured or murdered by a spouse, or driven to kill in self-defense.

Were the law to restrict access to marriage, it would make better sense to do so on the basis of an applicant's past abuses (domestic violence, for example, or the unrectified abuse of a prior partner's credit cards) or on the basis of clear evidence that the applicant lacks the willingness to respect basic rights (a record of criminal violence, for example) than to do so on the basis of the gender of one's proposed partner, which tells us nothing about that person's fitness to be granted legally enforceable intimate access to other human beings. Yet proponents of marriage for same-sex partners fondly cite the 1987 Supreme Court decision, *Turner v. Safley*,[7] that declared *un-Constitutional* the "arbitrary exclusion" of prisoners from marrying, as though that were a progressive move.[8] Perhaps it is for felons whose crimes were non-violent. I do not know which exclusions the law counts as arbitrary. But I know of no jurisdiction that prohibits felons convicted of violent crimes, even domestic abusers, when *not* in prison, from re-marrying as often as they like, provided they are not already married, are free of STDs, and so on. Proponents of marriage for same-sex partners might do better not to suggest that their case is analogous to that of felons.

My infamous potboiler, "Against Marriage and Motherhood,"[9] which argued against the political institutions of marriage and motherhood, urged lesbians and gays not to put energy into the battle for same-sex marriage, not to join heterosexuals in discriminating against those who are not married and in trapping abused partners in lethal relationships. I hinted that there might be a certain propriety, however, in heterosexuals, who benefit from the discrimination, putting *their* energies into the issue. Inheritance laws that specify what relationships one must bear to the deceased to inherit when there is no will (as is often the case with those who die young) and Social Security laws that specify what relationship one must bear to the deceased to qualify for death benefits are unjust to same-sex couples but can be profitable to heterosexual kin. It seems especially appropriate for heterosexuals who appreciate these injustices to work for their removal, to spend their ill-gotten gains in battles to undo the injustice.

But choosing to do this by fighting to gain legal regulation of marriage for same-sex partners leaves unaddressed equally serious injustices to people who choose not to marry but also have no affordable access to such things as health coverage or no way to leave Social Security death benefits to the party of their choice. It takes as givens practices that deserve to be challenged and undone. A more inclusive strategy would work to separate from marriage the auxiliary benefits that ideally the state would provide everyone but that are currently economically accessible to many only through employers and at the discretion of insurance companies, who are given free reign by the state to specify whatever relationship they like that one must bear to an employee in order to qualify. It is a virtue of Chauncey's treatment[10] of this subject that he makes clear these injustices and alternative ways to remove them. Ideally, we should work for equity in inheritance laws, Social Security, and the like. At least, it has to be admitted that appealing to health coverage and the like is a tainted argument for legal recognition of marriage for same-sex partners. Marriage should not have to be anyone's path to those benefits.

Yet it would not be an *altogether* bad thing if the state were to recognize same-sex marriages. Even for gays and lesbians who never married, just possessing the right in a society in which marriage is part of the basic structure of society would be laden with positive meaning, apart from auxiliary advantages and disadvantages of marriage. It would be more difficult for others to maintain that there is anything morally wrong with or abnormal about same-sex intimacy or to deny lesbians and gays other rights. It would be more difficult to maintain that lesbians and gays cannot be trusted to occupy positions of care-taking of the vulnerable, such as children or the elderly. Refusing to support legal recognition of same-sex marriage leaves these issues to be addressed in other ways. That is a cost, for they surely do have to be addressed.

A point of clarification. The denial of certain auxiliary benefits, such as health insurance for dependents, to same-sex partners is not only an *injustice*, in that it is an arbitrary (unjustified) inequality. It is also an *evil*, insofar as a reasonably foreseeable consequence is intolerable harm to some of those dependents. Thus it is both unjust and evil for insurance companies to deny coverage to dependents of gays and lesbians. I rely here on a distinction between evils and other wrongs, which I develop and defend elsewhere.[11] In broad outline, evils are culpable wrongs that foreseeably produce intolerable harms. Wrongs are not evils when they produce less serious harms, if they are harmful at all (in any sense of "harm" definable independently of "wrong"). Many wrongs (many inequities, for example) are not actually harmful, or not very. Petty theft is wrong, unjust, but not an evil. Murder and torture are evils.

The denial to same-sex couples of the right to marry is an injustice. But, unlike the denial of health coverage to dependents, it is not an evil, as long as non-married couples can cohabit and be left in peace to establish and live out their durable intimate relationships. That point may not be obvious, however. For it looks as though once the auxiliary benefits, such as health coverage for dependents, are attached to marriage, denying marriage to lesbians and gays produces the reasonably foreseeable intolerable harm of cutting their dependents off from those benefits. Evils, as I have defined them, have two basic components: culpable wrongdoing and intolerable harm, linked by reasonable foreseeability and a causal relationship. But every event has multiple causes. The morally relevant causal relationship is not always evident, and it may not be evident in this case. Which of the many causes of harm to dependents who lack health coverage is responsible for that harm? Which of them "produces" it, in the morally relevant sense?

The denial of access to marriage does have the consequence of cutting many dependents off from health insurance. But marriage law is simply the means used to deny such benefits to the dependents of lesbians and gays. The morally critical causal nexus is between denying the benefits and the harm, rather than between denying access to marriage (to which such benefits have been attached in some places, such as the U.S.) and the harm, for the following reasons.

First, the benefits are not essential to marriage; they can be detached from it and made more generally available. A state need not give insurance companies or employers the right to restrict health coverage to the dependents of only its married employees, nor need the state depend on private insurance companies or employers to provide health coverage.

Second, even if gays and lesbians could marry and thereby access those benefits, dependents of those who choose not to marry would still be exposed to the intolerable harms that flow from being cut off from such benefits. It could be justifiable for a state to allow such benefits to be attached (via employers and insurance companies) to marital status at such a cost only if marriage were a rational choice for anyone with dependents and if it would not be wrong for such a person to reject marriage. But not only is marriage not an option for everyone, it is not a rational choice for everyone for whom it is an option, not even everyone with dependents. It is wrong for the state to allow those benefits to be so attached to a status that is not available to everyone and that not everyone to whom it is available could rationally choose. Responsibility for the harm, therefore, lies in the denial of the benefits, rather than in the denial of the right to marry.

Although the denial of marriage to same-sex partners is not an evil, legal marriage itself *is* an evil, to the extent that it facilitates the infliction and coverup of reasonably foreseeable intolerable harm to those unlucky enough to find themselves trapped with violently abusive spouses.[12] What makes marriage an evil when it is not merely an injustice is that it hinders an abused spouse from exiting an abusive relationship before intolerable harm is done. An evil institution need not have as its purpose the infliction of intolerable harm. It is sufficient that intolerable harm be reasonably foreseeable, that there be no realistic way to prevent that harm short of abolishing the institution, and that there be people in a position to abolish the institution. American slavery did not have as its purpose to make slaves suffer cruelly and die young. Yet those harms were reasonably foreseeable, and there was no adequate way to protect slaves against them. But there were people who could have outlawed slavery. That is enough to make the institution evil. Marriage without unilateral divorce is in a similar position. There is no way to enforce laws against domestic cruelty without intolerable intrusion into the lives of spouses. The possibility of cruelty, unlike insurance benefits, is not detachable from the institution of marriage. The best one can do in an abusive marriage is divorce, when doing so is an option. Yet, unilateral divorce is not always an option, and even divorce may be insufficient when there are children.

The "foreverness," or at least indefiniteness, of the marriage commitment, and the presumption, backed by the power of the state, that the *burden of justification* lies on whoever would dissolve the union as long as one spouse wishes to keep it, have been central, historically, to distinguishing marriage from other intimate unions. Unilateral divorce, now available in some states, is a progressive move, bringing marriage closer to other civil unions. If there are no children, unilateral divorce may be sufficient to extricate an abused spouse from a legally binding relationship that gives the abuser intimate access. If there are children, matters are less simple. Laws governing guardianship are at present highly interwoven with marriage law. The marriage may be over, but there may still be a relationship giving an abuser a dangerous legal right of access that would never have existed without a history of marriage. If it is not necessary to establish abuse to get the divorce, it may still be necessary to establish abuse to prevent an abuser who is a legal guardian from retaining a legal right of access to the children, and through the children, in effect, often enough, access to oneself also if one remains their guardian. It is still in many cases impossible or nearly so to establish with objective evidence the facts of severe abuse (whether to oneself, the children, or both) that might lead a judge to prohibit an abuser from further contact.

But this is old ground. I have not seen reason to change my mind on marital cruelty issues. People who disagree tend to do so on empirical grounds, not philosophical ones. They tend to believe, on the basis of personal observation and despite voluminous evidence to the contrary, that domestic violence is not a great problem. Or, that it is not that difficult to prove. Or, that it is not so difficult to get out of an abusive relationship. Or, that marriage does not add significant obstacles to doing so. Or, that women who choose not to leave do so voluntarily.

My position has been not only that ideally the legal regulation of marriage would disappear but that, since that disappearance seems politically unlikely in the foreseeable future, we should at least not support legal marriage for anyone, gay or straight. Widespread worsening of the political scene during and since the 2004 U.S. presidential campaign may call for some modification in, or qualification or clarification of, that stance.

THE REALITY: A SET OF UNDESIRABLE OPTIONS

There are two plausible directions that modification of my prior position might take. One is to support a temporary battle for equality in the legal regulation of partnerships, whether same-sex or heterosex, as part of a general battle against arbitrary discrimination, but with the long-range objective of eventually abolishing all state regulation of intimate unions. The other direction is to try to get the marriage issue taken off the political agenda (whether one favors extending marriage or abolishing it) and turn our energies now to fighting evils that we may have a greater opportunity to address constructively, including the evil of people being left without health care in the wealthiest nation of the world, in the hope that when it becomes feasible to put marriage back on the agenda, our options will have improved. If we made progress with the issue of political torture by governments, for example, which is probably as widely condemned as it is practiced, we might find it easier to get constructive attention to the fact that marriage facilitates the private torture of women. Of these directions, I favor the second, taking marriage off the agenda for a while and turning our energies to other battles.

In today's political climate religious fundamentalism has become a force of significance. Appealing to the fundamentalist vote, political conservatives recently exploited the marriage issue to divert public attention from such widely recognized evils as political torture by governments and basic health issues, including environmental degradation. The marriage issue has been used to re-entrench homophobia, gain the support of an electorate for an overall political agenda that many might otherwise not have supported, and divert not only liberals but almost everyone from attending to such matters as the constitution of the Supreme Court, the immorality of U.S. failure to support the World Court, and other issues of global justice and U.S. foreign policy. For lesbians and gays, a result has been to make official in even more jurisdictions than before, and to re-entrench, our status as second class citizens.

There are two currently troubling issues. First, the marriage issue has been used by the political right to focus voters' attention away from volatile issues that are consequential for everyone, married or not, not just for lesbians and gays. Second, the marriage issue has backfired with truly frightening consequences to lesbians and gays in the U.S. We are worse off now than before, and the future appears grimmer.

To begin with the second issue, the spectre of gay marriage mobilized social conservatives to redefine marriage to explicitly exclude same-sex partners, and there is now the possibility of a Constitutional amendment to the same effect. Such initiatives probably would not have been taken even by conservatives had lesbians and gays not made marriage a public issue. Publicly embracing marriage in mass ceremonies and standing in long lines for marriage licences were all that was needed to mobilize the anti-gay vote, since such marriages, suddenly more than a theoretical possibility, make lesbian and gay life more visible and make it harder for fundamentalists to teach children that we are abnormal or immoral.

Given my views on marriage, some might wonder why I would not regard the conservative vote as a step forward. Marriages between same-sex partners are now officially and explicitly impossible in at least eleven states, since the November elections. Does that not mean less likelihood, at least for gays and lesbians, of being trapped in abusive relationships in those states?

Probably so. But excluding us is hardly a step toward the abolition of marriage. It is a step in the reverse direction, re-entrenching marriage in its traditional forms. Heterosexual victims of domestic violence continue to perish. Any gain for abused lesbian or gay partners may be out-weighed by the exclusion's larger implications regarding lesbian and gay citizenship. Arbitrary denials of the right to marry are nothing for marriage resisters to celebrate, because those denials contribute to defining people who are arbitrarily excluded as second-class citizens.

The Universal Declaration of Human Rights of 1948 states (art. 16, sect. 1):

> Men and women of full age, without any limitation due to race, nationality, or religion, have the right to marry and to found a family. They are entitled to equal rights as to marriage, during marriage, and at its dissolution.[13]

Although the *Declaration* does not explicitly mention the genders of partners, its statement is perfectly compatible with the presumption that those genders might be the same. The wording "men and women . . . have the right to marry" is utterly ambiguous between that reading and one that assumes heterosexual partners. Insofar as the gender-neutral reading is plausible, the denial of marriage to same-sex partners is a denial of human rights. If it is a human right from which gays and lesbians are excluded, we should contemplate seriously the possibility that we might also be denied other human rights. For the implication of that exclusion is that we are not fully human.

How can one not recall the Nuremberg Laws of 1935, which banned marriages between German citizens and anyone not a German citizen and went on to strip German Jews of their citizenship?[14] The Nuremberg Laws did not prohibit marriages among Jews, and the recent definitions of marriage do not, of course, prohibit gays and lesbians from entering into heterosexual marriages. But the law does not tell anyone else, within certain degrees of kinship, of a certain age, not already married to someone else, and free of STDs, whom they can or cannot marry. To that extent, the new definitions of marriage are analogous to the Nuremberg Laws that prohibited intermarriages. Nuremberg went further. It was a major step toward the Final Solution in destroying the legal personhood of Jews. Insofar as the restriction of marriage to heterosexual unions is an injury to the legal personhood of lesbians and gays, it is to be deplored independently of any value or disvalue that one may attach to marriage.

Must I now reverse my position on whether lesbians and gays should fight for marriage? Not necessarily. But there are serious costs in refusing to fight for same-sex marriage rights. Hence the attractiveness of the compromise of fighting for marriage now but with the long-range objective of eliminating the evils mentioned above. When explicit exclusions are in place regarding participation in unjust institutions that help to define the basic structure of society, there is a danger of contagion, that the exclusions will not be confined to just those practices but will spread to others, including practices that are in other respects just and desirable, such as being licensed to be a member of various professions. Supporting an evil practice by working to remove the arbitrary exclusion of lesbians and gays from it, then, needs to be weighed against risking the evil of a proliferation of exclusions if that one is not removed, which would further corrode the legal personhood of lesbians and gays.

Explicit arbitrary exclusions of lesbians and gays are dangerous, as others have long noted, for the same kinds of reasons that miscegenation laws were dangerous. Miscegenation laws explicitly banned interracial marriages in many states until the Supreme Court declared them un-Constitutional in 1967.[15] They were part of a larger pattern of discrimination that socially disfigured African-Americans, making it easier to discriminate against them in other areas. It took action by the highest court in the land to end those laws. Supreme Court support for gays and lesbians in any decade soon on this issue appears dismal.

Many critics have noted apparent analogies between marriage for same-sex partners and interracial marriage. Yet denial of marriage to same-sex partners is not quite analogous to miscegenation laws. Miscegenation was criminal. The case that led to the Supreme Court decision was preceded by an actual arrest and criminal charges against an interracial couple from Virginia who went to another state to marry and then returned home.[16] At present, lesbian or gay partners in the U.S. who marry (going to Canada, for example) are not vulnerable to criminal charges for having done so when they return home. But that could change.

When racially mixed marriages are not criminal but are subject to severe social penalties, existing laws against harassment and other crimes can be used to combat the discrimination. It is not necessary, in that case, to agitate for a new definition of marriage that explicitly recognizes interracial unions. But when anti-miscegenation laws exist, it becomes arguably imperative to fight for their removal, as long as marriage remains a basic social institution. Likewise, it can be argued, it becomes imperative to fight laws that explicitly prohibit same-sex marriage, or, what is for all practical purposes the same, situations in which no one with legal authority to do so will issue the needed licenses or certificates, or states that invalidate any such licenses or certificates.

The Supreme Court did not stop at finding un-Constitutional the *criminalization* of interracial marriage. It found un-Constitutional the *exclusion* of interracial partners from marrying, which had been done by the expedient of making such marriages criminal. It was not that the law explicitly defined marriage as the union of two persons of the same race. Interracial partners could and did marry, when they found someone willing to issue the license and someone to perform the relevant ceremony. They just risked being charged with a crime for having done so. It was something like abortion before the 1973 decision *Roe v. Wade*.[17] You could do it, if you could find someone willing to do the procedure. But that person risked being charged with a crime. The situation with lesbians and gays is different. It does not matter who we find willing to perform the ceremony. The result in most of the United States does not count as marriage. Short of abolishing marriage, there is no way to remove that exclusion without opening lesbian and gay intimate unions to legal regulation.

Yet a worry is that agitating for marriage in the current political climate may move religious fundamentalists to take advantage of their new-found power to go further and implement more exclusions of lesbians and gays from the basic structure of society. Consider who will be appointing the next several Supreme Court Justices.

It might be responded that, as feminists have learned about responding to rape, you do not necessarily get hurt worse for fighting back. *Au contraire*, fighting back may be your only hope of *not* getting raped. Those who discover they can get away with doing as they please are more likely to do it than those who meet with resistance. Consider how long it might have taken to abolish slavery or end segregation had people not been willing to endure things getting worse before they got better.

But, of course, the wisdom of your methods of resistance depends on whether you are confronting multiple or armed rapists or someone alone and unarmed. Religious fundamentalists confronting lesbians and gays today are like multiple and armed rapists. Here, there is something to be said for lying low, being realistic about where one can effectively channel one's energies.

Do I blame lesbians and gays who helped to make gay marriage a public political issue? One could as easily blame me for having urged lesbians and gays not to fight for marriage as feeding right into the conservative agenda. The best strategy, from hindsight, might have been to let the issue alone. The relatively liberal regime of President William Jefferson Clinton in the 1990s gave uptake to lesbian and gay demands, fostering hope that discriminatory social practices might change. As it turned out, "don't ask, don't tell" made things worse in the military than they were before, and improvement does not appear to be on the horizon.

But, it may be objected, if you find a practice unjust, should you not protest it? That depends. Not necessarily. The consequences of doing so are not irrelevant to the wisdom of doing so, and it is important not to contribute, if possible, to making the overall situation worse for decades to come. You can in many ways resist *supporting* a practice without protesting it publicly, even if others misread your silence as support. There are relatively quiet ways to refuse support: refuse to marry, to attend weddings or congratulate newlyweds, to give wedding gifts, etc., and patiently explain why when people ask out of sincere interest. If you teach, put the topic on the syllabus to raise consciousness regarding the philosophical issues. If you are already married, refuse, if you can afford to, to enjoy benefits wrongfully denied others, as John Stuart Mill refused to exercise rights the law unjustly gave him upon marrying Harriet Taylor.

If we were being shot for our sexual orientations, then, of course, we should protest publicly. We should always protest gay-bashing and other hate crimes. Perhaps likewise we should continue to protest against marriage in general, for the sake of those to whom it is fatal. But when we are arbitrarily denied the benefits of an already highly questionable (if not downright evil) institution, such as marriage, it may be better to focus our energies on basic issues that are more likely to gain enough support to make a difference, such as universal health coverage, preserving social security and making it more just, making our foreign policy more humane, fostering good relations with other nations, addressing world poverty and disease, and so on. Progress in these areas may or may not improve our social image as lesbians and gays. But it would benefit us as human beings, as well as benefitting countless others.

I take seriously the consequences of what we may do, because I am not a stoic. I think so-called "externals" matter and that they are not totally beyond our control. But neither am I a utilitarian: consequences are not everything. There is, further, a well-known problem with appeals to consequences in politics. Political consequences are so very difficult to predict with any reasonable degree of accuracy when power can shift as it can in a democracy, when myriads of individual choices, each somewhat unpredictable, determine outcomes. Thus, although it is fairly clear that marriage will not disappear in the foreseeable future, it is not clear, empirically, whether there is a greater likelihood of success in time to save lives in the project of removing the arbitrary exclusion from marriage of same-sex partners than there is of success in the projects of universal health coverage, making social security more just, making our foreign policy more humane, living in more environmentally sustainable ways, fostering good relations with other nations, and so on.

Progress on any of these projects looks grim. But progress on any or all of the latter issues would be an unambiguous move in the direction of justice. Removing the marriage exclusion, although it might save lives, would not be such an unambiguous move. For that reason, I conclude that it is probably better to put marriage on the back burner, at least for the next few years (if not longer). When we take it off at some propitious future moment, if efforts regarding universal health care and social security have meanwhile paid off, the option of phasing out marriage altogether (with appropriate grandparent clauses) may be both more feasible and more attractive. At any rate, we should have an improved set of options.[18]

NOTES

1. Rawls (*A Theory of Justice*, revised edition [Cambridge, Mass.: Harvard University Press, 1999]) lists "the monogamous family" (6) as an example of a major social institution that could be part of the basic structure of a society. In the United States, it seems fair to say that legal marriage is part of the basic structure, given how it is written into Social Security rules and so much else. On auxiliary benefits attached to legal marriage in the U.S., see George Chauncey (*Why Marriage? The History Shaping Today's Debate over Gay Equality* [New York: Basic Books, 2004], 71–77); Joan Callahan ("Speech That Harms: The Case of Lesbian Families," in Claudia Card, ed., *On Feminist Ethics and Politics* [Lawrence, Kan.: University Press of Kansas, 1999]); and Evan Wolfson (*Why Marriage Matters: America, Equality, and Gay People's Right to Marry* [New York: Simon and Schuster, 2004], 13–15). A good recent history of marriage, longer than Chauncey's, is Nancy F. Cott's *Public Vows: A History of Marriage and the Nation* (Cambridge, Mass.: Harvard University Press, 2000). A good recent anthology of short essays is Mary Lyndon Shanley, ed., *Just Marriage* (New York: Oxford University Press, 2004). A moral practically-oriented treatment is journalist E. J. Graff's *What Is Marriage For?* (Boston: Beacon Press, 2004).

2. Linda Lovelace, with Mike Grady, *Ordeal* (New York: Bell Publishing Company, 1983).

3. http://www.un.org/Overview/rights.html (accessed January 31, 2012).

4. Rawls, *Theory of Justice*, 7–8, 215–16, 308–9.

5. Chauncey, *Why Marriage?* 77–86.

6. See, for example, the story of the theft of the mother of Genghis Khan in J. McIver Weatherford, *Genghis Khan and the Making of the Modern World* (New York: Crown, 2004).

7. *Turner v. Safley* 482 U.S. 78 (1987).

8. Wolfson, *Why Marriage Matters*, 8–9.

9. *Hypatia* 11:3 (Summer 1996): 1–23.

10. Chauncey, *Why Marriage?*

11. *The Atrocity Paradigm: A Theory of Evil* (New York: Oxford University Press, 2002), 96-117.

12. For more extended discussion of the evil of terrorism in the home, see *The Atrocity Paradigm*, 139–65.

13. See also Eleanor Roosevelt et al., *Universal Declaration of Human Rights* in English, Spanish, French, Chinese, Russian, and Arabic (Bedford, Mass.: Applewood Books [no date]).

14. Israel Gutman ed., *Encyclopedia of the Holocaust* (New York: Macmillan, 1990), 1076-77.

15. *Loving v. Virginia* 388 U.S. 1 (1967).

16. Wolfson, *Why Marriage Matters*, 69–70.

17. *Roe v. Wade* 410 U.S. 113 (1973).

18. Thanks to Cheshire Calhoun, Victoria Davion, Holly Kantin, Francis Schrag, Russ Shafer-Landau, and audiences at the American Philosophical Association Eastern Division meetings (2004) and the University of Wisconsin Law School (2005) for helpful comments and questions.

STUDY QUESTIONS

1. How does Card define "evils" and how does she distinguish evils from other wrongs? Explain the role this difference plays in her argument against marriage. As you do so, clearly explicate—a worthwhile exegetical task—her entire argument.

2. Why does Card claim, "The denial to same-sex couples of the right to marry is an injustice. But, unlike the denial of health coverage to dependents, it is not an evil"? After all, don't same-sex couples who are prohibited from marrying suffer a wide variety of harms? Why must these harms be understood as "injustices" rather than as "evils"?

3. What is unilateral divorce? Would making it available everywhere (at least in the United States) make marriage no longer an *evil* institution? What implications do answers to this question have for Card's overall argument against marriage? Further, thinking along the lines of the First ("Universalizability") Formulation of Kant's Categorical Imperative (or a version of Rule Utilitarianism): if divorce is easily, unilaterally, and everywhere available, would that destroy marriage, making it no longer an institution at all (evil or otherwise)?

4. Even if divorce laws allowed unilateral divorces, this situation by itself would not avoid the necessity of proving that a spouse is so abusive as to warrant denying him or her access to the children. More is needed to rehabilitate marriage and protect children. Further, whether marriage still exists or has been fully jettisoned, would not the state need (justifiable) laws regulating the relationship between parents and children? Would the state as a result have any other obligations? Perhaps only the absence of children in a marriage or partnership is what fully eliminates the role of the state in marriage. What do you think? (A research project: look over historically important writings about the state and the family/marriage [including, but not limited to, John Stuart Mill and Harriet Taylor] to discover to what extent state interference in marriage has been, in the past, based solely or predominantly on the protection of children.)

5. Imagine Card and Cheshire Calhoun having coffee, wine, or fish-n-chips together and discussing each other's views on same-sex marriage. How would they reply to each other on both the philosophi-

cal and the political/practical levels? Might they come to agree on the latter even if they disagree on the former? What might transpire if Kurtz asks to join them?

TWELVE

What Is "Sexual Orientation"?

William S. Wilkerson

In this essay, **William S. Wilkerson** *raises some difficulties with the main-stream concept of "sexual orientation," which classifies people as heterosexual, homosexual, and bisexual and which assumes that people's sexual desires are fairly stable. Wilkerson argues that this concept of "sexual orientation" faces difficulty in accommodating sexual variations: for example, people whose sexual object choices are not based on sex/gender and people whose sexuality changes over time. The mainstream concept also faces difficulty in accounting for the different ways of understanding sexuality that cultures other than contemporary Western cultures have adopted. Wilkerson concludes by arguing that an "inter-pretive" model of sexuality allows us to have our cake and to eat it: on such a model we are able to explain how in some cultures people's sexual orientations are stable while also leaving conceptual room for new sexual possibilities.*

William S. Wilkerson is professor of philosophy at the University of Alabama in Huntsville. His research focuses on gay, lesbian, bisexual, transgender, and queer (GLBTQ) philosophy and the contemporary Continental tradition. He is the author of *Ambiguity and Sexuality: A Theory of Sexual Identity* (Palgrave Macmillan, 2007) and a coeditor of the forthcoming anthology *Beauvoir and Western Thought from Plato to Butler* (SUNY Press). "What Is Sexual Orientation?" is printed here for the first time. © 2012, William S. Wilkerson, who kindly gave permission for his new essay to be included in this volume.

> Most people find it difficult to grasp that whatever they like to do sexually will be thoroughly repulsive to someone else, and that whatever repels them sexually will be the most treasured delight of someone, somewhere.
>
> —Gayle Rubin, "Thinking Sex"

"Sexual orientation" is usually understood to refer to one's persistently recurring sexual desires for members of the sex that attracts one. In this

195

respect, it differs from "sexual identity," which refers to self-consciously living as a person with a particular sexual orientation. Although many people identify as gay, lesbian, or bisexual and live with that self-understanding, either privately or publicly, most identify as heterosexual. However, people need have neither a homosexual identity nor homosexual sex to have a homosexual orientation. Their orientation can be experienced as persisting feelings of attraction, sexual fantasies, or other private episodes.[1] When we speculate that people might be lesbian or gay before they come out, we usually speculate about their sexual orientation, not their identity.

Most think that sexual orientation is separate from the vicissitudes of historical and cultural change and independent of choice, and that everyone has a sexual orientation despite cultural and historical differences. Like traits such as intelligence, athleticism, or calm temperament, sexual orientation is regarded as part of a person's makeup. "Sexual orientation" thus names a psychological feature of people that precedes and guides the choices people make in life; the idea of *orientation* seems to imply a persistent and nonchosen direction in people's attitudes and desires.[2] Accordingly, sexual orientation explains why some people are attracted to people of the same sex while others are attracted to those of the opposite sex (and some to both).

Although not everyone regards sexual orientation this way, most do. Certainly mainstream gay and lesbian political movements reflect this view of sexual orientation when they claim that homosexuals and bisexuals are "born this way." In her excellent analysis of homophobia, Cheshire Calhoun notes that our culture assumes "that everyone necessarily has a determinable sexual orientation as part of their basic psychological makeup . . . there are no persons who lack a sexual orientation."[3] This view of sexual orientation also squares with the research into its biological basis, which considers it a persisting feature of a person's psychological makeup. Finally, this view is reflected in philosophical definitions of "sexual orientation": Edward Stein disregards both self-identification and behavior and thinks of sexual orientation as a "disposition" to engage in specific sexual acts with people of one or the other gender, thereby prioritizing people's desires and psychological features over their behavior. John Corvino also favors this view.[4]

I question three features of this concept of sexual orientation: its basis in sex, its stability, and its cross-cultural universality. First, sex: sexuality can involve many sorts of attractions, so that it appears that some people can be attracted to traits or features that have little or no connection to sex. Can sexual orientation help us understand these forms of sexuality? Second, stability: even if most people experience a consistent and stable attraction to one or another sex across their lives, some experience their sexuality as fluid and changing. Can the concept of sexual orientation handle both types, or are those with fluid sexualities not captured by it?

Finally, cross-cultural universality: sexual orientation purportedly exists across cultures and times, but, as I show below, sexual orientation might not be a universal feature of human existence but particular to our culture; it might result from how our particular culture has organized the experiences it calls sexual and might even result from the way individuals interpret their sexual feelings in light of their social situations.[5]

SEXUAL ORIENTATION, SEX, AND GENDER

In feminist thought, "gender" typically refers to both the socially visible presentation of oneself as either male or female and to the social role of male or female, while "sex" refers to the person's actual biological sex.[6] With this distinction in mind, we can ask a question not usually raised by your average person: does sexual orientation attach to sex, gender, or both? For even though, for example, gay men are usually attracted to people who are both sexually male and who present themselves as male, perhaps not all gay men are like that. A gay man could feel an attraction to a drag queen because he desires effeminate qualities in a man; putting it bluntly, he likes penises, but he likes them attached to very feminine gender presentation. We could say that, when it comes to sex, he's attracted to men, but when it comes to gender, he's attracted to femininity. Similarly a lesbian who is attracted to butch, masculine women could be attracted to female sex but also to male gender.

In these examples, we could argue that sex is the main attractor since both people are attracted to a particular *biological* sex, even though they desire this biological sex wrapped in the opposite gender. Certainly in the history of butch/femme relationships, attraction remained deeply intertwined with gender presentation, such that a femme was often attracted to *both* female sex and male gender presentation since she desired specifically butch women. So the orientation may really have been for masculine women (if the lesbian were femme) and feminine women (if the lesbian were butch).[7] In other words, the attraction could be for a particular sex/gender combination. Thus, if "sexual orientation" refers simply to attraction based on sex, it fails to capture such possibilities.

We can respond to these possibilities by broadening our concept of sexual orientation to encompass both sex and gender such that, for each person, we specify their orientation along an axis of sex and an axis of gender. Even if the mainstream concept of sexual orientation mostly ignores this distinction, this adjustment allows us to capture more fine-grained distinctions among people's sexual orientations. So there will be obvious cases: someone is gay if he is attracted to both male sex and male gender presentation, and someone is lesbian if she is attracted to both female sex and female gender presentation. Then there are less obvious cases that require us to decide: the femme attracted to butch women can also be a lesbian, with the qualification that she has some very specific desires about the gender presentation of her partners.

Going further, some people are intersex—they have physiological features of both genders—either naturally or as a result of elective surgery. (And, in this happy Internet age, we know that there is a minor pornography industry catering to those who sexually desire intersex people.) Do people who desire a body with a penis and female breasts desire males or females, gender or sex, or neither or both? If we say that they desire males, the common concept of sexual orientation would fail to explain the fact that they desire males with prominent female physical features. Similarly, if we say that they desire females, the common concept of sexual orientation would fail to explain the fact that they desire females with prominent male physical features.

We might solve this difficulty as follows: just as we broadened the concept of sexual orientation to include combinations of sex and gender, we can broaden it even further and say that those who desire intersex people have a unique sexual orientation built around ambiguously sexed bodies. However, in broadening it this far, we implicitly reject sexual orientation based solely on purportedly normal ideas of gender and sex. That is, the common understanding is that sexual orientation names attraction to people of a specific sex, but we have now seen that this concept is simply too narrow to capture the range of possible sex/gender combinations to which people can be attracted.

Moreover, as we keep adding different sexual possibilities, there seems to be no end to how many things we should include as objects of sexual orientations. We have already gone past the common belief that there are only two sexes to which one can be attracted to see that one can be attracted to various combinations of sexes and genders. But we can go even further: there are fetishists, zoophiles, narcissists—people with all kinds of sexual attractions that might not involve gender as the primary basis of attraction. Consider a foot fetishist who might be attracted to *both* men's and women's feet (as opposed to being attracted to men's feet because they are *men's* feet). Gender would then be less relevant than the object of the fetish. So are foot fetishists attracted to the sex first and the feet second, or are they attracted to *feet* and simply prefer men's to women's feet because, say, of their rougher skin or their larger size? In some cases, people might have an attraction to a sex that is at least coeval with their attraction to their object of the fetish, while in others people might be attracted simply to the object of their fetish rather than either sex. In both cases, we face difficulties in individuating the object of sexual attraction and difficulties with the connection between the object of sexual attraction and the sex of the person to whom one is attracted. What is the sexual orientation of the man who desires *men's* feet? Is he a homosexual or a homosexual-foot-fetishist? If the former, why neglect the fact that he likes feet? After all, men's feet *are* part of what he is sexually oriented toward. If the latter, then how narrowly or broadly are we to construe people's sexual orientations? Suppose he likes hairy feet. Is his sexual orientation a homosexual-hairy-foot-fetishist? And what is the sexual orientation of the man who desires feet regardless of sex and gender? He seems to have a persisting attraction to something that bears virtually no connection to sex or gender. So is he, simply, a "foot-sexual" (or even a "pede-sexual")? There might be orientations for feet, gentle temperaments, navels, or brown curly hair—sexual orientations could involve attraction to any kind of personal or bodily feature, or to things disconnected from human bodies altogether. Zoophiles desire sexual relations with animals; some fetishists actually have stable attractions to particular inanimate objects (shoes and underpants are popular examples, but we can imagine others).

Can sexual orientation handle all these possible cases? It could, but only if we broaden it to include not only sex, gender, and their combinations but also virtually any kind of stable sexual proclivity. Being attracted to a specific sex or gender would no longer be necessary for having a sexual orientation because somebody attracted only to, say, animals would not require human sex or gender for attraction. Attraction based on sex would still be sufficient for possessing a sexual orientation, but so would *any* stable sexual proclivity. Sexual orientation would just name whichever persisting psychosexual attraction a person feels. At this point, however, the concept of sexual orientation based on stable attraction loses its value since asserting the existence of all these sexual orientations amounts to saying that whatever attracts an individual over a period of time *is* his or her orientation. The concept gets so diluted that it loses the ability to explain particular features of human sexuality. This raises a dilemma: either we can retain the concept of orientation for all sexual proclivities, using it so broadly that it has no more explanatory power than the trivial claim that each individual has his or her own sexual proclivities (and this is putting aside asexual people), or we can restrict the concept to the narrow confines of attraction based on sex, in which case people with stable desires not directed towards sex will actually *lack* sexual orientations. The second horn of the dilemma is highly counterintuitive if, as Calhoun noted, our society assumes that *everybody* has a sexual orientation, while the first horn of the dilemma virtually eliminates the concept of sexual orientation by completely diluting it.[8]

Things are further complicated by the lives and experiences of bisexuals. How can they have an orientation if their sexuality lacks a consistent and persisting desire for one sex or gender? Consider the life of the French philosopher and novelist Simone de Beauvoir.[9] As a young student, she fell deeply in love with a young woman who died tragically, leaving Beauvoir to suffer a lifelong heartbreak, though she soon began her famous affair with the philosopher Jean-Paul Sartre. Even during this affair, she had occasional trysts with other women and men. Although the relationship with Sartre changed to friendship, she later had an intense sexual relationship with the American novelist Nelson Algren. The affair was doomed by circumstance, but only a few years later, she met a younger woman with whom she spent the rest of her life in companionship and love. Beauvoir flatly refused to define her sexuality, and her thinking about sexuality manifests genuine suspicion of the belief that we have deep, persistent desires for a specific sex.

Although Beauvoir's life may be an unusual example, it is possible that even people who identify as heterosexual or homosexual can have desires for, and engage in sex with, somebody outside their normal pattern. How should we understand sexual orientation if sex selection seems inconsistent in some cases? A common answer refers to the famous Kinsey scale: that sexual preference occurs along a continuum.[10] Although Alfred Kinsey's surveys of sexual activity of midcentury Americans are now dated, his scale has proved remarkably durable. Finding that few people had totally consistent sexual tendencies with respect to sex or gender (in other words, that few people had strictly heterosexual or homosexual activity), he proposed a continuum of sexuality from zero to six, with zero being exclusive heterosexuality and six being exclusive homosexuality. He claimed that one in ten men fell between a three and a five for a period of three years during their adult lives. In other words, they were predominantly having homosexual activity.[11] This one-in-ten figure has survived despite the fact that recent studies put the actual percentage of lifelong homosexual men and women much lower (around 4 percent for men and slightly lower for women).[12] The Kinsey scale allows us to make some conceptual room for sexual orientations based on sex that lack total consistency. Gay men and lesbians are fives and sixes, heterosexual men and women are zeros and ones, and bisexuals (e.g., Beauvoir) might be threes. An individual's sexual orientation is reflected in a persistent pattern of behavior: mostly boys, mostly girls, equally boys and girls, boys more than girls, and so on.

However, since bisexuals like Beauvoir feel attraction to people of both sexes, it is possible that their attraction is based on features other than gender. People who are attracted to *both* sexes might not be attracted to sex or gender *per se* but rather to other features of the person that bear no connection to gender. For example, Jane Litwoman, in an early essay on bisexuality, supports this possibility:

> The sexologist Kinsey has created a 0–6 scale in which people are rated as to their homo/heterosexuality. I think of myself as off the scale. . . . Gender is just not what I care about or even notice in a sexual partner. This is not to say I don't have categories of sexual attraction, that I judge each person as an individual—I have categories, but gender isn't one of them.[13]

Litwoman does not experience attraction based on sex at all but on other features of a person. Like Beauvoir, who saw both romantic and sexual relationships as expressions of a free desire to join with another in the project of becoming more whole people, Litwoman's sexuality functions much like the possible sexualities we discussed earlier. It is not built around sex. This does not deny that sex and gender are factors (surely, she *notices* them when she chooses sexual partners, and other bisexuals sometimes declare a preference for one sex), but it denies that sex or gender is always the determining factor in attraction. This is why Litwoman claims that she is entirely *off* a scale, such as Kinsey's, polarized by sex, since her dual attraction to people of both sex does not take sex itself as an aspect of attraction.

There are other reasons why Kinsey's scale does not help the mainstream concept of sexual orientation. First, the scale, as I discuss in the next section, is about sexual *behavior*, not the inner, psychic desires to which "sexual orientation" usually refers. Second, it is about the sex (male or female) of one's sexual partners. As such, the scale can at most capture "surface patterns" of behavior: it cannot capture the very particular sexual tastes we are discussing. Regardless of what attracts one person deeply and specifically, the scale only reveals patterns of selecting sexual partners from one of the two available sexes (or both in the case of bisexuals).

To summarize, the difficulty is that so many people's sexual lives do not fit the pattern of the popular concept of sexual orientation—a stable attraction based on sex or gender. In some of these cases, sexual orientation involves attraction to objects that are not related to sex or gender at all (zoophiles, for example), while in other cases, like fetishes, a person may be either attracted to sex first and the fetish object second, or the other way around. Finally, at least some bisexuals claim to be attracted not by sex but by people's other features.

SEXUAL ORIENTATION AND STABILITY

So far, we have focused on the question of whether the concept of sexual orientation based on sex or gender succeeds in explaining the great diversity of human sexual experience. The cases we raised show that this concept fails to capture the full range of human sexuality. Part of this failure arises from the fact that sexuality could be simply too various and individual, but it also arises from the assumption that sexual orientation names a stable feature of people's psychosexual make up: that it captures something about their psychology and sexuality that remains constant throughout most of their lives. Defining "sexual orientation" in terms of psychological disposition rather than behavior assumes this kind of stability. Because people's behaviors can be less consistent than their patterns of attraction (as Kinsey quickly discovered), behavior has been set aside as a defining feature of sexual orientation in both the philosophical literature[14] and the contemporary biological literature, as we will see below. Even the term "orientation" implies a lasting or enduring inclination.

Does sexual attraction indeed have the stability granted it by the concept of sexual orientation, or is it rather fluid and changing for individuals? This is a difficult question to answer, but one thing is clear: if we abandon stability, we have abandoned the concept of sexual orientation altogether since we would no longer be discussing persisting, recurring desires, which lie at the heart of the concept. We would then be left simply discussing behaviors or sexual interests over short periods of time, no longer seeing them as arising from any enduring feature of a person.

The answer to the question of sexual stability seems mixed. Most people in our society seem to experience their sexuality as fairly stable: gay men, lesbians, and heterosexuals usually claim to have feelings from an early age that persist through most of their lives. However, some people experience their sexuality as fluid. Beauvoir appears to have had such a fluid sexuality, and bisexuals often describe their sexuality in such terms. A well-known sociological study of bisexuals in the San Francisco Bay Area reports that a third to half of men and women experience major shifts in their sexual preferences, measured in terms of both psychological and behavioral factors.[15] It reports their attitude this way: "I experienced swings in my primary sexual interests between a Kinsey 6 to a 2 approximately every five years for the past fifteen years; I experienced changes in my sexual preferences from day to day, even moment to moment."[16] Quite aside from these rather striking examples, we may have noticed in our own lives that what attracts us sexually changes over time, even if the sex or gender remains stable as the primary object of attraction. At one point, we may prefer younger people, at another older, sometimes well-kempt, sometimes slovenly, sometimes heavy or thin; we might perhaps even cultivate a liking for sadism or masochism. This is especially true *if* sexual orientations are narrowly construed (e.g., *X* is a homosexual foot-fetishist, not simply a homosexual). For if so, then sexuality would indeed be, in many cases, fluid over time (e.g., *X* is still a homosexual but no longer a foot-fetishist). Human sexual desire can be quite multifarious, and what's hot at one time might be cold at another.

As proof of this, consider that Kinsey surveyed thousands of people and his results showed such inconsistency that he refused to countenance the idea of sexual orientation as a persistent desire.[17] He stated clearly that he was *not* measuring sexual orientation but rather measuring and cataloging *behaviors*. Those men who fell between three and five had sex mainly with other men over a three-year period but might have spent the rest of their lives having sex with women. Indeed, many have inaccurately used the Kinsey scale because Kinsey never meant to group people by *stable psychological orientations*. No doubt, we aren't bound by his ideas about his scale, but he created it because he realized that since many people's sexual behavior changes over time, it might not be fruitful to talk about sexual orientations.

Of course, Kinsey's work is dated, and there is recent biological research that appears to show that homosexuality, as a persistent desire for people of a particular gender, has a genetic or other biological basis. This research has received a lot of mainstream media attention and is popular among gays and lesbians because it purportedly proves that we are "born this way." If true, this research would support the claim that sexuality is not very fluid since it would present a scientifically justified case for a firm, biological foundation for sexual orientation. A full investigation of this literature goes beyond the scope of this essay, but it cannot rescue sexual orientation as a persistent, stable desire because it *assumes* its existence in just this form. All the famous researchers in the field (Dean Hamer, Simon LeVay, William Byne, Brian Mustanski, and J. Michael Bailey)[18] explicitly claim to study the opposite of what Kinsey studied. They do not investigate behaviors over short periods but persisting sexual orientations. They support this methodological decision by admitting that people's actual sexual behaviors are too fluid and unreliable and that a psychosexual sexual orientation remains stable across a person's lifetime, so it presents a better object of study.

This approach faces the difficulty that while behaviors are readily accessible, the inner psychology, fantasies, and orientations of subjects must be inferred indirectly. To solve this problem, most investigators screen their subjects to check whether they have genuine, enduring same-sex attractions (i.e., homosexual orientations). They must find some way to exclude those whose sexuality and sexual behavior are more like those of bisexuals and those with fluid sexualities. This aspect of their approach produces almost comically opposed results. For instance, Dean Hamer's famous early study *excluded* anybody who showed the slightest tendency towards bisexuality, while J. Michael Bailey's studies are infamous for *including* bisexuals on the assumption that true bisexuality does not really exist and that bisexuals are really homosexual.[19]

This part of their methodology shows that sexual orientation, as a persisting desire based on gender, does *not emerge* as a result of their data, but is the *filter* for the collection of the data. By grouping together a range of people who satisfy narrow criteria or by ignoring all the differences in people's reports of their sexual lives, scientists can certainly find evidence of a stable homosexual orientation, but only because they have either excluded or reinterpreted the experiences of those who do not fit the criterion of having a stable homosexual orientation. This does not show that the scientific studies produce false results, but it does show that they cannot be used to argue against the fluidity of human sexuality since they begin by disregarding or reinterpreting it. More important, by excluding people with fluid sexualities, these studies make plausible, in a back-handed way, the belief that they exist. Indeed, other empirical work has suggested that women, in contrast to men, tend to experience their sexuality as fluid and changing and that the tendency to think of sexual orientation on the model of male desire, which tends to be more stable, has led to the erasure of this difference (not surprisingly, most of the scientific studies have focused on male sexuality). [20]

So it is fair to conclude that empirical and anecdotal evidence shows that at least some people have fluid, changing sexualities. Does the concept of sexual orientation help us understand their sexuality? Again, no. Somebody whose sexuality changes over time and circumstance cannot have a persistent psychological disposition towards a particular sexual object or practice. Even if his or her sexual desires exhibit periods of relative stability, the periods have to be fairly long to have the kind of consistency necessary to the concept of sexual orientation.

We have seen, in the first section, that the common concept of sexual orientation fails to explain the sexualities of some people. With the addition of the possibility of sexual fluidity, the failure is more dramatic. For even if we agree that not all people feel attraction based on sex, gender, or combinations of the two, we might still think that *something* that is inner and persisting explains people's sexual proclivities, even though it might trivialize the concept of sexual orientation. But if some people's sexuality is not even stable, then we cannot speak of an orientation at all, not truthfully anyway. We are left simply with narratives about the particularities of a person's sexual life.

SEXUAL ORIENTATION, CULTURAL UNIVERSALITY, AND SOCIAL CONSTRUCTION

In academic discussions of sexuality, one important debate concerns whether sexual orientation is cross-cultural and universal or whether it varies with changing social and historical circumstances. *Social constructionism* is the view that sexuality varies with cultural variation. *Essentialism* is the view that sexuality is the same across cultures—specifically that people are basically divided into homosexuals, heterosexuals, and bisexuals. [21] Essentialism is thus in line with the common concept of sexual orientation.

According to social constructionism, the sexual identities we take for granted in contemporary America and Europe rarely appear in other times and places. The sociologist Stephen O. Murray documents a remarkable diversity of different sexual styles from around the world, with homosexual activity in men and women as part of many different sexual identity formations. [22] Some cultures treat sexual object choice as the result of gender difference: if I am a man attracted to men, it is because I am really a woman (or a third sex altogether), and my identity often has more to do with being a woman or a third sex than with my sexual behavior. Other cultures disregard sexual preference and desire in favor of sex role, whereby it is normal for some men to prefer sexually penetrating others (including other men) and abnormal for some men to strongly prefer being penetrated. In other cultures, homosexuality has a ritualized, professional, or spiritual role to play disconnected from its associations with sexuality, romance, and even the whole category of the erotic.[23]

The implications of these facts for the concept of sexual orientation depend on which version of social constructionism we endorse. I discuss three different versions: weak, strong, and interpretive social constructionism. Weak social constructionism claims that sexual identities and roles arise from social ways of responding to and organizing sexual desires and orientations so that different cultures organize sexual roles and identities in their particular ways. Though the social organization of these desires produces different sexual identities, sexual orientations are left untouched. This version of constructionism is thus compatible with at least some essentialist views because essentialists also recognize cultural variation in sexual roles and identities as a well-established fact (hence the adjective "weak"). Even if sexual *roles* and *identities* come in many shapes and forms, this would not deny the existence of underlying, fairly stable heterosexual, homosexual, and bisexual desires. The differences in the sexual lives found, for example, in Murray's work only show that different sexual roles and identities "channel" desires in different ways.[24] Weak social constructionism is thus compatible with the ordinary concept of sexual orientation.

More controversially, strong social constructionism argues that sexual *desire itself* also varies. This means that not all cultures and all ages have people with our taken-for-granted three-way division of sexual orientation. For example, people in another culture might have, instead of heterosexual or homosexual desire, a desire to penetrate or to be penetrated. Thus, desires are formed differently—are socially constructed—in different cultures and times, and there are many competing theories about how this process of desire construction happens.[25] The resulting view holds that sexual desires and identities remain fairly fixed *in* cultures but can vary *across* cultures, and that individuals with similar desires in a particular culture would experience their sexualities in basically the same way. This version of social constructionism implies that sexual orientations like ours need not exist in other cultures. Thus, sexual orientation need not have a universal status. Sexual orientation would result from the way a particular culture organizes its sexual practices and desires and would not exist apart from a particular combination of social factors. This strong social constructionism would then undercut the final feature we normally take to be part of the common concept of sexual orientation: its cultural universality.

Finally, interpretive social constructionism argues that, even if sexual desires remain the same across different cultures, individuals must engage in some self-interpretation of these feelings in light of social practices and that this self-interpretation changes the feelings themselves. Hence, the interpretive social constructionist disagrees with the strong social constructionist that individuals in particular cultures must experience similar sexual desires similarly, although given strong social pressures to interpret their desires in a particular way, they likely would. In making this argument, the interpretive constructionist relies on a philosophical tradition that assumes that a person's experiences do not come, as William James put it, "ticketed and labeled"—with their meanings and structures already given.[26] Only through a process of interacting with others and checking one's experiences against the linguistic and conceptual resources available in society do experiences come to have comprehensible meanings that one can use to understand and act on. I call this process "interpretive" because in it people begin with inchoate experiences, ones that suggest a plenitude of possible meanings, which must then be narrowed and understood in light of social categories. In doing this, the experiences themselves come to change as they come to be understood as an experience of "such and such."

This view about experience is plausible because many of our unconceptualized experiences are quite "thick" with possible meanings. To use an example relevant to sexual orientation, imagine a teenage boy who has strong feelings of attraction for another boy but who is unsure what these feelings mean. He might also simultaneously have feelings for some women. I use the word "feelings" here because the interpretive view will deny that we always begin with *desires* that are explicitly or obviously homosexual or heterosexual. Many coming-out stories include a long period of confusion such as this. What will this young man make of these feelings? First, he may not be certain *what* attracts him in each case. Does he like the other boy's masculinity, or his quick wit, or his intelligence? Are his feelings genuinely sexual or are they just a "warm fuzziness" he feels when he's around this particular boy? Similar questions arise about his feelings for girls. He experiences each of these feelings in the context of the other, such that he might compare these feelings to each other. Assuming that he lives in our society, he may well be aware that he could be gay, bisexual, or straight, but *which* possibility he chooses may not be obvious to him. Note that if he decides that his attraction to the boy is a sexual attraction to masculine features of the boy (his muscular body, his masculine comportment, his penis) and that this means that he is gay, he has interpreted his feelings and changed them in two respects. First, he has significantly *thinned* out his previously thick experiences by conceptualizing them and narrowing the range of their possible meanings. Second, by conceptualizing them and putting them into language, he has effectively changed them into the feelings that a gay person has; he has set aside his feelings for girls as secondary, perhaps just a result of social pressure to be heterosexual. Rather than the unconceptualized, thick, and ambiguous experiences, his interpretation has partially constructed them as feelings of a particular kind.

Interpretive social constructionism thus claims that sexual desire is partly inchoate and protean, such that we do not simply have straightforward sexual desires but something less clearly defined: feelings that can be interpreted in a variety of possible ways to fit different sexualities. Such a view would not only undercut the cross-cultural universality of sexual orientation, like strong social constructionism does, it would seem to radically undercut sexual orientation altogether. However, I would like to argue (and have argued)[27] that this is not the case. We can accept even this strong, interpretive social constructionism without embracing the apparent skepticism about sexual orientation it seems to imply.

SEXUALITY AS INTERPRETATION

To see how we can still retain sexual orientation based on sex or gender even with this interpretive view, consider religious identity. Christianity is a complex social phenomenon with a rich history, a specific set of values and mores, and a core group of beliefs, all of which are passed on and enforced by specific social groups, such as specific communities of believers and particular authority figures (pastors, priests, religious writers, and leaders). Being an individual Christian means adapting oneself to this social complex. Depending on the depth of a person's commitment to the social complex, the adaptation can have a deep and transforming effect on one's personality. Habits of action, thought, and perception can change as one sees the world as a Christian. This transformation accounts in part for the profundity of the conversion experience: people say they are different after conversion, and in some cases they genuinely are at a subpersonal or subconscious level. This means that both conscious, explicit understandings of one's self change and subconsciously one sees the world differently, adopts different habits, and *feels* differently about things. Christianity, as individually lived, is a self-transformation brought on by adaptation to specific cultural and historical traditions shared by communities of fellow believers. Keeping with the analogy, some people might try more than one religion or spiritual practice as they search for one that resonates with and makes sense of their vaguely felt spiritual needs.

Becoming Christian gives us another type of case in which we have rich, inchoate feelings that require interpretation to be understood. In the case of sexuality, feelings are capable of transformation and adaptation to social norms and roles. We would then declare ourselves gay or lesbian not because we have naturally given sexual orientations but because sexuality in our time is culturally organized around sexual orientations, be they homosexual or heterosexual, and we interpret our sexual feelings and experiences in light of these concepts, bringing our sexual selves in line to match. In much the same way, a person might have thick, inchoate spiritual needs that they cannot necessarily articulate but that resonate well with the particular beliefs, practices, and narratives of a particular religion. They adapt themselves to this religion and in the process come to understand their previously inchoate spiritual needs in light of its socially defined practices.

Both the religious and the sexual cases share the following structure: people have nonconceptualized feelings, some of which they can articulate, while others are inchoate and unclear. They spend time trying to understand them and rely on social ideals, roles, and identities to make sense of them.[28] In some cases, one might see that one obviously desires people of the same, or opposite, sex, but in many cases one might be less certain. In the latter cases, sexual orientation is not just a given and persistent desire for other men, women, or both; people have lots of desires that can be confusing to interpret, and they take on the project of a particular sexual orientation because it is the closest match. Identity and sexual orientation form together in the coming-out process. This view of sexual orientation thus brings it and sexual identity much closer together. People can develop an orientation based on their projected identity as much as they develop their identity based on feelings that they come to describe as an orientation.

Interpretive social constructionism thus both preserves and changes the common concept of sexual orientation: sexual orientation is neither a naturally occurring, persistent desire nor merely a concept that disregards the complexity of our desires (despite its practical use in some cases). Instead, it is a convergence of individual feelings, social constructs, and the interpretive choices individuals make about how to live their sexuality. Sexual orientation is more akin to an existential project than a psychological fact: it designates features of our existence that we take up and live in a particular social setting. People *do* have feelings, and some might have content that guides them toward some interpretations and away from others, but this content does not fully determine their sexual being.

This leads to an obvious objection: if there are feelings that fit with our current concept of sexual orientation, then the essentialist is right, and at least some people have sexual orientations as given, persisting desires for people of a particular sex or gender. Interpretive social constructionism regards sexual orientation as arising at the juncture of an individual's feelings and the social roles and cultural possibilities of their historical and geographical location. It thus admits that people have feelings that they match to their social surroundings. But surely, the objection continues, if some people have desires that lead them to adopt one rather than another sexual understanding and identity, then these desires have a meaning that could exist independently of social circumstances, and interpretation merely amounts to recognizing the truth of one's desires and experiences.

This objection claims that feelings are given and then subject to interpretation. But if feelings are subject to interpretation, then it must also be true that their meaning is not fully given; otherwise they would not be open to interpretation. Since there is something in the feeling that is subject to interpretation, there is something unclear and ambiguous in it, which the act of interpretation resolves through conceptualization. If its meaning is fully given, how could it change with context or even be construed in different ways? The objection asks us to accept the impossible: the interpretation of something that at the least requires no interpretation and that at the most *cannot* be interpreted.

At issue here is the larger philosophical question of the degree to which our experiences constrain the interpretations we make of them and the knowledge we gain from them. Three views are possible: our experiences totally constrain (determine, even) the interpretations we make of them. I find this view implausible for two reasons. First, it makes little sense to speak of determined interpretations since the interpretation of something implies the possibility that it could have been interpreted in another way, and second because our interpretations of feelings can and do change. Equally implausible is the second view that we can interpret any experience in any way. In between, there is the third view that experiences can suggest and constrain, without determining, our interpretations of them. This view is the most plausible. It fits well with familiar examples like interpreting literary works. A dense and thick work like *Moby Dick* supports many interpretations, but it does not support any interpretation at all. It is not, for example, a manual on how to assemble a tent. In the same way, the interpretive view of sexual orientation argues that a person's sexual feelings may guide his or her interpretation without determining it.

This account, then, allows that people's feelings may remain constant and that they may live out one particular sexual identity, which they regard as built from a particular sexual orientation. Yet it also allows for people whose sexuality focuses on other objects and sensations to find some other interpretive schemes that make sense of their own particular sexual proclivities. People can learn to understand their own sexuality as, perhaps, a fetish, or a desire for masochistic sensation, and they can find roles and communities that support and help them understand their specific sexuality. People might change their interpretation of their feelings or discover that their feelings may change, thus allowing that a person's sexuality can be fluid, even though such people could still tell a narrative about their changing sexual lives.

The interpretive view thus leaves us with interesting answers to the three questions we raised about the concept of sexual orientation: its basis in sex or gender, its stability, and its cross-cultural universality. In our current time and place, most people will interpret their sexuality in accordance with the prevailing concepts and roles in a society. In short, most people will settle on a sexual orientation based on sex and regard this as the natural feature of their psychosexual makeup because this is the prevailing concept, even if the interpretive view disputes that this sexual orientation is simply given as part of their psychosexual makeup. The interpretive view also implies that in cultures that organize their sexualities differently, people would organize and live their sexualities accordingly. So the interpretive view does not endorse the cross-cultural universality of the ordinary concept of sexual orientation and therefore does not require that sexuality be organized around sex or gender as our common concept of sexual orientation entails. Moreover, because an element of individual interpretation is always involved in the process of being sexual, there remains the possibility that in any particular culture some people might find other, more creative ways to interpret their feelings, thus realizing new sexual possibilities. Some individuals could even come to understand their sexuality as a fluid and changing process that defies any singular categorization. The interpretive view thus comports with the experience of those who have fluid and changing sexualities, although it does not claim, any more than the regular concept of sexual orientation does, that these people have sexual orientations since that concept remains tied to our prevailing understanding of it as a *stable* desire.

CONCLUSION

The concept of sexual orientation as an inner drive that is stable, that persists through times and cultures, and that is based on sex or gender faces some difficulties: How narrowly or broadly should we understand the concept so as to account for people's possibly diverse or fluid sexualities? Does it apply universally, given the possible truth of social constructionism, especially in its strong and interpretive versions? While there may be many ways to retain the concept in light of these questions and problems, none of them may seem ultimately satisfactory, and we may still have to wait for a better answer to the question: What is sexual orientation?[29]

NOTES

1. Ed Stein, in *The Mismeasure of Desire: The Science, Theory and Ethics of Sexual Orientation* (Oxford, U.K.: Oxford University Press, 1999), 23–70, discusses sexual orientation in terms of all these factors, as does much of the biological literature (see notes 18 and 19 below).

2. I do not endorse this view about choice. I merely mean to point out that the common view takes this stance on the status of choice in sexual orientation. See William Wilkerson, "Is It a Choice? Sexual Orientation as Interpretation," *Journal of Social Philosophy* 40:1 (2009): 97–116.

3. Cheshire Calhoun, *Feminism, the Family, and the Politics of the Closet: Lesbian and Gay Displacement* (Oxford, U.K.: Oxford University Press, 2000), 93.

4. John Corvino, "Orientation, Sexual," in *Sex from Plato to Paglia: A Philosophical Encyclopedia*, vol. 2, edited by Alan Soble (Westport, Conn.: Greenwood Press, 2006), 728–34, at 729–30.

5. I am not questioning the practical uses of the concept; we must often use the category of homosexuality (or heterosexuality) regardless of whether it captures deep facts about the particulars of people's sexual attractions, in, say, political action that seeks to change the discrimination against gay people or to stop the spread of HIV.

6. I am oversimplifying since this distinction has been criticized in different ways. For a nice summary of the history of this debate, see Linda Martín Alcoff, *Visible Identities: Race, Gender and the Self* (Oxford, U.K.: Oxford University Press, 2006), 153–55.

7. The history of these kinds of relationships can be found in Elizabeth Lapovsky Kennedy and Madeline Davis, *Boots of Leather, Slippers of Gold: The History of a Lesbian Community* (New York: Penguin, 1993). See also George Chauncey, "From Sexual Inversion to Homosexuality: The Changing Medical Construction of Sexual Boundaries," in *Passion and Power: Sexuality in History*, edited by Kathy Peiss, Christina Simmons, and Robert Padgug (Philadelphia, Penn.: Temple University Press), 87–117. The complexities of butch-femme (and butch-butch) sexual relationships are detailed in Gayle Rubin, "Of Catamites and Kings: Reflections on Butch, Gender, and Boundaries" in Gayle Rubin, *Deviations: A Gayle Rubin Reader* (Durham, N.C.: Duke University Press, 2011), 241–53, especially 246–47.

8. Others have objected that "sexual orientation" based on gender oversimplifies and therefore falsifies human sexuality. For example, Chris Cuomo writes, "the range of what drives us through the curves, scents, and swells of human intimacy cannot be captured by available woman/man/homo/hetero categories . . . sexuality is a realm of endless variety and particularity. Must it be something that provides an identity?" Chris Cuomo, *The Philosopher Queen: Feminist Essays on War, Love, and Knowledge* (Lanham, Md.: Rowman and Littlefield, 2003), 107.

9. This information can be found in a variety of sources, some in Deirdre Bair's *Simone de Beauvoir: A Biography* (New York: Summit Books, 1990), and some in Beauvoir's own *Diary of a Philosophy Student*, translated by Barbara Klaw, edited by Margaret Simons and Sylvie Le Bon de Beauvoir (Urbana-Champaign, Ill.: University of Illinois Press, 2006). Beauvoir fictionalized the story of her love affair with the American novelist Nelson Algren in her novel *The Mandarins*, translated by Leonard M. Friedman (New York: W.W. Norton, 1956). But the best discussion of her relationship to her sexuality is certainly Margaret Simons's "Lesbian Connections: Simone de Beauvoir and Feminism," in *Adventures in Lesbian Philosophy*, edited by Claudia Card (Bloomington, Ind.: Indiana University Press, 1985), 217–40.

10. Stein uses this scale in defining sexual orientation, *Mismeasure of Desire*, 47–49.

11. Alfred Kinsey, Wardell B. Pomeroy, and Clyde Martin, *Sexual Behavior in the Human Male* (Philadelphia, Penn.: W.B. Saunders Company, 1948), 612ff.

12. R. E. Fay, C. F. Turner, A. D. Klassen, and J. H. Gagnon, "Prevalence of Same-Gender Contact among Men," *Science* 243 (January 20, 1989): 343–48; S. M. Rogers and

C. F. Turner, "Male-Male Sexual Contact in the USA: Findings from Five Sample Surveys, 1970–1990," *Journal of Sex Research* 28:4 (1991): 491–519.

13. Jane Litwoman, quoted in Loraine Hutchins and Lana Kaahumanu, "Overview," in *Bi Any Other Name*, edited by Loraine Hutchins and Lana Kaahumanu (Los Angeles: Alyson Publications, 1991), 4–5. Carol A. Queen writes, "I hate hearing 'You just can't make up your mind.' I make up a decision each time I have sex. I choose to honor the purr in my cunt that says 'Gimme.' I choose the thrill of attraction and the promise of pleasure, the clit, the cock, the fire in the eyes" ("The Queer in Me," in *Bi Any Other Name*, 20).

14. Both Stein (*Mismeasure of Desire*, 41–44) and Corvino ("Orientation, Sexual," 728–29) reject behavioral definitions of "sexual orientation" because these definitions do not generally square with how we think of sexual orientation and because they face their own difficulties. Specifically, if we define "sexual orientation" behaviorally, sexual orientation lacks all stability and changes with the current behavior of any particular individual.

15. Martin S. Weinberg, Colin J. Williams, and Douglas Pryor, *Dual Attractions: Understanding Bisexuality* (Oxford, U.K.: Oxford University Press, 1994), 162–65.

16. Weinberg, Williams, and Pryor, *Dual Attractions*, 145.

17. Such interpretations and theories of homosexuality are, he writes, "most unfortunate, for they provide an interpretation in anticipation of any sufficient demonstration of the fact; and consequently they prejudice investigations of the nature and origin of homosexual activity" (Kinsey, *Sexual Behavior*, 612). This point proves remarkably prescient in light of later biological studies of homosexuality.

18. J. Michael Bailey et al., "Do Individual Differences in Sociosexuality Represent Genetic or Environmentally Contingent Strategies? Evidence from the Australasian Twin Registry," *Journal of Personality and Social Psychology* 78:3 (2000): 524–36; J. Michael Bailey and Richard Pillard, "A Genetic Study of Male Sexual Orientation," *Archives of General Psychiatry* 48:12 (1991): 1089–96; J. Michael Bailey, Richard Pillard, and Yvonne Agyei, "Heritable Factors Influencing Sexual Orientation in Women," *Archives of General Psychiatry* 50:3 (1993): 217–23; William Byne et al., "The Interstitial Nuclei of the Human Anterior Hypothalamus: An Investigation of Variation with Sex, Sexual Orientation, and HIV Status," *Hormones and Behavior* 40:2 (2001): 86–92; Dean Hamer et al., "A Linkage between DNA Markers on the X Chromosome and Male Sexual Orientation," *Science* 261 (July 16, 1993): 321–27; Dean Hamer and Peter Copeland, *The Science of Desire* (New York: Simon and Schuster, 1994); Simon LeVay, "A Difference in Hypothalamic Structure between Heterosexual and Homosexual Men," *Science* 253 (July 30, 1991): 1034–37; Brian Mustanski, Meredith Chivers, and J. Michael Bailey, "A Critical Review of Recent Biological Research on Human Sexual Orientation," *Annual Review of Sex Research* 12 (2002): 89–140.

19. G. Reiger, M. Chivers, and J. M. Bailey, "Sexual Arousal Patterns of Bisexual Men," *Psychological Science* 16:8 (2005): 579–84.

20. Lisa M. Diamond, *Sexual Fluidity: Understanding Women's Love and Desire* (Cambridge, Mass.: Harvard University Press, 2008).

21. The literature on this topic is vast. Some of the highlights include John Boswell, *Christianity, Social Tolerance, and Homosexuality* (Chicago: University of Chicago Press, 1990); John Boswell, "Revolutions, Universals, and Sexual Categories," in *Hidden from History: Reclaiming the Gay and Lesbian Past*, edited by Martin Duberman, Martha Vicinus, and George Chauncey (New York: NAL Books), 37–53; Michel Foucault, *The History of Sexuality*, vol. 1, translated by Robert Hurley (New York: Vintage Books, 1976); David Halperin, *One Hundred Years of Homosexuality* (New York: Routledge, 1990); David Halperin, *How to Do the History of Homosexuality* (Chicago: University of Chicago Press, 2002); and William Wilkerson, *Ambiguity and Sexuality* (New York: Palgrave Macmillan, 2007). All these authors argue either for some version of constructionism or present general introductions to the debate. Essentialism is defended by Raja Halwani, "Prolegomena to Any Future Metaphysics of Sexual Identity: Recasting the Essentialism and Social Constructionism Debate," in *Identity Politics Reconsid-*

ered, edited by Linda Martín Alcoff, Michael Hames-García, Satya P. Mohanty, and Paula M. L. Moya (New York: Palgrave Macmillan, 2005); and by Richard Mohr, *Gay Ideas* (Boston: Beacon Press, 1992).

22. Stephen O. Murray, *Homosexualities* (Chicago: Chicago University Press, 2000).

23. The claim that society has roles for people it would generally not acknowledge or wish to praise, as odd as it sounds, is quite common among sociologists who study deviance and deviance theory. The idea is that society can contain and monitor deviance by "channeling" it into specific roles that are nonetheless stigmatized. A classic text is Erving Goffman's *Stigma: Notes on the Management of Spoiled Identity* (Englewood Cliffs, N.J.: Prentice Hall, 1963).

24. John Boswell insists on this possibility for understanding social and sexual history (*Christianity, Social Tolerance, and Homosexuality*, 41–59), and Halwani's "Prolegomena" argues that essentialism is consistent with the variation in sexual roles across societies.

25. Theories for understanding this process include Gayle Rubin's argument that the creation of the sex/gender system involves deep social structures that both organize and create gender and sex roles. She combines both the social anthropology of Claude Lévi-Strauss with Freudian and Lacanian psychoanalysis to understand this process at both the social and individual level. See Gayle Rubin, "The Traffic in Women," in *Deviations: A Gayle Rubin Reader*, 33–65. Michel Foucault views the entire concept of human sexuality as a construct emerging out of contingent power relationships necessary to the creation of modern, ordered society. See *Abnormal: Lectures at the Collège de France 1974–1975*, edited by Valerio Marchetti and Antonella Salomoni, translated by Graham Burchell (New York: Picador, 2003), and *History of Sexuality*, vol. 1. George Chauncey sees the origin of modern gay and lesbian identity as bound up with social and economic transformations brought about by twentieth-century industrialization; see his *Gay New York: Gender, Urban Culture, and the Making of the Gay Male World, 1890–1940* (New York: Basic Books, 1994).

26. William James, *Pragmatism* (Sioux Falls, S.D.: NuVision Publications, 2007), 71. The discussion of whether or not experience has intrinsic content, how much this content constrains our understanding and conceptualization of it, and the related problem of the "given" has been large in the last century. For other important discussions, see Wilfrid Sellars, "Empiricism and Philosophy of Mind," in *Science, Perception, and Reality* (Atascadero, Calif.: Ridgeview Publishing, 1991), 127–96; John McDowell, *Mind and World* (Cambridge, Mass.: Harvard University Press, 1996), especially 3–24; Richard Rorty, *Philosophy and the Mirror of Nature* (Princeton: Princeton University Press, 1979), 182–92, and, in the Continental tradition, Maurice Merleau-Ponty, *Phenomenology of Perception*, translated by Donald Landes (New York: Routledge, 2012), especially the Introduction.

27. See Wilkerson, *Ambiguity and Sexuality* and "Is It a Choice?"

28. For a discussion of this kind of interpretive process, see Charles Taylor, "What Is Human Agency?" in *Human Agency and Language: Philosophical Papers*, vol. 1 (Cambridge: Cambridge University Press, 1985).

29. I would like to thank the editors—Raja Halwani, Nicholas Power, Alan Soble—along with Nicholas Jones, Chris Cuomo, Talia Mae Bettcher, and especially Andrew Cling for many helpful comments and suggestions on earlier drafts of this paper.

STUDY QUESTIONS

1. When discussing the sex/gender component of the mainstream concept of sexual attraction, Wilkerson uses both attraction "to" and attraction "based on" sex or gender. Is there a difference in the meaning of these expressions? How would the difference, if any,

affect the way we understand the mainstream concept of sexual orientation? How would it affect Wilkerson's argument?

2. Is there a way to philosophically analyze the concept of sexual orientation so that it is neither too broad (i.e., it succeeds in *not* including sexualities that preanalytically do not seem to warrant being called an orientation) nor too narrow (i.e., it succeeds in including all the sexualities that do warrant being classified as an orientation)?

3. What would Vernallis have to say to Wilkerson about bisexuals who are not attracted to others based on sex or gender (see her essay "Bisexual Marriage" in this volume)?

4. Explain the conceptual differences between strong social constructionism and interpretive social constructionism. How could one make a case that the latter is only a variation of the former, not a third version of social constructionism?

5. Explain the objection that Wilkerson raises against interpretive social constructionism and his reply to it. Is the reply convincing? Particularly, might interpretation get rid of epistemic ambiguity, as opposed to ambiguity in the very nature of experiences? How would this affect Wilkerson's argument?

6. Interpretive social constructionism claims that sexual desire is "partly inchoate and protean," but on what basis can it also claim that the feelings that we interpret (in light of our own and our culture's sexual constructs) and that form the basis of our sexual orientation are themselves sexual? What features would make such a "thin" (raw, uninterpreted, not yet conceptualized) experience a sexual one as opposed to a nonsexual one?

THIRTEEN

Bisexual Marriage

Kayley Vernallis

Kayley Vernallis *distinguishes between two types of bisexuals: (1) gender-specific bisexuals, who are attracted to people based on their gender and for that reason are attracted to both males/men and females/women, and (2) gender-nonspecific bisexuals, who are attracted to people based on their personality and character regardless of their gender. Vernallis argues that neither opposite-sex marriage rights nor same-sex marriage rights guarantee the equal treatment of gender-specific bisexuals, who desire to maintain concurrent relationships with both sexes or genders. If two central ideals of marriage are to allow the full expression of the sexuality of the spouses and, at the same time, to encourage and maintain sexual fidelity, then perhaps only foursome marriages—of two female bisexuals and two male bisexuals, all married to each other—would allow such bisexuals to uphold both of these ideals of marriage. Vernallis concludes with some remarks about how various sorts of plural marriages might benefit society.*

Kayley Vernallis is professor and chair of the philosophy department at California State University, Los Angeles. Her publications include "Tedium, Aesthetic Form, and Moral Insight in *Silverlake Life*," *Film and Philosophy* (2008); the entry "Bisexuality" in *Sex from Plato to Paglia: A Philosophical Encyclopedia*, edited by Alan Soble (2006), and "Bisexual Monogamy: Twice the Temptation but Half the Fun?" *Journal of Social Philosophy* (1999). "Bisexual Marriage" is printed here for the first time. © 2012, Kayley Vernallis, who kindly gave permission for this new essay to be included in this volume.

> Changing traditional attitudes toward homosexuality is in itself a mind-expanding experience for most people. But we shall not really succeed in discarding the straitjacket of our cultural beliefs about sexual choice if we fail to come to terms with the well-documented, normal human capacity to love members of both sexes.[1]
>
> —Margaret Mead

Is the legalization of same-sex marriage sufficient to include bisexuals? No; marriage equality for bisexuals requires what I call "bi-marriage"—a form of marriage that leaves room for plural marriages of three or four individuals, at least one member of which is not of the same gender as the others. I argue that, at least for some bisexuals, having sexual relationships with both men and women is just as central to the expression of their sexual identity as same-sex sexual relationships are to homosexuals and opposite-sex sexual relationships are to heterosexuals.

We have not heard much about bi-marriage. Why not? Perhaps because it is still commonly thought that bisexuality is not a real sexual orientation, that bisexuals are merely confused individuals or cowards, so marriage laws need not accommodate them.[2] Gays and lesbians might not advocate for bi-marriage perhaps because they believe that between straight and gay marriages, bisexuals would be covered.[3] Some feminists, such as myself, support bisexuals' right to form plural marriages, but they worry that they would then have no legal ground on which to exclude sexist polygamous practices. Others have not thought about bi-marriage all, but insofar as they have, they dismiss it as inherently unstable and hence not deserving of legal recognition. At the very least, I hope to show that bi-marriage is a topic we should take quite seriously.

In the first section, I explore the distinction between gender-specific bisexual attraction, which is attraction *on the basis of gender*, and gender-nonspecific attraction, which is *independent of gender*. In the second section, I argue that bisexuals have a right to bi-marriage only if (1) bisexual attraction is gender-specific and (2) bisexual relationships manifest the same core ideals we find in contemporary marriage. In the third section, I suggest that bi-marriage may benefit not just bisexuals but society as a whole.

BISEXUALITY AND ITS TWO FORMS

1. Bisexual Orientation

Bisexuality, like heterosexuality and homosexuality, is a sexual orientation. Sexual orientation is usually defined in terms of one or more of the following criteria: *behavior*—the gender of the people with whom one *has* sex; *sexual desire*—the gender of the people to whom one is *attracted* or whom one finds arousing; *fantasy*—the content of one's sexual *imaginings*; and *self-identification*—the *label* one uses to describe or think of oneself. While homosexuals and heterosexuals are oriented towards partners belonging to one gender, bisexuals are oriented towards partners belonging to both genders. It is important to identify temporal variations in bisexual relationships. For instance, we should distinguish between bisexual relationships that are simultaneous, in which at least three individuals are all in a relationship with each other; concurrent bisexual relationships, in which an individual has two *distinct* sexual relationships, one with a man and one with a woman, during the same period of his or her life; and serial bisexual relationships, in which an individual practices serial monogamy, alternating between same-sex and opposite-sex relationships.[4] Presumably, bi-marriage would be most appealing to individuals who manifest their sexual identity in simultaneous or concurrent bisexual relationships.

The distinction, however, that is most central to the justification of bi-marriage is between gender-specific bisexual attraction and gender-nonspecific sexual attraction. According to the gender-specific attraction model, bisexuals are sexually attracted to members of both genders *on the basis of their gender*. Thus, X might be attracted to Y partly in virtue of Y's having a penis and expectations about having sex with a man. On the second model of bisexuality, bisexuals are sexually attracted to members of both genders *independently of gender*. Note that when I first introduced bisexuality as one form of sexual orientation, I described bisexuals as *being attracted to both genders*. Although this characterization provides a simple way of distinguishing bisexuals from heterosexuals and homosexuals, it is important to see that it is ambiguous because there is more than one kind of attraction: some bisexuals are attracted to both genders and some are attracted to individuals irrespective of gender. So we need to clarify the differences between these models of bisexual attraction.[5]

2. Gender-Specific Bisexuality

Bisexuals who experience gender-specific attraction say that being able to sexually express themselves in gay *and* straight sexual relationships is crucial to their sense of sexual identity.[6] They are attracted to women as women, with their range of bodily traits (breasts, vagina, capacity to bear children, larger hip-to-waist ratio, etc.) and, often, with the character traits (warmth, empathy, etc.) associated with women. They are attracted to men as men, with the range of bodily traits (penis, facial and chest hair, physical strength, larger shoulder-to-waist ratio, etc.) and, often, the character traits (competitiveness, assertiveness, etc.) associated with men. They accept the duality of their attractions and feel richer in having both kinds of attraction.[7] Sexual desire for both genders does not mean that one has the same number of male and female partners in a lifetime, or even that one's attractions to men and women are equally strong, but it does mean that being attracted to *both* men and women is a defining feature of this form of bisexuality. Moreover, the behavior patterns of gender-specific bisexuals need not involve simultaneous sexual behavior with a man and a woman in the same bed at the same moment. One can have independent relationships with a man and a woman in the same general time frame of months or years. Call this the concurrent pattern of bisexual relationships. Finally, one's pattern of bisexual behavior can be expressed in serial (alternating) relationships with men and women. Call this the serial pattern of bisexual relationships.

Gender-specific bisexuals desire both men and women as potential sexual partners. Indeed, if they are forbidden to actualize their desires for one gender, they lose their opportunity to express their full sexual selves, thereby experiencing a loss of identity. The depth of that loss depends on how much their bisexual attraction is part of their identities. Sexual attraction might simply be the inducement of physiological arousal in one's sexual organs, but in gender-specific bisexuals, the object-directedness of their desires are important to who they are. Their satisfaction in sexual relationships is important in a way that goes beyond pleasure; they are integral to an individual's personality. In satisfying these desires one is, somehow, more authentic. After all, the satisfaction of desires is not peripheral to who someone is but is a form of self-cultivation and self-expression because it shapes the self and generates new desires whose character is conditioned by this dynamic process.

On this view (often called "expressivism"), the self is not given a fixed set of desires and character traits that one unveils or discovers. Instead, the intertwining of desire, action, and self-reflection constitute one's identity. This self-shaping is not done alone but with other people, socially (whether that relation is antagonistic or supportive). Of course, sometimes one's desires are not very important, as when one desires vanilla instead of chocolate ice cream. In contrast, sexuality and sexual object choice are more central to our identity and self-expression than ice cream preferences. As Freud writes, "The sexual behavior of a human being often *lays down the pattern* for all his other modes of reacting to life."[8]

But what is a person's identity? It is a dynamic but predictable structure for action and self-interpretation made up of a collection of traits, such as psychological dispositions, desires, habits, physiological tendencies, beliefs, commitments, and values. A trait is identity constituting if other traits depend on it—if it is manifested across several life spheres (e.g., work, leisure); it is resistant to conscious change; it can lead to the production of new traits through self-reflection and self-understanding; it leads others to label one as possessing that trait; it is dominant over other traits; and it tends to be dominant in stressful situations.[9] Typical traits that may be identity constituting include bodily traits such as weight, attractiveness, and athleticism; psychological traits such as self-doubt, shame, narcissism, and competitiveness; social-role traits such as being a prankster, leader, or enabler; and social-group traits generated by in-group and out-group expectations about ethnicity, race, gender, class, religion, and sexual orientation. Note that such traits need not be acknowledged or affirmed by the person who possesses them. Note also that most of us identify some traits as ideals, and that these idealized traits often play a complex role in relation to the traits we actually have.

For instance, one may have as an ideal the capacity to forgive, and commitment to this ideal may help dampen other more censorious tendencies, such as being judgmental. On the other hand, some ideals, such as being perfect, may contribute to strengthening the trait of shame—which can be particularly activated when one inevitably falls short of the ideal of perfection.

To say that sexuality and sexual orientation are central to our identities, then, is to say that our sexual desires, dispositions, activities, judgments, and ideals possess at least some of the structural and causal powers listed above. If one questions the legitimacy of one's desires, or if others characterize them as, for instance, sexually perverted, one may experience an identity crisis, which involves some loss of one's individuality or "me-ness." Alternatively, if one is prevented from manifesting one's sexual orientation, or even if one chooses to make a painful trade-off in the satisfaction of one's sexual object choice, one may experience a loss of self.[10]

Above, I characterized gender-specific bisexuals as desiring both men and women as sexual partners. In order to understand why it would be a loss of sexual flourishing for a gender-specific bisexual to be forbidden or to forgo making love with members of one gender, we need to know how that person experiences herself differently in same-gender, as opposed to opposite-gender, sexual interactions (or vice versa). It can't simply be reduced to having sex with different objects. If one's experience is the same, the objects are substitutable. To put it crudely, if there is no difference between having sex with members of one gender or the other, how could discontinuing sex with members of one gender constitute a real loss? But for gender-specific bisexuals, sex with male and female partners satisfies qualitatively different desires, and hence they incur a loss if they don't satisfy one of these types of desire. In contrast, the sexual desires of heterosexuals and homosexuals are confined to one gender, so they suffer no such loss.

This expressivist picture can explain the nature and significance of the gender-specific bisexual's loss. For, according to expressivism, in satisfying her sexual desires for women, the gender-specific bisexual experiences herself in a certain way. And in satisfying her sexual desires for men, the gender-specific bisexual experiences herself in yet another way. For example, consider a woman who feels that she is more dominant or masculine when making love with women and more passive and feminine when making love with men. Furthermore, she may feel proud that she can play both dominant and receptive roles. Playing both these roles in her sexual life may be central to her sexual identity and hence her personhood. When she cannot satisfy her desires for sex with the alternate gender, it is not just that she has lost a sexual object; it is as though one-half of her sexual self has gone to a nunnery, given how nonsubstitutable her self-expression in these kinds of experiences is.

3. Gender-Nonspecific Bisexuality

Gender-nonspecific bisexuals consider gender to be *irrelevant* to their sexual object choice, although their pattern of bisexual activity (simultaneous, concurrent, serial) may be just the same as for gender-specific bisexuals. The two forms of bisexuality are distinguished in terms of impulse, desire, and self-understanding. So both the ground of attraction and self-reflection play important roles in differentiating the two from each other. A bisexual woman's gender-nonspecific sexuality may be an important identity-constituting feature of who she is; however, it won't be essential to her identity that she expresses her sexuality with both men and women.

Gender-nonspecific bisexuals are likely to say that they are attracted to an individual's personality or that they "fall in love with the person." There is something very appealing about this form of bisexuality. It is more admirable to be drawn to a person on the basis of character (which we tend to regard as deep and as being under a person's control) rather than on the basis of bodily attractiveness (which we regard as superficial and as being less under a person's control). It also seems that gender-nonspecific bisexuals are not prejudiced. Unlike heterosexuals, homosexuals, and gender-specific bisexuals, they can see past not only people's bodily attractiveness and unattractiveness but also their gendered features. The best phrase to describe gender-nonspecific bisexual attraction is "character-based attraction."

I have two concerns about this form of bisexuality. First, it is unclear to what degree bodies are relevant to character-based attraction. If bodies are not relevant, then it cannot be characterized as a form of *sexual attraction*. Second, character is, at least to some degree, manifested in bodies, and societal expectations about character and gender make our sexual attractions more gender-laden than we think. This makes character-based attraction no longer what it claims to be. For what does it mean to say that sexual attraction is falling in love with a person, period, rather than a person as gendered?

Consider Erin, a gender-nonspecific bisexual, who describes her sexual attraction this way: "I fell in love with my college roommate Terry after spending so much time with her and seeing how caring and special she is. I didn't expect to become romantically involved with her. Sexual intimacy is just one aspect of our shared love and concern. It wouldn't matter to me whether Terry was a man or a woman. I love Terry as a person." This example relegates sexual attraction to being a byproduct of character attraction. *X*'s love for *Y*'s character is such that it eventually generates sexual desire for *Y* regardless of *Y*'s gender. The *only* thing that matters for generating sexual desire is the beloved's personality. Perhaps she hopes to enjoy her lover's body only as the body of her lover.

But is such a neutral description possible? I don't think so. If she doesn't eventually celebrate her lover's body as a gendered body that can give and receive sexual pleasure, then we cannot say that her connection to her lover's body is a sexual one at all.[11] The reason is that all of us, at least in our culture, have, to varying degrees, gendered body-specific attractions, which are also specific to the body's age, race, height, and other such physical features. One phenomenon that makes this apparent is how many of us experience being sexually attracted to "ideal sexual types." A slender but large-breasted woman with ⸱ pretty face is a common preferred sexual type for heterosexual men. A short, bald, pudgy man is not a typical sexual type for a heterosexual or bisexual woman.

I do not wish to deny that our sexual responsiveness is, to varying degrees, conditioned by our experience of a person's character. But a gender-neutral attitude is practically impossible to attain because *our sexual attractions are predominantly, if not always, gender-inflected.* For instance, we culturally project far more sexual attractiveness onto male novelists than female novelists.[12] What looks like commanding presence in a man often looks like overly aggressive—indeed, "ball-breaking"—behavior in a woman. Forthright sexiness in a man looks like slutty behavior in a woman. In a female Terry, caring may be attractive; in a male Terry, it may not be.

Gender-nonspecific bisexuals might accept these points. But they might point out that, unlike heterosexuals, homosexuals, and gender-specific bisexuals, primary sexual organs (e.g., penis, vagina) and secondary sexual ones (e.g., beard hair) are *not* the *determining* features in their sexual partner preference. Instead, they might note that their sexual attractions are robust but independent of gender-marked bodily features. Such a bisexual might say, "I don't care what my partners' primary and secondary sexual traits are, but I do care about whether they are small-bodied or graceful or athletic or youthful. Unlike penises and vaginas, these aren't gender-linked traits."

But this is wrong. A man is often considered to be in his prime at age fifty, but a woman almost never is. Physical grace in a man often translates to ponderous movement in a woman.[13] A small-bodied woman is petite, but a small-bodied man is . . . what? It is hard to think of a positive description. Gender cannot be *irrelevant* to sexual attraction if it is difficult to identify any gender-neutral bodily traits. There can be no genuinely gender-nonspecific sexual attraction that truly acknowledges the reality of bodies, at least as they are constituted by our current social world.[14] Gender-nonspecific bisexuals, then, have desires that, at best, can be seen as gender-semi-specific. Their preference for partners with athletic grace is best understood as a preference, generally implicit if not unconscious, for, say, fine athletic grace that is to some degree indexed to men, and for fine athletic grace that is to some degree indexed to women.

So gender-nonspecific bisexuals' preferences are not likely to be truly *gender-free*, even if they think they are. This should not surprise us.[15] We still live in a world dominated by gender dualisms (I address briefly at the end of this essay the role that gender-nonspecific bisexuals might play in breaking down these dualisms).

My main interest in this section has been to distinguish between gender-specific and gender-nonspecific forms of bisexuality. This is extremely important for understanding one dimension of bisexuality (sexual attraction) and because the two forms of attraction play very different roles in justifying bisexual marriage.[16] However, despite my serious doubts about whether the gender of one's partner can be truly irrelevant to sexual object choice, for the purposes of the next section I *assume* that for gender-nonspecific bisexuals it can in fact be irrelevant. So let's return, finally, to bisexuality and marriage. How do the models of gender-specific and gender-nonspecific bisexual attraction bear on the question of marriage rights? Do heterosexual and homosexual marriages protect all the rights that accrue to bisexuals in virtue of their sexual orientation?

BISEXUALITY AND MARRIAGE

1. Gender-Nonspecific Bisexual Attraction and the Ground for Marriage

If all bisexuals have gender-nonspecific attractions, and if only heterosexual marriage is legal, bisexuals suffer an injustice because it reduces their pool of potential candidates for marriage by half. Even worse, if one is a bisexual who is in love with an individual of the same gender and desires to marry that person, one suffers just as deep a personal loss in not being able to do so as a lesbian does if she cannot marry her same-gender lover. Of course, without the legalization of homosexual marriage, gays and lesbians cannot marry *any* of their potential romantic partners. But imagine Anna, a bisexual American citizen whose same-gender partner, Alejandra, is a Mexican citizen. Since the federal government currently does not recognize same-sex marriages, it might be impossible for Alejandra to live legally in the same country as Anna. Some gays and lesbians might claim, "Well, it is true that Anna is like us if gay marriage is illegal, since she can't marry and live with Alejandra. But there is a large pool of men she can choose from. We have, however, no pool of marriageable partners at all." But this comparison provides small consolation to the bisexual who is not able to be with the person she loves. Should we start distinguishing between and measuring degrees of personal and political loss to determine which losses involve injustice? Should we say that, for instance, banning gay marriage is worse than banning interracial marriage? (Heterosexual blacks had a pool of eligible, nonwhite partners when interracial marriage was illegal.) I wish to avoid these comparisons.

What if both heterosexual and homosexual marriages were legal? If both were legal, *there would be no need for bi-marriage if all bisexuals' attractions were gender-nonspecific* because gender-nonspecific bisexuals do not choose their partners on the basis of gender. The extension of marriage to include same-sex couples would provide a gender-nonspecific bisexual with all the legal protection necessary for the full expression of her sexual orientation. Laws that permit two individuals to marry without regard to gender will protect a gender-nonspecific bisexual no matter what the gender of the other marriage partner is.

2. Gender-Specific Bisexual Attraction and the Ground for Marriage

Will heterosexual and homosexual marriage laws fully protect gender-specific bisexuals? Recall that a gender-specific bisexual is attracted to both men and women. He desires women as women—for the distinctive character and bodily traits they possess. He also desires men as men—for *their* distinctive traits. For these bisexuals, their sexual identity is only expressed if they have sexual relationships with both men and women. If so, then neither option of heterosexual or homosexual marriage enables a gender-specific bisexual to fully realize his sexual identity because, as I argued above, one's experience of oneself is qualitatively different depending on whether one is in a relationship with a man or a woman. One may express different aspects not just of one's sexual identity but also of one's gender identity in these relationships. A loss of either homosexual or heterosexual relationships is potentially a partial loss of identity. This is the basis of my argument for bi-marriage, and it applies only to bisexuals whose desires are gender-specific. So from this point on I use "bisexual" to refer to this group. In the remainder of this section, I show that the temporal pattern of a bisexual's relationships bears on the argument for bi-marriage.

If a bisexual's orientation is expressed in serial relationships, her right to marry can be officially accommodated by legal heterosexual and homosexual marriage. For instance, she can marry a man for several years and then divorce him; she can then marry a woman for several years and then divorce her. And so on for the rest of her life. She may benefit from these serial marriages, but her spouses are not likely to benefit unless they are (1) heterosexuals or homosexuals who are happy to commit to a short-term marriage, or (2) bisexuals whose preferred timing of serial relationships matches hers. Besides, it is a rare thing—not to mention a bad idea—for anyone to enter a marriage while anticipating divorce. Indeed, it is one thing for people to fail to live up to the ideal of "till death do us part," but it is another thing to abandon that ideal from the get-go.[17]

If a bisexual's orientation is expressed in *concurrent* sexual relationships with men and women, her orientation will not be fully accommodated by heterosexual and homosexual marriage. Recall that concurrent relationships involve a person having two simultaneous sexual relationships independent of each other. It is not currently legal for a person to have two spouses—one through gay marriage and one through heterosexual marriage. Of course, some bisexuals in a heterosexual or a homosexual marriage (as well as some married heterosexuals and homosexuals) engage in "open marriages" in which both partners agree that one or both of them will have sexual and love relationships outside the marriage. Since gender-specific bisexuals can choose to be in open marriages, their sexual identities can be fulfilled in this way. However, heterosexuals and homosexuals do not need to resort to open marriages in order to fully express their sexual orientations. Given that we understand marriage as an expression of love and sexual fidelity, gender-specific bisexuals are presently denied the opportunity to jointly (1) fulfill their sexual identities and (2) participate in the fundamental ideal of fidelity in marriage. In this regard, they are not being treated equally to heterosexuals and would not be treated equally to homosexuals were homosexuals allowed to marry. It is not fair that bisexuals have to give up the full expression of their sexual orientation in order to be in a sexually exclusive marriage. This suggests that we ought to explore a rational grounding for bi-marriage, which I characterized earlier as the legal joining of three individuals, at least one of whom is of a different gender than the other two. In the next section I enumerate five ideals in contemporary marriage often employed in arguments for the extension of marriage to gays and lesbians and discuss their compatibility with bi-marriage.

3. Contemporary Marriage Ideals and Bi-Marriage

The following are contemporary marriage ideals:

- *Choice*. Marriage unions are the product of adult partners' rational choice, reflecting their individual desires, not dictated by the parents, the larger community, or, generally, people other than the partners to the marriage.
- *Mutuality*. Marriage is based upon mutual love, affection, and respect between spouses. If X is married to Y, then they love and respect each other mutually. It is not ideal that one partner seeks to marry for love while the other does so for money or status.
- *Commitment*. Marriage involves a serious commitment to long-term shared duties and responsibilities, including significant financial, medical, social, and legal ones.
- *Sexual Self-Expression*. Marriage supports forms of individual sexual expression and sexual intimacy that promote the stability of the marital relationship and the love, affection, and respect between the

spouses. Sexual exclusivity (or fidelity) helps achieve these goals. Although not all one's sexual desires need to be met in marriage, certainly basic forms of sexual self-expression should be realized.

- *Family Stability.* Although marriage does not require parenthood, if spouses choose to be parents, they should aim for emotional and financial stability that promotes social development in children. Even in the absence of children, stability is still a central feature of families that grows out of the first four ideals. When achieved, family members are readied to withstand adversity, support one another in old age, and so on.

The legalization of homosexual marriage rests on the claim that homosexuals should not be excluded from the institution of marriage simply because their sexual object choice differs from that of heterosexuals. Cultural acceptance of gay marriage is based on the fact that homosexual relationships, like heterosexual relationships, can attain the ideals identified above. Can bi-marriages attain them also? Certainly bisexuals are capable of making autonomous, rational choices about whom they want to marry, and they can be as committed to carrying out the financial, legal, and social duties associated with marriage as any other individuals. The ideals that seem to pose a challenge for bi-marriage triads are mutuality, sexual self-expression, and, perhaps, stability.

If marriage is to allow bisexuals to fully express their sexual identities, then we have a potential problem because it is not possible to simultaneously satisfy this requirement with the one that all members maintain sexual exclusivity in the marriage (by "sexual exclusivity" I mean that no one has sex with anyone outside the marriage and everyone in the marriage has one sexual outlet with at least one of the partners to the marriage). The individual who is the only man or woman in the triad cannot both fully satisfy his or her bisexual desires while also being sexually exclusive. If X is a woman, and both Y and Z are men, X cannot fully satisfy her bisexual *desires* after she marries unless she violates the requirement of sexual exclusivity by finding a female lover.

We can preserve sexual exclusivity and full sexual self-expression by making X a heterosexual woman. Now she has two bisexual male sexual partners, each of whom has both a female and a male partner. However, it would be odd for bi-marriage to logically require that (1) at least one of its members forgo full sexual self-expression or (2) at least one of its members be heterosexual. Both these solutions go against the spirit of bi-marriage, which is to extend to one group (bisexuals) the entitlements available to heterosexuals and homosexuals. For one thing, a heterosexual woman in a bi-marriage receives an additional entitlement that she wouldn't receive under traditional two-person monogamous marriages, namely, having two husbands with whom she has heterosexual sex. A parallel entitlement would be available for X were X the sole heterosexual man in a bi-marriage.

Problems also arise if we change the original case by making Z a heterosexual male and Y a bisexual female (X is still a heterosexual female). Z then has mutual relationships with X and Y, but X and Y do not have a relationship with each other. A similar problem arises if X is a homosexual female, Z is a heterosexual male, and Y is a bisexual female. For now Y has mutual relationships with X and Y, but X and Z do not have relations with each other. Although sexual exclusivity can be maintained in these cases, we unfortunately give up mutuality, the idea that each member loves, and is sexually intimate with, every other member.

Another solution is if the gender-minority member of the triad (say, X, a bisexual woman, in a marriage with Y and Z, two bisexual men) is willing to forgo sexual and love relations with members of her own sex in order to be in the marriage. The loss of her sexual flourishing might be offset by other gains. Still, she makes a sacrifice that heterosexual and homosexual individuals do not have to make when they choose to be sexually exclusive. This is significant because the moral justification for extending marriage to gays and then to bisexuals depends, at least in part, on the idea of a right to the forms of sexual flourishing that are distinctive to each kind of sexual orientation.

Critics of bi-marriage might claim that since its advocates deem it morally acceptable for the gender-minority individual in a married triad to forgo sexual intimacy with others of the same gender, there is no need for the state to make special accommodations for bi-marriage at all. For if closing off one class of sexual objects is morally acceptable in the case of a bisexual who is in a gender-minority position in a bi-marriage, it should be morally acceptable for bisexuals in traditional heterosexual or homosexual two-person marriages. The response to this is obvious. Although it is morally acceptable for one to willingly forgo some good, it does not follow that it is morally acceptable for this good to be taken from one. You might turn down health insurance from your employer because you have sufficient coverage under a spouse's policy and you would like to save your employer some money. But that doesn't mean that your employer can deny you insurance coverage. If you have a legal right and you choose to forgo that right, it does not follow that the state may not provide that right or may take it away from you. In relation to the issue at hand, while it is true that not every member of a bi-marriage can be bisexual and fully flourish sexually in a threesome bi-marriage, if a *particular* bisexual, X, is willing to forgo full bisexual flourishing in a particular marriage (say, X is a bisexual woman, and both Y and Z are bisexual men), she should still be *legally entitled* to form a different bi-marriage in which she can sexually fully flourish (with Y, a bisexual woman, and Z, a heterosexual man). She thus can have full sexual self-expression while achieving sexual fidelity in marriage. Indeed, in this arrangement, no bisexual has to forgo full sexual flourishing in marriage since the gender-minority individual is heterosexual. And the heterosexual satisfies both conditions of sexual self-expression and fidelity.

What could be better than this? What if X wants to marry only other bisexuals? *The only way to guarantee the bisexuality of each member, as well as the principles of sexual exclusivity and mutuality, is by expanding the marriage to four persons, with two partners from each gender.* Thus we have the following form of marriage: W and X, two bisexual men, and Y and Z, two bisexual women.[18]

The advantage of this proposal is that no member will need to sacrifice his or her bisexual identity, and hence all members will be theoretically equal to one another in their choices. On the other hand, this four-person model dictates that each member has two alternate-gender partners but only one same-gender partner. Although this ratio may not reflect some bisexuals' preferences, a foursome model doesn't deny any individual's capacity for sexual flourishing. In traditional polygamous marriages, stability is achieved through male power.[19] In bi-marriage, mutual love and sexual relationships among equals provide stability. Because all spouses love one another and are in sexually mutual relationships with one another, jealousy can be readily diffused; one can receive affirmation and self-reflection from more than one spouse, which can lead to a more realistic understanding of oneself.[20] Bi-marriages of foursomes will, at least in principle, make it possible for all members of the marriage to be bisexual, sexually flourish through sexual intimacy with members of both genders, have mutual sexual and love relationships, and be sexually exclusive. Of course, bi-marriage will face challenges. For instance, the more spouses there are, the harder it may be to come to consensus about what movie to see, which house to buy, and so forth. This poses challenges to stability, which makes good communication skills even more important.

Opponents of bi-marriage might say that bisexuals must first demonstrate a solid historical practice of bisexual marriage-like unions (bi-unions), and only then should society recognize bi-marriage. But very powerful social forces work against marriage-like bisexual threesomes and foursomes, so waiting for bi-unions to first prove their success is not in the offing. Moreover, the legalization of bi-marriage would foster social support for such unions.[21] Indeed, might bi-marriage even bring benefits to society at large? In the next and final section, I show how views of traditional heterosexual marriage arise out of a dualistic gender system, which devalues women and sexual minorities.[22] I then suggest how homosexuals, bisexuals, and others can challenge these binaries and hence contribute to stronger families and greater sexual freedom.

THE SOCIAL CONTRIBUTIONS OF
BISEXUALITY AND BI-MARRIAGE

Heterosexual marriage traditionally embodies false dualisms: (1) men and women are opposites; (2) these opposites complement one another in traditional marriage roles; and (3) homosexuality is the opposite of heterosexuality and is, at worst, a perversion, and at best, an exception to proper sexual relations. According to religious conservatives, God created gender, heterosexuality, and patriarchy. God made men physically strong and rational as well as driven toward autonomy, competition, and leadership. God made women physically weak, emotional, nurturing, and in need of protection and guidance. Gender-based traits complement each other in the traditional heterosexual marriage and are necessary to raising children. This conservative religious view is represented in the Danvers Statement (1988) published by the Council on Biblical Manhood and Womanhood.[23] A slightly more moderate view that does not mention religious values is expressed by David Blankenhorn, president of the Institute of American Values:

> Ultimately, the division of parental labor is the consequence of our biological embodiment as sexual beings and of the inherent requirements of effective parenthood. . . . Historically, the good father protects his family, provides for its material needs, devotes himself to the education of his children, and represents his family's interests in the larger world.[24]

Feminists and gay theorists have successfully challenged these traditional gender norms. In some heterosexual families, fathers now engage in childcare and mothers work outside the home. Among gay couples, both spouses often share work and family roles equally. As Susan Moller Okin notes, "Gay marriage has the potential to do more for gender equality than almost any other social change because it demonstrates that there aren't natural gender roles and a natural gendered division of labor within the family."[25] Bi-marriage can also contribute to gender equality. One spouse may stay home to care for children while the other spouses go to work. These roles may change year to year, thereby exhibiting the fluidity of such complex marriages of equal partners. Bi-marriage, even more than same-sex marriage, makes it harder to believe that there must be one spouse who truly "wears the pants" in the family.

The acceptance of homosexuality has made it far easier for straight-identified young men to give voice to and appreciate their emotional connection to other men, as Eric Anderson and Adi Adams show in a recent study of American male college athletes. One college soccer player says of his friend, "I love Dom . . . I mean I really love him. Call it a bromance if you want, but he's my boy . . . There's nothing I can't talk to him about."[26] Many of the young men said things like "we are all a little gay," but they did not refer to themselves or others as bisexual. I think that Margaret Mead is right that acknowledging same-sex love is an additional step in the acknowledgement of a rich capacity to love individuals of both sexes. This may be because far more of us have this capacity than we would like to admit.[27] Bi-marriage is a way for our culture to acknowledge the truth that emotional attachment, love, and commitment are just as integral to bisexuality as to other sexual orientations.

Obviously, the greatest challenge of bi-marriage—stable mutuality—is not made any easier by discrimination. We have few models or conventions to guide us in maintaining such marriages.[28] But as I suggested earlier, there are advantages to having more than one spouse or life-partner. One can better see oneself through the eyes of more than one other person because of the greater possibilities to correct distortions about oneself and others. The task of defining and delineating oneself in threesome or foursome marriages requires communication skills and sensitivities that might be instructive for all of us. Practical benefits for children in bi-marriages include greater financial stability from three or four parent incomes; better basic care for infants, as each adult has more time to sleep; and more adult attention for young children, which is linked to better school performance.[29]

I have argued that the main reason for extending marriage rights to bisexuals is the same reason why heterosexuals and homosexuals have the right to marry, namely, that marriage expresses a person's desires for love and sexual intimacy. However, the best way for marriage to fully express bisexuals' identities, especially the identities of gender-specific bisexuals, is in the form of foursomes. Thus, bi-marriage is both an extension of marriage and a radical reconceptualization of it.[30]

NOTES

1. Margaret Mead, "Bisexuality: A New Awareness," in *Aspects of the Present*, edited by Margaret Mead and Rhoda Metraux (New York: William Morrow and Company, in conjunction with Redbook Magazine, 1980), 269–75, at 271.

2. It is very common to think that men who identify as bisexual are closeted gays. Women in lesbian communities frequently deny the existence of bisexual women, "It just strikes me as . . . I just don't think bisexuality exists. There! As a legitimate category." Or they regard them as promiscuous, "When I think of 'bisexual' I think of bedhopping." Quoted by Amber Ault, "Hegemonic Discourse in an Oppositional Community: Lesbian Feminists and Bisexuality," *Critical Sociology* 20:2 (1994): 106–22, at 112, 117.

3. It is also true that gay and lesbian groups aren't rushing to defend bisexual marriage in the face of some social conservatives' claims that gay marriage will lead to something much worse: polygamy. For the conservative view, see Stanley Kurtz, "Beyond Gay Marriage: The Road to Polyamory," *Weekly Standard* 8:45 (August 4–11, 2003), reprinted in this volume. Gay and lesbian groups generally ignore these social conservatives.

4. This three-fold temporal distinction is introduced by Gary Zinik, "Identity Conflict or Adaptive Flexibility? Bisexuality Reconsidered," *Journal of Homosexuality* 11:1–2 (1985): 7–20.

5. A few psychological studies distinguish between gender-linked and non-gender-linked attraction. See, for instance, Michael W. Ross and Jay P. Paul, "Beyond Gender: The Basis of Sexual Attraction in Bisexual Men and Women," *Psychological Reports* 71 (1992): 1283–90.

6. Note that sexual attraction (desire, fantasy, and their related physiological and psychological constituents) does not tell the whole story of sexual orientation and identity. But, as we go along, I attempt to show the various connections sexual attraction can have to broader psychological identity and selfhood. For a discussion of sexual orientation, see John Corvino, "Orientation, Sexual," in *Sex from Plato to Paglia: A Philosophical Encyclopedia*, edited by Alan Soble (Westport, Conn.: Greenwood Press, 2006), 728–34, and William S. Wilkerson's essay in this volume.

7. Of course, many gender-specific bisexuals are attracted to manly women and feminine men.

8. Sigmund Freud, "'Civilized' Sexual Morality and Modern Nervous Illness," in *The Standard Edition of the Complete Psychological Works of Sigmund Freud*, vol. 9, translated by James Strachey (London: Hogarth, 1959), 181–204, at 198 (italics in original).

9. The last three traits come from Amelie Rorty and David Wong, "Aspects of Identity and Agency," in *Identity, Character, and Morality: Essays in Moral Psychology*, edited by Owen Flanagan and Amelie Oksenberg Rorty (Cambridge, Mass.: MIT Press, 1990), 19–36. These structural and functional characteristics of traits (for instance, predominance of a trait in stressful situations, strong causal effect on other traits, etc.) do not provide necessary and sufficient conditions for the constitution of identity. For instance, even if one's identity is centrally tied to one's physical appearance, thoughts about ruining one's hairdo will not be predominant in the stressful situation of saving a child from drowning. For some individuals, a sexual fetish for shoes might be a central yet compartmentalized trait. At best, we can identify a fairly loose set of conditions for identifying which traits can be said to contribute to identity.

10. I defend this claim in more detail in "Bisexual Monogamy: Twice the Temptation but Half the Fun?" *Journal of Social Philosophy* 30:3 (1999): 347–68.

11. In short, given how our society is presently structured, there are no gender-neutral personality traits and no gender-neutral bodies. A transgender individual will possess inflections of both, and those multiple inflections may be very sexually attractive to many individuals, including some gender-specific bisexuals. Individuals whose attractions seem especially close to being gender-nonspecific are, perhaps, pedophiles attracted to both very young girls and very young boys. Small body size, smooth skin, and lack of body odor may be the features that are most attractive in their eyes.

12. I owe this point to the novelist Michelle Huneven. Some female writers, such as Anaïs Nin and Erica Jong, are read as sexually attractive, but they can't compete with the "sexually potent" great writers such as Ernest Hemingway.

13. In fact, context matters quite a bit. A professional male ballet dancer will look incredibly graceful in the company of moderately trained female dancers.

14. Gender-nonspecific attraction may be even more difficult to attain if one's potential sexual partners are extremely unattractive. For some, sagging breasts in a man may be more disgusting than in a woman. I owe the general point to Raja Halwani.

15. It is similar to the case of those who espouse antiracist views yet unconsciously harbor racial prejudice. For a substantial list of articles on implicit attitudes, see http://projectimplicit.net/articles.php (accessed March 12, 2012). A typical article on race at the site is A. S. Baron and M. R. Banaji, "The Development of Implicit Attitudes: Evidence of Race Evaluations from Ages 6 to 10 and Adulthood," *Psychological Science* 17: 1 (2006): 53–58. If you would like to take the implicit attitudes test, see https://implicit.harvard.edu/implicit (accessed March 20, 2012). Can we devise an implicit-attitudes test for gender-nonspecific sexual attraction?

16. Basically, I have characterized these two forms of attraction as gender-relevant and gender-irrelevant. My argument for bi-marriage is strongest when it comes to those who take gender as extremely relevant, but it can apply to those for whom it is somewhat relevant.

17. On the other hand, serial bisexuals are not likely to do worse than other Americans in terms of the longevity of their marriages. The average length of marriages that end in divorce is about eight years; see http://www.census.gov/prod/2005pubs/p70-97.pdf (accessed March 4, 2012). Measuring the overall divorce rate is tricky, but the highest it has ever been is 41 percent as a measurement of all those ever married or ever divorced. Also see Dan Hurley's "Divorce Rate: It's Not as High as You Think," *New York Times* (April 19, 2005).

18. Will bisexuals most naturally express themselves and find solidarity best in relationships with other bisexuals? I don't know. Only the future will tell.

19. In traditional polygamous marriage, girls are commonly forced into marriage and many boys are ejected from the community. But it would be unfair, surely, to outlaw all marriages between more than two individuals simply in order to eliminate sexist polygamist practices; otherwise we ought to have already abandoned marriage altogether given its history of oppressing women in monogamous male-female marriages.

20. For these reasons I am not keen on bi-marriages that preserve the sexual expression of one's orientation but not the mutuality. Raja Halwani (personal correspondence) suggests the following scenario: R, a bisexual male, is married to S, a bisexual female. R is also married to P, a bisexual male, while S is married to T, a bisexual female. P is married to X, a heterosexual female, and T is married to Y, a heterosexual male. And while R is married to S and P, S and P are not married to each other. This is a marriage chain in which each member has two sexual partners (except X and Y). But why would S and P care about the other's interests? Wouldn't jealousy likely thrive? Would they be inclined to share P's assets if P dies? It is unlikely that stability can be achieved without mutuality.

21. Recall that one reason there hasn't been political pressure for bi-marriage is that homosexual and heterosexual marriage laws accommodate gender-nonspecific bisexuals' orientations.

22. See, for instance, Paula Rust, "Who Are We and Where Do We Go from Here?" in *Closer to Home: Bisexuality and Feminism*, edited by Elizabeth Reba Weise (Seattle: Seal Press, 1992), 281–310.

23. See http://www.cbmw.org/Resources/Articles/The-Danvers-Statement (accessed March 4, 2012). Only a few selected quotations from the Bible are included in the Danvers statement, but among them is Timothy 2:12–14 (English Standard Version): "I do not permit a woman to teach or to exercise authority over a man; rather she is to remain quiet."

24. David Blankenhorn, "The Unnecessary Father," excerpted from *Fatherless America*, Institute for American Values (New York: Basic Books, 1995), reprinted in *Applied Ethics: A Multicultural Approach*, 4th ed., edited by Larry May, Shari Collins-Chobanian, and Kai Wong (Upper Saddle River, N.J.: Pearson Prentice Hall, 2006), 380–88, at 385. Blankenhorn characterizes himself as a liberal democrat. At a recent federal trial, Blankenhorn was an expert witness in support of Proposition 8, the California proposition that made gay marriage illegal. Judge Walker ruled against the constitutionality of Proposition 8. See http://www.newyorker.com/online/blogs/newsdesk/perry-v-schwarzenegger (accessed March 4, 2012).

25. Susan Moller Okin, "Sexual Orientation, Gender, and Families: Dichotomizing Differences," *Hypatia* 11:1 (1996) 30–48, at 43. We can extend Okin's point. Because bi-marriage involves bisexuals whose identities are, in some ways, "and" or "in-between" identities, it may lead to greater acceptance of transgender, intersex, multiracial, and multiethnic individuals. We all gain from a social world where there is more room for "in-between," open, and evolving identities.

26. Eric Anderson and Adi Adams, "Aren't We All a Little Bisexual? The Recognition of Bisexuality in an Unlikely Place," *Journal of Bisexuality* 11:1 (2011): 3–22, at 13.

27. In 1948 Alfred Kinsey noted, "Nearly half (46%) of the population engages in both heterosexual and homosexual activities, or reacts to persons of both sexes, in the course of their adult lives." Alfred Kinsey, W. B. Pomeroy, and C. E. Martin, *Sexual Behavior in the Human Male* (Philadelphia, Penn.: W.B. Saunders, 1948), 656.

28. The Bloomsbury group in 1920s Britain provides perhaps the closest illustration.

29. See John McMurtry, "Monogamy: A Critique," *The Monist* 56:4 (1972): 587–99, for arguments in support of expanding the members of families.

30. Special thanks to Randal Parker, Raja Halwani, and Nicholas Power.

STUDY QUESTIONS

1. How do the following distinctions by Vernallis map onto each other: concurrent and serial bisexuality, concurrent patterns and alternating patterns of bisexual relationships, and gender-specific and gender-nonspecific bisexuality?

2. Is Vernallis correct to claim that "our sexual attractions are predominantly, if not always, gender-inflected"? What about those people who are attracted to transgendered people and to transsexuals?

3. How might Vernallis reply to the following objection: "Allowing foursome bisexual marriages would require major economic costs. Think of health insurance, resources devoted to divorces, weddings, and all the other things that come with marriage. It's not worth it"?

4. Assess the advantages and disadvantages of plural marriages. Are some of these advantages and disadvantages specifically due to the fact that the spouses are bisexuals or simply due to the fact that the marriage is plural?

5. Imagine Claudia Card and Cheshire Calhoun together having coffee, wine, or fish-and-chips, but this time joined by Kayley Vernallis. How would they reply to her on both the philosophical and the political/practical levels?

6. Consider the argument that because (or if) sexual fidelity is not always a good thing in ordinary two-person heterosexual marriage, it should not be an ideal of marriage. What implications does this have for Vernallis's conclusions about bi-marriage requiring room for plural marriages?

FOURTEEN

Trans Women and the Meaning of "Woman"

Talia Mae Bettcher

In this chapter, **Talia Mae Bettcher** *argues that two dominant models of trans-sexuality—the "Wrong Body Model" and the "Transgender Model"—are mis-guided. She provides the beginnings of a third model, a multiple-meaning view, which allows those trans people who wish to fit into the binaries of "man" and "woman" to do so without being pathologized. She argues that instead of start-ing with the mainstream or dominant meanings of the gender terms "man" and "woman," we ought to take equally seriously their meaning and usage in trans communities. Thus, expressions such as "trans woman" do not simply refer to controversial instances of "woman," and being a trans woman is not a strange type of woman, but a woman, period. This approach enables trans people to avoid accommodating themselves to the dominant usages of gender terms; they thereby reveal, at the same time, the political hegemony of the way these binaries are understood.*

Talia Mae Bettcher is professor of philosophy at California State University, Los Angeles. Among her articles are "Evil Deceivers and Make-Believers: Transphobic Violence and the Politics of Illusion" in *Hypatia* (2007) and "Trans Identities and First-Person Authority" in Laurie Shrage, ed., *"You've Changed": Sex Reassignment and Personal Identity* (2009). She coedited *Hypatia's* special issue *Transgender Studies and Feminism: Theory, Politics, and Gender Realities* (2009). She is also the author of *Berkeley's Philosophy of Spirit: Consciousness, Ontology, and the Elusive Subject* (2007). This essay is reprinted, revised, with the permission of Talia Mae Bettcher and the American Philosophical Association, from *The American Philosophical Associa-tion Newsletter on Philosophy and Lesbian, Gay, Bisexual, and Transgender Issues* 10:2 (Spring 2011): 2–5.

There is a familiar view of transsexuality that speaks of women trapped inside male bodies and men trapped inside female bodies. On this view—let's call it the "Wrong Body Model"—transsexuality is a misalignment between gender identity and sexed body. At its most extreme, the idea is that one's *real* sex, given by internal identity, is innate. It is on the basis of this identity that one affirms that one has always *really* belonged to a particular sex and has a claim to the surgical procedures that bring one's body into alignment with one's identity.[1] However, one of the problems with this account is that it naturalizes sex and gender differences in a troubling way. Christine Overall remarks, for example, "On this theory, gender is reified, at least for some individuals. As a member of the social group 'women,' I find this idea frightening."[2] As a (trans) woman and as a feminist, I find this idea frightening, too.

There is another view, explicitly political, that has developed over the past twenty years, which says that trans people challenge the traditional binary between man and woman. Because, on this view, trans people do not fit neatly into the two categories "man" and "woman," mainstream society attempts to force trans people into this system in order to make it appear that there is a sharp dichotomy between men and women (when trans people show that there is not). The medical establishment is but one way in which society makes trans people disappear. The forces of oppression aim at invisibility, and the strategy of resistance is to come out and make oneself visible.[3] On this view—let's call it the "Transgender Model"—it is not trans people who are the problem but society itself. One of the difficulties with this account is that many trans people don't view themselves as "beyond the binary" at all but as either men or women. Thus, the Transgender Model seems to invalidate the self-identities of some transsexual people.[4]

Due to problems with both models, I am interested in providing an alternative account that relies on a multiple-meaning view (it is not quite yet a model rivaling the above two, but the beginnings of one). Specifically, my aim is to develop an account that accommodates trans people who see themselves as situated in a binary category while avoiding the pathologization and naturalization of gender identity.[5] I aim to probe deeper into the Wrong Body Model and the Transgender Model and to use the results of this investigation to eventually develop a model both more plausible and more accommodating to the experiences of trans people. In this essay, I make a few preliminary moves in that direction.

My claim is that we can understand the gender identities of (at least some) trans people who situate themselves in a binary category to stand in a "meaning conflict" with more mainstream conceptions of what and who they are. Both the Wrong Body Model and the Transgender Model err in adopting what I call a "single-meaning position"; that is, they assume that a gender term has one meaning only. This leads them to presuppose the dominant meaning of gender terms while erasing resistant ones. Moreover, by presupposing the dominant meanings, both accounts end up accepting the marginal status of trans people. This leads them to try to justify the view that trans people are who they say they are. This is a bad place to start trans theory and politics, I argue, since non-trans people do not need to justify who they say they are in the same way: to accept this asymmetry is to effectively yield political ground from the very beginning. On the contrary, once we accept resistant, subcultural meanings, there is no need to defend the self-identifying claims of trans people. Instead, the power relations by which trans identities are institutionally enforced from without become fully visible.

My work is informed by my own experience as a (white) trans woman living in the trans activist subcultures of Los Angeles. There we've developed different gender practices (including the use of gender terms such as "woman" and "man") that do not always accord with more mainstream ones. It is my methodological starting point to take such practices seriously. As philosophers, we often rely on our intuitions about language use. This case is no different. It is just that my knowledge concerns a subculture that may seem foreign to some. My starting point is that in analyzing the meaning of terms such as "woman," it is inappropriate to dismiss alternative ways in which those terms are actually used in trans subcultures; such usage needs to be taken into consideration as part of the analysis. This is certainly the case when the question precisely concerns whether a trans person *counts* as a woman or a man.

THE SINGLE-MEANING POSITION

Consider a form of transphobia I call "the basic denial of authenticity." A central feature of it is "identity enforcement," whereby trans women are identified as "really men" and trans men are identified as "really women" (regardless of how we ourselves self-identify). Often this kind of identity enforcement (particularly through pronoun use) occurs repeatedly and runs against the trans person's own frequent requests to be treated otherwise. It can appear in mundane interactions between a trans person and a store clerk (e.g., repeated references to a trans woman as "sir") to cases in which a trans person is "exposed" as "really a man/woman, disguised as a woman/man" and subjected to extreme forms of violence and murder.[6]

Now consider the self-identifying claim "I am a trans woman." Frequently, in dominant cultural contexts, the expression "trans woman" is understood to mean "a man who lives as a woman." Is this a case in which an individual merely misunderstands the meaning of the expression? No, because that meaning is accepted by many people and, indeed, often by the media, law enforcement agencies, domestic violence and homeless shelters, and so forth. Yet when I use that expression ("I am a trans woman") in trans subcultures, it simply *does not* mean that. So it is fair to say that identity enforcement does not merely concern whether a gender category expression applies to a person but also what an expression even means. The enforcer thinks (in the case of the trans woman) that the category "man" applies while the category "woman" doesn't. So the enforcer thinks that if "trans woman" is truthfully said, it can't possibly mean that the person is a woman (and isn't actually a man). Instead, it must mean that the person is merely *pretending* to be a woman. "Trans" would flag something involving pretense and would perhaps have the force of "fake" (as in "fake woman").

There are two ways one might respond to the enforcer. The first involves accepting the single-meaning position; the second involves accepting the multiple-meaning position. In the single-meaning position, "woman" is taken to have a fixed meaning; it is taken for granted that there is *one* concept. The dispute between the enforcer and the trans woman hinges on whether the concept "woman" applies or doesn't apply to her. On this view, "trans" would qualify the term "woman" (taken in the standard meaning) as a particular kind (one who had been assigned male sex at birth, perhaps, who became a woman later). The disagreement concerning the meaning of "transgender" ("fake" versus "transitional") would then hinge on the correct applicability of the term "woman" (or "female"). So to the enforcer, "trans woman" means "man living as a woman" while to the trans woman, "trans woman" means "woman assigned to the male sex at birth." This obviously raises difficult questions about how we ought to analyze terms such as "woman" and "man."

Most people would define "woman" as "adult female human being" and "man" as "adult male human being," thereby considering the differences as biological. Yet many feminists have argued that "woman" picks out a *social* kind, role, or status.[7] If so, that would require an alternative analysis of "woman." Of course, even if we accept a biological definition, we would still have the difficulty of defining "female" and "male" because there are multiple features involved in sex determination (including chromosomal karyotype, gonadal structure, genital structure, reproductive capacity, and hormone levels), not to mention cases in which these features come apart. For example, a person with complete androgen insensitivity syndrome will have XY chromosomes and internal male gonads but a female phenotype. In such cases it may be very difficult to tell whether the person is male, female, or neither. Indeed, it seems plausible that there is no fact of the matter in such cases.

One way to accommodate this multiplicity of features in the single-meaning position is to take gender terms as expressing family resemblance concepts. An analysis of such concepts would not involve specifying their necessary and sufficient conditions but listing their various overlapping features (or family resemblances). This list would include the multiple features above. And one could easily add more cultural features to the list as well, thereby addressing the feminist insight that there is a significant social component to gender categories like "woman."

With this type of account in hand, one could show that at least *some* trans women meet enough of the conditions required for the application of the category "woman." One might point to hormone levels, surgically altered genitalia, and so forth to defend a claim to womanhood. The enforcer, by contrast, might point to karyotype and birth genitalia in order to defend a verdict of manhood. In such a conflict, the stakes concern which criteria are to weigh more in applying "woman." Notably, however, this strategy does not yield the kind of certainty one wants to validate a trans person's identity claims; at bottom we probably have a factually undecidable question. A trans woman in this case is, far from being a paradigm of womanhood, merely a marginal instance.[8] Whether she counts as a woman would depend on pragmatic and political considerations (concerns about *how best* to draw the line or about which criteria to use and how much weight they have). One might argue that in such hard cases it is best to consider self-identification (rather than karyotype) as decisive.[9] But that decision is not determined by a simple analysis of the concept "woman" but by the view that, in difficult cases, it is better to let people self-identify rather than pick a gender term for them. Despite the fact that the Transgender Model seems to ignore the self-identities of some transsexual people, it actually seems *to get it right* in positioning a postoperative trans woman problematically with respect to the binary. If a postoperative trans woman counts as a woman at all, it is not because she is a paradigmatic woman but because, while problematically positioned with regard to the binary categories, she is, owing to political considerations, *best viewed* as a woman.

The case is grimmer when we consider trans women who have not undergone genital reconstruction surgery and, particularly, those who have not undergone *any* bodily changes at all (hormone therapy, "top surgery," and the like). In terms of governmentally issued IDs, a trans woman who has not undergone *any* medical intervention is likely to not be allowed any changes (so her documentation will consistently say "male"). In cases of public sex segregation, including public change-rooms, domestic violence shelters, homeless shelters, shared hospital rooms, jail and prison housing, and same-sex searches by police officers and other security officials, she is likely viewed as "really male." To be sure, gender presentation may help secure that claim to womanhood. But that might not be enough. Certainly, it seems very hard to see how a trans woman could claim to be a veritable woman on the basis of gender identity *alone* (without such presentation). It even seems unclear how she can be recognized as "in-between" or "problematically positioned" with regard to the categories as the transgender model says. On the contrary, she would probably count as a "man" (just as the enforcer claims). The problem with the single-meaning position, then, is that it does not appear to do justice to trans people's self-identifying claims about their gender.

SEMANTIC CONTEXTUALISM

We can understand this disagreement differently if we understand it in terms of a more robust conflict over the very meaning of the term "woman." Already we have had to allow that the term "trans" means something different to the enforcer and to the trans woman: to the former it means "fake" and to the trans woman it might mean "transitional."[10] In the multiple-meaning account I propose, the same is true in the case of the term "woman." In order to bring out the details of my account, I contrast it with a view that is superficially similar to it, namely semantic contextualism. According to semantic contextualism, the extension of "woman" changes depending on the context. Jennifer Mather Saul considers a definition according to which "X *is a woman* is true in a context C [if and only if] X is human and relevantly similar (according to the standards at work in C) to most of those possessing all of the biological markers of female sex."[11]

On this definition, the term "woman" operates as an indexical: its content is determined by the specific context in which it is used since the standards for correct application of the concept contextually vary. However, despite this variability of content, the meaning of "woman" is still fixed in the sense that there is a single rule-governed way in which the content is determined. By analogy, while the indexical "I" changes its referent when different people utter it, the indexical still has a fixed "meaning" insofar as the referent is determined by the rule: "'I' refers to the person who utters it."[12] Because of this, I consider contextualism to endorse a single-meaning position.

In the account Saul considers, there can be a context C1 in which the relevant similarity (for correct application of the term "woman") involves "sincerely self-identifying as a woman" and another context C2 in which the relevant similarity involves "having XX chromosomes."[13] Thus, whether a trans woman counts as a woman depends on which standards are relevant in a given context. One of the benefits of this view is that it makes it possible for *any* trans woman (regardless of whether she has undergone medical procedures) to count as woman. It does this by allowing for contexts in which the standard of self-identification is salient in determining correct applicability. It also has the advantage that when trans women count as women in context C1, they do so for metaphysical reasons, that is, for reasons owing to the semantics of the term "woman" and the facts that obtain in the world of that context rather than for political reasons or decisions.

Despite these advantages, however, the account has problems. One major worry Saul raises with this account is that while it allows a trans woman to assert something true when she says, "I am a woman," it trivializes her assertion. For the enforcer is *also* correct. Explaining the worry, Saul says:

> The reason the trans woman's claims are true, on the contextualist view, is simply that there are a huge range of acceptable ways to use the term "woman" and the trans woman's way of using "woman" isn't ruled out . . . What the trans woman needs to do justice to her claim is surely not just the acknowledgement that her claim is true but also the acknowledgement that her opponent's claim is false.[14]

A second, related worry is that in questions concerning whether a trans woman is a woman, there does not seem to be room for metaphysical disagreement. First, note that this question is going to have to be context sensitive. That is, the question whether a trans woman is a woman must be relative to a given context. So the question comes down to which standards are applicable in a given context (say, for example, the context of restroom use). But the only way to make sense of the dispute is to see it as a political one. That is, the only way to arbitrate the dispute is by appealing to political and moral facts. Meditating on the word "woman" is probably not going to yield an answer. As Saul explains, "On my view of 'woman,' I cannot argue that the lawmakers are making a mistake about how the word 'woman' works. But what I can do is argue that they are morally and politically wrong to apply the standards that they do."[15] While trans women can claim womanhood as a metaphysical fact (relative to a context), in cases of controversy over which standards apply in a particular context, their status as women is once again decided by the political rather than the metaphysical.

Consider two additional concerns. First, there are no similar consequences for most non-trans women because most non-trans women are going to count as women *on almost any reasonable standard* (e.g., self-identification, karyotype, and reproductive capacity). Because of this, there is far less room for somebody to truthfully deny her womanhood (relative to some context). And in cases of dispute over which standards are relevant, most non-trans women count as women regardless of which standards are selected. That is, the question whether non-trans women count as women need not be decided by political decision (largely because the need for a decision would not arise). Most non-trans women would count as women across all or most contexts ("transcontextually"). In this sense, most non-trans women would count as paradigms of "woman." By contrast, trans women would not count as women transcontextually since there are obvious contexts when they do not count (e.g., when karyotype is salient), and so there are cases in which it is controversial whether trans women are women (it is controversial, that is, which standards to apply).

The second, related worry is that there will be certain contexts in which some trans women *do* count as men due to the fact that they have an XY karyotype, or a penis, or testes. A variation of an example Saul considers is the use of "woman" and "man" by the American Cancer Society when testing for prostate cancer. If it is decided that men of a certain age should be tested, then all trans women who are of that age would count as men in that specific context. The difficulty is that the trans women might not count themselves as men at all in *any* context, or they might not consider their prostates to undermine their claims to (trans) womanhood. Indeed, I know many trans women, for example, who are content with their "male genitalia." However, many do not consider them *male* genitalia in the first place, but the sort of genitalia congruent with transgender femaleness. Similarly, I know many trans men who have no interest in phalloplasty and who consider their genitalia (transgender) *male* genitalia. Often, what happens is that the social meaning commonly associated with a body part is, in a subcultural context, completely changed. In light of this, a trans woman might reasonably complain that testing for prostate cancer cannot be viewed in terms of testing only men (or males). Such a claim, she might argue, is transphobic in that it erases the existence of trans women by treating them as nothing but (non-trans) men. Instead, once trans women are taken seriously, the testing ought to be framed in terms of testing both non-trans men and trans women of a certain age. More simply, the testing could be done on *people* with prostates. That testicles, penises, XY karyotype, and prostates count as *male* in the first place is precisely what trans subcultures are *contesting*.

THE MULTIPLE-MEANING POSITION

As there are different gendered practices in different cultural contexts, the conflict over meaning exhibits itself in the contrast between dominant or mainstream culture and trans subcultures. This includes the practice of gender attribution. So a trans person can count as "really a man" according to dominant cultural practices while counting as a woman in friendlier trans subcultures.[16]

It is a fact that in some trans community contexts, the meanings of gender terms (such as "woman") are altered and their extensions broadened. This is a two-step process. First, "trans woman" is taken as a basic expression, not as a qualification of the dominant meaning of "woman." This means that whether someone is a trans woman does not depend primarily on questions about the applicability of the terms "man" and "woman." Recall that on the enforcer's view, "trans woman" means "fake woman" because "woman" does not apply to the individual (despite her "trying to pass herself off" as one). By contrast, on the family resemblance view, being a "trans woman" depends on one's counting as a woman *simpliciter*. On that view, it seems that only some trans women would count (and marginally so); as we saw above, trans women would have at best a mixture of family resemblance features and so would at best count as difficult cases. As to contextualism, there are at least two possibilities. The first is that when a trans woman does not count as a woman she also does not count as a "trans woman" (i.e., transitional woman). The second is that "trans woman" means "fake woman" in some contexts and "transitional woman" in others.

When I say that "trans woman" is basic I mean that it does not route through the question whether "woman" applies or not; that is, the criteria for the correct application of "trans woman" do not depend on the criteria governing the application of "woman." The criteria are roughly equivalent to the criteria governing "male-to-female trans person." Crudely, a person counts as a trans woman if she was assigned to the male sex at birth, currently lives as a woman, and self-identifies as a trans woman (or as a woman).[17] This means that "trans woman" applies *un-problematically* and *without qualification* to *all* self-identified trans women. For example, even if a trans woman has no surgical or hormonal changes in her body (while "living as a woman"), she can still count as a paradigm instance of "trans woman."

The second step is that being a trans woman is a sufficient condition for being a woman. "Woman" is then taken to apply to *both* trans and non-trans women (where "non-trans woman" is a person who counts as a woman but who does not count as a trans woman). We thereby end up with entirely new criteria for who is a woman (specified in the criteria for counting a person as a trans woman). And we end up with an extension of "woman" different from the one that refers to only non-trans women (and to trans women who have just enough features to be argued into the category). Indeed, we end up with a notion of "woman" on which a trans woman is a paradigmatic (rather than a borderline) case. Thus, the expression "non-trans woman" operates in the way that "woman" used to operate. "Woman," by contrast, now operates in such a way that it applies to trans women unproblematically. The same shift can occur with terms such as "female" and "male." Subculturally, what *counts* as male and female is broadened. So we can have trans women/females with penises and trans men/males with vaginas (although it is not clear even that terms such as "penis" and "vagina" would always be used in such cases). In such a context, a vagina would not necessarily be female and a penis would not necessarily be male.

The worry with this account is that it also (like the semantic contextualist approach but in a different way) trivializes the claims of trans women (and men). One might say, "*Of course* you're a teapot, if by 'teapot' we mean 'human being.' And *of course* you're a woman if by 'woman' we mean 'man who lives as a woman.'" The account, however, is no verbal trick but tracks a difference between cultural practices of gender and the relation of these practices to the interpretation of the body and self-presentation. Whether one is viewed as a "gender rebel" depends on interpretation. If one were viewed as a man, then one's gender presentation would be read as a form of "gender bending" if one wears a skirt. But if the same person were viewed as a woman, then her gender presentation would not be construed as misaligned with her status. The key is whether genitalia are viewed as necessary to one's normative gender status. Since in trans subcultural practices they are not, then in trans subculture a normative social status is reassigned in a very real way: what would count as gender non-normative (in the mainstream) is entirely normative (in the subculture).

This affects the way sex is segregated. To be sure, in trans subcultural formations there is no control over institutions (such as jail housing and strip-search requirements). But there can certainly be control over the way bodies may be subject to different privacy and decency boundaries. For example, "normally" a man's chest is not subject to taboos against nudity, but in trans subcultures, it might be read as a woman's chest or at least a chest that is subject to such taboos.

So this conflict of meaning is undergirded by a conflict in gender practice. And this gendered practice informs (and is informed by) a basic conception (or narrative) of how the world is composed of various different types of gendered people. There is a genuine dispute concerning two competing visions of gender. And the taken-for-granted assumption that the dominant cultural view is the only valid one can be seen as a kind of cultural arrogance bolstered by institutional power.

Consider someone who lives as a woman, sees herself as a woman, and has been sustained in a subculture that respects her intimacy boundaries, only to find that she is subject to violence because she is "really male." She goes through mainstream institutions (hospitals, jails) where she is housed as male, searched as male, and turned away from a shelter as male. This invalidation is not only of an individual's self-identity but also of an entire life that has been lived with dignity in a competing cultural world.[18] My point is that this conflict over meaning is deeply bound up with the distribution of power and the capacity to enforce a way of life, regardless of the emotional and physical damage done to the individual.

The multiple-meaning view allows us to avoid the difficulties that plague the family resemblance account, for according to my view, all trans women count as women and do so paradigmatically, not marginally. And trans women count as women not owing to a political decision that arises as a consequence of their status as "difficult cases" but owing to the metaphysical facts that accord with the very meaning of the word "man" and "woman" *as deployed in trans subcultures*. That is, from the perspective of trans subculture, the enforcer who denies that a trans woman is a woman would be *making an error* every bit as much as if he were to call a non-trans woman a man.

My view also avoids some of the difficulties that plague semantic contextualism. This might not be obvious since the multiple-meaning account might seem to be merely a version of it, given that it seems I have only added a new context-relative standard. In particular, one might worry that this account is open to the following objections that suggest its similarity to semantic contextualism. First, while it is true that from the perspective of trans subculture the enforcer is incorrect in denying that a trans woman is a woman, it is also true that from the perspective of dominant culture he is correct. Since the trans woman cannot claim that the enforcer's view is false, her self-identity claim is trivialized. In this way, the account is similar to semantic contextualism. Second, the decision regarding which perspective to take (the dominant or the resistant one) is a political one. So whether a trans woman counts as a woman is again a political decision. By contrast, a non-trans woman will count as a woman regardless of such political decisions; there is an asymmetry. Again, this is a problem that also plagued semantic contextualism. Replying to these objections helps show how my account differs from contextualism. I start with the first objection.

First, a trans woman can reject the entire dominant gender system as based on false beliefs about gender and gender practices that are harmful and even oppressive.[19] That is, while she might agree that she is not a woman in dominant culture, she can reject, on philosophical grounds, the entire system of gender that dominant cultures circulate. To see this, consider the following analogy. According to an evangelical account of "sinner," I would count as one. But it does not follow that I am one even though I might meet all the criteria of the evangelical account. In rejecting the claim that I'm a sinner, I'm rejecting the entire picture of the world in which that term has its definition fixed. Similarly, a trans woman can reject as false the claim that she is "really a man" by rejecting the entire system of gender in which that claim is true (on the grounds discussed above). This move does not work in the case of semantic contextualism, of course, since a trans woman who fails to accept that there are some contexts (e.g., karyotype-salient contexts) in which she is not a woman is simply wrong. On the multiple-meaning view, a trans woman can say that she is a woman in *all* legitimate contexts because those contexts in which she is not a woman occur in a dominant culture that has been rejected for the reasons mentioned above. She can argue that the very belief in contexts in which she counts as a man (for example, a context in which genital structure is relevant) rests on the assumption that penises *are* male and is therefore grounded in a vision that marginalizes trans women from the start.

Once we accept this response, we obviously also need to recognize that the shift in usage is *far more radical* than the mere introduction of a new contextually relative standard. It makes more sense to speak of a transformation in meaning or concept than to speak of a new contextually relative standard. Put another way, there are actually two concepts and two meanings of "womanhood." The two concepts (and the two meanings) are related in that the latter is the result of changes performed on the former. One starts with a particular concept and then expands it, for example, to include something that wasn't included in it before. This makes sense if we think of gender concepts as determined, in part, by underlying gender practices and conceptions of what a gendered world is. Once practice and conception seriously change, one can plausibly argue that the concepts change as well.

This allows us to reply to the second objection: we need not think that trans women only count as women on the basis of a political decision while non-trans women do not. Given that we can now speak of two concepts of "womanhood" (a dominant one and a resistant one), the question, "Are trans women really women?" does not get off the ground. Instead, we need to disambiguate the two concepts. A preoperative trans woman might be a woman-R ("woman" in the resistant sense) but not as a woman-D ("woman" in the dominant sense). She would be a woman-R and fail to be a woman-D not as a matter of political decision but metaphysically speaking. The political question, instead, concerns *which* concept we should take seriously, and this is connected to the larger question regarding which gendered vision of the world (if any) we commit to. Notably, these questions do not arise because of trans women counting as "difficult cases." And these questions *also* confront non-trans women. A non-trans woman who self-identifies as a woman-D can been seen as taking up a political stance that marginalizes trans women by endorsing a transphobic gendered view of the world. Or a feminist project that proceeds with the concept women-D could be viewed as anti-trans. In my account, the worry is not that non-trans women alone count as paradigmatic women. The worry, rather, is that a non-trans woman can avail herself of a concept (that is part of a larger gendered vision of the world) that marginalizes trans women. When a non-trans woman accepts this concept about what counts as a woman-D, this is the effect of privilege, not of it being the case that she is a paradigmatic woman while trans women are not.

So the multiple-meaning account I have outlined is not a variant of semantic contextualism, for it can *solve* the problems that confronted that account. Insofar as it squares with the reality of trans subcultural usage while addressing these problems, it seems to be the best account for our purposes. And by taking the multiple-meaning account seriously, we can now see some basic problems with both the Wrong Body Model and the Transgender Model.

STARTING POINTS FOR TRANS STORIES

This distinction between the single-meaning and multiple-meaning positions reveals something important about starting points in trans politics. Consider the question (among some non-trans feminists) whether trans women do or do not count as women. In raising such a question, trans women are viewed as difficult cases with respect to the category "woman." In this way, the inclusion of trans women in the category of "woman" is something in need of defense (unlike the taken-for-granted inclusion of non-trans women). Notably, this asymmetry, which places the womanhood of trans women in jeopardy, arises only if we assume the dominant understanding of "woman." If we assume a resistant understanding of "woman," no question arises since trans women are exemplars of womanhood. While it might sometimes be a useful strategy to assume a dominant understanding of "woman" in order to defend the inclusion of trans women (as difficult cases), an unquestioned assumption of the dominant understanding is a bad starting point in trans politics and theory. It ignores resistant meanings produced in trans subcultures, thereby leaving us scrambling to find a home in the dominant meanings, those meanings that marginalize us from the get-go.

Consider an analogy. When I teach an undergraduate course in the philosophy of gender, I examine arguments that purport to show the immorality of "homosexuality."[20] I try to show students why these arguments are unsound because it is important to debunk the (bad) arguments that harm lesbian, gay, bisexual, and transsexual (LGBT) people. However, in a graduate seminar in LGBT studies, I would not engage this issue because this would play into the hands of a heterosexist cultural asymmetry that places homosexuality in moral jeopardy while leaving the moral status of heterosexuality unquestioned—a questionable political starting point.

Similarly, it is a questionable political starting point to accept as valid the dominant understanding of gender categories that situate trans people as, at best, problematic cases. To be sure, it might be a useful strategy to adopt the dominant understanding in particular situations. But I worry about any theory designed to illuminate trans oppression or resistance that unreflectively accepts a dominant understanding of categories.

In the Wrong Body Model, one counts as a woman-D (at best) to some degree and with qualification, so long as an appropriate authority recognizes one as possessing the right gender identity and one undergoes, as much as possible, a transformative process to conform to the dominant concept of woman. A dominant understanding of the category is presupposed and an asymmetry is tacitly accepted whereby trans membership in the category requires justification. As a consequence, trans people who do not value genital reconstruction surgery are taken not to have the right gender identity, and they are delegitimated as "mere" cross-dressers. A result of the Wrong Body Model's affiliation with dominant meanings is that trans people who live their lives with dignity in different subcultural worlds of meaning are simply kicked to the curb.

The Transgender Model also marginalizes trans people. It presupposes a dominant understanding of the categories "man" and "woman" under which trans people fit only marginally or as difficult cases not easily categorized. Here, a trans person would be—at most—legitimized as a (marginal) woman through somehow arguing that she meets enough of the dominant criteria of membership. Similarly, a trans person could be legitimized as "in-between" by showing under which dominant categories the person falls and does not fall. In both cases, the dominant understanding is presupposed and the position of trans people vis-à-vis the categories is justified by pointing to the criteria of membership in *these categories* (unlike non-trans people who are accepted as paradigmatic of the dominant categories and therefore in no need of justification). Once we take resistant meanings seriously, however, it is no longer clear why a trans person who sees herself as a woman is only marginally so at best. And it is far from clear why certain bodies count as in-between. Once trans men and trans women are taken as paradigms of concepts like "man" and "woman," it becomes doubtful that their bodies are problematic or in-between. Perversely, then, the Transgender Model, like the Wrong Body Model, ends up dismissing the lived lives of trans people.

FINAL REMARKS

As I have framed it, there is a different and expanded notion of womanhood in trans subcultures. Although I have spoken as if there is only one understanding, this is misleading because trans subculture is generally replete with multiple and sometimes conflicting accounts of gender. After all, it is hard to be trans and avoid thinking a little bit about what a woman is, what a man is, what gender is, and the like. Gender terms ("trans," "transgender," "transsexual," "woman," etc.) simply won't stay put. Instead of understanding "trans woman" as a subcategory of an expanded category of womanhood, trans women may *also* be conceptualized as in-between with respect to the traditional categories where they do not count as women *simpliciter* (i.e., as non-trans women) who *are* seen as part of the binary. It is just not obvious how trans people are going to understand the term "woman" when they self-identify (or do not self-identify) with that term.

Such variability is not an "anything goes" approach. In trans subcultures, the use of these gender terms is subject to some constraint. Moreover, there is a fairly common linguistic practice. Claims about self-identity in (some) trans subcultures have the form of first-person, present-tense avowals of mental attitudes (e.g. "I am angry at you").[21] This means that the shift in meaning involves not only an expansion of the category but also a change in use, reflected in the grammar of first- and third-person assertions. It is no longer merely a question whether the category is truthfully predicated of the object in question. Instead, there is a first-person, present-tense avowal of gender. For example, the claim "I am a trans woman" may be an avowal of a deep sense of "who one is" (that is, of one's deepest values and commitments). And as such, this is the prerogative of the first person alone where defensible avowals of gender are presumptively taken as authoritative. Fundamental to this practice is the idea that gender categories do not merely apply (or fail to apply) on the basis of objective criteria but are adopted for personal and political reasons. For example, the category "trans woman" might be avowed or disavowed because the category does not speak to "who they are," because it does not fit or feel right. Alternatively, it might be avowed or disavowed on solely political grounds. Insofar as such considerations are fundamental to the very practice of gender attribution in these contexts, it is easy to see why this is such a shift from the dominant practice of gender attribution, which operates independently of such considerations. The shift makes room for the multiplicity of meaning by allowing first-person authority over both gender avowal and the very meaning of the avowal.

The point I have defended in this essay is that accounts that take for granted singular, fixed meanings of gender terms cannot plausibly provide a liberatory theory. Not only do such accounts go wrong by failing to square with the actual reality of the situation, namely the fact that central terms are used in trans contexts in multiple and contested ways; they actually undermine trans self-identifications by foreclosing the possibility of this multiplicity. These accounts do so, in part, because they aim to justify the categorization of trans people by appealing to the dominant meanings. This, I have argued, implies an acceptance of a marginalizing asymmetry between trans and non-trans people from the beginning. To provide a satisfying account of trans phenomena, gender marginalization cannot be accepted as a starting point. The demand for justification and the demand for illumination are not the same. We need new accounts, I believe, that don't begin with a *justification* for trans self-identity claims but that follow subcultural practice in taking the presumptive legitimacy of such claims for granted. This requires *recognizing* the multiplicity of resistant meanings rather than *acquiescing* to the dominant culture's erasure of them. In my view, it is the only way to yield illuminating accounts of trans phenomena that do not proceed from transphobic starting points.[22]

NOTES

1. For some examples, see Henry Rubin, *Self-Made Men: Identity and Embodiment among Transsexual Men* (Nashville, Tenn.: Vanderbilt University Press, 2003), 150–51. Not all transsexuals have endorsed this view.

2. Christine Overall, "Sex/Gender Transitions and Life-Changing Aspirations," in *"You've Changed": Sex Reassignment and Personal Identity*, edited by Laurie Shrage (Oxford, U.K.: Oxford University Press, 2009), 11–27, at 14. The worry is that culturally determined gender behavior, beliefs, and attitudes are often very harmful to women. So it is troublesome to treat them as natural or as essential because it makes them seem unchangeable and even suggests that this "is how it is meant to be."

3. This account glosses over significant differences among thinkers such as Kate Bornstein, Leslie Feinberg, and Sandy Stone. See Kate Bornstein, *Gender Outlaw: On Men, Women, and the Rest of Us* (New York: Routledge, 1994); Leslie Feinberg, *Stone Butch Blues: A Novel* (Los Angeles: Alyson Books, 1993); Sandy Stone, "The *Empire* Strikes Back: A Posttranssexual Manifesto," in *Body Guards: The Cultural Politics of Gender Ambiguity*, edited by Julia Epstein and Kristina Straub (New York: Routledge, 1991), 280–304. However, this account captures the general idea frequently assumed in discussions of trans issues. For a more in-depth discussion of the transgender paradigm, see Talia Mae Bettcher, "Feminist Perspectives on Trans Issues," http://plato.stanford.edu/entries/feminism-trans, *Stanford Encyclopedia of Philosophy*, edited by Edward N. Zalta (accessed March 10, 2012).

4. It is possible for variants of the Transgender Model to appeal to the notion of an innate gender identity. However, social constructionism about gender has definitely figured very prominently in this model.

5. By "naturalization" I mean that something cultural is treated as "natural" (that is, as independent of culture). In this case, I mean that gender identity is treated as innate. By "pathologization" I mean that something nonpathological is treated as though it is pathological.

6. For a more detailed account of the basic denial of authenticity, see Talia Mae Bettcher, "Appearance, Reality, and Gender Deception: Reflections on Transphobic Violence and the Politics of Pretence," in *Violence, Victims, and Justifications*, edited by Felix Ó Murchadha (Bern: Peter Lang, 2006), 175–200.

7. For a detailed discussion of the sex/gender distinction in feminist theory, see Mari Mikkola, "Feminist Perspectives on Sex and Gender," plato.stanford.edu/entries/feminism-gender, *Stanford Encyclopedia of Philosophy*, edited by Edward N. Zalta (accessed March 10, 2012).

8. For this style of approach, see C. Jacob Hale, "Are Lesbians Women?" *Hypatia* 11:2 (Spring 1996): 94–121; John Corvino, "Analyzing Gender," *Southwest Philosophy Review* 17:1 (2000): 173–80; Cressida Heyes, *Line Drawings: Defining Women through Feminist Practice* (Ithaca, N.Y.: Cornell University Press, 2000); and Jennifer McKitrick, "Gender Identity Disorder," in *Establishing Medical Reality: Essays in the Metaphysics and Epistemology of Biomedical Science*, edited by Harold Kincaid and Jennifer McKitrick (Dordrecht: Springer, 2007), 137–48.

9. See Corvino, "Analyzing Gender," 179, for this type of view.

10. I say "might" because I argue below that different trans women can mean different things by the expression "trans woman."

11. Jennifer Mather Saul, "Politically Significant Terms and the Philosophy of Language: Methodological Issues," in *Out from the Shadows: Analytical Feminist Contributions to Traditional Philosophy*, edited by Sharon L. Crasnow and Anita M. Superson (Oxford, U.K.: Oxford University Press, 2012), 195–216, at 201. Saul does not accept this account but uses it to develop the methodological point that very different considerations can inform analysis when the term is politically significant. For example, in analyzing "woman," Saul thinks that it is important to do justice to a trans woman's self-identity claims. Such intuitions are not easily explained away as they might be when we are not thinking of politically fraught cases precisely because so much more

seems to hinge on them. She then suggests that this is relevant to philosophers of language more generally. My point is less methodological, although I'm obviously concerned to take the claims of trans women seriously. My proposed account does justice to trans women's self-identity claims in a way that a semantic contextualist account does not. Besides, I do draw on trans subcultures' use of gendered language as crucial data in my analysis of gender terms. Taking seriously how trans people use the terms is often overlooked in analyses of these types.

12. My formulation of the rule is obviously too simple. But that doesn't matter for my purposes.

13. Saul, "Politically Significant Terms," 201, 203.

14. Saul, "Politically Significant Terms," 209–10.

15. Saul, "Politically Significant Terms," 204.

16. I am largely indebted to C. Jacob Hale for this type of view. See his "Leather Dyke Boys and Their Daddies: How to Have Sex without Men and Women," *Social Text* 52/53, 16:3–4 (1997): 223–36.

17. It is also possible to recognize somebody as a trans woman despite the fact that she has not yet "transitioned" and does not yet self-identify as a woman (or a trans woman) in case this person eventually transitions. Explaining this is actually quite tricky, however, so I won't worry about it in this paper. I am grateful to Jennifer Saul for pressing me to think about this more.

18. The notion of "world" originates in the work of María Lugones. My understanding of cultural conflicts over meaning is informed by her view. See her "Playfulness, 'World'-Travelling, and Loving Perception," *Hypatia: A Journal of Feminist Philosophy* 2:2 (Summer 1987): 3–19.

19. Here are some examples. One false belief is that gender terms only have single (dominant) meanings. Another is that all people are either "naturally" male or female. And, of course, there are many others that involve treating cultural phenomena as "natural" manifestations of gender. By "harmful gender practices" I mean to include those practices that involve treating trans people with violence and those that are sexist and sexually violent. For a discussion of these practices see Talia Mae Bettcher, "Evil Deceivers and Make-Believers: Transphobic Violence and the Politics of Illusion," *Hypatia: A Journal of Feminist Philosophy* 22:3 (Summer 2007): 43–65.

20. I have worries about the term "homosexuality" as it derives from a sexological framework in which same-sex sexuality is viewed as pathological.

21. For development of this view, see my "Trans Identities and First Person Authority," in *"You've Changed": Sex Reassignment and Personal Identity*, edited by Laurie Shrage (Oxford, U.K.: Oxford University Press, 2009): 98–120.

22. Parts of this essay were published as "Without a Net: Starting Points for Trans Stories," *American Philosophical Association LGBT Newsletter* 10:2 (Spring 2011): 2–5. I am grateful to the editor, William Wilkerson, for his comments. I am also grateful for the extremely helpful feedback by Raja Halwani and Nicholas Power in finalizing this version of the essay. I would also like to thank Jennifer Saul for her (always) insightful and constructive comments.

STUDY QUESTIONS

1. Clearly explain the differences between the single-meaning position and the multiple-meaning position. Explain also the variations in the single-meaning position. Compare and contrast these views with your own prior and pretheoretical understanding of your own sex or gender.

2. What is semantic contextualism? How does it differ from the multiple-meaning view, and why does Bettcher reject the former and accept the latter?

3. Think, in relation to semantic contextualism, what would count as a context. That is, how are we to identify and individuate contexts? Is this a problem that, in addition to the problems mentioned by Bettcher mentions, threatens the view?

4. Should the usage of gender terms in trans communities be taken, as Bettcher argues, on a par with the usage in mainstream communities? Imagine what Bettcher would say in response to the answer, "No, it should not, because trans communities are minorities."

5. How would Bettcher reply to the "anti-social-constructivist" objection that nothing about the world is implied by a word just because people mean something specific by that word? For example, suppose that some people use "rabbit" to mean "squirrel." Should we take this meaning seriously? How would such cases differ from how gender terms are used in trans communities?

6. Is deciding to accept subcultural meanings as being as equally valid as mainstream meanings a political decision? Investigate how the answer to this question affects Bettcher's view, according to which "trans women count as women not owing to a political decision."

7. Trace the implications, for her overall argument, of Bettcher's claim, made at the end of her essay, that trans communities use gender terms in "multiple and contested ways."

FIFTEEN

Trans Persons, Cisgender Persons, and Gender Identities

Christine Overall

In this essay, **Christine Overall** *argues that trans people are not so different from cisgendered people (people whose gender aligns with their sex at birth). One might believe that trans people are different from cisgendered people and thus are the "other" because trans people violate some conventional beliefs about sex and gender (that sex and gender are fixed or constant and always line up with each other). But Overall argues that trans people and cisgendered people are similar to each other in that (1) both are immersed in, and must contend with, a "system of compulsory gender"; (2) both have to negotiate how to maintain the gender identities they decide to adopt or keep; (3) both have to face risks and dangers if they decide to not conform to social requirements about sex and gender; and (4) both have similar tendencies when it comes to the continuity or discontinuity of their sex and gender. So, for example, a trans person whose sex at birth is male but who always felt female despite "his" assigned male gender exhibits the continuity of feeling female, much like a woman whose sex at birth is female and who has always felt "female" exhibits the continuity of feeling female. Because trans and cisgendered people are not so different from each other, this might help, argues Overall, in reducing the "otherness" of trans people.*

Christine Overall is professor of philosophy and holds a University Research Chair at Queen's University, Kingston, Ontario. Her research and teaching are in the areas of feminist philosophy, bioethics, philosophy of religion, and ethical and ontological questions about sex and gender. Her book *Aging, Death, and Human Longevity: A Philosophical Inquiry* (University of California Press, 2003) won awards from the Canadian Philosophical Association and the Royal Society of Canada. She has recently published *Why Have Children? The Ethical Debate* (MIT, 2012). "Trans Persons, Cisgender Persons, and Gender Identities" is published here for the first time. © 2012, Christine Overall, who kindly gave permission for her new essay to be included in this volume.

Sex (female or male) and gender (girl/woman or boy/man) are among the most important characteristics of human persons. Most people assume that (1) a person's sex is fixed and invariant; (2) gender is constant, although some variations in gender display may be recognized and permitted; and (3) a person's gender is congruent with the person's sex at birth; that is, girls and women are female while boys and men are male. Individuals who conform to these assumptions constitute the usually unnamed, default norm not only statistically but also normatively: it is considered healthy, normal, and inevitable for one's sex to be fixed and invariant, one's gender constant, and one's gender congruent with one's sex at birth. These individuals are *cisgendered*. A cisgendered person, then, is someone whose gender identity and gender presentation are conventionally congruent with her or his sex assigned at birth (usually on the basis of genitalia).

The existence of trans[1] individuals challenges all these assumptions. A trans person is someone whose gender identity (and usually[2] also gender presentation) is not conventionally congruent with the sex assigned at birth. A trans person's gender is not consistent with the individual's sex at birth; hence, (3) is violated. If the trans person undertakes significant bodily modifications, then (1) is violated. And (2) is violated because the person may start out, at least as a small child and sometimes into adulthood, with a gender presentation congruent with the sex at birth but then change gender presentation.

Because trans persons violate some or all of assumptions (1), (2), and (3), people generally believe that trans persons are very different from cisgendered persons and that trans persons' relationship to the characteristics of sex and gender is very different from that of cisgendered persons. Cisgendered persons—whose default status ensures that they are seldom labeled or identified as such—are presumed to be, with respect to their sex and gender, healthy, normal, unconflicted, and well-functioning. A trans person, by contrast, is thought to be someone who has a problem; with respect to their relationship to their sex and gender they are not healthy; they are abnormal, conflicted, and ill-functioning. The belief that there is this wide gulf between trans and cisgendered persons may be part of the basis for the "othering" of trans persons and the discrimination and oppression inflicted upon them.

This paper aims to dispel this belief about the alleged differences between cisgendered and trans persons by demonstrating the ways in which, with respect to their gender and sex identities, trans persons and cisgendered persons are similar. In making this case, I am not saying (1) that all trans persons—or all cisgendered persons, for that matter—are alike; (2) that there are no significant differences between trans persons and cisgendered persons; or (3) that social and political contexts are the same for both trans and cisgendered persons. I also refuse (4) to speak for trans persons, (5) to conflate trans persons with stereotypical male and female, and (6) to make trans identities a matter of medical illness.[3] Instead, this discussion arises, in part, from my thinking about what it means for *me* to be cisgendered, and my determination to call into question the only apparent normalcy of my own cisgenderism. I have attempted to do this by deliberately rejecting the notion of cisgenderism as the default condition and by trying to see some of the ways in which cisgendered people (whether they recognize these ways or not) are like trans persons with respect to how sex and gender operate in our lives. It is here, and here alone, that I want to claim that there is a significant general similarity between trans and cisgendered persons.

In order to see this similarity, it is first necessary to recognize that both gender and sex are social identities. By "social identity" I mean a shared understanding of who an individual is that is derived from the individual's membership in a group category.

GENDER AS SOCIAL IDENTITY

While the rigidity with which gender stereotypes is held continues to decline, there can be no denying that there are still gender-based differences in how we are expected to present ourselves and to act. Gender-validating forms of self-presentation include, first, forms of bodily styling, such as tattoos, make-up, hair (including length, color, condition, placement, and style), shaving, waxing, tanning, muscle building, the cultivation of "fitness," and various forms of so-called cosmetic surgery. Second, they include certain ways of dressing, talking, walking, sitting, running, throwing, and dancing.

Gender is socially required to be deeply definitive of each of us. Because of — and in some cases regardless of — our individual bodily configurations, a clear gender identification and presentation are socially compulsory; one does not have much, if any, choice about *whether* to have a gender, although one may have some choice about what kind of gender to have. Moreover, I think it is accurate to say that there are only two recognized, approved, and permissible genders in this culture. As everyone knows, gender is socially defined in terms of its association with sex (usually genitalia and so-called secondary sex characteristics like breasts and body hair distribution). The girl/woman gender is associated with female genitalia and secondary sex characteristics; the boy/man gender is associated with male genitalia and secondary sex characteristics. Sometimes, especially when people are trying to be what they think of as scientific, gender is defined in terms of its association with specific kinds and combinations of hormones or chromosomes. But in everyday practice, gender is mostly likely to be associated with relatively easily perceived genitalia and secondary sex characteristics. In that context, only two sets of genitalia and secondary sex characteristics are fully acknowledged and legitimated in popular culture in the West. Despite postmodern talk about multiple genders and doing gender in a thousand variations, and despite the fact that people do enact their gender in a variety of different ways depending on culture, socioeconomic class, race, religion, age, and sexuality, those enactments of gender are almost all categorizable into just two recognized and recognizable gender classes.[4]

Thus, if you look, for example, in any university classroom, any business meeting, any grocery store, any playground, you will quite readily be able to classify almost every single person as belonging to one gender class or the other. There is no conceptual, social, or material room in human society for a nongendered person. (An infant dressed only in a diaper is insufficiently gendered; hence the rush to dress the baby in supposedly gender-appropriate colors, symbols and styles.) And without a gender that is considered socially coherent and identifiable, one is almost unintelligible. We live in a culture of compulsory gender. Gender is not optional.

SEX AS SOCIAL IDENTITY

While gender is clearly a social identity, it is often thought that sex is thoroughly biological. But the very fact that there are such processes as sex transitions provides evidence that sex is indeed a social identity. It is by means of social processes, not biological determinism, that an individual's sex gets defined in historically specific ways and becomes almost always the most significant way of categorizing her or him (indeed, a necessary condition for personhood itself),[5] and that the genitalia are seen as representative or even determinative of who and what an individual is. In reality, however, what sex is thought to be varies from one society to another and one historical era to another; there is no ahistorical, acultural concept of sex. What it means to have a sex or to belong to a particular sex varies depending on which concatenation of body components—external genitalia, internal reproductive organs, hormones, gametes, or chromosomes—is believed to have metaphysical significance for sex identity.[6] For example, sometimes the sex identity of athletes who consider themselves to be female on the basis of their genitalia and participate in athletic events as women is challenged on the grounds that their chromosomes indicate that they are "really" male. In addition, what it means to have a sex also depends upon cultural understandings of the structure of and relationships between female and male genitalia. For example, Thomas Laqueur has shown that before the eighteenth century, males and females were thought to be two different forms of just one sex. Women were believed to have the same genitalia as men, with men's genitalia being outside the body and women's inside the body.[7] And what it means to have a sex also depends on how many sexes are assumed to exist, what the relationships among those sexes are thought to be (whether, for example, they are taken to vary as a matter of degree or of kind),[8] and whether or not the culture recognizes or denies the existence of genital and other physiological configurations that do not conform to the prevailing male or female social norm. Thus, having a sex can have more than one meaning in different times and places, and the significance of the sex that one has is open to social alteration. This is not to deny that sex is material or physical, or that one's sex may be experienced as real, demanding, and not subject to one's will. It is just to say that belonging to a particular sex is culture-specific.

Moreover, in the twenty-first century, one's sex can now be changed, and the ability to change it is the result of social factors, not biological ones. Thanks to scientific and medical research, genitals and breasts can be surgically enhanced, rebuilt, or removed altogether. So-called secondary sex characteristics such as hair distribution and muscle mass can be modified chemically via hormones. The body structure can be reshaped via fitness and nutrition regimes and even through the surgical reconstruction of bones.

A transition from one sex to another is, of course, undertaken not for its own sake but in order to enhance and express the person's gender identity by making the body more closely match the individual's sense of gender. Thus, an individual labeled a boy at birth may both identify and want to publicly present as a woman; the individual may then undergo surgery to create breasts or alter the genitalia to cohere with that felt sense of self. Individuals who undertake sex or gender transitions show, perhaps more than anyone else, that in important ways belonging to a sex is a social, not a biological, phenomenon; that one's sex is not inevitably fixed and immutable; and that one's genitalia (or any other body characteristics) do not inevitably represent, let alone determine through biological inevitability, who or what one is.

ACQUIRED AND ASPIRATIONAL IDENTITIES

For the purposes of my argument, I suggest that there are, generally speaking, two kinds of social identities. I call them "acquired identities" and "aspirational identities." An acquired identity is a notable personal characteristic that has been permanently ascribed or earned and requires no further action on the part of its possessor in order to be maintained. For example, one of my acquired identities is being the birth mother of two children. I gestated and delivered them, and whatever may happen in their lives or mine, I remain their birth mother.[9]

Other identities are not acquired but are ongoing and what I call "aspirational." An aspirational identity is a notable personal characteristic such that, if its possessor values it, she must maintain and reinforce it through ongoing action. One example is the identity of being a mother, not in the sense of having gestated and given birth but in the social sense of caregiver for one or more children. The individual who values her identity as a mother in the social sense must continue to engage in what are considered culturally appropriate mothering behaviors. If she fails to do so, she is in danger of losing her identity, as when people say, "She's no mother" or "She's not a real mother." Another example is being an artist. Being an artist is an aspirational identity (in most cases) because if the would-be artist does not practice her art and continue to generate works of art during her lifetime, people are likely to say, "She was an artist, but she gave it up." With respect to aspirational identities, their possessor is always at risk during her lifetime, if not of failure, then at least of inadequacy; the possessor of an aspirational identity must always and continually prove herself.[10]

To say that an identity is aspirational, however, is not to say that it is necessarily a matter of free choice. In a given culture, some aspirational identities may be compulsory, some may be voluntary, and others may be forbidden. These requirements and constraints may be enforced in the usual ways—through training, validation, reinforcement, the absence of other options, ridicule, shaming, and abuse. In addition, to say that an identity is aspirational is not to say that it is necessarily experienced as being freely chosen. One may aspire, throughout a period of one's life, to a particular identity while perhaps feeling compelled to do so. Moreover, to say that an identity is aspirational leaves open and does not resolve many further empirical issues that are specific to particular individuals, including, for example, how a particular aspiration is acquired, when a particular aspiration is acquired, whether the aspiration is held for a long time or a short time in one's life, how firmly and with how much commitment the aspiration is held, and how difficult it may be to act on the aspiration.

GENDER AS ASPIRATIONAL IDENTITY

In my sense of the term, gender is an aspirational identity. In that respect, it is the same for everyone. I call gender "aspirational" to acknowledge that gender identity is never complete and never finished; it is something that one renews each day. As Judith Butler convincingly shows, gender is an ongoing performance;[11] it is not a fixed characteristic, and certainly not a finished achievement, but rather an identity that can easily be called into question if one does not maintain it. Hence there are familiar accusations such as, "He's not a real man" and traditional prescriptions such as, "A true woman would. . . ."

One can aspire to exemplify a gender through the aforementioned bodily styling, self-presentation, and gendered activities, all of which must be ongoing for gender identity maintenance.[12] One learns how to aspire to one's gender through cultural tutelage that includes role models, advertising, media representations, parental socialization, peer pressure, gender-segregated activities and facilities, and so on. Gender is something at which one must work. Sometimes the work is pleasurable, sometimes it is not pleasurable, but it is always a matter of labor directed towards a goal that forever recedes from one's reach: the goal of being—of exemplifying—a fully appropriate manifestation of one gender or the other.

At least in theory it is possible to aspire to either of the two genders—the gender socially defined as congruent with one's sex or the gender socially defined as incongruent with it. What one aspires to may or may not match the social expectation of what a person with one's particular body should aspire to, and it may or may not match the gender assignment one was given at birth. A cisgendered person is someone who aspires to a gender identity that is socially considered to be consistent with her or his genitalia of birth and so-called secondary sex characteristics. A trans person is someone who does not aspire to a gender identity that is socially considered to be consistent with her or his genitalia of birth and so-called secondary sex characteristics.

Although I don't have room here to do justice to the subtleties of her ideas, I take from Talia Mae Bettcher the idea that every one of us, whether trans or cisgendered, has first-person authority (FPA) with respect to our gender. That is, all persons have the right to say what their gender is; other people are not entitled to determine one's gender or to tell another person that she is mistaken about her gender. As Bettcher explains, this is primarily a moral claim, not an epistemic one.[13] That is, it is not a statement about how we know what gender we are but rather a statement about who is entitled to legislate on our gender. One's gender is not so much something about which one has infallible knowledge[14] as it is something over which one has moral authority. That is, our FPA with respect to our gender is concerned with what we want ourselves to be, what we aspire to be. No one, I believe, is entitled to assign or impose a gender upon another functioning, autonomous human being. For this reason we should therefore assume that the assignment of gender to infants is at best provisional until the child reaches the age of being able to decide for herself or himself.[15]

TRANS AND CISGENDER: NOT SO DIFFERENT

The main contention of this essay is that with respect to sex and gender identities, trans persons and cisgendered persons are similar. We are now in a position to see what those similarities are. I shall describe four areas of similarity and then respond to what might seem to be an impediment to my claim about the similarity between trans persons and cisgendered persons.

1. Immersion in the System of Compulsory Gender

Even though some trans and cisgendered persons may be critical or skeptical of gender conventions, all trans and cisgendered persons are, of social necessity, deeply immersed in the system of compulsory gender. That immersion means that both trans and cisgendered persons are expected to validate their gender identity through all the means mentioned earlier—bodily styling; ways of dressing, talking, walking, sitting, running, throwing, and dancing; and gendered activities considered appropriate for men or for women.

In addition, both cisgendered and trans persons may in some cases decide to seek surgery in order to perform their gender identity (although the conditions, requirements, and criteria of access to such treatments are not the same for trans and cisgendered persons). For example, some trans people seek surgery in order to remove their genitalia or to surgically develop genitalia conventionally associated with persons of the gender to which they aspire. Similarly, some cisgendered women seek surgery to enlarge the size of their breasts or to reshape their genitalia (an operation called labiaplasty) in ways they believe to be desirable for authenticating and enhancing their membership in the gender to which they aspire. And some cisgendered men seek treatments and processes to enlarge their genitals. Moreover, some cisgendered and trans persons may seek hormonal treatments of various sorts in order to enhance their experiences or confirm their membership in the gender to which they aspire. For example, cisgendered women may use, at different times in their lives, contraceptive pills and so-called hormone replacement therapy. Cisgendered men may take testosterone. Trans men may take androgens and trans women may use estrogens and progestogens.

The growing demand by both cisgendered and trans persons for substances, operations, and processes to change the genitalia and secondary sex characteristics suggests that although sex is conventionally an identity that is *acquired* at birth (or even before, if fetal sex is identified through prenatal diagnostic tests) on the basis of visible genitalia, it is nonetheless becoming, in the service of achieving gender aspirations, more and more malleable for both trans and cisgendered persons. There is therefore reason to believe that sex is becoming, at least for some cisgendered and trans persons, an *aspirational* identity.

2. Constraints and Opportunities

Both trans and cisgendered persons also experience constraints upon, and find opportunities for, their gender aspirations. The constraints exist because, as I noted earlier, there are only two socially recognized, approved, and permissible genders in this culture, and their expression is still regulated. The opportunities arise, first, because trans people, and some cisgendered people, have the motivation, courage, and creativity to enact gender in ways that are not recognized, approved, and permissible from the point of view of mainstream society, and second because there are more and more cracks in the once-rigid façade of gender as a social institution, cracks that make gender nonconformity possible.

By definition, cisgendered persons aspire to a gender considered congruent with the socially recognized sex of their physical body. But the borderlines of what is considered congruent are still heavily patrolled and are inflected by expectations related to age, race, sexuality, and class. At the same time, with the relaxation over the last half-century of gender stereotypes, cisgendered persons have some freedom as to how they exemplify their gender; what kinds of gendered bodily styling, self-presentation, and activities they engage in; and what kind of man or woman they want to be.

Similarly, trans persons also have constraints and opportunities. For example, in addition to all the gender constraints that cisgendered people experience, some trans persons may be expected and required by the medical establishment to follow particularly strict gender norms considered consistent with the genitalia of members of the other sex in order to gain access to the medical treatments some may desire.[16] Moreover, trans persons' gender aspirations often confront what Bettcher calls "identity enforcement," a form of transphobia that explicitly denies and rejects the trans person's deeply felt identity in favor of what the enforcer believes is the individual's "real" identity.[17]

In terms of opportunities, some trans persons choose to identify explicitly as trans women or trans men, identities that are validated in their own right in trans subcultures and are not mere "qualification[s] of the dominant notion[s]" of woman or man.[18] Other trans persons reject what they see as the limitations associated with both genders as they are conventionally understood. Patrick Califia, for example, describes himself as "Not wanting to be female, but not having much enthusiasm for the only other option our society offers."[19] Similarly, Kate Bornstein says that she "identif[ies] as neither male nor female." She writes, "I know I'm not a man—about that much I'm very clear, and I've come to the conclusion that I'm probably not a woman either, at least not according to a lot of people's rules on this sort of thing."[20]

Similarly, a few trans persons may simply aim not to live as a member of one gender or another, not to exemplify a socially authorized version of manhood or womanhood, not to be gendered at all. In doing so, they challenge the nonoptional nature of the bi-gender system. A recent example is Australian norrie mAy-Welby [*sic*], who requested and received from the state of New South Wales an official certificate with the description "sex not specified." mAy-Welby was registered as male at birth, but at age 23 began hormone treatment and construction of a vagina. But mAy-Welby did not feel comfortable living as a female, ceased treatment, and decided to live as neither male nor female.[21] (mAy-Welby's change in legal status was subsequently revoked.)[22]

3. Dangers

These examples show that, as one would expect in a compulsory gender regime, both trans and cisgendered persons are subjected to constraints on their gender aspirations. At the same time, some, whether trans or cisgendered, seek and find ways to go beyond rote conformity. Nonetheless, most cultures make acting on one's gender aspirations relatively easy and safe for cisgendered persons and relatively difficult and dangerous for trans persons. So one obvious important difference between the situations of a cisgendered person and a transgendered person is that the trans person is much more likely to be at risk of harm for the sake of her gender aspirations than the cisgendered person is.

At least part of the reason for these risks is that there is a prevailing social requirement that gender identity should reflect and reveal genitalia (even while genitalia are kept hidden). Trans people violate one of the most fundamental social rules: that self-presentation must reflect genitalia of birth. Gender self-presentation conventionally functions to signal genitalia. As Bettcher puts it, "gender presentation literally *signifies* physical sex. If it is true that trans people who 'misalign' gender presentation with sexed body are deceivers or pretenders, then those who 'correctly' align presentation with body tell the truth."[23] Hence, whereas cisgendered persons are regarded as revealing and acting upon their "real" identity, trans persons may be regarded as deceptive and deliberately passing as someone they are not. The result is that they may be "punished" by bigots, identity enforcers who wish to push trans persons into what they (the bigots) regard as appropriate self-presentation and behavior.

The dangers trans persons face are serious. The risks and the realities of psychological and physical harm for the sake of one's gender choices make some gender aspirations much more difficult than others and hence require much greater courage and resilience. Yet it is also important to notice that some cisgendered persons may face comparable dangers. These include cisgendered women who reveal "too much" of the body, especially in cultures where women are expected to remain entirely concealed, cisgendered women who present as very "masculine," and cisgendered men who fail to present as sufficiently stereotypically "masculine." In different contexts, the extent of the risk of danger may depend not only on whether one is trans or cisgendered but on what sort of gender one aspires to and the material, political, and social conditions of the culture in which one lives. In most cases, the higher the degree of deviance and nonconformity, for both cisgendered and trans people, and the higher the extent of social pressure for gender conformity, the more danger the individual may incur.

4. Continuity and Discontinuity

It may appear that a difference between the cisgendered person and the trans person has to do with the continuity or discontinuity of their gender aspirations. There is continuity, it might be thought, in the cisgendered person's gender aspirations, whereas there is discontinuity in the gender aspirations of the trans person, who changes her gender presentation and behavior.

This belief is mistaken. In many cases both the continuity of cisgendered people's lives and the discontinuity of trans people's lives may be only apparent. Both cisgendered and transgendered persons may vary, over the course of their lives, in terms of their affiliation to their gender as assigned on the basis of their sex at birth and of their aspirational gender. For example, while some trans persons adopt their new gender identity part way through life, there are others who say they have always felt, or have felt for a long time, that the gender assigned to them on the basis of their genital characteristics was a mistake. They remember a lifetime of aspiring to and acting on a gender that is not consistent with the gender stereotype imposed on persons with their genitalia. Hence, ostensibly new manifestations of their gender are the result of aspirations that have been growing and developing for many years. For them, there is no discontinuity in aspirational gender, and their rejection of their assigned gender does not represent a change in aspiration but rather their taking action on their aspirational gender, which has not changed.

On the other hand, while some cisgendered persons never question the nature of their gender affiliation, others do. A cisgendered woman who does not reject her assigned label of "woman" may nonetheless change, maybe even substantially, her womanly aspirations. That is, over the course of her life, she may make big changes in the kind of woman she wants to be. I think this is the case, for example, with many women whose lives were profoundly changed by feminism at various points in its history. There have also been cases where persons with the assigned gender of woman have chosen to go off to war, to have a sexual relationship with a woman, to work in a "man's" occupation, or to get an education—all behaviors that were incompatible with their assigned gender at the time and therefore represent a kind of gender discontinuity, even when such individuals did not cease to identify as women. Thus, there may be continuity in some trans persons' gender aspirations and discontinuity in some cisgendered persons' gender aspirations.

The degree of affiliation and willingness to devote time and effort to one's gender may also vary. Both trans persons and cisgendered persons may vary, over their lifetimes, in the extent to which their gender is or is not central to their sense of self. While gender appears to be deeply defin-itive of human persons, not all of us regard our gender as authoritative statements about ourselves. Jacob Hale remarks, for example, that "moral and political values provide a better core for my sense of self than gen-dered subjectivity."[24] Ann Snitow says that feminism freed her from making gender her central affiliation. She remembers thinking, "Now I don't have to be a woman anymore. I need never become a mother. Being a woman has always been humiliating, but I used to assume there was no exit. Now the very idea of 'woman' is up for grabs. 'Woman' is my slave name; feminism will give me freedom to seek some other identity alto-gether."[25]

So cisgendered and transgendered persons do not necessarily and always differ, as groups, with respect to the continuity or discontinuity of their gender aspirations or the degree of their commitment to their gen-der.

BIOLOGICAL INFLUENCES ON GENDER IDENTITY

I now turn to what might seem to be an impediment to my claim about the similarities with respect to sex and gender between cisgendered per-sons and trans persons. Trans persons, it might be argued, are specially caused by their hormones or their brains to be trans. Trans persons re-ceive conflicting messages (one message from the configuration of their genitalia but another message from the brain, their hormones, and so on), and thus they are biologically motivated to act upon gender aspirations (even to the extent of modifying their bodies) that are incompatible with what their genitalia of birth would normally indicate.

However, the role of the body with respect to our gender aspira-tions—of any sort—is quite complex. We are embodied beings. How we are in the world, and the kinds of ways we feel, are at least in part a product of our bodies—their physical structure, their hormones, their capacities, their muscular development, their state of immaturity or ma-turity, their health, their impairments, and so on. Our bodies are shaped by our environments, and we also participate in shaping our bodies. Our bodies certainly give us certain proclivities, tendencies, wants, needs, weaknesses, and strengths. This fact applies to trans and cisgendered persons alike.

Since gender is thought to take its meaning from biological sex, our gender aspirations—whether we are trans or cisgendered—are perhaps reinforced by some bodily cues and undermined by others. What one aspires to is likely to be partly a function of what one's body is like and partly a function of one's socialization, always remembering that human beings are not merely passive recipients of socialization but are active participants with varying degrees of choice and autonomy. For if, as feminists have argued for at least four decades, gender is acquired or learned, then our bodies do not directly give us gender, although in a particular social context they may well make one gender easier and more comfortable to acquire than the other. On an ontological level, there is no fixed reality of gender. Because gender is aspirational, one is always working at it, and one is never finished with it. Gender is always a matter of doing, not just being.

I suggest that if hormones and brain structures influence gender aspirations in trans people, then they also influence gender aspirations in cisgendered people. It is an error to suppose that trans people are the objects of physiological influences but cisgendered people are not. True, trans people may experience conflicting messages from their bodies. But so do some cisgendered people, as is indicated by their varying affiliations to their gender identity, the changes in the degree to which gender is central to their lives, and their willingness to deviate from gender conformity. Cisgendered people who receive conflicting messages may choose to act on them (e.g., by engaging in certain activities considered not coherent with their assigned sex), or they may choose to ignore them. But it is a mistake to suppose that only trans people deal with conflicting messages about their sex and gender and that cisgendered persons never do.

I regard it as legitimate to ask empirical questions about why people—both trans *and* cisgendered—have the gender aspirations they have. Why, for example, are some cisgendered women conventionally feminine while other cisgendered women are not? Questions about the causes of gender aspirations are, however, empirical, and hence they are not ones that I have the expertise, experience, or evidence to answer. Nonetheless, I suspect that discovering the causes of gender aspirations, whether in trans or in cisgendered persons, would be no more and also no less complex than explaining the causes of other significant and life-defining human wants and aspirations. Why do some women deeply want to be mothers and others just as wholeheartedly do not? Why do some people feel called—sometimes very early on in life—to artistic pursuits, to athletics, or to spiritual activities? Why are some people ambitiously entrepreneurial whereas others are uncompetitive and nonmaterialistic?

Hence, I regard the claim that trans persons' gender aspirations are caused by specific brain or hormone patterns as inadequate, even if partially true, to show that trans persons' sex and gender identities are very different than those of cisgendered persons since I see no reason to suppose that cisgendered persons' gender aspirations are entirely independent of their brains and hormone patterns. Likewise, both trans and cisgendered persons are the products of gender socialization, while at the same time they must be recognized as agents, not mere patients, in the expression of their gender aspirations.

CONCLUSION

I have attempted to demonstrate what I consider to be the similarities, with respect to gender and sex identities, between trans persons and cisgendered persons. Contrary to the assumption that cisgendered and trans persons are very different and that hence to be trans is to be abnormal, disordered, and unhealthy, an examination of the gender aspirations of cisgendered and trans persons reveals significant similarities. It is because of the very nature of gender—a "nature" that is, I assume, mostly social—that there are so many important resemblances between trans and cisgendered persons.

Cisgenderism should not be considered the default human condition, a condition so obvious and normal as to be unnamable, and cisgendered people ought not to feel superior about their relationship to gender, for they are engaging in gender aspirational activities that are similar to those of trans persons. I hope that making this case helps to reduce the "othering" of trans persons by cisgendered persons and hence is a small step toward ending the oppression of trans people.[26]

NOTES

1. Although there is a linguistic distinction between "transgender" and "transsexual," I use the general term "trans" to refer to all individuals who go through transitions in sex or gender. I use the term "transition" to refer to the changes trans people undergo. Bobby Noble writes, "The pedantic distinction between 'transgender' and 'transsexual' cannot hold, especially for female to male transsexual men for whom surgeries are always already incomplete" ("Our Bodies Are Not Ourselves: Tranny Guys and the Racialized Class Politics of Embodiment," in *Trans/Forming Feminisms: Trans-Feminist Voices Speak Out*, edited by Krista Scott-Dixon [Toronto: Sumach Press, 2006], 95–104, at 102, note 2). That is, not all trans persons undertake surgery, and even when they do, not all trans persons follow the same path. Trans people vary in their choices about the types, degrees, and extent of body modification they want to undergo.

2. I say "usually" because for reasons such as danger and oppression trans persons sometimes do not self-present in the gender with which they identify.

3. See Jacob Hale, "Tracing a Ghostly Memory in My Throat: Reflections on FTM Feminist Voice and Agency," in *"You've Changed": Sex Reassignment and Personal Identity*, edited by Laurie J. Shrage (New York: Oxford University Press, 2009), 43–65; and Jacob Hale, "Suggested Rules for Non-Transsexuals Writing about Transsexuals, Transsexuality, Transsexualism, or Trans_____" (http://sandystone.com/hale.rules.html; accessed February 13, 2012).

4. Miqqi Alicia Gilbert, "Defeating Bigenderism: Changing Gender Assumptions in the Twenty-First Century," *Hypatia* 24:3 (2009): 93–112.

5. Naomi Scheman, "Queering the Center by Centering the Queer," in *Feminists Rethink the Self*, edited by Diana Tietjens Meyers (Boulder, Colo.: Westview Press, 1997), 124–62, at 132–33 and 140.

6. John Stoltenberg, *Refusing to Be a Man: Essays on Sex and Justice* (Portland, Ore.: Breitenbush Books, 1989), 30.

7. Thomas Laqueur, *Making Sex: Body and Sex from the Greeks to Freud* (Cambridge, Mass.: Harvard University Press, 1990).

8. See, for example, Marilyn Frye, *The Politics of Reality: Essays in Feminist Theory* (Freedom, Calif.: Crossing Press, 1983), 25, 38.

9. I am not claiming to be infallible about this identity. It is possible that I could learn that one of my children had been accidentally switched after birth with another infant. My point, instead, is that acquired identities attach to a person because of *past* actions, either her own or those of others, and there is nothing she need (or even can) do now in order to maintain those identities.

10. In some cases we can also distinguish between descriptive and normative aspirational identities, between being an *A* and being a good *A*. Being a professor is an aspirational identity; having passed all educational requirements and acquired an academic position, one must still work to maintain the identity by doing the job of professor with a minimum of competence. Being a good professor requires additional work to achieve excellence in teaching and research. Both being an *A* and being a good *A* require work in order to achieve and maintain the identity. If one slacks off enough, one will not only not be a good *A* but may even lose being an *A* altogether. However, in the case of gender as an aspirational identity, what matters for one's social survival is to succeed in earning and sustaining the descriptive label "woman" or "man." The terms "*good* woman" and "*good* man" (unlike "good professor") do not suggest special expertise in gender presentation, above and beyond mere competence, but instead are terms of moral approbation.

11. Judith Butler, *Gender Trouble* (New York: Routledge, Chapman and Hall, 1990).

12. Sandra Bartky, *Femininity and Domination: Studies in the Phenomenology of Oppression* (New York: Routledge, Chapman and Hall, 1990).

13. Talia Mae Bettcher, "Trans Identities and First-Person Authority," in *"You've Changed": Sex Reassignment and Personal Identity*, edited by Laurie J. Shrage (New York: Oxford University Press, 2009), 98–120, at 99.

14. Determining what aspiration to have is not a matter of consulting some primordial, infallible, indubitable sensation inside. If there is such a thing as feeling like a girl or feeling like a boy, that feeling is not the same as having a feeling of hunger, pain, or fatigue. For, like other social concepts, a girl has to learn what "girl" means before she can feel like a girl, but she does not have to learn what "hungry," "pain," or "tired" means in order to feel hungry, in pain, or tired.

15. What constitutes a degree of autonomy sufficient for determining one's gender is open to debate but is not a question that can be pursued at length here. Clearly a neonate is not capable of deciding her gender and should be assigned one provisionally. An eighteen-year-old is certainly capable of determining his gender and therefore has FPA with respect to that decision. Whether children and younger teens are sufficiently autonomous to possess FPA over their gender is complicated and depends on a variety of factors, including their developmental level, maturity, knowledge, and experience.

16. Dean Spade, "Mutilating Gender," in *The Transgender Studies Reader*, edited by Susan Stryker and Stephen Whittle (New York: Routledge, 2006), 314–32.

17. Talia Mae Bettcher, "Without a Net: Starting Points for Trans Stories," *American Philosophical Association Newsletter on Philosophy and Lesbian, Gay, Bisexual, and Transgender Issues* 10:2 (2011): 2–5, at 3.

18. Bettcher, "Without a Net," 3.

19. Patrick Califia, "Manliness," in *The Transgender Studies Reader*, edited by Susan Stryker and Stephen Whittle (New York: Routledge, 2006), 434–38, at 435.

20. Kate Bornstein, *Gender Outlaw: On Men, Women, and the Rest of Us* (New York: Random House, 1994), 4, 8.

21. "Sex Not Specified: Australia Leads the Way with Legal Document," *Scavenger* (www.thescavenger.net/glbsgdq/sex-not-specified-australia-leads-the-way-in-legal-document-756345-206.html; accessed February 13, 2012).

22. Jane Fae, "Australian Government Withdraws Non-Specified Gender Status," *Pink News: Europe's Largest Gay News Service* (http://www.pinknews.co.uk/2010/03/19/

australian-government-withdraws-non-specified-gender-status; accessed February 13, 2012).

23. Bettcher, "Trans Identities and First-Person Authority," 105, her emphasis.

24. Hale, "Tracing a Ghostly Memory in My Throat," 62, note 13.

25. Ann Snitow, "A Gender Diary," in *Conflicts in Feminism*, edited by Marianne Hirsch and Evelyn Fox Keller (New York: Routledge, 1990), 9–43, at 9.

26. For their comments and suggestions on earlier versions of this paper, I am grateful to the audiences at the Queen's University Department of Philosophy Colloquium Series, March 3, 2011, and at the annual meeting of the American Philosophical Association Central Division, Minneapolis, Minnesota, April 1, 2011. I also thank Raja Halwani and Nicholas Power for their detailed editing and very helpful comments.

STUDY QUESTIONS

1. Is it possible that one is (epistemically) mistaken about one's gender? How? Describe some examples of such mistakes. If a person could be mistaken about his or her gender, would this affect the claim (that Overall accepts from Bettcher) that a person has moral authority over his or her gender identity? Explain.

2. Cisgendered people, in Overall's view, face "comparable" risks and dangers to those facing trans people. In what ways are these risks and dangers comparable? Do you find her arguments convincing?

3. According to Overall, there are four crucial similarities between cisgendered and trans persons' identities. As with any claim about similarities between X and Y, there are also differences. These differences—depending on their number, nature, and strength—might make the similarities relatively unimportant. Are there any crucial differences between the identities of cisgendered and trans people?

4. Overall states, "Contrary to the assumption that cisgendered and trans persons are very different and that hence to be trans is to be abnormal, disordered, and unhealthy, an examination of the gender aspirations of cisgendered and trans persons reveals significant similarities." Does the existence of differences necessarily imply that being trans is "abnormal, disordered, and unhealthy"? What effect would your answer to this question have on the main points of Overall's essay?

5. In the section of her essay in which she confronts biological influences on gender identity, Overall correctly points out the empirical complexities in establishing the mechanisms by which cisgendered and transgendered "bodies give us certain proclivities, tendencies, wants, needs, weaknesses, and strengths." However, though it is true that "if hormones and brain structures influence gender aspirations in trans people, then they also influence gender aspirations in cisgendered people," does this response do justice to the com-

mon trans report that they always felt that they were a male brain in a female body (or a female brain in a male body)? (See the "Primer" available at http://transsexual.org/index.html for more details [accessed April 15, 2012].) How might Overall account for the dysphoria reported by the transgendered in such a way that it is definitive of the difference between the transgendered and the cisgendered?

III

Objectification and Consent—
the Theory

SIXTEEN

Sexual Morality and the Concept of Using Another Person

Thomas A. Mappes

The Second Formulation of the German philosopher Immanuel Kant's (1724–1804) famous Categorical Imperative (also called the "Formula of Humanity")—"always treat humanity, whether in your own person or in the person of any other, never simply as a means, but always at the same time as an end"—continues to frame philosophical discussions of the moral value of rational autonomy and our contemporary thoughts about the moral power of consent. Its proper application to sexual relations is the nexus of many essays in part III and part IV of this volume, beginning with the contribution of **Thomas A. Mappes** *, who sees Kant's views on objectification and using others for one's own goals as suggesting both necessary and sufficient conditions for morally licit sexual activity. On Mappes's (perhaps "libertarian") reading of the Second Formulation, sexual relations are morally permissible just in case they occur with the free and informed consent of the participants (a view not dissimilar from that of the utilitarian John Stuart Mill). Mappes examines different ways in which misinformation or deception (outright lies) as well as pressure or coercion (as in rape, for example) can poison sexual relations, and describes for our consideration a number of difficult or borderline cases. Mappes's remarks on the wrongness of sexual exploitation at the end of his essay are an interesting extension of his Kantian perspective.*

In order to do competent exegetical work in this area (to comprehend Kantian ethics, and the other essays in part III and part IV), one must study Kant's writings, especially his Lectures on Ethics *(trans. Peter Heath, ed. Peter Heath and J. B. Schneewind [Cambridge: Cambridge University Press, 1997]) and* The Metaphysics of Morals *(trans. Mary Gregor [Cambridge: Cambridge Univer-*

sity Press, 1991, 1996]). Other editions of these works are available, but these are undoubtedly currently the best.

Thomas Mappes is professor emeritus of philosophy, Frostburg State University in Maryland. He is the editor, with David DeGrazia, of *Biomedical Ethics*, 6th edition (McGraw-Hill, 2006), and the editor, with Jane S. Zembaty, of *Social Ethics: Morality and Social Policy*, 7th edition (McGraw-Hill, 2007). This essay is reprinted with the permission of the author from *Social Ethics: Morality and Social Policy*, 3rd edition (McGraw-Hill, 1987), pp. 248–62, edited by Thomas A. Mappes and Jane S. Zembaty. © 1985, Thomas A. Mappes.

The central tenet of *conventional* sexual morality is that nonmarital sex is immoral. A somewhat less restrictive sexual ethic holds that *sex without love* is immoral. If neither of these positions is philosophically defensible, and I would contend that neither is, it does not follow that there are no substantive moral restrictions on human sexual interaction. Any human interaction, including sexual interaction, may be judged morally objectionable to the extent that it transgresses a justified moral rule or principle. The way to construct a detailed account of sexual morality, it would seem, is simply to work out the implications of relevant moral rules or principles in the area of human sexual interaction.

As one important step in the direction of such an account, I will attempt to work out the implications of an especially relevant moral principle, the principle that it is wrong for one person to use another person. However ambiguous the expression "using another person" may seem to be, there is a determinate and clearly specifiable sense according to which using another person is morally objectionable. Once this morally significant sense of "using another person" is identified and explicated, the concept of using another person can play an important role in the articulation of a defensible account of sexual morality.

I. THE MORALLY SIGNIFICANT SENSE OF "USING ANOTHER PERSON"

Historically, the concept of using another person is associated with the ethical system of Immanuel Kant. According to a fundamental Kantian principle, it is morally wrong for A to use B *merely as a means* (to achieve A's ends). Kant's principle does not rule out A using B as a means, only A using B *merely* as a means, that is, in a way incompatible with respect for B as a person. In the ordinary course of life, it is surely unavoidable (and morally unproblematic) that each of us in numerous ways uses others as a means to achieve our various ends. A college teacher uses students as a means to achieve his or her livelihood. A college student uses instructors as a means of gaining knowledge and skills. Such human interactions, presumably based on the voluntary participation of the respective parties, are quite compatible with the idea of respect for persons. But respect for persons entails that each of us recognize the rightful authority of other persons (as rational beings) to conduct their individual lives as they see fit. We may legitimately recruit others to participate in the satisfaction of our personal ends, but they are used merely as a means whenever we undermine the voluntary or informed character of their consent to interact with us in some desired way. A coerces B at knife point to hand over $200. A uses B merely as means. If A had requested of B a gift of $200, leaving B free to determine whether or not to make the gift, A would have proceeded in a manner compatible with respect for B as a person. C deceptively rolls back the odometer of a car and thereby manipulates D's decision to buy the car. C uses D merely as a means.

On the basis of these considerations, I would suggest that the morally significant sense of "using another person" is best understood by reference to the notion of *voluntary informed consent*. More specifically, A immorally uses B if and only if A intentionally acts in a way that violates the requirement that B's involvement with A's ends be based on B's voluntary informed consent. If this account is correct, using another person (in the morally significant sense) can arise in at least two important ways: via *coercion*, which is antithetical to voluntary consent, and via *deception*, which undermines the informed character of voluntary consent.

The notion of voluntary informed consent is very prominent in the literature of biomedical ethics and is systematically related to the much-emphasized notion of (patient) autonomy. We find in the famous words of Supreme Court justice Cardozo a ringing affirmation of patient autonomy. "Every human being of adult years and sound mind has a right to determine what shall be done with his own body." Because respect for individual autonomy is an essential part of respect for persons, if medical professionals (and biomedical researchers) are to interact with their patients (and research subjects) in an acceptable way, they must respect individual autonomy. That is, they must respect the self-determination of the patient/subject, the individual's right to determine what shall be done with his or her body. This means that they must not act in a way that violates the requirement of voluntary informed consent. Medical procedures must not be performed without the consent of competent patients; research on human subjects must not be carried out without the consent of the subjects involved. Moreover, consent must be voluntary; coercion undermines individual autonomy. Consent must also be informed; lying or withholding relevant information undercuts rational decision making and thereby undermines individual autonomy.

To further illuminate the concept of using that has been proposed, I will consider in greater detail the matter of research involving human subjects. In the sphere of researcher-subject interaction, just as in the sphere of human sexual interaction, there is ample opportunity for immorally using another person. If a researcher is engaged in a study that involves human subjects, we may presume that the "end" of the researcher is the successful completion of the study. (The researcher may desire this particular end for any number of reasons: the speculative under-standing it will provide, the technology it will make possible, the eventu-al benefit of humankind, increased status in the scientific community, a raise in pay, etc.) The work, let us presume, strictly requires the use (employment) of human research subjects. The researcher, however, im-morally uses other people only if he or she intentionally acts in a way that violates the requirement that the participation of research subjects be based on their voluntary informed consent.

Let us assume that in a particular case participation as a research subject involves some rather significant risks. Accordingly, the researcher finds that potential subjects are reluctant to volunteer. At this point, if an unscrupulous researcher is willing to resort to the immoral using of other people (to achieve his or her own ends), two manifest options are avail-able—deception and coercion. By way of deception, the researcher might choose to lie about the risks involved. For example, potential subjects could be explicitly told that there are no significant risks associated with research participation. On the other hand, the researcher could simply withhold a full disclosure of risks. Whether pumped full of false informa-tion or simply deprived of relevant information, the potential subject is intentionally deceived in such a way as to be led to a decision that fur-thers the researcher's ends. In manipulating the decision making process of the potential subject in this way, the researcher is guilty of immorally using another person.

To explain how an unscrupulous researcher might immorally use an-other person via coercion, it is helpful to distinguish two basic forms of coercion.[1] "Occurrent" coercion involves the use of physical force. "Dis-positional" coercion involves the threat of harm. If I am forcibly thrown out of my office by an intruder, I am the victim of occurrent coercion. If, on the other hand, I leave my office because an intruder has threatened to shoot me if I do not leave, I am the victim of dispositional coercion. The victim of occurrent coercion literally has no choice in what happens. The victim of dispositional coercion, in contrast, does intentionally choose a certain course of action. However, one's choice, in the face of the threat of harm, is less than fully voluntary.

It is perhaps unlikely that even an unscrupulous researcher would resort to any very explicit measure of coercion. Deception, it seems, is less risky. Still, it is well known that Nazi medical experimenters ruthlessly employed coercion. By way of occurrent coercion, the Nazis literally forced great numbers of concentration camp victims to participate in ex-periments that entailed their own death or dismemberment. And if some concentration camp victims "volunteered" to participate in Nazi research to avoid even more unspeakable horrors, clearly we must consider them victims of dispositional coercion. The Nazi researchers, employing coer-cion, immorally used other human beings with a vengeance.

II. DECEPTION AND SEXUAL MORALITY

To this point, I have been concerned to identify and explicate the morally significant sense of "using another person." On the view proposed, A immorally uses B if and only if A intentionally acts in a way that violates the requirement that B's involvement with A's ends be based on B's voluntary informed consent. I will now apply this account to the area of human sexual interaction and explore its implications. For economy of expression in what follows, "using" (and its cognates) is to be understood as referring only to the morally significant sense.

If we presume a state of affairs in which A desires some form of sexual interaction with B, we can say that this desired form of sexual interaction with B is A's end. Thus A sexually uses B if and only if A intentionally acts in a way that violates the requirement that B's sexual interaction with A be based on B's voluntary informed consent. It seems clear then that A may sexually use B in at least two distinctive ways, (1) via coercion and (2) via deception. However, before proceeding to discuss deception and then the more problematic case of coercion, one important point must be made. In emphasizing the centrality of coercion and deception as mechanisms for the sexual using of another person, I have in mind sexual interaction with a fully competent adult partner. We should also want to say, I think, that sexual interaction with a child inescapably involves the sexual using of another person. Even if a child "consents" to sexual interaction, he or she is, strictly speaking, incapable of *informed* consent. It's a matter of being *incompetent* to give consent. Similarly, to the extent that a mentally retarded person is rightly considered incompetent, sexual interaction with such a person amounts to the sexual using of that person, unless someone empowered to give "proxy consent" has done so. (In certain circumstances, sexual involvement might be in the best interests of a mentally retarded person.) We can also visualize the case of an otherwise fully competent adult temporarily disordered by drugs or alcohol. To the extent that such a person is rightly regarded as temporarily incompetent, winning his or her "consent" to sexual interaction could culminate in the sexual using of that person.

There are a host of clear cases in which one person sexually uses another precisely because the former employs deception in a way that undermines the informed character of the latter's consent to sexual interaction. Consider this example. One person, A, has decided, as a matter of personal prudence based on past experience, not to become sexually involved outside the confines of a loving relationship. Another person, B, strongly desires a sexual relationship with A but does not love A. B, aware of A's unwillingness to engage in sex without love, professes love for A, thereby hoping to win A's consent to a sexual relationship. B's ploy is successful; A consents. When the smoke clears and A becomes aware of

B's deception, it would be both appropriate and natural for A to complain, "I've been used."

In the same vein, here are some other examples. (1) Mr. A is aware that Ms. B will consent to sexual involvement only on the understanding that in time the two will be married. Mr. A has no intention of marrying Ms. B but says that he will. (2) Ms. C has herpes and is well aware that Mr. D will never consent to sex if he knows of her condition. When asked by Mr. D, Ms. C denies that she has herpes. (3) Mr. E knows that Ms. F will not consent to sexual intercourse in the absence of responsible birth control measures. Mr. E tells Ms. F that he has had a vasectomy, which is not the case. (4) Ms. G knows that Mr. H would not consent to sexual involvement with a married woman. Ms. G is married but tells Mr. H that she is single. (5) Ms. I is well aware that Ms. J is interested in a stable lesbian relationship and will not consent to become sexually involved with someone who is bisexual. Ms. I tells Ms. J that she is exclusively homosexual, whereas the truth is that she is bisexual.

If one person's consent to sex is predicated on false beliefs that have been intentionally and deceptively inculcated by one's sexual partner in an effort to win the former's consent, the resulting sexual interaction involves one person sexually using another. In each of the above cases, one person explicitly *lies* to another. False information is intentionally conveyed to win consent to sexual interaction, and the end result is the sexual using of another person.

As noted earlier, however, lying is not the only form of deception. Under certain circumstances, the simple withholding of information can be considered a form of deception. Accordingly, it is possible to sexually use another person not only by (deceptively) lying about relevant facts but also by (deceptively) not disclosing relevant facts. If A has good reason to believe that B would refuse to consent to sexual interaction should B become aware of certain factual information, and if A withholds disclosure of this information in order to enhance the possibility of gaining B's consent, then, if B does consent, A sexually uses B via deception. One example will suffice. Suppose that Mr. A meets Ms. B in a singles bar. Mr. A realizes immediately that Ms. B is the sister of Ms. C, a woman that Mr. A has been sexually involved with for a long time. Mr. A, knowing that it is very unlikely that Ms. B will consent to sexual interaction if she becomes aware of Mr. A's involvement with her sister, decides not to disclose this information. If Ms. B eventually consents to sexual interaction, since her consent is the product of Mr. A's deception, it is rightly thought that she has been sexually used by him.

III. COERCION AND SEXUAL MORALITY

We have considered the case of deception. The present task is to consider the more difficult case of coercion. Whereas deception functions to undermine the *informed* character of voluntary consent (to sexual interaction), coercion either obliterates consent entirely (the case of occurrent coercion) or undermines the voluntariness of consent (the case of dispositional coercion).

Forcible rape is the most conspicuous, and most brutal, way of sexually using another person via coercion.[2] Forcible rape may involve either occurrent coercion or dispositional coercion. A man who rapes a woman by the employment of sheer physical force, by simply overpowering her, employs occurrent coercion. There is literally no sexual *interaction* in such a case; only the rapist performs an action. In no sense does the woman consent to or participate in sexual activity. She has no choice in what takes place, or rather, physical force results in her choice being simply beside the point. The employment of occurrent coercion for the purpose of rape "objectifies" the victim in the strongest sense of that term. She is treated like a physical object. One does not interact with physical objects; one acts upon them. In a perfectly ordinary (not the morally significant) sense of the term, we "use" physical objects. But when the victim of rape is treated as if she were a physical object, there we have one of the most vivid examples of the immoral using of another person.

Frequently, forcible rape involves not occurrent coercion (or not *only* occurrent coercion) but dispositional coercion.[3] In dispositional coercion, the relevant factor is not physical force but the threat of harm. The rapist threatens his victim with immediate and serious bodily harm. For example, a man threatens to kill or beat a woman if she resists his sexual demands. She "consents," that is, she submits to his demands. He may demand only passive participation (simply not struggling against him) or he may demand some measure of active participation. Rape that employs dispositional coercion is surely just as wrong as rape that employs occurrent coercion, but there is a notable difference in the mechanism by which the rapist uses his victim in the two cases. With occurrent coercion, the victim's consent is entirely bypassed. With dispositional coercion, the victim's consent is not bypassed. It is coerced. Dispositional coercion undermines the *voluntariness* of consent. The rapist, by employing the threat of immediate and serious bodily harm, may succeed in bending the victim's will. He may gain the victim's "consent." But he uses another person precisely because consent is coerced.

The relevance of occurrent coercion is limited to the case of forcible rape. Dispositional coercion, a notion that also plays an indispensable role in an overall account of forcible rape, now becomes our central concern. Although the threat of immediate and serious bodily harm stands out as the most brutal way of coercing consent to sexual interaction, we must not neglect the employment of other kinds of threats to this same end. There are numerous ways in which one person can effectively harm, and thus effectively threaten, another. Accordingly, for example, consent to sexual interaction might be coerced by threatening to damage someone's reputation. If a person consents to sexual interaction to avoid a threatened harm, then that person has been sexually used (via dispositional coercion). In the face of a threat, of course, it remains possible that a person will refuse to comply with another's sexual demands. It is probably best to describe this sort of situation as a case not of coercion, which entails the *successful* use of threats to gain compliance, but of *attempted* coercion. Of course, the moral fault of an individual emerges with the *attempt* to coerce. A person who attempts murder is morally blameworthy even if the attempt fails. The same is true for someone who fails in an effort to coerce consent to sexual interaction.

Consider now each of the following cases:

Case 1: Mr. Supervisor makes a series of increasingly less subtle sexual overtures to Ms. Employee. These advances are consistently and firmly rejected by Ms. Employee. Eventually, Mr. Supervisor makes it clear that the granting of "sexual favors" is a condition of her continued employment.

Case 2: Ms. Debtor borrowed a substantial sum of money from Mr. Creditor, on the understanding that she would pay it back within one year. In the meantime, Ms. Debtor has become sexually attracted to Mr. Creditor, but he does not share her interest. At the end of the one-year period, Mr. Creditor asks Ms. Debtor to return the money. She says she will be happy to return the money so long as he consents to sexual interaction with her.

Case 3: Mr. Theatregoer has two tickets to the most talked-about play of the season. He is introduced to a woman whom he finds sexually attractive and who shares his interest in the theater. In the course of their conversation, she expresses disappointment that the play everyone is talking about is sold out; she would love to see it. At this point, Mr. Theatregoer suggests that she be his guest at the theater. "Oh, by the way," he says, "I always expect sex from my dates."

Case 4: Ms. Jetsetter is planning a trip to Europe. She has been trying for some time to develop a sexual relationship with a man who has shown little interest in her. She knows, however, that he has always wanted to go to Europe and that it is only lack of money that has deterred him. Ms. Jetsetter proposes that he come along as her traveling companion, all expenses paid, on the express understanding that sex is part of the arrangement.

Cases 1 and 2 involve attempts to sexually use another person, whereas cases 3 and 4 do not. To see why this is so, it is essential to introduce a distinction between two kinds of proposals, viz., the distinction between *threats* and *offers*.[4] The logical form of a threat differs from the logical form of an offer in the following way. Threat: "If you *do not* do what I am proposing you do, I will bring about an *undesirable consequence* for you." Offer: "If you *do* what I am proposing you do, I will bring about a *desirable consequence* for you." The person who makes a threat attempts to gain compliance by attaching an undesirable consequence to the alternative of noncompliance. This person attempts to *coerce* consent. The person who makes an offer attempts to gain compliance by attaching a desirable consequence to the alternative of compliance. This person attempts not to coerce but to *induce* consent.

Since threats are morally problematic in a way that offers are not, it is not uncommon for threats to be advanced in the language of offers. Threats are represented as if they were offers. An armed assailant might say, "I'm going to make you an *offer*. If you give me your money, I will allow you to go on living." Though this proposal on the surface has the logical form of an offer, it is in reality a threat. The underlying sense of the proposal is this: "If you do not give me your money, I will kill you." If, in a given case, it is initially unclear whether a certain proposal is to count as a threat or an offer, ask the following question. Does the proposal in question have the effect of making a person *worse off upon noncompliance*? The recipient of an offer, upon noncompliance, is *not worse off* than he or she was before the offer. In contrast, the recipient of a threat, upon noncompliance, is *worse off* than he or she was before the threat. Since the "offer" of our armed assailant has the effect, upon noncompliance, of rendering its recipient worse off (relative to the preproposal situation of the recipient), the recipient is faced with a threat, not an offer.

The most obvious way for a coercer to attach an undesirable consequence to the path of noncompliance is by threatening to render the victim of coercion materially worse off than he or she has theretofore been. Thus a person is threatened with loss of life, bodily injury, damage to property, damage to reputation, etc. It is important to realize, however, that a person can also be effectively coerced by being threatened with the withholding of something (in some cases, what we would call a "benefit") to which the person is entitled. Suppose that A is mired in quicksand and is slowly but surely approaching death. When B happens along, A cries out to B for assistance. All B need do is throw A a rope. B is quite willing to accommodate A, "provided you pay me $100,000 over the next ten years." Is B making A an offer? Hardly! B, we must presume, stands under a moral obligation to come to the aid of a person in serious distress, at least when such assistance entails no significant risk, sacrifice of time, etc. A is entitled to B's assistance. Thus, in reality, B attaches an undesirable consequence to A's noncompliance with the proposal that A pay B $100,000. A is undoubtedly better off that B has happened along, but A is not rendered better off by B's proposal. Before B's *proposal*, A legitimately expected assistance from B, "no strings attached." In attaching a very unwelcome string, B's proposal effectively renders A worse off. What B proposes, then, is not an offer of assistance. Rather, B threatens A with the withholding of something (assistance) that A is entitled to have from B.

Since threats have the effect of rendering a person worse off upon noncompliance, it is ordinarily the case that a person does not welcome (indeed, despises) them. Offers, on the other hand, are ordinarily welcome to a person. Since an offer provides no penalty for noncompliance with a proposal but only an inducement for compliance, there is *in principle* only potential advantage in being confronted with an offer. In real life, of course, there are numerous reasons why a person may be less than enthusiastic about being presented with an offer. Enduring the presentation of trivial offers does not warrant the necessary time and energy expenditures. Offers can be both annoying and offensive; certainly this is true of some sexual offers. A person might also be unsettled by an offer that confronts him or her with a difficult decision. All this, however, is compatible with the fact that an offer is fundamentally welcome to a rational person in the sense that the *content* of an offer necessarily widens the field of opportunity and thus provides, in principle, only potential advantage.

With the distinction between threats and offers clearly in view, it now becomes clear why cases 1 and 2 do indeed involve attempts to sexually use another person whereas cases 3 and 4 do not. Cases 1 and 2 embody threats, whereas cases 3 and 4 embody offers. In case 1, Mr. Supervisor proposes sexual interaction with Ms. Employee and, in an effort to gain compliance, threatens her with the loss of her job. Mr. Supervisor thereby attaches an undesirable consequence to one of Ms. Employee's alternatives, the path of noncompliance. Typical of the threat situation, Mr. Supervisor's proposal has the effect of rendering Ms. Employee worse off upon noncompliance. Mr. Supervisor is attempting via (dispositional) coercion to sexually use Ms. Employee. The situation in case 2 is similar. Ms. Debtor, as *she* might be inclined to say, "offers" to pay Mr. Creditor the money she owes him *if* he consents to sexual interaction with her. In reality, Ms. Debtor is threatening Mr. Creditor, attempting to coerce his consent to sexual interaction, attempting to sexually use him. Though Mr. Creditor is not now in possession of the money Ms. Debtor owes him, he is *entitled* to receive it from her at this time. She threatens to deprive him of something to which he is entitled. Clearly, her proposal has the effect of rendering him worse off upon noncompliance. Before her proposal, he had the legitimate expectation, "no strings attached," of receiving the money in question.

Cases 3 and 4 embody offers; neither involves an attempt to sexually use another person. Mr. Theatregoer simply provides an inducement for the woman he has just met to accept his proposal of sexual interaction. He offers her the opportunity to see the play that everyone is talking about. In attaching a desirable consequence to the alternative of compliance, Mr. Theatregoer in no way threatens or attempts to coerce his potential companion. Typical of the offer situation, his proposal does not have the effect of rendering her worse off upon noncompliance. She now has a new opportunity; if she chooses to forgo this opportunity, she is no worse off. The situation in case 4 is similar. Ms. Jetsetter provides an inducement for a man whom she is interested in to accept her proposal of sexual involvement. She offers him the opportunity to see Europe, without expense, as her traveling companion. Before Ms. Jetsetter's proposal, he had no prospect of a European trip. If he chooses to reject her proposal, he is no worse off than he has theretofore been. Ms. Jetsetter's proposal embodies an offer, not a threat. She cannot be accused of attempting to sexually use her potential traveling companion.

Consider now two further cases, 5 and 6, each of which develops in the following way. Professor Highstatus, a man of high academic accomplishment, is sexually attracted to a student in one of his classes. He is very anxious to secure her consent to sexual interaction. Ms. Student, confused and unsettled by his sexual advances, has begun to practice "avoidance behavior." To the extent that it is possible, she goes out of her way to avoid him.

> *Case 5:* Professor Highstatus tells Ms. Student that, though her work is such as to entitle her to a grade of B in the class, she will be assigned a D unless she consents to sexual interaction.
>
> *Case 6:* Professor Highstatus tells Ms. Student that, though her work is such as to entitle her to a grade of B, she will be assigned an A if she consents to sexual interaction.

It is clear that case 5 involves an attempt to sexually use another person. Case 6, however, at least at face value, does not. In case 5, Professor Highstatus *threatens* to deprive Ms. Student of the grade she deserves. In case 6, he *offers* to assign her a grade that is higher than she deserves. In case 5, Ms. Student would be worse off upon noncompliance with Professor Highstatus's proposal. In case 6, she would not be worse off upon noncompliance with his proposal. In saying that case 6 does not involve an attempt to sexually use another person, it is not being asserted that Professor Highstatus is acting in a morally legitimate fashion. In offering a student a higher grade than she deserves, he is guilty of abusing his institutional authority. He is under an obligation to assign the grades that students earn, as defined by the relevant course standards. In case 6, Professor Highstatus is undoubtedly acting in a morally reprehensible way, but in contrast to case 5, where it is fair to say that he both abuses his institutional authority and attempts to sexually use another person, we can plausibly say that in case 6 his moral failure is limited to abuse of his institutional authority.

There remains, however, a suspicion that case 6 might after all embody an attempt to sexually use another person. There is no question that the literal content of what Professor Highstatus conveys to Ms. Student has the logical form of an offer and not a threat. Still, is it not the case that Ms. Student may very well feel threatened? Professor Highstatus, in an effort to secure consent to sexual interaction, has announced that he will assign Ms. Student a higher grade than she deserves. Can she really turn him down without substantial risk? Is he not likely to retaliate? If she spurns him, will he not lower her grade or otherwise make it harder for her to succeed in her academic program? He does, after all, have power over her. Will he use it to her detriment? Surely he is not above abusing his institutional authority to achieve his ends; this much is abundantly clear from his willingness to assign a grade higher than a student deserves.

Is Professor Highstatus naive to the threat that Ms. Student may find implicit in the situation? Perhaps. In such a case, if Ms. Student reluctantly consents to sexual interaction, we may be inclined to say that he has *unwittingly* used her. More likely, Professor Highstatus is well aware of the way in which Ms. Student will perceive his proposal. He knows that threats need not be verbally expressed. Indeed, it may even be the case that he consciously exploits his underground reputation. "Everyone knows what happens to the women who reject Professor Highstatus's little offers." To the extent, then, that Professor Highstatus intends to convey a threat in case 6, he is attempting via coercion to sexually use another person.

Many researchers "have pointed out the fact that the possibility of sanctions for noncooperation is implicit in all sexual advances across authority lines, as between teacher and student."[5] I do not think that this consideration should lead us to the conclusion that a person with an academic appointment is obliged in all circumstances to refrain from attempting to initiate sexual involvement with one of his or her students. Still, since even "good faith" sexual advances may be ambiguous in the eyes of a student, it is an interesting question what precautions an instructor must take to avoid unwittingly coercing a student to consent to sexual interaction.

Much of what has been said about the professor/student relationship in an academic setting can be applied as well to the supervisor/subordinate relationship in an employment setting. A manager who functions within an organizational structure is required to evaluate fairly his or her subordinates according to relevant corporate or institutional standards. An unscrupulous manager, willing to abuse his or her institutional authority in an effort to win the consent of a subordinate to sexual interaction, can advance threats and/or offers related to the managerial task of employee evaluation. An employee whose job performance is entirely satisfactory can be threatened with an unsatisfactory performance rating, perhaps leading to termination. An employee whose job performance is excellent can be threatened with an unfair evaluation, designed to bar the employee from recognition, merit pay, consideration for promotion, etc. Such threats, when made in an effort to coerce employee consent to sexual interaction, clearly embody the attempt to sexually use another person. On the other hand, the manager who (abusing his or her institutional authority) offers to provide an employee with an inflated evaluation as an inducement for consent to sexual interaction does not, at face value, attempt to sexually use another person. Of course, all of the qualifications introduced in the discussion of case 6 above are applicable here as well.

IV. THE IDEA OF A COERCIVE OFFER

In section III, I have sketched an overall account of sexually using another person *via coercion*. In this section, I will consider the need for modifications or extensions of the suggested account. As before, certain case studies will serve as points of departure.

> *Case 7:* Ms. Starlet, a glamorous, wealthy, and highly successful model, wants nothing more than to become a movie superstar. Mr. Moviemogul, a famous producer, is very taken with Ms. Starlet's beauty. He invites her to come to his office for a screen test. After the screen test, Mr. Moviemogul tells Ms. Starlet that he is prepared to make her a star, on the condition that she agree to sexual involvement with him. Ms. Starlet finds Mr. Moviemogul personally repugnant; she is not at all sexually attracted to him. With great reluctance, she agrees to his proposal.

Has Mr. Moviemogul sexually used Ms. Starlet? No. He has made her an offer that she has accepted, however reluctantly. The situation would be quite different if it were plausible to believe that she was, before acceptance of his proposal, *entitled* to his efforts to make her a star. Then we could read case 7 as amounting to his threatening to deprive her of something to which she was entitled. But what conceivable grounds could be found for the claim that Mr. Moviemogul, before Ms. Starlet's acceptance of his proposal, is under an obligation to make her a star? He does not threaten her; he makes her an offer. Even if there are other good grounds for morally condemning his action, it is a mistake to think that he is guilty of coercing consent.

But some would assert that Mr. Moviemogul's offer, on the grounds that it confronts Ms. Starlet with an overwhelming inducement, is simply an example of a *coercive offer*. The more general claim at issue is that offers are coercive precisely inasmuch as they are extremely enticing or seductive. Though there is an important reality associated with the notion of a coercive offer, a reality that must shortly be confronted, we ought not embrace the view that an offer is coercive merely because it is extremely enticing or seductive. Virginia Held is a leading proponent of the view under attack here. She writes:

> A person unable to spurn an offer may act as unwillingly as a person unable to resist a threat. Consider the distinction between rape and seduction. In one case constraint and threat are operative, in the other inducement and offer. If the degree of inducement is set high enough in the case of seduction, there may seem to be little difference in the extent of coercion involved. In both cases, persons may act against their own wills.[6]

Certainly a rape victim who acquiesces at knifepoint is forced to act *against her will*. Does Ms. Starlet, however, act against her will? We have said that she consents "with great reluctance" to sexual involvement, but she does not act against her will. She *wants* very much to be a movie star. I might want very much to be thin. She regrets having to become sexually involved with Mr. Moviemogul as a means of achieving what she wants. I might regret very much having to go on a diet to lose weight. If we say that Ms. Starlet acts against her will in case 7, then we must say that I am acting against my will in embracing "with great reluctance" the diet I despise.

A more important line of argument against Held's view can be advanced on the basis of the widely accepted notion that there is a moral presumption against coercion. Held herself embraces this notion and very effectively clarifies it:

> . . . although coercion is not always wrong (quite obviously: one coerces the small child not to run across the highway, or the murderer to drop his weapon), there is a presumption against it. . . . This has the standing of a fundamental moral principle. . . .
>
> What can be concluded at the moral level is that we have a *prima facie* obligation not to employ coercion.[7] [all italics hers]

But it would seem that acceptance of the moral presumption against coercion is not compatible with the view that offers become coercive precisely inasmuch as they become extremely enticing or seductive. Suppose you are my neighbor and regularly spend your Saturday afternoon on the golf course. Suppose also that you are a skilled gardener. I am anxious to convince you to do some gardening work for me and it must be done this Saturday. I offer you $100, $200, $300, . . . in an effort to make it worth your while to sacrifice your recreation and undertake my gardening. At some point, my proposal becomes very enticing. Yet, at the same time in no sense is my proposal becoming morally problematic. If my proposal were becoming coercive, surely our moral sense would be aroused.

Though it is surely not true that the extremely enticing character of an offer is sufficient to make it coercive, we need not reach the conclusion that no sense can be made out of the notion of a coercive offer. Indeed, there is an important social reality that the notion of a coercive offer appears to capture, and insight into this reality can be gained by simply taking note of the sort of case that most draws us to the language of "coercive offer." Is it not a case in which the recipient of an offer is in circumstances of genuine need, and acceptance of the offer seems to present the only realistic possibility for alleviating the need? Assuming that this sort of case is the heart of the matter, it seems that we cannot avoid introducing some sort of distinction between *genuine needs* and *mere wants*. Though the philosophical difficulties involved in drawing this distinction are not insignificant, I nevertheless claim that we will not achieve any clarity about the notion of a coercive offer, at least in this context, except in reference to it. Whatever puzzlement we may feel with regard to the host of borderline cases that can be advanced, it is neverthe-less true, for example, that I *genuinely need* food and that I *merely want* a backyard tennis court. In the same spirit, I think it can be acknowledged by all that Ms. Starlet, though she *wants* very much to be a star, does not in any relevant sense *need* to be a star. Accordingly, there is little plau-sibility in thinking that Mr. Moviemogul makes her a coercive offer. The following case, in contrast, can more plausibly be thought to embody a coercive offer.

> *Case 8:* Mr. Troubled is a young widower who is raising his three children. He lives in a small town and believes that it is important for him to stay there so that his children continue to have the emotional support of other family members. But economic times are tough. Mr. Troubled has been laid off from his job and has not been able to find another. His unemployment benefits have ceased and his relatives are in no position to help him financially. If he is unable to come up with the money for his mortgage payments, he will lose his rather modest house. Ms. Opportunistic lives in the same town. Since shortly after the death of Mr. Troubled's wife, she has consistently made sexual overtures in his direction. Mr. Troubled, for his part, does not care for Ms. Opportunistic and has made it clear to her that he is not interested in sexual involvement with her. She, however, is well aware of his present difficulties. To win his consent to a sexual affair, Ms. Opportunistic offers to make mortgage payments for Mr. Troubled on a continuing basis.

Is Ms. Opportunistic attempting to sexually use Mr. Troubled? The cor-rect answer is yes, even though we must first accept the conclusion that her proposal embodies an offer and not a threat. If Ms. Opportunistic were threatening Mr. Troubled, her proposal would have the effect of rendering him worse off upon noncompliance. But this is not the case. If he rejects her proposal, his situation will not worsen; he will simply remain, as before, in circumstances of extreme need. It might be objected at this point that Ms. Opportunistic does in fact threaten Mr. Troubled. She threatens to deprive him of something to which he is entitled, namely, the alleviation of a genuine need. But this approach is defensible only if, before acceptance of her proposal, he is entitled to have his needs alleviated *by her*. And whatever Mr. Troubled and his children are entitled to from their society as a whole—they are perhaps slipping through the "social safety net"—it cannot be plausibly maintained that Mr. Troubled is entitled to have his mortgage payments made *by Ms. Opportunistic*.

Yet, though she does not threaten him, she is attempting to sexually use him. How can this conclusion be reconciled with our overall account of sexually using another person? First of all, I want to suggest that nothing hangs on whether or not we decide to call Ms. Opportunistic's offer "coercive." More important than the label "coercive offer" is an appreciation of the social reality that inclines us to consider the label appropriate. The label most forcefully asserts itself when we reflect on what Mr. Troubled is likely to say after accepting the offer. "I really had no choice." "I didn't want to accept her offer but what could I do? I have my children to think about." Both Mr. Troubled and Ms. Starlet (in our previous case) *reluctantly* consented to sexual interaction, but I think it can be agreed that Ms. Starlet had a choice in a way that Mr. Troubled did not. Mr. Troubled's choice was *severely constrained by his needs*, whereas Ms. Starlet's was not. As for Ms. Opportunistic, it seems that we might describe her approach as in some sense exploiting or taking advantage of Mr. Troubled's desperate situation. It is not so much, as we would say in the case of threats, that she coerces him or his consent, but rather that she achieves her aim of winning consent by taking advantage of the fact that he is already "under coercion," that is, his choice is severely constrained by his need. If we choose to describe what has taken place as a "coercive offer," we should remember that Mr. Troubled is "coerced" (constrained) by his own need or perhaps by preexisting factors in his situation rather than by Ms. Opportunistic or her offer.

Since it is not quite right to say that Ms. Opportunistic is attempting to coerce Mr. Troubled, even if we are prepared to embrace the label "coercive offer," we cannot simply say, as we would say in the case of threats, that she is attempting to sexually use him via coercion. The proper account of the way in which Ms. Opportunistic attempts to sexually use Mr. Troubled is somewhat different. Let us say simply that she attempts to sexually use him *by taking advantage of his desperate situation*. The sense behind this distinctive way of sexually using someone is that a person's choice situation can sometimes be subject to such severe prior constraints that the possibility of *voluntary* consent to sexual interaction is precluded. A advances an offer calculated to gain B's reluctant consent to sexual interaction by confronting B, who has no apparent way of alleviating a genuine need, with an opportunity to do so, but makes this opportunity contingent upon consent to sexual interaction. In such a case, should we not say simply that B's need, when coupled with a lack of viable alternatives, results in B being incapable of *voluntarily* accepting A's offer? Thus A, in making an offer which B "cannot refuse," although not coercing B, nevertheless does intentionally act in a way that violates the requirement that B's sexual interaction with A be based upon B's voluntary informed consent. Thus A sexually uses B.

The central claim of this paper is that A sexually uses B if and only if A intentionally acts in a way that violates the requirement that B's sexual interaction with A be based on B's voluntary informed consent. Clearly, deception and coercion are important mechanisms whereby sexual using takes place. But consideration of case 8 has led us to the identification of yet another mechanism. In summary, then, limiting attention to cases of sexual interaction with a fully competent adult partner, A can sexually use B not only (1) by deceiving B or (2) by coercing B but also (3) by taking advantage of B's desperate solution.

NOTES

1. I follow here an account of coercion developed by Michael D. Bayles in "A Concept of Coercion," in J. Roland Pennock and John W. Chapman, eds., *Coercion: Nomos XIV* (Chicago: Aldine-Atherton, 1972), 16–29.

2. Statutory rape, sexual relations with a person under the legal age of consent, can also be construed as the sexual using of another person. In contrast to forcible rape, however, statutory rape need not involve coercion. The victim of statutory rape may freely "consent" to sexual interaction but, at least in the eyes of the law, is deemed incompetent to consent.

3. A man wrestles a woman to the ground. She is the victim of occurrent coercion. He threatens to beat her unless she submits to his sexual demands. Now she becomes the victim of dispositional coercion.

4. My account of this distinction largely derives from Robert Nozick, "Coercion," in Sidney Morgenbesser, Patrick Suppes, and Morton White, eds., *Philosophy, Science, and Method* (New York: St. Martin's Press, 1969), 440–72, and from Michael D. Bayles, "Coercive Offers and Public Benefits," *The Personalist* 55: 2 (Spring 1974), 139–44.

5. The National Advisory Council on Women's Educational Programs, *Sexual Harassment: A Report on the Sexual Harassment of Students* (August 1980), 12.

6. Virginia Held, "Coercion and Coercive Offers," in Pennock and Chapman, *Coercion: Nomos XIV*, 58.

7. *Ibid.*, 61, 62.

STUDY QUESTIONS

1. Some philosophers take the principle of free and informed consent so seriously that they apply it to all human activities. Thus, the moral considerations relevant to having sex with another person are no different from those that govern, say, playing tennis. (A version of this thesis can be found in Alan Goldman's "Plain Sex," in this volume.) But suppose someone says, "Any comparison between the informed consent I give in a hospital setting to that I give for sexual relations must be flawed, because sexual relations are significantly different in nature from medical procedures." Do you agree? How is sex different—if it is different—from the other ways we allow our bodies to be touched by others?

2. Mappes says that one person could sexually use another person by failing to disclose relevant facts to the other person prior to engaging in sexual activity. What specific facts are relevant? One possibility is Mappes's suggestion, that if I know that for you fact F would be relevant, would have an effect on your decision and consent, then I must not deceive you (by commission or omission) about F. Is this account adequate? Am I committed to disclosing *anything* about me that you might find relevant?

3. Suppose that X and Y are two gay men who meet in a venue where gay men have casual sexual encounters. Suppose also that X is HIV positive. Should X disclose his HIV status to Y if Y does not ask? What about if Y does ask? Does the fact that they are in a place where causal sex regularly occurs, and in which certain conventions are in place, have any bearing on this case? Think about how this issue might affect Mappes's principle.

4. In the movie *Indecent Proposal*, actors Woody Harrelson ("David") and Demi Moore ("Diana") play a young married couple who gamble away all their savings in Las Vegas. They then encounter a billionaire, John Gage (played by Robert Redford). John sexually desires Diana and offers David one million dollars to allow John to spend an evening with Diana. David and Diana eventually accept the offer. Who, if anyone, used whom here, according to Mappes? Who, if anyone, was morally culpable in this scenario? Would you take part in such an arrangement—as either David, John, or Diana?

5. On Mappes's view, should a client of a prostitute feel less guilt about hiring her, if he knows her to be hungry, than about hiring a prostitute he knows to be a drug addict? Try to get clear about Mappes's notion of "exploitation" and how it fits, logically, with the rest of his Kantian sexual ethics.

6. In Howard Klepper's "case 2" (see his "Sexual Exploitation and the Value of Persons," in this volume), Romeo brags to friends about

his sexual adventures with Juliet. By Mappes's lights, does Romeo dispositionally coerce Juliet into having sex, or does he simply disrespect her? Is Case 2 a case of (impermissible) sexual use at all?

7. Which of Mappes's cases do you think are realistic? Do you think some of them are far-fetched? If so, why?

SEVENTEEN

Sexual Exploitation and the Value of Persons

Howard Klepper

This essay by **Howard Klepper** *adds depth to Thomas Mappes's (see the previous chapter in this volume) interpretation and application of Immanuel Kant's Formula of Humanity. Though Klepper concurs with Mappes on the centrality of free and informed consent in making moral judgments about sexual activity, he argues that obtaining the consent of the other person prior to sex is not sufficient for morally proper sexual relations in a robust Kantian sense. For Klepper, a person can be treated sexually as a mere means (that is, wrongly) even if they have consented in a Mappesian way. In order to satisfy the Kantian requirement that we do not wrongly use another person sexually, we must—beyond getting their consent—be considerate of them and their needs. Our cultural norms demand that we treat sexual partners in a respectful and sensitive manner. (See a similar thesis, advanced but stated only briefly by Alan Goldman, in "Plain Sex," this volume, part I.) Kantian Christians would go further, insisting that if we really want to avoid merely using each other in sexual activity, we must be married (see, for example, Karol Wojtyła's* Love and Responsibility*). Klepper also makes some trenchant points about Kant's views on marriage and prostitution (on which, see also Alan Soble's "Sexual Use," the next chapter in this volume).*

Howard Klepper previously taught in the philosophy department and in the Strich School of Medicine of Loyola University, Chicago, and was a visiting fellow in the Biomedical Ethics Program at Stanford University. Now living in Berkeley, California, he makes, by hand, one-of-a-kind guitars (see www.klepperguitars.com). This essay is reprinted, with the permission of Howard Klepper and the publisher, Springer SBM B.V., from *Journal of Value Inquiry* 27, 3–4 (1993), 479–86. © 1993 Kluwer Academic.

In his *Lectures on Ethics,*[1] Kant gives us an application of his ethical theory to human sexual relations. Much of what he says there seems irrelevant and puritanical to the modern reader. For example, Kant condemns all sex outside of marriage, and he calls masturbation an abominable crime against nature.[2] It is not my purpose to defend these positions. But I think that Kant's discussion of the wrongfulness of using another person as a sexual object helps explain the wrongfulness of some kinds of sexual relations. In this essay I develop a Kantian account of sexual exploitation and suggest how to apply it to other exploitative relationships.

Kant's second formulation of the categorical imperative (the "Formula of Humanity") is often taken to be equivalent to a requirement that in our transactions with others, we do not deprive them of the opportunity for voluntary informed consent to their own actions. In our teaching we may conveniently answer a student's query as to what it means to treat another as a mere means, and not at the same time as an end, by saying that we do this if we induce another to act by coercion or deceit. We usually add that coercion includes threats as well as force, and that deceit includes withholding relevant information as well as lying. The virtue of this account is that coercion and deceit, while problematic, are easier to define and detect than the vaguer notion of respect for moral personhood. But I argue that this reduction of the Kantian imperative is incomplete, by showing how a person may be treated as a mere means sexually and otherwise in the absence of coercion or deceit.

The shortcomings of a reduction of the imperative to a ban on coercion or deceit may be illustrated by Thomas Mappes's essay, "Sexual Morality and the Concept of Using Another Person."[3] Mappes considers what moral rules govern sexual behavior in the context of general moral principles, by analysis of using another person sexually as a mere means. He defines the immoral use of another person, sexually or otherwise, as intentionally acting in a way that deprives the other person of voluntary informed consent. He further defines this as using coercion or deception to induce another to consent to an action.

Examples offered of deception by lying include denying having herpes, or being married, in order to get another to consent to a sexual relationship. Examples of deception by withholding information include failing to inform another of having a venereal disease, or being married, when there is good reason to believe that consent to sexual relations would be refused if that information were divulged.

Mappes considers coercion to present more difficult problems than deception, and he devotes the bulk of his essay to distinguishing coercive from noncoercive behavior. He discusses the distinction between threats and mere offers, concluding that taking advantage of another's desperate situation is coercion, even if threats and deception are not involved. For example, if Tom, a single father of two children, loses his job and is unable to make his mortgage payments, and Jane offers to pay the mortgage if Tom will enter into a sexual relationship with her, her behavior should be considered as treating Tom as a mere means.

Mappes's analysis is useful and correct as far as it goes. However, the concept of using another person sexually as a mere means is much broader than what is included in Mappes's account, which ends with the parties' agreement to have sex.[4] This is a description of immoral means of obtaining "consent" to a sexual relationship, but our moral obligations to others in sexual relationships do not end there. A person may be used sexually as a mere means during and after sexual acts as well. Consider the following case:

> *Case 1:* Romeo and Juliet have been out together on a few dates. They are sexually attracted to each other. Juliet willingly accepts Romeo's suggestion that they have sex together. During intercourse, Romeo makes no attempt to please or satisfy Juliet. After having an orgasm, he rolls over without a word and goes to sleep.

Case 1 is an uncontroversial instance, perhaps a paradigm instance, of using another person sexually, despite voluntary informed consent to engage in sex having occurred. Romeo has been selfish, rude, and inconsiderate. He has disregarded Juliet's value as a person and treated her as an object, a mere means to his ends. Our moral obligations to our sexual partners surely do not end with their voluntary informed consent. Closer to the truth is that they begin there. We have an ongoing obligation to be respectful and considerate of our sexual partners' needs. Like voluntary informed consent, this is not an obligation unique to sexual relationships. It applies to all our relationships with others, but the requirements imposed by this obligation increase with the intimacy of the relationship. The obligation applies with particular force to sexual relationships, because the intimacy of those relationships involves relinquishing defenses, which leaves people particularly vulnerable to feeling used. This obligation does not end with considerate lovemaking.

> *Case 2:* Romeo and Juliet begin a sexual relationship as before, but in this case both are generous and affectionate lovers. The next day, however, Romeo brags to his friends of his seduction of Juliet and gives them a lurid and detailed account of her sexual technique.

Case 2 is another instance of using another person sexually. Although the wrongful acts take place subsequent to the sexual acts, as in Case 1 their wrongfulness is based on a lack of respect and consideration for a sexual partner. The sexual character of the relationship, together with cultural conventions regarding privacy, renders the acts wrongful. In Western culture one shows disrespect for another by revealing intimate facts about the other's sexual behavior. For Romeo to give his friends a detailed account of the rest of his date with Juliet, exclusive of their sexual relations, would not be wrong. But the privacy of a person's sexual acts is a legitimate end for that person to seek, and to disregard that end does not respect the value of that person as an end in herself or himself.

A plausible response to the above cases is that they are instances of deceit. In Case 1 there was an implicit agreement on the part of Romeo to be concerned with Juliet's pleasure and satisfaction, and in Case 2 there was an implicit agreement to not make public intimate information that is conventionally considered to be private. If these are instances of deceit, the conclusion might be drawn that Mappes is wrong to say that coercion presents the more difficult and interesting instances of using another person sexually. That claim results from his focus on pre-sexual acts, in which implicit agreements as to how the partners will treat each other during and after sex have not yet become relevant. Once we take into our account the ways in which a person who has voluntarily consented to sex may be used sexually during and after the sexual acts, we have moved into an area in which the more difficult and interesting questions are those of deceit.

What would be the source of the implicit agreements in Cases 1 and 2? Juliet's having the relevant expectations about Romeo's conduct would by itself be insufficient. One party's unspoken expectations do not make for an implied agreement. For agreements to be implied in these cases means that both parties were aware of norms or standards of conduct, and that absent any explicit exclusion of these norms, it was reasonable to assume that they were incorporated into the parties' agreement. So, for implicit agreements to be binding, they must not be only expected by one party; the expectation must in a relevant sense be legitimate.

Does mutuality legitimate the expectation? An analogy to contract law is appropriate. The general legal rule is that a contractual term is implied where a reasonable person would infer it to exist, on the basis of the express agreements and observable behavior of the parties. A term may be taken as implied if it is customary and usual to the kind of agreement being made, and each party may reasonably assume that the other is aware of the custom and usage. That each party had the same unexpressed assumptions will not result in an implied agreement, despite the mutuality of the expectation, if a reasonable objective observer would not infer the agreement to exist under the circumstances. Thus, under the "objective" standard in contract law, mutual expectation is neither necessary nor sufficient to create an implied agreement. However, if neither party was aware of the custom and usage, no agreement occurred, under the doctrine of "mutual mistake."

Should we take an implicit agreement to engage in sexual behavior to morally legitimize that behavior? I think not. Our moral obligations are broader in scope than our legal ones. In what follows I argue that not only an implicit agreement, but also an explicit, voluntary, and informed agreement may be insufficient to justify behavior that amounts to using another person sexually by treating that person as a mere means to an end.

Let's get back to cases. Case 1 involves a norm within contemporary Western culture that sexual partners will be mutually concerned with each other's pleasure and feelings. Both partners will usually be aware of this norm and will be justified in taking the awareness to be mutual without explicit mention. Their agreement to have sex together will thus include an implicit agreement to attend to their partner's sexual satisfaction. Failure to keep this implicit agreement is a form of deceit, and therefore a conventional case of using another as a mere means. Two other possibilities are to be considered. The first is where one of the parties is unaware of the norm. Perhaps Romeo is a visitor from a culture in which men customarily are not concerned with mutuality in sex but regard a woman's sexual pleasure as unnecessary or even undesirable. Nonetheless, if Romeo were to be aware of Juliet's reasonable expectations and say nothing regarding his intent to honor those expectations, he would be deceitful by the standard we have set for implied agreements.

Second, let's suppose that Romeo is unaware of the sexual norms in Juliet's culture and that his unawareness is reasonable. In this case an objective reasonable observer would not take Romeo to have impliedly agreed to behave according to those sexual norms. In legal terms we might say that no agreement was made because of a mutual mistake of fact, that is, the parties did not agree as to the terms of their "contract," and this lack of agreement was not just subjective, but also would have been evident to an informed, objective observer. Does this mean that when Romeo behaves as in case 1 he has not used Juliet sexually? I think he has, despite the lack of an implied agreement to honor her expectations. Using another person as a mere means is not a culturally relative notion. We should instead say that in Romeo's home culture the norm is that men use women sexually as mere means to their ends. This is just an instance of the familiar truism that wrongful conduct does not become moral if everybody does it.

Even in the case where Juliet is aware of the norms of Romeo's culture, or is herself a member of that culture, so that we may take her to have impliedly agreed to his actions, I think that we would be entirely justified to say that Romeo had used Juliet sexually as a mere means. This further illustrates the difference between moral and legal notions. Legality has a relativistic dimension that morality does not share. Cultural conventions may determine the content of a lawful agreement; they do not thereby morally legitimize it. Put another way, the question whether Romeo has treated Juliet immorally is not settled by Romeo's behavior having been lawful, and even agreed upon.

The point may be further illustrated by variations on our cases. Suppose that in case 1, Juliet is aware that Romeo is a selfish and insensitive lover, but in spite of this (or, in a more perverse variant, because of it) chooses to have sex with him. Or, in case 2, suppose that Juliet is aware of Romeo's propensity to kiss and tell. This would not change the fact that Romeo treats Juliet as a mere means in these cases and uses her sexually.

If I am right about these cases, we must reject the interpretation of Kant's second formulation of the categorical imperative that equates treating another person as a mere means with using coercion or deceit. Neither is present in the variations on our cases just considered. Juliet gives voluntary informed consent, yet is treated as a mere means, as a sexual object.

More generally, treating another as a mere means includes treating the other as an object, and not at the same time as an intrinsically valuable moral subject; this is not negated even by the other's explicit consent to such treatment. A familiar example is slavery. The slave's voluntary informed consent to enter into the slavery relationship does not provide a moral justification for it. Similarly, consent to being abused or degraded does not render the abuse or degradation moral. (Although, with some limitations, it may make it legal. For example, consent is a defense to battery and rape, but not to murder and mayhem.)

Another aspect of the above variations on cases 1 and 2 is that both parties violate the Kantian imperative. This may be illustrated more clearly by examples involving prostitution relationships, where the behaviors of the parties are explicitly agreed to. Kant considered it to be "the depth of infamy"[5] to provide sexual services in exchange for money. He argues that a person's body is not property, which can be disposed of however that person wishes. The body is an inseparable part of a person, and because persons are priceless it cannot be treated as a mere thing that may be let out for hire.

Kant carried this idea further to claim that mutual satisfaction of sexual desire with no idea of material gain is also morally unacceptable. Here Kant's argument is that an agreement for mutual sexual satisfaction purports to be a contract to surrender only each person's body to the other, while retaining freedom over the other aspects of the person. But such a contract must necessarily be violated, because a part of the person cannot be separated from the whole; in a sexual relationship I necessarily use the whole person of my partner, thereby violating my agreement to use only a part, and making the person into a mere thing (which would be wrong even if it were agreed to).

Kant offers no justification for his claim that to have a right to use a part of a person is to have a right to use the whole person, though his argument depends on this claim. To surrender all of one's humanity to another, as in a relationship of slave to master, is wrong, but we have no good reason to see mutual consent to sexual relations as a surrender of the whole person, and thus contrary to the rational nature of humanity. Moreover, Kant's argument could extend, implausibly, to any agreement to sell one's labor to another. So we may reject Kant's claim that all sex outside of marriage is immoral. But I argue below that some kinds of prostitution relationships are immoral for Kantian reasons.

I am not claiming that all prostitution is necessarily exploitive or immoral. I leave that question open, as in some possible culture the sale of sexual services might not be either exploitive or degrading, and that even within contemporary Western culture a prostitution relationship might not involve treating another as a mere means to an end. I make here only the weaker claim that some prostitution agreements are cases of mutual exploitation. A typical example is case 3.

> *Case 3:* Romeo desires impersonal sex, in which he can use another person's body as a tool for his own pleasure. He meets Juliet, a prostitute, on a street corner. They negotiate an explicit agreement for the performance of sexual acts and go to a motel where they have sex in much the same fashion as in case 1. Juliet dislikes being used as Romeo's sexual object, but performs according to their contract, and considers her payment to be sufficient compensation.

We saw above that Kant's claim, that an agreement which gives another rights over a part of a person is necessarily an agreement for the surrender of all of that person, might lead to the conclusion that all agreements to hire out one person's services to another are immoral. A typical employment relationship, in which the employee is paid to perform work that he or she may not enjoy doing, is not necessarily an instance of mutual exploitation or of mutual treatment of another person as a mere means. A principled distinction between case 3 and other employment relationships is needed. What distinguishes case 3 from a common employer-employee relationship is that in case 3 it is Romeo's objective, a part of his ends or a second-order end, to treat another person as a mere means to his ends. Romeo might not want to find out that Juliet enjoyed her sexual acts with him; he may want a lack of mutuality. If in some employer-employee relationships the employee may feel used or degraded, that is normally incidental to such relationships, which could just as well (or better) exist without such feelings. But any employment relationship which has as the employer's purpose the denigration of the employee would similarly be wrongful regardless of the employee's voluntary informed consent, whether implicit or explicit.

We can also avoid the possibility that case 3 might be explained by Juliet's being coerced, in Mappes's sense, by Romeo taking advantage of her desperate economic situation. Let's suppose that economic need has not driven Juliet to prostitution. Perhaps she is supplementing an otherwise adequate income in order to obtain some luxury item she desires.

By hypothesis, Romeo intends to treat Juliet as a mere means in case 3. His purpose in hiring her is to treat her sexually as a mere object, and not as an end in herself. He exploits Juliet's willingness to be so treated. Juliet, for her part, has treated humanity *in her own person* as a mere means, by choosing, without necessity, to be so treated by Romeo. Kant might say that for a rational being to freely choose to be treated as a mere means and hence not as a free, rational being is contradictory. Moreover, a rational will would not voluntarily allow itself to be determined by the unfree, animal will of another. Juliet acts irrationally by Kantian standards. From a Kantian perspective such a choice must be motivated by sensuous inclination and hence be unfree.

Where Juliet is aware of the purpose that she be treated as a mere means by Romeo, her assent to that purpose determines that she is being treated as a mere means by both Romeo and herself. In such a case the exploitation is mutual. Juliet's end is to obtain money, and because Romeo's will is determined by irrational sensuous inclination he is unable to freely assent to her end. Juliet has used Romeo as a mere means to an end, by taking advantage of his lapse of rationality (in the Kantian sense).

We may now generalize the above conclusions. A person may be treated as a mere means not only by coercion and deceit, but also by any conduct intended to achieve the purpose of treating that person as an object and not at the same time an intrinsically valuable moral subject. The intention determines the treating as a mere means, not the success of the method by which it is carried out. Next, a person treats himself or herself as a mere means by voluntarily agreeing to be the object of conduct by which another intends to treat him or her as a mere means, where that intention is known. Last, such a relationship is mutually exploitative; a person who wishes to use another as a mere means cannot be acting from reason, in a Kantian sense, and therefore is in turn used as a mere means by another who consents to being so used.

These conclusions are drawn from cases of sexually using another as a mere means, but I see no problem in applying them elsewhere. They explain, for example, the wrongfulness many people intuitively saw in the dwarf-throwing contests that attracted media attention a few years ago.[6] Despite protests from the dwarfs involved that they were freely choosing to accept this employment as human projectiles, the sense shared by most observers, I think, was that a point of the game was that the dwarfs be treated as mere things. The dwarfs were being hired not just for the fact that they were projectiles of a desired shape or weight, but in order that human beings might be treated as non-rational, non-sentient objects. If those human projectiles did not see this, they did not do wrong, although we may be inclined to pity them. If they knew that their wrongful treatment was a purpose of the game, then they were wronging themselves and also exploiting their exploiters. This is explained by my interpretation of Kant's injunction against treating any person, including oneself, as a mere means to an end.

NOTES

1. Immanuel Kant, *Lectures on Ethics*, trans. L. Infield (London: The Century Co., 1930).
2. *Ibid.*, 166–67, 170.
3. Thomas Mappes, "Sexual Morality and the Concept of Using Another Person," in this volume.
4. Much philosophical writing on the subject of sex only discusses activity which precedes sexual acts. Thomas Nagel's seminal essay "Sexual Perversion" (in this volume) is typical in its focus on attraction and arousal. Nagel has been criticized for this truncated account (for example, Janice Moulton, "Sexual Behavior: Another Position," in this volume.)
5. Kant, *Lectures on Ethics*, 66.
6. "Little People Oppose Events in Which Dwarfs Are Objects," *New York Times*, 3 July 1992, p. 8, col. 1.

STUDY QUESTIONS

1. On what grounds does Klepper conclude that sexual relationships leave "people particularly vulnerable to feeling used"? What other sorts of relationships also, or are likely to, share these features? Does that make them wrong? Might sexual and other relationships have redeeming qualities that at least partially overcome these defects?

2. If, as Klepper claims, "intention determines the treating as a mere means," have I exploited a prostitute if my big-hearted intention is to enable her to buy food for her children? In general, do our intentions determine whether our actions are right or wrong, or are they relevant only in making judgments about our moral characters?

3. Consider the claim that "consent to being abused or degraded does not render the abuse or degradation moral." Would Mappes ("Sexual Morality and the Concept of Using Another Person," in this volume) or Kant agree or disagree (consult Alan Soble, "Sexual Use," in this volume)? Does the claim imply that consensual sadomasochistic sexual acts are immoral (if they involve consensual degradation)? Similarly, does the claim imply that it is immoral for a person to consent to being sexually used? What is morally wrong (if anything) when two mutually consenting adults consent to use and be used by each other sexually?

4. Klepper speaks about "our cultural norms" that obligate us to treat a lover "as an intrinsically valuable moral subject." Might we argue that these cultural norms are in need of revision? Are they written in stone? Our society, or large segments of it, apparently accepts or tolerates casual sex, extramarital sex, promiscuity, sadomasochism, and various kinds of sex work. Does this fact weak-

en Klepper's arguments that are grounded on what "our" norms are?

5. If we were to agree with Klepper that our moral obligations to our sexual partners only begin with free and informed consent and must be supplemented with other moral considerations, where do our obligations to others (or to ourselves) in sexual contexts come to an end? Why add only "show consideration" to the other person? Why not also claim that another necessary condition is that birth-control techniques not be employed? Or that the people must be married? Or heterosexual?

EIGHTEEN

Sexual Use

Alan Soble

If sexual desire is by its nature directed from one person toward another person as an object; if experiencing sexual desire and sexual arousal diminishes a person's rationality and autonomy; and if while engaging in sexual activity, people are essentially making use of each other as instruments of their own pleasure—then human sexual activity seems morally suspicious or, worse, morally wrong, in the absence of special overriding reasons (or excuses) that yield justifiable exceptions. This is what **Alan Soble** *calls the "Kantian Sex Problem." It cannot be solved merely by saying that we must engage in heterosexual activity to keep humanity going. Christians, including St. Paul and St. Augustine, were not persuaded of any theological requirement (given the grand narrative story that comprises Christianity) to keep earthly humanity going. The philosophical task is not to sidestep the problem by denying the Kantian account of the nature of sexual desire and sexual activity, or by denying the validity of the Second Formulation of Kant's Categorical Imperative (the Formula of Humanity), or by denying Kant's anthropology or ontology of the human person, i.e., our characteristic rational autonomy and our inherent worth or dignity. Rather, the task is to fashion a sexual ethics consistent with Kant's metaphysics of human sexuality, with his Second Formulation, and with his account of human dignity. This sexual ethics must entail that sexuality is not as morally pernicious as Kantian considerations suggest. While examining the literature on Kant and sex, Soble offers a typology of the various solutions that have been proposed in this literature. He critically discusses each type of solution and finds them lacking in some way or another. Soble also scrutinizes the writings of Kant, trying to make sense of the passages in which Kant himself tries to solve the problem that he created. An appendix has been added to this revision of Soble's essay. It contains a reply*

to yet another proposed solution to the Kantian sex problem, one that appeared in
print after this essay was first written and published.

I begin by describing the hideous nature of sexuality, in virtue of which sexual desire and activity are morally suspicious, or what we have been told about the foulness of sex by Immanuel Kant.[1] I then explain, given Kant's metaphysics of sex, why sexual activity apparently conflicts with the Second Formulation of the Categorical Imperative. I propose a typology of solutions to this problem and critically discuss recent philosophical ethics of sex that fall within the typology. I conclude with remarks about Kant's own solution.

THE NATURE OF SEX

On Kant's view, a person who sexually desires another person objectifies the other both before and during sexual activity. Manipulation and deception (primping, padding, making a good first impression) are so common as to seem natural to human sexual interaction.[2] The other's body, his or her lips, thighs, buttocks, and toes, are desired as the arousing parts they are, distinct from the person. As Kant says, about the genitals,

> sexuality is not an inclination which one human being has for another as such, but is an inclination for the sex of another. . . . [O]nly her sex is the object of his desires. . . . [A]ll men and women do their best to make not their human nature but their sex more alluring.[3]

Further, both the body and the compliant actions of the other person are tools (a means) that one uses for one's own sexual pleasure; to that extent the other person is a thing. Sexual activity itself is strange, not only by manifesting unwilled arousal and involuntary bodily movements, but also with its yearning to master, dominate, and consume the other's body. Sexual desire is a threat to the other's personhood, but the one under the spell of desire also loses hold of his or her own personhood. The person who desires another depends on the whims of that other for satisfaction, and becomes as a result a jellyfish, vulnerable to the other's demands and manipulations.[4] Merely being sexually aroused by another person can be experienced as coercive; similarly, a person who proposes an irresistible sexual offer may be exploiting another who has been made weak by sexual desire.[5] Moreover, a person who willingly complies with another person's request for a sexual encounter voluntarily makes an object of himself or herself. As Kant puts it, "For the natural use that one sex makes of the other's sexual organs is *enjoyment*, for which one gives oneself up to the other. In this act a human being makes himself into a thing."[6] And, for Kant, because those engaged in sexual activity make themselves into objects merely for the sake of sexual pleasure, both persons reduce themselves to animals. When

> a man wishes to satisfy his desire, and a woman hers, they stimulate each other's desire; their inclinations meet, but their object is not human nature but sex, and each of them dishonours the human nature of the other. They make of humanity an instrument for the satisfaction of their lusts and inclinations, and dishonour it by placing it on a level with animal nature.[7]

Finally, the power of the sexual urge makes it dangerous. Sexual desire is inelastic, relentless, the passion most likely to challenge reason and cause us to experience weakness of will (*akrasia*), compelling us to seek satisfaction even when doing so involves the risks of dark-alley gropings, microbiologically filthy acts, slinking around the White House, or impetuous marriage. Sexually-motivated behavior easily destroys our self-respect.

The sexual impulse, then, is morally dubious and, to boot, a royal pain. Kant thought that humans would be delighted to be free of such promptings:

> Inclinations . . . , as sources of needs, are so far from having an absolute value to make them desirable for their own sake that it must rather be the universal wish of every rational being to be wholly free from them.[8]

I am not sure that I believe all these claims about the nature of sexuality, but that is irrelevant, because many philosophers have with good reason taken them seriously. In some moods I might reply to Kant by muttering a Woody Allen-ish joke: "Is sex an autonomy-killing, mind-numbing, subhuman passion? Yes, but only when it's good." In this essay, however, I want to examine how sexual acts could be moral, if Kant's description is right.

SEX AND THE SECOND FORMULATION

Michael Ruse, the well-known philosopher of biology, has explained how a moral problem arises in acting on sexual desire:

> The starting point to sex is the sheer desire of a person for the body of another. One wants to feel the skin, to smell the hair, to see the eyes—one wants to bring one's own genitals into contact with those of the other. . . . This gets dangerously close to treating the other as a means to the fulfillment of one's own sexual desire—as an object, rather than as an end.[9]

We should add, to make Ruse's observation more comprehensively Kantian, that the desire to be touched, to be thrilled by the touch of the other, to be the object of someone else's desire, is equally a "starting point" that raises the moral problem.

Because this problem arises from the intersection of Kant's view of the nature of sexuality and Kant's ethics, let us review the Second Formulation: "Act in such a way that you always treat humanity, whether in your own person or in the person of any other, never simply as a means, but always at the same time as an end." Or "man . . . *exists* as an end in himself, *not merely as a means* for arbitrary use by this or that will: he must in all his actions, whether they are directed to himself or to other rational beings, always be viewed *at the same time as an end*."[10] The question arises: how can sexual desire be satisfied without merely using the other as an object and without treating the self as an object? How can sexual activity be planned and carried out while "at the same time" treating the other and the self as persons, treating their "humanity" as an end and confirming their autonomy and rationality? The Second Formulation directs us not to treat ourselves and others *merely* as means or objects. Permissible is treating another and ourselves as means as long as at the same time we are also treated as persons with dignity. Can this be done?

A person's providing free and informed consent to interactions with other persons is, in general for Kant, a necessary condition for satisfying the Second Formulation. It is not sufficient. In addition, treating someone as a person includes (among other things) taking on the other's ends (if these ends are permissible) as if they were one's own ends: "the ends of a subject who is an end in himself must, if this conception is to have its *full* effect in me, be also, as far as possible, *my* ends."[11] I must take on the other's ends for their *own* sake, not because doing so is effective in advancing my goals. It is further required that the other can take on my ends, my purpose, in my using him or her as a means:

> the man who has a mind to make a false promise to others will see at once that he is intending to make use of another man *merely as a means* to an end he does not share. For the man whom I seek to use for my

own purposes by such a promise cannot possibly agree with my way of behaving to him, and so cannot himself share the end of [my] action.[12]

Given Kant's metaphysics of sexuality, can all these requirements of the Second Formulation be satisfied in sexual interaction? That is the Kantian sex problem.

It should be noted that even though Kant advances these two conditions in addition to free and informed consent—I must take on your ends, and you must take on my ends—he apparently relaxes his standard for some situations, allowing one person to use another just with the free and informed consent of the used person, as long as one allows the used person to *retain* personhood or one does *not interfere* with his or her retaining personhood. This weaker test for satisfying the Second Formulation may be important in Kant's account of the morality of work-for-hire and of sexual relations.[13]

I now proceed to display a conceptual typology of various solutions to the Kantian sex problem, and discuss critically whether solutions that occupy different logical locations in the typology conform with the Second Formulation. There are five types of solution: behavioral internalism, psychological internalism, thin externalism, thick minimalist externalism, and thick extended externalism.

INTERNALIST SOLUTIONS

Internalist solutions to the sex problem advise us to modify the character of sexual activity so that persons engaged in it satisfy the Second Formulation. For internalists, restraints on how sexual acts are carried out, or restraints on the expression of the impulse, are required. Consent, then, is not sufficient for the morality of sexual acts, even if necessary. Note that one might fix a sexual act internally so that *qua* sexual act the act is unobjectionable, but it still might be wrong for other reasons; for example, it might be adulterous. There are two internalisms: *behavioral* internalism, according to which the physical components of sexual acts make the moral difference, and *psychological* internalism, according to which certain attitudes must be present during sexual activity.

Behavioral Internalism

Alan Goldman defines "sexual desire" as the "desire for contact with another person's body and for the pleasure which such contact produces. . . . The desire for another's body is . . . the desire for the pleasure that physical contact brings."[14] Because sexual desire is a desire for one's own pleasure, it is understandable that Goldman senses a Kantian problem. Thus Goldman writes that sexual activities "invariably involve at different stages the manipulation of one's partner for one's own pleasure" and thereby, he notes, seem to violate the Second Formulation—which, on Goldman's truncated rendition, "holds that one ought not to treat another as a means to such private ends." (In making the same point, Kant would have said "subjective," "discretionary," or "arbitrary" ends, instead of "private.") But Goldman suggests that from a Kantian perspective, "using other individuals for personal benefit," in sex or other interactions, is wrong "only when [the acts] are one-sided, when the benefits are not mutual." So, as a solution to the sex problem, Goldman proposes that

> Even in an act which by its nature "objectifies" the other, one recognizes a partner as a subject with demands and desires by yielding to those desires, by allowing oneself to be a sexual object as well, by giving pleasure or ensuring that the pleasures of the act are mutual.

This sexual moral principle—make sure to provide sexual pleasure for your partner—seems plausible and at least in spirit consistent with the Second Formulation.[15]

But *why* might one sexually please the other? (Pleasing the other person can be done, as Goldman recognizes, by actively doing something to the other, or by allowing the other person to treat us as an object, so that they do things to which we passively acquiesce.) One answer comes from sexual egoism or hedonism: pleasing the other is *necessary for or contributes to one's own pleasure.* How so? By inducing the other, through either the other's sexual arousal or gratitude, to furnish pleasure to oneself. Or because sexually pleasing the other satisfies one's desire to exert power or influence over the other. Or because in providing pleasure to the other we get pleasure by witnessing the effects of our exertions.[16] Or by causing the other to hold us in an esteem that heightens our arousal. Or because while giving pleasure to the other person we identify with his or her arousal and pleasure, which identification increases our own arousal and pleasure.[17] Or because pleasing the other alleviates or prevents guilt feelings, or doing so makes us feel good that we have kept a promise. Or. . . .

Another answer is that providing pleasure to the other can *and should* be done for the sake of pleasing the other, just because you know the other person has sexual needs and desires and hopes for their satisfaction. The sexual satisfaction of the other is an end in itself, is valuable in its own right, is not merely instrumentally valuable. It follows that in some circumstances you must be willing and ready to please the other person sexually when doing so does not contribute to your own satisfaction or even runs counter to it. Kant likes to focus on this sort of scenario in the *Groundwork*, cases that single out the motive of duty or benevolence from motives based on inclination.

I categorize Goldman as a behavioral internalist because all he insists on, in order to make sexual activity Kantianly morally permissible, is the *behavior* of providing pleasure for the other person. Goldman never claims that providing pleasure be done with a benevolent *motive* or purity of purpose. But this feature of his proposal is exactly why it fails, in its *own* terms. If providing pleasure to the other is a mechanism for attaining or improving one's own pleasure, providing pleasure to the other continues to treat the other merely as a means. Since giving pleasure to the other is instrumental in obtaining my pleasure, giving pleasure has not at all succeeded in internally *fixing* the nature of the sexual act. Providing pleasure can be a genuine internalist solution, by changing the nature of the sexual act, only if providing pleasure is an unconditional giving. Goldman's proposal thus fails to accommodate his own Kantian commitment. When Kant claims that we must treat the other as a person by taking on his or her ends as our own—by providing sexual pleasure, if that is his or her end—Kant does not mean that as a hypothetical, as if taking on the other's ends were a mechanism for getting the other person to allow us to treat him or her as a means. We must take on the other's ends as our own but not because doing so is useful for us in generating our own pleasure or achieving our own sexual goals. Sharing the ends of the other person means viewing those ends as valuable in their own right.

Further, for Kant, we may take on the ends of the other as our own only if the other's ends are themselves morally permissible: I may "make the other's ends my ends provided only that these are not immoral."[18] Given the objectification and use involved in sexual activity, as conceded by Goldman, the moral permissibility of the end of seeking sexual pleasure by means of another person has not yet been established for *either* party. We are not to make the other's ends our own ends if the other's ends are not, in themselves, already morally permissible, and whether the sexual ends of the other person *are* permissible is precisely the question at issue. Thus, to be told by Goldman that it is morally permissible for one person to objectify another in sexual activity if the other also objectifies the first, with the first's allowance, does not answer the question. Goldman's internalist solution attempts to change the nature of the sexual act, from what it is essentially to what it might be were we to embrace *slightly* better bedroom behavior, by avoiding raw selfishness. But this doesn't go far enough to fix the nature of sexual activity, if all that is required is that both parties add the giving of pleasure to an act that is by its nature, and remains, self-centered. Finally (and *perhaps* most important), Goldman ignores, in Kant's statement of the Second Formulation, that we must also respect the humanity *in one's own person*. To make oneself voluntarily an object for the sake of the other person's sexual pleasure, as Goldman recommends, only multiplies the use, does not eliminate it.

Goldman has, in effect, changed the problem from one of sexual objectification and use into one of distributive justice.[19] Sex is morally permissible, on his view, if the pleasure is mutual; the way to make sexual activity moral is to make it nonmorally good for both participants. Use and objectification remain, but they are permissible, on his view, because the objectification is reciprocal and the act is mutually beneficial. Even though in one sense Goldman makes sexual activity moral by making it *more* nonmorally good, for the *other* party, he also makes sexual activity moral by making it *less* nonmorally good, for the *self*, since one's sexual urgings must be restrained. What goes morally wrong in sexual activity, for Goldman, is that only one person experiences pleasure (or lopsidedly) and only one bears the burden of providing it. This is what Goldman means by saying that "one-sided" sexual activity is immoral. The benefits of receiving pleasure, and the burdens of the restraint of seeking pleasure and providing it to the other, must be passed around to everyone involved. This is accomplished, for Goldman, by a reciprocal distribution of being used as an object.

Suppose, instead, that both parties are expected to inject *unconditional* giving into an act that is essentially self-centered. Then both parties must buckle down more formidably, in order to restrain their impulses for their own pleasure and to provide pleasure to the other. But if altruistic giving were easy, given our natures, there would be less reason for thinking, to begin with, that sexual desire tends to use the other person in a self-interested way. To the extent that the sexual impulse is self-interested, as Goldman's definitions make clear, it is implausible that sexual urges could be controlled by a moral command to provide pleasure unconditionally. The point is not only that a duty to provide pleasure unconditionally threatens the nonmoral goodness of sexual acts, that it reduces the sexual excitement and satisfaction of both persons. Fulfilling such a duty, if we assume Goldman's account of sexual desire, may be unlikely or impossible.

Psychological Internalism

If Goldman wants to fix the sexual act internally, to change its nature, he must insist not merely on our performing behaviors that produce pleasure for the other, but on our producing pleasure for a certain reason. In this way, we move from behavioral to psychological internalism, which claims that sexual acts must be accompanied and restrained by certain attitudes, the presence of which ensure the satisfaction of the Second Formulation.

At one point in her essay "Defining Wrong and Defining Rape," Jean Hampton lays out a view that is similar to Goldman's, in which the occurrence of mutual pleasure alone solves the sex problem:

> when sex is as much about pleasing another as it is about pleasing oneself, it certainly doesn't involve using another as a means and actually incorporates the idea of respect and concern for another's needs.[20]

Providing sexual pleasure to the other person seems to Hampton to satisfy Kant's Second Formulation. But she goes beyond Goldman in attempting to understand the depth or significance of the sexual experience:

> one's humanity is perhaps never more engaged than in the sexual act. But it is not only present in the experience; more important, it is "at stake" in the sense that each partner puts him/herself in a position where the behavior of the other can either confirm it or threaten it, celebrate it or abuse it.[21]

This point is Kantian: sex is metaphysically and psychologically dangerous. Hampton continues:

> If this is right, then I do not see how, for most normal human beings, sexual passion is heightened if one's sexual partner behaves in a way that one finds personally humiliating or that induces in one shame or self-hatred or that makes one feel like a "thing." . . . Whatever sexual passion is, such emotions seem antithetical to it, and such emotions are markers of the disrespect that destroys the morality of the experience. . . . [W]hat makes a sexual act morally right is also what provides the groundwork for the experience of emotions and pleasures that make for "good sex."[22]

> If the wrongness of the act is a function of its diminishing nature, then that wrongness can be present even if, ex ante, each party consented to the sex. So . . . consent is *never by itself* that which makes a sexual act morally right. . . . Lovemaking is a set of experiences . . . which includes attitudes and behaviors that are different in kind from the attitudes and behaviors involved in morally wrongful sex.[23]

Hampton's thesis, as I understand it, is that sexual activity must be accompanied by certain humanity-affirming attitudes or emotions that manifest themselves in the sexual activity itself. Attitudes and emotions that repudiate humanity, that are disrespectful, are morally wrong and (because) destructive of mutual pleasure.[24] Hampton's psychological internalism seems fairly consistent with Kant's Second Formulation: for Hampton, consent may be necessary but it is not sufficient for behaving morally or respectfully toward another person sexually; giving pleasure to the other person, taking on their sexual ends, is required; and *why* the persons produce pleasure for each other is morally relevant. A paradox, however, looms here. Being willing to provide, selflessly, sexual pleasure for the other, and carrying out the appropriate acts, might not erase the fundamentally objectifying nature of sexual activity. In such acts one person makes himself the active yet selfless sexual partner of the other, and the other allows himself to be, if not relishes, being the center of such devoted sexual attention. Both people have taken Goldman's advice—make yourself a tool or an object for the other—to the limit.

There is a more serious (and non-paradoxical) problem in Hampton's position. Her view entails that at least some casual sex, in which both parties are out to satisfy their own randiness, is morally wrong, along with prostitution, because these sexual acts are not likely to be, in some robust sense, humanity-affirming. Sadomasochism would also seem to be morally wrong, on her view, because it involves what she sees as humanity-denying attitudes. Yet casual sex and prostitution, as objectifying and instrumental as they can be, and sadomasochistic sexual acts, as humiliating to one's partner as they can be, still often produce tremendous sexual excitement—contrary to what Hampton says about the psychological coincidence of the moral and nonmoral goodness of sexual acts. She believes, as does Goldman, that morally permissible sex involves mutual sexual pleasing, that the morality of sexual activity then depends in part on its nonmoral goodness and, further, that disrespectful attitudes destroy this mutual pleasure. Here, finally, is the problem: Are disrespectful attitudes morally wrong exactly because they destroy the other's sexual pleasure or simply because they are disrespectful? Ask this question in the context of Hampton's assessment of sadomasochism. If her argument is that disrespectful attitudes that occur during sexual encounters are morally wrong simply because they are disrespectful, sadomasochistic sexual activities are morally wrong even if they do, *contra* Hampton's intuition, produce pleasure for the participants. (In this case, Hampton may be better understood as what I later call an "externalist.") But if her argument is that disrespectful attitudes are wrong because or when they destroy the mutuality of the pleasure, then sadomasochism does not turn out to be morally wrong. (In this case, Hampton remains an internalist.)

Perhaps Hampton means that sexual activity is morally permissible only when it is *both* mutually pleasure-producing *and* incorporates humanity-affirming attitudes. This dual test for the morality of sexual encounters prohibits casual sex between strangers, prostitution, as well as sadomasochistic sexuality, no matter how sexually satisfying these activities are. In Hampton's essay, however, I could find no clear criterion of "humanity-affirming" other than "provides mutual pleasure." This is why she has trouble denying the permissibility of sadomasochism. Consider the lesbian sadomasochist Pat Califia on sadomasochism: "The things that seem beautiful, inspiring, and life-affirming to me seem ugly, hateful, and ludicrous to most other people."[25] As far as I can tell, Califia means "provides sexual pleasure" by "life-affirming." If so, no disagreement in principle exists between Hampton and Califia, if Hampton means "provides pleasure" by "humanity-affirming." What Hampton does not take seriously is Califia's point that brutal behaviors and humiliating attitudes that occur during sexual activity can make for mutually exciting and pleasurable sex.

EXTERNALIST SOLUTIONS

According to *externalism*, morality requires that we place restraints on when sexual acts are engaged in, with whom sexual activity occurs, or on the conditions in which sexual activities are performed. Properly setting the background context in which sexual acts occur enables us to satisfy the Second Formulation. One distinction among externalisms is that between *minimalist* externalism, which claims that morality requires that only the context of sexual activity be set, while the sexual acts may be whatever they turn out to be, and *extended* externalism, which claims that setting the context will also affect the character of the sexual acts. Another distinction among externalisms is that between *thin* externalism, according to which free and informed consent is both necessary and sufficient for the moral permissibility of sexual acts (with a trivial *ceteris paribus* clause), and *thick* externalism, which claims that something beyond consent is required for the morality of sexual activity.

Thin Externalism

Thomas Mappes argues that only weak contextual constraints are required for satisfying Kantian worries about sexual activity.[26] The giving of free and informed consent by the persons involved in a sexual encounter is both necessary and sufficient for the morality of their sexual activity, for making permissible the sexual use of one person by another person.[27] Consent is not sufficient for the morality of sexual acts *simpliciter*, because even though a sexual act might be morally permissible *qua* sexual act, it still might be, for example, adulterous. Mappes's position is a thin minimalist externalism. Indeed, thin externalism, defined as making consent both necessary and sufficient, must also be minimalist. This criterion of the morality of sexual activity is contentless, or fully procedural: it does not evaluate the form or the nature of the sexual act (what body parts are involved; in what manner the acts are carried out), but only the antecedent and concurrent conditions or context in which the sexual act takes place. In principle, the acts engaged in need not even produce pleasure, mutual or otherwise, for the participants, an implication that differs from Goldman's behavioral internalism.

Mappes, while developing his theory of sexual ethics, begins by repeating a point made frequently about Kantian ethics:

> According to a fundamental Kantian principle, it is morally wrong for A to use B *merely as a means* (to achieve A's ends). Kant's principle does not rule out A using B as a means, only A using B *merely* as a means, that is, in a way incompatible with respect for B as a person.

Then Mappes lays out his central thesis:

> A immorally uses B if and only if A intentionally acts in a way that
> violates the requirement that B's involvement with A's ends be based
> on B's voluntary informed consent.

For Mappes, the presence of free and informed consent—there is no deception and no coercive force or threats—satisfies the Second Formulation, because each person's providing consent ensures that the persons
involved in sexual activity with each other are not *merely* or *wrongfully*
using each other as means. Mappes intends that this principle be applied
to any activity, whether sexual or otherwise; he believes, along with
Goldman, that sexual activity should be governed by moral principles
that apply in general to human behavior.

Mappes spends almost all his essay discussing various situations that
might, or might not, involve violating the free and informed consent
criterion. He discusses which acts are deceptive, coercive (by force or
threat), or exploitative; sexual activity made possible by such maneuvers
are morally wrong. Some of these cases are intriguing, as anyone familiar
with the literature on the meaning and application of the free and informed consent criterion in the area of medical ethics knows. But, putting
aside for now the important question of the sufficiency of consent, not
everyone agrees that in sexual (or other) contexts free and informed consent is absolutely necessary. Jeffrie Murphy, for one, has raised some
doubts:

> "Have sex with me or I will find another girlfriend" strikes me (assum-
> ing normal circumstances) as a morally permissible threat, and "Have
> sex with me and I will marry you" strikes me (assuming the offer is
> genuine) as a morally permissible offer. . . . We negotiate our way
> through most of life with schemes of threats and offers . . . and I see no
> reason why the realm of sexuality should be utterly insulated from this
> very normal way of being human.[28]

Both "Have sex with me or I will find another girlfriend" and "Marry me
or I will never sleep with you again (or at all)" seem to be coercive yet
permissible threats.[29] Sexual activity obtained by the employment of
these coercions seems to involve immoral use, on Mappes's criterion.
Further, it is not difficult to imagine circumstances in which deception in
sexual contexts is not morally wrong (even if we ignore the universal
practice of the deceptive use of cosmetics and clothing). Mappes claims
that my *withholding* information from you, information that would influence your decision as to whether to have sexual relations with me, is
deception that makes any subsequent sexual activity between us morally
wrong. If I withhold the fact that I have an extraordinarily large or min-
uscule penis, and withholding that fact about my sexual anatomy plays a
role in your eventually agreeing to engage in sex with me, it is not obviously true that my obtaining sex through this particular deception-by-
omission is morally wrong. I suspect that such cases tend to show that we

cannot rely comprehensively on a consent criterion to answer all our pressing questions about sexual morality. Does the other person have a *right* to know the size of my penis while deliberating whether to have sex with me? What types of coercive threat do we have a *right* to employ in trying to achieve our goals? These significant questions cannot be answered by a free and informed consent criterion; they also suggest that reading the Second Formulation such that consent by itself can satisfy the Second Formulation is questionable.

Mappes provides little reason for countenancing his unKantian notion that the presence of free and informed consent is a sufficient condition for satisfying the Second Formulation, that is, for not treating another person merely as a means or not wrongfully using him or her. He does write that "respect for persons entails that each of us recognize the rightful authority of other persons (as rational beings) to conduct their individual lives as they see fit," which suggests the following kind of argument: Allowing the other's consent to control when the other may be used for my sexual ends is to respect that person by taking his or her autonomy, his or her ability to reason and make choices, seriously, while not to allow the other to make the decision about when to be used for my sexual ends is disrespectfully paternalistic. If the other's consent is granted sufficiency, that shows that I respect his or her choice of ends; or that even if I do not respect his or her particular choice of ends, at least I thereby show respect for his or her ends-making capacity or for his or her being a self-determining agent. Further, taking the other's consent as sufficient can be a way of taking on his or her sexual ends as my own ends, as well as his or her taking on my sexual ends in my proposing to use him or her. According to such an argument, perhaps the best way to read Kant's Second Formulation is as a pronouncement of moral libertarianism, or a quasi-libertarianism that also, as Mappes does, pays attention to situations that are ripe for exploitation.[30]

Even if the argument makes Kantian sense, Mappes's sexual principle seems to miss the point. The Kantian problem about sexuality is not, or is not only, that one person might make false promises, engage in deception, or employ force or threats against another person in order to gain sex. The problem of the objectification and use of both the self and the other arises for Kant even when, or especially when, both persons give perfectly free and informed consent. Thin externalism does not get to the heart of *this* problem. Perhaps no liberal philosophy that borders on moral libertarianism could even sense it as a problem; at any rate, no minimalist externalism could. The only sexual objectification that Mappes considers in his essay is that which arises with coercion, most dramatically in rape. Nothing in his essay deals with what Kant and other philosophers discern as the intrinsically objectifying nature of sexuality itself. As Goldman does, Mappes assimilates sexual activity to all other human activities, all of which are or should be governed by the same moral principles. Whether Mappes's proposal works will depend, then, in part on whether sex is not so different from other joint human activities that free and informed consent is not too weak a criterion in this area of life.

It is an interesting question why free and informed consent does not, for Kant, solve the sex problem. It seems so obvious to many today that Mappes's consent criterion solves the sex problem that we wonder what Kant was up to in his metaphysical critique of sexuality. Kant's rejection of Mappes's solution suggests that Kant perceived deeper problems in sexual desire and activity than Mappes and Goldman acknowledge. In *Lectures on Ethics*, Kant apparently accepts a Mappesian consent criterion regarding work-for-hire, but rejects it for sexual activity:

> Man [may], of course, use another human being as an instrument for his services; he [may] use his hands, his feet, and even all his powers; he [may] use him for his own purposes with the other's consent. But there is no way in which a human being can be made an Object of indulgence for another except through sexual impulse.[31]

For Kant, it seems that using another person in a work-for-hire situation is permissible, just with free and informed consent, as long as one does not undermine or deny the worker's humanity in any other way. But Kant finds something problematic about sexual interaction that does not exist during, say, a tennis game between two people or in a work-for-hire situation, while Mappes sees no moral difference between playing tennis with someone and playing with their genitals. This disagreement between philosophers who view sexual activity as something or as somehow special, and philosophers who lump all human interactions together, requires further thought.

Thick Externalism

Thick externalism claims that more stringent contextual constraints, beyond free and informed consent, are required for the morality of sexual activity. My central example is Martha Nussbaum's essay "Objectification," in which she submits that the Kantian sex problem is solved if sexual activity is confined to the context of an abiding, mutually respectful, and mutually regarding relationship. However, Nussbaum advances both a thick minimalist externalism and a thick extended externalism. That is, in her long and complex essay we find at least two theses: (1) a background context of an abiding, mutually respectful relationship makes noxious objectification during sexual activity morally *permissible*; and (2) a background context of an abiding, mutually respectful relationship turns what might have been noxious objectification into something *good* or even "wonderful," a valuable type of objectification in which autonomy is happily abandoned, a thesis she derives from her reading of D. H. Lawrence.

Thick Minimalist Externalism

In several passages, Nussbaum proposes a thick minimalist external-ism, according to which sexual objectification is morally permissible in the context of an abiding, mutually respectful relationship. Consider this modest statement of her general thesis:

> If I am lying around with my lover on the bed, and use his stomach as a pillow, there seems to be nothing at all baneful about this [instrumental objectification], provided that I do so with his consent . . . and without causing him pain, provided, as well, that I do so in the context of a relationship in which he is generally treated as more than a pillow. This suggests that what is problematic is not instrumentalization per se but treating someone *primarily* or *merely* as an instrument [for example, as a pillow]. The overall context of the relationship thus becomes funda-mental.[32]

We can modify this passage so that Nussbaum's general point about permissible instrumental objectification-in-context can be applied more directly to the Kantian sex problem:

> If I am lying around with my lover on the bed, and use his penis for my sexual satisfaction, there seems to be nothing at all baneful about this instrumental objectification, provided that I do so with his consent . . . and without causing him [unwanted] pain, provided, as well, that I do so in the context of a relationship in which he is generally treated as more than a penis. This suggests that what is problematic is not instru-mentalization per se but treating someone *primarily* or *merely* as an instrument [for example, as a penis]. The overall context of the relation-ship thus becomes fundamental.

Other passages in Nussbaum's essay also express her thick minimalist externalism: "where there is a loss in subjectivity in the moment of love-making, this can be and frequently is accompanied by an intense concern for the subjectivity of the partner *at other moments*."[33] Again: "When there is a loss of autonomy in sex, the context . . . can be . . . one in which, on the whole, autonomy is respected and promoted"[34] and "denial of autonomy and denial of subjectivity are objectionable if they persist throughout an adult relationship, but *as phases* in a relationship characterized by mutual regard they can be all right, or even quite wonderful."[35]

One of Nussbaum's theses, then, is that a loss of autonomy, subjectiv-ity, and individuality in sex, and the reduction of a person to his or her sexual body or its parts, in which the person is or becomes a tool or object, are morally acceptable if they occur within the background con-text of a psychologically healthy and morally sound relationship, an abiding relationship in which one's personhood—one's autonomy, sub-jectivity, and individuality—is generally acknowledged and respected. This solution to the sex problem seems plausible. It confirms the common (even if sexually conservative) intuition that one difference between morally permissible sexual acts and those that are wrongful because they are merely mutual use is the difference between sexual acts that occur in the context of a loving or caring relationship and those that occur in the absence of love, mutual care, or concern. Further, it appeals to our willingness to tolerate, exculpate, or bless (as the partners' own private business) whatever nastiness that occurs in bed between two people *as long as* the rest, and the larger segment, of their relationship is morally sound. The lovers may sometimes engage in objectifying sexual games, by role-playing boss and secretary, client and prostitute, or teacher and student (phases of their relationship in which autonomy, subjectivity, and individuality might be sacrificed), since *outside* these occasional sexual games, they do display respect for each other and abidingly support each other's humanity.

But this solution to the sex problem is inconsistent with Kant's Second Formulation, for that moral principle requires that a person be treated as an end *at the same time* he or she is being treated as a means. On Nussbaum's thick minimalist externalism, small, sexually vulgar chunks of a couple's relationship, small pieces of noxious sexual objectification, are morally permissible in virtue of the larger or more frequent heavenly chunks of mutual respect that comprise their relationship. But it is not, in general, right (except, perhaps, for some utilitarians) that my treating you badly today is either *justified* or *excusable* if I treated you admirably the whole day yesterday and will treat you more superbly tomorrow and the next day. As Nussbaum acknowledges, Kant insists that we ought not to treat someone *merely* as means, instrumentally, or as an object, but by that qualification Kant does not mean that treating someone as a means, instrumentally, or as an object at *some* particular time is morally permissible as long as he or she is treated with respect as a full person at *other* particular times.[36] That Nussbaum's thick minimalist externalist solution to Kant's sex problem violates the Second Formulation in this way is not the fault of the details of her account of the proper background context; the problem arises whether the background context is postulated to be one of abiding mutual respect and regard, or love, or marriage, or something else. Any version of thick minimalist externalism violates Kant's prescription that someone who is treated as a means must be treated *at the same time* as an end. Thick minimalist externalism fails because, unlike behavioral or psychological internalism, it makes no attempt to improve or fix the nature of sexual activity itself. It leaves sexual activity exactly as it was or would be, as essentially objectifying or instrumental, although it claims that even when having this character, it is morally permissible.

Thick Extended Externalism

Thick extended externalism tries to have it both ways: to justify sexual activity when it occurs within the proper context *and* to fix the nature of the sexual acts that occur in that context. So Nussbaum's second proposal would seem to stand a better chance of conforming with the Second Formulation. In explaining the thesis that sexual objectification can be a wonderful or good thing in the proper context, Nussbaum says that in Lawrence's *Lady Chatterley's Lover*,

> both parties put aside their individuality and become identified with their bodily organs. They see one another in terms of those organs. And yet Kant's suggestion that in all such focusing on parts there is denial of humanity seems quite wrong. . . . The intense focusing of attention on the bodily parts seems an *addition*, rather than a subtraction.[37]

Nussbaum means that being reduced to one's body or its parts is an addition to one's personhood, not a subtraction from it, *as long as* the background context of an abiding, mutually respectful relationship exists, as she assumes it did between Constance Chatterley and Oliver Mellors. Nussbaum is claiming that sexual objectification, the reduction of a person to his or her flesh, and the loss of individuality and autonomy in sexual activity, can be a wonderful or good aspect of life and sexuality. Being reduced to one's flesh, to one's genitals, supplements, or is an expansion or extension of, one's humanity, as long as it happens in a psychologically healthy and morally sound relationship.

Nussbaum goes so far in this reasoning as to make the astonishing assertion that "In Lawrence, being treated as a cunt is a permission to expand the sphere of one's activity and fulfillment."[38] In the ablutionary context of an abiding relationship of mutual respect, it is permissible and good for persons to descend fully to the level of their bodies, to become "cock" and "cunt," to become identified with their genitals, because in the rest of the relationship they are treated as *whole* persons. Or, more precisely, the addition of the objectification of being sexually reduced to their flesh *makes* their personhoods whole (it is, as Nussbaum writes, not a "subtraction"), as if without such a descent into their flesh they would remain partial, incomplete persons. This is suggested when Nussbaum writes, "Lawrence shows how a kind of sexual objectification . . . , how the very surrender of autonomy in a certain sort of sex act can free energies that can be used to make the self *whole and full*."[39] I suppose it is a metaphysical truth that to be whole and full, I must realize all my potentials. But some of my potential, it is not unreasonable to think, should not be realized, just because it would be immoral or stupid to do so. Shall I, a professor of philosophy, fulfill my humanity by standing on street corners in the Bronx and try homosexual tricking? I may supplement or try to attain the fullness of my humanity only in ways that are moral. Whether adding to my personhood the identification of myself with my genitals is moral is precisely the question at issue. Merely because reducing myself to my genitals is an "expansion" of myself and of my "sphere of . . . activity" does little to justify it.

In any event, one implication of Nussbaum's requirement of a background context of an abiding, mutually respectful relationship worries me, whether this background context is part of a thick minimalist or a thick extended externalism: casual sex turns out to be morally wrong. In the sexual activity that transpires between strangers or between those who do not have much or any mutual regard for each other, sexual objectification and instrumentalization make those sexual acts wrong, because there is no background context of the requisite sort that would either justify the sexual objectification or transform it into something good. Casual sex is a descent to the level of the genitals with nothing for the persons to hang on to, nothing that would allow them to pull themselves back up to personhood when their sexual encounter is over. (This is, in effect, what Kant claims about prostitution and concubinage.)[40] Nussbaum explicitly states this sexually conservative trend in her thought, and does not seem to consider it a weakness or defect of her account. Sounding like Kant, she writes:

> For in the absence of any narrative history with the person, how can desire attend to anything else but the incidental, and how can one do more than use the body of the other as a tool of one's own states? . . . Can one really treat someone with . . . respect and concern . . . if one has sex with him in the anonymous spirit? . . . [T]he instrumental treatment of human beings, the treatment of human beings as tools of the purposes of another, is always morally problematic; if it does not take place in a larger context of regard for humanity, it is a central form of the morally objectionable.[41]

Now, it is one thing to point out that Nussbaum's thick externalism is inimical to casual sex, or sex in the "anonymous spirit," for many would agree with her. Yet there is another point to be made. If noxious sexual objectification is permissible or made into something good only in the context of an abiding, mutually respectful relationship, then it is morally impermissible to engage in sexual activity in getting a relationship *underway*. The two persons may not engage in sexual activity early in their acquaintance, before they know whether they will come to have such an abiding and respectful relationship, because the sexual objectification of that premature sex could not be redeemed or cleansed; the requisite background context is missing. But, as some of us know, engaging in sexual activity, even when the persons do not know each other very well, often reveals to them important information about whether to pursue a relationship, whether to attempt to ascend to the abiding level. This is another aspect of Nussbaum's conservative turn: the persons must *first* have that abiding, mutually respectful relationship before engaging in sexual activity. It would be unconvincing to argue, in response, that sexual objectification in the early stages of their relationship is morally permissible, after all, because that sexual activity might contribute to the formation of an abiding, mutually respectful and regarding relationship that does succeed, later, in eliminating or cleansing the sexual objectification of the couple's sexual activity. That argument simply repeats in another form the dubious claim that morally bad phases or segments of a relationship are justified or excused in virtue of the larger or more frequent morally good segments of that relationship.

A similar problem arises in Nussbaum's discussion of sadomasochism. In response to her own question, "can sadomasochistic sexual acts ever have a simply Lawrentian character, rather than a more sinister character?" she replies:

> There seems to be no . . . reason why the answer . . . cannot be "yes." I have no very clear intuitions on this point, . . . but it would seem that some narrative depictions of sadomasochistic activity do plausibly attribute to its consensual form a kind of Lawrentian character in which the willingness to be vulnerable to the infliction of pain . . . manifests a more complete trust and receptivity than could be found in other sexual acts. Pat Califia's . . . short story ["Jessie"] is one example of such a portrayal.[42]

This is unconvincing. (It also sounds more like a Hamptonian psychological internalism than a thick externalism.) Califia describes in this lesbian sadomasochistic short story a first sexual encounter between two *strangers*, women, who meet at a party, an encounter about which neither knows in advance whether it will lead to a narrative history or an abiding relationship between them. In the sexual encounter described by Califia, there is no background context of an abiding, let alone mutually respectful, relationship. This means that the nature of their sexual activity *as sadomasochism* is irrelevant; the main point is that each woman, as a stranger to the other, must, on Nussbaum's own account, be merely using each other in the "anonymous spirit." Something Califia writes in "Jessie" makes a mockery of Nussbaum's proposal:

> I hardly know you—I don't know if you play piano, I don't know what kind of business it is you run, I don't know your shoe size—but I know you better than anyone else in the world.[43]

If Nussbaum wants to justify sadomasochistic sexual acts, she must say that, *in the context of an abiding, mutually regarding and respectful relationship*, either (1) sadomasochistic sexuality is permissible, no matter how humiliating or brutal the acts are to the participants (thick minimalist externalism), or (2) sadomasochistic sexuality is permissible because, in this background context, it can be a good or wonderful thing, an expansion of the couple's humanity (thick expanded externalism).

KANT'S SOLUTION

To provoke the reader's curiosity about Kant, I conclude with some pre-liminary remarks about Kant's solution to the sex problem. [44]

Kant argues in both the earlier *Lectures on Ethics* and the later *Metaphysics of Morals* that sexual activity is morally permissible only within a heterosexual, lifelong, and monogamous legal marriage. Hence Kant advances a thick externalism. (I will suggest that his externalism is minimalist.) Kant barely argues in these texts, or argues weakly, that marriage must be lifelong and heterosexual. [45] But Kant's argument that the only permissible sexual activity is married sexual activity is distinctive and presented forcefully. In the *Metaphysics of Morals*, he writes:

> There is only one condition under which this is possible: that while one person is acquired by the other *as if it were a thing*, the one who is acquired acquires the other in turn; for in this way each reclaims itself and restores its personality. But acquiring a member of a human being [i.e., access to or possession of the other's genitals and associated sexual capacities] is at the same time acquiring the whole person, since a person is an absolute unity. Hence it is not only admissible for the sexes to surrender and to accept each other for enjoyment under the condition of marriage, but it is possible for them to do so *only* under this condition. [46]

Sexual activity, with its essential sexual objectification, is morally permissible only in marriage, because only in marriage can each of the persons engage in sexual activity *without losing* their own personhood or humanity. In a Kantian marriage, each person is "acquired" by the other person (along with his or her genitals and sexual capacities) as if he or she were an object, and hence, by being acquired, loses his or her humanity (autonomy, individuality). But because the acquisition in marriage is reciprocal, each person *regains* his or her personhood (and hence does not lose it, after all). When I "surrender" myself to you, and you thereby acquire me, but you also "surrender" yourself to me, and I thereby acquire you, which "you" includes the "me" that you have acquired, we each surrender but then re-acquire ourselves. (I think this means that "I do" must be said simultaneously.)

There are many puzzles in Kant's solution. One is that Kant does not explicitly state in laying out his solution that through such a reciprocal surrender and acquisition the persons in some robust sense treat each other as persons or acknowledge each other's humanity as an end, in bed or otherwise. That is, after laying out his relentless criticism of sexual desire and activity, Kant never poses the question, "How might two people, married or not, treat themselves and each other as persons during sexual activity?" Kant is notorious for being stingy with examples, but why here? In fact, in only one place could I find, in a footnote in *Meta-*

physics of Morals, Kant using the language of the Second Formulation to speak about marriage:

> if I say "my wife," this signifies a special, namely a rightful, relation of the possessor to an object as a *thing* (even though the object is also a person). Possession (*physical* possession), however, is the condition of being able to *manage* . . . something as a thing, even if this must, in another respect, be treated at the same time as a person.[47]

But in neither the footnote nor the text does Kant explain what "in another respect" being treated as a person amounts to. The language of the Second Formulation is plainly here, including the crucial "at the same time," but not its substance. Further, in the text, Kant refrains from using the language of the Second Formulation:

> What is one's own here does not . . . mean what is one's own in the sense of property in the person of another (for a human being cannot have property in himself, much less in another person), but means what is one's own in the sense of usufruct . . . to make direct use of a person *as of* a thing, as a means to my end, but still *without infringing* upon his personality.[48]

It is permissible in *some* contexts to use another person as a means or treat as an object, merely with the other's free and informed consent, as long as one does not violate the humanity of the other in some other way, as long as one allows him or her otherwise to retain intact his or her personhood. The reciprocal surrender and acquisition of Kantian marriage, which involves a contractual free and informed agreement to exchange selves, *prevents* this (possibly extra) denial or loss of personhood. But this moral principle is far removed from the Second Formulation as Kant usually articulates it.

Kant's externalism, I submit, is minimalist: the objectification and instrumentality that attach to sexuality remain even in marital sexual activity. Hence not even Kant abides by the "at the same time" requirement of the Second Formulation in his solution to the sex problem. Nussbaum seems to recognize Kant's minimalism when she writes, "sexual desire, according to his analysis, drives out every possibility of respect. This is so even in marriage."[49] Raymond Belliotti finds, instead, thick extended externalism in Kant:

> Kant suggests that two people can efface the wrongful commodification inherent in sex and thereby redeem their own humanity only by mutually exchanging "rights to their whole person." The *implication* is that a deep, abiding relationship of the requisite sort ensures that sexual activity is not separated from personal interaction which honors individual dignity.[50]

But the "implication" is something Belliotti illicitly reads into Kant's texts. Kant no where says that in marriage, which is for him a contractual relationship characterized by mutual acquisition of persons as if they were objects (hardly a "deep, abiding relationship"), sexual activity "honors individual dignity." Belliotti reads Kant as if Kant were Nussbaum. When Kant asserts in the *Metaphysics* that sexual activity is permissible only in marriage, he speaks about the *acquisition* or *possession* of the other person by each spouse, and never mentions benevolence, altruism, or love. For similar reasons, Robert Baker and Frederick Elliston's view must be rejected. They claim that, according to Kant, "marriage transubstantiates immoral sexual intercourse into morally permissible human copulation by transforming a manipulative masturbatory relationship into one of altruistic unity."[51] But Kant never says anything about "altruism" in his account of marriage or of sex in marriage; no where does he claim that married persons come to treat each other as ends and respect their humanity in sexual activity by unconditionally providing sexual pleasure for each other. Indeed, Kant writes in the *Metaphysics* that "benevolence . . . deter[s] one from carnal enjoyment."[52] Further, both these readings of Kant are insensitive to the sharp contrast between Kant's glowing account of male friendship, in the *Lectures* and the *Metaphysics*, as a morally exemplary and fulfilling balance of love and respect, and Kant's dry account of heterosexual marriage, which makes marriage look like a continuation, or culmination, of the battle of the sexes. Kant never says about marriage anything close to this: "Friendship . . . is the union of two persons through equal mutual love and respect. . . . [E]ach participat[es] and shar[es] sympathetically in the other's well-being through the morally good will that unites them."[53]

Of course, the virtue of Belliotti's reading, and that of Baker and Elliston, is that if sexual activity can indeed be imbued with Kantian respect or "altruism," then the "at the same time" requirement of the Second Formulation is satisfied. But there is good evidence that Kant's own view is minimalist. When Kant writes in the *Lectures* that

> If . . . a man wishes to satisfy his desire, and a woman hers, they stimulate each other's desire; their inclinations meet, but their object is not human nature but sex, and each of them dishonours the human nature of the other. They make of humanity an instrument for the satisfaction of their lusts and inclinations, and dishonour it by placing it on a level with animal nature. . . .[54]

he intends this description to apply to sexual activity even in marriage, and not only to casual sex, prostitution, or concubinage. This point is confirmed by Kant's letter to C. G. Schütz, who had written to Kant to complain about Kant's similar treatment of sexuality in the later *Metaphysics*. To this objection offered by Schütz, "You cannot really believe that a man makes an object of a woman just by engaging in marital cohabitation with her, and vice versa," Kant concisely replies: "if the cohabitation is assumed to be *marital*, that is, *lawful*, . . . the authorization is already contained in the concept."[55] Note that Kant does not deny that objectification still occurs in marital sex; he simply says it is permissible, or authorized. Schütz makes the point another way: "married people do not become *res fungibiles* just by sleeping together," to which Kant replies: "An enjoyment of this sort involves at once the thought of this person as merely *functional*, and that in fact is what the reciprocal use of each other's sexual organs by two people *is*."[56]

Further, that marriage is designed and defined by Kant to be only about sexuality, about having access to the other person's sexual capacities and sexual body parts—for enjoyment or pleasure, not necessarily for reproduction—also suggests that his solution is minimalist. Consider Kant's definition of marriage in the *Metaphysics*: "Sexual union in accordance with principle is *marriage* (*matrimonium*), that is, the union of two persons of different sexes for lifelong possession of each other's sexual attributes."[57] There is no suggestion in this definition of marriage that Belliottian human, individual dignity will make its way into marital sexual activity (quite the contrary). Howard Williams tartly comments, about Kant's notion of marriage, that "sex, for Kant, seems simply to be a form of mutual exploitation for which one must pay the price of marriage. He represents sex as a commodity which ought only to be bought and sold for life in the marriage contract."[58] If sexual activity in marriage is, for Kant, a commodity, it has hardly been cleansed of its essentially objectionable qualities. Kant's view of marriage has much in common with St. Paul's (see 1 Cor. 7; *Metaphysics*, 179–80), in which each person has power over the body of the other spouse, and each spouse has a "conjugal debt" to engage in sexual activity with the other nearly on demand. That marriage is defined by Kant to be only about access to sex is what is astounding, even incomprehensible, to the contemporary mind, and may explain why modern philosophers are quick to attribute to Kant more congenial solutions to the sex problem.

Finally, a commonly neglected aspect of the Second Formulation, that one must *also* treat the humanity in one's own person as an end, is important in understanding Kant's solution to the sex problem. Duties to self are important for Kant, a fact overlooked by those philosophers (e.g., Mappes and Goldman) who emphasize its treat-the-other-as-an-end part. Notice the prominence of Kant's discussion of the duties to self in the *Lectures*. They are elaborately discussed early in the text, well before Kant discusses moral duties to others, and Kant in the *Lectures* launches into his treatment of sexuality immediately after he concludes his account of duties to self in general and before he, finally, gets around to duties to others. Allen Wood is one commentator on Kant who gets this right:

> [Kant] thinks sexual intercourse is "a degradation of humanity" because it is an act in which "people *make themselves* into an object of enjoyment, and hence into a thing" (VE 27:346). He regards sex as

permissible only within marriage, and even there it is in itself "a merely animal union" (MS 6:425).[59]

Kant makes it clear that a duty to treat the humanity in one's own person as an end is his primary concern in restricting sexual activity to marriage:

> there ar[ises] from one's duty to oneself, that is, to the humanity in one's own person, a right (*ius personale*) of both sexes to acquire each other as persons *in the manner of things* by marriage.[60]

For Kant, then, the crux of the argument about sex and marriage does not turn on a duty to avoid sexually objectifying the other, but to avoid the sexual objectification of the self. It would be an ironic reading of Kant to say that he claims that *my right to use you* in sexual activity in marriage arises from *my duty to myself*. What Kant is saying, without irony, is that as a result of the duty toward myself, I cannot enter into sexual relations with you unless I preserve my personhood; you, likewise, cannot enter into sexual relations with me unless you are able to preserve your personhood. Each of us can accomplish that goal only by mutual surrender and acquisition, the exchange of rights to our persons, genitals, and sexual capacities that constitutes marriage. It is not the right to use you sexually that is my goal, although I do gain that right. My goal is to preserve my own personhood in the face of the essentially objectifying nature of sexuality. But preserving my own personhood, as admirable as that might be, is not the same thing as treating you with dignity (or altruism) during marital sexual activity. Kant has still done nothing to accomplish that. Nor was that his intention.

METAPHILOSOPHICAL FINALE

Howard Williams has made a shrewd observation about Kant's solution to the sex problem:

> [A]n important premiss of Kant's argument is that sexual relations necessarily involve treating oneself and one's partner as things. . . . [T]o demonstrate convincingly that marriage is the only ethically desirable context for sex, Kant ought to start from better premises than these.[61]

Let me explain what is interesting here. Bernard Baumrin argues that if we want to justify sexual activity *at all*, we should start our philosophizing by conceding the worst: "I begin . . . by admitting the most damaging facts . . . that any theory of sexual morality must countenance," viz., that "human sexual interaction is essentially manipulative—physically, psychologically, emotionally, and even intellectually."[62] Starting with premises about sexuality any less ugly or more optimistic would make justifying sexual activity too easy. Williams's point is that if we want to justify the specific claim that sex is *permissible only in marriage*, starting with Kantian premises about the nature of sex makes *that* task too easy. If sex is in its essence wholesome, or if, as in Mappes and Goldman, sexual activity does not significantly differ from other activities that involve human interaction, then it becomes easier both to justify sexual activity and to justify sex outside of marriage. Those, including many Christian philosophers and theologians, who assume the worst about sexuality to begin with, gain an advantage in defending the view that sexuality must be restricted to matrimony.[63] This tactic is copied in a milder way by Nussbaum and Hampton, who reject casual sex. The convincing intellectual trick would be to assume the *best* about sex, that it is by its nature wholesome, and then argue, *anyway*, that it should be restricted to lifelong, monogamous matrimony and that casual sex is morally wrong. Perhaps the liberals Baumrin and Goldman are trying to pull off the reverse trick, in that they admit the worst about sexuality and still come out with a permissive sexual morality. But in admitting the worst, how do they avoid concluding, with Kant, that sexual activity is permissible only in the restrictive conditions of marriage? Perhaps they succeed, or think they do, only by reading the Second Formulation in a very narrow or easily satisfied way.

APPENDIX

1. I begin by suggesting that Joshua Schulz could have done a better job with his references and sources. This complaint, I argue, is not to pick nits. One book that Schulz draws on is my edited collection *The Philosophy of Sex: Contemporary Readings* (Rowman and Littlefield). But the edition he uses is the ancient first edition from 1980; in 2002 the book came out in its 4th edition. Schulz's essay would have been more reader-friendly had he employed the 4th edition, for it contains in one convenient place material that Schulz refers to in his article, including the essays by Alan Goldman, Thomas Mappes, and Martha Nussbaum, in addition to a chunk of Kant's *Vorlesung* (*Lectures on Ethics*), in which Kant lays out his dramatic views about sexuality. The 4th edition of *Philosophy of Sex* also contains a revised and expanded version of the essay I originally published in *Essays in Philosophy* in 2001 ("Sexual Use") and to which Schulz replies. Schulz's discussion of my views, and the views of the philosophers I discuss in my essay, would have benefited from his focusing on this revision. We have two reasons, so far, for worrying about Schulz's bibliographic procedures. Further, the 4th edition of *Philosophy of Sex* includes Irving Singer's "The Morality of Sex: Contra Kant" (reprinted from his *Explorations in Love and Sex* [Lanham, Md.: Rowman and Littlefield, 2002], pp. 1–20), which provides that which Schulz seeks in his essay (and, I will argue, never attains)—a "wholesome" or "optimistic" account of sexuality. It is

also a piece that approaches sexual desire and activity in a way much different from Kant.

There are other bibliographic curiosities in Schulz's essay. Given that Schulz's views about sexual desire and activity, or his version of Kant's views, rely on intentionality and the concept "person," given that he argues that the morally proper place for sexual expression is marriage, and given the last sentence of his essay ("Sexual desire . . . can be educated"), I was surprised that he ignores Roger Scruton's *Sexual Desire: A Moral Philosophy of the Erotic* (New York: Free Press, 1986). I was also surprised that someone who without apology or explanation uses the term "concupiscence" and invokes, in the pursuit of his philosophical goal, St. Paul's "remedy against sin" benefit of marriage (1 Cor. 7), overlooks Karol Wojtyla's *Love and Responsibility* (New York: Farrar, Straus and Giroux, 1981), in which the late Pope John Paul II attempts to merge Kant's Second Formulation of the Categorical Imperative (which he calls "the personalist norm") with Roman Catholicism. (What a shock, then, to find Schulz citing the Divine Debauchee, Georges Bataille.) He also slights the fine work done by Lara Denis (although stemming from a different perspective), which already improves Kant on sexuality, in particular her "From Friendship to Marriage: Revising Kant" (*Philosophy and Phenomenological Research* 63 [2001], pp. 1–28). Denis's "Kant on the Wrongness of 'Unnatural' Sex" (*History of Philosophy Quarterly* 16 [1999], pp. 225–48) is similarly useful. Elizabeth Brake's "Justice and Virtue in Kant's Account of Marriage" (*Kantian Review* 9 [2005], pp. 58–94) is relevant; it was published perhaps soon enough for Schulz to have acknowledged it. Both Denis and Brake have written more recent pieces on Kant; I mention them only to edify the reader and assist Schulz, knowing that he likely could not have taken them into account: Denis, "Sex and the Virtuous Kantian Agent" (in Raja Halwani, ed., *Sex and Ethics: Essays on Sexuality, Virtue and the Good Life* [London: Palgrave Macmillan, 2007], pp. 37–48); and Brake, "Kant, Immanuel" (in Alan Soble, ed., *Sex from Plato to Paglia: A Philosophical Encyclopedia* [Westport, Conn.: Greenwood Press, 2006], vol. 1, pp. 543–53). Another philosopher who has explored Kant's philosophy deeply (the way Schulz certainly does), while paying attention to Scruton and defending not-so-liberal sexual ethics, is Seiriol Morgan. Schulz would have benefited from consulting "Dark Desires" (*Ethical Theory and Moral Practice* 6:4 [2003], pp. 377–410) and "Sex in the Head" (*Journal of Applied Philosophy* 20:1 [2003], pp. 1–16), reprinted in this volume.

Allow me three more bibliographic points. Schulz claims that "sexual desire is always a desire *for* something under conditions: sexual desire, like all human desires, is intentional." I'm not sure that to say that sexual desire is a desire *for* something is equivalent to saying that sexual desire is "intentional," but the claim that sexual desire is *for* something—that sexual desire is "propositional"—has been powerfully denied by Jerome

Shaffer in his brilliant essay "Sexual Desire" (*Journal of Philosophy* 75:4 [1978], pp. 175–89; reprinted in Alan Soble, ed., *Sex, Love, and Friendship* [Amsterdam: Rodopi, 1997], pp. 1–12). Schulz's fascinating Kantian take on Adam and Eve might have been even more thoroughly Kantian (or more in keeping with what Kant wrote about that happy couple) had Schulz brought in Kant's "Conjectural Beginning of Human History" (1786; in Lewis White Beck, ed., *On History* [Indianapolis, Ind.: Bobbs-Merrill, 1963], pp. 53–68), which I discuss in "Kant and Sexual Perversion" (*Monist* 86 [2003], pp. 55–89). Finally, the impact of Schulz's reliance on "person" might have emerged more clearly had he considered Thomas Nagel's ontological use of "person" in describing human sexual arousal ("Sexual Perversion," in this volume) and how Sara Ruddick took this concept from Nagel and put a moral spin on it ("Better Sex," in Robert Baker and Frederick Elliston, eds., *Philosophy and Sex*, 2nd edition [Buffalo, N.Y.: Prometheus, 1984], pp. 280–99). The differences between Nagel's purely ontological and Ruddick's ontological-moral use of "person" are explored in my *Sexual Investigations* (New York: New York University Press, 1996), pp. 74–77, and in "Completeness, Sexual," *Sex from Plato to Paglia*, vol. 1, pp. 179–84.

2. I have been using "Kantian" without explanation. Schulz writes (in his note 21):

> [Alan] Goldman argues that . . . Kant's second formulation of the categorical imperative is *best interpreted exactly as Kant interprets it*: as a demand for "reciprocity in sexual relations," such that "even in an act which by its nature 'objectifies' the other, one recognizes a partner as a subject with demands and desires by yielding to those desires, by allowing oneself to be a sexual object as well, by giving pleasure or ensuring that the pleasures of the act are mutual" . . . . Goldman concludes that "It is this kind of reciprocity which forms the basis for morality in sex, which distinguishes right acts from wrong in this area as in others" . . . . [my ellipses and italics]

Is it true that Goldman's interpretation of the Categorical Imperative is exactly Kant's? That cannot be right. If it were, then Kant, as Goldman does, would bless casual sex as long as each person in the encounter tries to please, in reciprocal fashion, the other person (*but Kant doesn't*). Is it even true that Goldman claims that the Categorical Imperative is "best interpreted exactly as Kant interprets it"? No. What Goldman actually writes in his essay is that his interpretation is a "more realistic rendering" of the Categorical Imperative than Kant's. I don't know what Goldman means by the odd phrase "more realistic," but he's at least saying that Kant's interpretation of the Categorical Imperative requires modification (in a liberalizing direction). Goldman ends up with a *Kantian* view of sexual morality, or a Kantish view—a view *inspired by* Kant—but surely not a restatement of Kant's position. We get, in Goldman's account, only what Kant should have written, had he been more on his moral and anthropological toes. I think a rereading of this sort also occurs in Denis's essays on Kant, especially in "From Friendship to Marriage: Revising Kant." What I tried to do in "Sexual Use" was to stick faithfully to Kant. Schulz goes the route of Goldman and Denis. How far from Kant he travels and whether his elaborations are acceptable depend on his purpose: is he primarily doing exegesis, or is he formulating a philosophy in the "spirit" of Kant and so is not required to toe Kant's line?

3. Schulz's main contention in his essay is that he successfully responds to a challenge I posed in the "Metaphilosophical Finale" at the end of "Sexual Use." Schulz quotes part of the passage (ignore the minor discrepancies):

> If sex is, in its essence, wholesome, or if, as in Mappes and Goldman, sexual activity does not differ significantly from other human activities, it becomes easier to both justify sexual activity and to justify sex outside of marriage. Those, including many Christian philosophers, who assume the worst about sex gain an advantage in defending the view that sexuality must be restricted to matrimony. . . . The convincing intellectual trick would be to assume the *best* about sex, that it is by its nature wholesome, and then argue, *anyway*, that it should be restricted to marriage or that casual sex is wrong. (What might an optimistic account of sex look like)?

Then he announces, "I would like to perform the trick. I will argue that sex is by its nature wholesome (though not unconditionally so), and that sex should be restricted to marriage." I will argue that Schulz does not "perform the trick." The central reason is that he does not abide by the terms of the challenge; he does not begin with "optimistic" accounts of sexual desire and activity according to which "sex is by its nature wholesome." His (modified) Kantian definitions of sexual desire and activity are far from being the "best" assumptions about sex.

Schulz, in the culminating heart of his essay, provides a number of reasons for thinking that "marriage is the best context in which to pursue sexual goods insofar as it best minimizes the risk of objectification." I do not think this is true; nor do I think that Schulz has adequately defended it. His various arguments that marriage is the morally proper place for the expression of sexuality (it "should be restricted to marriage") are weak. But that is beside the point. Notice what Schulz is asserting: the value of restricting sex to marriage is that doing so minimizes objectification. But this assumes that there is something objectifying about sexuality itself that needs to be dealt with, overcome, or controlled. And to make that assumption is *not* to start with a "wholesome" view of sexuality. So Schulz has not performed the trick. He has, as I predicted in "Sexual Use," made things *too easy* on himself.

If marriage is touted because it has the power to attenuate the objectifying tendencies of sexual desire and activity, the challenge I posed at the end of "Sexual Use" has not been satisfied. The challenge was to assume the best about sex, that it is not especially associated with morally suspicious motives or attitudes, and then defend the claim that marriage is, anyway, the morally proper location for human sexuality. Kant assumes sex is by its nature objectifying and concludes that it ought to occur only in marriage. Schulz grants too much to Kant's premises and of course defends marriage as well, on the grounds that it overcomes objectification. What Shultz argues, and at most shows (which only supports my claim in "Sexual Use," not refutes it), is that if sex has objectifying tendencies, then sex in marriage or a Nussbaumian committed relationship has a better chance of attenuating the nastiness of sex, the objectification of self and other, than do other arrangements, for example, the bare mutual consent (of casual partners), as in Mappes, or mutual consent (of casual partners) supplemented with Goldmanian reciprocity.

Examine Schulz's revised Kantian definitions:

> P1': Human sexual desire is, in itself, the bodily appetite of a human person to use the body of a human person for the purpose of carnal satisfaction got through the use of their body's members.

> P2': Human sexual activity is any act in which each human person's body functions as the object of the other human person's sexual desire.

But what I meant by "wholesome" in "Sexual Use" was this: at least not, by its nature, selfish, self-centered, objectifying, or instrumental. Precisely these troublesome moral features are built right into Schulz's definitions of sexual desire and activity, the same way Kant does it: "in itself," "appetite," "to use," "for the purpose of . . . satisfaction," "functions as an object." In my essay, I asked, almost rhetorically, what an "optimistic" or "wholesome" account of sexuality would look like. There are some obvious candidates, but I did not mention them because they are, I suspect, false. Further, these "optimistic" accounts paint such a beautiful picture of human sexuality that they abundantly confirm my claim that if we start with a pretty picture of sex we will be hard pressed to defend the claim that marriage is the morally proper place for sex. Had Schulz begun with such a model and concluded through convincing arguments that marriage was morally the only or best place for sex, he would have met the challenge. Suppose (this is not Singer's view; for the details, see my "Hobbes, Thomas," in *Sex from Plato to Paglia*, vol. 1, pp. 454-60) that by its nature sexual desire was composed entirely of the desire to provide sexual pleasure to another person, a desire to satisfy the other merely for the other's sake. See? There could, on such an account of sexual desire, be no or little objection to casual sexual encounters, and marriage would seem not to be necessary or even relevant for loving, caring, respectful sexual activity.

NOTES

1. Kant's views on sexuality are in *Lectures on Ethics* [ca. 1780], trans. Louis Infield (Indianapolis, Ind.: Hackett, 1963), 162–71; and *The Metaphysics of Morals* [1797], trans. Mary Gregor (Cambridge: Cambridge University Press, 1996), 61–64, 126–28, 178–80.

2. Bernard Baumrin, "Sexual Immorality Delineated," in Robert Baker and Frederick Elliston, eds., *Philosophy and Sex*, 2nd edition (Buffalo, N.Y.: Prometheus, 1984), 300–311, at 300–302.

3. *Lectures*, 164.

4. "In desire you are compromised in the eyes of the object of desire, since you have displayed that you have designs which are vulnerable to his intentions" (Roger Scruton, *Sexual Desire: A Moral Philosophy of the Erotic* [New York: Free Press, 1986], 82).

5. See Virginia Held, "Coercion and Coercive Offers," in J. Roland Pennock and John W. Chapman, eds., *Coercion: Nomos VIX* (Chicago: Aldine, 1972), 49–62.

6. *Metaphysics*, 62.

7. *Lectures*, 164. Kant also suggests that sexuality can reduce humans *below* the level of animals, who in their instinctual innocence do not use each other sexually (122–23).

8. *Groundwork of the Metaphysic of Morals*, trans. H. J. Paton (New York: Harper Torchbooks, 1964), 95–96 (AK 4:428). St. Augustine agrees (*The City of God*, trans. Marcus Dods [New York: Modern Library, 1993], bk. 14, sec. 16, pp. 464–65).

9. *Homosexuality: A Philosophical Inquiry* (Oxford, U.K.: Blackwell, 1988), 185.

10. *Groundwork*, 96 (429); 95 (428).

11. *Groundwork*, 98 (430); see also *Metaphysics*, 199.

12. *Groundwork*, 97 (429). See Christine Korsgaard, "Creating the Kingdom of Ends: Reciprocity and Responsibility in Personal Relations," *Philosophical Perspectives* 6, *Ethics* (1992), 305–32.

13. C. E. Harris, Jr., seems to have this weaker version of the Second Formulation in mind when he claims that we are permitted to use another person in our interactions with him or her (e.g., a post office worker, doctor, professor) as long as, beyond using them for our purposes, we "do nothing to negate [their] status as a moral being," "do not deny him his status as a person," or "do not obstruct [their] humanity." Harris applies this principle to casual sex: as long as "neither person is overriding the freedom of the other or diminishing the ability of the other to be an effective goal-pursuing agent," it is permissible (*Applying Moral Theories*, 4th edition [Belmont, Calif.: Wadsworth, 2002], 153–54, 164).

14. "Plain Sex," 58, in this volume.

15. David Archard's position (and mistake) is similar to Goldman's. "If Harry has sex with Sue solely for the purpose of deriving sexual gratification from the encounter and with no concern for what Sue might get out of it, if Harry pursues this end single-mindedly and never allows himself to think of how it might be for Sue, then Harry treats Sue merely as a means to his ends. If, *by contrast*, Harry derives pleasure from his sex with Sue but also strives to attend to Sue's pleasure and conducts the encounter in a way that is sensitive to her needs, then Harry does not treat Sue merely as a means. . . . That the sexual relationship between Sue and Harry is consensual does not mean that neither one of them is treating the other merely as a means" (*Sexual Consent* [Boulder, Colo.: Westview, 1998], 41, italics added).

16. "The delight men take in delighting, is not sensual, but a pleasure or joy of the mind consisting in the imagination of the power they have so much to please" (Thomas Hobbes, "Human Nature, or the Fundamental Elements of Policy," in *The English*

Works of Thomas Hobbes, vol. IV, ed. Sir William Molesworth [Germany: Scientia Verlag Aalen, 1966], chap. 9, sec. 15, p. 48).

17. See Thomas Nagel, "Sexual Perversion," in this volume.

18. *Metaphysics*, 199.

19. See "Orgasmic Justice," in my *Sexual Investigations* (New York: New York University Press, 1996), 53–57.

20. Hampton, "Defining Wrong and Defining Rape," in Keith Burgess-Jackson, ed., *A Most Detestable Crime: New Philosophical Essays on Rape* (New York: Oxford University Press, 1999), 118–56, at 147.

21. Hampton, 147.

22. Hampton, 147–48.

23. Hampton, 150.

24. Alan Donagan's view (*The Theory of Morality* [Chicago: University of Chicago Press, 1977]) is similar. He praises "life-affirming and nonexploitative" sexuality; by contrast, "sexual acts which are life-denying in their imaginative significance, or are exploitative, are impermissible" (107, italics omitted). Donagan rejects sadomasochism, prostitution, and casual sex.

25. Califia, "Introduction," *Macho Sluts* (Los Angeles: Alyson Books, 1988), 9.

26. Thomas Mappes, "Sexual Morality and the Concept of Using Another Person," in this volume. Mappes's Kantian theory of sexual ethics counts as a solution to the Kantian sex problem, for he observes that "the domain of sexual interaction seems to offer ample opportunity for 'using' another person" (Mappes's introductory essay to chapter 4, "Sexual Morality," in Thomas A. Mappes and Jane S. Zembaty, eds., *Social Ethics: Morality and Social Policy*, 6th edition [New York: McGraw-Hill, 2002], 157–64, at 160; or see the 4th edition, 1992, 192; or the 5th, 1997, 153).

27. For another Kantian consent view, see Raymond Belliotti, "A Philosophical Analysis of Sexual Ethics," *Journal of Social Philosophy* 10:3 (1979): 8–11.

28. "Some Ruminations on Women, Violence, and the Criminal Law," in Jules Coleman and Allen Buchanan, eds., *In Harm's Way: Essays in Honor of Joel Feinberg* (Cambridge: Cambridge University Press, 1994), 209–30, at 218.

29. Alan Wertheimer argues that "Have sexual relations with me or I will dissolve our dating relationship" is *not* "a coercive proposal" (although it might still be wrong). See his "Consent and Sexual Relations," in this volume.

30. Mappes's free and informed consent test seems to imply that prostitution is permissible if the prostitute is not exploited, i.e., not taken advantage of in virtue of her economic needs. Baumrin's consent view seems to imply that prostitution is permissible, because either party may "discharge" the other's duty of providing sexual satisfaction ("Sexual Immorality Delineated," 303; see 305). But Goldman's position on prostitution is unclear. He does not advance a mere free and informed consent test, but lays it down that each person must make a sexual object of himself or herself for the sake of the pleasure of the other, or must provide sexual pleasure to the other so that their activity is mutually pleasurable. That seems to condemn prostitution, unless the client provides pleasure for the prostitute, or unless the prostitute's pleasure in receiving money makes their encounter sufficiently "mutual."

31. *Lectures*, 163. In several places I replaced "can" in Infield's translation with "may"; Kant's point is moral, not about natural or conceptual possibility.

32. "Objectification," *Philosophy and Public Affairs* 24:4 (1995): 249–91, reprinted in my *Philosophy of Sex*, 4th edition, 381–419 (the passage is on p. 394; references to "Objectification" are to POS4). In a slightly revised version of "Objectification" (*Sex and Social Justice* [New York: Oxford University Press, 1999], 213–39), Nussbaum changed "without causing him pain" to "without causing him unwanted pain" (223). That's a huge difference.

33. "Objectification," 401, italics added.

34. "Objectification," 401.

35. "Objectification," 411, italics added.

36. There is a similar problem of Kant exegesis in Baumrin's "Sexual Immorality Delineated." He claims that what is morally wrong, for Kant, is treating a person in *every* respect as a means. What is permissible, for Baumrin (or Baumrin's Kant), then, is treating a person as a means as long as the person is treated in (at least and perhaps only) *one* respect *not* as a means (300). What this means and whether it is compatible with the Second Formulation are unclear. Baumrin's rendition of the Second Formulation (he quotes Lewis White Beck's translation) does not include the phrase "at the same time" (310, note 1).

37. "Objectification," 400–401, italics added.

38. "Objectification," 405.

39. "Objectification," 402, italics added.

40. *Lectures*, 165–66.

41. "Objectification," 409, 410, 411. I am not able to explore here the tension between Nussbaum's rejecting sexuality in the "anonymous spirit" and her legal and moral defense of prostitution ("'Whether from Reason or Prejudice.' Taking Money for Bodily Services," *Sex and Social Justice*, 276-98; in this volume). See my discussions of Nussbaum in *Pornography, Sex, and Feminism* (Amherst, N.Y.: Prometheus, 2002), 72–78, 163–74; and in "Concealment and Exposure: A Mostly Temperate and Courageous Afterword," in Raja Halwani, ed., *Sex and Ethics: Essays on Sexuality, Virtue, and the Good Life* (New York: Palgrave Macmillan, 2007), 229–52, at 248–51.

42. "Objectification," 404. Nussbaum mistakenly calls Califia's short story "Jenny."

43. Califia, "Jessie," in *Macho Sluts*, 28–62, at 60. This was said by the top, Jessie, to her bottom, Liz, the morning after their sexual encounter.

44. Important accounts of Kant on sex include Vincent M. Cooke, "Kant, Teleology, and Sexual Ethics," *International Philosophical Quarterly* 31:1 (1991): 3–13; Onora O'Neill, "Between Consenting Adults," in *Constructions of Reason: Explorations of Kant's Practical Philosophy* (Cambridge: Cambridge University Press, 1989), 105–25; Susan Meld Shell, *The Embodiment of Reason: Kant on Spirit, Generation, and Community* (Chicago: University of Chicago Press, 1996) and *The Rights of Reason: A Study of Kant's Philosophy and Politics* (Toronto, Can.: University of Toronto Press, 1980); Irving Singer, *The Nature of Love*, vol. 2: *Courtly and Romantic* (Chicago: University of Chicago Press, 1984); and Keith Ward, *The Development of Kant's View of Ethics* (Oxford, U.K.: Blackwell, 1972).

45. I examine Kant's philosophical objections to homosexuality and, *a fortiori*, to homosexual marriage, in "Kant and Sexual Perversion," *Monist* 86:1 (2003): 57–92. See also Lara Denis, "Kant on the Wrongness of 'Unnatural' Sex," *History of Philosophy Quarterly* 16:2 (1999), 225–48.

46. *Metaphysics*, 62; *Lectures*, 167.

47. *Metaphysics*, 126*n*.

48. *Metaphysics*, 127; italics added.

49. "Objectification," 415, note 30.

50. *Good Sex: Perspectives on Sexual Ethics* (Lawrence, Kan.: University Press of Kansas, 1993), 100, italics added.

51. Baker and Elliston, "Introduction," *Philosophy and Sex*, 1st ed. (Buffalo, N.Y.: Prometheus, 1975), 8–9; 2nd edition (Buffalo, N.Y.: Prometheus, 1984), 17–18. Or see the "Introduction" in Robert B. Baker, Kathleen J. Wininger, and Frederick A. Elliston, eds., *Philosophy and Sex*, 3rd edition (Amherst, N.Y.: Prometheus, 1998), 23. These passages are missing from Robert B. Baker and Kathleen J. Wininger, eds., *Philosophy and Sex*, 4th edition (Amherst, N.Y.: Prometheus, 2009).

52. *Metaphysics*, 180. In her earlier translation of the *Metaphysics*, Gregor rendered this line "benevolence . . . stop[s] short of carnal enjoyment" (*The Doctrine of Virtue: Part II of the Metaphysic of Morals* [New York: Harper Torchbooks, 1964], 90).

53. *Metaphysics*, 215. Lara Denis attempts to rehabilitate Kant on marriage in "From Friendship to Marriage: Revising Kant," *Philosophy and Phenomenological Research* 63:1 (2001): 1–28.

54. *Lectures*, 164.

55. *Philosophical Correspondence: 1759–99*, trans. Arnulf Zweig (Chicago: University of Chicago Press, 1967), letter dated July 10, 1797, p. 235.

56. *Philosophical Correspondence*, 235-36; italics added to "is."

57. *Metaphysics*, 62.

58. *Kant's Political Philosophy* (New York: St. Martin's Press, 1983), 117.

59. *Kant's Ethical Thought* (Cambridge: Cambridge University Press, 1999), 2; italics added. Here is the line in the *Metaphysics* to which Wood refers ("MS 6:425"): "even the permitted bodily union of the sexes in marriage . . . [is] a union which is in itself merely an animal union" (179). This is more evidence that Kant's solution is minimalist.

60. *Metaphysics*, 64.

61. *Kant's Political Philosophy*, 117.

62. Baumrin, "Sexual Immorality Delineated," 301, 300.

63. Mary Geach (an offspring of Peter Geach and Elizabeth Anscombe) claims, as did Augustine and Jerome, that Christianity "encourages men and women to recognize the whoredom in their own souls. It is a decline from Christianity to see oneself as better than a prostitute if one is . . . given to masturbatory fantasies, or if one defiles ones [sic] marriage with contraception." Geach, not surprisingly, limits sexual activity to marriage ("Marriage: Arguing to a First Principle in Sexual Ethics," in Luke Gormally, ed., *Moral Truth and Moral Tradition: Essays in Honour of Peter Geach and Elizabeth Anscombe* [Dublin, Ire.: Four Courts Press, 1994], 177-93, at 178).

STUDY QUESTIONS

1. Explain Kantian doubts about the morality of sexuality, by invoking specifically the Second Formulation of the Categorical Imperative. Focus on two questions: (A) How does sexual desire, or how does the experience of sexual urges, compromise the morality of the agent in whom they occur? What is the effect of sexual passion on the agent's rational autonomy? (B) How does sexual activity compromise the morality of people who engage in this behavior? Take into account both threats to the humanity of the sexual agent as well as threats to the humanity of the agent's partner.

2. Be sure you understand Soble's criticisms of the attempts of several philosophers to solve the Kantian sex problem, including Alan Goldman, Jean Hampton, Thomas Mappes, Martha Nussbaum, and Joshua Schulz. How might each of these writers defend their proposals against the critical points made by Soble?

3. State and evaluate Kant's own solution to the Kantian sex problem. Do you think that the author is right to suggest that Kant's solution is a thick minimalist externalism? Also evaluate interpretations of Kant's solution offered on his behalf and in his name by other philosophers (e.g., Robert Baker and Frederick Elliston; Raymond Belliotti; search for others in the literature).

4. The "applied sexual ethics" topic of the morality of prostitution from a Kantian perspective is brought up in Soble's essay, both explicitly in several passages and implicitly between the lines. Dig

out these remarks on prostitution and compare them with the views of the writers who discuss prostitution in this volume.

5. Take seriously the joke, "Is sex an autonomy-killing, mind-numbing, subhuman passion? Yes, but only when it's good." Work out its personal, social, and ethical implications.

6. Define as carefully as possible the different types of solution to the Kantian sex problem. Are there any more beyond the types provided by the author?

NINETEEN

Why "Derivatization" Is Better Than "Objectification"

Ann J. Cahill

Ann J. Cahill *argues in this chapter that "objectification" is not a good conceptual tool for ethical analysis because its use assumes a mistaken view of what persons are, namely, that they are essentially nonbodily and autonomous. As a result, philosophers who use "objectification" as an instrument of ethical analysis misdiagnose what is wrong with those sexual encounters that are morally wrong and have a hard time making room for permissible sex. Cahill suggests a view of persons she calls "embodied intersubjectivity," according to which our bodies and our relationships with others are central to our personhood. Cahill thus suggests that instead of relying on the concept of objectification to understand what is wrong with some sexual relationships, we should rely on a different concept, "derivatization," which refers to the reduction of a person's subjectivity to that of another. To derivatize is to elide the differences between human beings and is, therefore, wrong. Avoiding derivatization in sexual encounters implies that we approach one another with wonder and humility, thereby not only making room for morally permissible sexual encounters but also celebrating them and our physicality.*

Ann Cahill is professor of philosophy at Elon University. She is the author of *Overcoming Objectification: A Carnal Ethics* (Routledge, 2010) and *Rethinking Rape* (Cornell University Press, 2001). Her research interests lie in the intersection of feminist theory and philosophy of the body, and she is currently undertaking a theoretical exploration of miscarriage. "Why 'Derivatization' Is Better Than 'Objectification'" is published here for the first time. © 2012, Ann J. Cahill, who kindly gave permission for her new essay to be included in this volume.

Feminists have long used the idea of objectification to explain why things like prostitution and pornography are wrong and harmful. It's easy to see how and why the idea of objectification works—if you can show how a certain practice or behavior treats a person like an object, you seem to have shown, almost by definition, that that practice or behavior is unethical. That is, it seems obvious that to treat a person as a thing is an act of disrespect and degradation.

Yet it is precisely that necessarily negative set of connotations that accompany objectification—especially sexual objectification—that I want to challenge. I want to argue that it is not always a sign of disrespect to treat a person as a thing and that the assumption that objectification is always bad relies on an understanding of the self that is contradictory to feminist values and concerns. In the face of this contradiction, I want to encourage feminist philosophers to reject objectification as a tool of ethical analysis and to build their critiques of phenomena like prostitution and pornography on different philosophical grounds.

Let's start with getting clear on the term itself. When feminists describe a certain action, set of behaviors, or representation as "objectifying," they almost always mean to point to ways in which the objectified individual or group is treated or represented as a *thing* as opposed to a *person*. For example, imagine a patient recovering in a hospital from surgery. If medical care givers focus exclusively on the medical aspects of the patient's recovery—checking blood pressure, adjusting medications, performing the necessary tests—without attending to the patient's emotional or psychological well-being (or lack thereof), feminists (as well as other philosophers) may describe the patient as being treated as a mere physical entity, a biological machine that needs fixing. To the extent that his personhood, that part of him that exists beyond the physical aspects of his illness, is being denied or ignored, he is therefore being objectified.

Sexual objectification, while still often described as treating someone like a thing (or, even more evocatively, like a "piece of meat"), combines the denial of personhood with a distinctive eroticism. So the woman walking down a busy street who becomes the target of sexualizing catcalls is not only being treated as less than a person, but she is also being treated as a *sex object* whose most important characteristic is her sexual attractiveness. What matters about a sex object is not her emotional complexity, educational background, family of origin, religious beliefs, or anything else. Of course, the actual person *does* have important other characteristics, but she is treated *as if* she does not—and that's what's wrong about sexual objectification.

It's important to note here that we're actually using the word "object" in two distinct ways. On the one hand, "object" means "material entity, one usually neither sentient nor conscious." In this sense, pens, tables, strawberries, and books are all objects. Such things do not have the kind of experiences that animate entities can have (like having emotions, making choices, and sensing). We call animate entities "subjects" as a way of distinguishing them from objects. Subjects and objects understood in this way are not just different from each other: they're organized into a hierarchy, where to be a subject is better than to be an object. That's why to objectify a person (subject) is to downgrade, disrespect, and insult him or her.

On the other hand, to be an "object" of something (attention, affection, anger, violence) is to be the (supposedly passive) recipient of the action of another. This meaning of "object" is particularly crucial in terms of feminist descriptions of "the male gaze," a term inaugurated by Laura Mulvey in the context of film theory.[1] The male gaze, Mulvey argued, frames and defines women as objects-to-be-looked-at-by-men, and while the male gaze need not only be taken up by men (women can view other women as objects-to-be-looked-at-by-men), it defines feminine (hetero) sexuality as limited to being-looked-at, being-desired, rather than itself looking or desiring. Subjects look, and objects are looked at. Again, these roles are hierarchized: the superior entity looks, the inferior entity is looked at.

Often, in feminist theory, the two ways of understanding objectification are combined, especially through the association of the body as primarily material and thus object-like. For example, Simone de Beauvoir draws important connections among woman's alleged inferiority to man, her sexual role vis-à-vis man, and her status as flesh.[2] Catharine MacKinnon draws these connections even more strongly; while de Beauvoir's analysis implies that woman can be liberated from these associations, MacKinnon's theories indicate that the objectifying forces in a patriarchal culture are so successful that to be a woman is necessarily to be passive and thing-like.[3] For MacKinnon, then, pornography doesn't merely *represent* women as objects; it actually *defines* and *creates* women as things. Pornography shapes sexuality in a way that requires women to be passive and dominated, and men to be active and dominating. And this is not just one way among many of understanding sexuality—pornography says that this is what sexuality *is*, this is what a sexual woman *does*, and (just as important) women are essentially and primarily *sexual* in precisely this way.

Beauvoir and MacKinnon are good examples of feminist theorists who provide explanations of how objectification works and how patriarchal cultures go about treating women as things. But they don't delve into any philosophical detail about *why* treating a person like a thing is unethical. That point is largely assumed and considered uncontroversial. Because it's this point that I challenge in this essay, we need to look at two feminist theorists who address it at length: Linda LeMoncheck and Martha Nussbaum. In unpacking their analyses, I show that the very idea of objectification relies on the assumptions about persons with which I disagree, namely (1) that the most essential elements of persons are non-bodily, and (2) that persons are essentially autonomous. If "objectification" assumes the truth of these claims, and those claims are both wrong and contrary to feminist values and goals, then feminism must turn to a concept other than objectification to critique ethically harmful practices. In the final section of this paper, I present just such an alternative concept: "derivatization."

LEMONCHECK AND NUSSBAUM ON OBJECTIFICATION

For LeMoncheck, the moral wrong in objectification is the belief that women are inferior to men; therefore, they do not deserve the treatment required by moral equality. It is no accident that the failure to recognize women as moral equals essentially reduces them to nonsubjects—that is, objects—because moral equality distinguishes persons from other beings and, importantly, from other kinds of bodies. "[I]t is only when women are regarded as inanimate objects, bodies, or animals, where their status as the moral equals of persons has been demeaned or degraded, that the expression 'sex objectification' is correctly used."[4] What holds together this category of "inanimate objects, bodies, or animals" is lack of personhood. Objectification, in one deft move, reduces women to things, and therefore nonpersons, robbing them of the respect that persons demand.

LeMoncheck's analysis obviously relies heavily on distinguishing between persons and nonpersons, a distinction that warrants a closer look. Following a fairly traditional, modern view of the person, LeMoncheck lists "distinctive human capacities,"[5] including sentience, self-awareness, rationality, self-determination, and reflective thought. These capacities make experiences such as self-respect and autonomy possible; they also, of course, make possible the loss of both, a possibility that results in the different and more extensive set of moral rights and responsibilities accorded to persons.

For LeMoncheck, "person" is a moral category whose members share capacities that are generally seen as nonbodily, that is, intellectually or cognitively derived. These capacities produce the familiar rights that many traditional political philosophies assign to persons (freedom from injury, exploitation, and stereotypes; the freedoms of self-determination and privacy). When a person's rights go unrecognized, are trampled upon or hindered, the person is humiliated, harmed, and degraded—that is, wronged. This is precisely the dynamic of sexual objectification:

> What is necessary to identify an incident as sex objectification is that the sex object be treated as an object, body, or animal but not also as the moral equal of persons. She is treated as if she lacked one or more of the distinctive human capacities upon which her rights to a certain level of well-being and freedom are based. . . . What this analysis suggests is that one can treat a woman as sexually attractive without treating her as a sex object, by treating her as a sexually attractive moral equal or person.[6]

Here, LeMoncheck clearly presents personhood as an essentially human characteristic to be added to the other traits that human beings share with animals (as well as other objects). Among the many possibilities of human interaction include two situations: treating another human being as a body but not as a moral equal, and treating him as a body *and* as a moral equal.

Thus, on LeMoncheck's analysis it is possible to objectify a person while recognizing that person's intellectual abilities, for example, or her capacity for mothering, or her familial relation to you—because one can still consider such a person less than a moral equal. But in considering her as less than a moral equal, she appears to be less of a person and perhaps not a real person at all. It is in this sense that she is in the category of "inanimate objects, bodies, and animals." The act of objectification, while not causing all personal characteristics of the objectified person to recede into nothingness, justifies approaching her as one who is inferior to the objectifier, worthy of less respect and less regard.

The fundamental distinction between persons and nonpersons is not itself rooted in sexuality. To be sexualized is not necessarily to be objectified; otherwise, sexuality itself becomes morally problematic, which LeMoncheck strenuously denies. Only when someone is sexually degraded to something less than a person does sexual treatment become unethical. Yet LeMoncheck also addresses the complex ways in which objectification affects the structure of (hetero)eroticism itself, both in men and women. Sexuality and degradation mix together in sexual objectification in at least two ways. First—and here LeMoncheck's analysis resonates with MacKinnon's—the degradation itself becomes erotic (almost certainly for the objectifier, and sometimes for the objectified). The objectified woman becomes sexy by becoming less-than-man and becomes inferior by virtue of becoming sexy. Second, the woman's sexuality is employed as a way to undermine her personhood, as it becomes "a kind of focus for her humiliation, embarrassment, and domination."[7] Persistent sexual objectification and dehumanization, then, limit women's ability to express freely their sexual desires, experiences, and delights. All feminine sexuality becomes pornography, and the feminine body itself comes to stand for that which is dirty and reprehensible about sex.[8]

The strategic use of feminine sexuality in the process of objectification and dehumanization explains a crucial confusion that has plagued feminists and nonfeminists, namely, that criticizing many examples of objectification seems tantamount to criticizing sexuality itself. LeMoncheck's analysis helps us to see how a general context of sexual objectification presents women with at most two choices: either be sexual and therefore be degraded and considered a moral unequal, or refuse to be sexual, thus limiting personal expression considerably. That is, the very way that (hetero)sexuality is commonly constructed makes it difficult for women to be recognized as *both* moral equals *and* sexual beings. It's precisely because degradation and feminine sexuality are so profoundly linked that critiquing the first raises the worry that such an ethics would render all sexual experiences and interactions unethical. But LeMoncheck's point is that as profound as that link is under current social and political conditions, it is not a necessary one: our understanding of heterosexuality need not require the dehumanization of women, and we can envision sexual practices and norms that no longer portray women as moral unequals.

Nussbaum also wants to avoid making sexuality itself a problem, even asking whether there may be instances of sexual objectification that might be not only morally acceptable but also positive, such as the affirming and delightful experiences of being viewed as sexually attractive.[9] In order to discern objectionable from nonobjectionable instances of objectification, says Nussbaum, we need to analyze the term "objectification" more deeply and pay better attention to the contexts in which objectification occurs.

Nussbaum's articulation of the moral error of objectification is familiar: "One is treating *as an object* what is really not an object, what is, in fact, a human being."[10] Like LeMoncheck's, Nussbaum's analysis rests upon a sharp distinction between persons and things, which raises two significant questions: what are the ways in which human beings treat objects, and which of these ways are problematic when applied to people?

Nussbaum identifies seven traits associated with objects that, if transferred to persons, may well be ethically problematic: instrumentality, lack of autonomy, inertness, fungibility, violability, ownership, and lack of subjectivity.[11] Not every object has each characteristic (there are, for example, irreplaceable objects and objects not subject to ownership), but every interaction with an object presumes and is predicated upon at least one of these traits. Nussbaum ultimately concludes that among these traits denial of autonomy and instrumentality are of particular importance because it is almost impossible to think of cases of inanimate objects "treated as autonomous" and because treating something autonomously "seems to entail treating it" in none of the other ways.[12] Even when we treat a given object as irreplaceable (say, the Hope diamond) or not properly capable of being owned (natural resources, perhaps), we do not consider it an autonomous subject with its own unique perspective, interests, set of goals, or capacity for decision making. Given that the lack of autonomy is the most consistent commonality among human beings' treatment of objects, to treat a person like an object (in an objectionable way) is most likely to deny that person's autonomy. Moreover, for Nussbaum, autonomy functions as perhaps the most defining element of moral equality among persons, so to deny a person's autonomy is to deny his personhood. Finally, it is virtually impossible to simultaneously accord autonomy to a being and perceive that being as a mere instrument of one's own ends. Similarly, to deny autonomy to someone makes it that much easier to treat her as a mere instrument.

Having established the ethical importance of autonomy and noninstrumentality, Nussbaum faces the problem that both instrumentality and denial of autonomy exist in positive bodily interactions, particularly positive sexual interactions. Mutually enjoyable sexual encounters tend to (or, at the very least, can) involve a certain loss of autonomy by which each person's experience is so deeply affected and shaped by the other's behavior that the individuals involved no longer experience themselves as self-contained, self-moving persons. Similarly, sexual arousal and satisfaction most often emanate from the interaction with another person's body; not only do lovers use each other's bodies in order to have a sexual experience, they often desire their bodies to be used in this way. Sexual activity, then, seems to involve instrumentality and denial of autonomy, the two traits that Nussbaum has described as most significant to personhood.

This philosophical conundrum should not be surprising, given Nussbaum's dependence on a framework developed by Kant, who, as Soble has demonstrated,[13] viewed sexual interactions with a profound ethical suspicion. Unlike Kant, Nussbaum recognizes that sexual experiences at least have the possibility of enhancing a person's well-being and sense of self. But how can experiences of objectification do so? Nussbaum appeals to context. If objectification takes place in a context that honors and supports each person's autonomy, then such "use" of the person's body may well be acceptable (it is assumed, of course, that the person so "used" has the freedom to deny such access to her body at any given point). And as long as that autonomy is consistently and reliably supported in the relationship as a whole, the loss of a sense of subjectivity that can occur in sexual encounters is not problematic.[14] One can even delight in the body parts of one's sexual partner without necessarily dehumanizing that individual as long as such an action is accompanied "with an intense regard for the person's individuality, which can even be expressed in a personalizing and individualizing of the bodily organs themselves."[15] For Nussbaum, then, treating one's sexual partner as an object can be perfectly acceptable—as long as the objectification occurs in a context that exists beyond the sexual encounter and in which the partners treat each other as individual, autonomous people. Without such a context, the objectified person is likely to be treated as a body without the accompanying characteristics of personhood.[16]

Nussbaum's appeal to context somewhat articulates—perhaps more so than LeMoncheck's—a sexual ethics that does not attempt to transcend or marginalize the body, even if, as Soble argues, it does so by violating some aspects of Kantian ethics. It leaves sexual persons the moral space in which to experience bodily pleasures without necessarily degrading each other's personhood. However, as I next argue, both approaches are encumbered by a Kantian framework that defines the person (and thus the moral value of the person) in nonbodily terms, which produces an ethically suspicious attitude toward the body. Moreover, these approaches assume that the person is fundamentally and appropriately autonomous and thus do not sufficiently take into account how encounters with the other are central to the subject itself.

WHAT'S WRONG WITH CURRENT THEORIES OF OBJECTIFICATION

My critique of LeMoncheck's and Nussbaum's analyses is based on a model of the person that I name "embodied intersubjectivity." This model appears in the work of several contemporary feminist philosophers.[17] It is a model grounded in feminist critiques of traditional theories of the self, theories which marginalize, ignore, or pathologize any individual or group who does not embody the ideal of the white, heterosexual, physically capable male. Approaching the self as necessarily embodied and intersubjective allows for a more inclusive and nuanced understanding of human personhood; however, as I demonstrate, adopting such a model reveals weaknesses in the theories of objectification that I summarized above.

Briefly, the model of embodied intersubjectivity improves upon dominant Western philosophies of the self in two ways. First, it repositions the body as central, rather than opposed, to the category of self or person. Too often, the body has been portrayed as at best an irrelevant aspect of personhood and at worst a hindrance to or distraction from its worthy elements (rationality, the soul, autonomy). And as long as the body takes up the subordinate position in the mind-body hierarchy, those persons more closely associated with the body (women and others) are deemed appropriately subordinate to those persons associated with the mind or soul (men, and sometimes others).

In contrast to this opposition between personhood and materiality, the model of embodied intersubjectivity makes the body central to human experience and activity. However important allegedly nonbodily traits such as rationality may be, such traits only and always arise in an embodied context. There is nothing about human subjectivity that can occur outside the realm of embodiment, which means that the body is neither tangential nor hostile to human personhood. Nor is it a mere substratum upon which the more salient layers of consciousness, rationality, and so forth are placed as forms of ethical upgrades. We are not persons *despite* our bodies, and we don't become better persons by denying or controlling our bodies (despite what all those women's magazines say!). We are persons (partly) because of our bodies; that is, our embodiment is as vital to our moral status as persons as it is to our experience.

Second, this approach seeks to recognize the vital role that relationships play in the formation of the self. In traditional models, defining personhood in terms of disembodied traits is deeply connected to understanding the person as first and foremost an individual. The ability to think and act on one's own (autonomy) is seen from this perspective as crucial to human dignity, and any encroachment upon that autonomy requires justification. Diana Meyers's critique of *homo economicus* might also be fairly leveled against the "natural man" of social theorists, whose existence precedes associations with other humans:

> In an eerie suspension of biological reality, selves are conceived as sufficient unto themselves. No one seems to be born and raised, for birth mothers and caregivers are driven offstage. . . . The self appears to materialize on its own, endowed with a starter set of basic desires, ready to select additional desires and construct overarching goals, and skilled in performing instrumental rationality tasks. . . . Since dependency is denied, no morally significant preconsensual or nonconsensual entanglements at the beginning or the end of life need be acknowledged. All affiliations are to be freely chosen, and all transactions are to be freely negotiated. The repudiation of feminine caregiving underwrites the illusion of independence, and the illusion of independence underwrites homo economicus's voluntarism.[18]

As Meyers points out, this critique does not amount to a total rejection of autonomy but rather to an understanding that both the self and the autonomy that selves enjoy emanate from relations with others. Rather than viewing the self as the building block of relations, this approach views relations as the condition of possibility of the self, without which the self cannot come into being. Feminists mean this quite literally: the human infant requires the care of another in order to develop the traits that mark the human self.

So the self who chooses, perceives, and acts is, by definition, the result of relations. Moreover, the importance of relations with regard to the human self does not end with infancy but persists: in all but the most extreme situations, human beings are continually engaged in relations with other human beings (and since even the hermit necessarily bears the physical, psychological, and emotional marks of previous relations, one could argue that the human self is never truly alone). To reorient the human self around relations in general is also to reframe our understanding of particular human identities. If human selves develop necessarily in the context of relations (all of which are socially and politically specific; while all human infants must be cared for to survive infancy, different human cultures vary widely in the ways in which they provide that care), then specific identities will be profoundly affected by the identities of others. I cannot disentangle who "I" am from the others with whom I have interacted. In brief, I am making two distinct points regarding the self and the importance of relations: one, that the *existence* of the self requires others, and two, that the *particular identity* of any given self is essentially shaped by the relations it has had and continues to have.

Conceptualizing the self as necessarily relational does not entail the notion that the self is utterly defined by relations or that we could predict what a specific self will become if it engages in certain types of relationships. Interactions and the selves that emerge from them are complex matters. And not every interaction is conducive to human flourishing; in fact, acts of violence can undermine the very humanness of persons.[19] However, such a model should cause us to question whether autonomy should enjoy the priority it has enjoyed in previous approaches. The other may sometimes be threatening and even dangerous—but remaining independent from the other is neither possible nor desirable, and moral dignity cannot be reduced to the ability to be free from such influences.

This, then, is the model of embodied intersubjectivity: an approach to the human subject that considers both the flesh and the other to be central to agency and any other crucial aspect of human existence. It is a model diametrically opposed to the analyses of objectification explored above, which rely (sometimes implicitly, sometimes explicitly)[20] on a Kantian definition of the person built around the twin poles of a disembodied rationality and autonomy.

And given their reliance on such a definition, it is no wonder that sexuality remains problematic. The problem that seems unsurpassable is that sexuality and sexual experiences can simultaneously involve the sense of being an object (both in the sense of being a physical entity, a body, and in the sense of being an object of another's gaze and attention) *and* an increased sense of flourishing as a human being. As long as the moral value of the human person is to be found in autonomy and disembodied traits, this combination is troubling and raises paradoxes that the variety of theorists mentioned in Soble's essay "Sexual Use" have tried to resolve. While I agree with Soble that such attempts ultimately fail, I argue that they fail not due to their incomplete or inconsistent adoption of Kantian principles but because those principles frame the question wrongly. Once one has established the self as marked by autonomy and nonbodily traits, sexuality and sexual interactions show up as in need of justification. If we start from a different insight—namely, that the self is fundamentally embodied and intersubjective—then sexuality and sexual interactions can be seen (under certain conditions) to have a role in enhancing one's sense of self.

Certainly, neither Nussbaum's appeal to context nor LeMoncheck's "dehumanization" accounts for an embodied sexuality as valuable to personhood. While LeMoncheck's can posit sexual encounters that do not *contradict* personhood (and thus are ethical), it can't explain how sexual encounters could *enhance* one's sense of being a human being of moral worth. Similarly, Nussbaum's appeal to context serves at best a redemptive function, a way of neutralizing sexuality's potential for undermining personhood.

Indeed, the construction of a positive sexual ethics has been an ongoing challenge for feminist philosophers. It is a crucial one, for if feminist theory is to provide a compelling account of human (inter)subjectivity, it must be able to explain the ways in which sexual encounters can promote a sense of well-being that is experienced as central to our very humanness but without being complacent towards genuinely ethically problematic sexual encounters, many of which stem from a hegemonic heterosexuality.

In other words, we should distinguish between sexual practices, experiences, and representations that *recognize* and *enhance* the embodied intersubjectivity of persons (thus increasing human flourishing, which is ethically laudable) from those that *reject* and *thwart* such embodied intersubjectivity. In the concluding "Metaphysical Finale" to "Sexual Use," Soble indicates that it is not particularly difficult to argue that (1) sex is problematic and therefore ought to be restricted to the institution of marriage (Kant's view), or (2) that sex is "wholesome" and therefore ought not to be restricted. "The convincing intellectual trick," according to Soble, "would be to assume the *best* about sex, that it is by its nature wholesome, and then argue, *anyway*, that it should be restricted to lifelong, monogamous matrimony and that casual sex is morally wrong." In fact, I am attempting to pull off a different intellectual trick entirely, one more in line with the concerns of feminist thinkers: arguing that sex can be understood as central to a flourishing sense of self but that there are sexual behaviors and practices that should nevertheless be considered ethically questionable. The theories of Luce Irigaray, as I next argue, provide an effective foundation for such a distinction and can help us to create a positive sexual ethics that is proudly carnal.

DERIVATIZATION

Instead of asking whether ethically questionable practices and norms treat persons as *objects*, we should ask whether they treat persons as *derivatives* of other persons. A new approach demands a new term: so rather than "objectification," I suggest that we use the concept of "derivatization" as a tool of ethical analysis. In this section, I provide a description of derivatization, detail its philosophical reliance on Irigaray's theory, and argue that it succeeds where "objectification" fails.

Grammatically, "derivatization" follows the structure of "objectification": if objectification is treating something that is not an object as an object, derivatization is treating something that is not a derivative as a derivative. When an individual or a group of individuals is derivatized, their subjectivity—their speech, their emotions, their choice of attire, and so forth—is reduced to and determined by the subjectivity of another. It is not that the derivatized individual or group is constructed or treated as utterly lacking in personhood because the derivatized person or group performs actions and demonstrates traits that only sentient, conscious entities could. However, those actions and traits ultimately (and in some cases entirely) refer back to another subject—so the derivatized subject is not its own person but is rather the kind of person that the derivatizing subject desires or needs.

In order to argue that it is wrong to derivatize another person, I need to argue that it is ethically necessary to approach human persons as *different* from one another, such that no person's being or identity should be understood as subsumed by that of another. On the one hand, this may appear to be an innocuous, and even uncontroversial claim; however, it's important to note that much of Western ethics is grounded not in a recognition of difference but of sameness. According to these approaches, human beings are equal, and thus worthy of moral consideration, by virtue of sharing certain universal traits that trump any distinctions among them. I am here suggesting quite a different approach, one that names difference as the ground and possibility of ethics. And in order to be consistent with my model of embodied intersubjectivity, I need to claim that this difference among human persons does not amount to autonomy by a different name. Again, Irigaray's theory of sexual difference is particularly helpful on both points.

From Irigaray's perspective, sexual difference—the fact that human beings come in (at least) two sexes, male and female—is an ontological fact, an inescapable element of human existence. There is no neutral, universal model of the human person. For Irigaray, human bodies are examples par excellence of this ineluctable diversity in that there is no one human body that can serve as a comprehensive representative of all human bodies (all human bodies are examples, at best, of one *kind* of human body). Irigaray's privileging of sexual difference above other differences (for example, differences in race or physical ability) is controversial and makes her vulnerable to a variety of philosophical critiques.[21] There is no doubt, for example, that Irigaray herself is primarily concerned with ethical questions surrounding heterosexual interactions and is at best uninterested in homosexual interactions. However, my interpretation of her theory emphasizes the *fact* of difference as ethically relevant and takes sexual difference to be emblematic but not exhaustive of the role of difference in general. I would therefore argue that Irigaray's disinterest in homosexual relations is contrary to the role that difference plays in her theory and that a more consistent attention to difference would recognize the ethical plurality of sexual relations as well as the non-necessity of heterosexuality itself (if men and women are truly ontologically distinct from each other, there is no necessity to their being sexual partners).

Irigaray further claims that the inequality under which women have suffered is the result of Western attempts to reduce this inescapable difference to sameness. This appears to be a contradictory claim: much feminist thought, particularly in the liberal tradition, argues that sexism often mistakenly focuses on and exaggerates the differences between men and women in order to argue that women are not worthy of men's rights and responsibilities. Irigaray, however, claims that the difference that patriarchy has regularly invoked is not qualitative but quantitative, which is to say, not a real difference at all. Women have been constructed as essentially similar to men but with fewer of the most important characteristics (e.g., rationality, independence, genius) most relevant when it comes to human moral worth. From the liberal perspective, patriarchy's mistake is to wrongly consider women to be less than human; from Irigaray's perspective, patriarchy's mistake is to consider humanness to be singular and to fail to recognize that difference is embedded at the most fundamental level of human existence.

To claim that difference is fundamental to human existence—to claim, as Irigaray does, that the human is always (at least) two—is to recognize that no one person, or even one group of persons, can represent the whole of humanity. There exists between men and women an irreducible difference that cannot (and should not) be overcome; any attempt to articulate a universal element of human identity necessarily results in either irrelevance (e.g., all humans being made out of cells) or oppression. Because no one standard can span qualitative difference, applying the same standard to diverse entities renders one of the two an inferior being. For example, if we define strength as upper-body strength, most women appear to be less strong than men—a result, based as it is in an allegedly neutral, but actually gendered, standard, that misrepresents women's strength by ignoring their stamina and lower-body strength.

This irreducible difference means that the sexes are not complementary parts that make up a unitary whole. In fact, for Irigaray, there is no "whole"—humanity is not marked by completeness but by dissimilarity. She argues that the theoretical demand for the universal, sex-neutral human being (a demand that runs consistently through Western thought) requires the denial of the ways in which women are *not* like men, and that it is this denial that must be rectified. Justice, then, depends on the idea that the sexes are ontologically distinct, not on the idea that women are the same as men.

To say that men and women are different from each other is not to say that they are incapable of engaging with each other in important, productive, and ethically valuable ways. In fact, for Irigaray, it is sexual difference itself that enables intersexual dialogue and engagement. Only when true difference is present can dialogue occur; without it, all that really transpires is monologue because to speak to someone who is defined by one's own being is ultimately to speak to oneself. To see this, imagine trying to argue with someone whose only goal is agreeing with you: such a conversation would be inauthentic and unproductive due to that person's refusal to take up a voice distinct from your own. Under Western patriarchy, women have played the roles demanded by the projections of men (primarily wives and mothers), and in that context, there has been little or no true engagement between men and women. Actual engagement between the sexes can only occur when women's being is recognized—by both men and women—as ontologically independent from the being of men.

For Irigaray, humanity always finds itself engaged in difference—even when that difference is assiduously denied. Recognizing that sexual difference cannot be transcended is the first step towards creating a real sexual equality, one that does not (as liberalism, Irigaray claims, does) require women to recreate themselves in the image of men. The foundational aspect of sexual difference demands that any kind of interaction between and among human beings must recognize the difference that makes it possible. Rather than search for ways in which human beings are similar or identical, Irigaray urges an ethics that embraces difference and its possibilities. We must assume that others are different, even in ways that we cannot imagine. If the other cannot be reduced to ourselves, we are ethically called to adopt an attitude of wonder, an attunement to the new possibilities that the other represents; and if we as individuals cannot represent the whole, we are ethically called to adopt an attitude of humility, a sense of our own necessary limitation. [22]

To deny the otherness of the sexes is to stagnate their relations, to doom them to the recitations of well-worn scripts. This pattern is most obvious in the construction of feminine sexuality:

> Desire manifests itself as quasi-mechanistic forces, functioning with no sensorial, sensual pleasure. Woman, assumed to have no libido of her own, devotes her energy to exacerbating [m]an's sexual tension, for which she becomes the site of discharge. In these abstract, stifling, disenchanted, not to say cynical, physical encounters, procreation remains the only tangible symptom of the existence of life and sensibility. Hence its value. [23]

Patriarchal society does not allow the flourishing of a distinctly female sexuality, so women are restricted to a sexuality centered on male needs and desires.

This reduction of women to what (heterosexual) men want and (think they) need is derivatization. It is an act of violence, degradation, and harm because women's being should not be subsumed under the subjectivity of men. Reducing women to men betrays women as sexually specific beings and makes it difficult, and sometimes impossible, for women to understand, explore, and experience their sexuality in a context free from the demands of heterosexual men.

A few examples of derivatization are useful, especially because, as with objectification, not all instances of derivatization involve sex or gender. Consider first a nonsexualized and nongendered example: a member of the wait staff at a high-end restaurant. He must adopt behaviors and attitudes that are most pleasant to the customer; so, even if the waiter is in a bad mood or finds a customer rude and obnoxious, he must convey a pleasant, accommodating manner. The waiter must be the kind of person with whom the customer wishes to interact (it is crucial for our discussion that the customer does in fact wish to interact with a *person*). Already we see the advantages of the notion of derivatization over the notion of objectification: if we claim that the waiter is objectified by the customer's unfairly superior position towards him, we would have to claim that the waiter is treated in ways importantly similar to the ways subjects commonly treat an inanimate object. But this is not true, because the actions that the waiter is compelled to undertake could only be undertaken by a subject. A more accurate way of interpreting the situation is to leave objectification out of the analysis and emphasize the ways in which the waiter is required to adopt a role entirely delimited by another subject: virtually everything the waiter does or says is reducible to the customer's desires and preferences. The derivatized waiter becomes a kind of extension of the customer's subjectivity, and so the ontological distinction between the two is denied and elided.

Consider next a more gendered example: the role of the traditional wife as defined by hegemonic patriarchy. The ideal wife—a stereotypical ideal, not an actual wife—is one whose subjectivity and personhood is subsumed by her husband's. In past decades and centuries, this subsuming was codified by law, which helps to explain why rape in marriage remained for so long a legal impossibility. While many aspects of marriage law that rely on gender inferiority have been challenged and changed, the cultural symbols that share those assumptions remain strong. The practice of married women taking their husband's surname continues in full force, brides are still "given away," and the wedding day is still a far more pivotal moment of transformation for the bride than for the groom. After the wedding day, the bride becomes the wife, and if she is a good one, she anticipates and fulfills the needs of the husband, ranging from the culinary to the sexual to the reproductive. Again, it is not that the ideal of the good wife is contrary to personhood itself but that the ideal constitutes a derivatized personhood: she must be the kind of person that he wants her to be.

Let's now consider a third example, one that brings sexuality more clearly to the fore: a woman who makes a living as an exotic dancer dresses and moves in sexually appealing ways to her heterosexual male customers. In developing her craft, she does not ask herself about her own sexual desires or what sorts of music and language she finds arousing. Instead, she models the representation of her sexuality on the sexual supplies of the heterosexual male. If she believes (or is told) that he finds schoolgirls sexy, she dons a short plaid skirt; if large breasts are all the rage, she considers implants, even if those implants reduce or obliterate the sexual sensations she can experience through her breasts. Derivatization is occurring because the point and motivation of all these decisions—decisions that shape what kind of subjectivity the dancer can inhabit and project—is male heterosexual desire. Importantly, the subjectivity of the feminine exotic dancer is entirely reducible to the subjectivity of her customers; she is a person, but while she is working as a dancer, she must have no subjective qualities that do not refer back to her customer's desires.

This example helps us to see that it is the totality of the demands of the job regarding her expressed subjectivity that is ethically problematic here. Every job, one could argue, requires an individual to consider the needs or concerns of the other. The doctor works so that the patient can be healthy, and the teacher is responsible in some crucial ways for the learning of the student. But neither the doctor nor the teacher needs to enact a subjectivity reducible to the other (the patient and the student, respectively) in order to do her job. What makes the medical and pedagogical interactions ethical, in fact, is a recognition that the parties involved in those interactions bring to them distinct knowledges and abilities that are nonreducible to each other. A doctor who understands her role as merely meeting a patient's stated needs, without reference to the doctor's own understandings of health and medicine, is negligent (as the recent trial of Michael Jackson's personal physician demonstrated!). And if the exotic dancer were seen as an expert on matters sexual, someone whom the client could view as an authority on matters important to the client, then perhaps the interaction would have a different ethical quality. But the most common form of exotic dancing in contemporary culture requires that the dancer project and enact a subjectivity entirely reducible to that of the viewer: she must be who he wants her to be, and who he wants her to be is entirely predictable from his own sexual desires. That she may adopt an entirely different subjectivity once she is off the job is not ethically relevant. Such changes in subjectivities are, within the model of embodied intersubjectivity, to be expected (subjects are different kinds of subjects in the context of different relations), but, more to the point, the fact that the dancer can move away from the derivatizing dynamic does not justify it. While she is being treated inappropriately as a derivative of another person's subjectivity, an ethical wrong is occurring. In addition, my analysis of the ethics of these situations does not rest on claims regarding whether sex workers do or do not choose their work freely. Economic and social conditions, in addition to personal preferences and talents, may all have a role to play in an individual choosing a variety of kinds of work. My concern here is whether that work necessarily entails ethical wrongs.

Finally, let's turn to one of Eve Ensler's *Vagina Monologues* for an example of a sexual interaction that is clearly nonderivatizing. In this monologue, the narrator describes her sexual encounter with Bob, who, as it turns out, loves to look at vaginas. The narrator, who regards her own vagina as irretrievably ugly, tries to beg off: does he really have to look? "I need to see you," Bob says, "I need to see what you look like," and in the looking, he delivers to the narrator an experience of her genitalia as positive, even glorious:

> He stayed looking for almost an hour, as if he were studying a map, observing the moon, staring into my eyes, but it was my vagina. In the light, I watched him looking at me, and he was so genuinely excited, so peaceful and euphoric, I began to get wet and turned on. I began to feel beautiful and delicious—like a great painting or a waterfall. Bob wasn't afraid. He wasn't grossed out. I began to swell, began to feel proud. Began to love my vagina. And Bob lost himself there and I was there with him, in my vagina, and we were gone.[24]

The sexual interaction between Bob and the narrator, while not limited to his viewing of her vagina, is positive and enhancing because Bob's gaze does not compare the narrator's vagina to some preexisting standard of beauty or acceptability. Because Bob's gaze does not organize the narrator's vagina according to his own fixed criteria—it is *particularity* that fascinates him, not some possibility of perfection—it is a nonderivatizing, affirming recognition of the narrator's sexual embodiment. An ethical analysis based on objectification would have us ask two questions of this clearly positive encounter, with the assumption that answering either in the affirmative would indicate an ethical problem: Is Bob treating the narrator's vagina as a thing? And is the narrator the passive recipient of an active gaze? When we approach this encounter through the lens of derivatization, however, we're able to see that Bob *does* treat the narrator's vagina as a thing (a material entity) and *does* subject it to an active gaze—and that both of these modes of viewing are not only ethically acceptable but in fact ethically praiseworthy because he does so with an attitude of wonder. Were he to approach her vagina to determine whether it matches up to his particular preference or some preexisting social ideal, he would be derivatizing her, and the encounter could not have had the self-enhancing quality that the narrator describes.

In the first three of these examples, it is clear who is being derivatized (the waiter, the wife, the dancer). Who exactly is doing the derivatizing is not as clear, however. Is it the individual taking up the other role in the pair (the customer, the husband)? Does it emanate from a society that shapes these roles in particular, defined ways? Does the derivatized person play a role in the derivatization? (Note that these questions would also arise with objectification.) In a word: yes. Derivatization is deeply implicated in social and political practices, and as such it doesn't have a singular, identifiable source. Representations can derivatize, economic relations can derivatize, individuals can derivatize and self-derivatize—and sometimes these actions can occur discretely while at other times they are concurrent. However, all acts of derivatization require a conceptual framework that makes the reduction of one person's subjectivity to another person's subjectivity coherent and possible.

Can derivatization be a matter of degrees? That is, can one be slightly or somewhat derivatized? In answering this question, I would want to distinguish between being derivatized and being influenced by an other. That is, as the model of embodied intersubjectivity clearly demonstrates, to have one's being influenced by an interaction with another is not ethically problematic. However, to enact a subjectivity, even temporarily, that is entirely reducible to another's wants or desires is at the very least ethically questionable. Attending the opera or a baseball game with a dearly beloved other out of generosity and good will rather than authentically felt interest does not constitute derivatization, nor does developing an appreciation for opera or baseball as a result of such excursions. But to *require* that one's partner actually become (or pretend to become) an opera or baseball lover does constitute derivatization and is ethically unjustifiable.

The question of autonomy remains: does this approach merely repackage autonomy, which I have already described as a problematic ground for ethical analysis? I think not. Irigaray's theory relies on the notion that one person's subjectivity is importantly different from another's. This difference is "ontological specificity" because the focus is on a person's *being*. But to say that a person's being, her identity and subjectivity, is nonreducible to another person's being is not to claim that a person ought to be seen as properly or ideally *independent* from the other. The phenomenon of sexual desire can help us to see this distinction clearly. It would make little sense to approach sexual desire as an independent experience, separable from the existence and actions of other human beings: what particular human beings sexually desire has much to do with the relations they have experienced, the social norms regarding sexuality that surround them, their understanding of their partners and their partners' desires, and so forth. Sexual desires are *intersubjective*. They are also specific: individuals have complex sets of sexual desires that can shift in relation to experiences but are not the predictable results of those experiences. Irigarian ethics recognizes the specificity of sexual desires while understanding them as necessarily open to transformation. The meaning or content of one's sexual desires cannot be fully explicated in terms of another person's sexual desires, but neither can it be explicated without reference to some others.

In highlighting the ethical significance of specificity, we no longer ask, "Are the persons involved in situation X acting autonomously, free from constraint or the influence of others?" Or, "Is the person being treated as an object rather than a subject?" Instead, we ask, "Do the relationships involved in phenomenon X sufficiently recognize and uphold the subjective specificity of the persons involved?" Note that despite the heterosexism of Irigaray herself, this question could be applied just as effectively to homosexual relations as to heterosexual relations. Sexual difference, while primary for Irigaray, is not the only difference that matters, and thus Irigaray's theory allows for the recognition of difference in same-sex relations as well.

Derivatization is more successful than objectification as a tool of ethical analysis. First, it does not risk vilifying physicality; indeed, Irigaray's ethics of sexual difference explicitly uses bodily differences among the sexes as a positive metaphor to ground ethics. Rather than being ethically questionable or puzzling, bodily interactions are paradigmatic examples of how difference allows for authentic engagement with the other. Second, in its refusal to give primary ethical weight to autonomy, derivatization does not construct the other in opposition to the self and thus does not view relations themselves with ethical suspicion. Third, derivatization allows us to understand how so-called sex objects are not, in fact, persons treated as objects but instead are subjects whose range of action and expression has been unethically restricted by the demands of heteronormative male desires. Taken together, these underpinnings of the notion of derivatization allow for ethical critiques that do not undermine an understanding of human beings as fundamentally embodied and essentially intersubjective.

Derivatization allows us to describe pornography as the representation of women not as "meat" or "merely bodies" but as women-for-men, stunted subjects whose rightful specificity is disallowed. It helps us to understand that some forms of artificial reproductive technology may pose ethical harms to women—not because they objectify those women but because they risk reifying the patriarchal norm of defining a woman in terms of her reproductive capacities (which are often framed as her ability to "give" a man a baby). But can derivatization sketch a positive account of sexuality, of how sexual and other bodily interactions can serve to enhance human experiences and of how bodily interactions can result in greater human flourishing (something that Kant couldn't do)?

Sexual interactions that do not derivatize require viewing the body of the other with a wonder marked by humility, without the use of a preexisting standard or set of demands. They would be imbued, then, with a sense of the unknown and the unpredictable. A nonderivatizing approach to sexuality and the other is not a theoretical hairshirt but quite the opposite: it honors and seeks sexual excitement and experience, based in an understanding of the sexual body as a material entity that is experienced, intersubjective, and always marked by difference. As Maurice Merleau-Ponty recognized,[25] the singular act of touch sets off a dizzying interplay of difference and intersection: to feel is distinct from being felt, and yet bodies can feel being felt, and bodies can often feel how the other body feels about being felt.

That experience of simultaneously feeling and being felt is a crucial element of identity and a flourishing sense of self. Thus, bodily encounters can make individuals feel more human, more valued, more alive, precisely as bodies-with-others—but only if these bodies are constructed and recognized as both sensing and differentiated. When feminine bodies are structured as sexual only to the degree to which they arouse other (heterosexual, male) bodies, their own ability to feel and to have sensation is deemed irrelevant. It is no wonder, then, that (as Deborah Tolman's research reminds us)[26] the girls and women who adopt hypersexualized identities are often sexually numb, absent of feeling, lacking a language of sensation that develops with experience and reflection. Similarly, those women deemed by society as improper objects of sexual attention (think mothers, or disabled women, or religious women) are denied their full, embodied intersubjectivity and are therefore harmed by *not* being seen as sex objects.

Adopting a stance of Irigarian wonder toward the body of the other does not require that every body be viewed as sexually appealing to every individual but requires a recognition of both limitation and openness. The recognition of limitation acknowledges that sexual subjects can desire this or that sort of person (and not others), or this or that sort of sexual experiences (and not others). The recognition of openness acknowledges that sexual desires and preferences are constantly in flux. That which is unappealing at one point in time can become appealing; that which is alluring can lose its allure. Entering into an ethical sexual relationship with another sexual subject entails simultaneously sharing one's desires and being willing to have those desires transformed by the relationship.

Wonder, embodiment, vulnerability, and intersubjectivity are all deeply intertwined. The sexual subject cannot fully know or contain the other and yet is radically open to transformation by means of interacting with the other. Sexual desire is both precursor and product of sexual interaction: sexual subjects come to such interactions already in process, always and inevitably in a state of becoming, marked by their sexual specificity but inseparable from their connections to others.

Vulnerability is the risking of one's known identity, the disorienting realization that what one is may be different than what one might become. To engage with the other, sexually or otherwise, in an authentic mode is to encounter oneself and the other as embodied processes, neither self-contained nor enduring, not reducible to each other and thus not ultimately knowable. A sexual ethics based in Irigarian wonder demands that all sexual subjects place their identity on the line—but it also requires that no identity be obviated by another. The danger of subjective obliteration is replaced by the positive possibility of subjective transformation, of having one's identity, preferences, desires, and practices be indelibly altered by an encounter with the other. To approach the other with wonder, with a sense of the unknowability of the other, is to simultaneously experience oneself as capable of profound alteration. Ethical sexual interactions, then, require all parties to have some subjective skin in the game.

NOTES

1. Laura Mulvey, *Visual and Other Pleasures* (Bloomington, Ind.: Indiana University Press, 1989).

2. Simone de Beauvoir, *The Second Sex*, translated by H.M. Parshley (New York: Vintage Books, 1974).

3. Catharine MacKinnon, *Feminism Unmodified: Discourses on Life and Law* (Cambridge, Mass.: Harvard University Press, 1987).

4. Linda LeMoncheck, *Dehumanizing Woman: Treating Persons as Sex Objects* (Totowa, N.J.: Rowman & Allanheld, 1985), 11. The question of nonhuman animals receives a similarly parenthetical treatment in the work of MacKinnon and Nussbaum. For discussions of the association of the feminine with the material, see Carol Adams, *The Sexual Politics of Meat: A Feminist-Vegetarian Critical Theory* (New York: Continuum, 1990); and Val Plumwood, *Feminism and the Mastery of Nature* (London and New York: Routledge, 1993). For an analysis of the relationship between that association and objectification, see my *Overcoming Objectification: A Carnal Ethics* (New York and London: Routledge, 2011), 65–66.

5. LeMoncheck, *Dehumanizing Woman,* 16–17.

6. LeMoncheck, *Dehumanizing Women*, 29.

7. LeMoncheck, *Dehumanizing Women*, 35.

8. LeMoncheck, *Dehumanizing Women*, 48.

9. Martha Nussbaum, "Objectification," *Philosophy and Public Affairs* 24:4 (1995): 249–91.

10. Nussbaum, "Objectification," 256–57, italics in the original.

11. Nussbaum, "Objectification," 257.

12. Nussbaum, "Objectification," 260.

13. "Sexual Use," in this volume.

14. Nussbaum, "Objectification," 276.

15. Nussbaum, "Objectification," 276.

16. See also Rae Langton's *Sexual Solipsism* (Oxford, U.K., and New York: Oxford University Press, 2009), which largely accepts Nussbaum's framing of the problem and resonates with MacKinnon's work as well. Interestingly, Langton adds to Nussbaum's list of ways that persons can problematically be treated as things the "idea of reducing someone to their body" (228). In "Objectification and Internet Misogyny," in *The Offensive Internet: Privacy, Speech, and Representation*, Saul Levmore and Martha C. Nussbaum, eds. (Cambridge, Mass.: Harvard University Press, 2010), Nussbaum herself seems to consider this a friendly amendment, yet I would argue that it undermines a central strength of Nussbaum's analysis, namely that it does not directly associate identification with the body as ethically problematic. Nussbaum's failure to recognize the relevance of her emphasis on the possibility of a nonobjectionable form of objectification, as opposed to Langton's failure to entertain that possibility, may indicate that their common allegiance to a Kantian model of the person trumps what would otherwise be significant differences in their approaches.

17. For a more extensive description of this model, see my *Rethinking Rape* (Ithaca, N.Y.: Cornell University Press, 2001).

18. Diana Meyers, "Feminist Perspectives on the Self," Stanford Encyclopedia of Philosophy, http://plato.stanford.edu/archives/spr2010/entries/feminism-self/ (accessed April 14, 2012).

19. See Susan Brison's *Aftermath: Violence and the Remaking of a Self* (Princeton, N.J.: Princeton University Press, 2002), and my *Rethinking Rape* for analyses of the particularly destructive harms of sexual violence.

20. See Evangelia Papadaki's "Sexual Objectification: From Kant to Contemporary Feminism," *Contemporary Political Theory* 6:3 (2007): 330–48.

21. For a discussion of some of the main critiques leveled against Irigaray, see my *Overcoming Objectification*, 39–42.

22. Luce Irigaray, *I Love to You: Sketch of a Possible Felicity in History*, translated by Alison Martin (New York: Routledge, 1996), 103.

23. Irigaray, 134.

24. Eve Ensler, *The Vagina Monologues* (New York: Villard), 57.

25. Maurice Merleau-Ponty, *The Visible and the Invisible*, translated by Alphonso Lingus (Evanston, Ill.: Northwestern University Press, 1968).

26. Deborah L. Tolman, *Dilemmas of Desire: Teenage Girls Talk about Sexuality* (Cambridge, Mass.: Harvard University Press, 2002).

STUDY QUESTIONS

1. What is Cahill's understanding of the concept of "objectification"? Is that understanding an accurate characterization of the way other scholars have interpreted the concept? What might a philosophical advocate of objectification (e.g., LeMoncheck, Nussbaum) say in response to Cahill's representations and critique of objectification and its usefulness?

2. Explain in detail the differences between objectification and derivatization (as acts or practices). In addition, while considering "objectification" and "derivatization" as concepts to be used in ethical analysis, what are the crucial differences between them?

3. How does Cahill reply to the objection that all (or almost all) types of work require some derivatization? Is (part of) her reply that the doctor and the teacher are not being derivatized? Or is it that they are being derivatized but that the derivatization, in their cases, is ethically permissible? (The same questions have been asked about objectification. See Alan Soble's discussion of Martha Nussbaum's account of objectification in "Sexual Use.") Indeed, according to Cahill, are all instances of derivatization morally wrong? Is she right or wrong? Provide your reasons.

4. Consider the "Bob" example. Cahill believes that the way Bob approaches the narrator's vagina is not only morally permissible but also "praiseworthy because he does so with an attitude of wonder. Were he to approach her vagina to determine whether it matches up to his particular preference, or some preexisting social ideal, he would be derivatizing her." This passage seems to imply that for any sexual encounter to be acceptable, the parties must approach

each other with "wonder," and if X sexually approaches Y because X desires Y ("matches" X's "particular preference"), the encounter is morally problematic. Evaluate this view.

5. In discussing the opera and baseball examples, Cahill writes, "to *require* that one's partner actually become (or pretend to become) an opera or baseball lover does constitute derivatization and is ethically unjustifiable." If so, what happens to derivatization in the exotic dancer and waiter examples, if they freely choose their professions? Or are they, somehow, required to choose them? What does "required" mean on Cahill's view?

6. Give examples of derivatization in sexual encounters in which there is actual physical contact between the parties (sexual intercourse, oral sex, and so forth).

7. If X masturbates while fantasizing about Y, is X derivatizing Y? If so, is X's masturbating ethically wrong? (See the analogous question about objectification, in the text at note number 14, in Alan Soble's "Jacking Off, Yet Again.")

TWENTY

Consent and Sexual Relations

Alan Wertheimer

It is often thought that moral questions about behavior, including sexual activity, can be appreciably if not finally answered by determining whether the participants consented. Although in this essay **Alan Wertheimer** *does not reject the moral power of consent or deny that consent can be "morally transformative," he does raise fascinating questions about consent: its nature, when it is present and absent, and its ultimate moral force. Wertheimer argues that it is too simple to deal with all sexual moral questions by referring to consent alone, that other moral factors and deliberations play an essential role. He presents a number of conundrums about the use of fraud or deception in sexual interactions as well as about the use of coercion and other sorts of pressures. In an intriguing section of his essay, Wertheimer suggests that whether and when "yes" means "yes" is a more important question than whether and when "no" means "no." He also discusses the novel idea that persons might, in some circumstances, have a moral duty to give consent to sexual relations. The very wording of this inquiry shows that other factors, beyond consent, must be brought to bear on questions in sexual ethics.*

Alan Wertheimer is professor emeritus of the University of Vermont and senior research scholar in the Department of Bioethics at the National Institutes of Health. He is the author of *Coercion* (Princeton University Press, 1987), *Exploitation* (Princeton University Press, 1996), and *Consent to Sexual Relations* (Cambridge University Press, 2003). This essay is reprinted with the permission of Alan Wertheimer and Cambridge University Press, from *Legal Theory* 2:2 (1996): 89–112. © 1996, Cambridge University Press.

I. INTRODUCTION

This essay has two broad purposes. First, as a political philosopher who has been interested in the concepts of coercion and exploitation, I want to consider just what the analysis of the concept of consent can bring to the question, what sexually motivated behavior should be prohibited through the criminal law?[1] Put simply, I shall argue that conceptual analysis will be of little help. Second, and with somewhat fewer professional credentials, I shall offer some thoughts about the substantive question itself. Among other things, I will argue that it is a mistake to think that sexual crimes are about violence rather than sex and that we need to understand just why the violation of sexual autonomy is a serious wrong. I shall also argue that the principle that "no means no" does not tell us when "yes means yes," and that it is the latter question that poses the most interesting theoretical difficulties about coercion, misrepresentation, and competence. In addition, I shall make some brief remarks concerning two questions about consent and sexual relations that lie beyond the criminal law: What "consent compromising behaviors" should be regarded as indecent, although not criminal? When *should* someone consent to sexual relations within an enduring relationship? (A word about notation. In what follows, A will represent a person who attacks B or makes a proposal to B, and it is B's consent that is at issue. A will always be male and B will always be female.)

II. CONSENT AND CONCEPTUAL ANALYSIS

A standard picture about this topic goes something like this. We start with the principle that the criminal law should prohibit behavior that seeks to obtain sexual relations without valid consent. To determine which specific behaviors should be prohibited by the criminal law, we must engage in a detailed philosophical analysis of the concept of consent (and related concepts). If such an analysis can yield the criteria of valid consent, we are then in a better position to identify the behaviors that should be prohibited.

I believe that this picture is mistaken. My central point in this section is that the questions (and their facsimiles)—What is consent? What is valid or meaningful consent?—are less important than they first seem. The concept of consent provides a useful template to organize many of the moral issues in which we are interested, but it cannot do much more than that. The question as to what behavior should be prohibited through the criminal law will be settled by moral argument informed by empirical investigation. Any attempt to resolve that question through an inquiry into the "essence" of consent or the conditions under which we can use the word "consent" will prove to be of only limited help.

A. Consent as Morally Transformative

Let us begin by noting that we are not interested in consent as a freestanding concept. Rather, we are interested in consent because consent *is morally transformative*; that is, it changes the moral relationship between A and B and between them and others.[2] B's consent may *legitimate* an action by A that would not be legitimate without B's consent, as when B's consent to surgery transforms A's act from a battery to a permissible medical procedure. B's consent to a transaction with A provides a reason for others not to interfere with that transaction, as when B's consent to let A put a tattoo on her arm gives C a reason to let them be. And B's consent may give rise to an *obligation*. If B consents to do X for A, B acquires an obligation to do X for A.

To say that B's consent is morally transformative is not to say that B's consent is either necessary or sufficient to change an "all things considered" moral judgment about A's or B's action. It may be legitimate for A to perform surgery on a delusional B without B's consent. It may be wrong for A to perform surgery on B with B's consent if the procedure is not medically indicated.[3] Similarly, we may think that exchanging money for sexual relations is wrong even if the prostitute consents to the exchange. But this does not show that the prostitute's consent is not morally transformative. After all, the prostitute's consent to sexual relations with A eliminates one very important reason for regarding A's behavior as wrong, namely, that A had sexual relations with B without her consent. B's consent is morally transformative because it provides a reason, although not a conclusive reason, for thinking that A's behavior is legitimate.

B. The Logic of Consent Arguments

To put the point of the previous section schematically, we are interested in the following sort of argument.

Major Premise: If B consents to A's doing X to B, then it is legitimate for A to do X to B.

Minor Premise: B has (has not) consented to A's doing X to B.

Conclusion: It is (is not) legitimate for A to do X to B.

Given the major premise, it seems that we must determine when the *minor premise* is true if we are going to know when the conclusion is warranted. For that reason, we may be tempted to think that an analysis of the concept of consent will identify the *criteria* or necessary and sufficient conditions of valid consent, and that empirical investigation can then (in principle) determine if those criteria are met. If the criteria are met, then the minor premise is true and the conclusion follows. If not, then the minor premise is false and the conclusion does not follow.

If things were only so simple. It is a mistake to think that we will be able to make much progress toward resolving the substantive moral and legal issues in which we are interested by philosophical resources internal to the concept of consent. In the final analysis, we are always going to have to ask: Given the facts that relate to issues of consent, how should we think about the moral and legal status of a transaction or relationship? In that sense, I am squarely in the camp that maintains that the concept of consent is fundamentally normative.

In suggesting that consent is essentially normative, I do not deny that it is possible to produce a morally neutral account of consent that would allow us to say when B consents by reference to specific empirical criteria. I do maintain that if we were to operate with a morally neutral account of consent, we would then have to go on to ask whether B's consent legitimates A's action, and that we will be unable to answer that question without introducing substantive moral arguments. A morally neutral account of consent would do little work in our moral argument. If we want consent to do more work in our moral argument, we must build some of our substantive moral principles into the account of consent that we deploy. We could say that B "really" consents only when B's consent token is morally transformative. In the final analysis, it does not matter much whether we adopt a thin, morally neutral, account of consent or a thick, morally laden, account of consent. Either way, the point remains that we will not be able to go from a morally neutral or empirical account of consent to moral or legal conclusions without introducing substantive moral arguments.

C. The Fallacy of Equivocation

Precisely because we can pack a lot or a little into our account of consent, it is all too easy for a "consent argument" to commit the fallacy of equivocation, in which the meaning of consent assumed by the major premise is not identical to the meaning of consent in the minor premise, and, thus, the conclusion does not follow even though both the major premise and minor premise may be true (given different meanings of consent). Consider a classic problem of political philosophy: Do citizens have a general (prima facie) obligation to obey the law? A standard argument goes like this:

Major Premise: One is obligated to obey the laws if one consents to do so.
Minor Premise: (Version 1): One who remains in his society rather than leaves thereby gives his consent to that society (Plato).[4]
Minor Premise: (Version 2): One who benefits from living in a society gives his consent to that society (Locke).[5]
Conclusion: One who does not leave his society or benefits from living in a society has an obligation to obey its laws.

Is either version of the minor premise true? The problem is this: There may be a linguistically plausible sense in which one who accepts the benefits of one's government has consented to that government or in which one who remains in one's society has consented to remain in that society. But, even if that were so, that will not resolve the problem of political obligation. We will have to determine if the type or strength of consent that figures in the major premise has been met in the minor premise. And it may not. Thus, we could agree with Plato that there is a sense in which one who does not leave his society gives his consent, while also agreeing with Hume that it is not the sort of *free* consent that would justify the ascription of a strong obligation to obey the law.[6] We can make a similar point about Locke's view.

The danger of equivocation arises with respect to two other concepts that will figure in our analysis: coercion and harm. Let us assume that one who is coerced into consenting does not give valid or morally transformative consent. When is consent coerced? Consider Harry Frankfurt's example:

> The courts may refuse to admit in evidence, on the grounds that it was coerced, a confession which the police have obtained from a prisoner by threatening to beat him. But the prisoner's accomplices, who are compromised by his confession, are less likely to agree that he was genuinely coerced into confession.[7]

Was the prisoner's confession coerced? There is no reason to think that there must be a single acceptable answer to this question. The answer to this question will depend on the sort of moral transformation that consent is meant to trigger. The sort of pressure to which the prisoner was subject may be sufficient to deprive his confession of legal validity. At the same time, and if there is anything like honor among thieves, the very same pressures may not be sufficient to excuse his betrayal of his accomplices. It will do no good to ask what appears to be a conceptual and empirical question: Was his confession coerced or not? Rather, we need to answer two moral questions: What sorts of pressures on prisoners to confess are sufficient to bar the introduction of the confession as evidence? What sorts of pressures on prisoners are sufficient to excuse the ascription of blame by those to whom the prisoner has obligations of silence?

A similar point can be made about the concept of harm. Suppose we start from the Millian principle that the state can justifiably prohibit only conduct that causes harm to others. The following questions arise: Does the psychic distress caused by offensive speech count as harmful? Does trespass that causes no physical damage to one's property constitute a harm? Does a Peeping Tom harm his target? Does he harm his target if she is unaware of his voyeurism? Clearly there is a sense in which psychic distress caused by offensive speech is harmful. As a matter of empirical psychology, it is simply untrue that "sticks and stones will break your bones, but names will never hurt you." And there is clearly a sense in which one has not been harmed by trespass that causes no physical damage, or by the Peeping Tom, particularly if the target is unaware of his voyeurism. But these observations will not tell us which activities can be legitimately prohibited by the state under the Millian principle.[8]

Once again, we have two choices. We could opt for a morally neutral or neurological account of harm, but then we will have to go on to ask whether harm so defined should or should not be prohibited, and whether some acts excluded by that definition can be legitimately prohibited. On the other hand, we could opt for a moralized account of harm, say, one in which one is harmed if one's rights are violated. On this view, we can maintain that the psychic distress caused by offensive speech does not count as a harm because it does not violate one's rights, whereas trespassing and voyeurism do count as harm because they violate one's rights to property and privacy. From this perspective, sexual offenses may cause a particularly serious harm because they violate an important right of the subject, not (solely) because they are physically or psychologically more damaging than nonsexual violence (although that may also be true).

III. A (BRIEF) THEORY OF CONSENT

With these anti-essentialist ruminations behind us, I shall sketch an account of consent in two stages. First, I shall consider the ontology of consent, the phenomena to which the template of consent calls our attention. Second, I shall consider what I shall call the "principles of consent," the conditions under which these phenomena are morally transformative.

A. The Ontology of Consent

First, morally transformative consent always involves a verbal or nonverbal action, some token of consent. Consent is performative rather than attitudinal. It might be objected that there is a plausible understanding of the word consent, in which mental agreement is sufficient to establish consent. I do not want to quibble over words. If one wants to insist that mental agreement is sufficient to establish consent, then I shall say that B's mental agreement to allow A to do X does not *authorize* or *legitimate* A's doing X in the absence of B's communication. If B has decided to accept A's business proposal and was about to communicate that decision to A when their call was disconnected, it would not be legitimate for A to proceed as if B had agreed. Similarly, that B actually desires sexual relations with A does not authorize A to have sexual relations with A if B has said "no."

Second, and to cover well-trod ground, B's consent token can be explicit or tacit, verbal or nonverbal. B gives verbal explicit agreement to A's proposal when B says "yes" or some equivalent. B may give nonverbal but explicit consent to A's proposal that they have sexual relations if B smiles and leads A into her bedroom. One gives tacit consent when silence or inaction is understood to constitute agreement. Thus if my department chair says, "Unless I hear from you, I'll assume that you can advise students at orientation," my silence is an indication that I am available. In general, it is of no fundamental importance whether consent is explicit or tacit, if it is understood that silence or inaction indicates consent, if there is a genuine opportunity for B to dissent, and if B's dissent will have moral force.

And that brings me to the third consideration. Consent will be valid or morally transformative only when certain conditions are met or, perhaps more helpfully, only in the absence of certain background defects. Those conditions will include, among other things, that B is competent to give consent, the absence of coercion, and also perhaps the absence of misrepresentation and concealment of important information. We could say that one who signs a contract at the point of a gun has not consented at all, or that her consent isn't sufficiently free to give rise to an obligation. Either way, her consent token will not be morally transformative.

B. The Principles of Consent

To put the argument in somewhat different terms, we do not start from the assumption that B's consent is morally transformative, in which case the question for philosophical analysis becomes whether B has or has not consented to A's action. Rather, the determination as to when consent is morally transformative is an *output* of moral theorizing rather than an *input*. Let us call the principles that define when a consent token is morally transformative the *principles of consent*.

The principles of consent may vary from context to context. To see this, consider four cases: (1) A physician tells his patient that she has breast cancer and that she should immediately undergo a mastectomy. He does not explain the risks of the procedure or other options. Because the patient trusts her physician, she signs a consent form. (2) A patient's leg is gangrenous and she must choose between amputation and death. She understands the alternatives, and, because she does not want to die, she signs the consent form. (3) A dance studio gets an elderly woman to contract to pay $20,000 for dance lessons by "a constant and continuous barrage of flattery, false praise, excessive compliments, and panegyric encomiums."[9] (4) A psychotherapist proposes that he and the patient have sexual relations. Because the patient has become sexually attracted to the psychotherapist, she enthusiastically agrees.

We might think that the woman's consent in (1) is not valid because the principles of consent for medical procedures require that the physician explain the risks and alternatives. In this case, valid or morally transformative consent must be *informed* consent. Yet, the principles of consent may also entail that the consent given in (2) is valid even though the patient reasonably believed that she had no choice but to agree, say, because the very real constraints on her decision were not the result of *illegitimate* pressures on her decision-making process. By contrast, the principles of consent might hold that the consent given in (3) is not valid or morally transformative because the dance studio acted illegitimately in procuring the woman's consent, even though she had more "choice" than in (2). And the principles of consent might hold that the consent given in (4) does not render it legitimate for the psychotherapist to have sexual relations with his patient, because he has a fiduciary obligation to refrain from sexual relations with his patient. Period. [10]

These are just intuitions. How do we determine the correct principles of consent for one context or another? At one level, the answer to these questions will ultimately turn on what is the best account of morality in general or the sorts of moral considerations relevant to this sort of problem. Somehow, I think we are unlikely to resolve that here. Suppose that the best account of the principles of consent reflect a commitment to impartiality, and that this commitment will be cashed out along consequentialist or contractarian lines. If we adopt a consequentialist outlook, we will want to examine the costs and benefits of different principles of consent and will adopt those principles that generate the best consequences—all things considered. From a contractarian perspective, we can think of the principles of consent as the outcome of a choice made under conditions of impartiality, perhaps as modeled by a Rawlsian veil of ignorance, although here, too, we will want to consider the costs and benefits of different principles (which is not to say that a contractarian will consider them in the way in which a consequentialist would). But the crucial and present point is that from either perspective, the point of moral theorizing is not to determine when one consents, per se. The task is to determine the principles for morally transformative consent.

IV. CRIMINAL OFFENSES

In this section, I want to bring the previous analysis to bear on the central question of this symposium: What sexually motivated behaviors should be regarded as criminal offenses? In considering this question, I shall bracket several related issues. First, I have nothing to say about the history of the law of rape. Second, I shall have little to say about problems of proof that arise because sexual offenses involve behavior that is frequently consensual, and because we operate in a legal context in which we are especially concerned to avoid the conviction of the innocent. Third, I shall not be concerned with questions as to the best interpretations of existing statutes. The question here is not, for example, whether Rusk was guilty under an existing statute if he caused his victim to fear being stranded in an unknown part of the city unless she engaged in sexual acts with him, but whether legislation should be designed so as to regard such behavior as a criminal offense[11] Finally, I shall have little to say about questions of culpability, the sorts of issues raised in the (in)famous case of *Regina v. Morgan*, in which several men claimed to believe that the wife of a friend consented to sexual relations with them even though she strongly objected at the time.[12] I am concerned with the question as to what conduct should be criminal, and not the conditions under which one might be justifiably excused from liability for such conduct.

A. Criminal Elements

In considering the question so posed, it will be useful to disaggregate some of the ways in which sexually motivated behavior might be seriously wrong.

First, a sexual offense involves a nonconsensual touching or bodily contact, that is, the elements of a standard battery. Nonconsensual touchings need not be violent or painful or involve the penetration of a bodily orifice.

Second, a sexual offense may involve a violent assault or battery, that is, physical contact that involves overpowering restraint of movement or physical pain or harm to the victim's body that lasts beyond the duration of the incident.

Third, a sexual offense may involve *threats* of violence. The perpetrator puts the victim in fear of harm to her life or body, and then uses that fear to obtain sexual relations. As the victim in *Rusk* put it, "If I do what you want, will you let me go?"

Fourth, sexual offenses may often involve harm or the fear of harms that *flow from* penetration as distinguished from the penetration itself, for example, unwanted pregnancy and sexually transmitted diseases.

Fifth, and of greatest relevance to this essay, is the moral and psychological harm associated with the fact that a sexual offense involves unwanted and nonconsensual penetration, that it "violates the interest in exclusive control of one's body for sexual purposes."[13]

B. Seriousness

The seriousness of a sexual offense may vary with the way in which these elements are combined. We can distinguish at least five sorts of sexual offense. Although reasonable people may disagree about the precise ranking, one view of their relative seriousness, in descending order of seriousness, looks like this: (1) sexually motivated assault with penetration and where violence is actually used to inflict harm or overcome resistance; (2) sexually motivated assault with penetration where violence is threatened but not used; (3) sexually motivated assault (where violence is used or threatened) where penetration does not occur ("attempted rape"); (4) penetration of the victim in the face of the victim's refusal to have sexual relations or her inability to consent to sexual relations, but without the use or threat of violence; (5) sexual battery or sexual harassment, where the victim is touched without her consent, but where penetration does not occur.

Before going further, let me make several points about this list. First, this list makes no distinction between cases in which the penetrator and victim are strangers and those in which they are acquaintances (or married). Second, this ordering does not draw a fundamental distinction between the *use* and *threat* of violence, an important departure from the traditional law of rape, in which actual violence and resistance to that violence were sometimes required. It is clearly a mistake to minimize the importance of threats. Consider a case in which A says something like this (perhaps using cruder language):

> You and I are going to play a game. We are going to have sex and I want you to act like you want it and are enjoying it. If you play the game, you won't be hurt. Indeed, I will do everything I know how to do to make the sex as pleasurable as possible. Otherwise, I will kill you with this gun.

Because B regards A's threat as credible, B goes along with A's game. This example indicates that the mere utterance of a phrase that would constitute valid consent if uttered in the absence of such threats ("Please do it!") does not constitute any kind of valid consent in the presence of such threats.[14]

For the purposes of this essay, the most interesting questions concern cases (3) and (4). A sexual offense may involve assault without what Dripps calls the "expropriation" of the victim's body (as in (3)) and may involve expropriation without the use or threat of violence (as in (4)). It might be argued that (4) is a more serious offense than (3) because nonconsensual sexual penetration is a greater harm than the use or threat of violence that does not result in penetration. If this is a plausible view, even if not the most widely held or correct view, we need to ask why nonconsensual penetration is such a serious wrong. Second, if it should be criminal to have sexual relations with someone who has refused sexual relations, if "no means no," we still need to ask when "yes means yes." We have already described a case in which a consent token ("Please do it!") does *not* mean yes. Other cases are more difficult.

A currently fashionable view maintains that rape is about violence not sex. That view might be resisted in two ways. It might be argued that rape is about sex because sex itself is about violence (or domination).[15] I have little to say about that view, except to note that even if there is a violent dimension to "ordinary" sex, there is still a distinction between the violence intrinsic to ordinary sex and the violence peculiar to what we have traditionally regarded as sexual crimes.

But I want to suggest that, for both empirical and moral reasons, it is crucial to see that sexual offense is at least partly about sex. First, there is considerable evidence that nonconsensual sexual relations are "a substitute for consensual sexual intercourse rather than a manifestation of male hostility toward women or a method of establishing or maintaining male domination."[16] Second, we cannot explain why the use or threat of violence to accomplish sexual penetration is more traumatic and a graver wrong than the use or threat of violence per se, except on the assumption that invasion of one's sexual being is a special sort of violation. Third, if women experience *non*violent but nonconsensual sex as a serious violation, this, too, can be explained only in the view that violation of a woman's sexual being is special. Consider, for example, the case in which A has sexual relations with an unconscious B. Some of the elements associated with a violent sexual assault would be lacking. There would be no fear, no overpowering of the will or experience of being coerced, and no experience of pain. Yet, even if B never discovers that A had sexual relations with her while she was unconscious, we might well think that B has been harmed or violated by A.[17]

The view that nonconsensual but nonviolent sex is a serious violation has been previously defended by several [authors]. Stephen Schulhofer argues that it should be a criminal offense to violate a person's sexual autonomy.[18] On Donald Dripps's "commodity" theory of sexual crime, the "expropriation" of another person's body for purposes of sexual gratification violates that person's interest in exclusive control over her body for sexual purposes.[19] Joan McGregor connects nonconsensual sexual relations to the invasion of privacy and the control of information about ourselves. She argues that nonconsensual sexual relations can be understood as violating an individual's right to control the "borders" of her relations with others.[20]

For present purposes, there is not much difference among these views. Although Dripps uses the avowedly "unromantic" language of commodity and expropriation, whereas Schulhofer and McGregor use the more philosophically respectable language of autonomy and control, these views are virtually extensionally equivalent.[21] They all maintain that it should be a criminal offense for A to engage in sexual penetration of B if B objects, whether or not A uses or threatens physical harm. It is true that Dripps would criminalize only the disregard of another's refusal to engage in sexual acts (except in cases in which the victim is unable to refuse) whereas Schulhofer and McGregor require a verbal or nonverbal yes. But this is of little practical import. If the law clearly states that B need only say "no" to render A liable to a criminal offense, then B's passivity will not be misunderstood.

Let us assume that this general view is correct. But why is it correct? Jeffrie Murphy suggests that it is not self-evident why the nonconsensual "penetration of a bodily orifice" is such a grave offense. He maintains that there is nothing that makes sexual assault "objectively" more serious than nonsexual assault, that the importance attached to penetration "is essentially cultural," and that if we did not "surround sexuality with complex symbolic and moral baggage," then nonconsensual sex would not be viewed as a particularly grave wrong.[22]

Murphy's science is probably wrong. A woman's abhorrence of non-consensual sex may be at least partially hard-wired. Evolutionary psychologists have argued that because reproductive opportunities for women are relatively scarce, it is genetically costly for a woman to have sex with a man whose attributes she could not choose and who shows "no evident inclination to stick around and help provide for the off-spring."[23] Thus, evolution would favor those women who were most disposed to abhor such sexual encounters. This is not to deny that there is great individual and cultural variability in the way in which people experience nonconsensual sexual relations. It is only to say that there is no reason to assume that culture is writing on a blank slate.

Yet, for our purposes, it does not really matter whether the best explanation for a woman's aversion to nonconsensual penetration is cultural or biological. The important question for moral and legal theory is whether the seriousness of a violation should be understood as *experience-dependent* or (at least partially) *experience-independent*. Although Murphy contrasts a "cultural" explanation of the wrongness of sexual crime with an "objective" explanation, what would an "objective" explanation look like? Murphy thinks that we need to explain why the penetration of an orifice is objectively more harmful than a punch in the nose. Fair enough. But then we also need to explain why physical injury is "objectively" worse than harm to our property or reputations or feelings or character. If the objective seriousness of harm is experience-*dependent*, there is nothing inherently special about physical injury, which Murphy takes to be the paradigm case of objective harm. After all, we could experience insults to our reputations as worse than physical injury and harm to our souls or character as a fate worse than death. On the other hand, if an objective account of harm is experience-*independent*, we would also need to explain why violations of sexuality are more serious than a punch in the nose. But here, once again, sexual harm is on a par with physical harm, for we would need to explain why harm to one's body is objectively more harmful than harm to one's property or reputation or soul.

I cannot produce an adequate account of the objective seriousness of sexual offense in this essay (and not just for lack of space), although the truth about that matter will affect the criminal penalties we are prepared to apply.[24] Although I am inclined to think that the character of this harm is at least partially experience-independent (that is, it would be a serious wrong even if it is not experienced that way), it should be noted that, even if it is experience-dependent, the criminal law is not designed to respond to the harm to the individual victim. Suppose, for example, that A rapes B, who, unbeknownst to A, actually embodies the alleged male fantasy: B wants to be raped. If the wrongness of a crime depends on the harm to the particular victim, then we might regard the rape of B as a lesser wrong. But, while the harm to a specific victim may affect the compensation owed to the victim in a civil action, the criminal law concerns harms to society and can be triggered even when there is no harm to a specific victim, as in an attempted crime in which no one is hurt. Similarly, even if the rape of a prostitute is a less serious offense because it does not involve the forcible taking of something that she regards as a "sacred and mysterious aspect of her self-identity," but merely the theft of a commodity that she normally trades for monetary gain, it does not follow that the criminal law should treat this rape as a less serious wrong.[25]

C. Defective Consent: When Does Yes Mean Yes?

Let us assume that the criminal law regards the disregard of a "no" (or the absence of a verbal or nonverbal "yes") as a basis for criminal liability. As we have seen, that would not resolve all of the problems. We have already seen that when B says "yes" in response to a threat of violence, her consent has no morally transformative power. The question arises, however, as to what other consent-eliciting behavior should be criminal. In this section, I want to focus on three ways in which B's consent token might be considered defective: (1) coercion; (2) misrepresentation or concealment; and (3) incompetence.

1. Coercion

Let us say that A coerces B to consent to engage in a sexual act when (a) A threatens to make B worse off if she does not perform that act and (b) it is reasonable to expect B to succumb to the threat rather than suffer the consequences.

It can be ambiguous as to whether condition (a) is met for two reasons. First, it can be ambiguous as to whether A threatens B at all. We do not say that a panhandler threatens B if he says, "Do you have any money to spare?" But does a large and tough-looking A threaten B when he says "I would appreciate it if you would give me your wallet," but issues no threat as to what he will do if B refuses? We are inclined to think that some nonverbal behaviors are reasonably understood as proposing to make B worse off if B refuses, and that it is also reasonable to expect A to understand this.

Let us assume that there is no misunderstanding as to the likely consequences of refusal. It can be ambiguous as to whether condition (a) is met because we must ask, "Worse off than what?" I have argued elsewhere that the crucial element in coercive proposals is that A proposes to make B worse off than she has a *right* to be vis-à-vis A or that A proposes to violate B's right, and not (as it might seem) that A proposes to make B worse off than her status quo.[26] Whereas the gunman's proposal—"Sign this contract or I will shoot you"—proposes to make B worse off than both her status quo baseline and her right-defined baseline, those baselines can diverge. If a drowning B has a right to be rescued by A, then A's proposal to rescue B only if she pays him $10,000 is a coercive proposal on this view because A proposes to make B worse off than her right-defined baseline, even though he proposes to make her better off than her status quo-defined baseline. On the other hand, A's proposal is not coercive on this view if A proposes to make B worse off than her status quo-defined baseline, but not worse off than her right-defined baseline ("Plead guilty to a lesser offense or I will prosecute you on the charge of which we both know you are guilty").

Consider six cases:

1. A says to B, "Have sex with me or I won't return your car keys and you will be left stranded in a dangerous area."
2. A says, "Have sexual relations with me or I will dissolve our dating relationship."
3. A, a professor, says, "Have sexual relations with me or I will give you a grade two grades lower than you deserve."
4. A, a professor, says, "Have sexual relations with me and I will give you a grade two grades higher than you deserve."
5. A, who owes B money, says, "Have sexual relations with me and I will repay the money that I owe you. Otherwise, ciao."
6. A, a jailer, says, "Have sexual relations with me and I will arrange your escape; otherwise you and I know that you will be executed by the state."[27]

On my view, A makes a coercive proposal in cases (1), (3), and (5), but not in cases (2), (4), and (6). In cases (1), (3), and (5), A proposes to make B worse off than she has a right to be if she refuses—to have her car keys returned, to receive the grade she deserves, to have her loan repaid. By contrast, in cases (2), (4), and (6), A does not propose to make B worse off than she has a right to be if she refuses. B has no right that A continue their dating relationship or a right to a higher grade than she deserves or not to be executed by the state (bracketing general objections to capital *punishment*).

To anticipate objections, I do not deny that it is wrong for A to make his proposal in (4) and (6) or (sometimes) in (2). A jailer violates his obligation to society if he helps a prisoner escape and commits an additional wrong if he trades that favor for sexual services. It is wrong for a professor to use his control over grades to obtain sexual favors. He violates his responsibility to his institution and to other students. Moreover, and perhaps unlike (6), A's proposal in (4) may entice B into accepting an arrangement that she will subsequently regret. In general, it is often wrong for A to make a "seductive offer" to B, that is, where A has reason to believe that it is likely that B will mistakenly perceive the (short-term) benefits of accepting the offer as greater than the (long-term) costs.

In any case, I do not say that A's proposals are coercive in (4) and (6) simply because, like (3), they create a choice situation in which B decides that having sexual relations with A is the lesser of two evils. After all, we could imagine that B, not A, initiates the proposals in (4) and (6) or is delighted to receive them, and it would be strange to maintain that B is coerced by a proposal that she initiates or is delighted to receive.

Now, consider (2) once again. B may regard the consequences of refusing A's proposal as devastating, as worse, for example, than receiving a lower grade than she deserves. It is also true that B's situation will be worse than her status quo if she refuses. Still, B cannot reasonably claim that she is the victim of "status coercion" or, more importantly, that her consent is not morally transformative.[28] And this [is] because A does not propose to violate B's rights if she refuses, for B has no right that A continue his relationship with B on her preferred terms.

The general point exemplified by (2) is that people make many decisions that they would not make if more attractive options were available to them. If I were independently wealthy, I might not choose to teach political philosophy for a living. If I were not at risk for losing my teeth, I would not consent to painful dental work. But it does not follow that I have been coerced into teaching or agreeing to have dental work performed. In principle, sex is no different. If B were wealthier or more attractive or more famous, she might not have to agree to have sexual relations with A in order to keep him in the relationship. Things being what they are, however, B might well decide that what she wants to do—all things considered—is to have sexual relations with A. It may be regrettable that people bargain with their sexuality, but there is no reason to regard bargaining *within the framework of one's rights* as compromising consent, at least in any way that should be recognized by the criminal law.

Let us now consider condition (b), which states that A coerces B only when it is reasonable to expect B to succumb to A's (admittedly coercive) threat rather than suffer the consequences or pursue a different course of action. Suppose that A proposes to tickle B's feet if she does not have sexual relations with him. I believe that A has made a coercive proposal to B, because A proposes to make B worse off than both her status quo baseline and her right-defined baseline. Still, if B decides to have sexual relations to avoid being tickled, I doubt that we would want to charge A with a criminal offense (unless, perhaps, A believed that B had an extreme aversion to being tickled). Here, we expect B to endure the consequences of A's coercive proposal rather than succumb to it.

Now, recall case (5). In my view, A has made a coercive proposal because A has proposed to violate B's right to be repaid if B refuses. But we might also say that B should sue A for breach of contract, and that we should not regard A's proposal as so compromising B's consent (because she has other legal options) that it should render A subject to a criminal charge.[29] We might disagree about this case. There are resources internal to the notion of coerced consent that allow us to go the other way. But it is moral argument, and not conceptual analysis, that will determine whether this is the sort of sexually motivated behavior that should be punished through the criminal law.

2. Fraud and Concealment

Suppose that A does not threaten B or propose to violate B's rights if she refuses to have sexual relations with A, but that B agrees to sexual relations with A only because B has certain beliefs about A that result from things that A has or has not said.

Consider:

1. A falsely declares that A loves B.
2. A falsely declares that he intends to marry B.
3. A falsely declares that he intends to dissolve the relationship if B does not consent (unlike (2), A is bluffing).
4. A fails to disclose that he has a sexually transmitted disease.
5. A fails to disclose that he has been having sexual relations with B's sister.

Has B given "valid" consent in these cases? We know that A has misrepresented or concealed important information in all of these cases. That is not at issue. The question is whether we should regard A's conduct as criminal.

There are several possibilities. If we were to extend the principle of *caveat emptor* to sexual relations, then there is arguably no problem in any of these cases. On the other hand, if we were to extend principles of criminal fraud or anything like the well-known medical principle of informed consent to the arena of sexual relations, then we could conclude that many representations that are now part and parcel of courtship should be illegal. I do not have anything close to a firm view about this matter. I think it entirely possible that, from either a contractualist or consequentialist perspective, we would choose a legal regime in which we treat the failure to disclose information about sexually transmitted diseases as criminal, but that we would not want to treat misrepresentation or failure to disclose information about one's feelings or marital intentions or other relationships as criminal offenses.[30] But that is only a guess. For now, I want only to stress that the question as to whether A should be criminally liable in any of these cases will be resolved by moral argument as to what parties who engage in sexual relations owe each other by way of intentional falsehood and disclosure of information, and not by an analysis of the concept of consent.

3. Competence

B can give valid or "morally transformative" consent to sexual relations with A only if B is sufficiently competent to do so. It is uncontroversial that B cannot consent to sexual relations with A if she is unconscious.[31] It is also relatively uncontroversial that B cannot give valid or morally transformative consent if she does not possess the appropriate mental capacities, say, because B is below an appropriate age or severely retarded.

The most interesting *theoretical* questions about competence arise with respect to (otherwise) competent adults who consent to sexual relations because they are under the influence of voluntarily consumed alcohol or some other judgment-distorting substance. Consider two possible positions about this issue. It might be argued that if a competent adult allows herself to become intoxicated, her initial competence flows through to any decisions she makes while less than fully competent. In a second view, A should be liable for a criminal offense if he engages in sexual relations with B when B's first indication of consent is given while intoxicated, even if B is responsible for having put herself in that position.[32]

I do not have a firm view as to what position we should adopt about this matter. But we should not say that A should not be held liable just because B has acted imprudently, or even wrongly, in allowing herself to become intoxicated. Although B's behavior may put her on the moral hook, it does not take A off the moral hook. Although B acts imprudently if she leaves her keys in an unlocked car, A still commits a theft if he takes it. We could adopt a similar view about sexual relations with an intoxicated B.

D. Benefits and Costs

I have argued that the principle that society should make it criminal for individuals to engage in sexual acts without the consent of the other party is highly indeterminate, that we must decide under what conditions consent is morally transformative. Suppose that we were to consider a choice between what I shall call a *permissive legal regime* (LR_P), under which A commits a sexual crime only when he uses violence or the threat of violence against B, and a *rigorous legal regime* (LR_R), say, one in which it is a criminal offense (1) to engage in sexual acts without the express consent of the other party, (2) to obtain that consent by proposing to violate a legal right of the other party, (3) to misrepresent or fail to disclose information about sexually transmitted diseases, (4) to engage in a sexual act with a party whose consent was first given when severely intoxicated, and so on. It is not important to define the precise contours of these two legal regimes. The point is that we are considering a choice between a (relatively) permissive and a (relatively) rigorous regime.

Which regime should we choose? I have suggested that we could model the choice along consequentialist lines, where we would calculate the costs and benefits associated with different sets of rules, or we could model the choice along contractualist lines, in which people would choose from behind a Rawlsian veil of ignorance. Suppose that we adopt the Rawlsian approach. To make progress on this issue, we must relax the veil. The contractors must know what life would be like for people under different sets of laws and norms, including the full range of information about the trade-offs between the costs and benefits of the two regimes. Here, as elsewhere, the contractors would know that there is no free and equal lunch. At the same time, the veil would be sufficiently thick to deprive them of information regarding their personal characteristics. They would not know whether they were male or female, a potential perpetrator or victim, or, say, their attitude toward sexual relations. They would not know whether *their* sexual lives would go better under one set of rules or another. I don't think we can say with any confidence what rules would be chosen under any of these models, but we might be able to say something about the sorts of benefits and costs they would have to consider.

On the assumption that LR_R would actually affect behavior in the desired direction, it would provide greater protection to the sexual autonomy of women and would promote an environment in which men come to consider "a woman's consent to sex significant enough to merit [their] reasoned attention and respect."[33] These are clear benefits. But there would be costs. Some of these costs would be endogenous to the legal system. LR_R may consume legal resources that would be better spent elsewhere. It may result in the prosecution or conviction of more innocent persons. LR_R may also generate some negative effects on the general structure of sexual and social relations. It may cause a decline in spontaneity and excitement in sexual relations. In addition, just as some persons enjoy the process of haggling over consumer transactions, some may enjoy the game of sexual negotiation, the haggling, bluffing, and concealment that have been a standard fixture of courtship. After all, whether coyness is biologically hard-wired or culturally driven, many women have long thought that it is better to (first) consent to sex after an initial indication of reluctance, lest they be viewed as too "easy" or "loose."[34] So B may suffer if A is too respectful of her initial reluctance. Finally, it is distinctly possible that some persons choose to become intoxicated precisely to render themselves less inhibited—the reverse of a standard Ulysses situation in which one acts *ex ante* to inhibit one's actions *ex post*.[35] So, if A were to comply with LR_R by refusing to have sexual relations with an intoxicated B, A would prevent B from doing precisely what B wanted to do.

Of course, to say that there is no free lunch does not mean that lunch isn't worth buying: The gains may be worth the costs. Whether that is so will depend, in part, on the way in which we aggregate the gains and costs. From a contractarian perspective, it is distinctly possible that we should give some priority to the interests of the worse off, that is, the potential victims of sexual offenses, rather than simply try to maximize the sum total of preference satisfaction or happiness or whatever. The weight of that priority will depend on the gravity of that violation, an issue that has not been settled. But I do not think we should be indifferent to numbers. If LR_R would work to the detriment of many and help but a few, that would make a difference. Still, here as elsewhere, we should be prepared to trade off considerable positive benefits to some persons in order to provide greater protection to those who would otherwise be harmed.

V. DECENT SEXUAL RELATIONS

Even if we were to expand the range of sexually motivated behaviors subject to criminal sanctions, the criminal law is a blunt instrument to be used relatively sparingly. There remains the question of what sort of behaviors should be regarded as indecent or seriously wrong. Is it seriously wrong for A to obtain B's consent to sexual relations by threatening to end a dating relationship? Is it less wrong if A is *warning* but not *threatening* B, that is, if A is not trying to manipulate B's behavior but is stating the truth, that he would not want to continue the relationship without sexual relations? Is it seriously wrong for A to falsely declare love in order to secure B's consent to sexual relations or to secure her consent while she is intoxicated?

I have no intention of trying to answer these questions in this essay. I do want to make a few remarks about the issues they present. First, there is no reason to think that the justified legal demands on our behavior are coextensive with the moral demands on our behavior. Just as we may have a (morally justified) legal right to engage in behavior that is morally wrong (for example, to give a lecture that the Holocaust is a hoax), we may have a morally justified legal right to produce another's consent to sexual acts in ways that are seriously wrong. Second, just as we might regard the principles of consent for the criminal law as the output of moral theorizing, we can regard the principles of consent for acting decently as the output of moral theorizing, although there would be a different mixture of benefits and costs. Third, this is not an issue without practical consequences. When millions of students are enrolled in sex education courses, it is a genuine question as to what principles we should teach them.

I think it fair to say that, at present, there is no consensus as to what constitutes immoral behavior in this arena. I believe that many people view the pursuit of sexual gratification in dating relationships along the lines of a "capitalist" model, in which all parties are entitled to try to press for the best deal they can get. On a standard (predominantly male) view of dating relationships, it is legitimate for A to seek B's consent to sexual relations, even if A believes B will come to regret that decision. Moreover, just as it is thought legitimate to misrepresent one's reservation price in a business negotiation (there is no assumption that one is speaking the truth when one says, "I won't pay more than $15,000 for that car"), one is entitled to misrepresent one's feelings or intentions. By contrast, in a fiduciary relationship, such as between physicians and patients, A has an obligation to act in the interests of his client rather than his own interests. A should not seek B's consent to a transaction if A believes it is not in B's interest to consent to that transaction.

It would probably be a mistake to apply a strong fiduciary model to sexual relations among competent adults. It might be argued that a paternalistic attitude toward another's sexual life would be rightly rejected as failing to respect the autonomy of the parties "to act freely on their own unconstrained conception of what their bodies and their sexual capacities are for."[36] This is all well and good as far as it goes, but it begs the question of how to understand autonomy, the pressures that it is reasonable for one to bring to bear on another's decision and whether one fails to respect another's autonomy when one fails to tell the truth and nothing but the truth about one's feelings, intentions, and other relationships. It may well turn out that some hybrid of these two models best captures A's moral responsibilities. Unlike the capitalist model, A must give considerable weight to B's interests, as well as his own. Unlike the fiduciary model, B's decision as to what serves her interests is in the driver's seat.

VI. WHEN SHOULD ONE CONSENT TO SEXUAL RELATIONS?

In this section, I want to open up a question that is frequently discussed among parties in enduring relationships but rarely mentioned in the academic literature: How should a couple deal with an asymmetrical desire for sexual relations? Let us assume that A desires sexual relations more frequently than B. Let us also assume that A and B agree that it is not permissible for A to have sexual relations with B when B does not consent. Their question—indeed, it is B's question—is whether she should consent to sexual relations when, other things being equal, she would prefer not to consent. In particular, they want to know if they could reasonably view the frequency of sexual relations or the distribution of satisfaction with their sexual lives as a matter to be governed by a principle of distributive justice. If, as Susan Moller Okin has argued, justice applies to some intra-familial issues, such as the control of economic resources and the distribution of household labor, does justice also apply to sex?[37]

It might be thought that it is wrong to think that B should ever consent to sexual relations when she does not want sex. But this simply begs the question, for people's "wants" are complex and multifaceted. Consider the problem that has come to be known as the "battle of the sexes." In one version of the problem, A and B both prefer to go to the movies together than to go alone, but each prefers to go to different types of movies. Their problem is to determine what movie they should see.[38] Although the "battle of the sexes" is usually used to exemplify a bargaining problem, I want to use the example to make a point about the character of one's "wants." For we can well imagine that A may not "want" to see B's preferred movie, other things being equal. Still, given that B really wants to see the movie and given that they most recently went to the movie that A preferred, A may genuinely want to see the movie that B prefers—all things considered.

It might be objected that "I want to do what you want to do" is fine for movies, but not sex. In this view, there are some "not wants" that are legitimate candidates for "all things considered wants," but the lack of a desire for sexual relations is not among them. In one variant of this view, sexual relations are radically different from other activities in which partners engage together because it would be self-defeating for partners to think that they are having sexual relations on this basis. A can enjoy the movie that he sees with B, although he knows that B would (otherwise) prefer to see something else, but A would not get satisfaction from sexual relations with B if A knows that B wants to have sexual relations only to satisfy or placate A's desire for sexual relations.

With some trepidation, I want to suggest that to think of sexual relations between partners in an enduring relationship as radically different from all other activities in which they engage "wildly misdescribes" their experience.[39] Sexual relations among such partners are simply not always viewed as sacred or endowed with greater mystery. But my point is not solely negative or deflationary. After all, to say that the most desirable form of sexual relations occurs within a loving relationship is also to say that sexual relations are a way of expressing affection and commitment, and not simply to express or satisfy erotic desire. It is, for example, entirely plausible that parties who have been fighting might engage in sexual relations as a way of demonstrating to themselves that the disagreement is relatively minor in the context of their relationship, that their love for each other is unshaken. In general, I see no reason to tightly constrain what count as legitimate reasons to want to engage in sexual relations—all things considered.

But what about distributive justice? Assume that A and B both understand that it is frustrating for A to forgo sexual relations when B does not desire sexual relations, whereas it is erotically unsatisfying for B to engage in sexual relations when she does not desire sexual relations—not awful or abhorrent, just unsatisfying. On some occasions, A would rather have sex than go to sleep, whereas B's utility function is the reverse. Given this situation, there are three possibilities: (1) A can absorb the burden of the asymmetry by forgoing sexual relations when B is not otherwise motivated to have sex; (2) B can absorb the burden of the asymmetry by consenting to have sexual relations whenever A desires to do so; or (3) A and B can share the burden of the asymmetry by agreeing that they will have sexual relations less often than A would (otherwise) prefer and more often than B would (otherwise) prefer. And B is trying to decide if she should choose (3). Note, once again, that the question is not whether B should consent to sexual relations that she does not want. Rather, she is trying to decide if she should want to have sexual relations—all things considered—when the things to be considered involve a commitment to fairness.

It might be objected that even if we do not tightly constrain the reasons that might legitimately motivate B to "want" to have sex with A, sexual relations lie beyond reasons based on justice or fairness. It might be maintained that a concern with fairness or justice arises only when interests conflict. As Hume remarked, justice has no place among married people who are "unacquainted with the *mine* and *thine*, which are so necessary and yet cause such disturbance in human society."[40] From this perspective, a conscious preoccupation with fairness in a marriage can be a symptom that the parties have failed to achieve the identity of interests that characterize a good marriage and may (causally) inhibit the formation of a maximally intimate relationship.[41] Love precludes a concern with justice, what Hume described as "the cautious, jealous virtue."[42]

I want to make several replies to this line of argument. First, and least important, there is obviously a limit to the identity of interests it is logically possible to achieve. If each party has an overall want to do what the other has a primary want to do, they will achieve an altruistic draw ("I want to do what you want to do." "But I want to do what you want to do."). And if each has an overall want to do what the other has an overall want to do, there will be no wants for the overall wants to get hold of.

Second, if we think that a good marriage is characterized by an identity of interests, this still leaves open the question as to how married partners should respond to the asymmetry of desire for sexual relations. Just as A might say, "I wouldn't want to have sexual relations if B doesn't want to," B might say, "If A wants to have sexual relations, then I want to have sexual relations." So if we reject the argument from distributive justice because it assumes that the interests of the parties conflict, there is no reason to think that the parties will settle on (1) rather than (2) or (3).

Third, I think it both unrealistic and undesirable to expect that the desires or interests of persons in the most successful intimate relationships will fully coincide. It is relatively, although not absolutely, easy for married partners not to distinguish between "mine" and "thine" with respect to property. It is much more difficult to achieve a communal view with respect to activities. Do loving spouses not care at all how many diapers they change? To which movies they go? Where they locate? Are they no longer loving if they do care? Indeed, it is not clear that it is even desirable for people to strive for a relationship in which their interests are so completely merged. It might be thought that a good marriage represents a "union" of autonomous individuals who do and should have goals and aspirations that are independent of their relationship.

From this perspective, a couple's concern with fairness simply reflects the fact that their desires are not identical, that they do not see why this fact should be denied or regretted, and that they want to resolve these differences in a fair way. As Susan Moller Okin puts it (albeit in a different context), "Why should we suppose that harmonious affection, indeed deep and long-lasting love, cannot co-exist with ongoing standards of justice?"[43] Indeed, I would go further. It might be argued that it is not merely that love can coexist with justice, but that to love another person is to want to be fair to them, or, more precisely, to want not to be unfair to them, for to love someone is typically to want to be more than fair to them, to be generous.

I have not actually argued that the distribution of satisfaction with one's sexual life in an enduring relationship is an appropriate topic for distributive justice. Although I have argued against several objections to the view that sexual relations are beyond the scope of justice, it is possible that other arguments would work. Moreover, even if the distribution of satisfaction with one's sexual life is an appropriate topic for a principle of justice, I make no suggestions here as to what the substance of a theory of justice in sexual relations would look like. It is entirely possible that such a theory would dictate that the parties choose something like (1) rather than (3) (I take it that (2) is a nonstarter). I only want to suggest that the topic may belong on the table.

NOTES

1. See Alan Wertheimer, *Coercion* (Princeton, N.J.: Princeton University Press, 1987) and *Exploitation* (Princeton, N.J.: Princeton University Press, 1996).

2. I borrow this phrase from Heidi Hurd's remarks at the conference at the University of San Diego Law School, which gave rise to this symposium.

3. For example, it may be wrong for a physician to accede to a beggar's request to have his leg amputated so that he can enhance his success as a beggar.

4. "You have never left the city, even to see a festival, nor for any other reason except military service; you have never gone to stay in any other city, as people do; you have had no desire to know another city or other laws; we and our city satisfied you. So decisively did you choose us and agree to be a citizen under us." Plato, *Crito*, in *The Trial and Death of Socrates*, trans. G. M. A. Grube (Indianapolis, Ind.: Hackett, 1975).

5. "[E]very man that hath any possession or enjoyment of any part of the dominions of any government doth thereby give his tacit consent, and is as far forth obliged to obedience to the laws of that government, during such enjoyment, whether this his possession be of land to him and his heirs for ever, or a lodging only for a week; or whether it be barely travelling freely on the highway . . ." John Locke, *Second Treatise Of Government*, chap. 8 (1690).

6. "Can we seriously say, that a poor person or artisan has a free choice to leave his country, when he knows no foreign language or manners, and lives, from day to day, by the small wages which he acquires? We may as well assert that a man, by remaining in a vessel, freely consents to the dominion of the master; though he was carried on board while asleep, and must leap into the ocean and perish, the moment he leaves her." David Hume, *Of the Original Contract* (1777).

7. Harry Frankfurt, "Coercion and Moral Responsibility," in *Essays on Freedom of Action*, ed. T. Honderich (London: Routledge & Kegan Paul, 1973), 65.

8. As Jeremy Waldron has put it, "[T]he question is . . . not what 'harm' really means, but what reasons of principle there are for preferring one conception to another . . . the question is not simply which is the better conception of harm, but which conception answers more adequately to the purposes for which the concept is deployed." *Liberal Rights: Collected Papers 1981-91* (Cambridge: Cambridge University Press, 1993). For a somewhat different view, see Frederick Schauer, "The Phenomenology of Speech and Harm," *Ethics* 103: 4 (1993): 635–53.

9. *Vokes v. Arthur Murray, Inc.*, 212 So. 2d 906 (1968), at 907.

10. See "Sexual Exploitation in Psychotherapy," chap. 6 in Wertheimer, *Exploitation*.

11. See *State v. Rusk*, 289 Md. 230, 424 A. 2d 720 (1981). The defendant had also intimidated the prosecutor by taking the keys to her car, disregarded her statement that she did not want to have sexual relations with him, and was said to have "lightly choked" her.

12. *Director of Public Prosecutions v. Morgan* (1975), 2 All E.R. 347.

13. Donald A. Dripps, "Beyond Rape: An Essay on the Difference between the Presence of Force and the Absence of Consent," *Columbia Law Review* 92: 7 (November 1992): 1780–1809, esp. 1797.

14. Indeed, it might be thought that this case is, in one way, more serious than those in which force is used to overcome the victim's resistance, namely, that it requires the victim to act inauthentically.

15. See Catharine MacKinnon, *Feminism Unmodified* (Cambridge, Mass.: Harvard University Press, 1987), 5–6.

16. See Richard A. Posner, *Sex and Reason* (Cambridge, Mass.: Harvard University Press, 1992), 384.

17. For a discussion of nonexperiential harm, see Joel Feinberg, *Harm to Others: The Moral Limits of the Criminal Law* (New York: Oxford University Press, 1984), chap. 2.

18. Stephen J. Schulhofer, "Taking Sexual Autonomy Seriously: Rape Law and Beyond," *Law and Philosophy* 11: 1-2 (1992): 35–94, esp. 70.

19. Dripps, "Beyond Rape," 1796*n*3.

20. Donald A. Dripps, "Force, Consent, and the Reasonable Woman," in *In Harm's Way: Essays in Honor of Joel Feinberg*, ed. J. L. Coleman and A. Buchanan (Cambridge: Cambridge University Press, 1994), 231–54, esp. 235. McGregor says that she borrows the notion of "border crossings" from Robert Nozick's *Anarchy, State and Utopia* (New York: Basic Books, 1974).

21. I think it no objection to the commodity (or any other) view of the law of sexual crimes that it "wildly misdescribes" the victim's experience. Robin West, "Legitimating the Illegitimate: A Comment on *Beyond Rape*," *Columbia Law Review* 93 (April 1993), 1442–48, esp. 1448. The question is whether a view provides a coherent framework for protecting the rights or interests that we believe ought to be protected. Indeed, it is an advantage of a "property" theory that it provides a basis for critiquing the traditional law of rape. That A takes B's property without B's consent is sufficient to show that A steals B's property. Force or resistance is not required.

22. See Jeffrie G. Murphy, "Some Ruminations on Women, Violence, and the Criminal Law," in Coleman and Buchanan, *In Harm's Way*, 214.

23. Robin Wright, "Feminists, Meet Mr. Darwin," *New Republic* (November 1994): 37. The evolutionary logic of nonconsensual sex is different for men. It is physically difficult to accomplish, and "the worst likely outcome for the man (in genetic terms) is that pregnancy would not ensue . . . hardly a major Darwinian disaster."

24. This is obviously true on a retributive theory of punishment, in which the level of punishment is related to the seriousness of the offense. But it is also true on a utilitarian theory, for the more serious the harm to the victim, the greater "expense" (in punishment) it makes sense to employ to deter such harms.

25. Murphy, "Some Ruminations on Women," 216*n*22.

26. Wertheimer, *Coercion*.

27. This is derived from a case introduced by Schulhofer, "Taking Sexual Autonomy Seriously," 70*n*18.

28. C. L. Muehlenhard and J. L. Schrag, "Nonviolent Sexual Coercion," in *Acquaintance Rape: The Hidden Crime*, ed. A. Parrot and L. Bechhofer (New York: Wiley, 1991), 115–28, esp. 119.

29. Don Dripps has suggested to me that case (5) is a variant on prostitution. In the standard case of prostitution, A proposes to pay B with A's money. In this case, A proposes to pay B with B's money.

30. As Stephen Schulhofer says, because there are "few pervasively shared intuitions" with regard to what constitutes serious misrepresentation as distinct from puffing or "story telling," the decisions as to "whether to believe, whether to rely and whether to assume the risk of deception . . . are often seen as matters to be left to the individual." "Taking Sexual Autonomy Seriously," 92*n*18.

31. It is less clear—and informal intuition (and pumping of friends) has done little to help—whether women would regard sexual relations while unconscious as worse than or not as bad as forcible sexual relations. One might think that it is worse to consciously experience an assault on one's bodily and sexual integrity, but it might also be thought that it is better to know what is happening to oneself than not to know.

32. I say "first" indication, because B could consent while sober to what she subsequently consents to while intoxicated.

33. Susan Estrich, *Real Rape* (Cambridge, Mass.: Harvard University Press, 1987), 98.

34. See the discussion of coyness in Robert Wright, *The Moral Animal* (Gloucester, Mass.: Peter Smith, 1994).

35. "Here are the keys to my car; don't let met drive home if I'm drunk." See, e.g., Thomas C. Schelling, "The Intimate Contest for Self-Command," in *Choice and Consequence* (Cambridge, Mass.: Harvard University Press, 1984), chap. 3.

36. Schulhofer, "Taking Sexual Autonomy Seriously," 70*n*18.

37. Susan Moller Okin, *Justice, Gender, and the Family* (New York: Basic Books, 1989).

38. See Brian Barry, *Theories of Justice* (Berkeley, Calif.: University of California Press, 1989), 116–17.

39. With apologies to Robin West.
40. David Hume, *A Treatise of Human Nature*, bk. III, sect. II.
41. I thank Pat Neal and Bob Taylor for pressing me on this point.
42. David Hume, *An Enquiry Concerning the Principles of Morals*, sect. III, pt. I, par. 3.
43. Okin, *Justice, Gender, and the Family*, 32n37.

STUDY QUESTIONS

1. What does Wertheimer mean when he calls consent "morally transformative"? Why does he claim that consent will *be* morally transformative, all things considered, only when certain conditions are met? What are these conditions?

2. Wertheimer discusses both sayings: "no means no" and "yes means yes." What do these expressions literally mean? What do they mean when particular people use them in particular contexts?

3. The legal philosopher Jeffrie Murphy believes that women's abhorrence to being raped is due to cultural conditioning and that, as a result, if we did not teach women certain things about sexuality, they would not experience being raped as such a grave harm. To the contrary, Wertheimer claims, women's abhorrence is "hardwired," that is, is due to women's biology as molded by natural and sexual selection. Who do you think is right here, and why? And what difference does it make, philosophically, legally, or politically? Is the spiritual and psychological repugnance of a strict Orthodox Jew or Muslim to pork biological or cultural? Does it matter, if someone shoves a piece of bacon, the forbidden meat, into his or her mouth? (See also the essay "How Bad Is Rape—II?" by H. E. Baber, in this volume.)

4. Is it morally wrong for a person A to say falsely to another person B "I love you" just so A can induce B to engage in sex? Should it be legally culpable fraud or deception? Is it morally wrong for a person A to say truly to another person B, "Have sex with me or find yourself some other boyfriend [girlfriend]" just so A can induce B to engage in sex? Should it be legally culpable coercion? Might that threat be, in some circumstances, morally suspicious exploitation? When? (See Thomas Mappes, "Sexual Morality and the Concept of Using Another Person," in this volume.)

5. In many marriages and relationships between two people, one person desires sexual activity from or with the other person more frequently than the second desires it with the first. Also, in many marriages and relationships one person desires a specific type of sexual activity that the second person finds distasteful or even immoral and prefers not to do. How would you propose to solve such conflicts—without suggesting that the two people get divorced or

split up? What helpful suggestions does Wertheimer make in his essay? What solution does he reject, and why?

TWENTY-ONE

The Harms of Consensual Sex

Robin West

In earlier chapters we encountered several lines of thought that opposed consent as the central moral standard of sexual activity. Opposition came from conservatives. Some Kantians, for example, argue that consent is not sufficient because consent does not prevent the participants from still treating each other as mere means. The conservative Thomistic Natural Law view is that marriage and openness-to-procreation are also required for sexual activity to be morally permissible. In this essay, legal scholar **Robin West** *finds fault with the consent criterion from a different perspective. She argues that consensual—but unwanted—sex often harms a woman in more subtle ways than do rape, assault, and harassment. West provides a compelling picture of the often unhappy circumstances under which much, though not all, everyday heterosexual activity occurs. Even when a woman employs her freedom and rationality in agreeing to sexual activity with a husband or boyfriend, if she is consenting to sexual contact that she does not genuinely desire, she may be undermining that same freedom and rationality. A lone, stringent consent standard, on West's view, is thereby an arrow in patriarchy's quiver. But West is not an uncritical feminist. She concludes by suggesting that feminist-liberal reforms of rape laws might have the unintended consequence of masking (by "legitimating") these subtle kinds of damage. She also wonders whether the radical feminist mantra that all heterosexual penetration perpetrates illicit sex trivializes the subtle harms done to the autonomy of women who consent to unwanted sexual activity.*

Robin West is professor of law at Georgetown University Law Center, where she teaches jurisprudence, torts, law and literature, and feminist legal theory. She is the author, most recently, of *Normative Jurisprudence: An Introduction* (Cambridge University Press, 2011), and of *Narrative, Authority, and Law* (University of Michigan Press, 1994), *Progressive Constitutionalism* (Duke University Press, 1995), *Caring for Justice* (New York University Press, 1997), *Re-Imagining Justice: Progressive Interpretations of Formal Equality, Rights, and the*

Rule of Law (Ashgate/Dartmouth 2003), and *Marriage, Sexuality, and Gender* (Paradigm Press, 2007). This essay is reprinted, with the permission of Robin West and The American Philosophical Association, from *The American Philosophical Association Newsletters* 94:2 (1995): 52–55.

Are consensual, non-coercive, non-criminal, and even non-tortious, heterosexual transactions ever harmful to women? I want to argue briefly that many (not all) consensual sexual transactions are, and that accordingly we should open a dialogue about what those harms might be. Then I want to suggest some reasons those harms may be difficult to discern, even by the women sustaining them, and lastly two ways in which the logic of feminist legal theory and practice itself might undermine their recognition.

Let me assume what many women who are or have been heterosexually active surely know to be true from their own experience, and that is that some women occasionally, and many women quite frequently, consent to sex even when they do not desire the sex itself, and accordingly have a good deal of sex that, although consensual, is in no way pleasurable. Why might a woman consent to sex she does not desire? There are, of course, many reasons. A woman might consent to sex she does not want because she or her children are dependent upon her male partner for economic sustenance, and she must accordingly remain in his good graces. A woman might consent to sex she does not want because she rightly fears that if she does not her partner will be put into a foul humor, and she simply decides that tolerating the undesired sex is less burdensome than tolerating the foul humor. A woman might consent to sex she does not want because she has been taught and has come to believe that it is her lot in life to do so, and that she has no reasonable expectation of attaining her own pleasure through sex. A woman might consent to sex she does not want because she rightly fears that her refusal to do so will lead to an outburst of violent behavior some time following—only if the violence or overt threat of violence is very close to the sexual act will this arguably constitute a rape. A woman may consent to sex she does not desire because she *does* desire a friendly man's protection against the very real threat of non-consensual violent rape by other more dangerous men, and she correctly perceives, or intuits, that to gain the friendly man's protection, she needs to give him, in exchange for that protection, the means to his own sexual pleasure. A woman, particularly a young woman or teenager, may consent to sex she does not want because of peer expectations that she be sexually active, or because she cannot bring herself to hurt her partner's pride, or because she is uncomfortable with the prospect of the argument that might ensue, should she refuse.

These transactions may well be rational—indeed in some sense they all are. The women involved all trade sex for something they value more than they value what they have given up. But that doesn't mean that they are not harmed. Women who engage in unpleasurable, undesired, but consensual sex may sustain real injuries to their sense of selfhood, in at least four distinct ways. First, they may sustain injuries to their capacities for self-assertion: the "psychic connection," so to speak, between pleasure, desire, motivation, and action is weakened or severed. *Acting* on the basis of our own felt pleasures and pains is an important component of forging our own way in the world—of "asserting" our "selves." Consenting to *un*pleasurable sex—acting in spite of displeasure—threatens that means of self-assertion. Second, women who consent to undesired sex may injure their sense of self-*possession*. When we consent to undesired penetration of our physical bodies we have in a quite literal way constituted ourselves as what I have elsewhere called "giving selves"—selves who cannot be violated, because they have been defined as (and define themselves as) being "for others." Our bodies to that extent no longer belong to ourselves. Third, when women consent to undesired and unpleasurable sex because of their felt or actual dependency upon a partner's affection or economic status, they injure their sense of autonomy: they have thereby neglected to take whatever steps would be requisite to achieving the self-sustenance necessary to their independence. And fourth, to the extent that these unpleasurable and undesired sexual acts are followed by contrary to fact claims that they enjoyed the whole thing—what might be called "hedonic lies"—women who engage in them do considerable damage to their sense of integrity.

These harms—particularly if multiplied over years or indeed over an entire adulthood—may be quite profound, and they certainly may be serious enough to outweigh the momentary or day-to-day benefits garnered by each individual transaction. Most debilitating, though, is their circular, self-reinforcing character: the more thorough the harm—the deeper the injury to self-assertiveness, self-possession, autonomy, and integrity—the greater the likelihood that the woman involved will indeed *not* experience these harms as harmful, or as painful. A woman utterly lacking in self-assertiveness, self-possession, a sense of autonomy, or integrity will not experience the activities in which she engages that reinforce or constitute those qualities *as harmful*, because she, to that degree, lacks a self-asserting, self-possessed self who *could* experience those activities as a threat to her selfhood. But the fact that she does not experience these activities as harms certainly does not mean that they are not harmful. Indeed, that they are not felt as harmful is a consequence of the harm they have already caused. This phenomenon, of course, renders the "rationality" of these transactions tremendously and even tragically misleading. Although these women may be making rational calculations in the context of the particular decision facing them, they are, by making those calculations, sustaining deeper and to some degree unfelt harms that undermine the very qualities that constitute the capacity for rationality being exercised.

Let me quickly suggest some reasons that these harms go so frequently unnoticed—or are simply not taken seriously—and then suggest in
slightly more detail some ways that feminist legal theory and practice
may have undermined their recognition. The first reason is cultural.
There is a deep-seated U.S. cultural tendency to equate the legal with the
good, or harmless: we are, for better or worse, an anti-moralistic, anti-
authoritarian, and anti-communitarian people. When combined with the
sexual revolution of the 1960s, this provides a powerful cultural explanation for our tendency to shy away from a sustained critique of the harms
of consensual sex. Any suggestion that legal transactions to which individuals freely consent may be harmful, and hence *bad*, will invariably be
met with skepticism—*particularly* where those transactions are sexual in
nature. This tendency is even further underscored by more contemporary
post-mortem skeptical responses to claims asserting the pernicious consequences of false consciousness.

Second, at least our legal-academic discourses, and no doubt academ-
ic-political discourses as well, have been deeply transformed by the "exchange theory of value," according to which, if I exchange A for B voluntarily, then I simply must be better off after the exchange than before,
having, after all, agreed to it. If these exchanges *are* the source of value,
then it is of course impossible to ground a *value* judgment that some
voluntary exchanges are harmful. Although stated baldly this theory of
value surely has more critics than believers, it nevertheless in some way
perfectly captures the modern zeitgeist. It is certainly, for example, the
starting and ending point of normative analysis for many, and perhaps
most, law students. Obviously, given an exchange theory of value, the
harms caused by consensual sexual transactions simply fade away into
definitional oblivion.

Third, the exchange theory of value is underscored, rather than significantly challenged, by the continuing significance of liberal theory and
ideology in academic life. To the degree that liberalism still rules the day,
we continue to valorize individual choice against virtually anything with
which it might seem to be in conflict, from communitarian dialogue to
political critique, and continue to perceive these challenges to individual
primacy as somehow on a par with threats posed by totalitarian statist
regimes.

Fourth, and perhaps most obvious, the considerable harms women
sustain from consensual but undesired sex must be downplayed if the
considerable pleasure men reap from heterosexual transactions is morally justified—*whatever* the relevant moral theory. Men do have a psychosexual stake in insisting that voluntariness alone ought be sufficient to
ward off serious moral or political inquiry into the value of consensual
sexual transactions.

Let me comment in a bit more detail on a further reason why these
harms seem to be underacknowledged, and that has to do with the logic

of feminist legal theory, and the efforts of feminist practitioners, in the area of rape law reform. My claim is that the theoretical conceptualizations of sex, rape, force, and violence that underscore both liberal and radical legal feminism undermine the effort to articulate the harms that might be caused by consensual sexuality. I will begin with liberal feminism and then turn to radical feminism.

First, and entirely to their credit, liberal feminist rape law reformers have been on the forefront of efforts to stiffen enforcement of the existing criminal sanction against rape, and to extend that sanction to include non-consensual sex, which presently is not cognizable legally as rape but surely should be. This effort is to be applauded, but it has the almost inevitable consequence of valorizing, celebrating, or, to use the critical term, "legitimating" consensual sexual transactions. If rape is bad *because* it is non-consensual—which is increasingly the dominant liberal-feminist position on the badness of rape—then it seems to follow that *consensual* sex must be good because it is consensual. But appearances can be misleading, and this one certainly is. That non-consensual transactions— rape, theft, slavery—are bad because non-consensual does *not* imply the value, worth or goodness of their consensual counterparts—sex, property, or work. It only follows that consensual sex, property, or work are not bad in the ways that non-consensual transactions are bad; they surely may be bad for some other reason. We need to explore, in the case of sex (as well as property and work), what those other reasons might be. Non-consensuality does not exhaust the types of harm we inflict on each other in social interactions, nor does consensuality exhaust the list of benefits.

That the liberal-feminist argument for extending the criminal sanction against rape to include non-consensual sex *seems* to imply the positive value of consensual sex is no doubt in part simply a reflection of the powers of the forces enumerated above—the cultural, economic, and liberal valorization of individualism against communal and authoritarian controls. Liberal feminists can obviously not be faulted for that phenomenon. What I want to caution against is simply the ever-present temptation to *trade* on those cultural and academic forces in putting forward arguments for reform of rape law. We need not trumpet the glories of consensual sex *in order* to make out a case for strengthening the criminal sanction against coercive sex. Coercion, violence, and the fear under which women live because of the threat of rape are sufficient evils to sustain the case for strengthening and extending the criminal law against those harms. We need not and should not supplement the argument with the unnecessary and unwarranted celebration of consensual sex—which, whatever the harms caused by coercion, does indeed carry its own harms.

Ironically, radical feminist rhetoric—which *is* aimed at highlighting the damage and harm done to women by ordinary, "normal" heterosexual transactions—*also* indirectly burdens the attempt to articulate the harms done to women by consensual heterosexual transactions, although it does so in a very different way. Consider the claim, implicit in a good deal of radical feminist writing, explicit in some, that "all sex is rape," and compare it for a moment with the rhetorical Marxist claim that "all property is theft." Both claims are intended to push the reader or listener to a reexamination of the ordinary, and both do so by blurring the distinction between consent and coercion. Both seem to share the underlying premise that that which is coerced—and perhaps only that which is coerced—is bad, or as a strategic matter, is going to be perceived as bad. Both want us to re-examine the value of that which we normally think of as good or at least unproblematic because of its apparent consensuality—heterosexual transactions in the first case, property transactions in the second—and both do so by putting into doubt the reality of that apparent consensuality.

But there is a very real difference in the historical context and hence the practical consequences of these two rhetorical claims. More specifically, there are two pernicious, or at least counter-productive, consequences of the feminist claim which are not shared, at least to the same degree, by the Marxist. First, and as any number of liberal feminists have noted, the radical feminist equation of sex and rape runs the risk of undermining parallel feminist efforts in a way not shared by the Marxist equation of property and theft. Marxists are for the most part not engaged in the project of attempting to extend the existing laws against *theft* so as to embrace non-consensual market transactions that are currently not covered by the laws against larceny and embezzlement. Feminists, however, *are* engaged in a parallel effort to extend the existing laws against rape to include all non-consensual sex, and as a result, the radical feminist equation of rape and sex is indeed undermining. The claim that all sex is in effect non-consensual runs the real risk of "trivializing," or at least confusing, the feminist effort at rape reform so as to include all truly non-consensual sexual transactions.

There is, though, a second cost to the radical feminist rhetorical claim, which I hope these comments have by now made clear. The radical feminist equation of rape and sex, no less than the liberal rape reform movement, gets its rhetorical force by trading on the liberal, normative-economic, and cultural assumptions that whatever is coercive is bad, and whatever is non-coercive is morally non-problematic. It has the effect, then, of further burdening the articulation of harms caused by consensual sex by forcing the characterization of those harms into a sort of "descriptive funnel" of non-consensuality. It requires us to say, in other words, that consensual sex is harmful, if it is, only because or to the extent that it shares in the attributes of non-consensual sex. But this might not be true—the harms caused by consensual sex might be just as important, just as serious, but nevertheless *different* from the harms caused by non-consensual sex. If so, then women are disserved, rather than served, by the equation of rape and sex, even were that equation to have the rhetorical effect its espousers clearly desire.

Liberal feminist rape reform efforts and radical feminist theory both, then, in different ways, undermine the effort to articulate the distinctive harms of consensual sex; the first by indirectly celebrating the value of consensual sex, and the latter by at least rhetorically denying the existence of the category. Both, then, in different ways, underscore the legitimation of consensual sex effectuated by non-feminist cultural and academic forces. My conclusion is simply that feminists could counter these trends in part by focusing attention on the harms caused women by consensual sexuality. Minimally, a thorough-going philosophical treatment of these issues might clear up some of the confusions on both sides of the "rape/sex" divide, and on the many sides of what have now come to be called the intra-feminist "sex wars," which continue to drain so much of our time and energy.

STUDY QUESTIONS

1. In arguing that a liberal consent criterion of morally permissible sexual activity does not adequately protect women, is West's position ultimately paternalistic, and in this way is itself injurious to women's autonomy? In claiming that more than a woman's agreement must be in place to allow her to avoid unwanted sex, are we not robbing her of the freedom to consent to sex on her own terms? Compare West's position with the possibly paternalistic Antioch University "Sexual Offense Policy" (see, for example, Leslie Francis's anthology *Date Rape* [University Park: Penn State University Press, 1996]), which has also been criticized for reducing autonomy even as it aims at promoting autonomy.

2. It is known that some women apply various kinds of strong or weak pressures on men (and women) to engage in sexual activity, without that pressure necessarily amounting to force or coercion that would make these sexual acts rape or nonconsensual. (See, for example, Peter Anderson and Cindy Struckman-Johnson, eds., *Sexually Aggressive Women: Current Perspectives and Controversies* [New York: Guilford, 1998].) Does this consensual but unwanted sexual activity harm men or reduce their autonomy? When and how? Might there be a difference between men and women in their ability to withstand the consequences of unwanted but consensual sex?

3. What if one partner in a couple desires to engage in sexual activity more than the other partner, but both desire sex in general? In many partnerships, this scenario seems rather the rule than the exception. What are the implications of this imbalance for West's

position? Contrast the arguments and conclusions reached by Alan Wertheimer about this scenario ("Consent and Sexual Relations," in this volume) to those advanced by West.

4. Is the presence of genuine sexual desire a more reliable moral criterion than consent to sexual activity? Granted, there are difficulties specifying what the consent criterion demands (here, learn to apply Wertheimer's vocabulary of "consent token" vs. "consent"), but what, in practice, does West's no-harm standard mean? Are there any conceptual or normative differences between West's view and that of Robin Morgan, who focuses on desire? "Rape exists any time sexual intercourse occurs when it has not been initiated by the woman, out of her own genuine affection and desire. . . . How many millions of times have women had sex 'willingly' with men they didn't want to have sex with? . . . How many times have women wished just to sleep instead or read or watch the Late Show? . . . Most of the decently married bedrooms across America are settings for nightly rape" ("Theory and Practice: Pornography and Rape," in *Going Too Far: The Personal Chronicle of a Feminist* [New York: Random House, 1977], 163–69, at 165–66).

5. After reading Lois Pineau's account of the ideal Kantian imperative regarding consent ("Date Rape: A Feminist Analysis," in this volume), think about whether genuinely "communicative sexuality" of the sort Pineau recommends would alleviate any or all of the harms West associates with women's consensual but unwanted sex—and *how*.

6. Is it possible that West's examples of consensual sexual activity are cases in which the woman does not really consent? Go through her examples and ask whether she has convincingly claimed or shown that the woman did consent. What are the implications for her thesis if in some of these cases the woman plausibly did not fully consent? Consider also this example: A woman who works in a flower shop is scheduled to be on duty on the eve of Valentine's Day, a busy night in the shop. She arrives at work two hours late because just as she was parking her car in the shop's lot, her boyfriend texts her and says he needs sex. She pulls out, drives forty-five minutes to his place, engages in sexual activity with him for thirty minutes, and then drives back to the shop. Why? She didn't want to make him angry with her. Did she consent to unwanted sexual activity to avoid a foul-humored boyfriend, or did the pressure she experienced mean that her "consent token" did not achieve the level of genuine consent?

TWENTY-TWO

Two Views of Sexual Ethics: Promiscuity, Pedophilia, and Rape

David Benatar

David Benatar *attempts to construct a disjunctive dilemma arising from two popular philosophical attitudes about sexuality. On one view (the "casual" philosophy of sex), sexual activity has intrinsic worth precisely as a source of pleasure. On the other view (the "significance" philosophy of sex), sexual activity has substantial instrumental value as an expression of love and commitment. If the value of sexual activity lies in the pleasure it produces, then casual sex is perfectly permissible. However, at least in principle, sometimes the value of the pleasure produced will outweigh the harm (a disvalue) that is done to unwilling people during rape or done to children in acts of pedophilia. (Utilitarian moral philosophy also faces this in-principle problem. Would it happen so frequently that we need to worry about it?) On the other hand, if the value of sexual activity lies in its significance (through love or commitment) and not in its pleasure, then rape and pedophilia are wrong, but casual sex and even mild promiscuity are also wrong. Given that the consequents of both conditionals are false (if sexual activity is about pleasure, then rape is in principle justifiable; if sex is about love or commitment, then casual sex is wrong)—rape is a paradigm case of a morally wrong sexual act; and casual sex, in the developed West, at least, largely escapes moral notice, let alone reprobation—these two philosophical positions, the "casual" and the "significance" views, are unacceptable as stated. The "casual" view has no power to prohibit sexual acts that are immensely pleasurable for one person yet harmful for another, while the "significance" view cannot morally bless what many people both engage in and approve of: sex without love. Benatar proceeds to ask whether there is some hybrid or intermediate philosophical position that is sufficiently permissive to allow casual sex and is also sufficiently*

restrictive to condemn rape and pedophilia. Because the child molester is contem-
porary culture's boogeyman, the embodiment of the darkest fears of many people,
Benatar's frank discussion of the source of our abhorrence of pedophilia is valu-
able.

David Benatar is professor of philosophy at the University of Cape Town, South Africa, and the author of *Better Never to Have Been: The Harm of Coming into Existence* (Oxford University Press, 2006). He has also edited *Ethics for Everyday* (McGraw-Hill, 2002) and *Life, Death, and Meaning: Key Philosophical Readings on the Big Questions* (Rowman & Littlefield, 2004). The essay is reprinted, with the permission of David Benatar and the journal, from *Public Affairs Quarterly* 16:3 (July 2002): 191–201.

The sexual revolution did not overthrow taboos about sex, but rather only restricted the number of practices regarded as taboo. Some sexual behaviors that were formally condemned are now tolerated or even endorsed. Others continue to be viewed with the opprobrium formerly dispensed to a broader range of sexual conduct. Promiscuity, for example, is widely accepted, but rape and pedophilia continue to be reviled.

On the face of it, this cluster of views—accepting promiscuity but regarding rape and pedophilia as heinous—seems perfectly defensible. I shall argue, however, that the view of sexual ethics that underlies an acceptance of promiscuity is inconsistent with regarding (1) rape as worse than other forms of coercion or assault, or (2) (many) sex acts with willing children as wrong at all. And the view of sexual ethics that would *fully* explain the wrong of rape and pedophilia would also rule out promiscuity. I intend this argument neither as a case against promiscuity nor as either a mitigation of rape or a partial defense of pedophilia. My purpose is to highlight an inconsistency in many people's judgments. Whether one avoids the inconsistency by extending or limiting the range of practices one condemns, will depend on which underlying view of the ethics of sex one accepts.

There are many views about the ethics of sex, but not all of these bear on the issues at hand. Consider, for instance, the view that a necessary condition of a sexual activity's being morally acceptable is that it carry the possibility of procreation.[1] While this view would be directly relevant to the practice of contraception, it would provide no way of morally judging promiscuity, pedophilia, or rape per se. Under some conditions, all of these practices would have procreative possibility.[2] Under others, none of them would. I shall restrict my attention to two views of sexual ethics that have special relevance to the three sexual practices I am considering.

TWO VIEWS OF SEXUAL ETHICS

The first of these is the view that for sex to be morally acceptable, it must be an expression of (romantic) love. It must, in other words, signify feelings of affection that are commensurate with the intimacy of the sexual activity. On this view a sexual union can be acceptable only if it reflects the reciprocal love and affection of the parties to that union. We might call this the significance view (or, alternatively, the love view) of sex, because it requires sex to signify love in order for it to be permissible.

On an alternative view of sexual ethics—what we might call the *casual view*—sex need not have this significance in order to be morally permissible. Sexual pleasure, according to this view, is morally like any other pleasure and may be enjoyed subject only to the usual sorts of moral constraints. A gastronomic delight, obtained via theft of a culinary delicacy, would be morally impermissible, but where no general moral principle (such as a prohibition on theft) applies, there can be no fault with engaging in gourmet pleasures. Having meals with a string of strangers or mere acquaintances is not condemnable as "casual gastronomy," "eating around," or "culinary promiscuity." Similarly, according to the casual view, erotic pleasures may permissibly be obtained from sex with strangers or mere acquaintances. There need not be any love or affection. (Nor need there always be pleasure. Just as a meal or a theatre performance might not be pleasurable and is not for that reason morally impermissible, so sex is not, nor ought be, always pleasurable.)

Both the significance view and the casual view are moral claims about when people *may* engage in sex. They are not descriptive claims about when people *do* engage in sex. Clearly both kinds of sex do occur. Sometimes sex does reflect love. Sometimes it does not.

IMPLICATIONS OF THE TWO VIEWS

A sexually promiscuous person is somebody who is casual about sex— somebody for whom sex is not (or need not be) laden with romantic significance. (As promiscuity is obviously a matter of degree, for most promiscuous people sex need not even be *tinged* with romantic significance.) This is not to say that the sexually promiscuous will have sex with simply anybody. Even the promiscuous can exercise some discretion in their choice of sexual partners just as the gastronomically "promiscuous" may be discriminating in the sort of people with whom they may wish to dine. The sexually promiscuous person is not one who is entirely undiscriminating about sexual partners, but rather somebody for whom romantic attachments are not a relevant consideration in choosing a sexual partner. It is thus clear why promiscuity is frowned upon by advocates of the significance view of sex. The promiscuous person treats as insignificant that which ought to be significant.

The significance view also has an explanation of why pedophilia is wrong. Children, it could be argued, are unable to appreciate the full significance that sexual activity should have.[3] This is not to suggest that children are asexual beings, but rather that they may lack the capacity to understand how sex expresses a certain kind of love. Having sex with a child is thus to treat the child as a mere means to attaining erotic pleasure without consideration of the mental states of which the provision of that pleasure should be an expression. Even if the child is sexually aroused, that arousal is not an expression of the requisite sorts of feelings. If the child is beyond infancy, the experience, in addition to being objectifying, may be deeply bewildering and traumatizing. The significance view of sex also provides an explanation of the special wrong of rape. On this view, raping people—forcing them to have sex—is not like forcing them to engage in other activities, such as going to the opera or to dinner. It is to compel a person to engage in an activity that should be an expression of deep affection. To forcibly strip it of that significance is to treat a vitally important component of sexual activity as though it were a mere trifle. It thus expresses extreme indifference to the deepest aspects of the person whose body is used for the rapist's gratification.

In defending promiscuous or casual sex, it has often been observed that not everybody thinks that sex must be an expression of love or affection. Many people, it is said, take the casual view of sex. For them, as I have said, sex is just another kind of pleasure and is permissible in the absence of love or affection. It is quite clear why this casual view does indeed entail the acceptability of promiscuous sex. What is often not realized, however, is that this view of sexual ethics leaves without adequate support the common judgments that are made about pedophilia and rape. I consider each of these two practices in turn.

If sex is morally just like other (pleasurable) activities and bears no special significance, why may it not be enjoyed with children? One common answer is that sex (with an adult)[4] can be harmful to a child. In the most extreme cases, including those involving physical force or those in which an adult copulates with a very small child, physical damage to the child can result. But clearly not all pedophilic acts are of this kind. Many, perhaps most, pedophilic acts are non-penetrative and do not employ physical force. Psychological harm is probably more common than physical damage. It is not clear, however, as a number of authors writing on this topic have noted, to what extent that harm is the result of the sexual encounter itself and to what extent it is the result of the secrecy and taboo that surrounds that sexual activity.[5] Insofar as a thorough embracing of the casual view of sex would eliminate those harms, the defender of this view cannot appeal to them in forming a principled objection to sexual interaction between adults and children. Because a society in which there were no taboos on pedophilia would avoid harm resulting from taboos on such activities and would simultaneously be inclusive of the pedophile's sexual orientation, it has everything to recommend it for defenders of the casual view.[6] At the most, advocates of this view can say that the current psychological harms impose temporary[7] moral constraints on sex with those children who, given their unfortunate puritanical upbringing or circumstances, would experience psychological trauma. Even such children may not be damaged by every kind of sexual interaction with an adult. For example, there is reason to believe that, where the child is a willing participant, the harm is either significantly attenuated or absent.[8]

Here it might be objected that although a child may sometimes appear to be a willing participant in sexual conduct with an adult, it is impossible for a child to give genuine consent to sexual activity.[9] For this reason, it might be argued, it is always wrong to engage in sexual relations with a child. Now, while this claim is entirely plausible on the significance view of sexual ethics, one is hard-pressed to explain how it is compatible with the casual view. What is it about sex, so understood, that a child is unable to consent to it? On this view, sex need carry no special significance and thus there is nothing that a child needs to understand in order to enter into a permissible sexual encounter. In response, it might be suggested that what a child needs to understand are the possible health risks associated with (casual) sex. That response, however, will not suffice to rule out all that those opposed to pedophilia wish to rule out. First, some sexual activities—most especially the noninvasive ones—do not carry significant health risks. Second, where children themselves are not thought competent to evaluate the risks of an activity, it is usually thought that a parent or guardian may, within certain risk limits, make the assessment on the child's behalf. Thus a parent may decide to give a child a taste of alcohol, allow a child to read certain kinds of books, or permit a child to participate in a sport that carries risks. If sex need be no more significant than other such activities, it is hard to see why its risks (especially when, as a result of safe sex, these are relatively small) and not those of the other activities (even when the latter are greater) constitute grounds for categorically excluding children and invalidating the consent which they or their parents give.

There is another consent-related objection that might be raised against pedophilia.[10] It might be argued that given the differences between adults and children, it is not possible for an adult and a child to understand one another's motives for wanting to have sex. The mutual unintelligibility of their motives makes it impossible for each party to know even roughly what the encounter means to the other and the absence of this information compromises the validity of the consent. Although this objection, like the previous one, is thoroughly plausible on the significance view, it lacks force on the casual view. Notice that the absence of mutual intelligibility of motives is not thought to be an objection to those activities with children, such as playing a game, that are not thought to carry the significance attributed to sex by the significance view. A child might be quite oblivious that the adult is playing the game only to give the child pleasure and that the adult may even be losing the game on purpose in order to enhance the child's pleasure or to build the child's sense of self-esteem. Yet, this is not thought to constitute grounds for invalidating a child's ability to consent to game playing with adults. The need for some mutual intelligibility of motive arises only if sex is significant.

Nor is it evident, on the casual view (unless it is coupled with a child-liberationist position), why children need consent at all. If a parent may pressure or force a child into participating in a sport (on grounds of "character-building"), or into going to the opera (on grounds of "learning to appreciate the arts"), why may a parent not coerce or pressure a child into sex? Perhaps a parent believes that treating sex as one does other aspects of life forestalls neurosis in the child and that gaining sexual experience while young is an advantage. If the evidence were sufficiently inconclusive that reasonable people could disagree about whether children really did benefit from an early sexual start, then those defenders of the casual view who also accept paternalism toward children would have to allow parents to decide for their children.

Whether or not interference with a child's freedom is justified, few people think that it is acceptable to interfere with the freedom of adults by, for example, forcing them to take up sport, go to the opera, or eat something (irrespective of whether it would be good for them). Those who accept this, even if they have the casual view of sexual ethics, have grounds for finding rape (of adults) morally defective. To rape people is to force them to do something that they do not want to do. Rape is an unwarranted interference with a person's body and freedom. The problem, for the defenders of the casual view is, that it need be no more serious an interference than would be forcing somebody to eat something, for example. Thus, although the casual view can explain why rape is wrong, it cannot explain why it is a special kind of wrong. One qualification needs to be added. Perhaps a proponent of the casual view could recognize that rape is especially wrong for those who do not share the casual view—that is, for those who believe (mistakenly, according to the casual view) that sex ought to be significant. A suitable analogy would be that of forcing somebody to eat a pork sausage. The seriousness of such an interference would be much greater if the person on whom one forced this meal were a vegetarian (or a Jew or a Muslim) than if he were not. A particular violation of somebody's freedom can be either more or less significant, depending on that person's attitudes. Although some may be willing to accept that rape is especially wrong only when committed against somebody who holds the significance view of sex, many would not. Many feminists, for example, have argued at length for the irrelevance, in rape trials, of a woman's sexual history. But if the casual view is correct, then her sexual history would be evidence—although not conclusive evidence—of her view of sexual ethics. This in turn would be relevant to determining how great a harm the rape was (but not to *whether* it was rape and thus to whether it was harmful). Raping somebody for whom sex has as little significance (of the sort under consideration) as eating a tomato would be like forcing somebody to eat a tomato. Raping somebody for whom sex is deeply significant would be much worse. Although a significance view of sex might also allow such distinctions between the severity of different rapes, it can at least explain why rape of anybody is more serious than forcing somebody to eat a tomato.

CHOOSING BETWEEN THE VIEWS

Is there any way of choosing between the significance and casual views of sex? Some might take the foregoing reflections to speak in favor of or against one of the views. Those who are convinced that promiscuity is morally permissible may be inclined to think that the casual view must be correct because it supports this judgment. Others, who believe that pedophilia is wrong and that rape is a special kind of evil and is unlike other violations of a person's body or autonomy, may think that the significance view is correct given that it can support these judgments.

There are other factors that are also relevant to evaluating each of these views of sexual ethics. Consider first those who speak in favor of the significance view. This view fits well with judgments most people make about forms of intimacy that, although not sexual practices themselves, are not unrelated to the intimacies of sex: (1) casually sharing news of one's venereal disease (a) with a mere acquaintance, or (b) with one's spouse or other close family members; (2) undressing (a) in the street, or (b) in front of one's spouse in the privacy of one's bedroom. Very few people would feel exactly the same about (a) as about (b) in either of these examples. This would suggest that most people think that intimacies are appropriately shared only with those to whom one is close, even if they disagree about just how close one has to be in order to share a certain level of intimacy. The significance view seems to capture an important psychological feature about humans. Although descriptive psychological claims do not entail normative judgments, any moral view that attempted to deny immutable psychological traits characteristic of all (or almost all) humans would be defective.

But are these psychological traits really universal or are they rather cultural products, found only among some peoples? There are examples of societies that are much less restrictive about sex (including sex with children) than is ours, just as there are societies in which there are many more taboos than in ours pertaining to food and eating. It is too easy to assume that the way we feel about sex and food is the way all people do. If so, and if others are better off for their more open views of sex, then the defender of the casual view may have a message of sexual liberation that would be worth heeding.[11] This is not to say that it would be an easy matter (even for an individual, let alone a whole society) to abandon a significance view and thoroughly embrace the casual view. But if the casual view is the preferable one, then even if it would be difficult to adopt it would nonetheless be a view to which people ought to strive. One way to do this would be to rear children with the casual view.

Whether viewing sex as significant is characteristic of all humanity or only of certain human cultures is clearly an empirical issue that psychologists, anthropologists, and others would be best suited to determine. This matter cannot be settled here. In the absence of such a determination and of a convincing argument for one or the other view of sexual ethics, the appropriate response is agnosticism (of the theoretical even if not the practical form). Neither form of agnosticism would permit one to follow *both* views—the one for the pedophilia and rape issues and the other for the promiscuity issue. At least at the theoretical level, the choices we make should be consistent if they are to avoid the comfortable acquiescence to whatever happen to be the current mores. Agnosticism about the correct view of sex, like agnosticism on any other issue, is not to be confused with indifference. One may care deeply about an issue while realizing that the available evidence is insufficient to make a judgment on it. Caring deeply, however, should not stand in the way of a dispassionate assessment of the evidence. There is a great danger that in matters pertaining to current sexual taboos, clear thinking will be in short supply.

Hybrids of the two views may be possible. For instance, it may be thought that sex is not quite like other pleasures, but neither need it be linked to the deepest forms of romantic love. On one such view, it might be sufficient that one *like*[12] (rather than love) somebody in order to copulate. However, no such mixed view would resolve our problem. Any view that took a sufficiently light view of sex that would justify promiscuity would have difficulty ruling out all pedophilia or classifying rape as the *special* wrong it is usually thought to be.

Nor do I think that a non-hybrid intermediate view will be able to drive a moral wedge between promiscuity, on the one hand, and rape and pedophilia, on the other. Such an intermediate view would (as the casual view does) deny that sex must be an expression of romantic affection, but (in common with the significance view) deny that sex is like other pleasures. Although I obviously cannot anticipate every possible way in which such a view might be developed, I find it hard to imagine how any version could distinguish promiscuity from rape and pedophilia. Consider two versions of an allegedly intermediate view that have been put to me.

The first of these[13] is that although sex need not be an expression of romantic affection, it is unlike other pleasures in that it is intimate or private. The latter part of this claim might be understood as being either descriptive or normative. The descriptive claim is that most people prefer to engage in sex (i) with intimates[14] or (ii) away from the view of others. The normative claim is that people *ought* to engage in sex only (i) with intimates or (ii) away from the view of others. If the basis for (some or other of) these claims is that sex is or ought to be a deep expression of a romantic affection, then the view under discussion is either support for or a disguised version of the significance view rather than an alternative intermediate view. I cannot think of other reasons why sex is morally permissible only *between intimates*, but perhaps there is some such reason why sex is or ought to be *private*. If there is, then there would be an intermediate view between the significance and casual views. But what would be wrong, on this intermediate view, with *private* sex between an adult and a willing child? And why would coerced private sex be worse than other kinds of coerced activities in private? I suspect that any plausible answer to these questions would have to appeal to the normative significance of sex as an expression of affection, and any such appeal could not lead to a special condemnation of rape and all pedophilia without also implying a condemnation of promiscuity.

The second version of an allegedly non-hybrid intermediate view that has been suggested to me is that sex is unlike other pleasures because it is "personally involving ([that is,] psycho-dynamically complex)" in ways that other pleasures are not.[15] However, it seems that any interpretation of the view that sex is personally involving would be, or would lend support to, a significance view of sex. It would surely be inappropriate, at least as a moral ideal, to engage in personally involving behaviors with those (such as mere acquaintances) with whom personal involvement (at the relevantly complex or deep level) is not really possible. If that is so, then I cannot see how the second non-hybrid intermediate view can succeed in driving a wedge between promiscuity on the one hand, and rape and pedophilia on the other.

The above conclusions should obviously be extremely troubling to those who approve of promiscuity but who abhor pedophilia and rape. My deliberations show, however, that this should provide little cause for self-satisfaction on the part of those who condemn promiscuity along with rape and all pedophilia. Their moral judgments about these practices may be consistent but it remains an open question whether they are consistently right or consistently wrong. Which it is will depend on which of the rival views of sexual ethics is better. Until that matter is resolved, adherents of both the significance view and the casual view have cause for unease.[16]

NOTES

1. My own view is that if the possibility of procreation has anything to do with the moral acceptability of sex, then the *absence* rather than the presence of such a possibility is a necessary condition for sex's moral acceptability. The foundation for this admittedly unusual view is my argument that coming into existence is always a harm and therefore to bring somebody into existence is always to inflict a harm. It follows that it is procreative rather than non-procreative sex that bears the burden of moral

justification. See my "Why It Is Better Never to Come Into Existence," *American Philosophical Quarterly* 34: 3 (July 1997), 345–55, and *Better Never to Have Been: The Harm of Coming into Existence* (Oxford University Press, 2006).

2. Sexual intercourse with a pre-pubescent child has no procreative possibility. Those opposed to pedophilia, at least in our society, include under the rubric of "pedophilia" not only sex with such children, but also with pubescent children, where procreation is a possibility. I assume, then, that the procreative condition is not the grounds on which they oppose pedophilia.

3. Adherents of the significance view need not take all pedophilia to be wrong. They might think that children (beyond a certain age) *can* understand the full significance of sex. I am thus claiming only that the significance view has a way of arguing that pedophilia is wrong, not that it has to argue in that way.

4. It is interesting that many of those who take pedophilia to be harmful do not have the same reprobation for sex between two people both of whom are (in the relevant sense) children.

5. Alfred Kinsey et al., *Sexual Behavior in the Human Female* (Philadelphia: W. B. Saunders Co., 1953), 120–121; Robert Ehman, "Adult-Child Sex," in *Philosophy and Sex* (New Revised [2nd] Edition), ed. Robert Baker and Frederick Elliston (Buffalo, N.Y.: Prometheus Books, 1984), 436; Igor Primoratz, *Ethics and Sex* (London: Routledge, 1999), 138. A commentator on my paper when I presented it at a conference claimed that there is much evidence to suggest that the harm does not result from the taboo. In support of this claim, she cited Anna Luise Kirkengen's *Inscribed Bodies: Health Impact of Childhood Sexual Abuse* (Dordrecht: Kluwer, 2001). I, however, am unable to find any support for her claim in this work. The book does deal with the adverse effects of sexual interactions with children. However, the question of whether it is the sexual interactions themselves or the taboos against them that cause harm is a specialized question that, as far as I can tell, is not addressed in this book. I mention the source in fairness to my commentator and for the benefit of those readers who wish to examine it for themselves.

6. Allen Buchanan has argued, in the context of a different debate, that the "morality of inclusion" requires that cooperative frameworks be made more inclusive where this is possible without unreasonable cost. (See his "The Morality of Inclusion," *Social Philosophy and Policy* 10: 2 (June 1996): 233–57.) Notice that even those ways of satisfying pedophilic preferences that do not involve actual children—such as child pornography that is either synthesized (that is, without using real models or actors) or is produced by adults being represented as children—are also abhorred, even where adult pornography is not. This suggests that the common abhorrence of pedophilia is not fully explained by the harm it is believed to do to the children involved.

7. That is, until the taboos can be eliminated.

8. T. G. M. Sandfort, "The Argument for Adult-Child Sexual Contact: A Critical Appraisal and New Data," in *The Sexual Abuse of Children: Theory and Research*, vol. 1, ed. William O'Donohue and James H. Geer (Hillsdale, N.J.: Lawrence Erlbaum Associates, 1992); Bruce Rind, Philip Tromovitch, and Robert Bauserman, "A Meta-Analytic Examination of Assumed Properties of Child Sexual Abuse Using College Samples," *Psychological Bulletin* 124: 1 (1998): 22–53.

9. See, for example, David Finkelhor, "What's Wrong with Sex between Adults and Children: Ethics and the Problem of Sexual Abuse," *American Journal of Orthopsychiatry* 49: 4 (1979): 692–97.

10. This objection was raised by an anonymous reviewer for *Public Affairs Quarterly*.

11. Of course, such benefits would have to be offset against the risks of sexually transmitted diseases, or steps would have to be taken within a sexual life governed by the casual view to minimize such risks.

12. In this context, "like" cannot mean "sexually attracted to," because that would be too weak to differentiate it from the pure hedonist view. Instead it would have to mean something like "have psychological affections-less-than-love for."

13. I am grateful to Raja Halwani for putting this to me and for suggesting that I raise and respond to the possibility of a non-hybrid intermediate view.

14. This appears not to be true of the promiscuous unless one stipulates that anybody with whom one has sex is thereby an intimate.

15. This view was suggested to me by an anonymous reviewer for *Public Affairs Quarterly*.

16. An earlier version of this paper was presented at a meeting of the Society for the Philosophy of Sex and Love at the Eastern Division meeting of the American Philosophical Association on December 30, 2001. The author is grateful to the University of Cape Town's Research Committee, as well as the International Science Liaison of the (South African) National Research Foundation for providing funding that enabled him to attend and participate in this meeting.

STUDY QUESTIONS

1. Defend the "casual" view against the charge, leveled by Benatar, that it is incompatible with the claim that sexual relations between an adult and a child as a partner are *always* wrong. Try to do so without cutting back on the moral permissibility of sex without love.

2. "Raping a person for whom sexual activity has merely the significance of eating a tomato would be like forcing someone to eat a tomato." Is this analogy psychologically apt or a misleading piece of rhetoric? Explain your answer. Pay attention, in your deliberations, to the issue of the evidentiary status of a claimant's sexual history in a rape trial (e.g., whether she has had a wildly promiscuous lifestyle or has spent many years working as a prostitute).

3. Benatar writes, "Because a society in which there were no taboos on pedophilia would avoid harm resulting from taboos on such activities and would simultaneously be inclusive of the pedophile's sexual orientation, it has everything to recommend it for defenders of the casual view." Is there any rationale for the mention of sexual orientation in this context? How could Benatar's point be made without employing this concept? What is the "sexual orientation" of which he speaks? Furthermore, is his claim true?

4. Benatar dismisses intermediate philosophies of sex that invoke privacy, intimacy, or the "personally involving" nature of sexuality. Relying on views of sexual ethics expressed elsewhere in this volume (for example, Alan Goldman, Alan Wertheimer, Robin West), try to demarcate some other sort of an intermediate view distinct from these, one that meets his objections.

5. According to Benatar, the "casual" view of sex has difficulty explaining the wrongness of pedophilia and the serious wrongness of rape. But does the "significance" view, according to which sexual activity is morally acceptable only if it expresses reciprocal love,

fare any better? Are rape and pedophilia not wrong, or less wrong, if the participants love each other?

6. Benatar closes by posing the question: Which of the rival views is better? What does "better" mean here? Would an explication or definition of "better" depend on which of the rival views one had prior commitments to? Or is there an independent, theory-neutral standard of "better" to which we might appeal in addressing this question?

IV

Objectification and Consent—
Applied Topics

TWENTY-THREE

"Whether from Reason or Prejudice": Taking Money for Bodily Services

Martha C. Nussbaum

In this provocative and erudite essay, **Martha Nussbaum** *offers an interesting approach to understanding prostitution by drawing analogies between the prostitute and other kinds of workers: the factory laborer, domestic servant, nightclub singer, philosophy professor, masseuse, and her hypothetical "colonoscopy artist." One of Nussbaum's points is that most people sell their bodies, or the use of them, for money, and we do not usually object to this circumstance in itself. Although Nussbaum does express doubts about the coherence of the moral criticism of prostitution, her focus here is largely legal: she attempts to refute, at length, seven arguments that have been proffered for the continuing criminalization of prostitution.*

Martha C. Nussbaum is Ernst Freund Professor of Law and Ethics at the University of Chicago. She is the author of *The Fragility of Goodness* (Cambridge University Press, 1986); *Sex and Social Justice* (Oxford University Press, 1999); *Upheavals of Thought: The Intelligence of Emotions* (Cambridge University Press, 2001); *Hiding from Humanity: Disgust, Shame, and the Law* (Princeton University Press, 2004); and *From Disgust to Humanity: Sexual Orientation and Constitutional Law* (Oxford University Press, 2010). Among her many significant journal articles are "Objectification," *Philosophy and Public Affairs* 24: 4 (1995): 249–91 (reprinted in Alan Soble, ed., *The Philosophy of Sex*, 3rd and 4th editions [Rowman and Littlefield, 1997, 2002]), and (with Kenneth Dover) "Platonic Love and Colorado Law: The Relevance of Ancient Greek Norms to Modern Sexual Controversies," *Virginia Law Review* 80: 7 (1994): 1515–1651. This essay is "'Whether from Reason or Prejudice': Taking Money for Bodily Services," from Nussbaum's *Sex and Social Justice* (Oxford University Press, 1999), 276–98. Original version published in *Journal of Legal Studies* 27: 2 (1998): 693–724. Reprinted with the permission of Martha C. Nussbaum and the University of Chicago Press. © 1998 by The University of Chicago. All rights reserved.

Taking leave of Binod, Durga slowly, deliberately walks towards the shack of Sukhlal the contractor, who stared at her even yesterday and flashed ten-rupee notes.

What else can one do, she argues to herself, except fight for survival? The survival of oneself, one's loved ones, and the hopes that really matter.

—Manik Bandyopadhyay, "A Female Problem at a Low Level" (1963)

If the story is about the peasant wife selling her body, then one must look for the meaning of that in the reality of peasant life. One can't look at it as a crisis of morality, in the sense one would in the case of a middle-class wife.

—Manik Bandyopadhyay, *About This Author's Perspective*

[Both epigraphs are translated from the Bangali by Kalpana Bardhan in *Women, Outcastes, Peasants, and Rebels: A Selection of Bengali Short Stories* (Berkeley: University of California Press, 1990). Bandyopadhyay (1908 56) was a leading Bengali writer who focused on peasant life and issues of class conflict.]

I. BODY SELLERS

All of us, with the exception of the independently wealthy and the unemployed, take money for the use of our body. Professors, factory workers, lawyers, opera singers, prostitutes, doctors, legislators—we all do things with parts of our bodies, for which we receive a wage in return.[1] Some people get good wages and some do not; some have a relatively high degree of control over their working conditions and some have little control; some have many employment options and some have very few. And, some are socially stigmatized and some are not.

The stigmatization of certain occupations may be well founded, based on convincing, well-reasoned arguments. But it may also be based on class prejudice, or stereotypes of race or gender. Stigma may also change rapidly, as these background beliefs and prejudices change. Adam Smith, in *The Wealth of Nations*, tells us that there are "some very agreeable and beautiful talents" that are admirable as long as no pay is taken for them, "but of which the exercise for the sake of gain is considered, whether from reason or prejudice, as a sort of publick prostitution." For this reason, he continues, opera singers, actors, and dancers must be paid an "exorbitant" wage, to compensate them for the stigma involved in using their talents "as the means of subsistence." "Should the publick opinion or prejudice ever alter with regard to such occupations," he concludes, "their pecuniary recompence would quickly diminish."[2] Smith was not altogether right about the opera market,[3] but his discussion is revealing for what it shows us about stigma. Today few professions are more honored than that of opera singer, and yet only two hundred years ago, that public use of one's body for pay was taken to be a kind of prostitution.

Looking back at that time, we now think that the judgments and emotions underlying the stigmatization of singers were irrational and objectionable, like prejudices against members of different classes and races. (I shall shortly be saying more about what I think those reasons were.) Nor do we see the slightest reason to suppose that the unpaid artist is a purer and truer artist than the paid artist. We think it entirely right and reasonable that high art should receive a high salary. If a producer of opera should take the position that singers should not be paid, on the grounds that receiving money for the use of their talents involves an illegitimate form of commodification and even market alienation of those talents, we would think that this producer was a slick exploiter, out to make a profit from the ill treatment of vulnerable and impressionable artists.[4] On the whole we think that far from cheapening or ruining talents, the presence of a contract guarantees conditions within which the artist can develop her art with sufficient leisure and confidence to reach the highest level of artistic production.[5]

It is widely believed, however, that taking money or entering into contracts in connection with the use of one's sexual and/or reproductive capacities is genuinely bad. Feminist arguments about prostitution, surrogate motherhood, and even marriage contracts standardly portray financial transactions in the area of female sexuality as demeaning to women and as involving a damaging commodification and market alienation of women's sexual and reproductive capacities.[6] The social meaning of these transactions is said to be both that these capacities are turned into objects for the use and control of men and also that the activities themselves are being turned into commodities, and thereby robbed of the type of value they have at their best.

One question we shall have to face is whether these descriptions of our current judgments and intuitions are correct. But even if they are, what does this tell us? Many things and people have been stigmatized in our nation's history, often for very bad reasons. An account of the actual social meaning of a practice is therefore just a door that opens onto the large arena of moral and legal evaluation. It invites us to raise Adam Smith's question: Are these current beliefs the result of reason or prejudice? Can they be defended by compelling moral arguments? And, even if they can, are these the type of moral argument that can properly be a basis for a legal restriction? Smith, like his Greek and Roman Stoic forebears, understood that the evaluations that ground emotional responses and ascriptions of social meaning in a society are frequently corrupt— deformed by self-interest, resentment, and mere unthinking habit. The task he undertook, in *The Theory of Moral Sentiments*, was to devise procedures and strategies of argument through which one might separate the rationally defensible emotions from the irrational and prejudiced. In so proceeding, Smith and the Stoics were correct. Social meaning does no work on its own: It offers an invitation to normative moral and political philosophy.

My aim in this essay will be to investigate the question of sexual "commodification" by focusing on the example of prostitution.[7] I argue that a fruitful debate about the morality and legality of prostitution should begin from a twofold starting point: from a broader analysis of our beliefs and practices with regard to taking pay for the use of the body, and from a broader awareness of the options and choices available to poor working women. The former inquiry suggests that at least some of our beliefs about prostitution are as irrational as the beliefs Smith reports about singers; it will therefore help us to identify the elements in prostitution that are genuinely problematic. Most, though not all, of the genuinely problematic elements turn out to be common to a wide range of activities engaged in by poor working women, and the second inquiry suggests that many of women's employment choices are so heavily constrained by poor options that they are hardly choices at all. I think that this should bother us—and that the fact that a woman with plenty of choices becomes a prostitute should not bother us provided there are sufficient safeguards against abuse and disease, safeguards of a type that legalization would make possible.

It is therefore my conclusion that the most urgent issue raised by prostitution is that of employment opportunities for working women and their control over the conditions of their employment. The legalization of prostitution, far from promoting the demise of love, is likely to make things a little better for women who have too few options to begin with.[8] The really helpful thing for feminists to ponder, if they deplore the nature of these options, will be how to promote expansion in the option set, through education, skills training, and job creation. These unsexy topics are not common themes in U.S. feminist philosophy, but they are inevitable in any practical project dealing with prostitutes and their female children.[9] This suggests that at least some of our feminist theory may be insufficiently grounded in the reality of working-class lives and too focused on sexuality as an issue in its own right, as if it could be extricated from the fabric of poor people's attempts to survive.

II. STIGMA AND WAGE LABOR

Why were opera singers stigmatized? If we begin with this question, we can move on to prostitution with expanded insight. Although we can hardly provide more than a sketch of the background here, we can confidently say that two common cultural beliefs played a role. First, throughout much of the history of modern Europe—as, indeed, in ancient Greece—there was a common aristocratic prejudice against earning wages. The ancient Greek gentleman was characterized by "leisure"—

meaning that he did not have to work for a living. Aristotle reproved the Athenian democracy for allowing such base types as farmers and craftsmen to vote, because, in his view, the unleisured character of their daily activities and their inevitable preoccupation with gain would pervert their political judgment, making them grasping and small-minded.[10] The fact that the Sophists typically took money for their rhetorical and philosophical teaching made them deeply suspect in the eyes of such aristocrats.[11] Much the same view played a role in the medieval Church, where it was controversial whether one ought to offer p᾽ ᾽osophical instruction for pay.[12] Bernard of Clairvaux, for example, held that taking fees for education is a "base occupation" (*turpis quaestus*). (Apparently he did not think this true of all wage labor but only where it involved deep spiritual things.)

Such views about wage labor remained closely linked to class privilege in modern Europe and exercised great power well into the twentieth century. Any reader of English novels will be able to produce many examples of the view that a gentleman does not earn wages, and that someone who does is too preoccupied with the baser things in life, and therefore base himself. Such views were a prominent source of prejudice against Jews, who, not having the same land rights as Christians, had no choice but to earn their living. Even in this century, in the United States, Edith Wharton shows that these attitudes were still firmly entrenched. Lily Bart, impoverished heroine of *The House of Mirth* (1905), is discussing her situation with her friend Gus Trenor. He praises the investment tips he has gotten from Rosedale, a Jewish Wall Street investments expert whose wealth has given him entry into the world of impoverished aristocrats who both use and despise him. Trenor urges Lily to encourage Rosedale's advances: "The man is mad to know the people who don't want to know him, and when a fellow's in that state, there is nothing he won't do for the first woman who takes him up." Lily dismisses the idea, calling Rosedale "impossible" and thinking silently of his "intrusive personality." Trenor replies: "Oh, hang it—because he's fat and shiny and has a shoppy manner! . . . A few years from now he'll be in it whether we want him or not, and then he won't be giving away a half-a-million tip for a dinner!" In the telling phrase "a shoppy manner," we see the age-old aristocratic prejudice against wage work, so deeply implicated in stereotypes of Jews as pushy, intrusive, and lacking in grace.

To this example we may add a moment in the film *Chariots of Fire* when the Jewish sprinter hires a professional coach to help him win. This introduction of money into the gentlemanly domain of sport shocks the head of his college, who suggests to him that as a Jew he does not understand the true spirit of English athletics. Genteel amateurism is the mark of the gentleman, and amateurism demands, above all, not earning or dealing in money. It may also imply not trying too hard, as if it were really one's main concern in life, but this attitude appears to be closely related to the idea that the gentleman does not need the activity because he has his living provided already; so the rejection of hard work is a corollary of the rejection of the tradesman. (Even today in Britain, such attitudes have not totally disappeared; people from aristocratic backgrounds frequently frown on working too hard at one's scholarly or athletic pursuits, as if this betrays a kind of base tradesmanly mentality.)

What is worth noting about these prejudices is that they do not attach to activities themselves, as such, but, rather, to the use of these activities to make money. To be a scholar, to be a musician, to be a fine athlete, to be an actor even, is fine—so long as one does it as an amateur. But what does this mean? It means that those with inherited wealth[13] can perform these activities without stigma, and others cannot. In England in the nineteenth century, it meant that the gentry could perform those activities, and Jews could not. This informs us that we need to scrutinize all our social views about money making and alleged commodification with extra care, for they are likely to embed class prejudices that are unjust to working people.

Intersecting with this belief, in the opera singer example, is another: that it is shameful to display one's body to strangers in public, especially in the expression of passionate emotion. The anxiety about actors, dancers, and singers reported by Smith is surely of a piece with the more general anxiety about the body, especially the female body, that has been a large part of the history of quite a few cultures. Thus, in much of India until very recently (and in some parts still), it is considered inappropriate for a woman of good family to dance in public; when Rabindranath Tagore included middle-class women in his theatrical productions early in the twentieth century, it was a surprising and somewhat shocking move. Similarly in the West: The female body should be covered and not displayed, although in some respects these conditions could be relaxed among friends and acquaintances. Female singers were considered unacceptable during the early history of opera; indeed, they were just displacing the *castrati* during Smith's lifetime, and they were widely perceived as immoral women.[14] Male actors, singers, and dancers suffered too; and clearly Smith means to include both sexes. Until very recently such performers were considered to be a kind of gypsy, too fleshy and physical, unsuited for polite company. The distaste was compounded by a distaste for, or at least a profound ambivalence about, the emotions that it was, and is, the business of these performers to portray. In short, such attitudes betray an anxiety about the body, and about strong passion, that we are now likely to think irrational, even though we may continue to share them at times; certainly we are not likely to think them a good basis for public policy.

When we consider our views about sexual and reproductive services, then, we must be on our guard against two types of irrationality: aristocratic class prejudice and fear of the body and its passions.

III. SIX TYPES OF BODILY SERVICE

Prostitution is not a single thing. It can only be well understood in its social and historical context. Ancient Greek *hetairai*, such as Pericles' mistress Aspasia, have very little in common with a modern call girl.[15] Even more important, within a given culture there are always many different types and levels of prostitution: In ancient Greece, the *hetaira*, the brothel prostitute, the streetwalker; in modern America, the self-employed call girl, the brothel prostitute, the streetwalker (and each of these at various levels of independence and economic success). It is also evident that most cultures contain a continuum of relations between women and men (or between same-sex pairs) that have a commercial aspect—ranging from the admitted case of prostitution to cases of marriage for money, going on an expensive date when it is evident that sexual favors are expected at the other end, and so forth. In most cultures, marriage itself has a prominent commercial aspect: The prominence of dowry murder in contemporary Indian culture, for example, testifies to the degree to which a woman is valued, above all, for the financial benefits one can extract from her family.[16] Let us, however, focus for the time being on contemporary America (with some digressions on India), on female prostitution only, and on explicitly commercial relations of the sort that are illegal under current law.

It will be illuminating to consider the prostitute by situating her in relation to several other women who take money for bodily services: (1) A factory worker in the Perdue chicken factory, who plucks feathers from nearly frozen chickens. (2) A domestic servant in a prosperous upper-middle-class house. (3) A nightclub singer in middle-range clubs, who sings (often) songs requested by the patrons. (4) A professor of philosophy, who gets paid for lecturing and writing. (5) A skilled masseuse, employed by a health club (with no sexual services on the side). (6) A person whom I'll call the "colonoscopy artist": She gets paid for having her colon examined with the latest instruments, in order to test out their range and capability.[17] By considering similarities and differences between the prostitute and these other bodily actors, we will make progress in identifying the distinctive features of prostitution as a form of bodily service.

Note that nowhere in this comparison am I addressing the issue of child prostitution or nonconsensual prostitution (e.g., young women sold into prostitution by their parents, forcible drugging and abduction, etc.). Insofar as these features appear to be involved in the international prostitution market, I do not address them here, although I shall comment on them later. I address only the type of choice to be a prostitute that is made by a woman over the age of consent, frequently in a situation of great economic duress.

The Prostitute and the Factory Worker

Both prostitution and factory work are usually low-paid jobs, but in many instances a woman faced with the choice can (at least over the short haul) make more money in prostitution than in this sort of factory work. (This would probably be even more true if prostitution were legalized and the role of pimps thereby restricted, though the removal of risk and some stigma might at the same time depress wages, to some extent offsetting that advantage for the prostitute.) Both face health risks, but the health risk in prostitution can be very much reduced by legalization and regulation, whereas the particular type of work the factory worker is performing carries a high risk of nerve damage in the hands, a fact about it that appears unlikely to change. The prostitute may well have better working hours and conditions than the factory worker; especially in a legalized regime, she may have much more control over her working conditions. She has a degree of choice about which clients she accepts and what activities she performs, whereas the factory worker has no choices but must perform the same motions again and again for years. The prostitute also performs a service that requires skill and responsiveness to new situations, whereas the factory worker's repetitive motion exercises relatively little human skill[18] and contains no variety.

On the other side, the factory worker is unlikely to be the target of violence, whereas the prostitute needs—and does not always get—protection against violent customers. (Again, this situation can be improved by legalization: Prostitutes in the Netherlands have a call button wired up to the police.) This factory worker's occupation, moreover, has no clear connection with stereotypes of gender—though this might not have been the case. In many parts of the world, manual labor is strictly segmented by sex, and more routinized, low-skill tasks are given to women.[19] The prostitute's activity does rely on stereotypes of women as sluttish and immoral, and it may in turn perpetuate such stereotypes. The factory worker suffers no invasion of her internal private space, whereas the prostitute's activity involves such (consensual) invasion. Finally, the prostitute suffers from social stigma, whereas the factory worker does not—at least among people of her own social class. (I shall return to this issue, asking whether stigma too can be addressed by legalization.) For all these reasons, many women, faced with the choice between factory work and prostitution, choose factory work, despite its other disadvantages.

The Prostitute and the Domestic Servant

In domestic service as in prostitution, one is hired by a client and one must do what that client wants, or fail at the job. In both, one has a limited degree of latitude to exercise skills as one sees fit, and both jobs require the exercise of some developed bodily skills. In both, one is at risk of enduring bad behavior from one's client, although the prostitute is more likely to encounter physical violence. Certainly both are traditionally professions that enjoy low respect, both in society generally and from the client. Domestic service on the whole is likely to have worse hours and lower pay than (at least many types of) prostitution, but it probably contains fewer health risks. It also involves no invasion of intimate bodily space, as prostitution (consensually) does.

Both prostitution and domestic service are associated with a type of social stigma. In the case of domestic service, the stigma is, first, related to class: It is socially coded as an occupation only for the lowest classes.[20] Domestic servants are in a vast majority of cases female, so it becomes coded by sex. In the United States, domestic service is very often racially coded as well. Not only in the South, but also in many parts of the urban North, the labor market has frequently produced a clustering of African-American women in these low-paying occupations. In my home in suburban Philadelphia in the 1950s and 1960s, the only African-Americans we saw were domestic servants, and the only domestic servants we saw were African-American. The perception of the occupation as associated with racial stigma ran very deep, producing difficult tensions and resentments that made domestic service seem to be incompatible with dignity and self-respect. (It need not be, clearly, and I shall return to this.)

The Prostitute and the Nightclub Singer

Both of these people use their bodies to provide pleasure, and the customer's pleasure is the primary goal of what they do.[21] This does not mean that a good deal of skill and art is not involved, and in both cases it usually is. Both have to respond to requests from the customer, although (in varying degrees depending on the case) both may also be free to improvise or to make suggestions. Both may be paid more or less and have better or worse working conditions, more or less control over what they do.

How do they differ? The prostitute faces health risks and risks of violence not faced by the singer. She also allows her bodily space to be invaded, as the singer does not. It may also be that prostitution is always a cheap form of an activity that has a higher better form, whereas this need not be the case in popular vocal performance (though of course it might be).[22] The nightclub singer, furthermore, does not appear to be participating in, or perpetuating, any type of gender hierarchy—although in former times this would not have been the case, singers being seen as "a type of publick prostitute" and their activity associated, often, with anxiety about the control of female sexuality. Finally, there is no (great) moral stigma attached to being a nightclub singer, although at one time there certainly was.

The Prostitute and the Professor of Philosophy

These two figures have a very interesting similarity: Both provide bodily services in areas that are generally thought to be especially intimate and definitive of selfhood. Just as the prostitute takes money for sex, which is commonly thought to be an area of intimate self-expression, so the professor takes money for thinking and writing about what she thinks—about morality, emotion, the nature of knowledge, whatever— all parts of a human being's intimate search for understanding of the world and oneself. It was precisely for this reason that the medieval thinkers I have mentioned saw such a moral problem about philosophizing for money: It should be a pure spiritual gift, and it is degraded by the receipt of a wage. The fact that we do not think that the professor (even one who regularly holds out for the highest salary offered) thereby alienates her mind, or turns her thoughts into commodities—even when she writes a paper for a specific conference or volume—should put us on our guard about making similar conclusions in the case of the prostitute.

There are other similarities: In both cases, the performance involves interaction with others, and the form of the interaction is not altogether controlled by the person. In both cases there is at least an element of producing pleasure or satisfaction (note the prominent role of teaching evaluations in the employment and promotion of professors), although in philosophy there is also a countervailing tradition of thinking that the goal of the interaction is to produce dissatisfaction and unease. (Socrates would not have received tenure in a modern university.) It may appear at first that the intimate bodily space of the professor is not invaded—but we should ask about this. When someone's unanticipated argument goes into one's mind, isn't this both intimate and bodily (and far less consensual, often, than the penetration of prostitute by customer)? Both performances involve skill. It might plausibly be argued that the professor's involves a more developed skill, or at least a more expensive training— but we should be cautious here. Our culture is all too ready to think that sex involves no skill and is simply "natural," a view that is surely false and is not even seriously entertained by many cultures.[23]

The salary of the professor, and her working conditions, are usually a great deal better than those of (all but the most elite) prostitutes. The professor has a fair amount of control over the structure of her day and her working environment, although she also has fixed mandatory duties, as the prostitute, when self-employed, does not. If the professor is in a nation that protects academic freedom, she has considerable control over what she thinks and writes, although fads, trends, and peer pressure surely constrain her to some extent. The prostitute's need to please her customer is usually more exigent and permits less choice. In this way, she is more like the professor of philosophy in Cuba than like the U.S. counterpart[24] —but the Cuban professor appears to be worse off, because she cannot say what she really thinks even when off the job. Finally, the professor of philosophy, if a female, both enjoys reasonably high respect in the community and also might be thought to bring credit to all women in that she succeeds at an activity commonly thought to be the preserve only of males. She thus subverts traditional gender hierarchy whereas the prostitute, while suffering stigma herself, may be thought to perpetuate gender hierarchy.

The Prostitute and the Masseuse

These two bodily actors seem very closely related. Both use a skill to produce bodily satisfaction in the client. Unlike the nightclub singer, both do this through a type of bodily contact with the client. Both need to be responsive to what the client wants, and to a large degree take direction from the client as to how to handle his or her body. The bodily contact involved is rather intimate, although the internal space of the masseuse is not invaded. The type of bodily pleasure produced by the masseuse may certainly have an erotic element, although in the type of "respectable" masseuse I am considering, it is not directly sexual.

The difference is primarily one of respectability. Practitioners of massage have fought for, and have to a large extent won, the right to be considered dignified professionals who exercise a skill. Their trade is legal; it is not stigmatized. And people generally do not believe that they degrade their bodies or turn their bodies into commodities by using their bodies to give pleasure to customers. They have positioned themselves alongside physical therapists and medical practitioners, dissociating themselves from the erotic dimension of their activity. As a consequence of this successful self-positioning, they enjoy better working hours, better pay, and more respect than most prostitutes. What is the difference, we might ask? One is having sex, and the other is not. But what sort of difference is this? Is it a difference we want to defend? Are our reasons for thinking it so crucial really reasons, or vestiges of moral prejudice? A number of distinct beliefs enter in at this point: the belief that women should not have sex with strangers; the belief that commercial sex is inherently degrading and makes a woman a degraded woman; the belief that women should not have to have sex with strangers if they do not want to, and in general should have the option to refuse sex with anyone they do not really choose. Some of these beliefs are worth defending and some are not. (I shall argue that the issue of choice is the really important one.) We need to sort them out and to make sure that our policies are not motivated by views we are not really willing to defend.

The Prostitute and the Colonoscopy Artist

I have included this hypothetical occupation for a reason that should by now be evident: It involves the consensual invasion of one's bodily space. (The example is not so hypothetical, either: Medical students need models when they are learning to perform internal exams, and young actors do earn a living playing such roles.)[25] The colonoscopy artist uses her skill at tolerating the fiber-optic probe without anesthesia to make a living. In the process, she permits an aperture of her body to be penetrated by another person's activity—and, we might add, far more deeply penetrated than is generally the case in sex. She runs some bodily risk, because she is being used to test untested instruments, and she will probably have to fast and empty her colon regularly enough to incur some malnutrition and some damage to her excretory function. Her wages may not be very good—for this is probably not a profession characterized by what Smith called "the beauty and rarity of talents," and it may also involve some stigma given that people are inclined to be disgusted by the thought of intestines.

And yet, on the whole, we do not think that this is a base trade, or one that makes the woman who does it a fallen woman. We might want to ban or regulate it if we thought it was too dangerous, but we would not be moved to ban it for moral reasons. Why not? Some people would point to the fact that it does not either reflect or perpetuate gender hierarchy, and this is certainly true. (Even if her being a woman is crucial to her selection for the job—they need to study, for example, both male and female colons—it will not be for reasons that seem connected with the subordination of women.) But surely a far greater part of the difference is made by the fact that most people do not think anal penetration by a doctor in the context of a medical procedure is immoral,[26] whereas lots of people do think that vaginal or anal penetration in the context of sexual relations is (except under very special circumstances) immoral, and that a woman who goes in for that is therefore an immoral and base woman.

IV. SEX AND STIGMA

Prostitution, we now see, has many features that link it with other forms of bodily service. It differs from these other activities in many subtle ways, but the biggest difference consists in the fact that it is, today, more widely stigmatized. Professors no longer get told that selling their teaching is a *turpis quaestus*. Opera singers no longer get told that they are unacceptable in polite society. Even the masseuse has won respect as a skilled professional. What is different about prostitution? Two factors stand out as sources of stigma. One is that prostitution is widely held to be immoral; the other is that prostitution (frequently at least) is bound up with gender hierarchy, with ideas that women and their sexuality are in need of male domination and control, and the related idea that women should be available to men to provide an outlet for their sexual desires. The immorality view would be hard to defend today as a justification for the legal regulation of prostitution, and perhaps even for its moral denunciation. People thought prostitution was immoral because they thought nonreproductive and especially extramarital sex was immoral; the prostitute was seen, typically, as a dangerous figure whose whole career was given over to lust. But female lust was (and still often is) commonly seen as bad and dangerous, so prostitution was seen as bad and dangerous. Some people would still defend these views today, but it seems inconsistent to do so if one is not prepared to repudiate other forms of nonmarital sexual activity on an equal basis. We have to grant, I think, that the most common reason for the stigma attaching to prostitution is a weak reason, at least as a public reason: a moralistic view about female sexuality that is rarely consistently applied (to premarital sex, for example), and that seems unable to justify restriction on the activities of citizens who have different views of what is good and proper. At any rate, it seems hard to use the stigma so incurred to justify perpetuating stigma through criminalization unless one is prepared to accept a wide range of laws that interfere with chosen consensual activities, something that most feminist attackers of prostitution rarely wish to do.

More promising as a source of good moral arguments might be the stigma incurred by the connection of prostitution with gender hierarchy. But what is the connection, and how exactly does gender hierarchy explain pervasive stigma? It is only a small minority of people for whom prostitution is viewed in a negative light because of its collaboration with male supremacy; for only a small minority of people at any time have been reflective feminists, concerned with the eradication of inequality. Such people will view the prostitute as they view veiled women, or women in *purdah*: with sympathetic anger, as victims of an unjust system. This reflective feminist critique, then, does not explain why prostitutes are actually stigmatized and held in disdain—both because it is not pervasive enough and because it leads to sympathy rather than to disdain.

The way that gender hierarchy actually explains stigma is a very different way, a way that turns out in the end to be just another form of the immorality charge. People committed to gender hierarchy and determined to ensure that the dangerous sexuality of women is controlled by men, frequently have viewed the prostitute, a sexually active woman, as a threat to male control of women. They therefore become determined either to repress the occupation itself by criminalization or, if they also think that male sexuality needs such an outlet and that this outlet ultimately defends marriage by giving male desire a safely debased outlet, to keep it within bounds by close regulation. (Criminalization and regulation are not straightforwardly opposed; they can be closely related strategies. Similarly, prostitution is generally conceived as not the enemy but the ally of marriage: The two are complementary ways of controlling women's sexuality.) The result is that social meaning is deployed in order that female sexuality will be kept in bounds carefully set by men. The stigma attached to the prostitute is an integral part of such bounding.

A valuable illustration of this thesis is given by Alain Corbin's valuable and careful study of prostitutes in France in the late nineteenth century.[27] Corbin shows that the interest in the legal regulation of prostitution was justified by the alleged public interest in reining in and making submissive a dangerous female sexuality that was always potentially dangerous to marriage and social order. Kept in carefully supervised houses known as *maisons de tolérance*, prostitutes were known by the revealing name of *filles soumises*, a phrase that most obviously designated them as registered, "subjugated" to the law, but that also connoted their controlled and confined status. What this meant was that they were controlled and confined so that they themselves could provide a safe outlet for desires that threatened to disrupt the social order. The underlying aim of the regulationist project, argues Corbin (with ample documentation), was "the total repression of sexuality."[28] Regulationists tirelessly cited St. Augustine's dictum: "Abolish the prostitutes and the passions will overthrow the world; give them the rank of honest women and infamy and dishonor will blacken the universe" (*De ordine* 2.4.12). In other words, stigma has to be attached to prostitutes because of the necessary hierarchy that requires morality to subjugate vice, and the male the female, seen as an occasion and cause of vice. Bounding the prostitute off from the "good woman," the wife whose sexuality is monogamous and aimed at reproduction, creates a system that maintains male control over female desire.[29]

This attitude to prostitution has modern parallels. One instructive example is from Thailand in the 1950s, when Field Marshal Sarit Thanarat began a campaign of social purification, holding that "uncleanliness and social impropriety . . . led to the erosion of social orderliness. . . ."[30] In theory, Thanarat's aim was to criminalize prostitution by the imposition of prison terms and stiff fines; in practice, the result was a system of medical examination and "moral rehabilitation" that shifted the focus of public blame from the procurers and traffickers to prostitutes themselves. Unlike the French system, the Thai system did not encourage registered prostitution, but it was similar in its public message that the problem of prostitution is a problem of "bad" women, and in its reinforcement of the message that female sexuality is a cause of social disruption unless tightly controlled.

In short, sex hierarchy causes stigma, commonly, not through feminist critique but through a far more questionable set of social meanings, meanings that anyone concerned with justice for women should call into question. For it is these same meanings that are also used to justify the seclusion of women, the veiling of women, the genital mutilation of women. The view boils down to the view that women are essentially immoral and dangerous and will be kept in control by men only if men carefully engineer things so that they do not get out of bounds. The prostitute, being seen as the uncontrolled and sexually free woman, is in this picture seen as particularly dangerous, both necessary to society and in need of constant subjugation. As an honest woman, a woman of dignity, she will wreck society. As a *fille soumise*, her reputation in the dirt, she may be tolerated for the service she provides (or, in the Thai case, she may provide an engrossing public spectacle of "moral rehabilitation").

All this diverts attention from some very serious crimes, such as the use of kidnapping, coercion, and fraud to entice women into prostitution. For these reasons, international human rights organizations, such as Human Rights Watch and Amnesty International, have avoided taking a stand against prostitution as such and have focused their energies on the issue of trafficking and financial coercion.[31]

It appears, then, that the stigma associated with prostitution has an origin that feminists have good reason to connect with unjust background conditions and to decry as both unequal and irrational, based on a hysterical fear of women's unfettered sexuality. There may be other good arguments against the legality of prostitution, but the existence of widespread stigma all by itself does not appear to be among them. As long as prostitution is stigmatized, people are injured by that stigmatization, and it is a real injury to a person not to have dignity and self-respect in her own society. But that real injury (as with the comparable real injury to the dignity and self-respect of interracial couples, or of lesbians and gay men) is not best handled by continued legal strictures against the prostitute and can be better dealt with in other ways (e.g., by fighting discrimination against these people and taking measures to promote their dignity). As the Supreme Court said in a mixed-race custody case, "Private biases may be outside the reach of the law, but the law cannot, directly or indirectly, give them effect."[32]

V. CRIMINALIZATION: SEVEN ARGUMENTS

Pervasive stigma itself, then, does not appear to provide a good reason for the continued criminalization of prostitution, any more than it does for the illegality of interracial marriage. Nor does the stigma in question even appear to ground a sound *moral* argument against prostitution. This is not, however, the end of the issue. There are a number of other significant arguments that have been made to support criminalization. With our six related cases in mind, let us now turn to those arguments.

(1) *Prostitution involves health risks and risks of violence.* To this we can make two replies. First, insofar as this is true, as it clearly is, the problem is made much worse by the illegality of prostitution, which prevents adequate supervision, encourages the control of pimps, and discourages health checking. As Corbin shows, regimes of legal but regulated prosti-

tution have not always done well by women: The health checkups of the *filles soumises* were ludicrously brief and inadequate.[33] But there is no reason why one cannot focus on the goal of adequate health checks, and some European nations have done reasonably well in this area.[34] The legal brothels in Nevada have had no reported cases of AIDS.[35] Certainly risks of violence can be far better controlled when the police are the prostitute's ally rather than her oppressor.

To the extent to which risks remain an inevitable part of the way of life, we must now ask what general view of the legality of risky undertakings we wish to defend. Do we ever want to rule out risky bargains simply because they harm the agent? Or do we require a showing of harm to others (as might be possible in the case of gambling, for example)? Whatever position we take on this complicated question, we will almost certainly be led to conclude that prostitution lies well within the domain of the legally acceptable, for it is certainly far less risky than boxing, another activity in which working-class people try to survive and flourish by subjecting their bodies to some risk of harm. There is a stronger case for paternalistic regulation of boxing than of prostitution, and externalities (the glorification of violence as example to the young) make boxing at least as morally problematic and probably more so. And yet I would not defend the criminalization of boxing, and I doubt that very many Americans would either. Sensible regulation of both prostitution and boxing, by contrast, seems reasonable and compatible with personal liberty.

In the international arena, many problems of this type stem from the use of force and fraud to induce women to enter prostitution, frequently at a very young age and in a strange country where they have no civil rights. An especially common destination, for example, is Thailand, and an especially common source is Burma, where the devastation of the rural economy has left many young women an easy mark for promises of domestic service elsewhere. Driven by customers' fears of HIV, the trade has focused on increasingly young girls from increasingly remote regions. Human rights interviewers have concluded that large numbers of these women were unaware of what they would be doing when they left their country and are kept there through both economic and physical coercion. (In many cases, family members have received payments, which then become a "debt" that the girl has to pay off.)[36] These circumstances, terrible in themselves, set the stage for other forms of risk and/or violence. Fifty to seventy percent of the women and girls interviewed by Human Rights Watch were HIV positive; discriminatory arrests and deportations are frequently accompanied by abuse in police custody. All these problems are magnified by the punitive attitude of the police and government toward these women as prostitutes or illegal aliens or both, although under both national and international law trafficking victims are exempt from legal penalty and are guaranteed safe repatriation to their country of origin. This situation clearly deserves both moral condemnation and international legal pressure, but it is made worse by the illegality of prostitution itself.

(2) *The prostitute has no autonomy; her activities are controlled by others.* This argument[37] does not distinguish prostitution from very many types of bodily service performed by working-class women. The factory worker does far worse on the scale of autonomy, and the domestic servant no better. I think this point expresses a legitimate moral concern. A person's life seems deficient in flourishing if it consists only of a form of work that is totally out of the control and direction of the person herself. Marx rightly associated that kind of labor with a deficient realization of full humanity and (invoking Aristotle) persuasively argued that a flourishing human life probably requires some kind of use of one's own reasoning in the planning and execution of one's own work.[38] But that is a pervasive problem of labor in the modern world, not a problem peculiar to prostitution as such. It certainly does not help the problem to criminalize prostitution—any more than it would be to criminalize factory work or domestic service. A woman will not exactly achieve more control and "truly human functioning" by becoming unemployed. What we should instead think about are ways to promote more control over choice of activities, more variety, and more general humanity in the types of work that are actually available to people with little education and few options. That would be a lot more helpful than removing one of the options they actually have.

(3) *Prostitution involves the invasion of one's intimate bodily space.* This argument[39] does not seem to support legal regulation of prostitution, provided that as the invasion in question is consensual—that is, that the prostitute is not kidnapped, or fraudulently enticed, or a child beneath the age of consent, or under duress against leaving if she should choose to leave. In this sense prostitution is quite unlike sexual harassment and rape, and far more like the activity of the colonoscopy artist—not to everyone's taste, and involving a surrender of bodily privacy that some will find repellant—but not for that reason necessarily bad, either for self or others. The argument does not even appear to support a moral criticism of prostitution unless one is prepared to make a moral criticism of all sexual contact that does not involve love or marriage.

(4) *Prostitution makes it harder for people to form relationships of intimacy and commitment.* This argument is prominently made by Elizabeth Anderson, in defense of the criminalization of prostitution.[40] The first question we should ask is, Is this true? People still appear to fall in love in the Netherlands and Germany and Sweden; they also fell in love in ancient Athens, where prostitution was not only legal but also, probably, publicly subsidized.[41] One type of relationship does not, in fact, appear to remove the need for the other—any more than a Jackie Collins novel removes the desire to read Proust. Proust has a specific type of value that is

by no means found in Jackie Collins, so people who want that value will continue to seek out Proust, and there is no reason to think that the presence of Jackie Collins on the bookstand will confuse Proust lovers and make them think that Proust is really like Jackie Collins. So, too, one supposes, with love in the Netherlands: People who want relationships of intimacy and commitment continue to seek them out for the special value they provide, and they do not have much trouble telling the difference between one sort of relationship and another, despite the availability of both.

Second, one should ask which women Anderson has in mind. Is she saying that the criminalization of prostitution would facilitate the formation of love relationships on the part of the women who were (or would have been) prostitutes? Or, is she saying that the unavailability of prostitution as an option for working-class women would make it easier for romantic middle-class women to have the relationships they desire? The former claim is implausible, because it is hard to see how reinforcing the stigma against prostitutes, or preventing some poor women from taking one of the few employment options they might have, would be likely to improve their human relations.[42] The latter claim might possibly be true (though it is hardly obvious), but it seems a repugnant idea, which I am sure Anderson would not endorse, that we should make poor women poorer so that middle-class women can find love. Third, one should ask Anderson whether she is prepared to endorse the large number of arguments of this form that might plausibly be made in the realm of popular culture—and, if not, whether she has any way of showing how she could reject those as involving an unacceptable infringement of liberty and yet allowing the argument about prostitution that she endorses. For it seems plausible that making rock music illegal would increase the likelihood that people would listen to Mozart and Beethoven; that making Jackie Collins illegal would make it more likely that people would turn to Joyce Carol Oates; that making commercial advertising illegal would make it more likely that we would appraise products with high-minded ideas of value in our minds; that making television illegal would improve children's reading skills. What is certain, however, is that we would and do utterly reject those ideas (we do not even seriously entertain them) because we do not want to live in Plato's *Republic*, with our cultural options dictated by a group of wise guardians, however genuinely sound their judgments may be.[43]

(5) *The prostitute alienates her sexuality on the market; she turns her sexual organs and acts into commodities.*[44] Is this true? It seems implausible to claim that the prostitute alienates her sexuality just on the grounds that she provides sexual services to a client for a fee. Does the singer alienate her voice, or the professor her mind? The prostitute still has her sexuality; she can use it on her own, apart from the relationship with the client, just as the domestic servant may cook for her family and clean her own

house.[45] She can also cease to be a prostitute, and her sexuality will still be with her, and hers, if she does. So she has not even given anyone a monopoly on those services, far less given them over into someone else's hands. The real issue that separates her from the professor and the singer seems to be the degree of choice she exercises over the acts she performs. But is even this a special issue for the prostitute, any more than it is for the factory worker or the domestic servant or the colonoscopy artist—all of whom choose to enter trades in which they will not have a great deal of say over what they do or (within limits) how they do it? Freedom to choose how one works is a luxury, highly desirable indeed, but a feature of few jobs that nonaffluent people perform.

As for the claim that the prostitute turns her sexuality into a commodity, we must ask what that means. If it means only that she accepts a fee for sexual services, then that is obvious, but nothing further has been said that would show us why this is a bad thing. The professor, the singer, the symphony musician—all accept a fee, and it seems plausible that this is a good state of affairs, creating spheres of freedom. Professors are more free to pursue their own thoughts now, as money makers, than they were in the days when they were supported by monastic orders; symphony musicians playing under the contract secured by the musicians' union have more free time than nonunionized musicians, and more opportunities to engage in experimental and solo work that will enhance their art. In neither case should we conclude that the existence of a contract has converted the abilities into things to be exchanged and traded separately from the body of the producer; they remain human creative abilities, securely housed in their possessor. So, if to "commodify"' means merely to accept a fee, we have been given no reason to think that this is bad.

If, on the other hand, we try to interpret the claim of "commodification" using the narrow technical definition of "commodity" used by the Uniform Commercial Code,[46] the claim is plainly false. For that definition stresses the "fungible" nature of the goods in question, and "fungible" goods are, in turn, defined as goods "of which any unit is, by nature or usage of trade, the equivalent of any other like unit." Although we may not think that the soul or inner world of a prostitute is of deep concern to the customer, she is usually not regarded as simply a set of units fully interchangeable with other units.[47] Prostitutes are probably somewhat more fungible than bassoon players but not totally so. (Corbin reports that all *maisons de tolérance* standardly had a repertory of different types of women, to suit different tastes, and this should not surprise us.) What seems to be the real issue is that the woman is not attended to as an individual, not considered a special, unique being. But that is true of many ways people treat one another in many areas of life, and it seems implausible that we should use that kind of disregard as a basis for criminalization. It may not even be immoral, for surely we cannot deeply know all the people with whom we have dealings in life, and many of those dealings are just fine without deep knowledge. So our moral question boils down to the question, Is sex without deep personal knowledge always immoral? It seems to me officious and presuming to use one's own experience to give an affirmative answer to this question, given that people have such varied experiences of sexuality.

In general, then, there appears to be nothing baneful or value debasing about taking money for a service, even when that service expresses something intimate about the self. Professors take a salary, artists work on commission under contract—frequently producing works of high intellectual and spiritual value. To take money for a production does not turn either the activity or the product (e.g., the article or the painting) into a commodity in the baneful sense in which that implies fungibility. If this is so, there is no reason to think that a prostitute's acceptance of money for her services necessarily involves a baneful conversion of an intimate act into a commodity in that sense. If the prostitute's acts are, as they are, less intimate than many other sexual acts people perform, that does not seem to have a great deal to do with the fact that she receives money, given that people engage in many intimate activities (painting, singing, writing) for money all the time without loss of expressive value. Her activity is less intimate because that is its whole point; it is problematic, to the extent that it is, neither because of the money involved nor because of the nonintimacy (which, as I have said, it seems officious to declare bad in all cases) but because of features of her working conditions and the way she is treated by others.

Here we are left with an interesting puzzle. My argument about professors and painters certainly seems to imply that there is no reason, in principle, why the most committed and intimate sex cannot involve a contract and a financial exchange. So why doesn't it, in our culture? One reply is that it quite frequently does, when people form committed relationships that include an element of economic dependence, whether one-sided or mutual; marriage has frequently had that feature, not always for the worse. But to the extent that we do not exchange money for sex, why don't we? In a number of other cultures, courtesans, both male and female, have been somewhat more common as primary sexual partners than they are here. Unlike quite a few cultures, we do not tend to view sex in intimate personal relationships the way we view an artist's creation of a painting, namely, as an intimate act that can nonetheless be deliberately undertaken as the result of an antecedent contract-like agreement. Why not? I think there is a mystery here, but we can begin to grapple with it by mentioning two features. First, there is the fact that sex, however prolonged, still takes up much less time than writing an article or producing a painting. Furthermore, it also cannot be done too often; its natural structure is that it will not very often fill up the entire day. One may therefore conduct an intimate sexual relationship in the way one would wish, not feeling that one is slighting it, while pursuing another line of work as one's way of making a living. Artists and scholars sometimes have to pursue another line of work, but they prefer not to. They characteristically feel that to do their work in the way they would wish, they ought to spend the whole day doing it. So they naturally gravitate to the view that their characteristic mode of creative production fits very well with contract and a regular wage.

This, however, still fails to explain cultural differences. To begin to grapple with these we need to mention the influence of our heritage of romanticism, which makes us feel that sex is not authentic if not spontaneous, "natural," and to some degree unplanned. Romanticism has exercised a far greater sway over our ideas of sex than over our ideas of artistic or intellectual production, making us think that any deal or antecedent arrangement somehow diminishes that characteristic form of expression.

Are our romantic ideas about the difference between sex and art good, or are they bad? Some of each, I suspect. They are problematic to the extent that they make people think that sex happens naturally, does not require complicated adjustment and skill, and flares up (and down) uncontrollably.[48] Insofar as they make us think that sex fits badly with reliability, promise keeping, and so forth, these ideas are certainly subversive of Anderson's goals of "intimacy and commitment," which would be better served, probably, by an attitude that moves sex in intimate personal relationships (and especially marriages) closer to the activity of the artist or the professor. On the other hand, romantic views also promote Anderson's goals to some degree, insofar as they lead people to connect sex with self-revelation and self-expression rather than prudent concealment of self. Many current dilemmas concerning marriage in our culture stem from an uneasy struggle to preserve the good in romanticism while avoiding the dangers it poses to commitment. As we know, the struggle is not always successful. There is much more to be said about this fascinating topic. But since (as I've argued) it leads us quite far from the topic of prostitution, we must now return to our primary line of argument.

(6) *The prostitute's activity is shaped by, and in turn perpetuates, male dominance of women.*[49] The institution of prostitution as it has most often existed is certainly shaped by aspects of male domination of women. As I have argued, it is shaped by the perception that female sexuality is dangerous and needs careful regulation; that male sexuality is rapacious and needs a "safe" outlet; that sex is dirty and degrading, and that only a degraded woman is an appropriate sexual object.[50] Nor have prostitutes standardly been treated with respect, or given the dignity one might think proper to a fellow human being. They share this with working-class people of many types in many ages, but there is no doubt that there are particular features of the disrespect that derive from male supremacy and the desire to lord it over women, as well as a tendency to link sex to

(female) defilement that is common in the history of Western European culture. The physical abuse of prostitutes and the control of their earnings by pimps—as well as the pervasive use of force and fraud in international markets—are features of male dominance that are extremely harmful and do not have direct parallels in other types of low-paid work. Some of these forms of conduct may be largely an outgrowth of the illegality of the industry and closely comparable to the threatening behavior of drug wholesalers to their—usually male—retailers. So there remains a question of how far male dominance as such explains the violence involved. But in the international arena, where regulations against these forms of misconduct are usually treated as a joke, illegality is not a sufficient explanation for them.

Prostitution is hardly alone in being shaped by, and reinforcing, male dominance. Systems of patrilineal property and exogamous marriage, for example, almost certainly do more to perpetuate not only male dominance but also female mistreatment and even death. There probably is a strong case for making the giving of dowry illegal, as has been done since 1961 in India and since 1980 in Bangladesh[51] (though with little success), for it can be convincingly shown that the institution of dowry is directly linked with extortion and threats of bodily harm, and ultimately with the deaths of large numbers of women.[52] It is also obvious that the dowry system pervasively conditions the perception of the worth of girl children: They are a big expense, and they will not be around to protect one in one's old age. This structure is directly linked with female malnutrition, neglect, noneducation, even infanticide, harms that have caused the deaths of many millions of women in the world.[53] It is perfectly understandable that the governments of India, Bangladesh, and Pakistan are very concerned about the dowry system, because it seems very difficult to improve the very bad economic and physical condition of women without some structural changes. (Pakistan has recently adopted a somewhat quixotic remedy, making it illegal to serve food at weddings—thus driving many caterers into poverty.) Dowry is an institution affecting millions of women, determining the course of almost all girl children's lives pervasively and from the start. Prostitution as such usually does not have either such dire or such widespread implications. (Indeed, it is frequently the product of the dowry system, when parents take payment for prostituting a female child for whom they would otherwise have to pay dowry.) The case for making it illegal on grounds of subordination seems weaker than the case for making dowry, or even wedding feasts, illegal, and yet these laws are themselves of dubious merit and would probably be rightly regarded as involving undue infringement of liberty under our constitutional tradition. (It is significant that Human Rights Watch, which has so aggressively pursued the issue of forced prostitution, takes no stand one way or the other on the legality of prostitution itself.)

More generally, one might argue that the institution of marriage as most frequently practiced both expresses and reinforces male dominance. It would be right to use law to change the most inequitable features of that institution—protecting women from domestic violence and marital rape, giving women equal property and custody rights and improving their exit options by intelligent shaping of the divorce law. But to rule that marriage as such should be illegal on the grounds that it reinforces male dominance would be an excessive intrusion upon liberty, even if one should believe marriage irredeemably unequal. So, too, I think, with prostitution: What seems right is to use law to protect the bodily safety of prostitutes from assault, to protect their rights to their incomes against the extortionate behavior of pimps, to protect poor women in developing countries from forced trafficking and fraudulent offers, and to guarantee their full civil rights in the countries where they end up—to make them, in general, equals under the law, both civil and criminal. But the criminalization of prostitution seems to pose a major obstacle to that equality.

Efforts on behalf of the dignity and self-respect of prostitutes have tended to push in exactly the opposite direction. In the United States, prostitutes have long been organized to demand greater respect, though their efforts are hampered by prostitution's continued illegality. In India, the National Federation of Women has adopted various strategies to give prostitutes more dignity in the public eye. For example, on National Women's Day, they selected a prostitute to put a garland on the head of the prime minister. Similarly, UNICEF in India's Andhra Pradesh has been fighting to get prostitutes officially classified as "working women" so that they can enjoy the child-care benefits local government extends to that class. As with domestic service, so here: Giving workers greater dignity and control can gradually change both the perception and the fact of dominance.

(7) *Prostitution is a trade that people do not enter by choice; therefore the bargains people make within it should not be regarded as real bargains.* Here we must distinguish three cases. First is the case in which the woman's entry into prostitution is caused by some type of conduct that would otherwise be criminal: kidnapping, assault, drugging, rape, statutory rape, blackmail, a fraudulent offer. Here we may certainly judge that the woman's choice is not a real choice, and that the law should take a hand in punishing her coercer. This is a terrible problem currently in developing countries; international human rights organizations are right to make it a major focus.[54]

Closely related is the case of child prostitution. Child prostitution is frequently accompanied by kidnapping and forcible detention; even when children are not stolen from home, their parents have frequently sold them without their own consent. But even where they have not, we should judge that there is an impermissible infringement of autonomy and liberty. A child (and, because of clients' fears of HIV, brothels now often focus on girls as young as ten)[55] cannot give consent to a life in prostitution; not only lack of information and of economic options (if parents collude in the deal) but also absence of adult political rights makes such a "choice" no choice at all.

Different is the case of an adult woman who enters prostitution because of bad economic options: because it seems a better alternative than the chicken factory, because there is no other employment available to her, and so on. This too, we should insist, is a case in which autonomy has been infringed but in a different way. Consider Joseph Raz's vivid example of "the hounded woman," a woman on a desert island who is constantly pursued by a man-eating animal.[56] In one sense, this woman is free to go anywhere on the island and do anything she likes. In another sense, of course, she is quite unfree. If she wants not to be eaten, she has to spend all her time and calculate all her movements in order to avoid the beast. Raz's point is that many poor people's lives are nonautonomous in just this way. They may fulfill internal conditions of autonomy, being capable of making bargains, reflecting about what to do, and so on. But none of this counts for a great deal, if in fact the struggle for survival gives them just one unpleasant option, or a small set of (in various ways) unpleasant options.

This seems to me the truly important issue raised by prostitution. Like work in the chicken factory, it is not an option many women choose with alacrity, when many other options are on their plate.[57] This might not be so in some hypothetical culture, in which prostitutes have legal protection, dignity and respect, and the status of skilled practitioner, rather like the masseuse.[58] But it is true now in most societies, given the reality of the (albeit irrational) stigma attaching to prostitution. But the important thing to realize is that this is not an issue that permits us to focus on prostitution in isolation from the economic situation of women in a society generally. Certainly it will not be ameliorated by the criminalization of prostitution, which reduces poor women's options still further. We may grant that poor women do not have enough options, and that society has been unjust to them in not extending more options while nonetheless respecting and honoring the choices they actually make in reduced circumstances.

How could it possibly be ameliorated? Here are some things that have actually been done in India, where prostitution is a common last-ditch option for women who lack other employment opportunities. First, both government and private groups have focused on the provision of education to women, to equip them with skills that will enhance their options. One group I recently visited in Bombay focuses in particular on skills training for the children of prostitutes, who are at especially high risk of becoming prostitutes themselves unless some action increases their options. Second, nongovernmental organizations have increasingly focused on the provision of credit to women, in order to enhance their employment options and give them a chance to "upgrade" in the domain of their employment. One such project that has justly won international renown is the Self-Employed Women's Association (SEWA), centered in Ahmedabad in Gujarat, which provides loans to women pursuing a variety of informal-sector occupations,[59] from tailoring to hawking and vending to cigarette rolling to agricultural labor.[60] With these loans, they can get wholesale rather than retail supplies, upgrade their animals or equipment, and so forth. They also get skills training and, frequently, the chance to move into leadership roles in the organization itself. Such women are far less likely to need to turn to prostitution to supplement their income. Third, they can form labor organizations to protect women employed in low-income jobs and to bargain for better working conditions—once again making this work a better source of income and diminishing the likelihood that prostitution will need to be selected. (This is the other primary objective of SEWA, which is now organizing hawkers and vendors internationally.) Fourth, they can form groups to diminish the isolation and enhance the self-respect of working women in low-paying jobs; this was a ubiquitous feature of both government and nongovernment programs I visited in India, and a crucial element of helping women deliberate about their options if they wish to avoid prostitution for themselves or their daughters.

These four steps are the real issue, I think, in addressing the problem of prostitution. Feminist philosophers in the United States do not write many articles about credit and employment;[61] they should do so far more. Indeed, it seems a dead end to consider prostitution in isolation from the other realities of working life of which it is a part, and one suspects that this has happened because prostitution is a sexy issue and getting a loan for a sewing machine appears not to be. But feminists had better talk more about getting loans, learning to read, and so forth if they want to be relevant to the choices that are actually faced by working women, and to the programs that are actually doing a lot to improve such women's options.

VI. TRULY HUMAN FUNCTIONING

The stigma traditionally attached to prostitution is based on a collage of beliefs most of which are not rationally defensible, and which should be especially vehemently rejected by feminists: beliefs about the evil character of female sexuality, the rapacious character of male sexuality, and the essentially marital and reproductive character of "good" women and "good" sex. Worries about subordination more recently raised by feminists are much more serious concerns, but they apply to many types of work poor women do. Concerns about force and fraud should be extremely urgent concerns of the international women's movement. Where these conditions do not obtain, feminists should view prostitutes as (usually) poor working women with few options, not as threats to the intimacy and commitment that many women and men (including, no doubt, many prostitutes) seek. This does not mean that we should not be concerned about ways in which prostitution as currently practiced, even in the absence of force and fraud, undermines the dignity of women, just as domestic service in the past undermined the dignity of members of a given race or class. But the correct response to this problem seems to be to work to enhance the economic autonomy and the personal dignity of members of that class, not to rule off-limits an option that may be the only livelihood for many poor women and to further stigmatize women who already make their living this way.

In grappling further with these issues, we should begin from the realization there is nothing per se wrong with taking money for the use of one's body. That's the way most of us live, and formal recognition of that fact through contract is usually a good thing for people, protecting their security and their employment conditions. What seems wrong is that relatively few people in the world have the option to use their body, in their work, in what Marx would call a "truly human" manner of functioning, by which he meant (among other things) having some choices about the work to be performed, some reasonable measure of control over its conditions and outcome, and also the chance to use thought and skill rather than just to function as a cog in a machine. Women in many parts of the world are especially likely to be stuck at a low level of mechanical functioning, whether as agricultural laborers or as factory workers or as prostitutes. The real question to be faced is how to expand the options and opportunities such workers face, how to increase the humanity inherent in their work, and how to guarantee that workers of all sorts are treated with dignity. In the further pursuit of these questions, we need, on balance, more studies of women's credit unions and fewer studies of prostitution.[62]

NOTES

1. Even if one is a Cartesian dualist, as I am not, one must grant that the human exercise of mental abilities standardly requires the deployment of bodily skills. Most traditional Christian positions on the soul go still further: Aquinas, for example, holds that souls separated from the body have only a confused cognition and cannot recognize particulars. So my statements about professors can be accepted even by believers in the separable soul.

2. Adam Smith, *The Nature and Causes of the Wealth of Nations*, I.x.b.25. Elsewhere, Smith points out that in ancient Greece acting was "as creditable . . . as it is discreditable now" (*Lectures on Rhetoric and Belles Lettres* ii.230).

3. He expresses the view that the relevant talents are not so rare, and that when stigma is removed, many more people will compete for the jobs, driving down wages;

this is certainly true today of acting, but far less so of opera, where "the rarity and beauty of the talents" remains at least one dominant factor.

4. Such arguments have often been used in the theater; they were used, for example, in one acting company of which I was a member, in order to persuade actors to kick back their (union-mandatory) salaries to the owners. This is fairly common in theater, where the union is weak and actors are so eager for employment that they are vulnerable to such arguments.

5. The typical contract between major U.S. symphony orchestras and the musicians' union, for example, guarantees year-round employment to symphony musicians, even though they do not play all year; this enables them to use summer months to play in low-paying or experimental settings in which they can perform contemporary music and chamber music, do solo and concerto work, and so forth. It also restricts hours of both rehearsal and performance during the performing season, leaving musicians free to teach students, attend classes, work on chamber music with friends, and in other ways to enrich their work. It also mandates blind auditions (i.e., players play behind a curtain)—with the result that the employment of female musicians has risen dramatically over the past twenty or so years since the practice was instituted.

6. See Elizabeth Anderson, *Value in Ethics and Economics* (Cambridge, Mass.: Harvard University Press, 1993) and "Is Women's Labor a Commodity?" *Philosophy and Public Affairs* 19 (1990): 71–92; Margaret Jane Radin, *Contested Commodities: The Trouble with the Trade in Sex, Children, Bodily Parts, and Other Things* (Cambridge, Mass.: Harvard University Press, 1996) and "Market-Inalienability," *Harvard Law Review* 100 (1987): 1849–1937; Cass R. Sunstein, "Neutrality in Constitutional Law (With Special Reference to Pornography, Abortion, and Surrogacy)," *Columbia Law Review* 92 (1992): 1–52, and *The Partial Constitution* (Cambridge, Mass.: Harvard University Press, 1993), 257–90. For contrasting feminist perspectives on the general issue of contract, see Jean Hampton, "Feminist Contractarianism," in Louise Antony and Charlotte Witt, eds., *A Mind of One's Own: Feminist Essays on Reason and Objectivity* (Boulder, Colo.: Westview, 1993), 227–55; and Susan Moller Okin, *Justice, Gender, and the Family* (New York: Basic Books, 1989).

7. I use this term throughout because of its familiarity, although a number of international women's organizations now avoid it for reasons connected to those in this essay, preferring the term "commercial sex worker" instead. For one recent example, see *Report of the Panel on Reproductive Health, National Research Council, Reproductive Health in Developing Countries: Expanding Dimensions, Building Solutions*, ed. Amy O. Tsui, Judith N. Wasserheit, and John G. Haaga (Washington, D.C.: National Academy Press, 1997), 30, stressing the wide variety of practices denoted by the term "commercial sex" and arguing that some studies show economic hardship as a major factor but some do not.

8. Among feminist discussions of prostitution, my approach is close to that of Sibyl Schwarzenbach, "Contractarians and Feminists Debate Prostitution," *New York University Review of Law and Social Change* 18 (1990–1): 103–29, and to Laurie Shrage, "Prostitution and the Case for Decriminalization," *Dissent* (Spring 1996): 41–45 (in which Shrage criticizes her earlier view expressed in "Should Feminists Oppose Prostitution?" *Ethics* 99 [1989]: 347–61).

9. To give just one example, the Annapurna Mahila Mandal project in Bombay offers job training and education to the daughters of prostitutes, in a residential school setting; they report that in five years they have managed to arrange reputable marriages for 1,000 such girls.

10. Aristotle, *Politics*, III.5 and VII.9–10.

11. See Plato, *Apology* 19D–20C, *Protagoras* (passim), *Gorgias* (passim).

12. I have profited here from reading an unpublished paper by Dan Klerman, "Slavery, Simony and Sex: An Intellectual History of the Limits of Monetary Relations."

13. Or those supported by religious orders.

14. Mrs. Elizabeth Billington, who sang in Arne's *Artaxerxes* in London in 1762, was forced to leave England because of criticisms of her morals; she ended her career in Italy. Another early *diva* was Maria Catalani, who sang for Handel (d. 1759), for example, in *Samson*. By the time of the publication of *The Wealth of Nations*, female singers had made great headway in displacing the castrati, who ceased to be produced shortly thereafter. For Smith's own attitudes to the female body, see *The Theory of Moral Sentiments* I.ii.1.3, where he states that as soon as sexual passion is gratified it gives rise to "disgust," and leads us to wish to get rid of the person who is their object, unless some higher moral sentiment preserves our regard for (certain aspects of) this person. "When we have dined, we order the covers to be removed; and we should treat in the same manner the objects of the most ardent and passionate desires, if they were the objects of no other passions but those which take their origin from the body." Smith was a bachelor who lived much of his life with his mother and did not have any lasting relationships with women.

15. Aspasia was a learned and accomplished woman who apparently had philosophical and political views; she is said to have taught rhetoric and to have conversed with Socrates. On the other hand, she could not perform any of the functions of a citizen, both because of her sex and because of her foreign birth. On the other hand, her son Pericles ["the younger"—eds.] was subsequently legitimated and became a general. More recently, it has been doubted whether Aspasia was in fact a *hetaira*, and some scholars now think her a well-born foreign woman. But other *hetairai* in Greece had good education and substantial financial assets; the two women recorded as students in Plato's Academy were both *hetairai*, as were most of the women attested as students of Epicurus, including one who was apparently a wealthy donor.

16. See chapter 3 of my *Sex and Social Justice* (New York: Oxford University Press, 1999).

17. As far as I know, this profession is entirely hypothetical, though not by any means far-fetched. It is clear, at any rate, that individuals' abilities to endure colonoscopy without anesthesia and without moving vary considerably, so one might well develop (or discover) expertise in this area.

18. It is probably, however, a developed skill to come to work regularly and to work regular hours each day.

19. Consider, for example, the case of Jayamma, a brick worker in Trivandrum, Kerala, India, discussed by Leela Gulati, *Profiles of Female Poverty* (Delhi: Hindustan Publishing Corp., 1981) and whom I met on March 21, 1997, when she was approximately sixty-five years old. For approximately forty years, Jayamma worked as a brick carrier in the brick-making establishment, carrying heavy loads of bricks on her head all day from one place to another. Despite her strength, fitness, and reliability, she could never advance beyond that job because of her sex, whereas men were quickly promoted to the less physically demanding and higher-paying tasks of brick molding and truck loading.

20. Indeed, this appears to be a ubiquitous feature: In India, the mark of "untouchability" is the performance of certain types of cleaning, especially those dealing with bathroom areas. Mahatma Gandhi's defiance of caste manifested itself in the performance of these menial services.

21. This does not imply that there is some one thing, pleasure, varying only by quantity, that they produce. With Mill (and Plato and Aristotle), I think that pleasures differ in quality, not only in quantity.

22. This point was suggested to me by Elizabeth Schreiber. I am not sure whether I endorse it: It all depends on whether we really want to say that sex has one highest goal. Just as it would have been right, in an earlier era, to be skeptical about the suggestion that the sex involved in prostitution is "low" because it is nonreproductive, so too it might be good to be skeptical about the idea that prostitution sex is "low" because it is nonintimate. Certainly nonintimacy is involved in many noncommercial sexual relationships and is sometimes desired as such.

23. Thus the *Kama Sutra*, with its detailed instructions for elaborately skilled performances, strikes most Western readers as slightly comic, because the prevailing romantic ideal of "natural" sex makes such contrivance seem quite unsexy.

24. We might also consider the example of a skilled writer who writes advertising copy.

25. See Terri Kapsalis, *Public Privates: Performing Gynecology from Both Ends of the Speculum* (Durham, N.C.: Duke University Press, 1997); and Kapsalis, "In Print: Backstage at the Pelvic Theater," *Chicago Reader* (April 18, 1997), 46. While a graduate student in performance studies at Northwestern, Kapsalis made a living as a "gynecology teaching associate," serving as the model patient for medical students learning to perform pelvic and breast examinations.

26. The same goes for vaginal penetration, according to Kapsalis: She says that the clinical nature of the procedure more than compensates for "society's queasiness with female sexuality."

27. Alain Corbin, *Women for Hire: Prostitution and Sexuality in France after 1850*, trans. Alan Sheridan (Cambridge, Mass.: Harvard University Press, 1990).

28. *Ibid.*, 29. Representative views of the authors of regulationism include the view that "[d]ebauchery is a fever of the senses carried to the point of delirium; it leads to prostitution (or to early death) . . ." and that "[t]here are two natural sisters in the world: prostitution and riot." *Ibid.*, 373.

29. For a more general discussion of the relationship between prostitution and various forms of marriage, see Richard Posner, *Sex and Reason* (Cambridge, Mass.: Harvard University Press, 1992), 130–33.

30. Sukanya Hantrakul, "Thai Women: Male Chauvinism à la Thai," *The Nation*, November 16, 1992, cited with further discussion in Asia Watch Women's Rights Project, *A Modern Form of Slavery: Trafficking of Burmese Women and Girls into Brothels in Thailand* (New York: Human Rights Watch, 1993).

31. See *A Modern Form of Slavery: The Human Rights Watch Global Report on Women's Human Rights* (New York: Human Rights Watch, 1995), 196–273, esp. 270–73. The pertinent international human rights instruments take the same approach, including the International Covenant on Civil and Political rights, the Convention on the Elimination of All forms of Discrimination against Women, and the Convention for the Suppression of Traffic in Persons and the Exploitation of the Prostitution of Others.

32. *Palmore v. Sidoti*, 466 U.S. 429 (1984).

33. See Corbin, *Women for Hire*, 90: In Paris, Dr. Clerc boasted that he could examine a woman every thirty seconds, and estimated that a single practitioner saw 400 women in a single twenty-four-hour period. Another practitioner estimated that the average number of patients per hour was fifty-two.

34. For a more pessimistic view of health checks, see Posner, *Sex and Reason*, 209, pointing out that they frequently have had the effect of driving prostitutes into the illegal market.

35. See Richard Posner, *Private Choices and Public Health: The AIDS Epidemic in an Economic Perspective* (Cambridge, Mass.: Harvard University Press, 1993), 149, with references.

36. See *Human Rights Watch Global Report*, 1–7.

37. See Anderson, *Value in Ethics and Economics*, 156: "Her actions under contract express not her own valuations but the will of her customer."

38. This is crucial in the thinking behind the "capabilities approach" to which I have contributed in *Women, Culture, and Development* and other publications. For the connection between this approach and Marx's use of Aristotle, see Martha C. Nussbaum, "Aristotle on Human Nature and the Foundations of Ethics," in *World, Mind, and Ethics: Essays on the Philosophy of Bernard Williams*, ed. J. E. J. Altham and R. Harrison (Cambridge: Cambridge University Press, 1993).

39. Made frequently by my students, not necessarily to support criminalization.

40. Anderson, *Value in Ethics and Economics*, 150–58; Anderson pulls back from an outright call for criminalization, concluding that her arguments "establish the legiti-

macy of a state interest in prohibiting prostitution, but not a conclusive case for prohibition," given the paucity of opportunities for working women.

41. See K. J. Dover, *Greek Homosexuality*, 2nd ed. (Cambridge, Mass.: Harvard University Press, 1978); and David Halperin, "The Democratic Body," in *One Hundred Years of Homosexuality and Other Essays on Greek Love* (New York: Routledge, 1990). Customers were all males, but prostitutes were both male and female. The evidence that prostitution was publicly funded is uncertain because it derives from comic drama, but it is clear that both male and female prostitution enjoyed broad public support and approval.

42. For a similar point, see Radin, "Market-Inalienability," 1921–25, and *Contested Commodities*, 132–36; Anderson refers to this claim of Radin, apparently as the source of her reluctance to call outright for criminalization.

43. I would not go quite as far as John Rawls, however, in the direction of letting the market determine our cultural options. He opposes any state subsidy to opera companies, symphony orchestras, museums, and so on, on the grounds that this would back a particular conception of the good against others. I think, however, that we could defend such subsidies, within limits, as valuable because they preserve a cultural option that is among the valuable ones, and that might otherwise cease to exist. Obviously much more argument is needed on this entire question.

44. See Radin, "Market-Inalienability"; and Anderson, *Value in Ethics and Economics*, 156: "The prostitute, in selling her sexuality to a man, alienates a good necessarily embodied in her person to him and thereby subjects herself to his commands."

45. On this point, see also Schwarzenbach, "Contractarians," with discussion of Marx's account of alienation.

46. See Richard Epstein, "Surrogacy: The Case for Full Contractual Enforcement," *Virginia Law Review* 81 (1995): 2327.

47. Moreover, the U.C.C. does not cover the sale of services, and prostitution should be classified as a service rather than a good.

48. It is well known that these ideas are heavily implicated in the difficulty of getting young people, especially young women, to use contraception.

49. See Shrage's earlier *Ethics* article; and Andrea Dworkin, "Prostitution and Male Supremacy," in *Life and Death* (New York: The Free Press, 1997).

50. An eloquent examination of the last view, with reference to Freud's account (which endorses it) is in William Miller, *The Anatomy of Disgust* (Cambridge, Mass.: Harvard University Press, 1997), Chapter 6.

51. The Dowry Prohibition Act of 1961 makes both taking and giving of dowry illegal; in Bangladesh, demanding, taking, and giving dowry are all criminal offenses. See Chapter 3 in *Sex and Social Justice*.

52. It is extremely difficult to estimate how many women are damaged and killed as a result of this practice; it is certainly clear that criminal offenses are vastly underreported, as is domestic violence in India generally, but that very problem makes it difficult to form any reliable idea of the numbers involved. See Indira Jaising, *Justice for Women* (Bombay: The Lawyers' Collective, 1996); and chapter 3 in my *Sex and Social Justice*.

53. See Amartya Sen and Jean Drèze, *Hunger and Public Action* (Oxford, U.K.: Clarendon Press, 1989), 52; and chapter 1 in my *Sex and Social Justice*. Kerala, the only Indian state to have a matrilineal property tradition, also has an equal number of men and women (contrasted with a 94:100 sex ratio elsewhere), and 97 percent both male and female literacy, as contrasted with 32 percent female literacy elsewhere.

54. See, for example, *A Modern Form of Slavery: Trafficking of Burmese Women; Human Rights Watch Global Report*, 1296–373; Amnesty International, *Human Rights Are Women's Right* (London: Amnesty International, 1995), 53–6.

55. See *Human Rights Watch Global Report*, 197, on Thailand.

56. Joseph Raz, *The Morality of Freedom* (Oxford, U.K.: Clarendon Press, 1986), 374.

57. See Posner, *Sex and Reason*, 132*n*43 on the low incidence of prostitution in Sweden, even though it is not illegal; his explanation is that "women's opportunities in the job market are probably better there than in any other country."

58. See Schwarzenbach, "Contractarians."

59. An extremely high proportion of the labor force in India is in the informal sector.

60. SEWA was first directed by Ela Bhatt, who is now involved in international work to improve the employment options of informal-sector workers. For a valuable description of the movement, see Kalima Rose, *Where Women Are Leaders: The SEWA Movement in India* (Delhi: Sage Publications, 1995).

61. But see, here, Schwarzenbach and Shrage (op. cit.). I have also been very much influenced by the work of Martha Chen, *A Quiet Revolution: Women in Transition in Rural Bangladesh* (Cambridge, Mass.: Schenkman, 1983) and "A Matter of Survival: Women's Right to Work in India and Bangladesh," in *Women, Culture, and Development*, ed. M. Nussbaum and J. Glover (Oxford, U.K.: Clarendon Press, 1995); and Bina Agarwal, *A Field of One's Own: Gender and Land Rights in South Asia* (Cambridge: Cambridge University Press, 1994); and also "Bargaining and Gender Relations: Within and Beyond the Household," FCND Discussion Paper No. 27, Food Consumption and Nutrition Division, International Food Policy Research Institute, Washington, D.C.

62. The author is grateful to students in her seminar on sexual autonomy and law for all that their discussions contributed to the formulation of these ideas, to Sibyl Schwarzenbach and Laurie Shrage for discussions that helped her think about how to approach this topic, and to Elizabeth Anderson, Gertrud Fremling, Richard Posner, Mark Ramseyer, Eric Schliesser, Elizabeth Schreiber, Stephen Schulhofer, Alan Soble, and Cass Sunstein for valuable comments on an earlier draft of this essay.

STUDY QUESTIONS

1. In explaining why prostitution is stigmatized, Nussbaum points out that it is commonly believed to be immoral. She then argues that "it seems inconsistent to do so [that is, object to prostitution morally] if one is not prepared to repudiate other forms of nonmarital sexual activity on an equal basis." Can you construct a moral position according to which prostitution is morally wrong yet noncommercial casual sex is morally permissible? Or is prostitution morally wrong, since casual or promiscuous sex, as Nussbaum argues elsewhere, is itself morally questionable? (See her "Objectification," *Philosophy and Public Affairs* 24: 4 (1995): 249–91; reprinted in Alan Soble, ed., *The Philosophy of Sex*, 3rd edition, 283–321, and 4th edition, 381–419.)

2. Nussbaum considers the claim, which could be used to support the criminalization of prostitution, that the acts of the prostitute "under contract express not her own valuations but the will of her customer." Nussbaum replies that in this regard the prostitute is in the same situation as most workers, that is, lack of control is a "pervasive problem of labor" in our society and others. What do you think of the alternative reply that many prostitutes firmly set the ground rules before they engage in sex with their clients and

thereby do not succumb to "the will of [the] customer"? Is it possible that at least some prostitutes have more control over the conditions of their work than many wage laborers? (See, for example, H. E. Baber, "How Bad Is Rape?—II" in this volume).

3. Isn't there something significant and morally relevant about sexual activity that might distinguish it from all the other examples of work, discussed by Nussbaum, in which people sell their bodies or the use of them? If not, why (as David Benatar might ask; see his "Two Views of Sexual Ethics: Promiscuity, Pedophilia, and Rape," in this volume) is rape considered to be such a morally atrocious act? If prostitution should not be stigmatized, as Nussbaum argues, does that provide any reason for lessening the stigmatization of rape or of being raped?

4. Is the analogy between prostitution and Nussbaum's "colonoscopy artist" a good or fair one? How would you (or Nussbaum) respond to someone who said, "The anus is not a sex organ, unlike the vagina; an inanimate instrument is not a body part, unlike the penis of a living male human being; and the purpose of colonoscopy artistry, for the consumer, is not the same as the purpose of prostitution, for the consumer"?

5. If Nussbaum is right that prostitution should be decriminalized, *ceteris paribus*, does this imply that the making of pornography should not be subject to criminal or civil sanctions? See Nicholas Power, "Cheap Thrills: A Call for More Pornography," in this volume.

TWENTY-FOUR

On Fucking Around

Raja Halwani

After discussing the definitions of "casual sex," "promiscuity," and "objectification" and examining some of the difficulties in these concepts, **Raja Halwani** *addresses the morality of objectification in connection with casual sex and promiscuity. He understands casual sex as "no-strings-attached" sex and promiscuity as frequent instances of casual sex (albeit with different partners within a short period of time). Assuming a pessimistic metaphysical view of sexual desire, Halwani argues that it is nearly impossible to defend casual sex and promiscuity against the accusation of objectification; even though a case can be made that casual sex and promiscuity do not necessarily involve objectification, they likely do. He concludes by suggesting that the wrongness of the objectification in casual sex and promiscuity might not be very serious and that both types of sexuality might, as a result, be morally permissible.*

Many people consider casual sex and promiscuity (CS&P) morally wrong, even if they admit that their practitioners find these activities pleasurable. CS&P are also thought to provide fertile ground for objectification, a philosophically thorny concept. After discussing issues of definition—philosophically interesting on their own—I discuss the ethics of CS&P as far as objectification is concerned. I argue that, even though the case can be made that they do not necessarily involve objectification, they are likely to objectify, given a particular and plausible view of sexual desire. However, I suggest that the wrongness of objectification can be overcome by other considerations, such that CS&P might in general be morally permissible.

DEFINITIONAL ISSUES

1. Casual Sex

Casual sex is sexual activity that occurs outside the context of a relationship. Often, but not always, the parties who engage in it seek only sexual pleasure. Typical examples include Internet hook-ups, bar hook-ups, sex between pornography actors, and anonymous encounters in gay bathhouses, gay or straight sex clubs, and straight swingers clubs.

However, it is difficult to define "casual sex" in terms of necessary and sufficient conditions; any proposed criterion that distinguishes casual from noncasual sex faces difficulties. Suppose that the criterion is that the intention be only for sexual pleasure. This sounds right since people who have casual sex usually do it only for sexual pleasure. But people in relationships (e.g., married couples, friends, couples in love) have sex often solely for sexual pleasure, yet the sex between them is not casual. So the criterion won't do as a sufficient condition. It is also not necessary because some people have casual sex not for sexual pleasure but for other reasons. For example, prostitutes do it for money, stressed individuals do it for release, and vain people do it to maintain their lofty self-image.

Here's a second criterion: that there is no marriage, love relationship, or committed relationship between the parties to the casual sex.[1] If such a relationship exists, the sex is not casual. If there is no such relationship, the sex is casual. Why emphasize marriage, love, and committed relationships, not other types of relationship? Because what matters is the right kind of commitment, whose very nature renders the activities between its parties—whether sexual or nonsexual—noncasual, such as love, marriage, deep friendship (acquaintances and work relationships are not such commitments). Is being in a relationship sufficient for the sex to be noncasual? It seems to be. We have seen above that even if the couple has sex for pleasure, being a couple is enough to make the sex noncasual. Moreover, even if they have a "quickie" before darting off to work, the sex still seems to be noncasual precisely because they are in a relationship. So being in a relationship seems to be sufficient for the sex to be noncasual.

But it does not seem to be necessary. Suppose that Fyodor and Leila meet in a bar, sparks fly (without the help of alcohol), and they go home and have sex with each other, each thinking that they have just met the love of their life, vowing to each other their eternal love. However, come morning, each says to him- or herself: "What was I thinking?" Did Fyodor and Leila have casual sex? If they did not because they intended the sex to be a prelude to a relationship, then we have an example of noncasual sex outside a committed relationship. So the proposed criterion is not necessary.

Here's a third criterion: that the parties to the sex act intend, hope, or desire (or something along these lines) that the sex act not lead to any commitment. If such an intention (or, more generally, mental state) exists, then the sex is casual. If it doesn't exist, then it is not casual. This criterion is the most plausible one. For if the parties to a sex act have such a mental state, it is hard to see how the ensuing sex is not casual. So it seems to be a sufficient condition. Moreover, it seems correct to think that if their sexual activity is casual, then such a mental state exists, so it seems to also be a necessary condition.

The plausible idea behind this criterion is captured by the phrase "no-strings-attached" (NSA) sex (hence the expression "NSA sex"). The idea is that the consent of the parties to the sexual act does not imply a commitment beyond the act—no commitment to love, to marriage, or to even seeing each other again for solely sexual purposes. However, the trick is how to clearly state this idea. Is it (1) that the consent implies no commitment beyond the act? Or is it (2) that the consent does not imply a commitment beyond the act? The first requires an explicit mental state on the part of the parties for no commitment, whereas (2) leaves things open and could be satisfied by the lack of any mental state. Though (2) is probably more common, I adopt (1) because it focuses on clear cases of casual sex, ruling out ambiguous ones (e.g., one or more parties having no clear mental states about the future).

But there are two complications. First, must *each* party to the sex act have such a mental state? Or is it enough that one or some do? What if X does not intend or want a commitment but Y does?[2] Second, *which* mental state should count? Suppose that Leslie and Pat know that they should not be in a committed relationship and so *intend* the sex between them to not lead to commitment. But suppose they also yearn for love so they *hope* that it does. Is the ensuing sex between them casual, because of their intention, or not, because of their hope?

Despite these complications, I define "casual sex" as "NSA sex, such that the consent of the parties implies no commitment beyond the act." The definition gives us what we need for our discussion.

2. Promiscuity

Obviously, having sex many times is crucial for understanding promiscuity. But with *whom* one has sex is also crucial. If John has sex twenty times a week with his partner (his marital spouse, the person he loves, or even his friend-with-benefits), we would be happy for him and hope that his partner's sexual drive matches his, but he would not be promiscuous. A promiscuous person has sex with *different* people, although a precise number is impossible to decide. The period of time is also important: having sex with ten different people during a period of twenty years is not much, but during one month is (again, the precise length of the period is impossible to decide). So the period of time during which one has sex, and with whom one has it, are crucial to whether someone is promiscuous.

What are the connections, if any, between casual sex and promiscuity? Perhaps promiscuity implies casual sex but not vice versa: someone who is promiscuous has, simply in virtue of that fact, casual sex because he has NSA sex (albeit a lot of it), but someone who has casual sex is not, simply in virtue of that fact, promiscuous because he might have casual sex very few times during his life (maybe even only once). But suppose that Nadia wants to be in a love relationship, but the (or one) way she tries to do so is by having sex with any man she thinks might be Mr. Right, only to be disappointed and to have to start over. Is Nadia promiscuous? Some might say "no" because she intends each sexual act to be the start, or part, of a new love relationship. Some might say "yes" because her intentions are irrelevant and because she has sex with many different men during a brief period of time. Is Nadia having casual sex? Again, some might say "no" because of her intentions, and some "yes" because none of the sex acts leads to, or ends up being part of, a love relationship. (On this essay's definition, Nadia is not having casual sex because she desires a commitment beyond the sexual act.) Now, *if* Nadia is promiscuous but is not engaging in casual sex, then promiscuity does not imply casual sex because someone could be promiscuous and not be having casual sex. Although it depends on the relevance of intentions (and hopes and other such mental states) to promiscuity and casual sex, the Nadia example is strong enough to shake our faith in the idea that promiscuous sex implies casual sex.

However, I set aside cases like Nadia's and focus on cases in which someone intends to engage in casual sex and on cases in which someone intends to be promiscuous (because she, e.g., does not want to be entangled in the complexities of love, likes sex, and likes sexual variety). I focus on these cases because, first, if CS&P are morally suspicious, then intentionally engaging in them is worse than unintentionally engaging in them, so we would be in the thick of the moral issues. Second, because as far as *only* objectification is concerned, whatever is morally wrong with someone who intentionally has casual sex would also be wrong with the person who is intentionally promiscuous (thus, the second person might, for non-objectification-related reasons, be ethically defective in ways the first person is not.) Any objectification-related differences between them would then be in terms of the number of ethical wrongs committed: a promiscuous person would engage in a lot more objectification than someone who has casual sex only a few times.

One final restriction: I focus on cases of CS&P in which the motive of the parties is to attain sexual pleasure (or to satisfy their sexual desires), not, say, to make money. This keeps the discussion manageable and confined to the type of cases people usually have in mind when they think of CS&P.

3. Objectification

The idea of objectification has its roots in Immanuel Kant's ethics. Kant thought that because of the very nature of sexual desire, the parties to a sex act use each other and themselves and then discard each other like "a lemon which has been sucked dry."[3] I return to Kant's views below because they are necessary for a discussion of CS&P.

To objectify a person is to treat him only as if an object. For example, Christa treats Tania as an object if she uses Tania as a chair while reading the newspaper. Objectification is a morally charged concept. To accuse someone of objectification is to accuse her of doing wrong. For to objectify someone is to treat him only as an object, thereby bringing him down from the level of being human or a person to the level of an object, thus degrading or dehumanizing him. Why? Because to be a person is to have a special property or quality that other objects (including plants and most, if not all, animals) lack and by virtue of which human beings are to be treated in morally special ways. This property might be dignity, rationality, autonomy, self-consciousness, being created in God's image, or something along these lines. To treat someone merely as an object is to bypass or neglect to treat him in accordance with this property, thereby degrading or dehumanizing him. Thus, it is to treat him in a morally wrong way.

Note three things. First, someone can intentionally *or* unintentionally bypass or neglect this special property, so someone can engage in objectification unintentionally or unawares. This does not mean that no wrong has been done, only that the objectifier is not to be blamed or held responsible (unless she should have known better). So *if* to have casual sex is necessarily to objectify the sexual partner, then one objectifies regardless of whether one intends to objectify (do not confuse intending to have casual sex with intending to objectify).

Second, if human beings are nothing but objects to begin with, albeit with a morally inflated name ("person"), then there is nothing wrong with objectification: we cannot act wrongly in treating an object merely as an object if it is nothing but an object to begin with.[4] Third, if human beings are not merely objects but are nonetheless *not* loftier than objects, then again objectification would not be wrong because by treating human beings as nothing but objects one would not be degrading them or lowering their status. Thus, for objectification to be wrong, we must (and will) assume that human beings are not mere objects (a plausible assumption) *and* that they have a morally higher status than objects (a controversial assumption).[5]

Two crucial questions immediately arise. First, is objectification only an issue of treatment? Can't we objectify someone only by regarding him—purely mentally viewing him—as merely an object?[6] Although it makes sense to speak about objectifying someone merely by regarding him as only an object, if the wrong of objectification is that it dehumanizes and degrades the person who is objectified, it is hard to see how merely regarding someone only as an object actually dehumanizes or degrades him. Mere regard reveals a moral defect or vice in the person who has this attitude, but it does not actually degrade the person so regarded. For actual degradation to occur, some form of treatment must occur. In any case, even if degradation occurs in mere regard, surely its meatiest and most important forms are those that result from treatment, so I shall continue to discuss objectification in terms of treatment.

The second question is: is the "only" in "to objectify a person is to treat him only as an object" needed to understand the wrong of objectification? Wouldn't *X* still be objectifying *Y*, thus doing something wrong, even if *X* does not treat *Y only* as an object? (Note that if *X* treats *Y* with respect and affection most of the time but during sex—or other situations—treats *Y* only as an object, *X* still objectifies *Y* during those times.)[7] To see whether treating someone as an-object-but-not-only-as-an-object is morally problematic, we should ask whether it is possible to treat someone as not an object at all, because if this is possible, then treating people as objects, whether "only" or not, would be morally defective given the better option of not treating them as objects at all.

One way of treating someone as an object is to treat her as an instrument or a tool for our purposes. Yet there seems no escape from this treatment in human interaction. For in virtually any example of human interaction—between grocer and shopper, salesperson and client, student and teacher, tenant and landlord, flight attendant and passenger, waiter and diner, and so on—we use people as tools: we use the grocer as a tool to obtain our groceries, the tenant to make an income, and so on. Even in interactions between friends and loved ones, about which we don't believe that people use each other as tools (e.g., a lover giving his beloved a gift), one might argue that the lover uses his beloved as a tool to attain his goals (of, e.g., giving her a gift: no beloved, no gift-giving).[8] We can then plausibly assume that treating each other as tools is unavoidable. (Perhaps those who believe that not every human interaction involves using people as tools should provide us with uncontroversial cases.) What we should aim for, then, is to treat them *not merely* as tools or objects.

However, one might claim that being used as a tool is only *one* way to be objectified. Are there not other ways in which we *can* avoid using people as objects altogether?

Martha Nussbaum lists seven different ways to objectify someone. Rae Langton adds three. I quote them at length (this is also useful for the discussion in part II). Nussbaum's list:

1. *Instrumentality.* The objectifier treats the object as a tool of his or her purposes.
2. *Denial of autonomy.* The objectifier treats the object as lacking in autonomy and self-determination.
3. *Inertness.* The objectifier treats the object as lacking in agency, and perhaps also in activity.
4. *Fungibility.* The objectifier treats the object as interchangeable (a) with other objects of the same type and/or (b) with objects of other types.
5. *Violability.* The objectifier treats the object as lacking in boundary integrity, as something that is permissible to break up, smash, break into.
6. *Ownership.* The objectifier treats the object as something owned by another, can be bought and sold, and so on.
7. *Denial of subjectivity.* The objectifier treats the object as something whose experience and feelings (if any) need not be taken into account.[9]

Langton's additional three:

8. *Reduction to body.* One treats [the person] as identified with his or her body, or body parts.
9. *Reduction to appearance.* One treats [the person] primarily in terms of how he or she looks, or how he or she appears to the senses.
10. *Silencing.* One treats [the person] as silent, lacking the capacity to speak.[10]

Other than instrumentality (already addressed), we can treat people as not objects at all in any of those ways. We need not treat others as incapable of making decisions (lacking autonomy and self-determination), as lacking in agency (inert), as interchangeable with others (fungible), as permissible to smash up (violable), as owned, as having no feelings and experience, and as reduced to body and appearance. If the above list is a list of ways of treating people as objects, then it is possible to not treat people as objects at all in any of these of ways.

But note that for each of these ways, the only way to treat someone as an object is by treating her *only* as an object. For example, I cannot treat someone as violable *while at the same time* treating her as inviolable: I cannot treat Omar as something permissible to cut up, lacerate, bounce up and down, and otherwise violate while simultaneously treating him as someone with boundaries that I should not overstep. Similar reasoning applies to the rest (again, excepting instrumentality).[11] Thus, even though we can avoid treating people in any of these ways as objects, if we do treat them as objects, we cannot simultaneously treat them as more than objects. Instrumentality is unique in this respect: as we shall see, it is possible to treat someone as an instrument but not only as an instrument.

Do not confuse "treating X as lacking in A," as the above ways state, with "justifiably overriding X's A." To justifiably override X's A is not to treat X as an object because the former is morally permissible, even sometimes required. For example, I may override X's inviolability by cutting off X's arm to save X's life. I may override X's capacity to speak to allow others to speak. I may reduce X to mere appearance if I am dressing X for X's role in a play. I may treat X as fungible if I approach X as a grocer, barista, or other service worker—as someone who agrees to compete with others in offering a service.

Thus, except for instrumentality, none of these eight ways undermines the definition of "objectification" as treating someone *only* as an object. We can then conclude that to objectify someone, one does indeed have to treat her *only* as an object. However, one type of objectification—instrumentality—can be avoided by treating the person as not only an object. Let's now see whether CS&P can avoid objectification.

MORAL ISSUES

1. Why CS&P Might Be Necessarily Objectifying

If objectification is always morally wrong and is a necessary feature of casual sex, casual sex is necessarily wrong. If promiscuity is multiple instances of casual sex with different people, promiscuity is also necessarily wrong. But why believe that objectification is a necessary feature of CS&P? The argument might go as follows. In engaging in CS&P, people have NSA sex for sexual pleasure. They thus use each other—they treat each other as objects, as tools—for the purpose of attaining this pleasure. Even if they provide each other with pleasure, they do so because (1) this gives them pleasure (the man performing oral sex on the woman finds giving oral sex pleasurable), (2) the receiver's pleasure enhances the provider's own pleasure (the man finds the woman's pleasure from receiving oral sex pleasurable), or (3) the provider desires that the receiver return the favor. They use each other for their selfish or self-interested (I gloss over the differences between these two) sexual pleasure. Thus, CS&P involve objectification: its parties use each other's bodies for the satisfaction of their sexual desires.

Supporting the above argument is a pessimist view of sexual desire according to which[12] (1) sexual desire targets people's bodies and body parts, thus coming dangerously close to making us view the people we sexually desire as objects (albeit live ones). (2) To satisfy sexual desire, we engage in all sorts of shenanigans, such as deception and lies ("Yes! I, too, loved *The English Patient!*") and dressing in ways to conceal our defects and highlight, if any, our assets (which might also be a form of deception). (3) Unless intruded upon by anxieties, worries, or—crucially—moral thoughts, sexual activity can be so pleasurable and consuming that parties to it lose control over themselves and lose "regard for the humanity of the other person."[13] (4) To satisfy sexual desire, we allow our reason to be subverted and we do irrational, stupid things both to get someone to have sex with us and during the sexual act (e.g., unsafe sex). Finally, (5) when we do attend to each other's desires, we do so, again, either because we find this pleasurable in itself or because we desire to receive sexual attention in return.

CS&P epitomize the above features of sexual desire. Precisely because CS&P are NSA sex whose goal is sexual pleasure, its parties (1) focus on and use the other's body and body parts to attain sexual pleasure; (2) more easily rationalize lies and deception because there is no future commitment to each other; (3) more easily give themselves up to sexual abandon because, again, there is no future commitment; (4) are more willing to put each other at risk for the same reason; and (5) if they do provide pleasure for each other, do so as a means to attaining their own sexual pleasure. So X attends to Y's pleasure because this gives X pleasure (X enjoys the activity, enjoys Y's pleasure in receiving the activity, or desires that Y return the favor). Indeed, attending to Y's pleasure *for Y's own sake* seems to require that X "snap out" of the grip of X's own sexual desire so that X can focus on Y and on Y's pleasure, which would kill or severely dampen X's sexual desire or pleasure, thereby defeating the very point of X's engaging in CS&P. So CS&P satisfy to the hilt the selfishness or self-interestedness of sexual desire. They are, then, necessarily objectifying.

If pessimism about sexual desire is true, what can the defender of CS&P say in their defense? Obviously, he can reject the pessimist view.[14] But to see whether CS&P objectify, we must accept the worst about sexual desire. If we don't, not only do we take the easy way out, we also cannot be sure that sexual desire is not objectifying (what if the pessimist about sex is correct?).

Instead, the defender of CS&P can adopt two argumentative strategies. First, he can argue that objectification is not a *necessary* feature of CS&P; whether CS&P objectify depends on whether they fall short of the conditions required to avoid objectification. Second, he can argue that even if CS&P objectify (whether because objectification is a necessary feature of CS&P or because it happens to be present in a particular act), other factors might override it such that the sexual act is not, overall, morally wrong. Let's start with the first strategy.

2. Why CS&P Are Not Necessarily Objectifying: First Attempt

Consider again Nussbaum and Langton's ways in which people can be objectified. Clearly, casual sex need not involve one partner treating the other as lacking in autonomy, as inert, as violable, as owned, and as lacking subjectivity. Indeed, it (usually) involves the exact opposite. For example, in taking into account Clark's sexual desires, Lois considers him to have autonomy, self-determination, and agency. Furthermore, she does not consider him to be violable because she attributes to him boundaries and integrity in two ways: first, by not treating Clark contrary to his desires and, second, precisely by treating him in accordance with his desires. Lois also, for the same reasons, does not treat Clark as an owned object. Finally, in taking his sexual desires and needs into account, she certainly does not treat him "as something whose experience and feelings . . . need not be taken into account."[15]

Moreover, because partners to casual sex can take each other's desires and wants into account, they do not treat each other as mere bodies, even though they usually focus on each other's bodies and even though they probably engage in casual sex *because* they like each other's physical appearance.[16] But it does not follow that objectification is occurring unless it also follows (which it does not) that from my focusing on a dancer's body or a chef's hands I objectify her.

They also, for similar reasons, don't treat each other as incapable of speaking.[17] And while the focus on each other's body could take the form of treating the other "primarily in terms of how they look," this need not imply objectification. Indeed, in signing up for casual sex, the partners expect and even want to be treated primarily in terms of their appearance: if individuals are proud of their shapely thighs, they might want their partners to pay sexual attention to them. For the same reasons, promiscuity need not involve objectification in any of the above ways.

This leaves us with instrumentality and fungibility. Consider fungibility first. Suppose that X goes to a bar in search of casual sex. In doing so, X treats the people in the bar as fungible, as interchangeable with others of the same type (potential sex partners for X). Yet no one should object that X is somehow treating one wrongly because, like merchants who compete for people's money, people in a bar often compete for others' sexual attention. They consent to being treated as interchangeable with other people of the same type.

With instrumentality, the argument also relies on consent. So long as the parties consent to the act, they do not treat each other merely as tools. Consent, that is, is sufficient to convert using someone merely as a means into using someone not merely as a means because in consenting to what Y desires, X respects Y's wishes. Thus, and to return to the grocer example, by, or in, paying him, we respect his wishes to be a seller, not someone to be abused and robbed. This seems to be true of CS&P. Like many nonsexual interactions, the partners respect each other's sexual needs, desires, and wishes. X is willing to perform oral sex on Y if Y desires it (X is even sometimes happy to!). Indeed, even if X uses Y only as a "piece of meat," X would not use Y only as a tool so long as X is complying with Y's desire to "Use me as a piece of meat!" For in doing Y's bidding, X seems to not be objectifying Y, that is, treating Y *merely* as an object. If anything, it seems to be a form of respect.

So runs the argument attempting to show why CS&P are not necessarily objectifying. In short, so long as the parties do not treat each other in all the possible ways of objectifying someone, or, if they do, do so with each other's consent, CS&P are not, in those cases, objectifying. Therefore, CS&P are not necessarily objectifying.

3. Why the First Attempt Fails

Given the pessimist view of sexual desire, the above defense of CS&P is problematic because it does not fully appreciate the problem with sexual desire, especially in regard to instrumentality.[18] Consider that while Kant agrees that consent is sufficient to render many human interactions nonobjectifying, he disagrees regarding sex. The reason is that sexual desire is pernicious (a pessimist view of sex) since it is the only human "inclination" that "is directed towards other human beings. They themselves, and not their work and services, are its Objects of enjoyment."[19] Sexual desire makes its object exactly that—an *object* of desire. Because by its nature sexual desire pushes human beings to disregard the humanity in each other (and in themselves), consent is *not enough* to make sexual activity nonobjectifying. Thus, if X and Y consent to a sexual act, they consent to an immoral activity. Indeed, each consents to two moral wrongs: X consents to objectify Y and to be objectified by Y (ditto for Y).[20]

To Kant, we must never treat people only as a means but always, at the same time, as an end. It is not fully clear what this means, but one crucial idea is that when dealing with other people we must *respect their morally permissible goals*. Often, this is satisfied simply by not hindering them. But sometimes we must *adopt* them: we must take on others' goals as our own. In Kant's words, "we make others our end" and we have a duty "to make the human being as such as an end."[21] We must help that person promote his or her goals for his or her sake, not for selfish, self-interested, or other reasons.

Now given the pessimist view of sexual desire, CS&P face two difficulties. First, if sexual desire makes us view our sexual partners as tools for its satisfaction, it is hard to see how partners to CS&P can adopt each other's sexual goals *for their own sakes*. Second, even if this is possible, it is hard to see why they *may*, let alone should, because if sexual desire is by nature objectifying, it is not a morally permissible goal that may be adopted. Thus, the defender of CS&P has her work cut out for her.

But here we should be careful. The reason usually given for why satisfying sexual desire is wrong is that sexual desire is objectifying—*X*'s satisfying *Y*'s sexual desire is wrong because it involves *X* objectifying *Y*. So if there were cases in which sexual desire can be satisfied without objectification, satisfying it in those cases would not be wrong. For example, if *X* can sexually satisfy *Y* for *Y*'s own sake, then *X* would not have objectified *Y* nor would have *Y* allowed him or herself to be objectified.

So whether sex is wrong hinges on *why* partners sexually satisfy each other's sexual desires—what their motives are. That is, the existence of the second difficulty hinges on the existence of the first. To see this point better, compare it to a nonsexual case. Suppose *Y*'s goal is to murder *Z*. Can *X* help *Y* attain *Y*'s goal for *Y*'s own sake? Yes. Should *X* do so? No, because murder is wrong regardless of *X*'s motives in helping *Y*. This is not so with sexual acts. There, if *X* can help *Y* attain *Y*'s sexual goals without objectifying *Y* (or *X* allowing him or herself to be objectified), the sole (or main) reason for thinking the goal of sexual satisfaction wrong is removed. So whether *X*'s satisfaction of *Y*'s sexual goals is wrong depends on whether *X* satisfies them for *Y*'s sake.

But the sexual pessimist is still on strong territory. As we have seen, the motives, given the nature of sexual desire, are selfish or self-interested (to attain sexual pleasure). Thus, in CS&P the partners cannot take on each other's goals for their own sakes; they thereby treat each other only as a means. Thus, CS&P are necessarily objectifying.[22]

4. Why CS&P Are Not Necessarily Objectifying: Second Attempt

We can get around this problem by distinguishing between the nature of sexual desire and particular cases of it. The idea is that even if sexual desire is by nature objectifying, this means only that it has to be especially guarded against, not that we must necessarily succumb to its pernicious nature. That is, that something is so-and-so by nature does not mean that its nature cannot be overcome (e.g., lions are by nature dangerous to human beings, but it does not mean that particular lions cannot be tamed). If true, this leaves the door open to cases in which sexual partners do not sexually objectify each other (or themselves).

What cases are these, and could some of them be of CS&P? Could *X* and *Y*, partners to a casual sex act, at least at some points during the act, attend to each other's sexual wants and pleasures for their own sake? Yes, because human beings do not always treat each other selfishly or self-interestedly. They can, and sometimes do, show concern for others even when in the grip of sexual desires or other powerful psychological forces. Kant himself gives an example of a man who, though his mind is clouded with sorrow, is able to attend to his duties to his fellow human beings.[23] The power of sexual desire, as overwhelming as it usually is, need not be so thoroughgoing that it blinds us always to the sexual needs of our partners. So, for example, realizing that Y enjoys receiving oral sex, X performs oral sex on Y for the sake of Y, not because X enjoys performing oral sex on Y, not because X sexually enjoys Y's pleasure, and not because X desires Y to reciprocate, but, say, because X is genuinely committed to the happiness of others, including Y's; because X is kind; because X happens to like Y and wants Y to have a good time; because X is fair, believing that because Y gave X pleasure, X should return the favor; or even because X happens to love Y. If X can do so, then X does not objectify Y (nor does Y allow himself to be objectified if Y agrees to allow X to sexually satisfy Y from these motives by X). Thus, because partners to casual sex can satisfy Kant's requirements for treating someone else as an end and not only as a means, casual sex is not *necessarily* objectifying. And if casual sex is not necessarily objectifying, then neither is promiscuous sex. For if promiscuous sex is frequently-engaged-in casual sex with different partners within a (short) period of time, partners to it could also attend to each other's sexual goals for their own sake; the frequency, variety, and time period of promiscuous sex are irrelevant to this (but see below).

That it is possible for X to attend to Y's sexual needs for the sake of Y says nothing, in and of itself, about X's sexual state of mind. In giving Y oral sex, X might or might not be enjoying it (and keep in mind that just because X enjoys sexually pleasing Y does not imply that X sexually pleases Y *because* X enjoys it), might or might not be disgusted by it, might or might not be indifferent to it. The point is that X performs oral sex on Y *for the sake of Y*. It concerns a type of reason or motive for performing oral sex, not X's sexual mental state. The pessimist about sexual desire (including Kant) claims that when X attends to Y's sexual goals, X does so for selfish or self-interested reasons. The defender of CS&P claims that this is not necessary, that it is possible for X to attend to Y's sexual goals for Y's own sake.[24] And if the Kantian or the pessimist thinks that such cases are impossible, she needs to show us why, given that human beings are capable of overcoming their powerful impulses in some cases.

5. Why the Second Attempt (Probably) Fails

Let's agree that it is possible for X to perform oral sex on Y for Y's own sake, from the motive of wanting to help Y attain sexual satisfaction for Y's sake (and that it is possible for Y to agree to this). Let's also agree that it is even possible that X sexually enjoys the act without thereby making X's motives morally suspect; as noted, we must not confuse X's sexually (or even nonsexually) enjoying something with X's reason for doing that thing. Still, it does not seem possible that X perform oral sex on Y from the motive of *sexual desire* without objectifying Y. That is, *if* what motivates X is sexual desire, as opposed to something else, the case is clinched, for X's sexual desire for Y precludes other motives that might render X's performing oral sex on Y nonobjectifying because to sexually desire Y *is* to desire Y as a body, as an object (on the Kantian pessimist view). Once X attends to Y's sexual needs *from* sexual desire, X objectifies Y. And when X attends to Y's sexual needs for their own sake, X does so *not* from sexual desire (we can tame the lion, but it would no longer be a lion). Indeed, Kant's charitable person who is able to help others despite his sadness does so from the motive of duty, not from sadness or the emotional state he is in. It seems, then, that sexual desire necessarily objectifies, and CS&P are in the thick of it. What needs to be shown to escape this conclusion is that one can act out of sexual desire and simultaneously attend to one's partner's sexual needs for the latter's own sake. I find this task difficult, though I don't deny its possibility (hence the "probably" in this subsection's title). I set it aside.

6. Why Casual Sex and Promiscuity Are Likely Objectifying

Even if it is true that CS&P need not necessarily objectify, this says nothing about how frequently they do and do not. This is an empirical issue, of course, but in all likelihood they *do* objectify. This is for three related reasons. First, human beings tend to be selfish and self-interested. At the very least, people's commitment to morality—if we can speak of commitment at all—is sporadic. This means that whether they act by taking on others' goals as their ends depends on their moods, emotions, what occupies them, and similar factors.[25] I have no evidence for this claim in the form of empirical studies (and I'm not sure what form such studies would take), but human history, the complexity of human psychology, and simply looking around give me very little confidence that people have strong moral fiber.

Second, because satisfying sexual desire is so pleasurable (that's what makes the desire so powerful), and because attending to one's partner's sexual goals for their own sake (usually, if not always) requires getting out of the grip of one's desire, the likelihood of people attending to each other's sexual goals for their own sakes decreases. That is, if X is in the grip of sexual desire, paying attention to Y for Y's sake means getting out of the desire's grip, which means not satisfying the desire, which means no pleasure for X. This defeats one of the main purposes of having sex.

Third, because the very point of CS&P is attaining sexual pleasure ("both parties are out to satisfy their own randiness," as Soble puts it[26]), and because by definition partners to CS&P lack future commitments to each other, the likelihood that they would act selflessly towards each other is close to zero. In all likelihood, they would use each other so as to satisfy their own sexual desires, including being more willing to deceive each other, to give themselves up to sexual abandon, and to take risks. And if paying more attention to others for their own sake means less sexual pleasure, partners to CS&P are not likely at all to pay sexual attention to each other for each other's sake; otherwise, why engage in CS&P to begin with? Imagine now *both* partners attending to each other's sexual wants for their own respective sakes, and you'll see how the sexual pleasure is entirely sucked out of the act. This is why it is also not likely that the partners would agree to being sexually satisfied by each other out of moral considerations, for this also defeats the point of sexual desire. Knowing that one sexually excites another is a crucial motive for engaging in sex, especially CS&P, because it heightens one's own sexual pleasure.

We must then face the fact that CS&P are likely rife with objectification. Indeed, the promiscuous person carries a very heavy moral burden because if avoiding objectification requires getting out of the grip of sexual desire to attend to her partner's sexual desires for their own sake, and if getting out of sexual desire's grip is difficult, the chances of one doing so become smaller and smaller the more one engages in casual sex with different people. The promiscuous person is then likely to engage in objectification quite frequently.

7. Two Possible Replies

At this point, defenders of CS&P have two options. The first is familiar: relax Kant's stringent requirements and argue that as long as the parties respect each other's wishes, desires, and boundaries, and as long as they attend to each other's sexual pleasure, even if for selfish or self-interested reasons, the sex is not objectifying. After all, when we pay the grocer we usually do so not for his own sake but for selfish or self-interested reasons (to get the groceries we want) without thereby doing something wrong. Why not, then, apply the same reasoning to sexual interaction? This option, basically, considers sexual desire and activity to be on a par with other human desires and activities. Thus, if consent is sufficient for these other activities, it also is for sexual ones.

This option abandons the pessimistic view of sexual desire, treating sexual desire as benign. For all we know, a benign view might be true, but by assuming it we do not address the worries of the pessimists and we take the easy way out.

The second option is to accept that CS&P are indeed objectifying but to argue that the immorality of objectification is not so serious as to require the parties to refrain from engaging in sexual activity, including CS&P.

How might one argue for this view? Let's first state the argument loosely. In teaching this issue over the years, my students tended to react as follows: "Okay. Sex has lots of objectification, and objectification is wrong. We get it. But so what? What is so horrible about sexual objectification?" What my students' reaction amounts to is that even though objectification is wrong, it is not so wrong as to require us to refrain from engaging in sex, including CS&P, when sex can be so pleasurable. Putting the argument less loosely, the idea is to first argue that even though sexual objectification is wrong, it is not a serious wrong (except in special cases, like rape), and to then argue that other factors compete with objectification's not-so-serious wrong, making sexual activity possibly morally permissible.

How is sexual objectification not a serious wrong? It is usually consensual, attentive, and not harmful. Contrast it with lying or coercion: they are serious moral wrongs because not only do they involve using others as mere means, but they also involve lack of consent and can, and often do, harm their victims. Not so with sexual objectification because, first, X and Y usually consent to the sexual activity, which, second, even though it involves the use of each other and of themselves as mere instruments, is not an activity that harms them (as when they consent to chop off each other's limbs) or harms other beings (as when they agree to rob a bank or to go cow tipping), especially if they take precautions (against, for example, STDs). Third, they are attentive to each other's sexual desires and needs (even if for selfish or self-interested reasons). So the wrong of sexual objectification, as real as it is, is not very serious.[27]

Second, there are good things about sex, including CS&P, that compete with the not-so-serious wrong of objectification, possibly rendering it overall morally permissible. First and most obviously, it is very pleasurable: there is pleasure in the very prospect of having sex, pleasure during the sexual activity itself (including foreplay), and pleasure in attaining orgasms (among other possible pleasures). Indeed, for many people who are not able to experience lofty pleasures (e.g., from reading classical Arabic poetry, contemplating Velázquez paintings, or drowning in the joyous seas of interpreting Wittgenstein), sexual pleasure is one of the few pleasures they have. Second, sexual activity is recreational, often providing (like other activities, such as solving jigsaw puzzles) needed entertainment, release, intense focus, and other forms of distraction from the humdrum or toil of everyday life. Third, for those people who do not desire or have time for monogamy, love, or a relationship, and for those who prefer sexual variety and the lack of love and sexual commitments, CS&P allow them to satisfy their sexual urges without the complications of relationships. Finally, according to some moral views, leading a rich, human life is important for human beings to flourish or live well. If sexual activity, undertaken moderately and in overall morally permissible ways, is part of such a life, then CS&P can contribute to it.[28]

The above four factors need not be the only ones, and they are not all of a moral nature (some are pleasure-related, some pragmatic). But the point is that if we couple the not-so-serious moral wrong of objectification with the above factors, sexual activity, including CS&P, might emerge as overall morally permissible.

CONCLUDING REMARKS

I have argued that on a pessimist view of sexual desire and given the point of CS&P (sexual pleasure), there is a strong case to be made that CS&P *necessarily* objectify and that even if they do not, they *likely* objectify. I have also suggested an argument that, despite the objectification, CS&P might be overall permissible. However, this does not mean that CS&P are morally in the clear because they can be wrong for other reasons. For example, casual sex can be wrong because it is adulterous, done from bad motives, or (if conservatives are correct) loveless. It can be wrong because the objectification is not overridden by other factors. Promiscuity might be wrong because it involves the overvaluation of sex. Thus, whether they are wrong in particular cases depends on all the relevant factors.[29]

NOTES

1. This is Albert Ellis's definition, "Casual Sex," *International Journal of Moral and Social Studies* 1:2 (1986): 157–69. For more on CS&P, see G. E. M. Anscombe, "Contraception and Chastity," *The Human World* no. 7 (1972): 9–30 (reprinted, revised, in *Ethics and Population*, edited by Michael Bayles [Cambridge, Mass.: Schenkman, 1976], 134–53); Frederick Elliston, "In Defense of Promiscuity," in *Philosophy and Sex*, 1st edition, edited by Robert Baker and Frederick Elliston (Buffalo, N.Y.: Prometheus, 1975), 223–43; Raja Halwani, *Virtuous Liaisons: Care, Love, Sex, and Virtue Ethics* (Chicago: Open Court, 2003), Chapter 3; Raja Halwani, "Casual Sex," in *Sex from Plato to Paglia: A Philosophical Encyclopedia*, edited by Alan Soble (Westport, Conn.: Greenwood Press, 2006), 136–42; Raja Halwani, "Casual Sex, Promiscuity, and Temperance," in *Sex and Ethics: Essays on Sexuality, Virtue, and the Good Life*, edited by Raja Halwani (New York: Palgrave Macmillan, 2007), 215–25; and Kristjan Kristjansson, "Casual Sex Revisited," *Journal of Social Philosophy* 29:2 (1998): 97–108.

2. There are four options, with varying degrees of cogency: (1) *X him* or *herself* is not having casual sex, though the *sex X* is having is casual (what would this mean?); (2) the sex-that-*X*-has is not casual, but the sex-that-*Y*-has is casual; (3) the sex is both casual and noncasual (a contradiction); and (4) there is no single answer because the answer is relative: to *X* the sex is not casual, to *Y* it is.

3. Kant, *Lectures on Ethics*, translated by Louis Infield (Indianapolis, Ind.: Hackett, 1963), 163.

4. Of course, humans are objects in that they are objects of this universe much like any other entity. They are also objects in a physical sense: they are made of the same stuff (the elements) that typical objects are made of. Each of these senses is compatible with humans' having a special property in virtue of which they should not be treated merely as objects are treated.

5. See Alan Soble, *Pornography, Sex, and Feminism* (Amherst, N.Y.: Prometheus, 2002), for an excellent discussion.

6. One philosopher who thinks that mere regard could be objectifying is Martha Nussbaum. See her example of "M" and "F" in "Feminism, Virtue, and Objectification," in *Sex and Ethics*, edited by Halwani, 49–62, at 54–55. See Alan Soble's reply, "Concealment and Exposure: A Mostly Temperate and Courageous Afterword," also in *Sex and Ethics*, 229–52, at 248–51. Another philosopher who thinks that mere regard could be objectifying is Rae Langton ("Autonomy-Denial in Objectification," in *Sexual*

Solipsism: Philosophical Essays on Pornography and Objectification [Oxford, U.K.: Oxford University Press, 2009], 223–40).

7. Nussbaum argues that objectification is permissible in relationships generally characterized by mutual respect; see "Objectification," *Philosophy and Public Affairs* 24:4 (1995): 249–91 (reprinted in *Philosophy of Sex: Contemporary Readings*, 4th edition, edited by Alan Soble [Lanham, Md.: Rowman and Littlefield, 2002], 381–419). For discussions of her views, see Alan Soble, "Sexual Use" (sections "Thick Minimalist Externalism" and "Thick Extended Externalism," in this volume); Patricia Marino, "The Ethics of Sexual Objectification: Autonomy and Consent," *Inquiry* 51:4 (2008): 345–64; Rae Langton, "Autonomy-Denial in Objectification"; and Raja Halwani, *Philosophy of Love, Sex, and Marriage: An Introduction* (New York: Routledge, 2010), 194–97.

8. This might stretch the concept of "tool" too much since we think of tools as things that, though needed to attain goals, are in principle replaceable by other things so long as the goal is attained, whereas we think that beloveds are not replaceable.

9. Nussbaum, "Objectification," 257. Her seventh way is not well-worded. There are cases in which it is permissible to not take someone's feelings and experiences into account. For example, X must set aside Y's fear of syringes in order to inject Y with the needed medicine. What Nussbaum intends, I suppose, is treating someone as if they lack feelings and experiences.

10. Langton, "Autonomy-Denial in Objectification," 228–29. In her three ways (and in her wording of Nussbaum's seventh), Langton changes Nussbaum's "objectifier" to "one" because the latter has a more neutral sense; in cases in which the object is an ordinary object (not a person), one is not being an objectifier (226, note 7).

11. I would be as confident about the ninth way were it not for the word "primarily"; in some cases — say, at a modeling agency — treating someone primarily in terms of how they look is perfectly appropriate. Then again, it is not clear what Langton means by "primarily."

12. See "The Analytic Categories of the Philosophy of Sex" (in this volume, 3–6), for Soble's discussion — which I freely (and thankfully) borrow and adapt — of the metaphysical sexual pessimists and the metaphysical sexual optimists. I focus on sexual desire and discuss sexual activity insofar as it results from sexual desire.

13. Soble, "Analytic Categories," 4.

14. There is an optimistic view of sexual desire (which Soble claims to find in the work of Irving Singer), according to which it is a force that can bring people together, bring them pleasure and joy, and is conducive to their well-being ("Analytic Categories," 5–6).

15. Nussbaum, "Objectification," 257.

16. Indeed, beyond paying attention to the quality that purportedly elevates people over objects, a few other things can destroy casual sexual activity. (Y: "Why are you suddenly asking me about my hobbies?" X: "I want to treat you as a full person, not as a hobby-less piece of meat." Y: [eyes rolling] "OMG.")

17. The silencing issue is complicated. Langton argues in several essays that sometimes pornography is causally implicated in rendering women silent; she means that their desires, particularly their refusals to engage in sex, are not heard (see *Sexual Solipsism*, especially "Speech Acts as Unspeakable Acts"). It is possible, then, that in casual sex women are not heard and are objectified in this sense. However, the objectification would not occur because the sex is casual but because women's silence cuts across many social areas.

18. Indeed, those who charge CS&P with necessary objectification should focus on instrumentality since CS&P need not involve the other objectifications.

19. Kant, *Lectures on Ethics*, 162. On Kant's views, see Thomas Mappes, "Sexual Morality and the Concept of Using Another Person" (in this volume); Lara Denis, "Kant on the Wrongness of 'Unnatural' Sex," *History of Philosophy Quarterly* 16:2 (1999): 225–48; Lara Denis, "Sex and the Virtuous Kantian Agent," in Halwani, ed., *Sex and Ethics*, 37–48; Soble, "Sexual Use"; and Halwani, *Philosophy of Love, Sex, and Marriage*, 200–10.

20. For Kant, marriage is the only solution to sexual objectification. I do not discuss his solution because it is problematic; see Lara Denis, "From Friendship to Marriage: Revisiting Kant," *Philosophy and Phenomenological Research* 63:1 (2001): 1–28. Soble, however, thinks that Kant's solution is coherent; see "Sexual Use" (in this volume, section "Kant's Solution").

21. Kant, *Metaphysics of Morals* 6:393 and 6:395, translated and edited by Mary J. Gregor, in *Practical Philosophy* (Cambridge: Cambridge University Press, 1996). These remarks by Kant are made in the context of his argument for beneficence as a duty (thanks to Alan Soble for showing me his e-mail exchange with Lara Denis about this issue, and to Denis for allowing, but not merely allowing, her brain to be picked by Soble). See also Onora O'Neill, "Between Consenting Adults," in *Constructions of Reason: Explorations of Kant's Practical Philosophy* (Cambridge: Cambridge University Press, 1989), 105–25.

22. Note an interesting result: sexual acts done *not* from sexual desire need not be morally wrong on this view because they would not stem from the manipulative, overpowering, and pernicious impulse of sexual desire. Thus, when sex workers have sex with clients from nonsexual desires, when spouses oblige and have sex with their spouses when they do not desire sex, when gorgeous Ahmad has sex with Matt because he wants Matt to have a taste of heaven, and so forth—these sexual acts, if wrong, are not wrong on the ground that they are objectifying. As Soble makes the point hyperbolically: "Casual sex, even a cold fuck, even a bought fuck, is less a threat to one's autonomy" because the pernicious overpowering influence of sexual desire is absent (*Pornography, Sex, and Feminism*, 182).

23. *Grounding for the Metaphysics of Morals* 4:398, translated by James W. Ellington (Indianapolis, Ind.: Hackett, 1981).

24. Note that X can attend to Y's sexual goals neither for selfish reasons nor for reasons related to Y's goals: X might believe that God or Caligula commanded X to do so.

25. This is one reason Kant refused to ground morality in human nature.

26. Soble, "Sexual Use," in this volume, 309–10.

27. One might object that (1) the genuineness of consent is problematic because the agreement is warped by the power of sexual desire. This may be true; however, because the consent is usually to a harmless activity, a warped judgment might not be a general serious issue, but serious only in particular cases (e.g., fellatio in the Oval Office). One might object that (2) this argument brings in consequentialist reasons into a nonconsequentialist, Kantian framework. But neither Kant himself nor his followers shun consequentialist considerations (their concern is to decide when and to what extent they are morally relevant). Further, Kant or no Kant, harm is an important moral factor that needs to be taken into account in assessing the overall morality of action or types of actions.

28. Compare this view to Kant's marriage solution to objectification, in which, according to Soble, "Kant does not deny that objectification still occurs in marital sex; he simply says it is permissible, or authorized" ("Sexual Use," 323). On temperate and moderate CS&P, see Halwani, *Virtuous Liaisons*, chapter 3; Halwani, "Casual Sex, Promiscuity, and Temperance."

29. Thanks to Patricia Marino and Nicholas Power for comments on an earlier draft. Special thanks to Alan Soble, whose trenchant comments showed me the need to change my arguments and conclusions.

STUDY QUESTIONS

1. Are rape, bestiality, and necrophilia examples of casual sex? How would you go about answering this question? What are the impli-

cations of your answers for understanding "casual sex" as "no-strings-attached" sexual activity?

2. Given Halwani's definition of "objectification," can one objectify animals? Would your answer require a revision in Halwani's definition? In the case of mammals who are not as linguistically competent as humans, might their consent rest more on behavioral cues (they seem to enjoy the activity) than on verbal messages?

3. Would adopting different definitions of "casual sex" and "promiscuity" change our (and Halwani's) moral conclusions about them? At the metaphilosophical level, would a "yes" answer imply that the moral evaluations are already (and at least partially) packed into the definitions of "casual sex" and "promiscuity"? Would such definitions be accurate insofar as they are reports about "moral facts"?

4. Suppose we accept a metaphysically optimistic view of sex. Would this strongly support the conclusion that objectification does not occur in CS&P? Or might it, instead, provide equally strong reasons for not engaging in CS&P because they do not achieve the optimistic model of ideal sexuality?

5. Sex workers engage in casual sex and promiscuity, and their usual motive is to earn money in exchange for sexual services. Do sex workers (e.g., prostitutes) sexually objectify their clients, both seeing them merely as sources of income and treating them the same way? Do they objectify their clients by manipulating their sexuality and taking advantage of their clients' sexual desire and hence sexual vulnerability? Do prostitutes allow themselves to be sexually objectified by their clients, who may be taking advantage of the prostitute's need for money? However, to what extent are these moral faults, when they exist, due to the nature of the sexual interactions as casual and promiscuous?

6. How serious is the wrong of objectification, or on what does the seriousness of objectification rest? Is Halwani right to suggest that in some circumstances objectification is not serious enough to be the overriding or ruling moral consideration? (Martha Nussbaum claims in "Objectification" [note 7] that using a lover's body as a pillow is either not objectification or an innocuous case of objectification.) If sexual desire is as perniciously powerful as the metaphysical pessimists make it out to be, to what extent can a philosopher rely, as Halwani does and as sexual liberals tend to do, on the presence of genuine consent as mitigating, overriding, the wrongfulness of objectification? We are faced here with a perennial and seemingly intractable question: does it make moral or conceptual sense that a person may consent to be (sexually) used? Start with the essay by Thomas Mappes in this volume, and then consider several others.

TWENTY-FIVE

Date Rape: A Feminist Analysis

Lois Pineau

In this essay, **Lois Pineau** *shows how the mythology surrounding rape enters into a criterion of "reasonableness" that operates through the legal system to make women vulnerable to unscrupulous sexual victimization. She explores the possibility for changes in legal procedures and presumptions that would better serve women's interests by leaving them less vulnerable to sexual violence. Achieving these goals requires a reformulation of the criterion of consent in terms of what is reasonable from a woman's point of view, which relies not on a "contractual" model of sexual interactions but on what Pineau calls a "communicative" model of sexual interactions. Pineau's essay spawned a great deal of constructive philosophical and legal literature on date and acquaintance rape. Its fundamental ideas were incorporated into Antioch University's famous "Sexual Offense Policy" (on which see, for example, Alan Soble's essay in* The Philosophy of Sex, *5th ed., pp. 459–77).*

Lois Pineau left philosophy to study law in 1994. She has been a member of the criminal defense bar in Toronto, Canada since 1999. She continues to be interested in political and legal philosophy and ethics, particularly in the area of mental health. This essay was awarded the Fred Berger Memorial Prize of the American Philosophical Association in 1991 as the best article in the philosophy of law. It first appeared in *Law and Philosophy* 8:2 (1989): 217–43. © Kluwer Academic Publishers. Reprinted here by permission of Kluwer Academic Publishers.

The feminist recognition that dominant ideologies reinforce conceptual frameworks that serve patriarchal interests lies behind what must now be seen as a revolution in political analysis, one which for the first time approaches the problems that women face from a woman's point of view. One of those problems is the ongoing difficulty of dealing with a society that practices and condones violence against women. This is particularly the case with date rape.

Date rape is nonaggravated sexual assault, nonconsensual sex that does not involve physical injury, or the explicit threat of physical injury. But because it does not involve physical injury, and because physical injury is often the only criterion that is accepted as evidence that the *actus reas* is nonconsensual, what is really sexual assault is often mistaken for seduction. The replacement of the old rape laws with the new laws on sexual assault has done nothing to resolve this problem.

Rape, defined as nonconsensual sex, usually involving penetration by a man of a woman who is not his wife, has been replaced in some criminal codes with the charge of sexual assault.[1] This has the advantage both of extending the range of possible victims of sexual assault, the manner in which people can be assaulted, and replacing a crime which is exclusive of consent, with one for which consent is a defense.[2] But while the consent of a woman is now consistent with the conviction of her assailant in cases of aggravated assault, nonaggravated sexual assault is still distinguished from normal sex solely by the fact that it is not consented to. Thus the question of whether someone has consented to a sexual encounter is still important, and the criteria for consent continues to be the central concern of discourse on sexual assault.[3]

However, if a man is to be convicted, it does not suffice to establish that the *actus reas* was consensual. In order to be guilty of sexual assault a man must have the requisite *mens rea*, i.e., he must either have believed that his victim did not consent or that she was probably not consenting.[4] In many common law jurisdictions a man who sincerely believes that a woman consented to a sexual encounter is deemed to lack the required *mens rea*, even though the woman did not consent, and even though his belief is not reasonable.[5] Recently, strong dissenting voices have been raised against the sincerity condition, and the argument made that *mens rea* be defeated only if the defendant has a reasonable belief that the plaintiff consented.[6] The introduction of legislation which excludes "honest belief" (unreasonable sincere belief) as a defense, will certainly help to provide women with greater protection against violence. But while this will be an important step forward, the question of what constitutes a reasonable belief, the problem of evidence when rapists lie, and the problem of the entrenched attitudes of the predominantly male police, judges, lawyers, and jurists who handle sexual assault cases, remains.

The criteria for *mens rea*, for the reasonableness of belief, and for consent are closely related. For although a man's sincere belief in the consent of his victim may be sufficient to defeat *mens rea*, the court is less likely to believe his belief is sincere if his belief is unreasonable. If his belief is reasonable, they are more likely to believe in the sincerity of his belief. But evidence of the reasonableness of his belief is also evidence that consent really did take place. For the very things that make it reasonable for *him* to believe that the defendant consented are often the very things that incline the court to believe that she consented. What is often missing is the voice of the woman herself, an account of what it would be reasonable for *her* to agree to, that is to say, an account of what is reasonable from *her* standpoint.

Thus, what is presented as reasonable has repercussions for four separate but related concerns: (1) the question of whether a man's belief in a woman's consent was reasonable; (2) the problem of whether it is reasonable to attribute *mens rea* to him; (3) the question of what could count as reasonable from the woman's point of view; (4) the question of what is reasonable from the court's point of view. These repercussions are of the utmost practical concern. In a culture which contains an incidence of sexual assault verging on epidemic, a criterion of reasonableness which regards mere submission as consent fails to offer persons vulnerable to those assaults adequate protection.

The following statements by self-confessed date rapists reveal how our lack of a solution for dealing with date rape protects rapists by failing to provide their victims with legal recourse:

> All of my rapes have been involved in a dating situation where I've been out with a woman I know. . . . I wouldn't take no for an answer. I think it had something to do with my acceptance of rejection. I had low self-esteem and not much self-confidence and when I was rejected for something which I considered to be rightly mine, I became angry and I went ahead anyway. And this was the same in any situation, whether it was rape or it was something else.[7]

> When I did date, when I was younger, I would pick up a girl and if she didn't come across I would threaten her or slap her face then tell her she was going to fuck—that was it. But that's because I didn't want to waste time with any come-ons. It took too much time. I wasn't interested because I didn't like them as people anyway, and I just went with them just to get laid. Just to say that I laid them.[8]

There is, at this time, nothing to protect women from this kind of unscrupulous victimization. A woman on a casual date with a virtual stranger has almost no chance of bringing a complaint of sexual assault before the courts. One reason for this is the prevailing criterion for consent. According to this criterion, consent is implied unless some emphatic episodic sign of resistance occurred, and its occurrence can be established. But if no episodic act occurred, or it did not occur, and the defendant claims that it didn't, or if the defendant threatened the plaintiff but won't admit it in court, it is almost impossible to find any evidence that would support the plaintiff's word against the defendant. This difficulty is exacerbated by suspicion on the part of the courts, police, and legal educators that even where an act of resistance occurs, this act should not be inter-

preted as a withholding of consent, and this suspicion is especially upheld where the accused is a man who is known to the female plaintiff.

In Glanville Williams's classic textbook on criminal law we are
warned that where a man is unknown to a woman, she does not consent
if she expresses her rejection in the form of an episodic and vigorous act
at the "vital moment." But if the man is known to the woman she must,
according to Williams, make use of "all means available to her to repel
the man."[9] Williams warns that women often welcome a "mastery advance" and present a token resistance. He quotes Byron's couplet,

> A little still she strove, and much repented
> And whispering "I will ne'er consent" — consented

by way of alerting law students to the difficulty of distinguishing real
protest from pretense.[10] Thus, while in principle, a firm unambiguous
stand, or a healthy show of temper ought to be sufficient, if established,
to show nonconsent, in practice the forceful overriding of such a stance is
apt to be taken as an indication that the resistance was not seriously
intended, and that the seduction had succeeded. The consequence of this
is that it is almost impossible to establish the defendant's guilt beyond a
reasonable doubt.

Thus, on the one hand, we have a situation in which women are
vulnerable to the most exploitive tactics at the hands of men who are
known to them. On the other hand, almost nothing will count as evidence
of their being assaulted, including their having taken an emphatic stance
in withholding their consent. The new laws have done almost nothing to
change this situation. Yet clearly, some solution must be sought. Moreover, the road to that solution presents itself clearly enough as a need for
a reformulation of the criterion of consent. It is patent that a criterion that
collapses whenever the crime itself succeeds will not suffice.

The purpose of this paper is to develop such a criterion, and I propose
to do so by grounding this criterion in a conception of the "reasonable."
Part of the strength of the present criterion for consent lies in the belief
that it is reasonable for women to agree to the kind of sex involved in
"date rape," or that it is reasonable for men to think that they have
agreed. My argument is that it is not reasonable for women to consent to
that kind of sex, and that there are furthermore, no grounds for thinking
that it is reasonable. Since what we want to know is when a woman has
consented, and since standards for consent are based on the presumed
choices of reasonable agents, it is what is reasonable from a woman's
point of view that must provide the principal delineation of a criterion of
consent that is capable of representing a woman's willing behavior. Developing this line of reasoning further, I will argue that the kind of sex to
which it would be reasonable for women to consent suggests a criterion
of consent that would bring the kind of sex involved in date rape well
within the realm of sexual assault.

THE PROBLEM OF THE CRITERION

The reasoning that underlies the present criterion of consent is entangled in a number of mutually supportive mythologies which see sexual assault as masterful seduction, and silent submission as sexual enjoyment. Because the prevailing ideology has so much informed our conceptualization of sexual interaction, it is extraordinarily difficult for us to distinguish between assault and seduction, submission and enjoyment, or so we imagine. At the same time, this failure to distinguish has given rise to a network of rationalizations that support the conflation of assault with seduction, submission with enjoyment. I therefore want to begin my argument by providing an example which shows both why it is so difficult to make this distinction, and that it exists. Later, I will identify and attempt to unravel the lines of reasoning that reinforce this difficulty.

> The woman I have in mind agrees to see someone because she feels an initial attraction to him and believes that he feels the same way about her. She goes out with him in the hope that there will be mutual enjoyment and in the course of the day or evening an increase of mutual interest. Unfortunately, these hopes of *mutual* and *reciprocal* interest are not realized. We do not know how much interest she has in him by the end of their time together, but whatever her feelings she comes under pressure to have sex with him, and she does not want to have the kind of sex he wants. She may desire to hold hands and kiss, to engage in more intense caresses or in some form of foreplay, or she may not want to be touched. She may have reasons unrelated to desire for not wanting to engage in the kind of sex he is demanding. She may have religious reservations, concerns about pregnancy or disease, a disinclination to be just another conquest. She may be engaged in a seduction program of her own which sees abstaining from sexual activity as a means of building an important emotional bond. She feels she is desirable to him, and she knows, and he knows that he will have sex with her if he can. And while she feels she doesn't owe him anything, and that it is her prerogative to refuse him, this feeling is partly a defensive reaction against a deeply held belief that if he is in need, she should provide. If she buys into the myth of insistent male sexuality she may feel he is suffering from sexual frustration and that she is largely to blame.
>
> We do not know how much he desires her, but we do know that his desire for erotic satisfaction can hardly be separated from his desire for conquest. He feels no dating obligation, but has a strong commitment to scoring. He uses the myth of "so hard to control" male desire as a rhetorical tactic, telling her how frustrated she will leave him. He becomes overbearing. She resists, voicing her disinclination. He alternates between telling her how desirable she is and taking a hostile stance, charging her with misleading him, accusing her of wanting him, and being coy, in short of being deceitful, all the time engaging in rather aggressive body contact. It is late at night, she is tired and a bit queasy

from too many drinks, and he is reaffirming her suspicion that perhaps she has misled him. She is having trouble disengaging his body from hers, and wishes he would just go away. She does not adopt a strident angry stance, partly because she thinks he is acting normally and does not deserve it, partly because she feels she is partly to blame, and partly because there is always the danger that her anger will make him angry, possibly violent. It seems that the only thing to do, given his aggression, and her queasy fatigue, is to go along with him and get it over with, but this decision is so entangled with the events in process it is hard to know if it is not simply a recognition of what is actually happening. She finds the whole encounter a thoroughly disagreeable experience, but he does not take any notice, and wouldn't have changed course if he had. He congratulates himself on his sexual prowess and is confirmed in his opinion that aggressive tactics pay off. Later she feels that she has been raped, but paradoxically tells herself that she let herself be raped.

The paradoxical feelings of the woman in our example indicate her awareness that what she feels about the incident stands in contradiction to the prevailing cultural assessment of it. She knows that she did not want to have sex with her date. She is not so sure, however, about how much her own desires count, and she is uncertain that she has made her desires clear. Her uncertainty is reinforced by the cultural reading of this incident as an ordinary seduction.

As for us, we assume that the woman did not want to have sex, but just like her, we are unsure whether her mere reluctance, in the presence of high-pressure tactics, constitutes nonconsent. We suspect that submission to an overbearing and insensitive lout is no way to go about attaining sexual enjoyment, and we further suspect that he felt no compunction about providing it, so that on the face of it, from the outside looking in, it looks like a pretty unreasonable proposition for her.

Let us look at this reasoning more closely. Assume that she was not attracted to the kind of sex offered by the sort of person offering it. Then it would be *prima facie* unreasonable for her to agree to have sex, unreasonable, that is, unless she were offered some pay-off for her stoic endurance, money perhaps, or tickets to the opera. The reason is that in sexual matters, agreement is closely connected to attraction. Thus, where the presumption is that she was not attracted, we should at the same time presume that she did not consent. Hence, the burden of proof should be on her alleged assailant to show that she had good reasons for consenting to an unattractive proposition.

This is not, however, the way such situations are interpreted. In the unlikely event that the example I have described should come before the courts, there is little doubt that the law would interpret the woman's eventual acquiescence or "going along with" the sexual encounter as consent. But along with this interpretation would go the implicit understanding that she had consented because when all was said and done, and when the "token" resistances to the "masterful advances" had been made she had wanted to after all. Once the courts have constructed this interpretation, they are then forced to conjure up some horror story of feminine revenge in order to explain why she should bring charges against her "seducer."

In the even more unlikely event that the courts agreed that the woman had not consented to the above encounter, there is little chance that her assailant would be convicted of sexual assault.[11] The belief that the man's aggressive tactics are a normal part of seduction means that *mens rea* cannot be established. Her eventual "going along" with his advances constitutes reasonable grounds for his believing in her consent. These "reasonable" grounds attest to the sincerity of his belief in her consent. This reasonableness means that *mens rea* would be defeated even in jurisdictions which make *mens rea* a function of objective standards of reasonableness. Moreover, the sympathy of the court is more likely to lie with the rapist than with his victim, since if the court is typical, it will be strongly inclined to believe that the victim had in some way "asked for it."

The position of the courts is supported by the widespread belief that male aggression and female reluctance are normal parts of seduction. Given their acceptance of this model, the logic of their response must be respected. For if sexual aggression is a part of ordinary seduction, then it cannot be inconsistent with the legitimate consent of the person allegedly seduced by this means. And if it is normal for a woman to be reluctant, then this reluctance must be consistent with her consent as well. The position of the courts is not inconsistent just so long as they allow that some sort of protest on the part of a woman counts as refusal. As we have seen, however, it frequently happens that no sort of protest would count as a refusal. Moreover, if no sort of protest, or at least if precious few count, then the failure to register these protests will amount to "asking for it," it will amount, in other words, to agreeing.

The court's belief in "natural" male aggression and "natural" female reluctance has increasingly come under attack by feminist critics who see quite correctly that the entire legal position would collapse if, for example, it were shown empirically that men were not aggressive, and that women, at least when they wanted sex, were. This strategy is of little help, however, so long as aggressive men can still be found, and relics of reluctant women continue to surface. Fortunately, there is another strategy. The position collapses through the weakness of its internal logic. The next section traces the several lines of this logic.

RAPE MYTHS

The belief that the natural aggression of men and the natural reluctance of women somehow make date rape understandable underlies a number of prevalent myths about rape and human sexuality. These beliefs maintain their force partly on account of a logical compulsion exercised by them at an unconscious level. The only way of refuting them effectively, is to excavate the logical propositions involved, and to expose their misapplication to the situations to which they have been applied. In what follows, I propose to excavate the logical support for popular attitudes that are tolerant of date rape. These myths are not just popular, however, but often emerge in the arguments of judges who acquit date rapists, and policemen who refuse to lay charges.

The claim that the victim provoked a sexual incident, that "she asked for it," is by far the most common defense given by men who are accused of sexual assault.[12] Feminists, rightly incensed by this response, often treat it as beneath contempt, singling out the defense as an argument against it. On other fronts, sociologists have identified the response as part of an overall tendency of people to see the world as just, a tendency which disposes them to conclude that people for the most part deserve what they get.[13] However, an inclination to see the world as just requires us to construct an account which yields this outcome, and it is just such an account that I wish to examine with regard to date rape.

The least sophisticated of the "she asked for it" rationales, and in a sense, the easiest to deal with, appeals to an injunction against sexually provocative behavior on the part of women. If women should not be sexually provocative, then, from this standpoint, a woman who is sexually provocative deserves to suffer the consequences. Now it will not do to respond that women get raped even when they are not sexually provocative, or that it is men who get to interpret (unfairly) what counts as sexually provocative.[14] The question should be: Why shouldn't a woman be sexually provocative? Why should this behavior warrant any kind of aggressive response whatsoever?

Attempts to explain that women have a right to behave in sexually provocative ways without suffering dire consequences still meet with surprisingly tough resistance. Even people who find nothing wrong or sinful with sex itself, in any of its forms, tend to suppose that women must not behave sexually unless they are prepared to carry through on some fuller course of sexual interaction. The logic of this response seems to be that at some point a woman's behavior commits her to following through on the full course of a sexual encounter as it is defined by her assailant. At some point she has made an agreement, or formed a contract, and once that is done, her contractor is entitled to demand that she satisfy the terms of that contract. Thus, this view about sexual responsibility and desert is supported by other assumptions about contracts and agreement. But we do not normally suppose that casual nonverbal behavior generates agreements. Nor do we normally grant private persons the right to enforce contracts. What rationale would support our conclusion in this case?

The rationale, I believe, comes in the form of a belief in the especially insistent nature of male sexuality, an insistence which lies at the root of natural male aggression, and which is extremely difficult, perhaps impossible to contain. At a certain point in the arousal process, it is thought, a man's rational will gives way to the prerogatives of nature. His sexual need can and does reach a point where it is uncontrollable, and his natural masculine aggression kicks in to assure that this need is met. Women, however, are naturally more contained, and so it is their responsibility not to provoke the irrational in the male. If they do go so far as that, they have both failed in their responsibilities, and subjected themselves to the inevitable. One does not go into the lion's cage and expect not to be eaten. Natural feminine reluctance, it is thought, is no protection against a sexually aroused male.

This belief about the normal aggressiveness of male sexuality is complemented by common knowledge about female gender development. Once, women were taught to deny their sexuality and to aspire to ideals of chastity. Things have not changed so much. Women still tend to eschew conquest mentalities in favor of a combination of sex and affection. Insofar as this is thought to be merely a cultural requirement, however, there is an expectation that women will be coy about their sexual desire. The assumption that women both want to indulge sexually, and are inclined to sacrifice this desire for higher ends, gives rise to the myth that they want to be raped. After all, doesn't rape give them the sexual enjoyment they *really* want, at the same time that it relieves them of the responsibility for admitting to and acting upon what they want? And how then can we blame men, who have been socialized to be aggressively seductive precisely for the purpose of overriding female reserve? If we find fault at all, we are inclined to cast our suspicions on the motives of the woman. For it is on her that the contradictory roles of sexual desirer and sexual denier have been placed. Our awareness of the contradiction expected of her makes us suspect her honesty. In the past, she was expected to deny her complicity because of the shame and guilt she felt at having submitted.[15] This expectation persists in many quarters today, and is carried over into a general suspicion about her character, and the fear that she might make a false accusation out of revenge, or some other low motive.[16]

But if women really want sexual pleasure, what inclines us to think that they will get it through rape? This conclusion logically requires a theory about the dynamics of sexual pleasure that sees that pleasure as an emergent property of overwhelming male insistence. For the assumption that a raped female experiences sexual pleasure implies that the person who rapes her knows how to cause that pleasure independently of any information she might convey on that point. Since her ongoing protest is inconsistent with requests to be touched in particular ways in particular places, to have more of this and less of that, then we must believe that the person who touches her knows these particular ways and places instinctively, without any directives from her.

Thus we find, underlying and reinforcing this belief in incommunicative male prowess, a conception of sexual pleasure that springs from wordless interchanges, and of sexual success that occurs in a place of meaningful silence. The language of seduction is accepted as a tacit language: eye contact, smiles, blushes, and faintly discernible gestures. It is, accordingly, imprecise and ambiguous. It would be easy for a man to make mistakes about the message conveyed, understandable that he should mistakenly think that a sexual invitation has been made, and a bargain struck. But honest mistakes, we think, must be excused.

In sum, the belief that women should not be sexually provocative is logically linked to several other beliefs, some normative, some empirical. The normative beliefs are that (1) people should keep the agreements they make (2) that sexually provocative behavior, taken beyond a certain point, generates agreements (3) that the peculiar nature of male and female sexuality places such agreements in a special category, one in which the possibility of retracting an agreement is ruled out, or at least made highly unlikely, (4) that women are not to be trusted, in sexual matters at least. The empirical belief, which turns out to be false, is that male sexuality is not subject to rational and moral control.

DISPELLING THE MYTHS

The "she asked for it" justification of sexual assault incorporates a conception of a contract that would be difficult to defend in any other context and the presumptions about human sexuality which function to reinforce sympathies rooted in the contractual notion of just deserts are not supported by empirical research.

The belief that a woman generates some sort of contractual obligation whenever her behavior is interpreted as seductive is the most indefensible part of the mythology of rape. In law, contracts are not legitimate just because a promise has been made. In particular, the use of pressure tactics to extract agreement is frowned upon. Normally, an agreement is upheld only if the contractors were clear on what they were getting into and had sufficient time to reflect on the wisdom of their doing so. Either there must be a clear tradition in which the expectations involved in the contract are fairly well known (marriage), or there must be an explicit written agreement concerning the exact terms of the contract and the expectations of the persons involved. But whatever the terms of a contract, there is no private right to enforce it. So that if I make a contract with you on which I renege, the only permissible recourse for you is through due legal process.

Now it is not clear whether sexual contracts can be made to begin with, or if so, what sort of sexual contracts would be legitimate. But assuming that they could be made, the terms of those contracts would not be enforceable. To allow public enforcement would be to grant the state the overt right to force people to have sex, and this would clearly be unacceptable. Granting that sexual contracts are legitimate, state enforcement of such contracts would have to be limited to ordering nonsexual compensation for breaches of contract. So it makes no difference whether a sexual contract is tacit or explicit. There are no grounds whatsoever that would justify enforcement of its terms.

Thus, even if we assume that a woman has initially agreed to an encounter, her agreement does not automatically make all subsequent sexual activity to which she submits legitimate. If during coitus a woman should experience pain, be suddenly overcome with guilt or fear of pregnancy, or simply lose her initial desire, those are good reasons for her to change her mind. Having changed her mind, neither her partner nor the state has any right to force her to continue. But then if she is forced to continue she is assaulted. Thus, establishing that consent occurred at a particular point during a sexual encounter should not conclusively establish the legitimacy of the encounter.[17] What is needed is a reading of whether she agreed throughout the encounter.

If the "she asked for it" contractual view of sexual interchange has any validity, it is because there is a point at which there is no stopping a sexual encounter, a point at which that encounter becomes the inexorable outcome of the unfolding of natural events. If a sexual encounter is like a slide on which I cannot stop halfway down, it will be relevant whether I enter the slide of my own free will, or am pushed.

But there is no evidence that the entire sexual act is like a slide. While there may be a few seconds in the "plateau" period just prior to orgasm in which people are "swept" away by sexual feelings to the point where we could justifiably understand their lack of heed for the comfort of their partner, the greater part of a sexual encounter comes well within the bounds of morally responsible control of our own actions. Indeed, the available evidence shows that most of the activity involved in sex has to do with building the requisite level of desire, a task that involves the proper use of foreplay, the possibility of which implies control over the form that foreplay will take. Modern sexual therapy assumes that such control is universally accessible, and so far there has been no reason to question that assumption. Sexologists are unanimous, moreover, in holding that mutual sexual enjoyment requires an atmosphere of comfort and communication, a minimum of pressure, and an ongoing check-up on one's partner's state. They maintain that different people have different predilections, and that what is pleasurable for one person is very often anathema to another. These findings show that the way to achieve sexual pleasure, at any time at all, let alone with a casual acquaintance, decidedly does not involve overriding the other person's express reservations and providing them with just any kind of sexual stimulus.[18] And while we do not want to allow science and technology a voice in which the voices of particular women are drowned, in this case science seems to concur with women's perception that aggressive incommunicative sex is not what they want. But if science and the voice of women concur, if aggressive seduction does not lead to good sex, if women do not like it or want it, then it is not rational to think that they would agree to it. Where such sex takes place, it is therefore rational to presume that the sex was not consensual.

The myth that women like to be raped, is closely connected, as we have seen, to doubt about their honesty in sexual matters, and this suspicion is exploited by defense lawyers when sexual assault cases make it to the courtroom. It is an unfortunate consequence of the presumption of innocence that rape victims who end up in court frequently find that it is they who are on trial. For if the defendant is innocent, then either he did not intend to do what he was accused of, or the plaintiff is mistaken about his identity, or she is lying. Often the last alternative is the only plausible defense, and as a result, the plaintiff's word seldom goes unquestioned. Women are frequently accused of having made a false accusation, either as a defensive mechanism for dealing with guilt and shame, or out of a desire for revenge.

Now there is no point in denying the possibility of false accusation, though there are probably better ways of seeking revenge on a man than accusing him of rape. However, we can now establish a logical connection between the evidence that a woman was subjected to high-pressure aggressive "seduction" tactics, and her claim that she did not consent to that encounter. Where the kind of encounter is not the sort to which it would be reasonable to consent, there is a logical presumption that a woman who claims that she did not consent is telling the truth. Where the kind of sex involved is not the sort of sex we would expect a woman to like, the burden of proof should not be on the woman to show that she did not consent, but on the defendant to show that contrary to every reasonable expectation she did consent. The defendant should be required to convince the court that the plaintiff persuaded him to have sex with her even though there are no visible reasons why she should.

In conclusion, there are no grounds for the "she asked for it" defense. Sexually provocative behavior does not generate sexual contracts. Even where there are sexual agreements, they cannot be legitimately enforced either by the State, or by private right, or by natural prerogative. Secondly, all the evidence suggests that neither women nor men find sexual enjoyment in rape or in any form of non-communicative sexuality. Third-ly, male sexual desire is containable, and can be subjected to moral and rational control. Fourthly, since there is no reason why women should not be sexually provocative, they do not "deserve" any sex they do not want. This last is a welcome discovery. The taboo on sexual provocative-ness in women is a taboo both on sensuality and on teasing. But sensual-ity is a source of delight, and teasing is playful and inspires wit. What a relief to learn that it is not sexual provocativeness, but its enemies, that constitutes a danger to the world.

COMMUNICATIVE SEXUALITY: REINTERPRETING THE KANTIAN IMPERATIVE

The present criterion of consent sets up sexual encounters as contractual events in which sexual aggression is presumed to be consented to unless there is some vigorous act of refusal. As long as we view sexual interac-tion on a contractual model, the only possibility for finding fault is to point to the presence of such an act. But it is clear that whether or not we can determine such a presence, there is something strongly disagreeable about the sexual aggression described above.

In thinking about sex we must keep in mind its sensual ends, and the facts show that aggressive high-pressure sex contradicts those ends. Con-sensual sex in dating situations is presumed to aim at mutual enjoyment. It may not always do this, and when it does, it might not always succeed. There is no logical incompatibility between wanting to continue a sexual encounter, and failing to derive sexual pleasure from it.[19]

But it seems to me that there is a presumption in favor of the connec-tion between sex and sexual enjoyment, and that if a man wants to be sure that he is not forcing himself on a woman, he has an obligation either to ensure that the encounter really is mutually enjoyable, or to know the reasons why she would want to continue the encounter in spite of her lack of enjoyment. A closer investigation of the nature of this obligation will enable us to construct a more rational and a more plau-sible norm of sexual conduct.

Onora O'Neill has argued that in intimate situations we have an obli-gation to take the ends of others as our own, and to promote those ends in a non-manipulative and non-paternalistic manner.[20] Now it seems that in honest sexual encounters just this is required. Assuming that each person enters the encounter in order to seek sexual satisfaction, each person engaging in the encounter has an obligation to help the other seek his or her ends. To do otherwise is to risk acting in opposition to what the other desires, and hence to risk acting without the other's consent.

But the obligation to promote the sexual ends of one's partner implies the obligation to know what those ends are, and also the obligation to know how those ends are attained. Thus, the problem comes down to a problem of epistemic responsibility, the responsibility to know. The solution, in my view, lies in the practice of a communicative sexuality, one which combines the appropriate knowledge of the other with respect for the dialectics of desire.

So let us, for a moment, conceive of sexual interaction on a communicative rather than a contractual model. Let us look at it the way I think it should be looked at, as if it were a proper conversation rather than an offer from the Mafia.

Conversations, when they are proper conversations, as opposed to lectures, diatribes, or interrogations, illustrate the logical relation between communicative interaction and treating someone as an end in herself in O'Neill's sense. This logical relation can be illustrated by the difference in kind between a typical contract and a proper sort of conversation, a difference that derives primarily from the different relation each bears to the necessity for cooperation. The difference is this: typically, where contracts are concerned, cooperation is primarily required as a means to some further end set by the contract. In proper conversations, as I shall define them here, cooperation is sought as an end in itself.

It is not inimical to most contracts that the cooperation necessary for achieving its ends be reluctant, or even hostile. Although we can find fault with a contractor for failing to deliver goods or services, we do not normally criticize her for her attitude. And although there are situations where we employ people on the condition that they be congenial, even then we do not require that their congeniality be the real thing. When we are having a proper conversation, however, we do, typically, want the real thing. In conversation, the cooperation with the other is not just a means to an interesting conversation; it is one of the ends we seek, without which the conversation ceases to satisfy.

The communicative interaction involved in conversation is concerned with a good deal more than didactic content and argument. Good conversationalists are intuitive, sympathetic, and charitable. Intuition and charity aid the conversationalist in her effort to interpret the words of the other correctly and sympathy enables her to enter into the other's point of view. Her sensitivity alerts her to the tone of the exchange. Has her point been taken good-humouredly or resentfully? Aggressively delivered responses are taken as a sign that *ad hominems* are at work, and that the respondent's self-worth has been called into question. Good conversationalists will know to suspend further discussion until this sense of self-worth has been reestablished. Angry responses, resentful responses, bored responses, even over-enthusiastic responses require that the emotional ground be cleared before the discussion be continued. Often it is better to change the topic, or to come back to it on another day under different circumstances. Good conversationalists do not overwhelm their respondents with a barrage of their own opinions. While they may be persuasive, the forcefulness of their persuasion does not lie in their being over-bearing, but rather in their capacity to see the other's point of view, to understand what it depends on, and so to address the essential point, but with tact and clarity.

Just as communicative conversationalists are concerned with more than didactic content, persons engaged in communicative sexuality will be concerned with more than achieving coitus. They will be sensitive to the responses of their partners. They will, like good conversationalists, be intuitive, sympathetic, and charitable. Intuition will help them to interpret their partner's responses; sympathy will enable them to share what their partner is feeling; charity will enable them to care. Communicative sexual partners will not overwhelm each other with the barrage of their own desires. They will treat negative, bored, or angry responses, as a sign that the erotic ground needs to be either cleared or abandoned. Their concern with fostering the desire of the other must involve an ongoing state of alertness in interpreting her responses.

Just as a conversationalist's prime concern is for the mutuality of the discussion, a person engaged in communicative sexuality will be most concerned with the mutuality of desire. As such, both will put into practice a regard for their respondent that is guaranteed no place in the contractual language of rights, duties, and consent. The dialectics of both activities reflect the dialectics of desire insofar as each person's interest in continuing is contingent upon the other person wishing to do so too, and each person's interest is as much fueled by the other's interest as it is by her own. Each respects the subjectivity of the other not just by avoiding treading on it, but by fostering and protecting the quality of that subjectivity. Indeed, the requirement to avoid treading on the subjectivity of the other entails the obligation to respect the dialectics of desire.[21] For in intimacy there is no passing by on the other side. To be intimate just is to open up in emotional and personal ways, to share personal knowledge, and to be receptive to the openness of the other. This openness and sharing normally take place only in an atmosphere of confidence and trust. But once availed of this knowledge, and confidence, and trust, one has, as it were, responsibility thrust upon one, the responsibility not to betray the trust by misusing the knowledge. And only by respecting the dialectics of desire can we have any confidence that we have not misused our position of trust and knowledge.

CULTURAL PRESUMPTIONS

Now it may well be that we have no obligation to care for strangers, and I do not wish to claim that we do. Nonetheless, it seems that O'Neill's point about the special moral duties we have in certain intimate situations is supported by a conceptual relation between certain kinds of personal relationships and the expectation that it should be a communicative relation. Friendship is a case in point. It is a relation that is greatly underdetermined by what we usually include in our sets of rights and obligations. For the most part, rights and obligations disappear as terms by which friendship is guided. They are still there, to be called upon, in case the relationship breaks down, but insofar as the friendship is a friendship, it is concerned with fostering the quality of the interaction and not with standing on rights. Thus, because we are friends, we share our property, and property rights between us are not invoked. Because we are friends, privacy is not an issue. Because we are friends we may see to each other's needs as often as we see to our own. The same can be said for relations between lovers, parents and dependent children, and even between spouses, at least when interaction is functioning at an optimal level. When such relations break down to the point that people must stand on their rights, we can often say that the actors ought to make more of an effort, and in many instances fault them for their lack of charity, tolerance, or benevolence. Thus, although we have a right to end friendships, it may be a reflection on our lack of virtue that we do so, and while we cannot be criticized for violating other people's rights, we can be rightfully deprecated for lacking the virtue to sustain a friendship.

But is there a similar conceptual relation between the kind of activity that a date is, and the sort of moral practice which it requires? My claim is that there is, and that this connection is easily established once we recognize the cultural presumption that dating is a gesture of friendship and regard. Traditionally, the decision to date indicates that two people have an initial attraction to each other, that they are disposed to like each other, and look forward to enjoying each other's company. Dating derives its implicit meaning from this tradition. It retains this meaning unless other aims are explicitly stated, and even then it may not be possible to alienate this meaning. It is a rare woman who will not spurn a man who states explicitly, right at the onset, that he wants to go out with her solely on the condition that he have sexual intercourse with her at the end of the evening, and that he has no interest in her company apart from gaining that end, and no concern for mutual satisfaction.

Explicit protest to the contrary aside, the conventions of dating confer on it its social meaning, and this social meaning implies a relationship which is more like friendship than the cutthroat competition of opposing teams. As such, it requires that we do more than stand on our rights with regard to each other. As long as we are operating under the auspices of a dating relationship, it requires that we behave in the mode of friendship and trust. But if a date is more like a friendship than a business contract, then clearly respect for the dialectics of desire is incompatible with the sort of sexual pressure that is inclined to end in date rape. And clearly, also, a conquest mentality which exploits a situation of trust and respect for purely selfish ends is morally pernicious. Failure to respect the dialectics of desire when operating under the auspices of friendship and trust is to act in flagrant disregard of the moral requirement to avoid manipulative, coercive, and exploitive behavior. Respect for the dialectics of desire is *prima facie* inconsistent with the satisfaction of one person at the expense of the other. The proper end of friendship relations is mutual satisfaction. But the requirement of mutuality means that we must take a communicative approach to discovering the ends of the other, and this entails that we respect the dialectics of desire.

But now that we know what communicative sexuality is, and that it is morally required, and that it is the only feasible means to mutual sexual enjoyment, why not take this model of what is reasonable in sexual interaction? The evidence of sexologists strongly indicates that women whose partners are aggressively uncommunicative have little chance of experiencing sexual pleasure. But it is not reasonable for women to consent to what they have little chance of enjoying. Hence it is not reasonable for women to consent to aggressive noncommunicative sex. Nor can we reasonably suppose that women have consented to sexual encounters which we know and they know they do not find enjoyable. With the communicative model as the norm, the aggressive contractual model should strike us as a model of deviant sexuality, and sexual encounters patterned on that model should strike us as encounters to which *prima facie* no one would reasonably agree. But if acquiescence to an encounter counts as consent only if the acquiescence is reasonable, something to which a reasonable person, in full possession of knowledge relevant to the encounter, would agree, then acquiescence to aggressive noncommunicative sex is not reasonable. Hence, acquiescence under such conditions should not count as consent.

Thus, where communicative sexuality does not occur, we lack the main ground for believing that the sex involved was consensual. Moreover, where a man does not engage in communicative sexuality, he acts either out of reckless disregard, or out of willful ignorance. For he cannot know, except through the practice of communicative sexuality, whether his partner has any sexual reason for continuing the encounter. And where she does not, he runs the risk of imposing on her what she is not willing to have. All that is needed then, in order to provide women with legal protection from "date rape" is to make both reckless indifference and willful ignorance a sufficient condition of *mens rea* and to make communicative sexuality the accepted norm of sex to which a reasonable woman would agree.[22] Thus, the appeal to communicative sexuality as a norm for sexual encounters accomplishes two things. It brings the aggressive sex involved in "date rape" well within the realm of sexual assault, and it locates the guilt of date rapists in the failure to approach sexual relations on a communicative basis.

THE EPISTEMOLOGICAL IMPLICATIONS

Finding a proper criterion for consent is one problem, discovering what really happened, after the event, when the only eye witnesses give conflicting accounts is another. But while there is no foolproof way of getting the unadulterated truth, it can make a significant difference to the outcome of a prosecution, what sort of facts we are seeking. On the model of aggressive seduction we sought evidence of resistance. But on the new model of communicative sexuality what we want is evidence of an ongoing positive and encouraging response on the part of the plaintiff. This new goal will require quite different tactics on the part of the cross-examiners, and quite different expectations on the part of juries and judges. Where communicative sexuality is taken as the norm, and aggressive sexual tactics as a presumption against consent, the outcome for the example that I described above would be quite different. It would be regarded as sexual assault rather than seduction.

Let us then consider a date rape trial in which a man is cross-examined. He is asked whether he was presuming mutual sexual enjoyment. Suppose he answers in the negative. Then he would have to account for why he persisted in the face of her voiced reluctance. He cannot give as an excuse that he thought she liked it, because he believes that she did not. If he thought that she had consented even though she didn't like it, then it seems to me that the burden of proof would lie with him to say why it was reasonable to think this. Clearly, her initial resistance, her presumed lack of enjoyment, and the pressure tactics involved in getting her to "go along" would not support a reasonable belief in consent, and his persisting in the face of her dissatisfaction would surely cast doubt on the sincerity of his belief in her consent.

But suppose he answers in the affirmative. Then the cross-examiner would not have to rely on the old criteria for non-consent. He would not have to show either that she had resisted him, or that she was in a fearful or intimidated state of mind. Instead he could use a communicative model of sexuality to discover how much respect there had been for the dialectics of desire. Did he ask her what she liked? If she was using contraceptives? If he should? What tone of voice did he use? How did she answer? Did she make any demands? Did she ask for penetration? How was that desire conveyed? Did he ever let up the pressure long enough to see if she was really that interested? Did he ask her which position she preferred? Assuming that the defendant does not perjure himself, he would lack satisfactory answers to these questions. But even where the defendant did lie, a skilled cross-examiner who was willing to go into detail could probably establish easily enough when the interaction had not been communicative. It is extraordinarily difficult to keep up a consistent story when you are not telling the truth.

On the new criterion, the cross-examination focuses on the communicative nature of the ongoing encounter, and the communicative nature of an encounter is much easier to establish than the episodic act of resistance. For one thing, it requires that a fairly long, yet consistent story be told, and this enables us to assess the plausibility of the competing claims in light of a wider collection of relevant data. Secondly, in making noncommunicative sex the primary indicator of coercive sex it provides us with a criterion for distinguishing consensual sadomasochism from brutality. For even if a couple agree to sadomasochistic sex, bondage and whippings and the rest of it, the court has a right to require that there be a system of signals whereby each partner can convey to the other whether she has had enough.[23] Thirdly, the use of a new criterion of communicative sexuality would enable us to introduce a new category of nonaggravated sexual assault which would not necessarily carry a heavy sentence but which would nonetheless provide an effective recourse against "date rape."[24]

CONCLUSION

In sum, using communicative sexuality as a model of normal sex has several advantages over the "aggressive-acquiescence" model of seduction. The new model ties the presumption that consensual sex takes place in the expectation of mutual desire much more closely to the facts about how that desire actually functions. Where communicative sex does not occur, this establishes a presumption that there was no consent. The importance of this presumption is that we are able, in criminal proceedings, to shift the burden of proof from the plaintiff, who on the contractual model must show that she resisted or was threatened, to the defendant who must then give some reason why she should consent after all. The communicative model of sexuality also enables us to give a different conceptual content to the concept of consent. It sees consent as something more like an ongoing cooperation than the one-shot agreement which we are inclined to see it as on the contractual model. Moreover, it does not matter, on the communicative model, whether a woman was sexually provocative, what her reputation is, what went on before the sex began. All that matters is the quality of communication with regard to the sex itself.

But most importantly, the communicative model of normal sexuality gives us a handle on a solution to the problem of date rape. If noncommunicative sexuality establishes a presumption of nonconsent, then where there are no overriding reasons for thinking that consent occurred, we have a criterion for a category of sexual assault that does not require evidence of physical violence or threat. If we are serious about date rape, then the next step is to take this criterion as objective grounds for establishing that a date rape has occurred. The proper legislation is the shortest route to establishing this criterion.

There remains, of course, the problem of education. If we are going to change the rules about what is socially acceptable in sexual relations, then it is only fair to let the public know. In a mass media society, this is not hard to do. A public information campaign will spread the news in no time at all. The real problem is the reluctance of the mass media to deal with questions of sexual relations and sexual intimacy. Its politicians are still curiously reluctant to stand up to an increasingly small sector of society that is unwilling to admit, despite all the evidence to the contrary, that anyone but well-meaning husbands and wives ever have sex. I would not be surprised if this sort of puritanical holdout were the very source of the problem of rape. Certainly, sexual ignorance must contribute significantly to the kind of social environment conducive to rape.

NOTES

1. G. Geis and R. Geis, "Rape Reform: An Appreciative-Critical Review," *Bulletin of the American Academy of Psychiatry and the Law* 6:3 (1978): 301–12. Also see Michael Davis, "Setting Penalties: What Does Rape Deserve?" *Law and Philosophy* 3:1 (1984): 61–110.

2. Under Common Law a person cannot consent to aggravated assault. Also, consent may be irrelevant if the victim was unfit to consent. See Davis, "Setting Penalties," 104–5.

3. Discussion Paper No. 2, *Rape and Allied Offenses: Substantive Aspects*. Law Reform Commission of Victoria (August 1986).

4. In a recent Australian case a man was convicted of being an accomplice to a rape because he was reckless in determining whether the woman raped by his friend was consenting. The judge ruled that his "reckless indifference" sufficed to establish *mens rea*. This ruling was possible, however, only because unreasonable belief is not a rape defense in Australia. *Australian Law Review* 71, 120. [We have been unable to verify this reference—eds.]

5. This is true, at present, in jurisdictions which follow the precedent set by *Morgan v. Morgan*. [*DPP v. Morgan* (1975) 2 All ER 411; (1975) 61 Cr App R 136 (U.K.)—eds.] In this case, four men were acquitted of rape because they sincerely thought that their victim had consented, despite their admitting that she had protested vigorously. See Mark Thornton's "Rape and *Mens Rea*," *Canadian Journal of Philosophy*, Supp. Vol. 8 (1982): 119–46.

6. *Ibid.*

7. *Why Men Rape*, Sylvia Levine and Joseph Loenig, eds. (Toronto, Can.: Macmillan, 1980), 83.

8. *Ibid.*, 77.

9. Glanville Williams, *Textbook of Criminal Law*, 2nd edition (London: Stevens and Sons, Ltd., 1983), 238.

10. *Ibid.*

11. See Jeanne C. Marsh, Alison Geist, and Nathan Caplan, *Rape and the Limits of Law Reform* (Boston: Auburn House, 1982), 32. According to Marsh's study on the impact of the Michigan reform of rape laws, convictions were increased for traditional conceptions of rape, i.e., aggravated assault. However, date rape, which has a much higher incidence than aggravated assault, has a very low rate of arrest and an even lower one of conviction.

12. See Marsh, *Rape and the Limits of Law Reform*, 61, for a particularly good example of this response. Also see John M. MacDonald, "Victim-Precipitated Rape," in his *Rape: Offenders and Their Victims* (Springfield, Ill.: Charles C. Thomas, 1971), 78–89, for a good example of this response in academic thinking. Also see Amir Menachim, *Patterns in Forcible Rape* (Chicago: University of Chicago Press, 1972), 259.

13. See Eugene Borgida and Nancy Brekke, "Psychological Research on Rape Trials," in *Rape and Sexual Assault*, Ann Wobert Burgess, ed. (New York: Garland Press, 1985), 314. Also see M. J. Lerner, "The Desire for Justice and Reactions to Victims," *Altruism and Helping Behaviour*, J. Macauly and L. Berkowitz, eds. (New York: Academic Press, 1970).

14. As, for example, Lorenne Clark and Debra Lewis do in *Rape: The Price of Coercive Sexuality* (Toronto, Can.: The Women's Press, 1977), 152–53.

15. See Sue Bessner, *The Laws of Rape* (New York: Praeger, 1984), 111–21, for a discussion of the legal forms in which this suspicion is expressed.

16. *Ibid.*

17. A speech-act like, "OK, let's get it over with," is taken as consent, even though it is extracted under high pressure, the sex that ensues lacks mutuality, and there are no ulterior reasons for such an agreement. See Davis, "Setting Penalties," 103. Also see Carolyn Schafer and Marilyn Frye, "Rape and Respect," in *Women and Values: Readings in Recent Feminist Philosophy*, Marilyn Pearsall, ed. (Belmont, Calif.: Wadsworth, 1986), 188–96, at 189, for a characterization of the common notion of consent as a formal speech-act.

18. It is not just women who fail to find satisfaction in the "swept away" approach to sexual interaction. Studies of convicted rapists, and of conquest-oriented men, indicate that men are frequently disappointed when they use this approach as well. In over half of aggravated sexual assaults penetration fails because the man loses his erection. Those who do succeed invariably report that the sex experienced was not enjoyable. This supports the prevailing view of sexologists that men depend on the positive response of their partners in order to fuel their own responsive mechanisms. See A. N. Groth, *Rape and Sexual Assault*. [Does Pineau mean either A. N. Groth, "The Rapist's View," in Ann Burgess, ed., *Violence through a Forensic Lens* (King of Prussia, Penna.: Nursing Spectrum, 2000); or A. N. Groth. "The Rapist's View," in Ann Burgess and Lynda Holmstrom, eds., *Rape: Crisis and Recovery* (R. J. Brady, 1979)?—eds.]. Also see *Why Men Rape*, Sylvia Levine and Joseph Koenig, eds., or consult any recent manual on male sexuality.

19. Robin Morgan comes perilously close to suggesting that there is when she defines rape as any sexual encounter that is not initiated by a woman out of her own heartfelt desire. See *Going Too Far* (New York: Random House, 1968), 165.

20. Onora O'Neill, "Between Consenting Adults," *Philosophy and Public Affairs* 14:3 (1985): 252–77.

21. The sort of relationship I have in mind exemplifies the "feminist" approach to ethics argued for by Nel Noddings, *Caring: A Feminine Approach to Ethics* (Berkeley, Calif.: University of California Press, 1984). In particular, see her discussion of teaching as a "duality," 195.

22. As now seems to be the case in Australian law. See note 4.

23. The SAMOIS justification of sadomasochism rests on the claim that sadomasochistic practices can be communicative in this way. See the collective's book *Coming to Power* (Boston: Alyson Publications, 1981).

24. See sections 520e, Act No. 266, State of Michigan. Sexual assault in the fourth degree is punishable by imprisonment of not more than two years or a fine of not more than $500, or both.

STUDY QUESTIONS

1. In criticizing beliefs that people have about sexuality, Pineau attributes to them the notion that "sexually provocative behavior, taken beyond a certain point, generates agreements" (that is, an agreement on the part of the woman to engage in sexual activity, or a promise to do so). That was written by Pineau in 1989. Do you think it is (still) true? Is it true of more subtle forms of flirting or of any flirting at all? Go further: what if a woman gives consent to sexual activity. Has she made a firm and binding commitment? May she later retract her consent? When and when not?

2. Pineau claims that there is such a thing as "*not* the sort of sex we would expect a woman to like." If a woman engages in that sort of sex, she goes on to argue, the presumption is that she did not consent and her male partner has the burden of proving that she did consent. Are you able to provide examples of this kind of sexual activity? Do you find plausible what Pineau says about this sort of sexual activity? Perhaps Alan Wertheimer would claim that women are hard-wired not to like certain kinds of sexual activity (see "Consent and Sexual Relations," in this volume). What might these be? On the other hand, what happens to Pineau's thesis if sexual likes and dislikes are fully the result of socialization? Does Pineau require the notion of what would not be liked by the "reasonable" woman?

3. If, as Pineau claims, in a sexual encounter each party has a (Kantian) moral obligation to help the other attain his or her sexual goals, how sexually pleasurable will the sexual act be for the parties? More generally, is "communicative" sexuality as pleasurable as sexuality that does not abide by Pineau's restrictions? Does this matter? Does her argument turn on the claim that safety and avoiding violence offset the possible loss of sexual pleasure?

4. Pineau sometimes uses the phrase "aggressive noncommunicative sexuality" and sometimes the phrase "noncommunicative sexuality." Does she use them interchangeably? *Are* they interchangeable? Suppose that there is noncommunicative but nonaggressive sexuality. How would such sexual encounters fit into Pineau's analysis?

5. Give a detailed example of (or imagine how) casual sexual relations between two strangers would go. Is it possible that sexual encounters between strangers are *more* susceptible to the moral faults discussed by Pineau, or can causal sex between strangers conform sufficiently to her communication model? Does she seem to think that sexual relations between people who know each other (as in acquaintance rape) are *equally* susceptible?

6. Might men and women, in general, have different preferences for types of sexual activities, with men preferring more aggressive sex? How would we be able to find out the truth of such a claim? And how would it, if true, affect Pineau's arguments and conclusions? (See the essay by Joan Mason-Grant, "Pornography as Embodied Practice," in this volume, for the role that pornography might play in shaping men's sexual desires.)

TWENTY-SIX

How Bad Is Rape?—II

H. E. Baber

Borrowing a sophisticated philosophical account of the concept of "harm" from Joel Feinberg, **H. E. Baber** *compares the harms resulting from being raped with the harms endured by women obliged to perform menial labor and comes to a surprising conclusion. In her arguments, Baber uses economic data about the conditions of ordinary working women to aid her argument that while rape is certainly bad, it is not as bad as the pink-color jobs that many of these women occupy, the sorts of occupational sex segregation that feminism also fights against. Baber's answer to this question (which also arises in Martha Nussbaum's "'Whether from Reason or Prejudice': Taking Money for Bodily Services," in this volume) has colossal implications for where and how feminist political and social activism should proceed.*

H. E. Baber received her Ph.D. from Johns Hopkins University and is professor of philosophy at the University of San Diego. She has published in the areas of analytic metaphysics, philosophical theology, and feminism. She is the author of *The Multicultural Mystique: The Liberal Case against Diversity* (Prometheus, 2008) and is coeditor of *Globalization and International Development* (Broadview, 2012). This essay is an extensively revised version of an essay that originally appeared in *Hypatia* 2:2 (1987): 125–38. It appears here with the permission of H. E. Baber. © 2012, H. E. Baber.

Rape is bad. This is uncontroversial.[1] It is one of the many wrongs committed against women. But *how* bad is rape—more particularly, how bad is it vis-à-vis other gender-based offenses?[2] I shall argue that while rape is bad, the work that most women employed outside the home are compelled to do is more seriously harmful because doing such work damages the most fundamental interests of the victim, what Joel Feinberg calls "welfare interests," whereas rape typically does not.[3]

It may be suggested that the very question of which of these evils is the more serious is misconceived insofar as the harms they induce are so different in character as to be incommensurable. Nevertheless, for practical purposes we are often obliged to weigh interests in diverse goods against one another and to compare harms of different kinds. Feminists do not have endless resources: we cannot fight on all fronts. Women are disadvantaged in a variety of ways, but given that feminist resources are limited, our priority should be to address those harms that affect the most women and that are most serious. Currently four out of ten women work in female-dominated occupations—those whose incumbents are at least 75 percent female[4] : far more than the number of women who are raped. Most womenswork is poorly paid, offers no prospect of advancement and is, above all, agonizingly boring. I argue the harm that such work does to women is more serious than the harm of being raped.

Feinberg's account of how we may assess the relative seriousness of various harms, in *Harm to Others* and elsewhere, provides a rational basis for such comparisons and for my consideration of the relative seriousness of rape and work. In addition, my comparison of these harms brings to light a lacuna in Feinberg's discussion, which I propose to fill by providing an account of the way in which the duration of a harmed state contributes to its seriousness.

WHY RAPE IS BAD

Rape is bad because it constitutes a serious harm to the victim. To harm a person is to thwart, set back, or otherwise interfere with his interests. Understood in this sense, "harm" is not synonymous with "hurt." We typically have an interest in avoiding chronic, distracting physical pain and psychic anguish insofar as we require a certain degree of physical and emotional well-being to pursue our projects; hence hurts are often harmful. But there are hurts that are not harmful, such as root canal work, and, arguably, harms that are not hurtful. Our interests extend to states of affairs beyond immediate experience. I have an interest, for example, in my reputation so that if I am slandered I am harmed even if, being altogether unaware of what is being said about me, I am not hurt. Gossip can harm me, even if it has no material consequences for my life, insofar as I have an interest in others' speaking and thinking well of me. Harms are thus to be understood in terms of the interests or stakes that persons have in states of affairs.

Virtually everyone has an interest in avoiding involuntary contact with others, particularly unwanted contacts that are intimate or invasive. Being raped violates this interest. Hence, quite apart from any further consequences it may have for the victim or for others, it constitutes a harm. In addition, people have an interest in not being used as mere means for the benefit of others, an interest that is violated by rape. Finally, all persons can be presumed to have an interest in going about their business free of restriction and interference. Rape, like other crimes of violence, thwarts this interest. Since rape sets back some of the victim's most important interests, the victim of rape is in a harmed condition.

The condition of being raped is a *harmful* condition as well as a *harmed* condition to the extent that it generates further harms—anxiety, feelings of degradation, and other psychological states that may interfere with the victim's pursuit of other projects. In these respects rape is no different from other violent crimes. The victim of assault or robbery is violated, and this in and of itself constitutes a harm. In addition, being assaulted or robbed is harmful insofar as victims of assault and robbery tend to suffer from fears and psychological traumas as a result of their experience, which may interfere with their pursuit of other projects.

There is a tendency to exaggerate the *harmfulness* of rape, that is, to make much of the incapacitating psychological traumas that some victims suffer as a result of being raped. One motive for such claims is the recognition that the harm of rape *per se* is often underestimated and hence that, in some quarters, rape is not taken as seriously as it ought to be taken. Rape has not been treated in the same way as other violent crimes. A person, whether male or female, who is mugged is not asked to produce witnesses, to provide evidence of his good character, or to display bodily injuries as evidence of his unwillingness to surrender his wallet to his assailant. In the past, however, the burden of proof has been placed wrongfully on the victims of rape to show their respectability and their unwillingness, the assumption being that (heterosexual) rape is merely a sexual act rather than an act of violence and that sex acts can be presumed to be desired by the participants unless there is strong evidence to the contrary. Writers who stress the traumas rape victims suffer cite the deleterious consequences of rape in response to such assumptions.

It is, however, quite unnecessary to exaggerate the harmfulness of rape to explain its seriousness. Women are not merely sexual resources whose wants and interests can be ignored—and women do not secretly want to be raped. Like men, women have an important interest in not being used or interfered with; hence being raped is a harm. Even if it did not hurt the victim physically or psychologically or tend to bring about any *further* harms, it would still be a harm in and of itself. A person who is assaulted or robbed does not need to produce evidence of the psychological trauma he suffers as a consequence in order to persuade others that he has been harmed. We recognize that, quite apart from the consequences, the act of assault or robbery is itself a harm. The same is true of rape. If we recognize rape for what it is, a violent crime against the person, we shall not take past sexual activity as evidence that the victim has not "really" been raped any more than we should take a history of habitual charitable contributions as evidence that the victim of mugging has not "really" been robbed, neither shall we feel compelled to stress the psychological consequences of rape: rape is in and of itself a harm.

If this is made clear, there is no compelling reason to harp on the suffering of rape victims. Furthermore, it may on balance be undesirable to do so. First, making much of the traumas rape victims allegedly suffer tends to reinforce the pervasive sexist assumption that women are cowards who break under stress and are incapable of dealing with physical danger or violence. Secondly, representing such traumas as the normal, expected consequences of rape does a disservice to victims who might otherwise be considerably less traumatized by their experience.

THE RELATIVE SERIOUSNESS OF HARMS

Everyone agrees that rape is bad. The disagreement is over how bad. This raises a more general question, namely that of ranking harms with regard to their relative seriousness.

Given our understanding of harm as the thwarting of an individual's interests and our assumption that a person's interests extend beyond immediate experience, it will not do to rank harms strictly according to how unpleasant they are for the victim or the extent to which they decrease his *felt* satisfaction. A person is harmed when his interests are impeded regardless of whether he suffers as a consequence. Persons have an interest in liberty, for example, and are harmed when deprived of liberty even if they do not *feel* frustrated as a consequence. The advice of stoics has a hollow ring, and projects for "adjusting" people to severely restrictive conditions strike most of us as unacceptable precisely because we recognize that even if self-cultivation or conditioning can prevent us from *feeling* frustrated when our most fundamental interests are thwarted, such practices cannot prevent us from being harmed.

The seriousness of a harm is determined by the importance of the interest that is violated within the network of the victim's interests.

> Some interests are more important than others in the sense that harm to them is likely to lead to greater damage to the whole economy of personal (or as the case may be, community) interests than harm to the lesser interest will do, just as harm to one's heart or brain will do more damage to one's bodily health than an "equal degree" of harm to less vital organs. Thus, the interest of a standard person in X may be more important than his interest in Y in that it is, in an analogous sense, more "vital" in his whole interest network than is his interest in Y. A person's welfare interests tend to be his most vital ones, and also to be equally vital.[5]

A person's "welfare interests" are those that are typically most vital in a personal system of interests, for instance, interests in minimally decent health and the absence of chronic distracting pain, a tolerable environment, economic sufficiency, emotional stability, the absence of intolerable stress, and minimal political liberty—all those things that are required for the "standard person" to pursue any further projects effectively.

> These are interests in conditions that are generalized means to a great variety of possible goals and whose joint realization, in the absence of very special circumstances, is necessary for the achievement of more ultimate aims. . . . When they are blocked or damaged, a person is very seriously harmed indeed, for in that case his more ultimate aspirations are defeated too; whereas setbacks to a higher goal do not to the same degree inflict damage on the whole network of his interests.[6]

Three points should be noted here. First, we decide which interests are to count as welfare interests by reflecting upon the needs and capacities of the "standard person." Some people are more capable than the standard person—and we have all heard their inspirational stories *ad nauseam*. The standard person, however, cannot be expected to produce saleable paintings with a brush held in his mouth if paralyzed nor can the standard person be expected to overcome grinding poverty and gross discrimination to achieve brilliant success at the very pinnacle of the corporate ladder. Our interests in physical integrity and a minimally decent standard of living are therefore welfare interests.

Second, welfare interests are interests in having minimally tolerable amounts of good things, just enough to enable their possessors to pursue ulterior interests. Empirical questions may be raised as to what sort of environment is "tolerable" to the standard person, what degree of political liberty he needs to pursue his goals and how much material security he requires: there are borderline cases. Nevertheless it is clear that a person who lives under conditions of extreme political oppression, always on alert for the midnight visit of the secret police, or one who spends most of his time and energy scratching to maintain the minimal material conditions for survival is effectively blocked from pursuing other ends. Persons have an interest in having more of goods such as health, money, and political liberty than they require for the pursuit of their ulterior interests since such surplus goods are a cushion against unforeseen reverses. In hard times, a middle-class family may have to cut its entertainment and clothing budget—a working-class family, however, may be reduced to chill penury while the truly poor are forced out onto the street. Our interest in having money, health, and the like in excess of the tolerable minimum is not however a *welfare* interest.

Finally, it should be noted that "welfare interests, taken together, make a chain that is no stronger than its weakest link." There are few, if any, tradeoffs possible among welfare interests: an excess of one good cannot compensate for the lack of a minimally tolerable level of another. "All the money in the world won't help you if you have a fatal disease, and great physical strength will not compensate for destitution or imprisonment,"[7] nor, one might add, will fringe benefits, company picnics, impressive titles, or even high pay compensate for dull, demeaning work in an all-but-intolerable environment.

The greatest harms that can come to persons are those that affect their most vital interests. To maim or cripple a person is to do him a great harm since one's interest in physical health is a very vital interest, indeed, a welfare interest. Stealing a sum of money from a rich man is less harmful than stealing the same sum of money from a pauper because depriving a person of his means of survival sets back a welfare interest whereas depleting his excess funds does not.

Now in light of these considerations it should be apparent, first, that rape is a serious harm but, secondly, that it is not among the most serious harms that can befall a person. It is a serious offense because everyone has an interest in liberty construed in the broadest sense not merely as freedom from state regulation but as freedom to go about one's business without interference. Whenever a person's projects are impeded, whether by a public agency or a private individual, he is, to that extent, harmed. Rape interferes with a person's freedom to pursue his own projects and is, to that extent, a harm. It does not, however, render a person altogether incapable of pursuing his ulterior interests. Having a certain minimally tolerable amount of liberty is a welfare interest without which a person cannot pursue any further projects. While rape diminishes one's liberty, it does not diminish it to such an extent that the victim is precluded from pursuing other projects which are in his interest.

No doubt most rape victims, like victims of violent crime generally, are traumatized. Some rape victims indeed may be so severely traumatized that they incur long-term, severe psychological injury and are rendered incapable of pursuing other projects. For the standard person, however, for whom sexuality is a peripheral matter on which relatively little hangs, being raped, though it is a serious harm, does not violate a welfare interest. There is no evidence to suggest that most rape victims are permanently incapacitated by their experiences, nor that in the long run their lives are much poorer than they otherwise would have been. Again, this is not to minimize the harm of rape: rape is a serious harm. Nevertheless, some harms are more serious and, in the long run, more harmful.

TIMES, INTERESTS, AND HARMS

What can be worse than rape? A number of tragic scenarios come to mind: (1) A person is killed in the bloom of youth, when he has innumerable projects and plans for the future. Intuitively death is always a bad thing, though it is disputed whether it is a harm, but clearly untimely death is a grave harm insofar as it dooms the victim's interest in pursuing a great many projects. (2) A person is severely maimed or crippled. The interests of a person who is mentally or physically incapacitated are thwarted as the range of options available to him in his impaired state is severely limited. (3) A person is destitute, deprived of food, clothing, and shelter. Here one thinks of the victims of famine in Africa or street people reduced to sleeping in doorways in our otherwise affluent cities. Persons in such circumstances have not the resources to pursue their ulterior interests. (4) A person is enslaved. He is treated as a mere tool for the pursuit of his master's projects and deprived of the time and resources to pursue his own. Each of these misfortunes is worse than rape. And the list could be continued.

All these harmed conditions are chronic rather than episodic. They occupy large stretches of persons' histories—or, in the case of untimely death, obliterate large segments of their *projected* histories. To this extent such harmed conditions interfere more with the pursuit of other projects that are conducive to persons' well-being than does rape.

It is not entirely clear from Feinberg's discussion how the temporal extent of harms figure into calculations of their relative seriousness. Feinberg suggests that transitory hurts, whether physical or mental, do not harm the interests of the standard person, for whom the absence of pain is not a focal aim, whereas chronic, distracting pain and emotional instability set back persons' most vital interests because they prevent them from pursuing their goals and projects.[8] Nevertheless, intense pain, however transitory, may be all-encompassing and completely distracting for the extent of its duration. It is not entirely clear from Feinberg's discussion, however, why, given his account of interests and harms, we should not be forced to conclude that some transitory hurts are harms not because they violate an interest in not being hurt but because they preclude the victim from pursuing other interests, albeit for a very short time. Indeed, it is not clear why we should not be compelled to regard some very transitory pains, traumas, and inconveniences as set-backs to welfare interests. If we agree that being imprisoned for a number of years impedes a welfare interest because it precludes the prisoner from pursuing his ulterior interests while imprisoned, why should we not say that being locked in the bathroom for twenty minutes is a harm of equal, if not greater, magnitude though of shorter duration? After all, while locked in the bathroom, I am, if anything, in a worse position to pursue my ulterior interests than I should be if I were in prison.

Intuitively, however, the duration of a harmed state figures importantly in assessments of its seriousness. Being locked in the bathroom for twenty minutes is not, we think, a great harm of short duration—it is simply a trivial harm insofar as it makes no significant difference to the victim's total life plan. Being imprisoned for several years, on the contrary, does make an important difference to the victim's biography: all other things being equal, it precludes him from realizing a great number of aims that he should otherwise have accomplished. All is not as it was after the prisoner has served his sentence. After his release, the prisoner has much less time to accomplish his ends. A large chunk of his life has been blanked out, and most likely his total life history will be poorer for it. A person who has been falsely imprisoned may be "compensated" after a fashion with a monetary settlement, but we all recognize that this does not really set things right: he has, after all, lost that many years off of his life, and as a consequence he will *never* achieve a great many things that he would otherwise have achieved. Imprisonment impedes a welfare interest.

Short-term or episodic harms, however, rarely undermine welfare interests since, typically, people's focal aims are timeless in that timing is not essential to their realization. I can no longer make-a-million-by-age-thirty—a temporally tagged goal—though I still can make a million. Of course I would prefer to have the million sooner than later. If, however, my aim is merely to make a million at some time or other, I can afford to sit tight. Though the circumstances that prevail at some times may be more conducive to the achievement of my goal than those that prevail at other times, it is not essential to the satisfaction of my desire that it occur at any special time. My aim is not essentially time-bound.

Because most of persons' focal aims are not time-bound, persons by and large can afford to sit tight. Barring the occasional Man from Porlock, our interests are not seriously set back by transitory pains or other relatively short-lived distractions. A momentary twinge may prevent me from starting to write my paper at 12:05. No matter: I shall start it at 12:06, and the delay is unlikely to have any significant effect on my total opus. My interest is in producing a certain body of work during my lifetime, and this interest is sufficiently robust to withstand a good many temporary setbacks. Nevertheless, while most people's interests are relatively robust, insofar as they are not time-bound, they are not impregnable. Long-term or chronic distractions can seriously impede even those interests that are not time-bound. If I suffer from chronic, distracting pain or emotional instability for a number of years, I may *never* write my paper or realize many of my other ambitions. Art is long but life, alas, is short.

When it comes to assessing the relative seriousness of various harms, we consider them with respect to their tendency to interfere with our typically "timeless" aims. The most serious harms are those that interfere with the greatest number of interests for the longest time, those that are most likely to prevent us from ever achieving our goals. The greatest harms, those that damage welfare interests, therefore, are those that bring about harmed states that are chronic rather than episodic.

WOMENSWORK IS WORSE THAN RAPE

On this account, being obliged to work is, for most people, a very serious harm indeed because work is chronic rather than episodic: it occupies a large part of the worker's waking life for a long time. For the fortunate few, work in and of itself contributes to well-being. For most workers, however, work provides few satisfactions. For the least fortunate, whose jobs are dull, routine, and regimented, work provides no satisfactions whatsoever, and the time devoted to work prevents them from pursuing any other projects that might be conducive to their well-being.

As a matter of fact, women figure disproportionately though not exclusively in this group. In 2008, 3,550,000 Americans, most of them women, worked as cashiers. As the Bureau of Labor Statistics' *Occupational Outlook Handbook* notes, "Most cashiers work indoors, usually standing in booths or behind counters. Often they are not allowed to leave their workstations without supervisory approval."[9] About 2.3 million Americans, most of them women, worked as customer service representatives. They did their work in call centers, taking orders and handling complaints while supervisors monitored their calls. "Call centers," the *Occupational Outlook Handbook* notes, "may be crowded and noisy, and work may be repetitious and stressful, with little time between calls." These occupations are typical of the work most women are forced to do: sedentary and physically constrained, repetitive, boring, and closely supervised.[10]

As a result of discrimination in employment, most women are compelled to take boring, underpaid, dead-end jobs like these and, as a consequence, to spend a substantial part of their waking lives at tedious, regimented, mind-killing toil. A great many men have equally appalling jobs. And anyone, whether male or female, who spends a good deal of time at such work is in a more seriously harmed state than one who is raped. Women however have an additional grievance insofar as such jobs fall disproportionately to them as a consequence of unfair employment practices, which have persisted into the twenty-first century.[11]

To be compelled to do boring womenswork is to be harmed in the most serious way. Doing such work impedes a welfare interest: it deprives the worker of the minimal degree of freedom requisite for the pursuit of a number of other interests. As with other such deprivations, the harm done cannot be undone by other benefits. The time workers spend at their jobs deprives them of the freedom necessary to the effective pursuit of their other projects. For this there can be no true compensation. Rape, like all crimes against the person, is bad in part because it deprives the victim of some degree of freedom; being compelled to work is worse in this regard insofar as it chronically deprives the victim of the minimal amount of freedom requisite to the pursuit of other important interests, which are conducive to well-being.

Work is worse than rape in other respects as well. Pink-collar workers, like rape victims, are used as mere means to the ends of others, but arguably, workers are violated in a way that is more detrimental to their interests. Rape merely violates the victims' sexual integrity. The work that most women do violates their integrity as intellectual beings. Routine clerical work, which falls almost exclusively to women, prevents workers from thinking about other matters: they are fettered intellectually. Such work occupies the mind just enough to dominate the worker's inner life but not enough to be of any interest. Since persons have a greater stake in their mental and emotional lives than they do in their sexuality, being "raped" intellectually, the condition of most women in the labor force, violates a more vital interest than being raped sexually.

There are indeed certain disanalogies between the harms of rape and pink-collar work. First, persons have a right not to be raped, but they do not have a right to avoid unpleasant work. Second, while rapists clearly harm their victims, it is not so clear that employers, particularly if they have not engaged in unfair hiring practices, harm their employees. Third, on the face of it, whereas rape victims are coerced, workers freely choose their occupations. Finally, it will be suggested that the work most women do is not so grim as I have suggested. None of these suggestions, however, undermines the central thesis of this paper, namely that doing pink-collar work is worse than being raped.

First, I have not argued that being compelled to do unpleasant work is a *wrong* but only that it is a *harm*, and a grave one. People do not have an absolute right to not be harmed in any way, so to be harmed is not necessarily to be wronged. It may be, in some cases, that the advancement of the interests of others outweighs the harm that comes to the victim so that, on balance, the harm to the victim does not constitute an injustice or a wrong. As consumers, all of us, men and women alike, have an interest in retaining women as a source of cheap clerical and service work. It may be that, on balance, our interest as consumers in getting goods and services on the cheap outweighs the interest of women as potential workers in not being exploited—though I doubt it. If, however, this is so, then the exploitation of women in these positions is not a wrong, even though it is a harm.

Second, to be in a harmed state is not necessarily to be harmed by some moral agent. On Feinberg's account, natural disasters—and not merely persons who omit to aid victims—cause harm. One can be harmed by impersonal forces—by hurricanes, wildfires, or floods—or by the innocent, blameless actions of others. To suggest that workers are seriously harmed by the work they do is not to say that their employers are blameworthy, even if they are causally responsible for workers' coming to harm.

Third, most women in the pink-collar sector are compelled to work. For most, career housewifing is not an option: few men are willing to provide lifelong financial support to women. Labor force participation, like rape, is coercive. Admittedly, intuitions about what constitutes coercion differ, so, for example, some suggest that a woman who cannot display bruises or wounds as evidence of a serious struggle has not really been forced to have sex with her assailant: even with a knife to her throat a woman is still free to choose death rather than dishonor. Nevertheless, most of us would recognize this as a case of coercion and, by the same reasoning, should recognize that for most women entry into the labor force is coerced. A woman without any other adequate means of support is forced to work.

Fourth, growing sociological literature on women in the workforce, observation, and personal experience all suggest that the work most women do is every bit as miserable as I have suggested. But it is not just work itself that does harm. Workers are also harmed to the extent that most work precludes their pursuit of other ends. Even if some workers are numbed to the hurt of work *per se*, all endure the harm insofar as their interests are impeded and their lives are impoverished.

Elite public intellectuals, politicians, and professors who speak about social justice are among the privileged few whose "work" is inherently satisfying and who do not recognize what work is like for most people, who do not speak because they have no voice—that is, because no one will listen (as Lao Tzu said, "Those who speak don't know and those who know don't speak"). For most women and men, work is nothing but drudgery that sets back their interests and harms them. Nonelite women, however, are locked into a narrower range of occupations than their male counterparts because of ongoing discrimination in employment. It is disturbing that while most of us are trapped in boring, underpaid, dead-end pink-collar jobs, feminist activists have by and large focused their attention on other issues. The harmfulness of work is not simply a woman's issue: many men are forced to do dull, demeaning, often dangerous work, and anyone, whether male or female, who spends a good deal of time doing boring work is in a more seriously harmed state than one who is raped. It is disturbing that there is so little recognition of the harmfulness of work.

POSSIBILITIES: A POSTSCRIPT

From the beginnings of second-wave feminism in the past century to the present, activists concerned with promoting the interests of women have focused on sexuality issues—primarily reproductive rights, including access to contraception and the availability of legal abortion, and also pornography, rape, and domestic violence. These are important issues, and for the most part activists have been on the side of right: abortion should certainly be legal, available, and affordable; rape and domestic violence are criminal acts and should of course be taken seriously. I have suggested, however, that these issues are not as important as discrimination in employment and occupational sex segregation.

Occupational sex segregation gets little attention because it is of less concern to women with four-year college degrees or higher, the feminist "base," than it is for the other roughly two-thirds of women in the U.S. population since sex segregation decreases with educational attainment.[12] The U.S. maintains a three-gender system: men, women, and Us. For Us, the most highly educated third of the population, there are unisex positions in business and the professions as doctors, lawyers, professors, politicians, and managers. There are far fewer unisex jobs for high school graduates or individuals who have had "some college." Blue-collar occupations remain overwhelmingly male. In 2010, according to the U.S. Bureau of Labor Statistics, only 0.1 percent of brickmasons, blockmasons, and stonemasons; 1.4 percent of carpenters; 1.5 percent of electricians; and 1.6 percent of automotive service technicians and mechanics were female.[13] In a great many trades the percentage of women is so low that the Bureau of Labor Statistics simply indicates that women's presence is negligible without recording a figure. These occupations include locksmiths and safe repairers, air traffic controllers, ambulance drivers, jewelers and precious stone and metal workers, etchers and engravers, and furniture finishers. Interestingly, most of the jobs in which women are greatly underrepresented do not require significant upper-body strength—the only characteristic that would likely disqualify many women.

Occupational sex segregation is not entirely a reflection of women's (informed) preferences: a 2010 briefing paper by the Institute for Women's Policy Research reports that "there is considerable research suggesting that occupational choice is often constrained, by socialization, lack of information, or more direct barriers to entry, to training or work in occupations where one sex is a small minority of the workforce."[14] As a consequence, working-class women are squeezed into a narrow range of traditional pink-collar service-sector jobs, where overcrowding depresses wages.[15]

Upper-middle-class women by and large do not see the possibility that they, or their daughters, might be forced to do boring, underpaid, dead-end womenswork as a real and present danger. When they go through the supermarket check-out, they do not imagine what it is like to spend one's working day confined to that 2-foot-by-2-foot space performing the same repetitive task over and over and over again without any challenge or possibility of achievement: they do not think "that could easily be me." When they order merchandise by phone, they do not imagine what it is like to work in a call center, confined to a carrel, working under close supervision, taking orders, doing the same routine task over and over and over again: they do not think "that could easily be me." They cannot, for the most part, imagine what life is like for most working-class women—scanning groceries, waitressing, keying in data, taking phone orders: trapped, constrained and bored, with their backs to the wall and no way out. But they can easily imagine facing an unplanned pregnancy or being a victim of street crime. When a woman is raped, every woman thinks, "that could easily be me." The preoccupations of upper-middle-class women, concerns about the bad things that could, realistically, happen to them, shape the projects and priorities of feminist activism.[16]

Whether for good or ill, nothing is more important to the quality of a person's life than work. Most of us spend more time at work than we do at any other activity. Work dominates our life and our consciousness, and the work we do determines our social and economic status. Moreover, the worst jobs, those that are the most boring, those that involve tedious, repetitive tasks, physical constraint, and close supervision, are also poorly paid and offer little scope for advancement. Women are overrepresented in these occupations.

Most work, particularly the work that the majority of women do, is more seriously harmful to individuals who do it than sexual assault. Realistically, women's job options are still limited: most women who have not caught the brass ring, who do not compete in the high end of the labor market where the most highly educated men and women apply for unisex positions in management and the professions, are *de facto* confined to boring, underpaid pink-collar womenswork. Feminists have not paid enough attention to occupational sex segregation, wage gaps, discrimination and its remedies, and other bread-and-butter issues because they are not pressing for us and because, unlike sexuality issues, they are not sexy. Sex, violence, and crime are interesting; poverty and drudgery are not.[17]

Women are still effectively locked out of blue-collar jobs; most of us are stuck in boring, underpaid, dead-end pink-collar jobs. It is very difficult to generate much sympathy for feminist activism when it has done little to oppose sex segregation in employment which, I have argued, undermines women's quality of life more than any of the other disadvantages and injustices we face. Most of us spend our days keying in data, answering phones, scanning groceries, and doing all the other tedious drudge work that has always been women's lot, but feminists don't seem to give a damn. It is hard not to see this as a betrayal. Being raped is bad. But being a Walmart cashier is much, much worse.[18]

NOTES

1. Everyone agrees that rape is bad. The core meaning of "rape" is "forcible or fraudulent sexual intercourse especially imposed on women" (*The Little Oxford Dictionary*). But, given the elaborate and confusing rules of sexual etiquette that have traditionally figured in human courtship rituals, it has not always been clear what constituted fraud or coercion in these matters. In particular, it has been assumed that female coyness is simply part of the courtship ritual so that women who acquiesce to the sexual demands of acquaintances under protest are merely playing the game and thus have not in fact been forced into anything. That is to say, it is assumed that under such conditions the sexual act is not an instance of rape at all, hence that a woman who claims she has been raped in such circumstances is disingenuous and may be assumed to have malicious motives. It is to these assumptions that women should object—not to my suggestion that rape is a less serious harm than has commonly been thought. What sexists underestimate is not the seriousness of rape but rather the frequency with which it occurs.

2. Joan McGregor addresses the question of *how* bad rape is in *Is It Rape? On Acquaintance Rape and Taking Women's Consent Seriously* (Aldershot, U.K.: Ashgate Publishing, 2005). For further discussion see Alan Soble's review of McGregor in *Law and Philosophy* 25: 6 (November, 2006): 663–72.

3. My argument rests on the assumption that for most of us very little hangs on sexuality issues—that for most of us in modern Western industrial or postindustrial societies our focal aims, and hence our interests, are not much affected by sexual activities, whether voluntary or involuntary. In spite of popular acceptance of Freudian doctrines, this does seem to be the case. In a society where people's most important aims were tied up with sexual activities, things would be different, and rape would be even more serious than it is among us. Imagine, for example, a society in which women were excluded entirely from the workforce and marriage was their only economic option, so that a woman's sexuality, like the cowboy's horse, was her only means of livelihood; imagine that in this society sexual purity were highly valued (at least for women) and a woman who was known to be "damaged goods," for whatever reason, was as a result rendered unmarriageable and subjected to constant humiliation by her relatives and society at large. In such circumstances rape would indeed violate a welfare interest and would be among the most serious of crimes, rather like horse theft in the Old West. There are no doubt societies in which this is the case. It is not, however, the case among us.

Again, some people may regard their sexual integrity as so intimately wrapped up with their self-concept that they would be violated in the most profound way if forced to have sexual intercourse against their will. There are no doubt persons for whom this is the case. It is not, however, the case for the standard person. Admittedly, this is an empirical conjecture. But we do recognize that it is the case for the standard male person, and the assumption that women are different seems to be a manifestation of the sexist assumption that women are primarily sexual beings.

4. Ariane Hegewisch, Hannah Liepmann, Heffret Hayes, and Heidi Hartmann, "Separate and Not Equal? Gender Segregation in the Labor Market and the Gender Wage Gap." Briefing Paper, Washington, D.C.: Institute for Women's Policy Research, September 2010, p. 1.

5. Joel Feinberg, *Harm to Others* (Oxford, U.K.: Oxford University Press, 1984), 204–5.

6. Feinberg, *Harm to Others*, 37.

7. Feinberg, *Harm to Others*, 57.

8. Feinberg, *Harm to Others*, 45ff.

9. Bureau of Labor Statistics, *Occupational Outlook Handbook, 2010–11 Edition* (Washington, D.C.: United States Department of Labor Statistics), http://www.bls.gov/oco (accessed February 14, 2012).

10. Bureau of Labor Statistics, *Occupational Outlook Handbook.*

11. See Hegewisch et. al., "Separate and Not Equal," 14. While women's labor force participation increased dramatically during the past forty years, and women have entered a number of traditionally male occupations, occupational sex segregation has remained unchanged since the 1990s.

Hegewisch et al. write,

> The "Index of Dissimilarity" provides an analytical tool for assessing which occupational trends are typical for the labor market as a whole. The Index measures how many women or men would have to change occupations to achieve the same gender composition in each occupation as in the civilian labor force overall. . . . The index ranges from 0 (complete integration) to 1. . . . The Index for all workers fell from 0.68 in 1972 to 0.50 in 2002, when it was at its lowest point, a dip of 26 percent. Yet, in 2009 and most of the years since 1996, the index has hovered around 0.51. The trend towards integration appears to have stalled; there has been no further progress towards occupational gender balance.

12. See Hegewisch et al., "Separate and Not Equal," 13.

13. Bureau of Labor Statistics, *Occupational Outlook Handbook.*

14. See Hegewisch et al., "Separate and Not Equal," 13.

15. This is economist Barbara Bergmann's "overcrowding hypothesis." See her "Occupational Segregation, Wages and Profits When Employers Discriminate by Race and Sex," *Eastern Economic Journal* 1:2 (1974): 103–10.

16. See H. E. Baber, "Worlds, Capabilities, and Well-Being," in *Ethical Theory and Moral Practice* 13:4 (2010): 377–92. On the account of well-being proposed there, mere possibilities—possibilities that are never realized—can affect our well-being for good or for ill. Having options, even if we do not exercise them, contributes to our well-being: freedom broadly construed is in and of itself of value. By the same token, mere possibilities can make us worse off. I will not spend my days scanning groceries or keying in data, but I escaped by the skin of my teeth: because I am a woman the possible worlds in which I am a cashier, a customer service representative, or a data entry operator are close by, and the proximity of these possible worlds makes me worse off. Moreover, because having options is in and of itself of value, whether we exercise them or not, my lack of options makes me worse off. Because I am a woman, I have no viable fallback positions—jobs that I would find minimally tolerable. As a woman, *de facto*, I would not be able to get a job working construction, driving a tow truck, cleaning out cars at a dealership, or doing any of a range of unskilled "men's jobs" that most people, including me, would prefer to avoid but which aren't as unpleasant as comparable "women's jobs" and which, in any case, many women would prefer to pink-collar jobs if they could get them. During World War II, women in great numbers flocked to traditionally male jobs without any special persuasion or social engineering. They were simply informed that these jobs were, at least temporarily, open to women. For a discussion of women's entry into these jobs during World War II, see Maureen Honey, *Creating Rosie the Riveter: Class, Gender, and Propaganda during World War II* (Amherst, Mass.: University of Massachusetts Press, 1984). Currently, working-class women do not apply for traditionally male jobs because they believe with justification that they will not be taken seriously and will likely be embarrassed if they apply.

17. For over a decade, from December 1998 to its final resolution by the Supreme Court in 2011, a class-action sex-discrimination suit against Walmart, America's largest private employer, worked its way through the courts. No one noticed. Feminist activists were occupied with sexier matters. Meanwhile, the one-and-a-half million women involved in the case, who had worked at Walmart confined to boring, dead-end womenswork, lost their case. It isn't hard to see why most younger women are "not feminists but . . ." or why working-class women by and large do not think that feminism has anything to offer them.

18. I am grateful to Raja Halwani, Lila Luce, and Lori Watson for comments on an earlier draft of this paper.

STUDY QUESTIONS

1. "External costs" are those that are borne by those outside a contract, such as when it is claimed that a landlord's renting a shop space to an adult video store would harm the nearby stores. Are there external costs to rape that Baber fails to consider? Do all women (and men) pay a price for the rape of one woman? Read Susan Brison's essay "Surviving Sexual Violence" (in this volume) before answering this question.

2. Alan Wertheimer (in this volume, "Consent and Sexual Relations") distinguishes between "neurological" and "moralized" accounts of harm. In a neurological account of harm, a rape victim's particular amount of trauma and distress count as harms, while only in a moralized account is a rape victim's loss of bodily integrity in itself a harm. Which claims of Baber depend on which of these accounts?

3. Extend Baber's account of the harmfulness of rape to the harmfulness of prostitution. Is prostitution as a full-time job better than being a full-time cashier at Walmart? Take into account also Martha Nussbaum's evaluation of prostitution as a job and teaching as a job (see "'Whether from Reason or Prejudice': Taking Money for Bodily Services," in this volume).

4. What philosophical (or rhetorical?) advantage is gained by Baber's immediately changing the question from "How bad is rape?" to "How bad is rape vis-à-vis other gender-based offenses"? Does her wording create an unfair advantage, or is it perfectly acceptable?

5. Baber quotes with approval Joel Feinberg's claim that there cannot typically be tradeoffs between competing "welfare interests." But think about whether her ranking of, for example, a woman's having to take a "boring, underpaid, dead-end job" as worse than being raped implicitly assumes such a tradeoff.

6. Baber uses the following facts in making her case: "Most cashiers work indoors, usually standing in booths or behind counters. Often they are not allowed to leave their workstations without supervisory approval." They "spend one's working day confined to that 2-foot-by-2-foot space performing the same repetitive task over and over and over again." Discuss the similarities and differences with the situation of veal calves, who are "kept in small wooden . . . crates which prevent movement and inhibit muscle growth. . . . They are fed an iron deficient diet to keep their flesh . . . appealing to the consumer. [They are] alone and deprived of light for a large portion of their *four-month* lives" (www.animal

ssuffering.com/resources/facts/factory-farming.php).

7. Baber defines rape as "forcible or fraudulent sexual intercourse especially imposed on women." Something is missing from this definition: that rape occurs when the woman (or other victim) does not consent. (See Lois Pineau's "Date Rape: A Feminist Analysis," in this volume.) Whether, or to what extent, rape should be defined in terms of "force" or in terms of "lack of consent" is an important issue that philosophical and legal scholars have been investigating. (See, for example—as a bare beginning—the references mentioned in Baber's note 2.) Is it possible that taking an alternative definition of "rape" seriously would lead us to assess Baber's various claims differently?

8. Robin West describes (in this volume) "The Harms of Consensual Sex." How bad are the harms of consensual, unwanted sex vis-à-vis the harms of rape understood as nonconsensual sex? Shouldn't nonconsensual, unwanted sex be more harmful to women than consensual, unwanted sex? If so, does this make the harmfulness of rape, on Baber's view, greater than she estimates it to be?

TWENTY-SEVEN

Surviving Sexual Violence

Susan J. Brison

In this chapter, **Susan J. Brison** *provides a powerful narrative of her own rape and its aftermath. In an unusually personal story of trauma and recovery, she confronts a number of philosophical issues regarding personal identity and the nature of memory, conceptual questions over how to categorize (and honestly discuss) rape's devastating effects, moral challenges raised by the sexism and cultural taboos surrounding rape, and legal obstacles to effective yet nondiscriminatory measures we can take to protect women.*

Susan J. Brison teaches philosophy and women's and gender studies at Dartmouth College and is the author of *Aftermath: Violence and the Remaking of a Self* (2002) and coeditor of *Contemporary Perspectives on Constitutional Interpretation* (1993). She has published articles on free speech controversies and on sexual violence in academic journals as well as in newspapers and magazines such as the *New York Times*, the *San Francisco Chronicle*, and the *Guardian*. This chapter is the essay "Surviving Sexual Violence: A Philosophical Perspective," *Journal of Social Philosophy* 24:1 (1993): 5–22. Reprinted with the permission of Susan J. Brison, the *Journal of Social Philosophy*, and Blackwell Publishing, Ltd. The essay also appeared in *Aftermath: Violence and the Remaking of a Self* (Princeton University Press, 2002), 2–12 and 129–31.

On July 4, 1990, at 10:30 in the morning, I went for a walk along a peaceful-looking country road in a village outside Grenoble, France. It was a gorgeous day, and I didn't envy my husband, Tom, who had to stay inside and work on a manuscript with a French colleague of his. I sang to myself as I set out, stopping to pet a goat and pick a few wild strawberries along the way. About an hour and a half later, I was lying face down in a muddy creek bed at the bottom of a dark ravine, struggling to stay alive. I had been grabbed from behind, pulled into the bushes, beaten, and sexually assaulted. Feeling absolutely helpless and entirely at my assailant's mercy, I talked to him, calling him "sir." I tried to appeal to his humanity, and, when that failed, I addressed myself to his self-interest. He called me a whore and told me to shut up.

Although I had said I'd do whatever he wanted, as the sexual assault began I instinctively fought back, which so enraged my attacker that he strangled me until I lost consciousness. When I awoke, I was being dragged by my feet down into the ravine. I had often, while dreaming, thought I was awake, but now I was awake and convinced I was having a nightmare. But it was no dream. After ordering me, in a gruff, Gestapo-like voice, to get on my hands and knees, my assailant strangled me again. I wish I could convey the horror of losing consciousness while my animal instincts desperately fought the effects of strangulation. This time I was sure I was dying. But I revived, just in time to see him lunging toward me with a rock. He smashed it into my forehead, knocking me out, and eventually, after another strangulation attempt, he left me for dead.

After my assailant left, I managed to climb out of the ravine, and was rescued by a farmer who called the police, a doctor, and an ambulance. I was taken to emergency at the Grenoble hospital where I underwent neurological tests, x-rays, blood tests, and a gynecological exam. Leaves and twigs were taken from my hair for evidence, my fingernails were scraped, and my mouth was swabbed for samples. I had multiple head injuries, my eyes were swollen shut, and I had a fractured trachea, which made breathing difficult. I was not permitted to drink or eat anything for the first thirty hours, although Tom, who never left my side, was allowed to dab my blood-encrusted lips with a wet towel. The next day, I was transferred out of emergency and into my own room. But I could not be left alone, even for a few minutes. I was terrified my assailant would find me and finish the job. When someone later brought in the local paper with a story about my attack, I was greatly relieved that it referred to me as *Mlle M. R.* and didn't mention that I was an American. Even by the time I left the hospital, eleven days later, I was so concerned about my assailant tracking me down that I put only my lawyer's address on the hospital records.

Although fears for my safety may have initially explained why I wanted to remain anonymous, by that time my assailant had been apprehended, indicted for rape and attempted murder, and incarcerated without possibility of bail. Still, I didn't want people to know that I had been sexually assaulted. I don't know whether this was because I could still hardly believe it myself, because keeping this information confidential was one of the few ways I could feel in control of my life, or because, in spite of my conviction that I had done nothing wrong, I felt ashamed.

When I started telling people about the attack, I said, simply, that I was the victim of an attempted murder. People typically asked, in horror, "What was the motivation? Were you mugged?" and when I replied, "No, it started as a sexual assault," most inquirers were satisfied with that as an explanation of why some man wanted to murder me. I would have thought that a murder attempt plus a sexual assault would require more, not less, of an explanation than a murder attempt by itself. (After all, there are two criminal acts to explain here.)

One reason sexual violence is taken for granted by many is because it is so very prevalent. The FBI, notorious for underestimating the frequency of sex crimes, notes that, in the United States, a rape occurs on an average of every six minutes.[1] But this figure covers only the reported cases of rape, and some researchers claim that only about 10% of all rapes get reported.[2] Every 15 seconds, a woman is beaten.[3] The everydayness of sexual violence, as evidenced by these mind-numbing statistics, leads many to think that male violence against women is natural, a given, something not in need of explanation and not amenable to change. And yet, through some extraordinary mental gymnastics, while most people take sexual violence for granted, they simultaneously manage to deny that it really exists—or, rather, that it could happen to them. We continue to think that we—and the women we love—are immune to it, provided, that is, that we don't do anything "foolish." How many of us have swallowed the potentially lethal lie that if you don't do anything wrong, if you're just careful enough, you'll be safe? How many of us have believed its damaging, victim-blaming corollary: if you are attacked, it's because you did something wrong? These are lies, and in telling my story I hope to expose them, as well as to help bridge the gap between those of us who have been victimized and those who have not.

Sexual violence and its aftermath raise numerous philosophical issues in a variety of areas in our discipline. The disintegration of the self experienced by victims of violence challenges our notions of personal identity over time, a major preoccupation of metaphysics. A victim's seemingly justified skepticism about everyone and everything is pertinent to epistemology, especially if the goal of epistemology is, as Wilfrid Sellars put it, that of feeling at home in the world. In aesthetics, as well as in philosophy of law, the discussion of sexual violence in- or as- art could use the illumination provided by a victim's perspective. Perhaps the most important issues posed by sexual violence are in the areas of social, political, and legal philosophy, and insight into these, as well, requires an understanding of what it's like to be a victim of such violence.

One of the very few articles written by philosophers on violence against women is Ross Harrison's "Rape—A Case Study in Political Philosophy."[4] In this article Harrison argues that not only do utilitarians need to assess the harmfulness of rape in order to decide whether the harm to the victim outweighs the benefit to the rapist, but even on a rights-based approach to criminal justice we need to be able to assess the benefits and harms involved in criminalizing and punishing violent acts such as rape. In his view, it is not always the case, contra Ronald Dworkin, that rights trump considerations of utility, so, even on a rights-based account of justice, we need to give an account of why, in the case of rape, the pleasure gained by the perpetrator (or by multiple perpetrators, in the case of gang-rape) is always outweighed by the harm done to the victim. He points out the peculiar difficulty most of us have in imagining the pleasure a rapist gets out of an assault, but, he asserts confidently, "There is no problem imagining what it is like to be a victim. . . ."[5] To his credit, he acknowledges the importance, to political philosophy, of trying to imagine others' experience, for otherwise we could not compare harms and benefits, which he argues must be done even in cases of conflicts of rights in order to decide which of competing rights should take priority. But imagining what it is like to be a rape victim is no simple matter, since much of what a victim goes through is unimaginable. Still, it's essential to try to convey it.

In my efforts to tell the victim's story—my story, our story—I've been inspired and instructed not only by feminist philosophers who have refused to accept the dichotomy between the personal and the political, but also by critical race theorists such as Patricia Williams, Mari Matsuda, and Charles Lawrence, who have incorporated first person narrative accounts into their discussions of the law. In writing about hate speech, they have argued persuasively that one cannot do justice to the issues involved in debates about restrictions on speech without listening to the victims' stories.[6] In describing the effects of racial harassment on victims, they have departed from the academic convention of speaking in the impersonal, "universal," voice and relate incidents they themselves experienced. In her groundbreaking book, *The Alchemy of Race and Rights*,[7] Williams describes how it felt to learn about her great-great-grandmother who was purchased at age 11 by a slave owner who raped and impregnated her the following year. And in describing instances of everyday racism she herself has lived through, she gives us imaginative access to what it's like to be the victim of racial discrimination. Some may consider such first person accounts in academic writing to be self-indulgent, but I consider them a welcome antidote to scholarship that, in the guise of "universality," tends to silence those who most need to be heard.

Philosophers are far behind legal theorists in acknowledging the need for a diversity of voices. We are trained to write in an abstract, universal voice and to shun first-person narratives as biased and inappropriate for academic discourse. Some topics, however, such as the impact of racial and sexual violence on victims, cannot even be broached unless those affected by such crimes can tell of their experiences in their own words. Unwittingly further illustrating the need for the victim's perspective, Harrison writes, elsewhere in his article on rape, "What principally distinguishes rape from normal sexual activity is the consent of the raped woman."[8] There is no parallel to this in the case of other crimes, such as theft or murder. Try "What principally distinguishes theft from normal gift-giving is the consent of the person stolen from." We don't think of theft as "coerced gift-giving." We don't think of murder as "assisted suicide minus consent." Why not? In the latter case, it could be because assisted suicide is relatively rare (even compared with murder) and so it's odd to use it as the more familiar thing to which we are analogizing. But in the former case, gift-giving is presumably more prevalent than theft (at least in academic circles) and yet it still sounds odd to explicate theft in terms of gift-giving minus consent (or coerced philanthropy). In the cases of both theft and murder, the notion of violation seems built into our conceptions of the physical acts constituting the crimes, so it is inconceivable that one could consent to the act in question. Why is it so easy for a philosopher such as Harrison to think of rape, however, as "normal sexual activity minus consent"? This may be because the nature of the violation in the case of rape hasn't been all that obvious. Witness the phenomenon of rape jokes, the prevalence of pornography glorifying rape, the common attitude that, in the case of women, "no" means "yes," that women really want it.[9]

Since I was assaulted by a stranger, in a "safe" place, and was so visibly injured when I encountered the police and medical personnel, I was, throughout my hospitalization and my dealings with the police, spared the insult, suffered by so many rape victims, of not being believed or of being said to have asked for the attack. However, it became clear to me as I gave my deposition from my hospital bed that this would still be an issue in my assailant's trial. During my deposition, I recalled being on the verge of giving up my struggle to live when I was galvanized by a sudden, piercing image of Tom's future pain on finding my corpse in that ravine. At this point in my deposition, I paused, glanced over at the police officer who was typing the transcript, and asked whether it was appropriate to include this image of my husband in my recounting of the facts. The gendarme replied that it definitely was and that it was a very good thing I mentioned my husband, since my assailant, who had confessed to the sexual assault, was claiming I had provoked it. As serious as the occasion was, and as much as it hurt to laugh, I couldn't help it, the suggestion was so ludicrous. Could it have been those baggy Gap jeans I was wearing that morning? Or was it the heavy sweatshirt? My maddeningly seductive jogging shoes? Or was it simply my walking along minding my own business that had provoked his murderous rage?

After I completed my deposition, which lasted eight hours, the police officer asked me to read and sign the transcript he'd typed to certify that it was accurate. I was surprised to see that it began with the words, *"Comme je suis sportive . . ."* ("Since I am athletic . . .")—added by the police to explain what possessed me to go for a walk by myself that fine morning. I was too exhausted by this point to protest "No, I'm not an athlete, I'm a philosophy professor," and I figured the officer knew what he was doing, so I let it stand. That evening, my assailant was formally indicted. I retained a lawyer, and met him along with the investigating magistrate, when I gave my second deposition toward the end of my hospitalization. Although what occurred was officially a crime against the state, not against me, I was advised to pursue a civil suit in order to recover unreimbursed medical expenses, and, in any case, I needed an advocate to explain the French legal system to me. I was told that since this was an "easy" case, the trial would occur within a year. In fact, the trial took place two and a half years after the assault, due to the delaying tactics of my assailant's lawyer who was trying to get him off on an insanity defense. According to Article 64 of the French criminal code, if the defendant is determined to have been insane at the time, then, legally, there was "*ni crime, ni délit*"—neither crime nor offense. The jury, however, did not accept the insanity plea and found my assailant guilty of rape and attempted murder.

As things turned out, my experience with the criminal justice system was better than that of most sexual assault victims. I did, however, occasionally get glimpses of the humiliating insensitivity victims routinely endure. Before I could be released from the hospital, for example, I had to undergo a second forensic examination at a different hospital. I was taken in a wheelchair out to a hospital van, driven to another hospital, taken to an office where there were no receptionists and where I was greeted by two male doctors I had never seen before. When they told me to take off my clothes and stand in the middle of the room, I refused. I had to ask for a hospital gown to put on. For about an hour the two of them went over me like a piece of meat, calling out measurements of bruises and other assessments of damage, as if they were performing an autopsy. This was just the first of many incidents in which I felt as if I was experiencing things posthumously. When the inconceivable happens, one starts to doubt even the most mundane, realistic perceptions. Perhaps I'm not really here, I thought, perhaps I did die in that ravine. The line between life and death, once so clear and sustaining, now seemed carelessly drawn and easily erased.

For the first several months after my attack, I led a spectral existence, not quite sure whether I had died and the world went on without me, or whether I was alive but in a totally alien world. Tom and I returned to the States, and I continued to convalesce, but I felt as though I'd somehow outlived myself. I sat in our apartment and stared outside for hours, through the blur of a detached vitreous, feeling like Robert Lowell's newly widowed mother, described in one of his poems as mooning in a window "as if she had stayed on a train / one stop past her destination."[10]

My sense of unreality was fed by the massive denial of those around me—a reaction I learned is an almost universal response to rape. Where the facts would appear to be incontrovertible, denial takes the shape of attempts to explain the assault in ways that leave the observers' worldview unscathed. Even those who are able to acknowledge the existence of violence try to protect themselves from the realization that the world in which it occurs is their world and so they find it hard to identify with the victim. They cannot allow themselves to imagine the victim's shattered life, or else their illusions about their own safety and control over their lives might begin to crumble. The most well-meaning individuals, caught up in the myth of their own immunity, can inadvertently add to the victim's suffering by suggesting that the attack was avoidable or somehow her fault. One victims' assistance coordinator, whom I had phoned for legal advice, stressed that she herself had never been a victim and said that I would benefit from the experience by learning not to be so trusting of people and to take basic safety precautions like not going out alone late at night. She didn't pause long enough during her lecture for me to point out that I was attacked suddenly, from behind, in broad daylight.

We are not taught to empathize with victims. In crime novels and detective films, it is the villain, or the one who solves the murder mystery, who attracts our attention; the victim, a merely passive pretext for our entertainment, is conveniently disposed of—and forgotten—early on. We identify with the agents' strength and skill, for good or evil, and join the victim, if at all, only in our nightmares. Though one might say, as did Clarence Thomas, looking at convicted criminals on their way to jail, "but for the grace of God, there go I,"[11] a victim's fate prompts an almost instinctive "it could never happen to me." This may explain why there is, in our criminal justice system, so little concern for justice for victims— especially rape victims. They have no constitutionally protected rights *qua* victims. They have no right to a speedy trial or to compensation for damages (although states have been changing this in recent years), or to privacy vis-à-vis the press. As a result of their victimization, they often lose their jobs, their homes, their spouses—in addition to a great deal of money, time, sleep, self-esteem, and peace of mind. The rights to "life, liberty, and the pursuit of happiness," possessed, in the abstract, by all of us, are of little use to victims who can lose years of their lives, the freedom to move about in the world without debilitating fear, and any hope of returning to the pleasures of life as they once knew it.

People also fail to recognize that if a victim could not have anticipated an attack, she can have no assurance that she will be able to avoid one in the future. More to reassure themselves than to comfort the victim, some deny that such a thing could happen again. One friend, succumbing to the gambler's fallacy, pointed out that my having had such extraordinary bad luck meant that the odds of my being attacked again were now quite slim (as if fate, although not completely benign, would surely give me a break now, perhaps in the interest of fairness). Others thought it would be most comforting to act as if nothing had happened. The first card I received from my mother, while I was still in the hospital, made no mention of the attack or of my pain and featured the "bluebird of happiness," sent to keep me ever cheerful. The second had an illustration of a bright, summery scene with the greeting: "Isn't the sun nice? Isn't the wind nice? Isn't everything nice?" Weeks passed before I learned, what I should have been able to guess, that after she and my father received Tom's first call from the hospital they held each other and sobbed. They didn't want to burden me with their pain—a pain that I now realize must have been greater than my own.

Some devout relatives were quick to give God all the credit for my survival but none of the blame for what I had to endure. Others acknowledged the suffering that had been inflicted on me, but as no more than a blip on the graph of God's benevolence—necessary, fleeting, evil, there to make possible an even greater show of good. An aunt, with whom I had been close since childhood, did not write or call at all until three months after the attack, and then sent a belated birthday card with a note saying that she was sorry to hear about my "horrible experience" but pleased to think that as a result I "will become stronger and will be able to help so many people. A real blessing from above for sure." Such attempts at a theodicy discounted the horror I had to endure. But I learned that everyone needs to try and make sense, in however inadequate a way, of such senseless violence. I watched my own seesawing attempts to find something for which to be grateful, something to redeem the unmitigated awfulness: I was glad I didn't have to reproach myself (or endure others' reproaches) for having done something careless, but I wished I had done something I could consider reckless so that I could simply refrain from doing it in the future. For some time I was glad I did not yet have a child, who would have to grow up with the knowledge that even the protector could not be protected, but I felt an inexpressible loss when I recalled how much Tom and I had wanted a baby and how joyful were our attempts to conceive. It was difficult to imagine getting pregnant, because it was so hard to let even my husband near me, and because I felt it would be harder still to let a child leave my side.

It might be gathered, from this litany of complaints, that I was the recipient of constant, if misguided, attempts at consolation during the first few months of my recovery. This was not the case. It seemed to me that the half-life of most people's concern was less than that of the sleeping pills I took to ward off flashbacks and nightmares—just long enough to allow the construction of a comforting illusion that lulls the shock to sleep. During the first few months after my assault, my close friends, my sister, and my parents were supportive, but most of the aunts, uncles, cousins, and friends of the family notified by my parents almost immediately after the attack didn't phone, write, or even send a get well card, in spite of my extended hospital stay. These are all caring, decent people who would have sent wishes for a speedy recovery if I'd had, say, an appendectomy. Their early lack of response was so striking that I wondered whether it was the result of self-protective denial, a reluctance to mention something so unspeakable, or a symptom of our society's widespread emotional illiteracy that prevents most people from conveying any feeling that can't be expressed in a Hallmark card.

In the case of rape, the intersection of multiple taboos—against talking openly about trauma, about violence, about sex—causes conversational gridlock, paralyzing the would-be supporter. We lack the vocabulary for expressing appropriate concern, and we have no social conventions to ease the awkwardness. Ronald de Sousa has written persuasively about the importance of grasping paradigm scenarios in early childhood in order to learn appropriate emotional responses to situations.[12] We do not learn—early or later in life—how to react to a rape. What typically results from this ignorance is bewilderment on the part of victims and silence on the part of others, often the result of misguided caution. When, on entering the angry phase of my recovery period, I railed at my parents: "Why haven't my relatives called or written? Why hasn't my own brother phoned?" They replied, "They all expressed their concern to us, but they didn't want to remind you of what happened." Didn't they realize I thought about the attack every minute of every day and that their inability to respond made me feel as though I had, in fact, died and no one had bothered to come to the funeral?

For the next several months, I felt angry, scared, and helpless, and I wished I could blame myself for what had happened so that I would feel less vulnerable, more in control of my life. Those who haven't been sexually violated may have difficulty understanding why women who survive assault often blame themselves, and may wrongly attribute it to a sex-linked trait of masochism or lack of self-esteem. They don't know that it can be less painful to believe that you did something blameworthy than it is to think that you live in a world where you can be attacked at any time, in any place, simply because you are a woman. It is hard to go on after an attack that is both random—and thus completely unpredictable—and not random, that is, a crime of hatred towards the group to which you happen to belong. If I hadn't been the one who was attacked on that road in France, it would have been the next woman to come along. But had my husband walked down that road instead, he would have been safe.

Although I didn't blame myself for the attack, neither could I blame my attacker. Tom wanted to kill him, but I, like other rape victims I came to know, found it almost impossible to get angry with my assailant. I think the terror I still felt precluded the appropriate angry response. It may be that experiencing anger towards an attacker requires imagining oneself in proximity to him, a prospect too frightening for a victim in the early stages of recovery to conjure up. As Aristotle observed in the *Rhetoric*, Book I, "no one grows angry with a person on whom there is no prospect of taking vengeance, and we feel comparatively little anger, or none at all, with those who are much our superiors in power."[13] The anger was still there, however, but it got directed towards safer targets:

my family and closest friends. My anger spread, giving me painful shoot-
ing signs that I was coming back to life. I could not accept what had
happened to me. What was I supposed to do now? How could everyone
else carry on with their lives when women were dying? How could Tom
go on teaching his classes, seeing students, chatting with colleagues . . .
and why should he be able to walk down the street when I couldn't?

The incompatibility of fear of my assailant and appropriate anger towards him became most apparent after I began taking a women's self-
defense class. It became clear that the way to break out of the double bind
of self-blame versus powerlessness was through empowerment—physical as well as political. Learning to fight back is a crucial part of this
process, not only because it enables us to experience justified, healing
rage, but also because, as Iris Young has observed in her essay "Throwing Like a Girl," "women in sexist society are physically handicapped,"
moving about hesitantly, fearfully, in a constricted lived space, routinely
underestimating what strength we actually have.[14] We have to learn to
feel entitled to occupy space, to defend ourselves. The hardest thing for
most of the women in my self-defense class to do was simply to yell
"No!" Women have been taught not to fight back when being attacked, to
rely instead on placating or pleading with one's assailant—strategies that
researchers have found to be least effective in resisting rape.[15]

The instructor of the class, a survivor herself, helped me through the
difficult first sessions, through the flashbacks and the fear, and showed
me I could be tougher than ever. As I was leaving after one session, I saw
a student arrive for the next class—with a guide dog. I was furious that,
in addition to everything else this woman had to struggle with, she had
to worry about being raped. I thought I understood something of her fear
since I felt, for the first time in my life, like I had a perceptual deficit—not
the blurred vision from the detached vitreous, but, rather, the more haz-
ardous lack of eyes in the back of my head. I tried to compensate for this
on my walks by looking over my shoulder a lot and punctuating my
purposeful, straight-ahead stride with an occasional pirouette, which
must have made me look more whimsical than terrified.

The confidence I gained from learning how to fight back effectively
not only enabled me to walk down the street again, it gave me back my
life. But it was a changed life. A paradoxical life. I began to feel stronger
than ever before, and more vulnerable, more determined to fight to
change the world, but in need of several naps a day. News that friends
found distressing in a less visceral way—the trials of the defendants in
the Central Park jogger case, the controversy over *American Psycho*, the
Gulf war, the Kennedy rape case, the Tyson trial, the fatal stabbing of law
professor Mary Joe Frug near Harvard Square, the ax murders of two
women graduate students at Dartmouth College (also neglected by all
but the local press since the victims were black and from Ethiopia)—
triggered debilitating flashbacks in me. Unlike survivors of wars or earth-

quakes, who inhabit a common shattered world, rape victims face the cataclysmic destruction of their world alone, surrounded by people who find it hard to understand what's so distressing. I realized that I exhibited every symptom of post-traumatic stress disorder—dissociation, flashbacks, hypervigilance, exaggerated startle response, sleep disorders, inability to concentrate, diminished interest in significant activities, and a sense of a foreshortened future.[16] I could understand why children exposed to urban violence have such trouble envisioning their futures. Although I had always been career-oriented, always planning for my future, I could no longer imagine how I would get through each day, let alone what I might be doing in a year's time. I didn't think I would ever write or teach philosophy again.

The American Psychiatric Association's *Diagnostic and Statistical Manual* defines post-traumatic stress disorder, in part, as the result of "an event that is outside the range of usual human experience."[17] Because the trauma is, to most people, inconceivable, it's also unspeakable. Even when I managed to find the words and the strength to describe my ordeal, it was hard for others to hear about it. They would have preferred me to just "buck up," as one friend urged me to do. But it's essential to talk about it, again and again. It's a way of remastering the trauma, although it can be retraumatizing when people refuse to listen. In my case, each time someone failed to respond I felt as though I were alone again in the ravine, dying, screaming. And still no one could hear me. Or, worse, they heard me, but refused to help.

I now know they were trying to help, but that recovering from trauma takes time, patience, and, most of all, determination on the part of the survivor. After about six months, I began to be able to take more responsibility for my own recovery, and stopped expecting others to pull me through. I entered the final stage of my recovery, a period of gradual acknowledgement and integration of what had happened. I joined a rape survivors' support group, I got a great deal of therapy, and I became involved in political activities, such as promoting the Violence against Women Act (which was eventually passed by congress in 1994).[18] Gradually, I was able to get back to work.

When I resumed teaching at Dartmouth in the fall of 1991, the first student who came to see me in my office during freshman orientation week told me that she had been raped. The following spring, four Dartmouth students reported sexual assaults to the local police. In the aftermath of these recent reports, the women students on my campus were told to use their heads, lock their doors, not go out after dark without a male escort. They were advised: just don't do anything stupid.

Although colleges are eager to "protect" women by hindering their freedom of movement or providing them with male escorts, they continue to be reluctant to teach women how to protect themselves. After months of lobbying the administration at my college, we were able to convince them to offer a women's self-defense and rape prevention course. It was offered in the winter of 1992 as a physical education course, and nearly 100 students and employees signed up for it. Shortly after the course began, I was informed that the women students were not going to be allowed to get P.E. credit for it, since the administration had determined that it discriminated against men. I was told that granting credit for the course was in violation of Title IX, which prohibits sex-discrimination in education programs receiving federal funding—even though granting credit to men for being on the football team was not, even though Title IX law makes an explicit exception for P.E. classes involving substantial bodily contact, and even though every term the college offers several martial arts courses, for credit, that are open to men, geared to men's physiques and needs, and taken predominantly by men. I was told by an administrator that, even if Title IX permitted it, offering a women's self-defense course for credit violated "the College's non-discrimination clause—a clause which, I hope, all reasonable men and women support as good policy."

The implication that I was not a "reasonable woman" didn't sit well with me as a philosopher, so I wrote a letter to the appropriate administrative committee criticizing my college's position that single-sex sports, male-only fraternities, female-only sororities, and pregnancy leave policies are not discriminatory, in any invidious sense, while a women's self-defense class is. The administration finally agreed to grant P.E. credit for the course, but shortly after that battle was over, I read in the *New York Times* that "a rape prevention ride service offered to women in the city of Madison and on the University of Wisconsin campus may lose its university financing because it discriminates against men."[19] The dean of students at Wisconsin said that this group—the Women's Transit Authority—which has been providing free nighttime rides to women students for nineteen years, must change its policy to allow male drivers and passengers. These are, in my view, examples of the application of what Catharine MacKinnon refers to as "the stupid theory of equality."[20] To argue that rape prevention policies for women discriminate against men is like arguing that money spent making university buildings more accessible to disabled persons discriminates against those able-bodied persons who do not benefit from these improvements.[21]

Sexual violence victimizes not only those women who are directly attacked, but *all* women. The fear of rape has long functioned to keep women in their place. Whether or not one agrees with the claims of those, such as Susan Brownmiller,[22] who argue that rape is a means by which *all* men keep *all* women subordinate, the fact that all women's lives are restricted by sexual violence is indisputable. The authors of *The Female Fear*, Margaret Gordon and Stephanie Riger, cite studies substantiating what every woman already knows—that the fear of rape prevents women from enjoying what men consider to be their birthright. Fifty percent of women never use public transportation after dark because of fear of rape. Women are eight times more likely than men to avoid walking in their own neighborhoods after dark, for the same reason.[23] In the seminar on Violence against Women which I taught for the first time in the spring of 1992, the men in the class were stunned by the extent to which the women in the class took precautions against assault every day—locking doors and windows, checking the back seat of the car, not walking alone at night, looking in closets on returning home. And this is at a "safe," rural New England campus.

Although women still have their work and leisure opportunities unfairly restricted by their relative lack of safety, paternalistic legislation excluding women from some of the "riskier" forms of employment (e.g. bartending)[24] has, thankfully, disappeared, except, that is, in the military. We are still debating whether women should be permitted to engage in combat, and the latest rationale for keeping women out of battle is that they are more vulnerable than men to sexual violence. Those wanting to limit women's role in the military have used the reported indecent assaults on two female American prisoners of war in Iraq as evidence for women's unsuitability for combat.[25] One might as well argue that the fact that women are much more likely than men to be sexually assaulted on college campuses is evidence that women are not suited to post-secondary education. No one, to my knowledge, has proposed returning Ivy League colleges to their former all-male status as a solution to the problem of campus rape. Some have, however, seriously proposed enacting after-dark curfews for women, in spite of the fact that men are the perpetrators of the assaults. This is yet another indication of how natural it still seems to many people to address the problem of sexual violence by curtailing women's lives. The absurdity of this approach becomes apparent once one realizes that a woman can be sexually assaulted anywhere, at any time—in "safe" places, in broad daylight, even in her own home.

For months after my assault, I was afraid of people finding out about it—afraid of their reactions and of their inability to respond. I was afraid that my professional work would be discredited, that I would be viewed as biased, or, even worse, not properly philosophical. Now I am no longer afraid of what might happen if I speak out about sexual violence. I'm much more afraid of what will continue to happen if I don't. Sexual violence is a problem of catastrophic proportions—a fact obscured by its mundanity, by its relentless occurrence, by the fact that so many of us have been victims of it. Imagine the moral outrage, the emergency response we would surely mobilize, if all of these everyday assaults occurred at the same time or were restricted to one geographical region. But why should the spatiotemporal coordinates of the vast numbers of sexual assaults be considered to be morally relevant? From the victim's point of view, the fact that she is isolated in her rape and her recovery, combined with the ordinariness of the crime that leads to its trivialization, makes the assault and its aftermath even more traumatic.

As devastating as sexual violence is, however, I want to stress that it is possible to survive it, and even to flourish after it, although it doesn't seem that way at the time. Whenever I see a survivor struggling with the overwhelming anger and sadness, I'm reminded of a sweet, motherly, woman in my rape survivors' support group who sat silently throughout the group's first meeting. At the end of the hour she finally asked, softly, through tears: "Can anyone tell me if it ever stops hurting?" At the time I had the same question, and wasn't satisfied with any answer. Now I can say, yes, it does stop hurting, at least for longer periods of time. A year after my assault, I was pleased to discover that I could go for fifteen minutes without thinking about it. Now I can go for hours at a stretch without a flashback. That's on a good day. On a bad day, I may still take to my bed with lead in my veins, unable to find one good reason to go on.

Our group facilitator told us that first meeting: "You will never be the same. But you can be better." I protested that I had lost so much: my security, my self-esteem, my love, and my work. I had been happy with the way things were. How could they ever be better now? As a survivor, she knew how I felt, but she also knew that, as she put it, "When your life is shattered, you're forced to pick up the pieces, and you have a chance to stop and examine them. You can say 'I don't want this one anymore' or 'I think I'll work on that one.'" I have had to give up more than I would ever have chosen to. But I have gained important skills and insights, and I no longer feel tainted by my victimization. Granted, those of us who live through sexual assault aren't given ticker tape parades or the keys to our cities, but it's an honor to be a survivor. Although it's not exactly the sort of thing I can put on my résumé, it's the accomplishment of which I'm most proud.

Two years after the assault, I could speak about it in a philosophical forum. There I could acknowledge the good things that came from the recovery process—the clarity, the confidence, the determination, the many supporters and survivors who have brought meaning back into my world. This was not to say that the attack and its aftermath were, on balance, a good thing or, as my aunt put it, "a real blessing from above." I would rather not have gone down that road. It has been hard for me, as a philosopher, to learn the lesson that knowledge isn't always desirable, that the truth doesn't always set you free. Sometimes, it fills you with incapacitating terror and, then, uncontrollable rage. But I suppose you should embrace it anyway, for the reason Nietzsche exhorts you to love your enemies: if it doesn't kill you, it makes you stronger.

People ask me if I'm recovered now, and I reply that it depends on what that means. If they mean "am I back to where I was before the attack"? I have to say, no, and I never will be. I am not the same person who set off, singing, on that sunny Fourth of July in the French countryside. I left her in a rocky creek bed at the bottom of a ravine. I had to in order to survive. I understand the appropriateness of what a friend described to me as a Jewish custom of giving those who have outlived a brush with death new names. The trauma has changed me forever, and if I insist too often that my friends and family acknowledge it, that's because I'm afraid they don't know who I am.

But if recovery means being able to incorporate this awful knowledge into my life and carry on, then, yes, I'm recovered. I don't wake each day with a start, thinking: "this can't have happened to me!" It happened. I have no guarantee that it won't happen again, although my self-defense classes have given me the confidence to move about in the world and to go for longer and longer walks—with my two big dogs. Sometimes I even manage to enjoy myself. And I no longer cringe when I see a woman jogging alone on the country road where I live, although I may still have a slight urge to rush out and protect her, to tell her to come inside where she'll be safe. But I catch myself, like a mother learning to let go, and cheer her on, thinking, may she always be so carefree, so at home in her world. She has every right to be.

NOTES

1. Federal Bureau of Investigation, *Uniform Crime Reports for the United States*, 1989, 6.

2. Robin Warshaw notes that "[g]overnment estimates find that anywhere from three to ten rapes are committed for every one rape reported. And while rapes by strangers are still underreported, rapes by acquaintances are virtually nonreported. Yet, based on intake observations made by staff at various rape counseling centers (where victims come for treatment, but do not have to file police reports), 70–80 percent of all rape crimes are acquaintance rapes" (*I Never Called It Rape* [New York: Harper & Row 1988], 12).

3. National Coalition against Domestic Violence, fact sheet, in "Report on Proposed Legislation S.15: The Violence against Women Act," 9. On file with the Senate Judiciary Committee.

4. In *Rape: An Historical and Cultural Enquiry*, edited by Sylvana Tomaselli and Roy Porter (New York: Basil Blackwell, 1986), 41–56. Another, much more perceptive, article is Lois Pineau's "Date Rape: A Feminist Analysis," *Law and Philosophy* 8:2 (1989): 217–43 [reprinted in this volume]. In addition, an excellent book on the causes of male violence was written by a scholar trained as a philosopher, Myriam Miedzian, *Boys Will Be Boys: Breaking the Link between Masculinity and Violence* (New York: Doubleday, 1991). Philosophical discussions of the problem of evil, even recent ones such as that in Robert Nozick, *The Examined Life: Philosophical Meditations* (New York: Touchstone, 1989), don't mention the massive problem of sexual violence. Even Nel Noddings' book, *Women and Evil* (Berkeley, Calif.: California University Press, 1989), which is an "attempt to describe evil from the perspective of women's experience," mentions rape only twice, briefly, and in neither instance from the victim's point of view.

5. Harrison, "Rape," 51.

6. See especially Patricia Williams's discussion of the Ujaama House incident in *The Alchemy of Race and Rights* (Cambridge, Mass.: Harvard University Press, 1991, 110, 116), Mari Matsuda, "Public Response to Racist Speech: Considering the Victim's Story" (*Michigan Law Review* 87:8 [1989]: 2320–81), and Charles R. Lawrence, III, "If He

Hollers, Let Him Go: Regulating Racist Speech on Campus" (*Duke Law Journal* 1990:3 [1990]: 431–83).

7. *The Alchemy of Race and Rights, passim.*

8. Harrison, "Rape," 52.

9. As the authors of *The Female Fear* note: "The requirement of proof of the victim's nonconsent is unique to the crime of forcible rape. A robbery victim, for example, is usually not considered as having 'consented' to the crime if he or she hands money over to an assailant [especially if there was use of force or threat of force]" (Margaret T. Gordon and Stephanie Riger, *The Female Fear: The Social Cost of Rape* [Chicago: University of Illinois Press, 1991], 59).

10. *Selected Poems* (New York: Farrar, Straus and Giroux, 1977), 82.

11. Quoted in *The New York Times*, September 13, 1991, p. A18. Although Judge Thomas made this statement during his confirmation hearings, Justice Thomas's actions while on the Supreme Court have belied his professed empathy with criminal defendants.

12. *The Rationality of Emotion* (Cambridge, Mass.: MIT Press, 1987).

13. Translated by W. Rhys Roberts, in *The Complete Works of Aristotle*, vol. 2, edited by Jonathan Barnes, 2181–82 (Princeton, N.J.: Princeton University Press, 1984). I thank John Cooper for drawing my attention to this aspect of Aristotle's theory of the emotions.

14. In *Throwing Like a Girl and Other Essays in Feminist Philosophy and Social Theory* (Indianapolis, Ind.: Indiana University Press, 1990), 153.

15. Pauline B. Bart and Patricia H. O'Brien, "Stopping Rape: Effective Avoidance Strategies," *Signs: Journal of Women in Culture and Society* 10:1 (1984): 83–101.

16. For a clinical description of post-traumatic stress disorder (PTSD), see the *Diagnostic and Statistical Manual of Mental Disorders*, 4th ed. (Washington, D.C.: American Psychiatric Association, 1994). Excellent discussions of the recovery process undergone by rape survivors can be found in Morton Bard and Dawn Sangrey, *The Crime Victim's Book* (New York: Brunner/Mazel, 1986); Helen Benedict, *Recovery: How to Survive Sexual Assault—for Women, Men, Teenagers, Their Friends and Families* (Garden City, N.Y.: Doubleday, 1985); Judith Lewis Herman, *Trauma and Recovery* (New York: Basic Books, 1992); and Ronnie Janoff-Bulman, *Shattered Assumptions: Towards a New Psychology of Trauma* (New York: The Free Press, 1992). I have also found it very therapeutic to read first-person accounts by rape survivors such as Susan Estrich, *Real Rape* (Cambridge, Mass.: Harvard University Press, 1987) and Nancy Ziegenmeyer, *Taking Back My Life* (New York: Summit, 1992).

17. *Diagnostic and Statistical Manual of Mental Disorders*, 3rd ed., revised (Washington, D.C.: American Psychiatric Association, 1987), 247. *DSM-IV* no longer refers to the precipitating event in this way. Instead, it refers to "an extreme traumatic stressor" (424).

18. I was particularly interested in that section of the act which classified gender-motivated assaults as bias crimes. (This section of the act was, unfortunately, struck down by the U.S. Supreme Court in the spring of 2000.) From the victim's perspective this reconceptualization is important. What was most difficult for me to recover from was the knowledge that some man wanted to kill me simply because I am a woman. This aspect of the harm inflicted in hate crimes (or bias crimes) is similar to the harm caused by hate speech. One cannot make a sharp distinction between physical and psychological harm in the case of PTSD sufferers. Most of the symptoms are physiological. I find it odd that in philosophy of law, so many theorists are devoted to a kind of Cartesian dualism that most philosophers of mind rejected long ago. (See Susan Brison, "Speech, Harm, and the Mind-Body Problem in First Amendment Jurisprudence," *Legal Theory* 4:1 [1998]: 39–61.)

19. *New York Times*, April 19, 1992, p. 36.

20. She characterized a certain theory of equality in this way during the discussion after a Gauss seminar she gave at Princeton University, April 9, 1992.

21. For an illuminating discussion of some of the ways in which we need to treat people differently in order to achieve genuine equality, see Martha Minow, *Making All the Difference: Inclusion, Exclusion, and American Law* (Ithaca, N.Y.: Cornell University Press, 1990).

22. *Against Our Will: Men, Women, and Rape* (New York: Bantam, 1975).

23. Gordon and Riger, *The Female Fear*, 23.

24. As recently as 1948, the U. S. Supreme Court upheld a state law prohibiting the licensing of any woman as a bartender (unless she was the wife or daughter of the bar owner where she was applying to work). *Goesaert v. Cleary* 335 U.S. 464 (1948).

25. *New York Times*, June 19, 1992, pp. 1, A13.

STUDY QUESTIONS

1. Brison mentions the idea that rape can lead to the "disintegration" of the self. After paying attention to what she says about this issue in her essay (e.g., "This was just the first of many incidents in which I felt as if I was experiencing things posthumously"), explain what this claim means and how it might bear on philosophical discussions of personal identity.

2. Commenting on first-person accounts—not the usual academic style in which philosophers write—Brison says, "I consider them a welcome antidote to scholarship that, in the guise of 'universality,' tends to silence those who most need to be heard." What does Brison mean by "universality"? And how might such first-person accounts enrich the usual academic discussions about rape? Might they do so also for discussions about prostitution and pornography? Are there other examples?

3. Brison seems to believe that characterizing "rape" as "sexual activity without consent" does not make much sense, much like characterizing "theft" as "coerced gift-giving" and "murder" as "assisted suicide minus consent" does not make sense. Assess this claim. How might one argue that although the latter two characterizations don't make sense the first does? Moreover, how are we to characterize (or even define) "rape" if we reject the idea that it is nonconsensual sexual activity? Consult Alan Wertheimer's essay in this volume, "Consent and Sexual Relations," while you are answering this question.

4. Explain and evaluate Brison's argument that providing women's defense courses (in college) for credit is not a form of discrimination against men.

5. Brison writes, "It has been hard for me, as a philosopher, to learn the lesson that knowledge isn't always desirable, that the truth doesn't always set you free." What knowledge and truth is Brison referring to, exactly? Are there other examples of knowledge and truths that one is better off without?

6. Given Brison's essay, how bad is rape? Does Brison's case amount to a refutation of H.E. Baber's claims in "How Bad Is Rape?—II" (in this volume). More generally, how do the two essays philosophically "speak to" each other?

TWENTY-EIGHT

Pornography as Embodied Practice

Joan Mason-Grant

The writings of Andrea Dworkin and Catharine MacKinnon are well known for their forceful criticisms of both pornography and sexual practices. In this essay, **Joan Mason-Grant** *revisits some of the themes found in the writings of Dworkin and MacKinnon. She argues, in particular, that pornography should not be understood as "speech" (which had earlier been insisted upon by other scholars, both pro-pornography and anti-pornography advocates). Examining pornography as a vehicle for the expression of ideas, in Mason-Grant's view, leads social theoreticians astray from comprehending pornography and its relationship to socialized sexuality. Pornography, she claims, is better understood as an "embodied practice" that shapes pernicious and women-subordinating forms of sexuality. This perspective allows an illuminating account of pornography and sexuality that has the potential to lead to a liberated sexuality. For a discussion of Mason-Grant, among other matters, see the essay in this volume by Nicholas Power, "Cheap Thrills: A Call for More Pornography."*

Joan Mason-Grant received her B.A. in philosophy in June 1982 and then, from the University of Western Ontario, her Ph.D. in philosophy in October 1998. She died from cancer in May 2009. Mason-Grant was an assistant professor at King's University College (U.W.O.), where she taught women's studies and social justice and peace studies. She also worked with Ontario's Middlesex-London Health Unit Teen Sexuality Coalition. This essay is reprinted from her book *Pornography Embodied: From Speech to Sexual Practice* (Rowman and Littlefield, 2004), and is reprinted by the permission of the publisher.

We live in interesting times, sexually speaking. We in the West often think of ourselves as sexually liberated, and in many ways we are. In school, we talk openly about AIDS and other sexually transmitted diseases, and teach our children how to put condoms on bananas. We talk directly about birth control, at least in those educational contexts not yet recuperated by feverishly fearful moral conservatives. Women are now recognized as beings with sexual desires and capable of sexual autonomy. Homosexual relationships are on the way to being brought into the fold of socially and legally recognized love relationships. Victorian skirts have been lifted, so to speak, and the sexual revolution appears to have taken hold in a rollicking, widespread, open embrace of sexuality. Still, all is not well in the land of sexual liberation. The bodies of women and children, and some men, have been re-commodified to an extent that is disturbing. Rigid gender scripts have been reinstated to an astonishing degree through this commodification. And, as is predictable in capitalist economies, the commodification process has been accompanied by an interesting discourse about "choice" and "liberation," buzzwords that often mask underlying power relations that systematically deny certain groups of people the experience of real choice or real liberation.

The debate over pornography contains all these contradictions. In this essay, I seek to open a space, in the context of the pornography debate, for a critical exploration of the widespread assumption that the pervasiveness of pornography is a sign of liberation, and I seek to do so by challenging the long-held conceptualization of pornography as speech.

In the realm of pornography (I speak of the readily accessible, heterosexual mainstream pornography),[1] the road to sexual liberation has been opened up almost exclusively by appeal to the idea of "freedom of speech." One of the tasks in this essay is to explain how pornography has come to be seen as "speech" and thereby found its protection not only from law but from social critique generally. I believe the well-entrenched "liberal" idea that pornography is speech has shut down fruitful critical discussion of the material role of mainstream pornography in our sexual lives.

As a counterpoint to this understanding of pornography, I revisit the fundamentals of the much maligned (and, I believe, much misunderstood) analysis of pornography first worked out by Andrea Dworkin and then taken up by Catherine MacKinnon.[2] The crux of this analysis is the claim that pornography is not merely the representation or expression of ideas, that is, "speech," but a *material practice* of subordination. Dworkin and MacKinnon are most well known, infamously perhaps, for their construction in 1992 of a civil rights ordinance that attempted to codify their conceptualization of pornography within the law. Their aim was to shift the legal response to pornography from the paternalistic criminal code of a patriarchal state to the realm of civil litigation so that individuals who believed themselves to have been "subordinated" through pornography's material practices—its production, distribution, or consumption— could seek redress from those who materially profit from the subordination. In my view, ironically, the ordinance and the legal debate it generated have actually consolidated and strengthened the general view, even among radical thinkers, that pornography is speech. In the wake of this debate, the innovative conceptual substance of the Dworkin-MacKinnon analysis of pornography has been distorted, obscured, often rendered virtually unrecognizable and, what is most frustrating, left undeveloped. The constructive aim of this essay is to bring critical awareness back to the core insight of that analysis—that pornography is a series of irreducibly embodied *practices* that work quite differently from political speech—and to begin to elaborate the concept of pornography as a practice in order to better understand how mainstream pornography contributes to a profoundly impoverished, overly objectifying and, yes, subordinating sexual know-how.

THE LEGAL QUESTION AND THE SPEECH PARADIGM

Before I proceed, I feel compelled to state a couple of things categorically: First, I am opposed to state censorship (so was Andrea Dworkin).[3] Second, I do not think *looking* at pornography "causes" violence. This oversimplified characterization of the relationship between pornography and subordination is a symptom of the speech paradigm, which I critique in this essay. I feel called to state these facts clearly in advance of my argument because contemporary discussion of pornography tends to get absorbed into an over-determined conservative-versus-liberal binary opposition that has an astonishing power to prevent people from hearing what is actually being said.

The key reason for this rigid binary construction of the pornography debate is the preoccupation with the legal question of whether the state should have prohibitive laws regarding pornography.[4] Whenever the issue of pornography arises, it comes with the baggage of age-old questions about the extent of state intervention in and control of individual lives in matters of morality. In the case of pornography, the long-standing "conservative" view is that public communication of and about explicit sexuality is a threat to community moral standards. In this view, the state is understood to be the guardian of the moral fabric of society; laws proscribing and prohibiting "obscenity" are therefore justified. By contrast, the "liberal" view is that the expression of explicit sexuality is, at worst, merely offensive and, at best, a healthy release of sexual desire from the regulative confines of repression; in either case, liberals think that the use of pornography is none of the state's business. So a limit on repressive state or institutional power is taken to be essential to individual freedom and self-determination. Since the constitutionally-based guarantee to freedom of speech has been effectively established as a limit to state power, especially in the United States, "freedom of speech" is universally aligned with emancipatory values.

The dominance of the legal question in the pornography debate has put in place a number of false dichotomies, composed of several false alignments: Those who are procensorship, conservative, anti-sex, anti-pornography are lined up against those who are anticensorship, liberal, pro-sex, pro-pornography. The frigid and uptight side has to face off with those who are liberal and open and sexually liberated, and those who have a stake in keeping state power at bay have come to have a stake in the conceptualization of pornography as "speech." This makes it politically difficult to admit the possibility that the practices of pornography (production, distribution, and consumption) work quite differently from political speech, that they might be realms of systemic oppression as powerful and damaging as, though different in nature than, the oppression sometimes wielded by the state, and that the freedoms granted by constitutional guarantees to free speech may, in fact, exacerbate those oppressions, profoundly restricting the real autonomy and self-determination of entire groups of people. These are insights integral to the analysis of pornography Dworkin and MacKinnon developed. However, the dominance of the speech paradigm, girded up by fear of state oppression, has made it strangely difficult for critics of their work to assess these ideas on their own terms.

PORNOGRAPHY AS SPEECH: RONALD DWORKIN

A central premise of my argument is that the speech paradigm predominates in contemporary debate over pornography. I use the phrase "speech paradigm" to mean the general view of communication that takes political speech as its model. Ronald Dworkin[5] offers an argument that I take to be a well-formulated example of a liberal defense of pornography as speech that tacitly accepts the speech paradigm as a way to conceptualize pornography.

Ronald Dworkin's arguments[6] coincide with current First Amendment law in the United States regarding pornography and, I submit, with a significant range of public discourse and sentiment. The legal orientation and the popular sentiment I have in mind was expressed quite clearly, for example, in the Oliver Stone movie *The People vs. Larry Flynt*:

> At the heart of the First Amendment is the recognition of the fundamental importance of the free flow of ideas. Freedom to speak one's mind is not only an aspect of individual liberty, but essential to the quest for truth and the vitality of society as a whole. In the world of debate about public affairs, many things done with motives that are less than admirable are nonetheless protected by the First Amendment.[7]

The movie depicts the legal challenges of Larry Flynt, publisher of *Hustler* magazine, in fighting for First Amendment protection against applications of obscenity law. The power of the film lies in the antihero figure of

Flynt, who is at once the object of our disgust (for there is little in the film that recommends him as a person of good character) and a kind of flag-bearer for the principle of free speech in a liberal democracy.

Ronald Dworkin's defense of Larry Flynt's right, even responsibility, to speak would look like this: Ronald Dworkin and others in society may not like Larry Flynt or the content of *Hustler*, but to constrain Flynt's liberty to publish *Hustler* is to limit his freedom *on the basis that his way of life is inherently less worthy than others*. The intriguing aspect of Ronald Dworkin's argument is that it derives from the principle of *equality* and not, as one might expect of a liberal, the principle of individual liberty. Equality, for Ronald Dworkin, is a matter of treating people's suffering and frustration with equal concern and *treating people's differing views about the good life with equal respect in the law*. His arguments about pornography tend to emphasize the latter aspect of this principle of equality over the former, which he calls the "right to moral independence." To preserve the principle of equality, the State must refrain from enforcing a certain conception of the good life and suppressing others. Laws censoring or otherwise prohibiting pornography would be laws enforcing a certain conception of the good life and, thereby, would violate the right of equality. So even if the public overwhelmingly called for the prohibition of pornography (a utilitarian justification for censorship laws) the principle of equality would trump this majority preference. On this argument, the right to publish, buy, and read pornography is understood to both derive from and protect equality.

Are there any circumstances in which the right to moral independence might be overridden? In his early discussions of pornography Ronald Dworkin considers only moralist criticisms or concerns about pornography that express preferences about the good life. In his later writings on the subject, he responds to the feminist argument that pornography is "not a moral issue"[8] but a question of harm. Ronald Dworkin allows that speech can justifiably be limited if it can be shown to constitute a *clear and present danger* or *cause* harm, that is, limited *if* certain forms of pornography could be shown to "significantly increase the danger that women will be raped or physically assaulted." However, he dismisses this possibility as academic speculation because, in his estimation, there has been no persuasive evidence of such a causal link between pornography and violence. He does consider the further claim that pornography "denies [women] the right to be their own masters by recreating them, for politics and society, in the shapes of male fantasy" and that it thereby produces a climate in which women cannot exercise their liberty because they "are perceived and understood unauthentically [*sic*]."[9] He acknowledges that this is a potentially powerful argument, for the systematic reconstruction of women's public identity may infringe on their capacity to fulfill their responsibility to express their views. However, he quickly dispenses with this argument by first reducing it to the narrowly causal claim that pornography is largely responsible for, rather than a core practice of, this subordinating reconstruction of identity and then arguing that this seems "strikingly implausible."

> Sadistic pornography is revolting, but it is not in general circulation, except for its milder, soft-porn manifestations. It seems unlikely that it has remotely the influence over how women's sexuality or character or talents are conceived by men, and indeed by women, that commercial advertising and soap operas have. Television and other parts of popular culture use sexual display and sexual innuendo to sell virtually everything, and they often show women as experts in domestic detail and unreasoned intuition and nothing else. The images they create are subtle and ubiquitous, and it would not be surprising to learn, through whatever research might establish this, that they indeed do great damage to the way women are understood and allowed to be influential in politics. Sadistic pornography, though much more offensive and disturbing, is greatly overshadowed by these dismal cultural influences as a causal force.[10]

Having conceded the strength of the argument that women's positive liberty might be infringed by the systematic reconstruction of their public identity, and having recognized the force of these other forms of cultural expression, Ronald Dworkin might as easily have concluded not only that pornography is subordinating to women but that these other forms of expression also deserve effective intervention. It might seem that the extent to which contempt for women saturates society would count as unacceptable "suffering and frustration" under the "right to equal concern" feature of the principle of equality. In short, he could conclude that this systemic sexism violates the principle of equality on all fronts. He does not.

IDEAL VERSUS SUBSTANTIVE SYSTEMS: EQUALITY, SOCIAL POWER, AND SPEECH

Ronald Dworkin's arguments about pornography are focused on the legal question of whether a prohibitive policy toward pornography can be justified. My interest here is not in the legal question. As I indicated, I am opposed to state censorship. Rather, my interest is in how the argument over pornography undertaken within this particular theater of law commits Ronald Dworkin, and many other liberals, to certain scripts about the nature of equality, social power, and speech and, by implication, about the *nature* of pornography. Because the tyranny of state power preoccupies Ronald Dworkin, he seems unable to seriously engage on its own terms the idea that pornography is a material practice that may be subordinating.

I maintain that Ronald Dworkin cannot move in this direction because he works within a particular framework involving abstract conceptions of equality, social power, and speech. Ronald Dworkin's project is idealist and normative. He is concerned to elaborate an *ideal* system, that is, a system of principle that constitutes a liberal political theory within which specific political decisions can be justified. In this formal project, the abstract principle of equality defines the system. Because he derives specific liberties such as free speech from the principle of equality, he assumes that equality is always already a constitutive feature of this system. The integrity of the system, its coherence and consistency, is of utmost concern.

Herein lies a fundamental conceptual and methodological conflict with the approach to questions of equality undertaken by social critics such as Dworkin and MacKinnon. They are concerned first and foremost with *substantive* systems—social systems, economic systems, meaning systems—that operate on the ground, as it were, in the messy negotiations of everyday life. Substantive systems are not made up of abstract principles. They are made up of people engaged in concrete practices with one another, people who understand themselves and others in terms of socially and politically charged categories. Dworkin and MacKinnon presume that substantive equality does not in fact exist even in our liberal society that holds equality as a cherished, constitutionally enshrined principle. So their approach to analyzing issues of equality is contextual and diagnostic; their task is to understand *how* sex/gender *in*equality works in such a social context, how it is lived out in everyday life, and why so many people do not perceive it as inequality.

Differing concepts of social power are intertwined with the notions of equality in these different approaches. For Dworkin and MacKinnon, equality is an irreducibly substantive matter: If it does not exist in the concrete practices of social life, this is because of an imbalance in social power. As MacKinnon writes, "In this approach, an equality question is a question of the distribution of power. . . . The question of equality, from the standpoint of what it is going to take to get it, is at root a question of hierarchy."[11]

It might be said that Ronald Dworkin also sees equality as a question of the distribution of social power, for the principle of equality properly adhered to prevents social inequality from seeping into policy making. But for him, social power is characterized quite narrowly as the power of one group (the majority preference) to enforce its conception of the good life on others (those in the minority) through the mechanism of state power. In his work, the problem of social power metamorphoses into the problem of state power. Dworkin and MacKinnon, by contrast, are concerned with actual disparities in social power.

Finally, these contesting notions of equality and social power manifest themselves in, and shed light on, differing conceptions of speech tacitly at work in these competing arguments. Ronald Dworkin states that pornography is no different than "speech directly advocating that women occupy inferior roles."[12] He apparently takes the analogy between pornography and such speech to be self-evident, for he offers no argument for it. Like political speech, the words and images of pornography represent ideas, or express a point of view. While pornography may indeed be powerful enough to provoke or excite certain feelings, such as disgust, it nonetheless depends, like any other speech, on "mental intermediation" for its effects.[13] The principle of the right to moral independence requires that people be allowed to *make up their own minds* about its rightness or wrongness, truth or falsity.

In this view, words and images are understood to be conveyors of ideas that, in the "marketplace of ideas," can be expressed and contemplated, offered and tested out, like so many heads of lettuce or widgets, by independent, fully mature, rational consumers and then accepted or rejected on their merits. Here, "thought" is presumed to be conscious, considered, and rational, and "ideas" and "meanings" are decidedly immaterial. This is the dominant way of understanding "speech" in contemporary liberalized countries. As Dworkin notes, "The general view . . . is that writers think up ideas or words and then other people read them and all this happens in the head, a vast cavern somewhere north of the eyes. It is all air, except for the paper and ink, which are simply banal. Nothing happens."[14]

Within this conceptual framework, words and images are passive conveyors of ideas. They can represent, refer, or connote, but they do not themselves "do" anything. People do things. The ideas represented or expressed in words and images cannot be said to be "ours" unless or until we consciously accept them. They may offend our sensibilities, they may give us a stomachache, but they do not shape our consciousness, or seep into our own way of thinking or acting, unless and until we (consciously) adopt them as our own. Words and images are thus safely at a distance from action by the process of mental intermediation, which is, of course, presumed to be private, personal, and internal.

On this way of looking at things, the claim that pornography is itself subordinating is prima facie implausible. Yet, this is precisely the claim that theorists such as Dworkin and MacKinnon seem to want to press:

> Pornography contains ideas, like any other social practice. But the way it works is not as a thought or through its ideas as such, at least not in the way thoughts and ideas are protected as speech. Its place in abuse requires understanding it more in active than in passive terms, as constructing and performative rather than as merely referential or connotative.[15]

The model of speech tacitly ascribed to by Ronald Dworkin may work fine for political speech. But in the Dworkin-MacKinnon analysis, pornographic practices are critically different from someone explicitly asserting that women are inferior to men. Making sense of this difference requires understanding that the entire system of pornographic practices, including the use of pornographic materials for sex, consists in a series of embodied, material practices that contribute to the making and unmaking of meanings about sexuality, gender, race, ability, class, sexual power, control, self-esteem, and so on.

PORNOGRAPHY: SYSTEMIC PRACTICES OF SUBORDINATION

As indicated, the approach of Dworkin and MacKinnon is diagnostic, part of a critical investigation into extant inequalities manifested in phenomena ranging from economic and political inequality to harassment, child sexual assault, sexual violence, and femicide. Pornography emerges in their investigations not as the causal root of these inequalities but as a "core constitutive practice"[16] of gender inequality and "a major social force for institutionalizing . . . second class status for women."[17] As Dworkin writes,

> Pornography originates in a real social system in which women are sexually colonized and have been for hundreds of centuries. Pornography—whether as a genre or as industry or as aid to masturbation—originates in that system, flourishes in that system, and *has no meaning or existence outside that system*.[18]

On this approach, "pornography" is inadequately understood if reduced to the materials, the words and images, typically presumed to be denoted by the term. Rather, pornographic materials can be understood only within the context of a vast network of related and mutually constitutive material practices, including the production and consumption of pornography. The production of pornographic materials involves material activities among human beings, especially in modern pornography, which requires the bodies of real women and men. The pornography industry is linked to the modeling industry and is tied also to prostitution, sexual slavery, and sex tourism. Many, not all, women are coerced behind the scenes to perform in pornographic scenes they are not comfortable doing and to show themselves enjoying them. Many women report taking drugs or dissociating to get through this work. In short, pornography production makes use of the sexual relations of power that it is in the business of depicting as sexy. Similarly, the consumption of pornographic materials also occurs in materially real contexts, amidst sexual relations of power. For example, in addition to being used as sexual arousal or masturbation material, pornography also is used as a blueprint for sexual activity between partners, or as a tool in sex crimes ranging from the production of child pornography to sexual assault and sexual murder. It is also used in the workplace, to intimidate women. The key point, here, is that the social relations performed in pornographic materials are already at work in the world—in the production of the materials, in the structure of the sex industry, in modes of sexual practice—and they are legitimated and further entrenched when they are enacted through sexual activity involving the use of pornographic materials.

So pornographic materials exemplify a social logic that is already real in the world. What is this social logic?[19] On Dworkin and MacKinnon's analysis, mainstream heterosexual pornography fuses the eroticization of domination and subordination with the social construction of gender, race, class, and ability. Always primed for sex, the female or feminized performer is offered not as a fully developed character but as cunt, ass, tits—the object of desire. Her looked-at, freely displayed body parts are the catalyst to masculine arousal. More than this, female carnality is presented as the irresistible source of masculine desire, exerting a sexual "I must" that grips males from within, compelling them to act. This power of female sexuality over male desire explains the central eroticized dynamic of mainstream pornography: The sexual actor gendered "male" must pursue and conquer the actor gendered "female" who, while always prepared to be "taken," often coyly or aggressively resists. This dynamic restores masculine control, at once explaining and excusing male sexual dominance as a response to an insistent itch. This gendered dynamic is racialized within pornographic materials: the darker skinned the female actor, the more carnal and untamed her sexual desire tends to be (and the less valuable her life); the darker skinned the masculine actor, the more powerful his ability to overcome. Disabled women are hypersexualized, their particular disability offered as the fetishized vehicle of their compliance or their masochism. The sexual dynamic in mainstream pornography is one of overt or implied struggle, involving either flight and capture or, more subtly, resistance and subduing and possession. The resolution of the sexual tension, the closing act of the performance, is male ejaculation, the male spent and satisfied. Mainstream heterosexual pornography presents these relations in narrowly conceived scripts that are repeated over and over. They can thus be seen as regulative norms that establish what counts as normal and perverse, sexy and asexual, identifying the paths of access to social viability as a sexual actor.

Dworkin and MacKinnon emphasize the interrelatedness of all the practices of pornography, from the conditions of its production and distribution to its consumption. However, their claims about the consumption of pornography have drawn the sharpest resistance, principally because of the dominance of the speech paradigm. Discussion about the use of pornographic materials for sex routinely bumps up against the legal defense of pornography as speech and, as a result, tends to be protected from critical scrutiny by all, save conservative moralists. However, on Dworkin and MacKinnon's analysis, the use of pornography is nothing like engaging in political speech. Rather, the use of pornographic materials is sexual activity—a performed, *embodied practice.* Dworkin writes, "Pornography happens. . . . The man's ejaculation is real."[20] Similarly, MacKinnon argues:

> Pornography is masturbation material. It is used as sex. It therefore is sex. . . . With pornography, men masturbate to women being exposed, humiliated, violated, degraded, mutilated, dismembered, bound, gagged, tortured, and killed. . . . What is real here is not that the materials are pictures, but that they are part of a sex act. The women are in two dimensions, but the men have sex with them in their own three-dimensional bodies, not in their minds alone. Men come doing this.[21]

On this account, the consumption of pornographic materials is not adequately conceptualized as a disembodied, cognitive, contemplative, information-processing activity. Rather, it is a material activity, distinctly sexual and irreducibly embodied. While it involves representations, it is not "reading about" sex, as though the sex were elsewhere. *It is sex.* In using mainstream, mass-market pornographic materials for sex, consumers *bodily experience* inequality, the objectification of the female body, violence, and brutality as pleasureful, erotic, and orgasmic.

WE BECOME WHAT WE PRACTICE BEING: THE PRACTICE PARADIGM

In place of the dominant speech paradigm, we need an alternative "practice paradigm" that better captures and elaborates more complexly the embodied activity of using pornographic materials for sex. In *Pornography Embodied*, I work out a phenomenological account of the relationship between routinized bodily practices and the formation of our practical know-how. Too involved to reproduce here, I can nonetheless provide a summary of its central points. I draw on the work of Drew Leder who, in *The Absent Body*, provides a complex and dynamic account of corporeality that shows how the social and organic are intertwined phenomenologically.[22] His account links the production of agency—our ability to act intelligibly in the world—with the bodily practices in which we engage. As he describes it, the structure of our practices is incorporated at the level of the lived body and sedimented in the form of tacit personal know-how. This account links our capacity for functional competence to the tacitness of our practiced bodies. The knowledge acquired through the process of incorporation is not propositional knowledge or abstract ideas, but a robustly practical, functional know-how. The process of incorporation operates over time and below the level of conscious awareness. The value of this account for understanding the use of pornography for sex is that it suggests how the reiterative enactment of certain repetitive scripts of sexuality works at the level of personal experience, explains why we are often unaware of these processes, and makes them available to critical scrutiny.

Sexual desire is often thought of as belonging to an essentially presocial, inherent, or "given" realm. Like hunger, sexual desire seems to be a force that grips us from within, exerting an "I must," demanding satisfaction. Arising from the organic dimension of our being, hunger and sexual desire are experienced as belonging to a realm outside personal mastery and quite apart from social influence. A fundamental implication of the account of incorporation referred to above is that it is a mistake to conclude from the experiential fact that processes and powers of the organic body exceed our direct control that they are uninfluenced by our activities and practices. Through the ongoing processes of incorporation characteristic of our embodied beings, the social norms that structure our practices become intertwined with the organic, and agency and personal know-how are so constituted. For example, a moment's reflection makes clear that the yearnings driven by hunger *are* shaped by the systemic norms of eating practices. Do you yearn for Kraft dinner when you are hungry? Or beans and rice, or raw fish, or whale blubber, or venison, or home-cooked organic veggie stew? The trajectory taken by our desire for food is intimately bound up with the social norms and practices through which we have learned about eating. Sexual desire is only a different kind of hunger. It is surely organic, arising as part of our biological being. But it takes shape within the social context in which we come to maturity as sexual beings.[23]

Importantly, the social norms of eating and of sex are not principally communicated to us as ideas or opinions. They are modeled, performed, acted out, rehearsed, from our earliest days. The notion of incorporation suggests that, over time, that which is repetitively acted out—practiced—seeps into one's organismic ground, coming to shape not only our habits, but our desires and yearnings, and our personal know-how. Incorporation happens not in a flash, but over time, through a bodily history of structured repetition. This suggests that, as a given form of sexuality is acted out, rehearsed, it seeps into our organismic ground, shaping sexual desire and pleasure, shaping perception and expectation, and thereby shaping the way one interacts sexually with others.

THE USE OF PORNOGRAPHY AND THE CULTIVATION OF SEXUAL KNOW-HOW

Andrea Dworkin calls pornography a form of *sexual pedagogy*. The use of pornographic materials for sex is very often the sexual activity that first unlocks the mysterious and urgent world of sexuality to young people who are newly sexually alive and curious. Dworkin says that pornography is "exceptionally effective precisely because it is not just mental; it is physiologically real to [its users], and they learn in their bodies about women from the pornography in a way that it doesn't matter what they think. They can think one thing, but what they do is something else."[24] This "learning in their bodies" is aptly captured by the account of incorporation outlined above. Using the framework of this account, we can now fruitfully ask just what sort of sexual know-how the use of mainstream heterosexual pornography for sex cultivates.

If the use of mainstream heterosexual pornography is a practice routinely engaged in as one comes to sexual maturity, its users will *experience* sexual desire, arousal, and satiation in its terms. That is, their desire and pleasure will plausibly become calibrated to the values of gendered, racialized, and classed dominance, subordination, and objectification that mainstream pornography makes available as sex. The transgressive quality of using pornography for sex intensifies this experience, making the social logic that is the vehicle of sexual arousal seem not just normal but *natural*; in a world where sexual desire and pleasure are typically regarded as unanalyzable brute facts, whatever feels sexy must *naturally be* sexy. Sexual pleasure becomes an indicator of some underlying human nature: If domination and subordination feel good, they must be a natural part of human nature. Of course, the social relations that predominate in mainstream pornography are not limited to mainstream pornography. They are also pervasive in the larger culture. Surely the cultural prevalence of these norms bolsters rather than mitigates the force of mainstream pornography that, in turn, consolidates their normalizing force.

The corporeal practice of using pornographic materials for sex thus consists in a kind of erotic rehearsal of the social logic they contain.[25] The norms of sexuality thus experienced, supported and reiterated by other cultural practices, become incorporated into the functional base of one's sexual agency. Over time, they become the tacit basis of a personal sexual know-how that is experienced as natural and normal. In this way, mainstream pornography contributes to what one sexually knows how to do, shaping perceptions and expectations of oneself and others.

In fact, this analysis leads to the observation that it is not just the content of pornography that is concerning but the very situation of using pornographic materials as a way of practicing sex. The catalyst to sexual arousal in pornography is a two-dimensional, anonymous "other," and the key mode of interaction is voyeurism. That is, in using pornography, one is "having sex" with or in relation to, a two-dimensional rather than a three-dimensional "other." Despite the apparent realism of modern porn—real bodies, real orifices—the figures in pornography are completely unburdened by character or relationship development; the performers are reduced to their essential sexual parts: genitals or breasts. This provides the users of pornography an ease of access to sex objects that are otherwise either off limits or more complicated to access when they are attached to fully human, flesh-and-blood beings. Further, the only sense engaged in the "interaction" with the sexual other of pornography is vision. Now, there is nothing wrong with "looking" as a part of sexual interaction. But I worry that the prevalence of "looking" as a predominant form of sexual practice, instituted in pornography, establishes voyeurism as a predominant way of interacting sexually with others. This strips the situation of the mutuality of perception and concern demanded in respectful relationships with flesh-and-blood others, especially relationships involving intimate bodily interaction.

So what pornography does is to provide an opportunity, over and over, to have sex with another without actually having to directly interact with, or be accountable to, the sexual other. Indeed, the "reality" of the other (a photograph, a video) presents a real person who apparently loves being merely an object of arousal. In the routine use of porn, the cycle of erotic desire, arousal, and satiation is organized arrogantly, with exclusive concern for the needs, desires, and involvement of the user. Now, thinking again of the explorations of youth, if the use of porn for sex routinely precedes sex in the flesh with fully human others, it makes sense to me that such users will be practiced in an objectifying, self-absorbed form of sexuality without ever having had to attend to the needs, desires, feelings, or interests of another.

Here the link to a good deal of prostitution and sex tourism is obvious. For example, research on the travel postings to the World Sex Guide from Western men returning from Thailand make clear how much of their sexual experience there is dependent on their ability to view the women they fuck as merely objects, merely commodities they buy. These postings reveal a thoroughgoing market mentality. They provide extensive information about money, quantified descriptions of the sexual activity, and advice about how to be on guard against the possibility of being overcharged or robbed. And it's not that sex tourists don't know about the context of poverty in which the trade thrives in Thailand. But this is represented, in good business fashion, as an opportunity for getting the most bang for the buck.

REVOLUTIONIZING PRACTICE

There is a deep irony in the contemporary sex scene. The sexual practice of using mainstream, mass-market pornography for sex, which many are inclined to think of as "sexually liberated," is, in fact, a repetitive rehearsal of an exceedingly impoverished sexual script. There is little that is creative, expressive, fully human or "free" down this road. If this were the only objection, we could just ignore pornography like we ignore a bad book. But the analysis offered here also shows that, insofar as this script serves as a widespread training ground for sexual know-how, it is likely to perpetuate subordinating forms of sexuality.

The cultivation of sexual know-how is a powerful process—intimate and personal. Our sexual desires and our ways of being sexual are formed under conditions we are rarely encouraged to scrutinize and in which we come to have a great personal stake. Thrown into the normalized relations of sexuality predominant in this culture, we are somewhat at their mercy as we mature into sexually alive persons. The nature of incorporation illuminates the intransigence of our learned sexual know-how; we all come to have a deeply personal stake in practices that may not only be impoverished, but subordinating. While it's true that we *experience* sexual desires as innate, as "just the way I am," it is possible to critically unpack these desires, ask of them where they came from and whether they may be rooted in social relations that are subordinating. Such a process can be authentically liberating, opening the possibility of reshaping our desire by actually leaving off some practices, and cultivating others. This is not easy work. Revolutionizing practice needs the cultural support of a community of people with the courage, maturity, and creativity to engage these issues openly, to disrupt entrenched ways of talking about them, and to take up the challenge of looking below the level of everyday conscious awareness into our own habitual sexual practices.

NOTES

1. Much is made about the inability to define precisely what is meant by [the word] "pornography." The drive to define [it] precisely is a legalistic project. In my work, I am interested in practical know-how. Most any person familiar with the cultural conventions of where they live could go out and buy pornography or readily find it on the Internet without suffering any deep definitional anxieties. The analysis of this essay and the book on which it is based focus on mainstream, mass-market pornography that is widely available and principally targeted to men or heterosexual couples.

2. Andrea Dworkin's work on pornography includes *Woman Hating* (New York: Dutton, 1974); *Pornography: Men Possessing Women* (New York: 1979); *Intercourse* (New York: Free Press, 1987); and *Letters from a War Zone* (Brooklyn, N.Y.: Lawrence Hill Books, 1993). Catherine MacKinnon's work includes, most prominently, *Feminism Unmodified: Discourses on Life and Law* (Cambridge, Mass.: Harvard University Press, 1987) and *Only Words* (Cambridge, Mass.: Harvard University Press, 1993).

3. Andrea Dworkin, "Against the Male Flood: Censorship, Pornography and Equality," in *Letters from a War Zone*, 272.

4. See the Appendix in my *Pornography Embodied* (Rowman and Littlefield, 2004) for a detailed account of this legal history.

5. To avoid confusion between the two Dworkins, I will use "Dworkin" by itself to denote Andrea Dworkin and I will use Ronald Dworkin's full name when referring to him.

6. See Ronald Dworkin, *Taking Rights Seriously* (Cambridge, Mass.: Harvard University Press, 1977); "Do We Have a Right to Pornography?" in his *A Matter of Principle* (Cambridge, Mass.: Harvard University Press, 1985); "Liberty and Pornography," *New York Review of Books* (August 15, 1991): 12–15; "The Coming Battles over Free Speech,"

New York Review of Books (June 11, 1992): 55–58, 61–64; and "Women and Pornography," *New York Review of Books* (October 21, 1993): 36–42.

7. Oliver Stone, Janet Young, and Michael Hausman, producers, *The People vs. Larry Flynt* (Columbia Pictures, 1996). The quotation is a paraphrased version of Chief Justice Rehnquist's court decision in *Hustler Magazine v. Falwell*, 485 US 46 (1988).

8. MacKinnon, "Not A Moral Issue," in *Feminism Unmodified*, 146–62. Ronald Dworkin focuses his critique entirely on MacKinnon's work, virtually ignoring the conceptual groundwork laid by Dworkin.

9. Ronald Dworkin, "Liberty and Pornography," 14.

10. Ronald Dworkin, "Liberty and Pornography," 14.

11. MacKinnon, "Difference and Dominance: On Sex Discrimination," in *Feminism Unmodified*, 40.

12. Ronald Dworkin, "Liberty and Pornography," 14.

13. The phrase is Judge Frank Easterbrook's. See *American Booksellers Association, Inc. v. Hudnut*, 771 F2d 323 (1985), 328.

14. Dworkin, "Against the Male Flood," 255.

15. MacKinnon, *Only Words*, 21.

16. MacKinnon, "Not A Moral Issue" and "Francis Biddle's Sister: Pornography, Civil Rights, and Speech," in *Feminism Unmodified*, 149 and 173, respectively.

17. MacKinnon, "On Collaboration," in *Feminism Unmodified*, 201.

18. Dworkin, *Letters from a War Zone*, 237.

19. See chapter 1 of *Pornography Embodied* for a detailed explication of this analysis.

20. Dworkin, *Pornography*, xxxviii (1989 reprint).

21. MacKinnon, *Only Words*, 21.

22. Drew Leder, *The Absent Body* (Chicago: University of Chicago Press, 1990).

23. Despite the misunderstandings of some, this analysis fits with the constructivism of both Dworkin and MacKinnon. Both theorists ascribe to a "general theory of sexuality" in which sexuality is not considered to be "an inborn force inherent in individuals" but "social and relational, constructing and constructed of power." MacKinnon writes, "[Desire] is taken for a natural essence or presocial impetus but is actually *created* by the social relations, the hierarchical relations, in question. This process *creates the social beings we know as women and men*, as their relations create society" (MacKinnon, "Desire and Power," in *Feminism Unmodified*, 49–54, at 49).

24. Dworkin, in Cindy Jenefsky (with Ann Russo), *Without Apology: Andrea Dworkin's Art and Politics* (Boulder, Colo.: Westview Press, 1998), 58.

25. While we can talk of a predominant social logic within mainstream pornography, this social logic is not all-determining. All systems of meaning harbor constitutive instabilities, hence the possibility of change. I discuss this at length in chapter 5 of *Pornography Embodied*.

STUDY QUESTIONS

1. In her opening paragraph, Mason-Grant says that people in the Western world are sexually liberated in many ways, and gives this example: "Women are now recognized as beings with sexual desires and capable of sexual autonomy." Do you find this historical claim ("now," ca. 2000, as opposed to earlier times) to be accurate? It implies that there had been a time when women were not recognized as having sexual desires. Can you provide reasons to think the claim true or false? If you think the claim true, can you point to the dates around which women were (finally) recognized in the West as having sexual desires? Consider, in marshaling evidence

for and against Mason-Grant's claim, Western literature, e.g., the Old Testament, Sappho's fragments, ancient Greek mythology (Zeus, Hera, Tiresias), the Roman poets (Ovid, Catallus), the writings of the Church Fathers (Augustine, Aquinas), Chaucer's *Canterbury Tales*, and Boccaccio's *Decameron*.

2. Mason-Grant uses the expressions "real choice," "real liberation," and "real autonomy." Are you clear about the difference between "real" liberation and "fake" liberation? What is accomplished substantively (or rhetorically) by attaching "real" to these words? Is "real" in these expressions being used the same way it is used by Mason-Grant in her expressions "real bodies," "real orifices," "real women, "and "real persons"? What is a "fake" orifice or a "fake" person?

3. Mason-Grant states several times that she is opposed to state censorship of pornography or its state-enforced legal prohibition. Yet the MacKinnon-Dworkin ordinance, as Mason-Grant points out, was meant to open up legal space for individual *civil* action against the producers, distributors, and consumers of pornography. Does Mason-Grant defend this legal tactic or is she sympathetic to it? Is this tactic in effect backhanded legal regulation of pornography? Does not resorting to civil courts still rely on state interference, which Mason-Grant claims to disdain?

4. One of MacKinnon's criticisms of pornography reproduced by Mason-Grant is this: "With pornography, men masturbate to women being exposed, humiliated, violated, degraded, mutilated, dismembered, bound, gagged, tortured, and killed." Mason-Grant, too, in her essay seems to emphasize this sort of brutal pornography. Is this type of pornography representative of the genre, or have some critics of pornography exaggerated its extent among available sexual materials? Is the type of man who masturbates while gazing on this sort of pornography representative of men? If brutal pornography is a very small part of the genre, and if the type of man who enjoys it is relatively uncommon, what happens to the case against pornography advanced, on these grounds, by MacKinnon and Mason-Grant?

5. Mason-Grant claims that "the social norms of . . . sex are . . . modeled, performed, acted out, rehearsed, from our *earliest* days," which implies—even if we ignore Freudian ideas about events from infancy and very early childhood being the determinants of our sexualities—that our sexualities are already being laid down well before we go to school or church, well before we read, watch television, and so forth. Yet she also claims that "the use of pornographic materials for sex is very often the sexual activity that first unlocks the mysterious and urgent world of sexuality to young people," that is, that exposure to pornography after our "earliest

days" is a significant element in the formation of our (or boys' and men's) sexualities. Do you sense a contradiction here or, at least, a puzzle? What is the empirical psychological or sociological evidence that pornography is "very often," as she claims, implicated in the formation of the awakening sexuality of teenagers? Is her claim true to your own experiences? (A research exercise: browse through Mason-Grant's *Pornography Embodied*, including the bibliography, for empirical evidence of pornography's influence on sexuality. If you are interested, also consult Rae Langton's essays on pornography, looking for empirical evidence about its causal effects.)

TWENTY-NINE

Cheap Thrills: A Call for More Pornography

Nicholas Power

In this essay, **Nicholas Power** *replies to the arguments critical of pornography by three leading feminists from across the spectrum of radical to liberal feminism. In doing so, Power relies on the Engage-Image-Equivalence Principle to argue that their views assume an* a priori *and sex-negative appraisal of human sexuality and sexually explicit materials. His criticisms target the views of Joan Mason-Grant (see her "Pornography as Embodied Practice," in this volume), which he claims provide a one-sided view of pornography's pedagogy. He concludes with a phenomenology of Internet pornography, arguing that it is currently benign, on the whole, and potentially positive.*

Feminist views on pornography remain divided a generation after Catherine MacKinnon's *Only Words* and her outrageous claim that pornography had "emerged as a tool of genocide" in the Serbian rapes of Bosnian women.[1] Led by cultural critics and legal activists, one arm of feminism now provides a full-on defense of pornography as liberationist expression.[2] Many feminists within philosophy, however, are to this point reluctant to embrace pornography as a force in contemporary sexuality as both a source of sexual pleasure and an entry point into sexual exploration and practice. In order to properly locate their objection to pornography, I work through many of its animadversions—that pornography turns men into rapists, for instance—and grapple with complex topics in obscenity law and sexual ethics. I reject a broad range of feminist attempts to locate misogynist features in pornography, locate an anti-male bias in their arguments, and conclude by making a case for more, not less, pornography.[3] In general terms, I recommend to feminism the conclusion of a recent comparison of states with varying circulation rates of pornography: "pornography and gender equality both flourish in politically tolerant societies."[4]

I. ANTI-PORNOGRAPHY FEMINISM

The reasons why a minority of feminists doesn't embrace pornography will take some unraveling, so let us back up to so-called anti-pornography feminism's initial confrontation with its widespread dissemination in the U.S. To recount an oft-told story, Catherine MacKinnon and Andrea Dworkin oriented their legal response around two sorts of potential victims of pornography: women abused by men aroused by pornography and actors abused in producing it. To provide statutory protection to these victims, they defined pornography this way:

> Pornography is the graphic sexually explicit subordination of women through pictures and/or words that also includes one or more of the following: (i) women are presented dehumanized as sexual objects, things or commodities; or (ii) women are presented as sexual objects who enjoy pain or humiliation; or (iii) women are presented as sexual objects who experience sexual pleasure in being raped; or (iv) women are presented as sexual objects tied up or cut up or mutilated or bruised or physically hurt; . . . or (ix) woman are presented in scenarios of degradation, injury, torture, shown as filthy or inferior, bleeding, bruised, or hurt in a context that makes these conditions sexual.[5]

On a charitable reading, this definition links pornographic depictions of sex to subordination and the harms suffered by those who engage in these actual sexual practices.[6] Whether the link is conceptual (note the "peculiar" use of the "is" of identity which opens the quote[7]) or causal, this version of the feminist thesis claims that pornography contributes to an ideology that subordinates, debases, and devalues women and hence is in violation of our society's standing commitments to equal respect and to the dignity of all, regardless of gender.

One-quarter of a century's worth of research has demonstrated, beyond any doubt, that the availability of pornography is inversely related to the amount of sexual violence inflicted upon women and that its consumption may actually soften sexist attitudes, and both public opinion and law have turned away from anti-pornography feminism's sex-negative views.[8] For now, however, we are trying to charitably understand their stance on pornography, as its one-sided view of pornography will reemerge in the views of more moderate and even liberal feminists.

What's important to keep in mind is that anti-pornography feminists, along with some religious conservatives, see pornography as a frontline in a broader culture war. For this minority of feminists, it is part and parcel of a patriarchal assault on female standing. Christians crusading against pornography see it as a symptom of liberal value neutrality and moral decay.[9] Surprisingly enough, there is a "lowest common denominator" of sorts to the sexual ethics of anti-pornography feminists, liberal defenders of porn, and Christians crusading against pornography (about which no more will be said here).[10]

Each of these opposing constituencies assumes a simple principle: if you may (are permitted to) sexually do it, in real life, then you can picture it, post it, and share it; whereas, if you may not (or ought not), then you can't (or ought not). Alan Soble, the Benthamite liberal, who is no friend of anti-pornography feminism, still finds "probably correct" the claim that, "It is permissible to make an image of a sexual act if and only if it is permissible to do that act, or it is wrong to make an image of a sexual act if and only if it is wrong to engage in that act" and goes on to group anti-pornography feminists and conservatives together in saying, "their narrow judgments as to what is permissible in pornography derive, then, from their narrow judgments of what it is permissible to do sexually."[11]

It is this equivalent evaluation of sexual acts and sexual images—we can call it the "Engage-Image-Equivalence Principle," or EIEP for short—that allows Dworkin to make an *a priori* identification of pornography with actual harms done to women: "Pornography, unlike obscenity, is a discrete, identifiable system of sexual exploitation."[12] MacKinnon likewise attempts to distance her objection to pornography from obscenity law—a topic I return to below—and restates a version of EIEP: while pornography "has been legally framed as a vehicle for the expression of ideas," she correctly points out that "pornography is masturbation material." However, she continues with an inference that, it must be said, needs force: "It [pornography] is used as sex. It therefore is sex." She continues:

> With pornography, men masturbate to women being exposed, humiliated, violated, degraded, mutilated, dismembered, bound, gagged, tortured and killed. In the visual materials, they experience this *being done* by watching it *being done*. What is real here is not that the materials are pictures, but that they are part of a sex act.[13]

Applying EIEP to such materials, however, allows us to isolate the *a priori* basis of radical feminism's charge. Of course, we can safely ignore her talk of mutilation, dismemberment, torture, and killing as these are impermissible and are absent from any online or print pornography sources that I am aware of; a few first-person reports of torture aside, this sort of pornography is the creation of MacKinnon's imagination. (I don't mean to diminish these sorts of intolerable abuse or deny that women bear more than their share of them, but no opponent of pornography has been able to cite any example of an image of it being marketed or used as pornography, or of course any such act as being the result solely of an abuser's having watched pornography.) On the other hand, men (and women) do masturbate to images of women (and men) being exposed, and in MacKinnon's and Dworkin's opinions, being "humiliated, violated," and "degraded." However, the sorts of sexual activities typically depicted in mainstream pornography—oral sex within heterosexual and online pornography, or sadomasochistic bondage—need not be considered humiliating or degrading and have become standard fare in American bedrooms.

Only an *a priori* rejection of such sex acts, applied to, as opposed to being derived from, an empirical (*a posteriori*) analysis of explicit depictions of them, would justify the moral estimation of anti-pornography feminism. Those feminists who deem these categories of sex acts to be humiliating or degrading are assuming (1) that the majority of those consensually participating in them are deluded (deluded, in part by an ideology which pornography perpetuates, a claim I examine below), and (2) that the humiliation or degradation of that sex act is maintained or transferred to a depiction of that act. Both assumptions are dubious, the latter one especially so, as Alan Soble makes clear:

> Consider a photograph of a woman licking an erect penis, or the act itself. Perhaps she is in control or in charge. She is responsible for her pleasure, she can stop inconsiderately, or nibble the wrong way or cause distraction, or break the spell by coughing and pausing to pick a pubic hair out of her mouth. . . . Or perhaps he is in control. . . . Or they are experimenting. . . . Or they are playing boss and secretary, president and intern. . . . Multiple interpretations of fellatio are possible that are not fixed by the surface content of a depiction of the act.[14]

The "polysemicity" of images is a general principle of aesthetics that can't be gainsaid as being true of features somehow unique to sexually explicit imagery, and EIEP implies that anti-pornography feminism's biased interpretation of pornography as subordinating goes through to their negative appraisal of these acts themselves. Neither acts nor images inherently subordinate, I conclude, though I explore below the possibility that their use can.

Anti-pornography feminism is starkly at odds with a hard-fought and still tenuous legal tradition that has both extended free speech protections to modes of sexual expression that some might deem offensive, and that has secured for men and women, gay and straight, "sweeping guarantees of personal autonomy in matters of sex."[15] The autonomy protections secured under this liberal body of law are perhaps best expressed by David Richards: "Legal enforcement of a particular sexual ideal fails . . . to accord due respect to individual autonomy."[16] Consuming pornography has come to be seen as a private matter, and if there are no external costs associated with it—costs that are borne by someone besides the consumer and dealer—then this should be seen as a logical extension of liberal justice.

II. JOAN MASON-GRANT'S ILLIBERALISM

Some feminist critics of pornography focus on the masturbatory use that men make of it and call upon a strategy that is close to definitive of feminist philosophy and ethics, one recently articulated by Martha Nussbaum (who we'll discuss in detail below). They will make the case that as do other areas of liberal justice, EIEP neglects the chasm between abstract principle and contextual practice, between the intimate contexts in which people actually have sex compared to those commercial ones in which they consume it. (This is another way of saying that the feminist critique of pornography is *ideological*, which is to say that pornography distorts its true meaning and serves hidden interests.) On such a view, EIEP masks the features characteristic of pornographic representations of sex and stacks the deck in favor of its defenders, who have a ready reply to the charge, say, that pornographic images objectify women: namely, that sex itself necessarily involves a degree of objectification, as Kant teaches us.[17]

Joan Mason-Grant makes this case and argues that EIEP only appears germane to a moral estimation of pornography because it blurs the line between acts and images, just as the courts have done in adopting the "speech paradigm" as in what she calls the "pornography as speech paradigm."[18] The Seventh U.S. Circuit Court accepted the MacKinnonesque argument that pornography "fosters . . . bigotry and contempt" that "harm women's opportunities for equality and rights" and yet concludes (correctly on my view, solipsistically, on Mason-Grant's) that it doesn't do this in the real world but only in the mind of the viewer of pornography: "All of these unhappy effects depend on mental intermediation. Pornography affects how people see the world, their fellows, and social relations."[19]

On Mason-Grant's view, this ignores the definitive feature of typical pornography today: it is an embodied and discriminatory sexual practice of men. Pornography is not simply speech and is not just ideas, as her summary of the dispute between the liberal and "Dworkin-MacKinnon" critique makes clear:

> In this [liberal] view, words and images are understood to be conveyors of ideas that, in the "marketplace of ideas," can be expressed and contemplated, offered and tested out, like so many heads of lettuce or widgets, by independent, fully mature, rational consumers and then accepted or rejected on their merits. . . . Within this conceptual framework, words and images are passive conveyors of ideas. They can rep-

resent, refer, or connote, but they do not themselves "do" anything. People do things. Words and images are thus safely at a distance from action by the process of mental intermediation, which is, of course, presumed to be private, personal, and internal. On this way of looking at things, the claim that pornography is itself subordinating is prima facie implausible. . . . But in the Dworkin-MacKinnon analysis, pornographic practices are critically different from someone explicitly asserting that women are inferior to men. Making sense of this difference requires understanding that the entire system of pornographic practices, including the use of pornographic materials for sex, consists in a series of embodied, material practices that contribute to the making and unmaking of meanings about sexuality, gender, race, ability, class, sexual power, control, self-esteem, and so on.[20]

These claims about embodied "pornographic practices" are beside the point. The court's *modus tollens* — "If pornography is what pornography does, so is other speech, but speech is not what it does, so pornography is not what it does" — is left unchallenged whether we are talking about "passive conveyors of ideas" or "embodied" practices. Flag burning is surely a material practice but has semantic content which warrants its protection as free expression; it's precisely because "doing" can connote that "liberalized" countries don't draw a bright line between expression and conduct, such as that between sadomasochistic sex and pornography. What remains of Mason-Grant's objection can only consist in her final claim that "the entire system of pornographic practices" presents a "repetitive rehearsal of an exceedingly impoverished sexual script," to which we can all agree while keeping in mind how utterly "impoverished" our parents' collections of *Playboy* were, and while holding out hope for the pornography of tomorrow.[21]

I can find little evidence to support the remainder of Mason-Grant's speculations, however, such as that through an extended and unchecked use of pornography, a user's sexual "desire and pleasure will plausibly become calibrated to the values of gendered, racialized, and classed dominance, subordination, and objectification that mainstream pornography makes available as sex."[22] Similarly, she claims that "mainstream pornography" is somehow "linked to the modeling industry, and is tied also to prostitution, sexual slavery, and sex tourism" and that these materials "restore masculine control, at once explaining and excusing male sexual dominance as a response to an insistent itch," all of which is indicative of "a social logic that is already real in the world . . . the eroticization of domination and subordination with the social construction of gender, race, class and ability."[23] Such "calibrations," "links," "ties," and "indicatives" are too vague to persuade anyone not already convinced. Besides, if the social logic of eroticized subordination is "already real in the world," we can no longer isolate the harms of pornography *per se*, and we are left with EIEP intact and with Mason-Grant's disapproval of what she sees in it.

Having said this, we should concede Mason-Grant's general claim that pornography (including the sexist and racist stereotypes and characterizations frequently found there) help to define for viewers what counts as normal and perverse, sexy and asexual. This educational dimension is properly emphasized by Mason-Grant while she mostly avoids making the sorts of absurdly strong claims that are typical of many opponents to pornography.[24] Sexual desire is undeniably influenced by cultural norms, and it is hardly controversial to claim that "mainstream pornography *contributes* to what one sexually knows how to do, shaping perceptions and expectations of oneself and others."[25] None of this, however, negates the Seventh Circuit's claim that "mental intermediation" is the proper locus of these concerns, and hence our focus will soon turn to pornography's male consumer.

Regardless of the vagueness of "contributes to" here—I'd wager that a recent summer of Hollywood romantic comedies contributes as much to a patriarchal "social logic" as pornography does[26] —my main reservation to Mason-Grant's overall conclusion is her biased neglect of contrary views of porn's pedagogical potential.[27] When I survey my students over their use of porn, they report a much more positive appraisal, and the empirical evidence suggests that the effect of pornography, even on underage viewers, is largely mediated by the values that people bring to the materials.[28] In addition, regular consumption of pornography doesn't play a significant role in reported levels of intimacy or sexual satisfaction of the consumer or his or her partner.[29] Sallie Tisdale's alternative reading of pornography is the one I would recommend be put alongside Mason-Grant's.[30] Because she enjoys pornographic material, Tisdale feels as though she is viewed as a "damaged woman, a heretic"; while the rest of society tells her the material she enjoys is bad, "pornography tells me the opposite: that *none* of my thoughts are bad, that anything goes."[31] As Tisdale imagines herself in the shoes (or lack thereof) of the female porn star who is bound, tied up, and submissive, she feels like a free woman in her fantasies. Recognizing that her own rape fantasies are only as shameful as she allows them to be, she expands her libertine attitude to all women: "by letting go of judgments I hold against myself, and my desires, I let go of the judgments about the desires and the acts of others."[32]

III. MARTHA NUSSBAUM'S LIBERAL FEMINISM

What Tisdale and the vast majority of Americans, feminist or not, want to see in the public policies surrounding pornography is that its use be considered private and harmless. Only pornography that depicts children is consistently deemed offensive in Western societies, and its regulation is thus deemed appropriate, there being no way to produce such materials without harming children, the thinking goes.[33] There is no harm in pornographic representations of sex in and of themselves. Besides this, Tisdale provides a glimpse of the potential of sexual self-analysis that forms the basis of my positive arguments for more pornography. Before we get there, however, let's consider what Martha Nussbaum, a leading liberal feminist, has to say about Tisdale's take on shameful materials.

Nussbaum's objection to pornography is at once more guarded and yet more foundational than MacKinnon's or Mason-Grant's, for its conclusion is that, "In short: the legal definition of obscenity actively colludes with misogyny, has the root concepts of misogyny embedded in it."[34] This is the clearest way to state the "ideological" character of the feminist objection to pornography mentioned above, and though it is more thoroughgoing than the causal objections we have to this point canvassed, it is in tension with Nussbaum's other commitments. Nussbaum argues forcefully that laws and morality are firmly and irrevocably grounded upon the emotions (of anger and resentment, mostly) and that this is as it should be. Thus, she departs from the opposition to pornography on the basis of disgust, on the grounds that male disgust for the female body is apparently the misogynistic message put forth in pornography. As she says: "the morally significant issues . . . are of human dignity, objectification, and subordination. Disgust has nothing to do with it." Disgust, like shame, has historically been linked to "group-based thinking" as this emotion has a social construction unlike others, and so Nussbaum finds it an unstable ground for law.[35]

Like John Stuart Mill, Nussbaum argues that only an expected and imminent harm is a possible ground for the legal regulation of conduct, but as a cognitivist about the emotions in general, she is committed to states of disgust amounting to judgments that assent to "value-laden appearances" we make of our environment. She cites the work of Paul Rozin, whose core definition of disgust is "revulsion at the prospect of (oral) incorporation of an offensive object."[36] Indeed, in an earlier work she says, "Disgust plays a valuable role in motivating the avoidance of genuinely harmful substances."[37] However, while disgust over the unavoidable presence of its "primary objects" such as noxious odors or filthy bathroom facilities in prison can be suitable bases for antinuisance laws, "socially-mediated" disgust as in a "homosexual provocation defense" cannot, as it (like shame) is based ultimately on a transcendent view of human nature in which our inherent animality is irrationally rejected. We should be indignant over the harms reflected in pornography, not disgusted by its content, on this view. In this way, Nussbaum argues that U.S. obscenity law and its focus on offensive materials serves to ideologically mask the misogynistic content of pornography.

One might come away from Nussbaum's views with the impression that she's on Tisdale's side. Just as only a homophobe would claim to be disgusted by witnessing a homosexual act, so those who, *a priori*, consider sex disgusting would on these grounds object to pornography, and as Nussbaum-the-Millian says, too bad:

> Even if some citizens in a liberal society continue to believe that sex is disgusting, the presence of sexually explicit materials in society is no more harmful to them than the presence of texts defending a religion different from their own. They can simply avoid those materials, and, at most, demand that they not be easily available to children, or displayed in public in a way that accosts unwilling viewers.[38]

However, Nussbaum strikes a more Rawlsian note when she disapproves of pornography (on all-too-familiar grounds), for she continues:

> The issue that a society committed to the equality of its female citizens should take seriously is the issue of subordination, humiliation, and associated harms. These aspects of pornography threaten core elements of a liberal society, elements on which citizens who otherwise differ in religion or comprehensive vision of life can agree. Much pornography, it is no news to say, depicts sexuality in a way designed to reinforce misogynistic stereotypes, portraying women as base and deserving of abuse, as wanting and asking for abuse, and as outlets for the male's desire to humiliate and abuse.[39]

I agree that subordination should be taken seriously, and if pornography subordinated women, then it could and should be deemed unprotected speech, legally (and morally) akin to hate speech. However, the question remains: must we view "much pornography" as reinforcing misogynistic stereotypes? If these aspects of pornography threaten equality, dignity, and other important values only insofar as they reinforce preexisting false and dangerous beliefs about women, then Nussbaum leaves us where we started, at EIEP, and misogynist content can be "bracketed" as socially mediated disgust and shame. That is, if pornographic subordination is a "value-laden" judgment some viewers make of its content, then their sexual ethic differs from Tisdale's, and depictions of sexual activity can be "screened off," so to speak, as factors that reinforce misogynistic stereotypes, which are properly seen to be a result of some viewers' mental intermediation. Nussbaum simply assumes that pornographic images depict abuse and other unethical acts; she adopts an *a priori* view of the meaning of such imagery.

This is the only reading of Nussbaum that squares her Millian understanding of harm with claims on commercial sex she makes in a more recent work.[40] Here, her goal is to move us from a politics of disgust to a politics of humanity, and she cites with approval a long list of court rulings, stemming from *Lawrence v. Texas*, which in 2003 struck down Texas's antisodomy laws and which protects "conduct that belongs to a private sphere of personal decision making."[41] Included on this list is *Stanley v. Georgia*, which protected, on free speech and due process grounds, the use of pornography insofar as it was confined to the home. In fact, Nussbaum wants the Court to go further and clarify the private-public distinction here along classical Millian lines, in which "self-regarding" and "secluded" acts, even commercial ones as in adult theaters and sex clubs, should all be unregulated.[42] Hence she applauds the extension of these laws to permit sex in the consensual confines of a private sex club, and, I infer, sex acts involving bondage with a female "sub" in a sadomasochistic sex club. These acts are now out of harm's way, on her view. Therefore, if on her view they are also harmless, then all of us, even those of us who, in her words, "otherwise differ in religion or comprehensive vision of life," must permit them. If they aren't, then the threat to self-respect and dignity that Nussbaum worries about does not adhere to aspects of sexually explicit images and pornography itself but to an *a priori* appraisal of the sex engaged therein. If EIEP were applied to the explicit images, they would be in the clear. A feminist analysis again misses the mark, and we are free to conclude that there is nothing inherently wrong with typical consumers watching typical pornography.[43]

Nussbaum's main conclusion is that pornography should not be seen as obscene, and hence regulable, because classifying sex and carnality as obscene is part and parcel of the misogynistic logic that feminists struggle against. I think of all the false conceits of feminist views on pornography, the greatest is this narcissistic one, which is blind to the objectification of men in pornography and to the priority of fantasy in watching it. The female body is not the only available object of disgust in the typical viewer's experience of pornography, contrary to what Nussbaum suggests, and thus her argument that disgust could only ground misogynistic laws is blocked. The shock some feel in the presence of pornography may stem from human sexuality itself displayed in such an outlandish and contrived way.[44]

This is Joel Feinberg's consistently Millian view of why pornography can seem offensive to some. Twenty years before Nussbaum, he could already point to an "honor roll" of scholars—none of them noted feminists, mind you—who avoid the "pernicious error" of identifying the obscene with the pornographic.[45] Feinberg answers his own question—"how can sex (of all things) be obscene?"—by pointing to both a "moral sensibility" not against sex but against "unsubtly shameless and open" depictions of sex and an amoral desire to avoid being "spatially or psychologically close to the physiological organs and processes deemed 'private' in our culture."[46] Such an analysis is consistent with what we shall find on the Internet pornography sites I discuss below. The important point is that female sexuality is not, on this view, what shocks and offends us, so to claim that our legal concept of obscenity has misogynistic roots is simply false. Nussbaum calls *Lawrence* "an achievement of the moral imagination" on behalf of the Supreme Court justices, but it also represents a political achievement by gays and lesbians who weren't ashamed of their own sex lives.[47] Tisdale isn't ashamed of her fantasies regarding sexually explicit materials, and neither should anyone else be. Nussbaum also concedes that "the idea of diffuse public harms in connection with sex-related businesses has extraordinary tenacity, generating restrictions that cannot be justified by solid evidence."[48] Apparently so, and I feel safe in concluding that she would want to join me in extending the liberal Millian safeguards of sexual freedom to pornographic websites so as to ameliorate the past's "socially mediated" disgust over sex of all sorts.

IV. INTERNET PORNOGRAPHY

Pornography is sexual fantasy and provides access to sexual pleasure otherwise unavailable or unaffordable for many. This is, indeed, its primary redeeming feature, one which some in the men's movement have begun to describe in libertarian language of freedoms, as in men have a right to virtual sex, over and above the objections of the "sexual trade unionists" (i.e., anti-pornography feminists).[49] Putting this "men's rights" argument aside for now—though Susan Faludi's "backlash" thesis predicts it will strengthen over time[50] —the liberal defender of pornography can't rest content on EIEP. If pornography is defensible, its place in our sexual pedagogy and practices must be also. In particular, liberals must offer a defense of the Internet pornography phenomenon of the last decade or so; they can't ignore what psychologists have come to call its "triple-A engine" effect of accessibility, affordability, and anonymity, a "concept that encapsulates essential differences between standard, historically marketed sexual materials (general pornography) and Internet pornography, and indicates the latter's potential for virulence" and its apparent potential for causing novel harms to women.[51]

Let's therefore take a closer look at Internet pornography and see if an application of EIEP can defend its content and pervasive use. Its most striking feature is its sheer diversity; it caters to men and women, hetero-, homo- and pansexual; to those with traditional, deviant, and even perverse tastes; as well as to those curious about interracial, intergenerational, and even interspecies sex, and provides much of this dizzying spectacle free of charge to anyone with Internet access. To the struggles of the various subpopulations of sexual (and racial and national) minorities making their presence felt with increasing vivacity, the LGBT and intersexed, for instance, such pansexual pluralism can be seen as a positive force (even as much of it, at least to this point, reinforces stereotypes within hetero culture).[52] This pluralism comes with a cost, however; the democratized production of this content makes regulation concerning the safety of its actors difficult to maintain. Los Angeles County has stringent codes governing the pornography industry, but the young woman (of Niceville, Florida, whom I happen to know personally) who makes films in her parents' house, uploads them to her own website, and uses an anonymous PayPal account to enroll customers, is left on her own, as are the popular "amateur" pornographers (foreign and domestic) who sell their materials to corporations such as YGBT.

These legitimate yet hardly intrinsic worries aside, however, the pornography sites most conducive to the feminist counterargument include Hustler's Barely Legal series (reputed to have grossed $10 million).[53] On the surface, such straight pornography depicts male sexual prowess and features men busily catering to female sexual desire; the man is a tool and his face rarely appears at all. He is reduced to a part and thus objectified as much as, if not more than, the female. Though the tool's orgasm is the "money shot," as this is enough to show—and is indeed *required* to show—the viewer that what he has just witnessed was "real," it's her expressions of being turned on that are the really elusive goal of the producer, as it is of a lover. The transparent features of sex—arousal and release—are, or appear to be anyway, more easily and reliably accomplished for male actors than for the typical viewer, and this is surely part of its appeal as fantasy.[54] Its appeal as transgressive fantasy to the male majority of its users requires more digging, however. Jean Baudrillard makes the case that all pornography, no matter how hard or soft, is the ultimate medium of masculinity, but not because it has anything to do with patriarchal oppression. Instead, pornography is hypermasculine because it makes sex hyperreal, more detailed and better than the real thing:

> Pornography is the quadrophonics of sex. It adds a third and fourth track to the sexual act. It is the hallucination of detail that rules. . . . End of the secret. What else does pornography do, in its sham vision, than reveal the inexorable, microscopic truth of sex?[55]

I agree that the appeal tinged with revulsion typical consumers report is better captured on this account than on the feminist one, even if more needs to be said. Many pornographic images help to sustain an image of masculine control, undoubtedly, but that no longer needs to be seen as misogyny, and their value lies in helping to ultimately show men and women that such control, in the real world, is a fantasy.[56]

That Internet pornography is pure fantasy, utterly divorced from the real relations between real men and real women, is a fact that cannot be overstated. It also explains why EIEP is only "*probably* correct" when applied to today's Internet pornography, for although its content and use are morally defensible, EIEP is largely besides the point here. Men (and women) turn to it for fantasy materials, as the exotic is the erotic, but only as it remains exotic and inapplicable to real sexual relations.[57] Why today's man would seek out the particular sorts of material he does—often with sadomasochistic themes, so that "facials" seem to outnumber "cream-pies," for instance—has been best analyzed by Alan Soble's broadly Marxist account. He offers an alternative to Dworkin's explanation of the "temporal coincidence" that the pornography explosion began at the same time as the women's movement. What she calls a male "backlash" Soble attributes to the fact that "feminist ideology, from moderate to radical, spread into households, schools, and workplaces, leaving the consciousness of very few women untouched."[58] This ongoing revolution—in a growing list of fields and job markets, my female students will earn, on average, more than their male conspecifics—has resulted in women displacing men in the specific roles assigned both genders in capitalist production, as well as in their economic and legal freedom from men. This, in turn, results in women's "unwillingness to accommodate to male sexuality."[59] Soble inverts Dworkin's "backlash" thesis, in other words, and concludes that "men consume pornography, not to reassert patriarchal power over women in the real world, but to recoup a sense of power in a fantasy world, and that this is a response to their perception that they have lost sexual power."[60] I see support for such a view in many of the personal narratives of men who make use of pornography's cheap thrills.[61]

Men may resent much of Internet pornography's reduction of masculine sexuality to cum, but they can resist this by approaching it as Tisdale does: with "all the curiosity of the anthropologist and the frank hope of the voyeur" and, above all, without shame.[62] The problem with today's pornography is not, to repeat, that it leads to sexual violence against women or that it contributes to harmful sexual desires or misogynistic attitudes in the men who consume it; the problem with pornography is that it's too pornographic! It's too close a simulacrum of fantasy and too easily transforms unconscious fears into visually attainable desires. Until we adjust our libidos to its vivacity, it will attract and repel in equal measure and reflect male fantasies of power and potency as well as anxieties and fears over the same. Until we internalize the "probable correctness" of EIEP and see pornography as a means of "mapping the limits of our shame," as Tisdale puts it, we can't approach explicit depictions of sex as dispassionately as required to appease the sorts of feminist worries I reviewed above.[63] Beyond these aesthetic and psychological complaints, I am skeptical of any other normative appraisal of pornography itself and am confident that in time we will learn to use this technology in ways properly befitting *eros*.[64]

NOTES

1. "The world has never seen sex used this consciously, this cynically, this elaborately, this openly, this systematically, with this degree of technological and psycho-

logical sophistication, as a means of destroying a whole people. . . . With this war, pornography emerges as a tool of genocide" (Catherine MacKinnon, "Turning Rape into Pornography," *MS.* [July–August 1993], 22–40, at 27). See Drucilla Cornell's "Introduction" to her *Feminism and Pornography* (Oxford, U.K.: Oxford University Press, 2000), 1–15, for further discussion. The reason I call this claim "outrageous" emerges later.

2. Nadine Strossen's *Defending Pornography: Free Speech, Sex, and the Fight for Women's Rights* (New York: New York University Press, 2000) and Wendy McElroy's *XXX: A Woman's Right to Pornography* (New York: St. Martin's Press, 1995) are leading examples.

3. Even if I largely do so in the weak-kneed sense that "the solution to (often) offensive pornography is more pornography."

4. Larry Baron, "Pornography and Gender Equality: An Empirical Analysis," *Journal of Sex Research* 27:3 (1990): 363–80, at 363. It should be noted, though, that he uses the circulation rates of soft-porn magazines as the measure of pornography consumption.

5. *Pornography and Civil Rights: A New Day for Women's Equality*, by Andrea Dworkin and Catherine A. MacKinnon (Minneapolis, Minn.: Organizing Against Pornography, 1988). Helen Longino similarly defines pornography as the verbal or pictorial representations of sexual behavior that recommend or endorse degradation ("Pornography, Oppression, and Freedom" in Susan Dwyer, ed., *The Problem of Pornography* [Belmont, Calif.: Wadsworth, 1995], 34–47, at 35–36). Alan Soble's critique of Longino is rich; see chapter 6 of *Sexual Investigations* (New York: New York University Press, 1996), especially 220–23.

6. Less charitable readings abound. A useful place for philosophers to begin is the debate between Melinda Vadas and William Parent, reprinted in Robert M. Stewart's *Philosophical Perspectives on Sex and Love* (Oxford, U.K.: Oxford University Press, 1995), 56–70. (See notes 7 and 26 below.) When MacKinnon says that pornography is a tool of genocide (see note 1, above), she means that the use of rape by Serbian forces is the moral equivalent of pornographic sex; it is porn-in-action, on her view. This is an outrageous, biased, and self-serving extension of the meaning of "pornography."

7. Vadas defends what she admits is a "peculiar" analysis of pornography in her "A First Look at the Pornography/Civil Rights Ordinance: Could Pornography Be the Subordination of Women?" reprinted in Stewart, *Philosophical Perspectives on Sex and Love*, 56–65, at 57.

8. The literature here is vast, and I refer to more below, but a fairly thorough overview, especially of measures of community attitudes toward pornography, is provided in Milton Diamond's "Pornography, Public Acceptance, and Sex Related Crime: A Review," *International Journal of Law and Psychiatry* 32:1 (2009): 304–14.

9. "Hope for freedom and transformation" for the "countless Christian men" who "struggle with the addictive power of porn" is offered by biopsychologist William M. Struthers in *Wired for Intimacy: How Pornography Hijacks the Male Brain* (Downers Grove, Ill.: InterVarsity Books, 2009), back cover. (It doesn't deserve a quote from its hoary insides, I'm afraid.) Research shows a stronger link between sexual offenders being raised in a repressive religious setting compared to their having watched pornography, by the bye; see Michael Goldstein and Harold Kant, *Pornography and Sexual Deviance: A Report of the Legal and Behavioral Institute* (Berkeley, Calif.: University of California Press, 1973).

10. Which is unfortunate, as religiosity is the single most explanatory variable in determining a person's attitudes towards pornography. Evolutionary psychologists pinpoint competing mating strategies at work in today's adult U.S. population, the adoption of one or the other being responsible for a range of behaviors such as church attendance and childbearing and a corresponding range of attitudes towards adultery, abortion, and the like. See J. Weeden, A. B. Cohen, and D. T. Kenrick, "Religious Attendance as Reproductive Support," *Evolution & Human Behavior* 29:6 (2008): 327–34. And, as Richard Posner points out,

The more fundamental point, however, which explains why pornography should be unproblematic when the status of women is either very low (ancient Greece) or very high (modern Denmark) but deeply problematic when it is intermediate, as in cultures dominated by the great monotheistic religions, is that only in these cultures is sex a morally charged subject. There cannot be a concept of the obscene, as I am using the term, in a society in which sex is a morally indifferent subject, like eating; erotic representations have no shock value in such a society.(*Sex and Reason* [Cambridge, Mass.: Harvard University Press, 1992], 365.)

11. Soble, *Pornography, Sex, and Feminism* (Amherst, N.Y.: Prometheus, 2002), 174.

12. Dworkin, "Against the Male Flood: Censorship, Pornography, and Equality," in Cornell, ed., *Feminism and Pornography*, 19–38, at 26.

13. Mackinnon, "Only Words," in Cornell, ed., *Feminism and Pornography*, 94–120, at 100–101. All emphasis is in the original.

14. Soble, *Pornography, Sex, and Feminism*, 29.

15. To borrow conservative Stanley Kurtz's disapproving characterization, "Beyond Gay Marriage: The Road to Polyamory" (in this volume, 157).

16. David A. J. Richards, *Sex, Drugs, Death, and the Law* (Totowa, N.J.: Rowman & Littlefield, 1982), 99.

17. Soble, "Sexual Use" (in this volume).

18. Joan Mason-Grant's main work in this area is *Pornography Embodied: From Speech to Sexual Practice* (Lanham, Md.: Rowman & Littlefield, 2004). Before her death she contributed an excerpt of her book, entitled "Pornography as Embodied Practice," to Alan Soble and Nicholas Power, eds., *Philosophy of Sex*, 5th ed. (Lanham, Md.: Rowman & Littlefield, 2008), which is also reprinted in this volume. All page references are to the current reprint.

19. It is worthwhile to quote the court more fully, as the notion of "mental intermediation" will reappear below:

> Therefore we accept the premises of this legislation. Depictions of subordination tend to perpetuate subordination. The subordinate status of women in turn leads to affront and lower pay at work, insult and injury at home, battery and rape on the streets. . . . Yet this simply demonstrates the power of pornography as speech. All of these unhappy effects depend on mental intermediation. Pornography affects how people see the world, their fellows, and social relations. If pornography is what pornography does, so is other speech. (*American Booksellers, Inc. v. Hudnut*, 771 F2d 323 [1985], 329.)

20. Mason-Grant, 528–29.

21. Mason-Grant, 534.

22. Mason-Grant, 533.

23. Mason-Grant, 530.

24. Pamela Paul's *Pornified: How Pornography Is Damaging Our Lives, Our Relationships, and Our Families* (New York: Henry Holt, 2006) is typical of this literature, and strictly anecdotal.

25. Mason-Grant, 533, emphasis added.

26. Parent calls "intractable" the "problem of distinguishing causal claims from claims that watching or reading pornography simply reinforces preexisting negative attitudes toward women" ("A Second Look at Pornography and the Subordination of Women," in Stewart, ed., *Philosophical Perspectives on Sex and Love*, 66–70, at 68). Though commonplace in the literature, these causal attribution errors, in some treatments, become galling. Sociologist Gail Dines's *Pornland* (Boston: Beacon Press, 2010) is subtitled *How Porn Has Hijacked Our Sexuality*, and yet she says (*concedes*, in what ranks as the most banal analysis of the field I have yet to come across):

> As boys grow up to be men, they are inundated with messages from the media, messages that both objectify women's bodies and depict women as

sex objects who exist for male pleasure. These images are part and parcel of the visual landscape and hence are unavoidable. . . . What pornography does is take these cultural messages about women and present them in a succinct way that leaves little room for multiple interpretations. . . . [G]onzo pornography, particularly . . . delivers a clear message to men, who have already developed a somewhat pornographic gaze by virtue of being brought up in a society filled with sexist pop culture images. [86]

If our media, visual landscape, culture, and society inundates, supplies, presents, and delivers messages, images, and narratives that pornography takes and clarifies or makes succinct, then Dines shouldn't imply that pornography itself has hijacked our sexuality.

27. It should be pointed out that a recent Swiss study found no link between exposure to pornography and risky sexual behavior among adolescents; see Marie-Thérèse Luder et al., "Associations between Online Pornography and Sexual Behavior among Adolescents: Myth or Reality?" *Archives of Sexual Behavior* 40:5 (2011): 1027–35. A Canadian study found a positive effect: Todd G. Morrison, Anomi Bearden, Rebecca Harriman, Melanie A. Morrison, and Shannon R. Ellis, "Correlates of Exposure to Sexually Explicit Material among Canadian Post-secondary Students," *Canadian Journal of Human Sexuality* 13:3–4 (2004): 143–56.

28. Michael Flood reviews studies of children eleven to seventeen exposed (sometimes accidentally) to pornography and concludes that "porn is a poor sex educator" ("The Harms of Pornography Exposure among Children and Young People," *Child Abuse Review* 18 (November 2009): 384–400, at 394.) Of course it is, when the children exposed to it report feeling "sick" and "embarrassed"! I could find no reference to harms, other than being "upset," traceable to pornography exposure in any of the studies he analyzes. (Given that half of all seventeen-year-old males in the U.S. are sexually active, I doubt that many of them were upset.)

29. Most recently, among Croatian men; see Aleksandar Stulhofer, Vesna Busko, and Ivan Landripet, "Pornography, Sexual Socialization, and Satisfaction among Young Men," *Archives of Sexual Behavior* 39:1 (February 2010): 168–78.

30. "Talk Dirty to Me" originally appeared in *Harper's Magazine* (February 1992): 37–46, and was reprinted in Soble and Power, eds., *Philosophy of Sex*, 5th ed., 419–32. All page references are to the latter.

31. Tisdale, 427.

32. Tisdale, 428.

33. Diamond ("Pornography, Public Acceptance, and Sex Related Crime") reports that in the U.S., even in its "reddest" states, "The only feature of a community standard that could be found, and still seems to hold today, is an intolerance for any materials in which children or minors are involved either as actors, participants, part of production or viewers" (308). Obviously, child pornography is typically deemed impermissible due to a much more direct application of the harm principle, as minors and children, in our society at present, are deemed to be harmed even by viewing sex. Attitudes may differ in Japan, where nude minors, in sites such as Saki's Room, have a significant presence (Katrien Jacobs, *Netporn: DIY Web Culture and Sexual Politics* [Lanham, Md.: Rowman & Littlefield, 2007], 39). In addition, at times this application of obscenity law is often stretched to cover cases where harm is hard to find, such as the "Hensen affair," in which a leading Sydney art gallery was prosecuted for displaying a nude photo of a six-year-old girl. In light of the media storm over the case, Lawyers Gareth Griffith and Kathryn Simon wrote a "briefing paper" for the New South Wales Parliament in which they assert, without argument, the extravagant claim that "the very act of accessing child pornography makes the offender a party to child sexual abuse" (available online in section 2.5 at http://parliament.nsw.gov.au/prod/parlment/publications.nsf/key/ChildPornographyLaw [accessed April 6, 2012]). And although the production of child pornography in some jurisdictions poses a real danger to real children in real life, the 300 percent rise in the length of the average federal sentence for its mere possession over the last fourteen years can hardly be justified as a means

of mitigating this harm. See Kristin Carlson, "Commentary, Strong Medicine: Toward Effective Sentencing of Child Pornography Offenders," *Michigan Law Review* 27 (2010), http://www.michiganlawreview.org/assets/fi/109/carlson.pdf (accessed April 6, 2012).

34. Martha Nussbaum, *Hiding from Humanity: Disgust, Shame, and the Law* (Princeton, N.J.: Princeton University Press, 2004), 139.

35. Nussbaum, *Hiding from Humanity*, 146.

36. Nussbaum, *Hiding from Humanity*, 87.

37. Nussbaum, *Upheavals of Thought: The Intelligence of Emotions* (Cambridge, U.K.: Cambridge University Press, 2001), 205.

38. Nussbaum, *Hiding from Humanity*, 139.

39. Nussbaum, *Hiding from Humanity*, 139.

40. Nussbaum, *From Disgust to Humanity: Sexual Orientation and Constitutional Law* (Oxford, U.K.: Oxford University Press, 2010).

41. Nussbaum, *From Disgust to Humanity*, 193.

42. Nussbaum, *From Disgust to Humanity*, 196.

43. For further discussion of Nussbaum's Rawlsian and Millian commitments, see David Archard, "Disgust, Offensiveness, and the Law," *Journal of Applied Philosophy* 25:4 (2008): 314–21.

44. David Benatar may have a similar point in mind in his online review of Nussbaum's book: "The psychologists to whom Professor Nussbaum refers do indeed think that the objects of true disgust are always either animals or animal products. But does it follow that disgust is a way of hiding from humanity? It may instead be a way of acknowledging our humanity and expressing our repugnance at its inherent animality. On this view, it is not disgust itself but rather its bounds—the absence of disgust, or greater disgust, about more of ourselves—that constitutes the hiding" (http://www.riverwoodcenter.org/poc/view_doc.php?id=2321&type=book&cn=216 [accessed April 6, 2012]).

45. Joel Feinberg, "Obscenity, Pornography, and the Arts," reprinted in *Philosophy of Sex and Love: A Reader*, edited by Robert Trevas, Arthur Zucker, and Donald Borchert (Upper Saddle River, N.J.: Prentice Hall, 1997), 286–297, at 296, note 2.

46. Feinberg, "Obscenity, Pornography, and the Arts," 295.

47. Nussbaum, *From Disgust to Humanity*, 89.

48. Nussbaum, *From Disgust to Humanity*, 192.

49. A common theme of the blogosphere; see, for example, http://theantifeminist.com/ (accessed April 17, 2012).

50. Susan Faludi, *Backlash: The Undeclared War against American Women* (New York: Crown, 1991), 40–41; see also Alan Soble, *Pornography: Marxism, Feminism, and the Future of Sexuality* (New Haven, Conn.: Yale University Press, 1986), 82–84, whose view is discussed below.

51. See Thomas P. Kalman, "Clinical Encounters with Internet Pornography," *Journal of the American Academy of Psychoanalysis and Dynamic Psychiatry* 36:4 (2008): 593–618, at 610.

52. Heather Butler notes that in representing lesbian sex, "cinema can also easily represent dildo sex" in which "orgasm does not seem to be a preoccupation" ("What Do You Call a Lesbian with Long Fingers? The Development of Lesbian and Dyke Pornography," in Linda Williams, ed., *Porn Studies* [Durham, N.C.: Duke University Press, 2004], 167–97, at 187). In that same anthology, Williams's own "Skin Flicks on the Racial Border: Pornography, Exploitation, and Interracial Lust" (271–308) concludes, in part, that "the very taboos that once effectively policed the racial barrier now work in the service of eroticizing its transgression" (286).

53. See the commendable encyclopedia entry on pornography by Lori Gruen in Soble, ed., *Sex From Plato to Paglia: A Philosophical Encyclopedia* (Westport, Conn.: Greenwood Press, 2006), vol. 2, 811–23. The $10 million figure is reported at p. 815.

54. Consider this, admittedly anecdotal, evidence from Susannah Breslin's blog, "Letters from Men Who Watch Pornography" (http://lettersfromwatchers.blogspot.com/ [accessed April 6, 2012]):

> Pornography is a crutch, something I lean on in times of need, in dry spells, in times of wanting to feel better about myself, to take my mind off my worries of sexual inadequacy.

And this:

> Pornography was my last refuge I guess; I can get the sexual urges out of my system with a minimum of time and money and effort and go back to being a good little zombie at my job. In porn I like seeing women who are enjoying themselves, it doesn't even matter how attractive they are, as long as they can portray an honest appearance of true sexual joy on screen, and I can pretend that I am there with them and they enjoy my company. I always just wanted to be loved, and yet I could never break through the wall of mistrust surrounding me. Porn at least gives me a semi-satisfying illusion.

55. Jean Baudrillard, *Seduction*. Translated by Brian Singer (New York: St. Martin's Press, 1990), 31.

56. A Freudian and Oedipal fantasy, argues Cornell ("Pornography's Temptation," in *Feminism and Pornography*, 551–68, at 558).

57. I mean "inapplicable" in the sense in which Michael Slote uses it to analyze the perverse: "the ordinary notions of a monster and of an unnatural (or perverted) act are for similar reasons inapplicable to reality" ("Inapplicable Concepts," *Philosophical Studies* 28:4 [1975]: 265–71, at 265.

58. Soble, *Pornography: Marxism, Feminism, and the Future of Sexuality*, 85.

59. Soble, *Pornography: Marxism, Feminism, and the Future of Sexuality*, 86.

60. Soble, *Pornography: Marxism, Feminism, and the Future of Sexuality*, 87.

61. Such as this contribution to Breslin's blog:

> And while I am still aware of the inherent pathetic quality of being a man alone at my age, I would much rather be the connoisseur of an under-appreciated form of entertainment continuing to transcend the aesthetic limits hitherto placed upon it by forces of official history than a harried everyman, harangued by the burdens of emotional turmoil, personality conflict, atrophying sexual energy, and ludicrously inexcusable asinine conversations and circular arguments. . . . Women do not find me attractive enough for anything other than a gilded chair in the Friend Zone. And it is a development about which I can do nothing. So rather than dwell and ferment in my own isolation, I can use porn to have the "good parts" of a relationship while evading the burdens of engaging in a relationship with someone that will inevitably, statistically fail.

62. Tisdale, 421.

63. Tisdale, 421.

64. For helpful comments on prior versions of this essay, I'd like to thank Alan Soble, Raja Halwani, my colleagues at UWF—Sally Ferguson and Steven Hood—members of the Florida Philosophical Association, especially Brook Sadler and Scott Kimbrough, and last but not least, the student members of UWF's Socratic Society.

STUDY QUESTIONS

1. State the main conclusion of Power's argument. Then trace, through the essay, his arguments for that conclusion. Along the way, make sure to state and explain EIEP and the role it plays in Power's argument.

2. Power calls the feminist critique of pornography "ideological." What does that term mean in this context? If Power is correct in considering the feminist critique ideological, might feminism consider his defense of pornography similarly ideological (in fact, as patriarchal)? Does feminism have any other persuasive responses to his criticism?

3. What does Power mean by the assertion that some anti-pornography feminists reject pornography *a priori* (a term that has various applications in philosophy)? How does this assertion differ from Alan Soble's polysemicity thesis, briefly discussed by Power?

4. According to Power, supporters and defenders of pornography can reply to the charge that pornography is guilty of objectification by pointing out that human sexuality itself already and "necessarily involves objectification." Is this a successful or cogent defense of pornography? Try to answer this question also by using EIEP.

5. What does Power mean by "Internet pornography is pure fantasy"? Is it free of ambiguity, vagueness, and other problems? So: Is Power correct to claim (1) that Internet pornography *is* pure fantasy and (2) that this fact explains why "EIEP is largely besides the point here"?

6. Is Power correct to claim that the polysemicity of images is "a general principle of aesthetics"? Assuming that by "aesthetics" he means "the philosophy and the study of art," might art images differ in important ways from pornographic ones when it comes to polysemicity?

7. In "Why 'Derivatization' Is Better than 'Objectification'" (in this volume), Ann Cahill suggests that a female exotic dancer is subject to derivitization because her subjectivity is reducible to the subjectivity of her male customers. Apply her analysis to female actors in heterosexual pornography, and construct an argument either for or against the claim that derivatization also occurs there despite (or in light of) what Power says about pornography's being cheap.

A Bibliography of the Philosophy of Sex

GENERAL

Abramson, Paul R. *Sex Appeal: Six Ethical Principles for the 21st Century*. Oxford, U.K.: Oxford University Press, 2010.

Abramson, Paul R., and Steven D. Pinkerton, eds. *Sexual Nature Sexual Culture*. Chicago: University of Chicago Press, 1995.

Alexander, W. M. "Philosophers Have Avoided Sex." *Diogenes* 72 (Winter 1970): 56–74. Reprinted in *The Philosophy of Sex*, 2nd ed., edited by Alan Soble. Savage, Md.: Rowman & Littlefield, 1991, 3–19.

———. "Sex and Philosophy in Augustine." *Augustinian Studies* 5 (1974): 197–208.

Ariès, Philippe, and André Béjin, eds. *Western Sexuality: Practice and Precept in Past and Present Times*. New York: Blackwell, 1985.

Atkinson, Ronald. *Sexual Morality*. London: Hutchinson, 1965.

Atkinson, Ti-Grace. *Amazon Odyssey*. New York: Links Books, 1974.

Baker, Robert, and Frederick Elliston, eds. *Philosophy and Sex*, 1st ed. Buffalo, N.Y.: Prometheus, 1975; 2nd ed., 1984.

Baker, Robert B., and Kathleen J. Wininger, eds. *Philosophy and Sex*, 4th ed. Amherst, N.Y.: Prometheus, 2009.

Baker, Robert B., Kathleen J. Wininger, and Frederick A. Elliston, eds. *Philosophy and Sex*, 3rd ed. Amherst, N.Y.: Prometheus, 1998.

Beemyn, Brett, and Mickey Eliason, eds. *Queer Studies: A Lesbian, Gay, Bisexual, and Transgender Anthology*. New York: New York University Press, 1996.

Belliotti, Raymond. *Good Sex: Perspectives on Sexual Ethics*. Lawrence, Kan.: University Press of Kansas, 1993.

Bernard, Michael E. "Sex." In *Rationality and the Pursuit of Happiness: The Legacy of Albert Ellis*, 127–54. Chichester, U.K.: Wiley-Blackwell, 2011.

Blackburn, Simon. *Lust: The Seven Deadly Sins*. New York: Oxford University Press, 2004.

Bristow, Joseph. *Sexuality*, 2nd ed. London: Routledge, 2011.

Browne, Jude, ed. *The Future of Gender*. Cambridge: Cambridge University Press, 2007.

Bruce, Michael, and Robert M. Stewart, eds. *College Sex-Philosophy for Everyone: Philosophers with Benefits*. Chichester, U.K.: Wiley-Blackwell, 2010.

Brundage, James A. *Law, Sex, and Christian Society in Medieval Europe*. Chicago: University of Chicago Press, 1987.

Bullough, Vern L., and Bonnie Bullough. *Sexual Attitudes: Myths and Realities*. Amherst, N.Y.: Prometheus, 1995.

———, eds. *Human Sexuality: An Encyclopedia*. New York: Garland, 1994.

Buss, David M. *The Evolution of Desire*. New York: Basic Books, 1994.

Butler, Judith. *Bodies that Matter: On the Discursive Limits of "Sex"* (New York: Routledge, 1993).

———. *Gender Trouble: Feminism and the Subversion of Identity*. New York: Routledge, 1990.

———. *Undoing Gender*. New York: Routledge, 2004.

Califia, Pat. *Public Sex: The Culture of Radical Sex*. Pittsburgh, Penn.: Cleis Press, 1994.

Califia, Patrick. *Speaking Sex to Power: The Politics of Queer Sex.* San Francisco, Calif.: Cleis Press, 2002.

Carr, David. "Freud and Sexual Ethics." *Philosophy* 62:241 (1987): 361–73.

Colker, Ruth. "Feminism, Sexuality, and Authenticity." In *At the Boundaries of Law,* edited by Martha A. Fineman and Nancy S. Thomadsen, 135–47. New York: Routledge, 1991.

———. "Feminism, Sexuality, and Self: A Preliminary Inquiry into the Politics of Authenticity." *Boston University Law Review* 68:1 (1988): 217–64.

Davis, Murray. *Smut: Erotic Reality/Obscene Ideology.* Chicago: University of Chicago Press, 1983.

Devine, Philip E., and Celia Wolf-Devine, eds. *Sex and Gender: A Spectrum of Views.* Belmont, Calif.: Wadsworth, 2003.

Diamond, Jared. *Why Is Sex Fun? The Evolution of Human Sexuality.* New York: Basic Books, 1997.

Dufourmantelle, Anne. *Blind Date: Sex and Philosophy,* translated by Catherine Porter. Urbana, Ill.: Illinois University Press, 2007.

Duggan, Lisa, and Nan D. Hunter. *Sex Wars: Sexual Dissent and Political Culture.* New York: Routledge, 1995.

Dworkin, Andrea. *Intercourse.* New York: Free Press, 1987.

Eadie, Jo, ed. *Sexuality: The Essential Glossary.* London: Arnold, 2004.

English, Deirdre, Amber Hollibaugh, and Gayle Rubin. "Talking Sex: A Conversation on Sexuality and Feminism." *Socialist Review* 11:4 (1981): 43–62.

Epstein, Louis M. (1948) *Sex Laws and Customs in Judaism.* New York: Ktav, 1967.

Farley, Margaret. "Sexual Ethics." In *Encyclopedia of Bioethics,* vol. 5, revised edition, edited by Warren Reich, 2365–75. New York: Simon & Schuster Macmillan, 1995.

Feder, Ellen K., Karmen MacKendrick, and Sybol S. Cook, eds. *A Passion for Wisdom: Readings in Western Philosophy on Love and Desire.* Upper Saddle River, N.J.: Prentice Hall, 2004.

Ferber, Abby L., Kimberly Holcomb, and Tre Wentling, eds. *Sex, Gender, and Sexuality: The New Basics.* New York: Oxford University Press, 2009.

Firestone, Shulamith. *The Dialectic of Sex: The Case for Feminist Revolution.* New York: Bantam Books, 1970.

Foucault, Michel. *The History of Sexuality.* Vol. 1, *An Introduction.* New York: Vintage, 1976.

———. *The History of Sexuality.* Vol. 2, *The Use of Pleasure.* New York: Pantheon, 1985.

———. *The History of Sexuality.* Vol. 3, *The Care of the Self.* New York: Vintage, 1986.

Fuchs, Eric. *Sexual Desire and Love: Origins and History of the Christian Ethic of Sexuality and Marriage,* translated by Marsha Daigle. New York: Seabury, 1983.

Fuchs, Wolfgang. "Love and Lust after Levinas and Lingis." *Philosophy Today* 52:1 (2008): 45–51.

Garry, Ann. "Why Are Love and Sex Philosophically Interesting?" *Metaphilosophy* 11:2 (1980): 165–77. Reprinted in Alan Soble, ed., *The Philosophy of Sex,* 2nd ed. Savage, Md.: Rowman and Littlefield, 1991, pp. 21–36.

Gilbert, Paul. *Human Relationships: A Philosophical Introduction.* Oxford, U.K.: Blackwell, 1991.

Gruen, Lori, and George F. Panichas, eds. *Sex, Morality, and the Law.* New York: Routledge, 1997.

Gudorf, Christine E. *Body, Sex, and Pleasure: Reconstructing Christian Sexual Ethics.* Cleveland, Ohio: Pilgrim Press, 1994.

Halwani, Raja. *Philosophy of Love, Sex, and Marriage: An Introduction.* New York: Routledge, 2010.

Hamilton, Christopher. "Sex." In *Living Philosophy: Reflections on Life, Meaning, and Morality,* 125–41. Edinburgh, U.K.: Edinburgh University Press, 2002. Reprinted in *The Philosophy of Sex,* 5th ed., edited by Alan Soble and Nicholas Power. Lanham, Md.: Rowman & Littlefield, 2008, pp. 99–116.

Hock, Roger R. *Human Sexuality*. Upper Saddle River, N.J.: Pearson/Prentice Hall, 2007.

Hunter, J. F. M. *Thinking about Sex and Love*. New York: St. Martin's, 1980.

Irigaray, Luce. *This Sex Which Is Not One*, translated by Catherine Porter. Ithaca, N.Y.: Cornell University Press, 1985; original publication, 1997.

Jackson, Stevi, and Sue Scott, eds. *Feminism and Sexuality: A Reader*. New York: Columbia University Press, 1996.

Jagger, Jill. *Judith Butler: Sexual Politics, Social Change and the Power of the Performative*. London: Routledge, 2008.

Jeffreys, Sheila. *Anticlimax: A Feminist Perspective on the Sexual Revolution*. New York: New York University Press, 1990.

Jordan, Mark D. *The Ethics of Sex*. Oxford, U.K.: Blackwell, 2002.

Jung, Patricia Beattie, Mary E. Hunt, and Radhika Balakrishnan, eds. *Good Sex: Feminist Perspectives from the World's Religions*. New Brunswick, N.J.: Rutgers University Press, 2001.

Kahr, Brett. *Who's Been Sleeping in Your Head? The Secret World of Sexual Fantasy*. New York: Basic Books, 2008.

Kalbian, Aline. *Sexing the Church: Gender, Power, and Contemporary Catholic Ethics*. Bloomington, Ind.: Indiana University Press, 2005.

Kaplan, Morris. *Sexual Justice: Democratic Citizenship and the Politics of Desire*. New York: Routledge, 1997.

Kolnai, Aurel. *Sexual Ethics: The Meaning and Foundations of Sexual Morality*, edited and translated by Francis Dunlop. Aldershot, U.K.: Ashgate, 2005.

Kuefler, Matthew, ed. *The History of Sexuality Sourcebook*. Peterborough, Ont.: Broadview Press, 2007.

Laqueur, Thomas. *Making Sex: Body and Gender from the Greeks to Freud*. Cambridge, Mass.: Harvard University Press, 1990.

Laumann, Edward O., John H. Gagnon, Robert T. Michael, and Stuart Michaels. *The Social Organization of Sexuality: Sexual Practices in the United States*. Chicago: University of Chicago Press, 1994.

Lebacqz, Karen, ed., with David Sinacore-Guinn. *Sexuality: A Reader*. Cleveland, Ohio: Pilgrim Press, 1999.

Leidholdt, Dorchen, and Janice C. Raymond, eds. *The Sexual Liberals and the Attack on Feminism*. New York: Teachers College Press, 1990.

LeMoncheck, Linda. *Loose Women, Lecherous Men: A Feminist Philosophy of Sex*. New York: Oxford University Press, 1997.

Lomardo, Marc. "James Baldwin's Philosophical Critique of Sexuality." *Journal of Speculative Philosophy* 23:1 (2009): 40–50.

MacKinnon, Catharine A. *Feminism Unmodified: Discourses on Life and Law*. Cambridge, Mass.: Harvard University Press, 1987.

Maglin, Nan Bauer, and Donna Perry, eds. *"Bad Girls"/"Good Girls": Women, Sex, and Power in the Nineties*. New Brunswick, N.J.: Rutgers University Press, 1996.

Marcuse, Herbert. (1955) *Eros and Civilization: A Philosophical Inquiry into Freud*. Boston: Beacon Press, 1966.

Marietta, Don E., Jr. *Philosophy of Sexuality*. Armonk, N.Y.: M. E. Sharpe, 1997.

McWhorter, Ladelle. *Bodies and Pleasures: Foucault and the Politics of Sexual Normalization*. Bloomington, Ind.: Indiana University Press, 1999.

Money, John. *The Adam Principle. Genes, Genitals, Hormones, and Gender: Selected Readings in Sexology*. Buffalo, N.Y.: Prometheus, 1993.

Nagel, Thomas. *Concealment and Exposure and Other Essays*. Oxford, U.K.: Oxford University Press, 2002.

Nelson, James B. *Embodiment: An Approach to Sexuality and Christian Theology*. Minneapolis, Minn.: Augsburg, 1978.

Nelson, James B., and Sandra P. Longfellow, eds. *Sexuality and the Sacred: Sources for Theological Reflection*. Louisville, Ky.: Westminster John Knox, 1994.

Nozick, Robert. "Sexuality." In *The Examined Life.* New York: Simon and Schuster, 1989, pp. 61–67.

Nye, Robert A., ed. *Sexuality.* Oxford, U.K.: Oxford University Press, 1999.

Pagels, Elaine. *Adam, Eve, and the Serpent.* New York: Vintage, 1988.

Paglia, Camille. *Sexual Personae: Art and Decadence from Nefertiti to Emily Dickinson.* New Haven, Conn.: Yale University Press, 1990.

Peiss, Kathy, Christina Simmons, and Robert Padgug, eds. *Passion and Power: Sexuality in History.* Philadelphia, Penn.: Temple University Press, 1989.

Posner, Richard A. *Sex and Reason.* Cambridge, Mass.: Harvard University Press, 1992.

Primoratz, Igor. *Ethics and Sex.* London: Routledge, 1999.

———, ed. *Human Sexuality.* Aldershot, U.K.: Dartmouth, 1997.

Punzo, Vincent. *Reflective Naturalism: An Introduction to Moral Philosophy.* New York: Macmillan, 1969.

Radakovich, Anka. *Sexplorations: Journeys to the Erogenous Frontier.* New York: Crown, 1997.

Ranke-Heinemann, Uta. *Eunuchs for the Kingdom of Heaven: Women, Sexuality and the Catholic Church.* New York: Penguin, 1990.

Reeve, C. D. C. *Love's Confusions.* Cambridge, Mass.: Harvard University Press, 2005.

Richter, Alan. *Dictionary of Sexual Slang.* New York: John Wiley & Sons, 1993.

Richter, Duncan. "Sex." In *Anscombe's Moral Philosophy.* Lanham, Md.: Lexington Books, 2011, pp. 139–66.

Robinson, Paul. *The Freudian Left: Wilhelm Reich, Geza Roheim, Herbert Marcuse.* New York: Harper and Row, 1969.

———. *The Modernization of Sex: Havelock Ellis, Alfred Kinsey, William Masters and Virginia Johnson.* New York: Harper and Row, 1976.

Rogers, Eugene F., Jr., ed. *Theology and Sexuality: Classic and Contemporary Readings.* Oxford, U.K.: Blackwell, 2002.

Rubin, Gayle S. "Thinking Sex: Notes for a Radical Theory of the Politics of Sexuality." In *Pleasure and Danger: Exploring Female Sexuality,* edited by Carole S. Vance, 267–319. London: Routledge and Kegan Paul, 1984.

Rubin, Lillian B. *Erotic Wars: What Happened to the Sexual Revolution?* New York: Farrar, Straus and Giroux, 1990.

Russell, Bertrand. *Marriage and Morals.* London: George Allen and Unwin, 1929.

Scruton, Roger. *Sexual Desire: A Moral Philosophy of the Erotic.* New York: Free Press, 1986.

Seidman, Steven. *Embattled Eros.* New York: Routledge, 1992.

———. *The Social Construction of Sexuality.* New York: W. W. Norton, 2010.

Shelp, Earl E., ed. *Sexuality and Medicine.* Vol. 1, *Conceptual Roots.* Dordrecht: Reidel, 1987.

———. *Sexuality and Medicine.* Vol. 2, *Ethical Viewpoints in Transition.* Dordrecht: Reidel, 1987.

Singer, Irving. *The Goals of Human Sexuality.* New York: Schocken Books, 1973.

———. *Sex: A Philosophical Primer.* Lanham, Md.: Rowman & Littlefield, 2001.

Soble, Alan. "Philosophy of Sex." In *Encyclopedia of Philosophy,* 2nd ed., vol. 7, edited by Donald Borchert, 521–32. New York: Macmillan/Thomson, 2006.

———. *The Philosophy of Sex and Love: An Introduction.* St. Paul, Minn.: Paragon House, 1998.

———. *The Philosophy of Sex and Love: An Introduction,* 2nd ed. St. Paul, Minn.: Paragon House, 2008.

———. *Sexual Investigations.* New York: New York University Press, 1996.

———, ed. *Eros, Agape, and Philia: Readings in the Philosophy of Love.* New York: Paragon House, 1989; reprinted with corrections St. Paul, Minn.: Paragon House, 1999.

———, ed. *The Philosophy of Sex: Contemporary Readings,* 1st ed. Totowa, N.J.: Rowman & Littlefield, 1980; 2nd ed., Savage, Md.: Rowman & Littlefield, 1991; 3rd ed., Lanham, Md.: Rowman & Littlefield, 1997; 4th ed., Lanham, Md.: Rowman & Littlefield, 2002.

————, ed. *Sex from Plato to Paglia: A Philosophical Encyclopedia.* Westport, Conn.: Greenwood, 2006.

————, ed. *Sex, Love, and Friendship.* Amsterdam: Rodopi, 1997.

Soble, Alan, and Nicholas Power, eds. *The Philosophy of Sex: Contemporary Readings.* 5th ed. Lanham, Md.: Rowman & Littlefield, 2008.

Solomon, Lewis D. *The Jewish Tradition, Sexuality, and Procreation.* Lanham, Md.: University Press of America, 2002.

Solomon, Robert C., and Kathleen M. Higgins, eds. *The Philosophy of (Erotic) Love.* Lawrence, Kan.: University Press of Kansas, 1991.

Stafford, J. Martin. *Essays on Sexuality and Ethics.* Solihull, U.K.: Ismeron, 1995.

Stein, Edward, ed. *Forms of Desire.* New York: Routledge, 1992.

Stewart, Robert M., ed. *Philosophical Perspectives on Sex and Love.* New York: Oxford University Press, 1995.

Stimpson, Catharine R., and Ethel Spector Person, eds. *Women: Sex and Sexuality.* Chicago: University of Chicago Press, 1980.

Stuart, Elizabeth, and Adrian Thatcher, eds. *Christian Perspectives on Sexuality and Gender.* Grand Rapids, Mich.: Eerdmans, 1996.

Sullivan, Clayton. *Rescuing Sex from the Christians.* New York: Continuum, 2006.

Swidler, Arlene, ed. *Homosexuality and World Religions.* Valley Forge, Penn.: Trinity Press, 1993.

Taverner, William J., and Ryan W. McKee, eds. *Taking Sides: Clashing Views in Human Sexuality.* New York: McGraw-Hill, 2010.

Thurber, James, and E. B. White. *Is Sex Necessary?* New York: Harper and Brothers, 1929.

Tiefer, Leonore. *Sex Is Not a Natural Act and Other Essays,* 2nd ed. Boulder, Colo.: Westview, 2004; original publication, 1995.

Trevas, Robert, Arthur Zucker, and Donald Borchert, eds. *Philosophy of Sex and Love: A Reader.* Upper Saddle River, N.J.: Prentice-Hall, 1997.

Vance, Carole S. ed. *Pleasure and Danger: Exploring Female Sexuality.* London: Routledge and Kegan Paul, 1984.

Verene, Donald, ed. *Sexual Love and Western Morality,* 1st ed. New York: Harper and Row, 1972; 2nd ed. Boston: Jones and Bartlett, 1995.

Vlemnick, Jens de, and Eran Dorfman, eds. *Sexuality and Psychoanalysis: Philosophical Criticisms.* Leuven, Bel.: Leuven University Press, 2010.

Warnke, Georgia. *Debating Sex and Gender.* New York: Oxford University Press, 2011.

Weber, Jonathan. "Sex." *Philosophy* 84:2 (2009): 233-50.

Weeks, Jeffrey. *Invented Moralities: Sexual Values in an Age of Uncertainty.* New York: Columbia University Press, 1995.

————. *The Languages of Sexuality.* Milton Park, U.K.: Routledge, 2011.

————. *Sexuality and Its Discontents.* London: Routledge and Kegan Paul, 1985.

————. *The World We Have Won: The Remaking of Erotic and Intimate Life.* London: Routledge, 2007.

Weeks, Jeffrey, and Janet Holland, eds. *Sexual Cultures: Communities, Values and Intimacy.* New York: St. Martin's, 1996.

West, David. *Reason and Sexuality in Western Thought.* Cambridge, Mass.: Polity, 2005.

Whiteley, C. H., and Winifred N. Whiteley. *Sex and Morals.* New York: Basic Books, 1967.

Williams, Mary E., ed. *Sex.* Farmington Hills, Mich.: Greenhaven Press, 2006.

Wilson, Edward O. "Sex." In *On Human Nature.* Cambridge, Mass.: Harvard University Press, 1978, pp. 125–54.

Wilson, John. *Love, Sex, and Feminism: A Philosophical Essay.* New York: Praeger, 1980.

Wojtyła, Karol [Pope John Paul II]. *Love and Responsibility.* New York: Farrar, Straus and Giroux, 1981.

CONCEPTUAL ANALYSIS

Benn, Piers. "Is Sex Morally Special?" *Journal of Applied Philosophy* 16:3 (1999): 235–45.

Boswell, John. "Revolutions, Universals, and Sexual Categories." *Salmagundi*, Nos. 58–59 (Fall 1982/Winter 1983): 89–113.

De Cecco, John P. "Definition and Meaning of Sexual Orientation." *Journal of Homosexuality* 6:4 (1981): 51–67.

Diorio, Joseph A. "Feminist-constructionist Theories of Sexuality and the Definition of Sex Education." *Educational Philosophy and Theory* 21:2 (1989): 23–31.

Farrell, Daniel M. "Jealousy." *Philosophical Review* 89:4 (October 1980): 527–59.

———. "Jealousy and Desire." In *Love Analyzed*, edited by Roger E. Lamb, 165–88. Boulder, Colo.: Westview, 1997.

Fausto-Sterling, Anne. *Sexing the Body: Gender Politics and the Construction of Sexuality*. New York: Basic Books, 2000.

Frye, Marilyn. "Lesbian 'Sex.'" In *Willful Virgin: Essays in Feminism 1976–1992*. Freedom, Calif.: Crossing Press, 1992, pp. 109–19.

Giles, James. *The Nature of Sexual Desire*. Westport, Conn.: Praeger, 2004; and Lanham, Md.: University Press of America, 2008.

———. "Sartre, Sexual Desire, and Relations with Others." In *French Existentialism: Consciousness, Ethics, and Relations with Others*, edited by James Giles, 155–73. Amsterdam: Rodopi, 1999.

———. "A Theory of Love and Sexual Desire." *Journal for the Theory of Social Behavior* 24:4 (1995): 339–57.

Gray, Robert. "Sex and Sexual Perversion." *Journal of Philosophy* 75:4 (1978): 189–99.

Jacobsen, Rockney. "Arousal and the Ends of Desire." *Philosophy and Phenomenological Research* 53:3 (1993): 617–32.

Klein, Fritz, Barry Sepekoff, and Timothy Wolf. "Sexual Orientation: A Multi-Variable Dynamic Process." *Journal of Homosexuality* 11:1–2 (1985): 35–50.

Koertge, Noretta. "Constructing Concepts of Sexuality: A Philosophical Commentary." In *Homosexuality/Heterosexuality: Concepts of Sexual Orientation*, edited by David McWhirter, Stephanie Sanders, and June Reinisch, 387–97. New York: Oxford University Press, 1990.

Martin, Christopher F. J. "Are There Virtues and Vices that Belong Specifically to the Sexual Life?" *Acta Philosophica* 4:2 (1995): 205–21.

Moore, Gareth. "Sexual Needs and Sexual Pleasures." *International Philosophical Quarterly* 35:2 (1995): 193–204.

Morgan, Seiriol. "Sex in the Head." *Journal of Applied Philosophy* 20:1 (2003): 1–16.

Padgug, Robert. "Sexual Matters: On Conceptualizing Sexuality in History." *Radical History Review* 20 (Spring/Summer 1979): 3–23.

Randall, Hilary E., and E. Sandra Byers. "What Is Sex? Students' Definitions of Having Sex, Sexual Partner, and Unfaithful Sexual Behaviour." *Canadian Journal of Human Sexuality* 12:2 (2003): 87–96.

Ruddick, Sara. "Better Sex." In *Philosophy and Sex*, 2nd ed., edited by Robert Baker and Frederick Elliston, 280–99. Buffalo, N.Y.: Prometheus, 1984.

Sanders, Stephanie A., Brandon J Hill, William L. Yarber, Cynthia A. Graham, Richard A. Crosby, and Robin R. Milhausen. "Misclassification Bias: Diversity in Conceptualisations about Having 'Had Sex.'" *Sexual Health* 7:1 (2010): 31–34.

Sanders, Stephanie, and June Reinisch. "Would You Say You 'Had Sex' If . . . ?" *Journal of the American Medical Association* 281:3 (January 20, 1999): 275–77.

Shaffer, Jerome A. "Sexual Desire." *Journal of Philosophy* 75:4 (1978): 175–89. Reprinted in *Sex, Love, and Friendship*, edited by Alan Soble, 1–12. Amsterdam: Rodopi, 1997.

Shrage, Laurie. "Do Lesbian Prostitutes Have Sex with Their Clients? A Clintonesque Reply." *Sexualities* 2:2 (1999): 259–61.

Solomon, Robert. "Sexual Paradigms." *Journal of Philosophy* 71:11 (1974): 336–45.

Sullivan, John P. "Philosophizing about Sexuality." *Philosophy of the Social Sciences* 14:1 (1984): 83–96.

Taylor, Roger. "Sexual Experiences." *Proceedings of the Aristotelian Society* 68 (1967–1968): 87–104. Reprinted in *The Philosophy of Sex*, 1st ed., edited by Alan Soble, 59–75. Totowa, N.J.: Rowman & Littlefield, 1980.

Thomas, Keith. "The Double Standard." *Journal of the History of Ideas* 20:2 (1959): 195–216.

SEXUAL PERVERSION

Baltzly, Dirk. "Peripatetic Perversions: A Neo-Aristotelian Account of the Nature of Sexual Perversion." *The Monist* 85:1 (2003): 3–29.

Bullough, Vern L., and Bonnie Bullough. *Sin, Sickness, and Sanity: A History of Sexual Attitudes.* New York: Garland, 1977.

Conrad, Peter, and Joseph W. Schneider. *Deviance and Medicalization: From Badness to Sickness.* St. Louis, Mo.: Mosby, 1980; expanded edition, Philadelphia, Penn.: Temple University Press, 1992.

Davidson, Arnold. "Conceptual History and Conceptions of Perversions." In *Philosophy and Sex*, 3rd ed., edited by Robert B. Baker, Kathleen J. Wininger, and Frederick A. Elliston, 476–86. Amherst, N.Y.: Prometheus, 1998.

———. "Sex and the Emergence of Sexuality." *Critical Inquiry* 14:1 (1987): 16–48.

Denis, Lara. "Kant on the Wrongness of 'Unnatural' Sex." *History of Philosophy Quarterly* 16:2 (1999): 225–48.

De Sousa, Ronald. "Norms and the Normal." In *Freud: A Collection of Critical Essays*, edited by Richard Wollheim, 196–221. Garden City, N.Y.: Anchor Books, 1974.

Eggington, William. *Perversity and Ethics.* Stanford, Calif.: Stanford University Press, 2006.

Freud, Sigmund. "Three Essays on the Theory of Sexuality." In *The Standard Edition of the Complete Psychological Works of Sigmund Freud*, vol 7., translated and edited by James Strachey, 125–45. London: Hogarth Press, 1953–1974; original publication, 1905.

Gates, Katharine. *Deviant Desires: Incredibly Strange Sex.* New York: Juno Books, 2000.

Gert, Bernard. "A Sex Caused Inconsistency in DSM-III-R: The Definition of Mental Disorder and the Definition of Paraphilias." *The Journal of Medicine and Philosophy* 17:2 (1992): 155–71.

Gert, Bernard, and Charles M. Culver. "Defining Mental Disorder." In *The Philosophy of Psychiatry: A Companion*, edited by Jennifer Radden, 415–25. New York: Oxford University Press, 2004.

Gray, Robert. "Sex and Sexual Perversion." *Journal of Philosophy* 75:4 (1978): 189–99.

Humber, James. "Sexual Perversion and Human Nature." *Philosophy Research Archives* 13 (1987–1988): 331–50.

Irvine, Janice M. *Disorders of Desire: Sex and Gender in Modern American Sexology.* Philadelphia, Penn.: Temple University Press, 1990.

———. "Reinventing Perversion: Sex Addiction and Cultural Anxieties." *Journal of the History of Sexuality* 5:3 (1995): 429–50.

Kadish, Mortimer R. "The Possibility of Perversion." *Philosophical Forum* 19:1 (1987): 34–53. Reprinted in *The Philosophy of Sex*, edited by Alan Soble, 2nd ed. Savage, Md.: Rowman & Littlefield, 1991, pp. 93–116.

Kaplan, Louise J. *Female Perversions: The Temptations of Emma Bovary.* New York: Anchor Books, 1991.

Ketchum, Sara Ann. "The Good, the Bad, and the Perverted: Sexual Paradigms Revisited." In *The Philosophy of Sex*, 1st ed., edited by Alan Soble, 139–57. Totowa, N.J.: Rowman & Littlefield, 1980.

Kupfer, Joseph. "Sexual Perversion and the Good." *The Personalist* 59:1 (1978): 70–77.

Levinson, Jerrold. "Sexual Perversity." *The Monist* 86:1 (2003): 30–54.

Levy, Donald. "Perversion and the Unnatural as Moral Categories." *Ethics* 90:2 (1980): 191–202. Reprinted (revised and expanded) in *The Philosophy of Sex*, 1st ed., edited by Alan Soble, 169–89. Totowa, N.J.: Rowman & Littlefield, 1980.

Miller, Kristie. "On the Concept of Sexual Perversion." *The Philosophical Quarterly* 60:241 (2010): 808–30.

Milligan, Tony. "The Wrongness of Having Sex with Animals." *Public Affairs Quarterly* 25:3 (2011): 241ff.

Neu, Jerome. "Freud and Perversion." In *The Cambridge Companion to Freud*, edited by Jerome Neu, 175–208. Cambridge, U.K.: Cambridge University Press, 1991.

———. "What Is Wrong with Incest?" *Inquiry* 19:1 (1976): 27–39.

Oliver, Kelly. "Innocence, Perversion, and Abu Ghraib." *Philosophy Today* 51:3 (2007): 343–56.

Penney, James. *The World of Perversion: Psychoanalysis and the Impossible Absolute of Desire.* Albany, N.Y.: SUNY Press, 2006.

Priest, Graham. "Sexual Perversion." *Australasian Journal of Philosophy* 75:3 (1997): 360–72.

Primoratz, Igor. "Sexual Perversion." *American Philosophical Quarterly* 34:2 (1997): 245–58.

Rosen, Raymond C., and Sandra R. Leiblum, eds. *Case Studies in Sex Therapy.* New York: Guilford Press, 1995.

Roudinesco, Élisabeth. *Our Dark Side: A History of Perversion*, translated by David Macey. Cambridge, Mass.: Polity, 2009.

Slote, Michael. "Inapplicable Concepts and Sexual Perversion." In *Philosophy and Sex*, 1st ed., edited by Robert Baker and Frederick Elliston, 261–67. Buffalo, N.Y.: Prometheus, 1975.

Soble, Alan. "Kant and Sexual Perversion." *The Monist* 86:1 (2003): 57–92.

———. "Paraphilia and Distress in DSM-IV." In *The Philosophy of Psychiatry: A Companion*, edited by Jennifer Radden, 54–63. New York: Oxford University Press, 2004.

Solomon, Robert. "Sex and Perversion." In *Philosophy and Sex*, 1st ed., edited by Robert Baker and Frederick Elliston, 268–87. Buffalo, N.Y.: Prometheus, 1975.

Spiecker, Ben, and Jan Steutel. "Paedophilia, Sexual Desire and Perversity." *Journal of Moral Education* 26:3 (1997): 331–42.

Steele, Valerie. *Fetish: Fashion, Sex and Power.* New York: Oxford University Press, 1996.

Szasz, Thomas S. "The Product Conversion—From Heresy to Illness." In *The Manufacture of Madness: A Comparative Study of the Inquisition and the Mental Health Movement.* New York: Harper and Row, 1970, pp. 160–79.

Vannoy, Russell. "The Structure of Sexual Perversity." In *Sex, Love, and Friendship*, edited by Alan Soble, 358–71. Amsterdam: Rodopi, 1997.

Zilney, Laura J., and Lisa Anne Zilney. *Perverts and Predators: The Making of Sexual Offending Laws.* Lanham, Md.: Rowman & Littlefield, 2009.

MASTURBATION

Bennett, Paula, and Vernon A. Rosario, eds. *Solitary Pleasures: The Historical, Literary, and Artistic Discourses of Autoeroticism.* New York: Routledge, 1995.

Budapest, Zsuzsanna E. "Self-Blessing Ritual." In *Womanspirit Rising: A Feminist Reader in Religion*, edited by Carol P. Christ and Judith Plaskow, 269–72. San Francisco, Calif.: Harper and Row, 1979.

Burger, John R. *One-Handed Histories: The Eroto-Politics of Gay Male Video Pornography.* New York: Haworth, 1995.

Cornog, Martha, ed. *The Big Book of Masturbation: From Angst to Zeal.* San Francisco: Down There Press, 2003.

Dodson, Betty. "How I Became the Guru of Female Sexual Liberation." In *Personal Stories of "How I Got Into Sex": Leading Researchers, Sex Therapists, Educators, Prosti-*

tutes, Sex Toy Designers, Sex Surrogates, Transsexuals, Criminologists, Clergy, and More . . . , edited by Bonnie Bullough, Vern L. Bullough, Marilyn A. Fithian, William E. Hartman, and Randy Sue Klein, 122–30. Amherst, N.Y.: Prometheus, 1997.

———. *Liberating Masturbation: A Meditation on Self-Love.* New York: Betty Dodson, 1978.

Elders, M. Joycelyn. "The Dreaded M Word. It's Not a Four-Letter Word." *Nerve,* June 26, 1997, www.nerve.com/dispatches/elders/mword (accessed March 3, 2012).

Engelhardt, H. Tristram Jr. "The Disease of Masturbation: Values and the Concept of Disease." *Bulletin of the History of Medicine* 48 (Summer 1974): 234–48. Reprinted in *Contemporary Issues in Bioethics,* edited by T. Beauchamp and L. Walters, 109–13. Encino, Calif.: Dickenson, 1978.

Fortunata, Jacqueline. "Masturbation and Women's Sexuality." In *The Philosophy of Sex,* 1st ed., edited by Alan Soble, 389–408. Totowa, N.J.: Rowman & Littlefield, 1980.

Francis, John J. "Masturbation." *Journal of the American Psychoanalytic Association* 16:1 (1968): 95–112.

Groenendijk, Leendert F. "Masturbation and Neurasthenia: Freud and Stekel in Debate on the Harmful Effects of Autoeroticism." *Journal of Psychology and Human Sexuality* 9:1 (1997): 71–94.

Haynes, James. "Masturbation." In *Human Sexuality: An Encyclopedia,* edited by Vern Bullough and Bonnie Bullough, 381–85. New York: Garland, 1994.

Hershfield, Jeffrey. "The Ethics of Sexual Fantasy." *International Journal of Applied Philosophy* 23:1 (2009): 27–49.

Jordan, Mark D. "Masturbation, or Identity in Solitude." In *The Ethics of Sex.* Oxford, U.K.: Blackwell, 2002, pp. 95–104.

Kielkopf, Charles. "Masturbation: A Kantian Condemnation." *Philosophia* 25:1–4 (1997): 223–46.

Laqueur, Thomas. *Solitary Sex: A Cultural History of Masturbation.* New York: Zone Books, 2003.

Moore, Gareth. "Natural Sex: Germain Grisez, Sex, and Natural Law." In *The Revival of Natural Law: Philosophical, Theological and Ethical Responses to the Finnis-Grisez School,* edited by Nigel Biggar and Rufus Black, 223–41. Aldershot, U.K.: Ashgate, 2000.

Neu, Jerome. "An Ethics of Fantasy?" *Journal of Theoretical and Philosophical Psychology* 22:2 (2002): 137–57.

Sarnoff, Suzanne, and Irving Sarnoff. *Sexual Excitement/Sexual Peace: The Place of Masturbation in Adult Relationships.* New York: M. Evans, 1979.

Satlow, Michael L. "'Wasted Seed': The History of a Rabbinic Idea." *Hebrew Union College Annual* 65 (1994): 137–69.

Soble, Alan. "Kant and Sexual Perversion." *The Monist* 86:1 (2003): 57–92.

Tiefer, Leonore. "Review of Suzanne Sarnoff and Irving Sarnoff, Sexual Excitement/ Sexual Peace: The Place of Masturbation in Adult Relationships." *Psychology of Women Quarterly* 8:1 (1983): 107–9.

COMPUTERS AND THE INTERNET

Adeney, Douglas. "Evaluating the Pleasures of Cybersex." *Australasian Journal of Professional and Applied Ethics* 1:1 (1999): 69–79.

Attwood, Feona, ed. *Porn.com: Making Sense of Online Pornography.* New York: Peter Lang, 2010.

Ben-Ze'ev, Aaron. *Love Online: Emotions on the Internet.* Cambridge: Cambridge University Press, 2004.

Collins, Louise. "Emotional Adultery: Cybersex and Commitment." *Social Theory and Practice* 25:2 (1999): 243–70.

———. "Is Cybersex Sex?" In *The Philosophy of Sex*, 5th ed., edited by Alan Soble and Nicholas Power, 117–31. Lanham, Md.: Rowman & Littlefield, 2008.

Cooper, Al, ed. *Cybersex: The Dark Side of the Force*. New York: Brunner-Routledge, 2000.

———. *Sex and the Internet: A Guide Book for Clinicians*. New York: Brunner-Routledge, 2002.

Hughes, Donna M. "The Use of New Communications and Information Technologies for Sexual Exploitation of Women and Children." *Hastings Women's Law Journal* 13:1 (2002): 129–48.

Kessler, Suzanne J. *Lessons from the Intersexed*. Piscataway, N.J.: Rutgers University Press, 1998.

Kiesbye, Stefan, ed. *Sexting*. Detroit, Mich.: Greenhaven Press, 2011.

Levmore, Saul, and Martha C. Nussbaum, eds. *The Offensive Internet: Privacy, Speech, Representation*. Cambridge, Mass.: Harvard University Press, 2010.

Levy, Neil. "Virtual Child Pornography: The Eroticization of Inequality." *Ethics and Information Technology* 4:4 (2002): 319–23.

Maheu, Marlene M., and Rona B. Subotnik. *Infidelity on the Internet: Virtual Relationships and Real Betrayal*. Naperville, Ill.: Sourcebooks, 2001.

Parikka, Jussi, and Tony D. Sampson, eds. *The Spam Book: On Viruses, Porn, and Other Anomalies from the Dark Side of Digital Culture*. Cresskill, N.J.: Hampton Press, 2009.

HOMOSEXUALITY AND QUEER ISSUES

Arroyo, Christopher. "Same-Sex Marriage, 'Homosexual Desire,' and the Capacity to Love." *International Journal of Applied Philosophy* 25:2 (2011): 171–86.

Bailey, Cathryn. "Embracing the Icon: The Feminist Potential of the Trans Bodhisattva, Kuan Yin." *Hypatia* 24:3 (2009): 178–96.

Baird, Robert M., and M. Katherine Baird, eds. *Homosexuality: Debating the Issues*. Amherst, N.Y.: Prometheus, 1995.

Ball, Carlos A. *The Morality of Gay Rights: An Exploration in Political Philosophy*. New York: Routledge, 2003.

Barry, Peter Brian. "Same-Sex Marriage and the Charge of Illiberality." *Social Theory and Practice* 37:2 (2011): 333–57.

Berlatsky, Noah, ed. *Homosexuality*. Detroit, Mich.: Greenhaven Press, 2011.

Bersani, Leo. "Is the Rectum a Grave?" *October* No. 43 (Winter 1987): 197–222.

Bettcher, Talia Mae. "Appearance, Reality, and Gender Deception: Reflections on Transphobic Violence and the Politics of Pretence." In *Violence, Victims, and Justifications*, edited by Felix Ó Murchadha, 175–200. Bern: Peter Lang, 2006.

———. "Evil Deceivers and Make-Believers: Transphobic Violence and the Politics of Illusion." *Hypatia* 22:3 (2007): 43–65.

———. "Trans Identities and First-Person Authority." In *"You've Changed": Sex Reassignment and Personal Identity*, edited by Laurie Shrage, 98–210. Oxford, U.K.: Oxford University Press, 2009.

———. "Without a Net: Starting Points for Trans Stories." *American Philosophical Association Newsletter on Philosophy and Lesbian, Gay, Bisexual, and Transgender Issues* 10:2 (Spring 2011): 2–5.

Bloodsworth-Lugo, Mary K., and Carmen Lugo-Lugo. *Containing (un)American Bodies: Race, Sexuality, and Post-9/11 Construction of Citizenship*. Amsterdam: Rodopi, 2010.

Boswell, John. *Christianity, Social Tolerance, and Homosexuality*. Chicago: University of Chicago Press, 1980.

———. *Same-Sex Unions in Premodern Europe*. New York: Villard, 1994.

Bradshaw, David. "A Reply to Corvino." In *Same Sex: Debating the Ethics, Science, and Culture of Homosexuality*, edited by John Corvino, 17–30. Lanham, Md.: Rowman & Littlefield, 1997.

Browne, Kath, Jason Lim, and Gavin Brown, eds. *Geographies of Sexualities: Theory, Practices and Politics*. Aldershot, U.K.: Ashgate, 2007.

Buccola, Nicholas. "Finding Room for Same-Sex Marriage: Toward a More Inclusive Understanding of a Cultural Institution." *Journal of Social Philosophy* 36:3 (2005): 331–43.

Byne, William, and Edward Stein. "Ethical Implications of Scientific Research on the Causes of Sexual Orientation." *Health Care Analysis* 5:2 (1997): 136–48.

Calhoun, Cheshire. *Feminism, the Family, and the Politics of the Closet: Lesbian and Gay Displacement*. Oxford, U.K.: Oxford University Press, 2000.

———. "Separating Lesbian Theory from Feminist Theory." *Ethics* 104:3 (1994): 558–81.

Califia, Patrick. *Sex Changes: The Politics of Transgenderism*. San Francisco: Cleis Press, 2003.

Callahan, Joan. "Same-Sex Marriage: Why It Matters—At Least for Now." *Hypatia* 24:1 (2009): 70–80.

Callahan, Sidney. "Why I Changed My Mind: Thinking about Gay Marriage." *Commonweal* (April 22, 1994): 6–8.

Card, Claudia. *Lesbian Choices*. New York: Columbia University Press, 1995.

———. *On Feminist Ethics and Politics*. Lawrence, Kan.: University Press of Kansas, 1999.

———, ed. *Adventures in Lesbian Philosophy*. Bloomington, Ind.: Indiana University Press, 1985.

Cárdenas, Micha. *Trans Desire*. New York: Atropos Press, 2010.

Colene Hume, Maggi. "Sex, Lies, and Surgery: The Ethics of Gender-Reassignment Surgery." *Dialogue* 53:2–3 (2011): 140-48.

Colter, Ephen Glenn, Wayne Hoffman, Eva Pendleton, Alison Redick, and David Serlin, eds. *Policing Public Sex: Queer Politics and the Future of AIDS Activism*. Boston: South End Press, 1996.

Conrad, Ryan, ed. *Against Equality: Queer Critiques of Gay Marriage*. Lewiston, Maine: Against Equality Publishing Collective, 2010.

Cooley, D. R. "Non-Heterosexuals in Heterosexual Marriages as a Form of Spousal Abuse." *International Journal of Applied Philosophy* 21:2 (2007): 161–79.

Corvino, John. "Analyzing Gender." *Southwest Philosophy Review* 17:1 (2000): 173–80.

———. "Homosexuality and the Moral Relevance of Experience." In *Ethics in Practice*, 2nd ed., edited by Hugh LaFollette, 241–50. Oxford, U.K.: Blackwell, 2001.

———. "Homosexuality and the PIB Argument." *Ethics* 115:3 (2005): 501–34.

———, ed. *Same Sex: Debating the Ethics, Science, and Culture of Homosexuality*. Lanham, Md.: Rowman & Littlefield, 1997.

Corvino, John, and Maggie Gallagher. *Debating Same-Sex Marriage*. New York: Oxford University Press, 2012.

Crompton, Louis. *Homosexuality and Civilization*. Cambridge, Mass.: Harvard University Press, 2003.

Currah, Paisley, and Lisa Jean Moore. "'We Won't Know Who You Are': Contesting Sex Designations in New York City Birth Certificates." *Hypatia* 24:3 (2009): 113–35.

Currah, Paisley, Richard M. Juang, and Shannon Price Minter, eds. *Transgender Rights*. Minneapolis, Minn.: University of Minnesota Press, 2006.

Daper, Heather, and Neil Evans. "Transsexualism and Gender Reassignment Surgery." In *Cutting to the Core: Exploring the Ethics of Contested Surgeries*, edited by David Benatar, 97–110. Lanham, Md.: Rowman & Littlefield, 2006.

Dean, Craig R. "Fighting for Same Sex Marriage." In *Gender Basics*, edited by Anne Minas, 275–77. Belmont, Calif.: Wadsworth, 1993, pp. 275–77.

Diamond, Lisa M. *Sexual Fluidity: Understanding Women's Love and Desire*. Cambridge, Mass.: Harvard University Press, 2009.

Dover, Kenneth. *Greek Homosexuality*, updated and with a new postscript. Cambridge, Mass.: Harvard University Press, 1989; original publication 1978.

Dreger, Alice Domurat. *Hermaphrodites and the Medical Invention of Sex.* Cambridge, Mass.: Harvard University Press, 1998.

Elliot, Patricia. *Debates in Transgender, Queer, and Feminist Theory: Contested Sites.* Farnham, U.K.: Ashgate, 2010.

Elliston, Frederick. "Gay Marriage." In *Philosophy and Sex*, 2nd ed., edited by Robert Baker and Frederick Elliston, 146–66. Buffalo, N.Y.: Prometheus, 1984.

Eskridge, William N., Jr. *The Case for Same-Sex Marriage: From Sexual Liberty to Civilized Commitment.* New York: Free Press, 1996.

Feit, Mario. *Democratic Anxieties: Same-Sex Marriage, Death, and Citizenship.* Lanham, Md.: Lexington Books, 2011.

Ferguson, Ann. "Gay Marriage: An American and Feminist Dilemma." *Hypatia* 22:1 (2007): 39–57.

Finnis, John. "Law, Morality, and 'Sexual Orientation'." *Notre Dame Law Review* 69:5 (1994): 1049–76.

———. "Natural Law and Unnatural Acts." In *Human Sexuality*, edited by Igor Primoratz, 5–27. Aldershot, U.K.: Dartmouth, 1997.

———. "The Wrong of Homosexuality." *The New Republic* (November 15, 1993), 12–13. Reprinted in *The Philosophy of Sex*, 5th ed., edited by Alan Soble and Nicholas Power, 135–39. Lanham, Md.: Rowman & Littlefield, 2008.

Freeman, M. D. A. "Not Such a Queer Idea: Is There a Case for Same Sex Marriages?" *Journal of Applied Philosophy* 16:1 (1999): 1–17.

Friedman, Lauri S., ed. *Gay Marriage.* Detroit, Mich.: Greenhaven Press, 2010.

Galupo, M. Paz, ed. *Bisexuality and Same-Sex Marriage.* London: Routledge, 2009.

Garber, Marjorie. *Bisexuality and the Eroticism of Everyday Life.* New York: Routledge, 2000.

———. *Vice Versa: Bisexuality and the Eroticism of Everyday Life.* New York: Simon and Schuster, 1995.

Garrett, Jeremy. "Public Reasons for Private Vows: A Response to Gilboa." *Public Affairs Quarterly* 23:3 (2009): 261ff.

Gilbert, Miqqi Alicia. "Defeating Bigenderism: Changing Gender Assumptions in the Twenty-first Century." *Hypatia* 24:3 (2009): 93–112.

Gilboa, David. "Same-Sex Marriage in a Liberal Democracy: Between Rejection and Recognition." *Public Affairs Quarterly* 23:3 (2009): 245–60.

———. "Marriages, Services, and Contracts: A Reply to Garrett." *Public Affairs Quarterly* 23:4 (2009): 325–36.

Glick, Elisa. "Feminism, Queer Theory, and the Politics of Transgression." *Feminist Review* 64 (Spring, 2000): 19–45.

Gray, John Scott. "Rawls's Principle of Justice and Its Application to the Issue of Same-Sex Marriage." *Southern African Journal of Philosophy* 23:2 (2004): 158–70. Reprinted in *Philosophy and Sex*, 4th ed., edited by Robert B. Baker and Kathleen Wininger, 197–212. Amherst, N.Y.: Prometheus Books, 2009.

Hale, C. Jacob. "Are Lesbians Women?" *Hypatia* 11:2 (1996): 94–121.

———. "Leather Dyke Boys and Their Daddies: How to Have Sex without Men and Women." *Social Text* 16:3–4 (1997): 223–36.

———. "Tracing a Ghostly Memory in My Throat: Reflections on FTM Feminist Voice and Agency." In *"You've Changed": Sex Reassignment and Personal Identity*, edited by Laurie Shrage, 43–65. Oxford, U.K.: Oxford University Press, 2009.

Hall, Donald E., and Maria Pramaggiore, eds. *Representing Bisexualities: Subjects and Cultures of Fluid Desire.* New York: New York University Press, 1996.

Halperin, David M. *One Hundred Years of Homosexuality.* New York: Routledge, 1990.

Hamer, Dean, and Peter Copeland. *The Science of Desire.* New York: Simon and Schuster, 1994.

Herdt, Gilbert. *Sambia Sexual Culture: Essays from the Field.* Chicago: University of Chicago Press, 1999.

Heyes, Cressida J. "Changing Race, Changing Sex: The Ethics of Self-Transformation." *Journal of Social Philosophy* 37:2 (2006): 266–82.

Hines, Sally. *TransForming Gender: Transgender Practices of Identity, Intimacy and Care*. Bristol, U.K.: Policy Press, 2007.

Hines, Sally, and Tam Sanger, eds. *Transgender Identities: Towards a Social Analysis of Gender Diversity*. New York: Routledge, 2010.

Hope, Debra A., ed. *Contemporary Perspectives on Lesbian, Gay, and Bisexual Identities*. New York: Springer, 2009.

Hutchins, Loraine, and Lana Kaahumanu, eds. *Bi Any Other Name*. Los Angeles: Alyson Publications, 1991.

Jordan, Jeff. "Is It Wrong to Discriminate on the Basis of Homosexuality?" *Journal of Social Philosophy* 25:1 (1995): 39–52. Reprinted in *Philosophy and Sex*, 3rd ed., edited by Robert B. Baker, Kathleen J. Wininger, and Frederick A. Elliston, 177–89. Amherst, N.Y.: Prometheus Books, 1998; and 4th ed., edited by Robert B. Baker and Kathleen J. Wininger, 184–96. Amherst, N.Y.: Prometheus Books, 2009.

Jordan, Mark D. *Recruiting Young Love: How Christians Talk about Homosexuality*. Chicago: University of Chicago Press, 2011.

Jung, Patricia, and Ralph Smith. *Heterosexism: An Ethical Challenge*. Albany, N.Y.: State University of New York Press, 1993.

Kheshti, Roshanak. "Cross-Dressing and Gender (Tres)Passing: The Transgender Move as a Site of Agential Potential in the New Iranian Cinema." *Hypatia* 24:3 (2009): 158–77.

Klesse, Christian. *The Spectre of Promiscuity: Gay Male and Bisexual Non-Monogamies and Polyamories*. Aldershot, U.K.: Ashgate, 2007.

Koppelman, Andrew. "The Decline and Fall of the Case against Same-Sex Marriage." *University of St. Thomas Law Journal* 2:1 (2004): 5–32.

———. *The Gay Rights Question in Contemporary American Law*. Chicago: University of Chicago Press, 2002.

———. "Homosexual Conduct: A Reply to the New Natural Lawyers." In *Same Sex: Debating the Ethics, Science, and Culture of Homosexuality*, edited by John Corvino, 44–57. Lanham, Md.: Rowman & Littlefield, 1997.

———. "Homosexuality and Infertility." In *The Philosophy of Sex*, 5th ed., edited by Alan Soble and Nicholas Power, 141–54. Lanham, Md.: Rowman & Littlefield, 2008.

———. *Same Sex, Different States: When Same-Sex Marriages Cross State Lines*. New Haven, Conn.: Yale University Press, 2006.

Lane, Riki. "Trans as Bodily Becoming: Rethinking the Biological as Diversity, Not Dichotomy." *Hypatia* 24:3 (2009): 136–57.

Lee, Patrick K. "Marriage, Procreation, and Same-Sex Unions." *The Monist* 91:3–4 (2008): 422–38 (with a reply by Adéle Mercier [439–441] and a rejoinder by Lee [442–45]).

Lee, Rosa. *Why Feminists Are Wrong: How Transsexuals Prove Gender Is Not a Social Construction*. Philadelphia: Xlibris Corp., 2006.

LeVay, Simon. *Queer Science*. Cambridge, Mass.: MIT Press, 1996.

———. *The Sexual Brain*. Cambridge, Mass.: MIT Press, 1993.

Levin, Michael. "Homosexuality, Abnormality, and Civil Rights." *Public Affairs Quarterly* 10:1 (1996): 31–48.

———. "Why Homosexuality Is Abnormal." *The Monist* 67:2 (1984): 251–83.

Mann, Bonnie. "Gay Marriage and the War on Terror." *Hypatia* 22:1 (2007): 247–51.

March, Andrew F. "What Lies Beyond Same-Sex Marriage? Marriage, Reproductive Freedom and Future Persons in Liberal Public Justification." *Journal of Applied Philosophy* 27:1 (2010): 39–58.

Mayo, David. "An Obligation to Warn of HIV Infection?" In *Sex, Love and Friendship*, edited by Alan Soble, 447–53. Amsterdam: Rodopi, 1997.

Mead, Margaret. "Bisexuality: A New Awareness." In *Aspects of the Present*, edited by Margaret Mead and Rhoda Metraux, 271–86. New York: William Morrow, 1980.

Mercier, Adéle. "On the Nature of Marriage: Somerville on Same-Sex Marriage." *The Monist* 91:3–4 (2008): 407–21.

Mohr, Richard D. "The Case for Gay Marriage." *Notre Dame Journal of Law, Ethics, and Public Policy* 9 (1995): 215–39.

———. *Gay Ideas*. Boston: Beacon Press, 1992.

———. *Gays/Justice*. New York: Columbia University Press, 1988.

———. *The Long Arc of Justice: Lesbian and Gay Marriage, Equality, and Rights*. New York: Columbia University Press, 2005.

———. *A More Perfect Union*. Boston: Beacon Press, 1994.

Moore, Gareth. "Natural Sex: Germain Grisez, Sex, and Natural Law." In *The Revival of Natural Law: Philosophical, Theological and Ethical Responses to the Finnis-Grisez School*, edited by Nigel Biggar and Rufus Black, 223–41. Aldershot, U.K.: Ashgate, 2000.

———. *A Question of Truth: Christianity and Homosexuality*. New York: Continuum, 2003.

Murphy, Timothy F. "Homosexuality and Nature: Happiness and the Law at Stake." *Journal of Applied Philosophy* 4:2 (1987): 195–204.

———, ed. *Gay Ethics: Controversies in Outing, Civil Rights, and Sexual Science*. Binghamton, N.Y.: Haworth, 1994.

Myerson, Marilyn, Sara L. Crawley, Erica Hesch Anstey, Justine Kessler, and Cara Okopny. "Who's Zoomin' Who? A Feminist, Queer Content Analysis of 'Interdisciplinary' Human Sexuality Textbooks." *Hypatia* 22:1 (2007): 92–113.

Nagle, Jeanne. *Same-Sex Marriage: The Debate*. New York: Rosen Publishing, 2010.

Namaste, Viviane. "Undoing Theory: The 'Transgender Question' and the Epistemic Violence of Anglo-American Feminist Theory." *Hypatia* 24:3 (2009): 11–32.

Neu, Jerome. "Sexual Identity and Sexual Justice." *Ethics* 108:3 (1998): 586–96. Reprinted in *The Philosophy of Sex*, 5th ed., edited by Alan Soble and Nicholas Power, 213–25. Lanham, Md.: Rowman & Littlefield, 2008.

Nussbaum, Martha. "Platonic Love and Colorado Law: The Relevance of Ancient Greek Norms to Modern Sexual Controversies." *Virginia Law Review* 80:7 (1994): 1515–1651.

———. *From Disgust to Humanity: Sexual Orientation and Constitutional Law*. Oxford, U.K.: Oxford University Press, 2010.

Ouellette, Alicia. "Moral Reasoning in Judicial Decisions on Same-Sex Marriage." In *Philosophy and Sex*, 4th ed., edited by Robert B. Baker and Kathleen J. Wininger, 168–83. Amherst, N.Y.: Prometheus Books, 2009.

Penney, James. *The World of Perversion: Psychoanalysis and the Impossible Absolute of Desire*. Albany, N.Y.: SUNY Press, 2006.

Perry, Michael J. "Same-Sex Unions." In *The Political Morality of Liberal Democracy*. Cambridge, U.K.: Cambridge University Press, 2010, pp. 138–55.

Polikoff, Nancy D. *Beyond Gay and Straight Marriage: Valuing All Families under the Law*. Boston: Beacon Press, 2008.

Prager, Dennis. "Homosexuality, the Bible, and Us—A Jewish Perspective." *The Public Interest*, No. 112 (Summer 1993): 60–83.

Pronk, Pim. *Against Nature? Types of Moral Argumentation Regarding Homosexuality*. Grand Rapids, Mich.: W. B. Eerdmans, 1993.

Quinn, Carol, ed. *American Philosophical Association Newsletter on Philosophy and Lesbian, Gay, Bisexual, and Transgender Issues* 4:1 (Fall 2004) [Issue on Same-Sex Marriage] .

Rajczi, Alex. "A Populist Argument for Legalizing Same-Sex Marriage." *The Monist* 91:3–4 (2008): 475–505.

Reamer, Frederic G., ed. *AIDS & Ethics*. New York: Columbia University Press, 1991.

Rich, Adrienne. "Compulsory Heterosexuality and Lesbian Existence." In *Blood, Bread and Poetry*. New York: W. W. Norton, 1986, pp. 23–75; original publication, 1980.

Richards, David A. J. *Women, Gays, and the Constitution: The Grounds for Feminism and Gay Rights in Culture and Law*. Chicago: University of Chicago Press, 1998.

Robinson, Paul. *Gay Lives: Homosexual Autobiography from John Addington Symonds to Paul Monette*. Chicago: University of Chicago Press, 1999.

Robson, Ruthann. "A Mere Switch or a Fundamental Change? Theorizing Transgender Marriage." *Hypatia* 22:1 (2007): 58–70.

Rosario, Vernon A., ed. *Science and Homosexualities*. New York: Routledge, 1997.

Ross, Michael W., and Jay P. Paul. "Beyond Gender: The Basis of Sexual Attraction in Bisexual Men and Women." *Psychological Reports* 71:3 (1992): 1283–90.

Rubin, Henry. *Self-Made Men: Identity and Embodiment among Transsexuals*. Nashville, Tenn.: Vanderbilt University Press, 2003.

Ruse, Michael. *Homosexuality: A Philosophical Inquiry*. New York: Blackwell, 1988.

Sadler, Brook J. "Rethinking Civil Unions and Same-Sex Marriage." *The Monist* 91:3–4 (2008): 578–605.

Samons, Sandra L. *When the Opposite Sex Isn't: Sexual Orientation in Male-to-Female Transgender People*. New York: Routledge, 2009.

Schaff, Kory. "Equal Protection and Same-Sex Marriage." *Journal of Social Philosophy* 35:1 (2004): 133–47.

———. "Kant, Political Liberalism, and the Ethics of Same-Sex Relations." *Journal of Social Philosophy* 32:3 (2001): 446–62.

Scheman, Naomi. "Queering the Center by Centering the Queer." In *Feminists Rethink the Self*, edited by Diana Tietjens Meyers, 124–62. Boulder, Colo.: Westview Press, 1997.

Scott-Dixon, Krista. "Public Health, Private Parts: A Feminist Public-Health Approach to Trans Issues." *Hypatia* 24:3 (2009): 33–55.

Shotwell, Alexis, and Trevor Sangrey. "Resisting Definition: Gendering through Interaction and Relational Selfhood." *Hypatia* 24:3 (2009): 55–76.

Shrage, Laurie, ed. *"You've Changed": Sex Reassignment and Personal Identity*. Oxford, U.K.: Oxford University Press, 2009.

Snorton, C. Riley. "'A New Hope': The Psychic Life of Passing." *Hypatia* 24:3 (2009): 77–92.

Snyder, Jane M. *Lesbian Desire in the Lyrics of Sappho*. New York: Columbia University Press, 1997.

Soble, Alan. "Kant and Sexual Perversion." *The Monist* 86:1 (2003): 57–92.

Spriggs, Merle, and Julian Savulescu. "The Ethics of Surgically Assigning Sex for Intersex Children." In *Cutting to the Core: Exploring the Ethics of Contested Surgeries*, edited by David Benatar, 79–96. Lanham, Md.: Rowman & Littlefield, 2006.

Stafford, J. Martin. "Love and Lust Revisited: Intentionality, Homosexuality and Moral Education." *Journal of Applied Philosophy* 5:1 (1988): 87–100.

———. "The Two Minds of Roger Scruton." *Studies in Philosophy and Education* 11 (1991): 187–93.

Stein, Edward. *The Mismeasure of Desire: The Science, Theory, and Ethics of Sexual Orientation*. Oxford: Oxford University Press, 2001.

———. "The Relevance of Scientific Research about Sexual Orientation to Lesbian and Gay Rights." *Journal of Homosexuality* 27:3–4 (1994): 269–308.

Storms, Michael D. "Theories of Sexual Orientation." *Journal of Personality and Social Psychology* 38:4 (1980): 783–92.

Storr, Merl, ed. *Bisexuality: A Critical Reader*. London: Routledge, 1999.

Strasser, Mark. *Legally Wed*. Ithaca, N.Y.: Cornell University Press, 1997.

———. *On Same-Sex Marriage, Civil Unions, and the Rule of Law: Constitutional Interpretation at the Crossroads*. Westport, Conn.: Praeger, 2002.

Strasser, Mark Philip, Traci C. West, Martin Dupuis, and William A. Thompson, eds. *Defending Same-Sex Marriage*. Westport, Conn.: Praeger, 2007.

Stroll, Avrum. "A Defense of Same-Sex Marriage." *Public Affairs Quarterly* 23:4 (2009): 343–56.

Stryker, Susan, and Stephen Wittle, eds. *The Transgender Studies Reader*. New York: Routledge, 2006.

Sullivan, Andrew. *Love Undetectable: Reflections on Friendship, Sex, and Survival*. New York: Knopf, 1998.

———. *Virtually Normal: An Argument about Homosexuality*. New York: Knopf, 1995.

———, ed. *Same-Sex Marriage: Pro and Con*. New York: Vintage, 2004.

Thomas, Laurence M., and Michael E. Levin. *Sexual Orientation and Human Rights.* Lanham, Md.: Rowman & Littlefield, 1999.

Vacek, Edward. "A Christian Homosexuality?" *Commonweal* (December 5, 1980), 681–84.

Vernallis, Kayley. "Bisexual Monogamy: Twice the Temptation but Half the Fun?" *Journal of Social Philosophy* 30:3 (1999): 347–68.

Vernon, Jim. "Free Love: A Hegelian Defense of Same-Sex Marriage Rights." *The Southern Journal of Philosophy* 47:1 (2009): 69–89.

Wardle, Lynn D., ed. *What's the Harm? Does Legalizing Same-Sex Marriage Really Harm Individuals, Families, or Society?* Lanham, Md.: University Press of America, 2008.

Wardle, Lynn D., Mark Strasser, William C. Duncan, and David Orgon Coolidge, eds. *Marriage and Same-Sex Unions: A Debate.* Westport, Conn.: Praeger, 2003.

Wedgwood, Ralph. "Same-Sex Marriage: A Philosophical Defense." In *Philosophy and Sex*, 3rd ed., edited by Robert B. Baker, Kathleen J. Wininger, and Frederick A. Elliston, 212–30. Amherst, N.Y.: Prometheus Books, 1998.

Weinberg, Martin S., Colin J. Williams, and Douglas Pryor. *Dual Attraction: Understanding Bisexuality.* Oxford: Oxford University Press, 1994.

Weise, Elizabeth Reba, ed. *Closer to Home: Bisexuality and Feminism.* Seattle: Seal Press, 1992.

Weithman, Paul J. "Natural Law, Morality, and Sexual Complementarity." In *Sex, Preference, and Family: Essays on Law and Nature*, edited by David M. Estlund and Martha C. Nussbaum, 227–46. New York: Oxford University Press, 1997.

Wellington, A. A. "Why Liberals Should Support Same-Sex Marriage." *Journal of Social Philosophy* 26:3 (1995): 5–32.

Wilkerson, William S. *Ambiguity and Sexuality: A Theory of Sexual Identity.* New York: Palgrave Macmillan, 2007.

———. "Is It a Choice? Sexual Orientation as Interpretation." *Journal of Social Philosophy* 40:1 (2009): 97–116.

Williams, Craig A. *Roman Homosexuality: Ideologies of Masculinity in Classical Antiquity.* New York: Oxford University Press, 1999.

Williams, Reginald. "Same-Sex Marriage and Equality." *Ethical Theory and Moral Practice* 14:5 (2011): 589–95.

Wittig, Monique. *The Lesbian Body* [*Le Corps Lesbien*], translated by David LeVay. Boston: Beacon Press, 1973.

Zylan, Yvonne. *States of Passion: Law, Identity, and the Social Construction of Desire.* Oxford: Oxford University Press, 2011.

CONTRACEPTION AND ABORTION

Anscombe, G. E. M. "Contraception and Chastity." *The Human World* no. 7 (1972), 9–30. Reprinted (with criticisms and a rebuttal) in *Ethics and Population*, edited by Michael Bayles, 134–53. Cambridge, Mass.: Schenkman, 1976.

———. "You Can Have Sex without Children." In *Ethics, Religion and Politics*. Minneapolis: University of Minnesota Press, 198, pp. 82–96.

Archard, David, and David Benatar, eds. *Procreation and Parenthood: The Ethics of Bearing and Rearing Children.* Oxford: Oxford University Press, 2010.

Beckwith, Francis J. *Defending Life: A Moral and Legal Case against Abortion Choice.* New York: Cambridge University Press, 2007.

Beis, Richard H. "Contraception and the Logical Structure of the Thomist Natural Law Theory." *Ethics* 75:4 (1965): 277–84.

Berlatsky, Noah, ed. *Abortion.* Farmington Hills, Mich.: Greenhaven Press, 2011.

Boonin-Vail, David. "A Defense of 'A Defense of Abortion': On the Responsibility Objection to Thomson's Argument." *Ethics* 107:2 (1997): 286–313.

Brake, Elizabeth. "Fatherhood and Child Support: Do Men Have a Right to Choose?" *Journal of Applied Philosophy* 22:1 (2005): 55–73.

Brody, Baruch. "Thomson on Abortion." *Philosophy and Public Affairs* 1:3 (1972): 335–40.

Cahill, Lisa Sowle. "Grisez on Sex and Gender: A Feminist Theological Perspective." In *The Revival of Natural Law: Philosophical, Theological and Ethical Responses to the Finnis-Grisez School*, edited by Nigel Biggar and Rufus Black, 242–61. Aldershot, U.K.: Ashgate, 2000.

Callahan, Daniel. *Abortion: Law, Choice, and Morality*. New York: Macmillan, 1970.

Callahan, Joan C. "The Fetus and Fundamental Rights." *Commonweal* (April 11, 1986): 203–7. Reprinted, revised, in *The Ethics of Abortion: Pro-Life vs. Pro-Choice*, revised ed., edited by Robert M. Baird and Stuart E. Rosenbaum, 249–62. Buffalo, N.Y.: Prometheus, 1993.

Callahan, Sidney. "Abortion and the Sexual Agenda." *Commonweal* (April 25, 1986): 232–38. Reprinted in *The Ethics of Abortion: Pro-Life vs. Pro-Choice*, revised ed., edited by Robert M. Baird and Stuart E. Rosenbaum, 111–21. Buffalo, N.Y.: Prometheus, 1993; and in *Philosophy of Sex*, 3rd ed., edited by Alan Soble, 151–64, and 4th ed., 177–90.

Cohen, Carl. "Sex, Birth Control, and Human Life." In *Philosophy and Sex*, 2nd ed., edited by Robert Baker and Frederick Elliston, 185–99. Buffalo, N.Y.: Prometheus, 1984.

Cohen, Howard. "Abortion and the Quality of Life." In *Feminism and Philosophy*, edited by Mary Vetterling-Braggin, Frederick Elliston, and Jane English, 429–40. Totowa, N.J.: Rowman & Littlefield, 1977.

Corea, Gena. *The Mother Machine: Reproductive Technologies from Artificial Insemination to Artificial Wombs*. New York: Harper and Row, 1986.

Dadlez, E. M., and William L. Andrews. "Federally Funded Elective Abortion: They Can Run, but They Can't Hyde." *International Journal of Applied Philosophy* 24:2 (2010): 169–84.

Denis, Lara. "Abortion and Kant's Formula of Universal Law." *Canadian Journal of Philosophy* 37:4 (2007): 547–80.

Diorio, Joseph A. "Contraception, Copulation Domination, and the Theoretical Barrenness of Sex Education Literature." *Educational Theory* 35:3 (1985): 239–54.

Dworkin, Ronald. *Life's Dominion: An Argument about Abortion, Euthanasia, and Individual Freedom*. New York: Knopf, 1993.

Finnis, John M. "Law, Morality, and 'Sexual Orientation.'" *Notre Dame Law Review* 69:5 (1994): 1049–76.

———. "Natural Law and Unnatural Acts." In *Human Sexuality*, edited by Igor Primoratz, 5–27. Aldershot, U.K.: Dartmouth, 1997.

Geach, Mary. "Marriage: Arguing to a First Principle in Sexual Ethics." In *Moral Truth and Moral Tradition: Essays in Honour of Peter Geach and Elizabeth Anscombe*, edited by Luke Gormally, 177–93. Dublin: Four Courts Press, 1994.

Grisez, Germain, Joseph Boyle, John Finnis, William E. May, and John C. Ford. *The Teaching of "Humanae vitae": A Defense*. San Francisco: Ignatius Press, 1988.

Hanrahan, Rebecca. "The Decision to Abort." *International Journal of Applied Philosophy* 21:1 (2007): 25–41.

Holbrook, Daniel. "All Embryos Are Equal? Issues in Pre-implantation Genetic Diagnosis, IVF Implantation, Embryonic Stem Cell Research, and Therapeutic Cloning." *International Journal of Applied Philosophy* 21:1 (2007): 43–53.

Hopkins, Patrick D. "Can Technology Fix the Abortion Problem? Ectogenesis and the Real Issues of Abortion." *International Journal of Applied Philosophy* 22:2 (2008): 311–26.

Hull, Richard T., ed. *Ethical Issues in the Reproductive Technologies*. Amherst, N.Y.: Prometheus, 2005; original publication, 1990.

John Paul II (Pope). "*Evangelium vitae*." *Origins* 24:42 (1995): 689–727.

Kaczor, Christopher. *The Ethics of Abortion: Women's Rights, Human Life, and the Question of Justice*. New York: Routledge, 2011.

Kamm, Frances Myrna. *Creation and Abortion: A Study in Moral and Legal Philosophy*. Oxford: Oxford University Press, 1992.

Kornegay, R. Jo. "Hursthouse's Virtue Ethics and Abortion: Abortion Ethics without Metaphysics?" *Ethical Theory and Moral Practice* 14:1 (2011): 51–71.

Lee, Patrick. *Abortion and Unborn Human Life*, 2nd ed. Washington, D.C.: Catholic University Press of America, 2010.

Lindemann, Hilde. "'. . . But *I* Could Never Have One': The Abortion Intuition and Moral Luck." *Hypatia* 24:1 (2009): 41–55.

Lowe, Pam. "Contraception and Heterosex: An Intimate Relationship." *Sexualities* 8:1 (2005): 75–92.

Luper, Steven. "Abortion." In *The Philosophy of Death*. Cambridge: Cambridge University Press, 2009, pp. 197–218.

Manninen, Bertha Alvarez. "Pleading Men and Virtuous Women: Considering the Role of the Father in the Abortion Debate." *International Journal of Applied Philosophy* 21:1 (2007): 1–24.

Marquis, Don. "Abortion Revisited." In *The Oxford Handbook of Bioethics*, edited by Bonnie Steinbock, 395–415. Oxford: Oxford University Press, 2007.

———. "Why Abortion Is Immoral." *Journal of Philosophy* 86:4 (1989): 183–202.

Martin, Christopher F. J. "Are There Virtues and Vices That Belong Specifically to the Sexual Life?" *Acta Philosophica* 4:2 (1995): 205–21.

Merino, Noël, ed. *Birth Control*. Farmington Hills, Mich.: Greenhaven Press, 2011.

Meyers, Chris. *The Fetal Position: A Rational Approach to the Abortion Issue*. Amherst, N.Y.: Prometheus Books, 2010.

Murphy, Timothy F. "Abortion and the Ethics of Genetic Sexual Orientation Research." *Cambridge Quarterly of Healthcare Ethics* 4:4 (1995): 340–50.

Napier, Stephen, ed. *Persons, Moral Worth, and Embryos: A Critical Analysis of Pro-Choice Arguments*. Dordrecht, Netherlands: Springer, 2011.

Nicholson, Susan T. *Abortion and the Roman Catholic Church*. Knoxville, Tenn.: Religious Ethics, 1978.

Noonan, John T. *Contraception: A History of Its Treatment by the Catholic Theologians and Canonists*, enlarged ed. Cambridge, Mass.: Harvard University Press, 1986.

———, ed. *The Morality of Abortion*. Cambridge, Mass.: Harvard University Press, 1970.

Oshana, Marina. "Autonomy and the Partial-Birth Abortion Act." *Journal of Social Philosophy* 42:1 (2011): 46–60.

Paden, Roger. "Abortion and Sexual Morality." In *Sex, Love, and Friendship*, edited by Alan Soble, 229–36. Amsterdam: Rodopi, 1997.

Paul VI (Pope). "*Humanae vitae*." *Catholic Mind* 66 (September 1968): 35–48. Reprinted in *Philosophy and Sex*, 2nd ed., edited by Robert Baker and Frederick Elliston, 167–83. Buffalo, N.Y.: Prometheus, 1984, pp. 167–83.

Perry, Michael J. "Abortion." In *The Political Morality of Liberal Democracy*. Cambridge: Cambridge University Press, 2010, pp. 123–37.

Pius XI (Pope). "On Christian Marriage" [*Casti connubii*]. *Catholic Mind* 29:2 (1931): 21–64.

Rapaport, Elizabeth, and Paul Segal. "One Step Forward, Two Steps Backward: Abortion and Ethical Theory." In *Feminism and Philosophy*, edited by Mary Vetterling-Braggin, Frederick Elliston, and Jane English, 408–16. Totowa, N.J.: Littlefield Adams, 1977.

Reiman, Jeffrey. "Abortion, Infanticide, and the Asymmetric Value of Human Life." *Journal of Social Philosophy* 27:3 (1996): 181–200. Reprinted in *Philosophy and Sex*, 3rd ed., edited by Robert B. Baker, Kathleen J. Wininger, and Frederick A. Elliston, 261–78. Amherst, N.Y.: Prometheus Books, 1998.

Roberts, Melinda A. *Abortion and the Moral Significance of Merely Possible Persons: Finding Middle Ground in Hard Cases*. Heidelberg, Germany: Springer, 2010.

Shrage, Laurie. *Moral Dilemmas of Feminism: Prostitution, Adultery, and Abortion.* New York: Routledge, 1994.

Silverstein, Harry. "On a Woman's 'Responsibility' for the Fetus." *Social Theory and Practice* 13:1 (1987): 103–19.

Smith, Holly M. "Intercourse and Moral Responsibility for the Fetus." In *Abortion and the Status of the Fetus,* edited by W. B. Bondeson, H. T. Engelhardt Jr., S. F. Spicker, and D. H. Winship, 229–45. Dordrecht, Netherlands: Reidel, 1983.

Soble, Alan. "More on Abortion and Sexual Morality." In *Sex, Love, and Friendship,* edited by Alan Soble, 239–44. Amsterdam: Rodopi, 1997.

Solomon, Robert. "Sex, Contraception, and Conceptions of Sex." In *Thirteen Questions in Ethics,* 2nd ed., edited by G. Lee Bowie, Meredith W. Michaels, and Kathleen Higgins. 95–107. Fort Worth, Tex.: Harcourt Brace, 1992.

Steffen, Lloyd, ed. *Abortion: A Reader.* Eugene, Ore.: Wipf & Stock, 2010.

Steinbock, Bonnie. *Life before Birth: The Moral and Legal Status of Embryos and Fetuses,* 2nd ed. New York: Oxford University Press, 2011.

Teichman, Jenny. "Intention and Sex." In *Intention and Intentionality: Essays in Honour of G. E. M. Anscombe,* edited by Cora Diamond and Jenny Teichman, 147–61. Ithaca, N.Y.: Cornell University Press, 1979.

Thomson, Judith Jarvis. "A Defense of Abortion." *Philosophy and Public Affairs* 1:1 (1971): 47–66.

Tooley, Michael, Celia Wolf-Devine, Philip E. Devine, and Alison M. Jaggar. *Abortion: Three Perspectives.* New York: Oxford University Press, 2009.

Watt, E. D. "Professor Cohen's Encyclical." *Ethics* 80 (1970): 218–21.

Whitehead, Mary Beth, and Loretta Schwartz-Nobel. *A Mother's Story: The Truth about the Baby M Case.* New York: St. Martin's Press, 1989.

Wilcox, John T. "Nature as Demonic in Thomson's Defense of Abortion." *The New Scholasticism* 63:4 (1989): 463–84.

Willis, Ellen. "Abortion: Is a Woman a Person?" In *Beginning to See the Light.* New York: Knopf, 1981, pp. 205–11. Reprinted in *Powers of Desire: The Politics of Sexuality,* edited by Ann Snitow, Christine Stansell, and Sharon Thompson, 471–76. New York: Monthly Review Press, 1983; and in *Philosophy of Sex,* 3rd ed., edited by Alan Soble, 165–69, and 4th ed., 191–95.

Wilson, George B. "Christian Conjugal Morality and Contraception." In *Population Ethics,* edited by Francis X. Quinn, 98–108. Washington, D.C.: Corpus, 1968.

Wolf-Devine, Celia. "Abortion and the Feminine Voice." *Public Affairs Quarterly* 3:3 (1989): 81–97. Reprinted in *The Problem of Abortion,* 3rd ed., edited by Susan Dwyer and Joel Feinberg, 160–74. Belmont, Calif.: Wadsworth, 1997; and in *Sex and Gender: A Spectrum of Views,* edited by Philip E. Devine and Celia Wolf-Devine, 163–72. Belmont, Calif.: Wadsworth, 2003.

Yeung, Anthony. "Abortion and the Potential Person Argument." In *New Essays in Applied Ethics: Animal Rights, Personhood and the Ethics of Killing,* edited by Hon-Lam Li and Anthony Yeung, 132–52. Basingstoke, U.K.: Palgrave Macmillan, 2007.

Zaner, Richard M. "A Criticism of Moral Conservatism's View of *In Vitro* Fertilization and Embryo Transfer." *Perspectives in Biology and Medicine* 27:2 (1984): 201–12.

SEX, LOVE, AND MARRIAGE

(For Same-Sex Marriage, See Homosexuality and Queer Issues)

Almond, Brenda. *The Fragmenting Family.* Oxford: Clarendon Press, 2006.

Anapol, Deborah M. *Love without Limits: The Quest for Sustainable Intimate Relationships.* San Rafael, Calif.: IntiNet Resource Center, 1992.

———. *Polyamory in the 21st Century: Love and Intimacy with Multiple Partners.* Lanham, Md.: Roman & Littlefield, 2010.

Archard, David, and David Benatar, eds. *Procreation and Parenthood: The Ethics of Bearing and Rearing Children*. Oxford, U.K.: Oxford University Press, 2010.

Barash, David P., and Judith Eve Lipton. *The Myth of Monogamy: Fidelity and Infidelity in Animals and People*. New York: Henry Holt, 2001.

Barker, Meg, and Darren Langdridge, eds. *Understanding Non-Monogamies*. New York: Routledge, 2011.

Barnhart, J. E. and Mary Ann Barnhart. "Marital Faithfulness and Unfaithfulness." *Journal of Social Philosophy* 4:2 (1973): 10–15.

Barnhart, Joseph E., and Mary Ann Barnhart. "The Myth of the Complete Person." In *Feminism and Philosophy*, edited by Mary Vetterling-Braggin, Frederick Elliston, and Jane English, 277–90. Totowa, N.J.: Rowman & Littlefield, 1977.

Bayles, Michael D. "Marriage, Love, and Procreation." In *Philosophy and Sex*, 2nd ed., edited by Robert Baker and Frederick Elliston, 130–45. Buffalo, N.Y.: Prometheus Books, 1984; 3rd ed., edited by Robert B. Baker, Kathleen J. Wininger, and Frederick A. Elliston, 116–29. Amherst, N.Y.: Prometheus Books, 1998.

Benatar, David. *Better Never to Have Been: The Harm of Coming into Existence*. Oxford: Clarendon Press, 2006.

Bradley, Gerard V. "What's in a Name? A Philosophical Critique of 'Civil Unions' Predicated upon a Sexual Relationship." *The Monist* 91:3–4 (2008): 606–31.

Brake, Elizabeth. "Is Divorce Promise-Breaking?" *Ethical Theory and Moral Practice* 14:1 (2011): 23–39.

———. "Justice and Virtue in Kant's Account of Marriage." *Kantian Review* 9 (March 2005): 58–94.

———. "Marriage, Morality, and Institutional Value." *Ethical Theory and Moral Practice* 10:3 (2007): 243–54.

———. "Minimal Marriage: What Political Liberalism Implies for Marriage Law." *Ethics* 120:2 (2010): 302–37.

———. *Minimizing Marriage: Marriage, Morality, and the Law*. New York: Oxford University Press, 2012.

Brooks, Thom. "The Problem with Polygamy." *Philosophical Topics* 37:2 (2009): 109–22.

Brophy, Brigid. "Monogamy." In *Don't Never Forget: Collected Views and Reviews*. London: Jonathan Cape, 1966, pp. 28–31.

Carr, David. "Chastity and Adultery." *American Philosophical Quarterly* 23:4 (1986): 363–71.

Cave, Eric M. "Harm Prevention and the Benefits of Marriage." *Journal of Social Philosophy* 35:2 (2004): 233–43.

Cicovacki, Predrag. "On Love and Fidelity in Marriage." *Journal of Social Philosophy* 24:3 (1993): 92–104.

Clark, Elizabeth A. "'Adam's Only Companion': Augustine and the Early Christian Debate on Marriage." *Recherches Augustiniennes* 21 (1986): 139–62.

Collins, Louise. "Emotional Adultery: Cybersex and Commitment." *Social Theory and Practice* 25:2 (1999): 243–70.

Connelly, R. J. "Philosophy and Adultery," in *Adultery in the United States*, edited by Philip E. Lampe, 131–64. Amherst, N.Y.: Prometheus Books, 1987, pp. 131-64.

Constantine, Larry L., and Joan M. Constantine. *Group Marriage: Marriages of Three or More People, How and When They Work*. New York: Macmillan, 1973.

Cott, Nancy. *Public Vows: A History of Marriage and the Nation*. Cambridge, Mass.: Harvard University Press, 2000.

Curzer, Howard J. "An Aristotelian Critique of the Traditional Family." *American Philosophical Quarterly* 47:2 (2010): 135–48.

Denis, Lara. "From Friendship to Marriage: Revising Kant." *Philosophy and Phenomenological Research* 63:1 (2001): 1–28.

Diorio, Joseph. "Sex, Love, and Justice: A Problem in Moral Education." *Educational Theory* 31:3–4 (1982): 225–35. Reprinted in *Eros, Agape, and Philia*, edited by Alan Soble, 273–88. St. Paul, Minn.: Paragon House, 1989.

Ellis, Albert. *The Civilized Couple's Guide to Extramarital Adventure.* New York: Wyden, 1972.

Finnis, John M. "The Good of Marriage and the Morality of Sexual Relations: Some Philosophical and Historical Observations." *American Journal of Jurisprudence* 42 (1997): 97–134.

———. "Marriage: A Basic and Exigent Good." *The Monist* 91:3–4 (2008): 388–407.

Francoeur, Robert T., Martha Cornog, and Timothy Perper. *Sex, Love, and Marriage in the 21st Century: The Next Sexual Revolution.* San Jose, Calif.: toExcel, 1999.

Garrett, Jeremy R. "History, Tradition, and the Normative Foundations of Civil Marriage." *The Monist* 91:3–4 (2008): 446–74.

———. "Marriage Unhitched from the State: A Defense." *Public Affairs Quarterly* 23:2 (2009): 161ff.

———. "Why the Old Sexual Morality of the New Natural Law Undermines Traditional Marriage." *Social Theory and Practice* 34:4 (2010): 591–622.

Geach, Mary. "Marriage: Arguing to a First Principle in Sexual Ethics." In *Moral Truth and Moral Tradition: Essays in Honour of Peter Geach and Elizabeth Anscombe,* edited by Luke Gormally, 177–93. Dublin: Four Courts Press, 1994.

Geach, Mary Catherine. "Lying with the Body." *The Monist* 91:3–4 (2008): 523–57.

Gregor, Thomas. "Sexuality and the Experience of Love." In *Sexual Nature Sexual Culture,* edited by P. Abramson and S. Pinkerton, 330–50. Chicago: University of Chicago Press, 1995.

Gregory, Paul. "Against Couples." *Journal of Applied Philosophy* 1:2 (1984): 263–68.

———. "Eroticism and Love." *American Philosophical Quarterly* 25:4 (1988): 339–44.

Halwani, Raja. "Virtue Ethics and Adultery." *Journal of Social Philosophy* 29:3 (1998): 5–18. Reprinted in *Ethics for Everyday,* edited by David Benatar, 226–39. Boston: McGraw-Hill, 2002.

Higgins, Kathleen Marie. "How Do I Love Thee? Let's Redefine a Term." *Journal of Social Philosophy* 24:3 (1993): 105–11.

Ketchum, Sara Ann. "Liberalism and Marriage Law." In *Feminism and Philosophy,* edited by Mary Vetterling-Braggin, Frederick Elliston, and Jane English, 264–76. Totowa, N.J.: Rowman & Littlefield, 1977.

Lankford, Ronald D. Jr., ed. *Polygamy.* Detroit, Mich.: Greenhaven Press, 2009.

Lesser, A. H. "Love and Lust." *Journal of Value Inquiry* 14:1 (1980): 51–54.

Lodge, David. "Sick with Desire." *New York Review of Books* (July 5, 2001): 28–32.

Margolis, Joseph, and Clorinda Margolis. "The Separation of Marriage and Family." In *Feminism and Philosophy,* edited by Mary Vetterling-Braggin, Frederick Elliston, and Jane English, 291–301. Totowa, N.J.: Rowman & Littlefield, 1977.

Marquis, Don. "What's Wrong with Adultery?" In *What's Wrong? Applied Ethicists and Their Critics,* edited by David Boonin and Graham Oddie, 231–38. New York: Oxford University Press, 2005.

Martin, Mike W. "Adultery and Fidelity." *Journal of Social Philosophy* 25:3 (1994): 76–91.

McCluskey, Colleen. "An Unequal Relationship between Equals: Thomas Aquinas on Marriage." *History of Philosophy Quarterly* 24:1 (2007): 1–18.

McMurtry, John. "Monogamy: A Critique." *The Monist* 56:4 (1972): 587–99. Reprinted in *Philosophy and Sex,* 2nd ed., edited by Robert Baker and Frederick Elliston, 107–18. Buffalo, N.Y.: Prometheus Books, 1984.

———. "Sex, Love, and Friendship." In *Sex, Love, and Friendship,* edited by Alan Soble, 169–93. Amsterdam: Rodopi, 1997.

Mendus, Susan. "Marital Faithfulness." *Philosophy* 59:228 (1984): 243–52. Reprinted in *Eros, Agape, and Philia,* edited by Alan Soble, 235–44. New York: Paragon House, 1989; and in *Philosophy and Sex,* 4th ed., edited by Robert B. Baker and Kathleen J. Wininger, 116–26. Amherst, N.Y.: Prometheus Books, 2009.

Morris, John C. *First Comes Love? The Changing Face of Marriage.* Cleveland, Ohio: Pilgrim Press, 2007.

O'Driscoll, Lyla. "On the Nature and Value of Marriage." In *Feminism and Philosophy,* edited by Mary Vetterling-Braggin, Frederick Elliston, and Jane English, 249–63.

Totowa, N.J.: Rowman & Littlefield, 1977. Reprinted in *Philosophy of Sex and Love: A Reader*, edited by Robert Trevas, Arthur Zucker, and Donald Borchert, 130–37. Upper Saddle River, N.J.: Prentice Hall, 1997.

Overall, Christine. *Why Have Children? The Ethical Debate*. Cambridge, Mass.: The MIT Press, 2012.

Prusak, Bernard G. "The Costs of Procreation." *Journal of Social Philosophy* 42:1 (2011): 61–75.

Rapaport, Elizabeth. "On the Future of Love: Rousseau and the Radical Feminists." *Philosophical Forum* 5:1–2 (1973/74): 185–205. Reprinted in *The Philosophy of Sex*, 1st ed., edited by Alan Soble, 369–88. Totowa, N.J.: Rowman & Littlefield, 1980; and *The Philosophy of (Erotic) Love*, edited by Robert C. Solomon and Kathleen M. Higgins, 372–90. Lawrence, Kan.: University Press of Kansas, 1991.

Rosewarne, Lauren. *Cheating on the Sisterhood: Infidelity and Feminism*. Santa Barbara, Calif.: Praeger/ABC-CLIO, 2009.

Rubin, Roger H. "Alternative Lifestyles Revisited, or Whatever Happened to Swingers, Group Marriages, and Communes?" *Journal of Family Issues* 22:6 (2001): 711–16.

Sclater, Shelley Day, Fatemeh Ebtehaj, Emily Jackson, and Martin Richards, eds. *Regulating Autonomy: Sex, Reproduction and Family*. Oxford, U.K.: Hart Publishing, 2009.

Scruton, Roger. "Meaningful Marriage." In *Political Philosophy: Arguments for Conservatism*. London: Continuum, 2007, pp. 81–102.

Shanley, Mary Lyndon, ed. *Just Marriage*. New York: Oxford University Press, 2004.

Shrage, Laurie. *Moral Dilemmas of Feminism: Prostitution, Adultery, and Abortion*. New York: Routledge, 1994.

Small, Meredith F. *What's Love Got to Do with It? The Evolution of Human Mating*. New York: Anchor, 1995.

Stafford, J. Martin. "Love and Lust Revisited: Intentionality, Homosexuality and Moral Education." *Journal of Applied Philosophy* 5:1 (1988): 87–100.

———. "On Distinguishing between Love and Lust." *Journal of Value Inquiry* 11:4 (1977): 292–303.

Steinbock, Bonnie. "Adultery." In *The Philosophy of Sex*, 2nd ed., edited by Alan Soble, 187–92. 2nd ed. Savage, Md.: Rowman & Littlefield, 1991.

Sunstein, Cass, and Richard H. Thaler. "Privatizing Marriage." *The Monist* 91:3–4 (2008): 377–87.

Taylor, Richard. *Having Love Affairs*. Buffalo, N.Y.: Prometheus, 1982.

———. *Love Affairs: Marriage and Infidelity*. Amherst, N.Y.: Prometheus, 1997.

Vannoy, Russell. "Can Sex Express Love?" In *Sex, Love, and Friendship*, edited by Alan Soble, 247–57. Amsterdam: Rodopi, 1997.

———. *Sex without Love: A Philosophical Exploration*. Buffalo, N.Y.: Prometheus, 1980.

Vernallis, Kayley. "Bisexual Monogamy: Twice the Temptation but Half the Fun?" *Journal of Social Philosophy* 30:3 (1999): 347–68.

Walsh, Anthony. "Love and Sex." In *Human Sexuality: An Encyclopedia*, edited by Vern Bullough and Bonnie Bullough, 369–73. New York: Garland, 1994.

Wardle, Lynn D., Mark Strasser, William C. Duncan, and David Orgon Coolidge, eds. *Marriage and Same-Sex Unions: A Debate*. Westport, Conn.: Praeger, 2003.

Wasserstrom, Richard. "Is Adultery Immoral?" In *Philosophy and Sex*, 2nd ed., edited by Robert Baker and Frederick Elliston, 93–106. Buffalo, N.Y.: Prometheus, 1984.

Weaver, Bryan R. "Marriage and the Norm of Monogamy." *The Monist* 91:3–4 (2008): 506–22.

Westlund, Andrea C. "The Reunion of Marriage." *The Monist* 91:3–4 (2008): 558–77.

Wilson, Mike. *Divorce*. Detroit, Mich.: Greenhaven Press, 2009.

Wojtyla, Karol (Pope Paul John II). *Love and Responsibility*, translated by H. T. Willetts. New York: Farrar, Straus, and Giroux, 1981; 2nd printing 1994.

Wreen, Michael J. "What's Really Wrong with Adultery." In *The Philosophy of Sex*, 2nd ed., edited by Alan Soble, 179–86. Savage, Md.: Rowman & Littlefield, 1991.

KANTIAN SEXUAL ETHICS (AND OBJECTIFICATION)

Anderson, Clelia Smyth, and Yolanda Estes. "The Myth of the Happy Hooker: Kantian Moral Reflections on a Phenomenology of Prostitution." In *Violence against Women: Philosophical Perspectives*, edited by Stanley G. French, Wanda Teays, and Laura M. Purdy, 152–58. Ithaca, N.Y.: Cornell University Press, 1998.

Baker, Robert B. "'Pricks' and 'Chicks': A Plea for 'Persons.'" In *Philosophy and Sex*, 1st ed., edited by Robert B. Baker and Frederick A. Elliston, 45–64. Buffalo, N.Y.: Prometheus, 1975. Reprinted in *Philosophy and Sex*, 3rd ed., edited by Robert B. Baker, Kathleen J. Wininger, and Frederick A. Elliston, 281–97. Amherst, N.Y.: Prometheus, 1998, along with "'Pricks' and 'Chicks': A Postscript after Twenty-Five Years," 297–305.

Baron, Marcia. "Love and Respect in the *Doctrine of Virtue*." In *Kant's Metaphysics of Morals: Interpretive Essays*, edited by Mark Timmons, 391–408. New York: Oxford University Press, 2002.

Baumrin, Bernard. "Sexual Immorality Delineated." In *Philosophy and Sex*, 2nd ed., edited by Robert B. Baker and Frederick A. Elliston, 300–311. Buffalo, N.Y.: Prometheus, 1984; original publication, 1975.

Belliotti, Raymond. *Good Sex: Perspectives on Sexual Ethics*. Lawrence, Kan.: University Press of Kansas, 1993.

Bencivegna, Ermanno. "Kant's Sadism." *Philosophy and Literature* 20:1 (1996): 39–46.

Brake, Elizabeth. "Justice and Virtue in Kant's Account of Marriage." *Kantian Review* 9 (March 2005): 58–94.

Brecht, Bertolt. "On Kant's Definition of Marriage in *The Metaphysic of Ethics*," translated by John Willet. In *Poems 1913–1956*, revised ed., edited by John Willett and Ralph Manheim, with Erich Fried, 312. New York: Methuen, 1987; original publication, 1938.

Cahill, Ann J. *Overcoming Objectification: A Carnal Ethics*. New York: Routledge, 2011.

Cooke, Vincent M. "Kant, Teleology, and Sexual Ethics." *International Philosophical Quarterly* 31:1 (1991): 3–13.

Denis, Lara. "From Friendship to Marriage: Revising Kant." *Philosophy and Phenomenological Research* 63:1 (2001): 1–28.

———. "Kant on the Wrongness of 'Unnatural' Sex." *History of Philosophy Quarterly* 16:2 (1999): 225–48.

Freud, Sigmund. "On the Universal Tendency to Debasement in the Sphere of Love." In *The Standard Edition of the Complete Psychological Works of Sigmund Freud*, vol. 11, edited by James Strachey, 177–90. London, U.K.: The Hogarth Press, 1953–1974; original publication, 1912.

Gregor, Mary J. *Laws of Freedom: A Study of Kant's Method of Applying the Categorical Imperative in the Metaphysik der Sitten*. New York: Barnes and Noble, 1963.

Hampton, Jean. "Defining Wrong and Defining Rape." In *A Most Detestable Crime: New Philosophical Essays on Rape*, edited by Keith Burgess-Jackson, 118–56. New York: Oxford University Press, 1999.

Haslanger, Sally. "On Being Objective and Being Objectified." In *A Mind of One's Own: Feminist Essays on Reason and Objectivity*, edited by Louise Antony and Charlotte Witt, 85–125. Boulder, Colo.: Westview, 1993.

Herman, Barbara. "Could It Be Worth Thinking about Kant on Sex and Marriage?" In *A Mind of One's Own*, edited by Louise Antony and Charlotte Witt, 49–67. Boulder, Colo.: Westview, 1993.

Kant, Immanuel. *Lectures on Ethics*, translated by Peter Heath, edited by Peter Heath and J. B. Schneewind. Cambridge: Cambridge University Press, 1997; original publication, 1792–1794.

———. *The Metaphysics of Morals*, translated by Mary Gregor. Cambridge: Cambridge University Press, 1991; revised ed., 1996; original publication 1797–1798.

Kielkopf, Charles. "Masturbation: A Kantian Condemnation." *Philosophia* 25:1–4 (1997): 223–46.

Kneller, Jane. "Kant on Sex and Marriage Right." In *The Cambridge Companion to Kant and Modern Philosophy*, edited by Paul Guyer, 447–76. Cambridge: Cambridge University Press, 2006.

Korsgaard, Christine M. "Creating the Kingdom of Ends: Reciprocity and Responsibility in Personal Relations." *Philosophical Perspectives* 6 (1992): 305–32.

Landau, Iddo. "Two Notions of Objectification." *Philosophy Today* 51:3 (2007): 312–19.

Langton, Rae. *Sexual Objectification: Philosophical Essays on Pornography and Objectification*. Oxford: Oxford University Press, 2009.

LeMoncheck, Linda. *Dehumanizing Women: Treating Persons as Sex Objects*. Totowa, N.J.: Rowman & Allanheld, 1984.

Madigan, Timothy. "The Discarded Lemon: Kant, Prostitution and Respect for Persons." *Philosophy Now* 21 (Summer/Autumn 1998): 14–16. Reprinted in *Prostitution: On Whores, Hustlers, and Johns*, edited by James E. Elias, Vern L. Bullough, Veronica Elias, and Gwen Brewer, 107–11. Amherst, N.Y.: Prometheus, 1998, pp. 107–11.

Marino, Patricia. "The Ethics of Sexual Objectification: Autonomy and Consent." *Inquiry* 51:4 (2008): 345–64.

Morgan, Seiriol. "Dark Desires." *Ethical Theory and Moral Practice* 6:4 (2003): 377–410.

Moscovici, Claudia. *From Sex Objects to Sexual Subjects*. New York: Routledge, 1996.

Mosser, Kurt. "Kant and Feminism." *Kant-Studien* 90:3 (1999): 322–53.

Nussbaum, Martha C. "Objectification." *Philosophy and Public Affairs* 24:4 (1995): 249-91. Reprinted in *Philosophy of Sex*, 3rd ed., edited by Alan Soble, 283–321, and 4th ed., 381–419. Revised in her *Sex and Social Justice*. New York: Oxford University Press, 1999, pp. 213–39.

O'Neill, Onora. "Between Consenting Adults." *Philosophy and Public Affairs* 14:3 (1985): 252–77. Reprinted in *Constructions of Reason: Explorations of Kant's Practical Philosophy*. Cambridge: Cambridge University Press, 1989, pp. 105–25.

———. "Kantian Ethics." In *A Companion to Ethics*, edited by Peter Singer, 175–85. Oxford, U.K.: Blackwell, 1991.

Papadaki, Evangelia. "Sexual Objectification: From Kant to Contemporary Feminism." *Contemporary Political Theory* 6:3 (2007): 330–48.

Sample, Ruth. "Sexual Exploitation and the Social Contract." *Canadian Journal of Philosophy*, "Feminist Moral Philosophy," Supp. Vol. 28 (2003): 189–217.

Sartre, Jean-Paul. (1943) *Being and Nothingness: An Essay on Phenomenological Ontology*, translated by Hazel E. Barnes. New York: Philosophical Library, 1956.

Schaff, Kory. "Kant, Political Liberalism, and the Ethics of Same-Sex Relations." *Journal of Social Philosophy* 32:3 (2001): 446–62.

Singer, Irving. "Benign Romanticism: Kant, Schlegel, Hegel, Shelly, Byron." In *The Nature of Love*, vol. 2: *Courtly and Romantic*. Chicago: University of Chicago Press, 1984, pp. 376–431.

———. "The Morality of Sex: Contra Kant." *Critical Horizons* 1:2 (2000): 175–91. Reprinted in *Explorations in Love and Sex*. Lanham, Md.: Rowman and Littlefield, 2001, pp. 1–20; and *The Philosophy of Sex*, 4th ed., edited by Alan Soble, 259–72.

Soble, Alan. "Kant and Sexual Perversion." *The Monist* 86:1 (2003): 57–92.

Sparshott, Francis. "Kant without Sade." *Philosophy and Literature* 21:1 (1997): 151–54.

Waldron, Jeremy. "When Justice Replaces Affection: The Need for Rights." *Harvard Journal of Law and Public Policy* 11: (1988): 625–47.

VIRTUE ETHICS

Carr, David. "Two Kinds of Virtue." *Proceedings of the Aristotelian Society* 84 (1984–1985): 47-61.

Geach, Peter T. *The Virtues*. Cambridge: Cambridge University Press, 1977.

Halwani, Raja. "Ethics, Virtue." In *Sex from Plato to Paglia: A Philosophical Encyclopedia*, edited by Alan Soble, 279–85. Westport, Conn.: Greenwood Press, 2006.

———. "Virtue Ethics and Adultery." *Journal of Social Philosophy* 29:3 (1998): 5–18. Reprinted in *Ethics for Everyday*, edited by David Benatar, 226–39. Boston: McGraw-Hill, 2002.

———. "Virtue Ethics, Casual Sex, and Objectification." In *Philosophy of Sex*, 5th ed., edited by Alan Soble and Nicholas Power, 337–49. Lanham, Md.: Rowman & Littlefied, 2008.

———. *Virtuous Liaisons: Care, Love, Sex, and Virtue Ethics*. Chicago: Open Court, 2003.

———, ed. *Sex and Ethics: Essays on Sexuality, Virtue, and the Good Life*. New York: Palgrave, 2007.

Martin, Christopher F. J. "Are There Virtues and Vices That Belong Specifically to the Sexual Life?" *Acta Philosophica* 4:2 (1995): 205–21.

Morgan, Seiriol. "Dark Desires." *Ethical Theory and Moral Practice* 6:4 (2003): 377–410.

Putman, Dan. "Sex and Virtue." *International Journal of Moral and Social Studies* 6:1 (1991): 47–56.

CASUAL SEX AND PROMISCUITY

Barker, Meg, and Darren Langdridge, eds. *Understanding Non-Monogamies*. New York: Routledge, 2010.

Birkhead, Tim. *Promiscuity: An Evolutionary History of Sperm Competition*. Cambridge, Mass.: Harvard University Press, 2000.

Ellis, Anthony. "Casual Sex." *International Journal of Moral and Social Studies* 1:2 (1986): 157–69.

Elliston, Frederick. "In Defense of Promiscuity." In *Philosophy and Sex*, 1st ed., edited by Robert Baker and Frederick Elliston, 223–43. Buffalo, N. Y.: Prometheus, 1975.

Groneman, Carol. *Nymphomania: A History*. New York: Norton, 2000.

Halwani, Raja. "Casual Sex." In *Sex from Plato to Paglia: A Philosophical Encyclopedia*, edited by Alan Soble, 136–42. Westport, Conn.: Greenwood Press, 2006.

———. "Casual Sex, Promiscuity, and Temperance." In *Sex and Ethics: Essays on Sexuality, Virtue, and the Good Life*, edited by Raja Halwani, 215–25. New York: Palgrave, 2007.

———. "Virtue Ethics, Casual Sex, and Objectification." In *Philosophy of Sex*, 5th ed., edited by Alan Soble and Nicholas Power, 337–49. Lanham, Md.: Rowman & Littlefied, 2008.

Klesse, Christian. *The Spectre of Promiscuity: Gay Male and Bisexual Non-Monogamies and Polyamories*. Aldershot, U.K.: Ashgate, 2007.

Kristjansson, Kristjan. "Casual Sex Revisited." *Journal of Social Philosophy* 29:2 (1998): 97–108.

Ley, David J. *Insatiable Wives: Women Who Stray and the Men Who Love Them*. Lanham, Md.: Rowman & Littlefield, 2009.

Wolf, Naomi. *Promiscuities: The Secret Struggle for Womanhood*. New York: Random House, 1997.

RAPE, POWER, AND CONSENT

Abdullah-Khan, Noreen. *Male Rape: The Emergence of a Social and Legal Issue*. Basingstoke, U.K.: Palgrave Macmillan, 2008.

Alcoff, Linda Martín. "Discourses of Sexual Violence in a Global Framework." *Philosophical Topics* 37:2 (2009): 123–39.

Anderson, Peter B., and Cindy Struckman-Johnson, eds. *Sexually Aggressive Women: Current Perspectives and Controversies*. New York: Guilford, 1998.

Archard, David. "Informed Consent: Autonomy and Self-Ownership." *Journal of Applied Philosophy* 25:1 (2008): 19–34.

———. "'A Nod's as Good as a Wink': Consent, Convention, and Reasonable Belief." *Legal Theory* 3:3 (1997): 273–90.

———. *Sexual Consent.* Boulder, Colo.: Westview, 1998.

———. "The Wrong of Rape." *The Philosophical Quarterly* 57:228 (2007): 374–93.

Belliotti, Raymond. "A Philosophical Analysis of Sexual Ethics." *Journal of Social Philosophy* 10:3 (1979): 8–11.

Bogart, John H. "On the Nature of Rape." *Public Affairs Quarterly* 5 (1991): 117–36. Reprinted in *Philosophical Perspectives on Sex and Love,* edited by Robert M. Stewart, 168–80. New York: Oxford University Press, 1995.

Bourke, Joanna. *Rape: Sex, Violence, History.* Emeryville, Calif.: Shoemaker & Hoard, 2007.

Brison, Susan J. *Aftermath: Violence and the Remaking of a Self.* Princeton, N.J.: Princeton University Press, 2002.

Burgess, Ann Wolbert, ed. *Rape and Sexual Assault: A Research Handbook.* New York: Garland, 1985.

Burgess-Jackson, Keith. *Rape: A Philosophical Investigation.* Aldershot, U.K.: Dartmouth, 1996.

———, ed. *A Most Detestable Crime: New Philosophical Essays on Rape.* New York: Oxford University Press, 1999.

Cahill, Ann J. *Rethinking Rape.* Ithaca, N.Y.: Cornell University Press, 2001.

Calhoun, Laurie. "On Rape: A Crime against Humanity." *Journal of Social Philosophy* 28:1 (1997): 101–9.

Card, Claudia. "Rape as a Terrorist Institution." In *Violence, Terrorism, and Justice,* edited by R. G. Frey and Christopher Morris, 296–319. New York: Cambridge University Press, 1991.

———. "Rape as a Weapon of War." *Hypatia* 11:4 (1996): 5–18.

Caringella, Susan. *Addressing Rape Reform in Law and Practice.* New York: Columbia University Press, 2009.

Cave, Eric M. "Unsavory Seduction." *Ethical Theory and Moral Practice* 12:3 (2009): 235–45.

Cowling, Mark, and Paul Reynolds, eds. *Making Sense of Sexual Consent.* Aldershot, U.K.: Ashgate, 2004.

Dadlez, E. M., William L. Andrews, Courtney Lewis, and Marissa Stroud. "Rape, Evolution, and Pseudoscience: Natural Selection in the Academy." *Journal of Social Philosophy* 40:1 (2009): 75–96.

Davis, Michael. "Setting Penalties: What Does Rape Deserve?" *Law and Philosophy* 3:1 (1984): 61–110.

Doniger, Wendy. "Sex, Lies, and Tall Tales." *Social Research* 63:3 (1996): 663–99.

DuToit, Louise. *A Philosophical Investigation of Rape: The Making and Unmaking of the Feminine Self.* New York: Routledge, 2009.

Estrich, Susan. "Rape." In *Feminist Jurisprudence,* edited by Patricia Smith, 158–87. New York: Oxford University Press, 1993.

———. *Real Rape: How the Legal System Victimizes Women Who Say No.* Cambridge, Mass.: Harvard University Press, 1987.

Foa, Pamela. "What's Wrong with Rape." In *Feminism and Philosophy,* edited by Mary Vetterling-Braggin, Frederick Elliston, and Jane English, 347–59. Totowa, N.J.: Rowman & Littlefield, 1977. Reprinted in *Philosophy and Sex,* 3rd ed., edited by Robert B. Baker, Kathleen J. Wininger, and Frederick A. Elliston, 583–93. Amherst, N.Y.: Prometheus Books, 1998.

Francis, Leslie P., ed. *Date Rape: Feminism, Philosophy, and the Law.* State College, Penn.: Pennsylvania State University Press, 1996.

French, Stanley G., Wanda Teays, and Laura M. Purdy, eds. *Violence against Women: Philosophical Perspectives.* Ithaca, N.Y.: Cornell University Press, 1998.

Golash, Deirdre. "Power, Sex, and Friendship in Academia." *Essays in Philosophy* 2:2 (January 2001), http://commons.pacificu.edu/eip/vol2/iss2/8 (accessed March 4, 2012). Reprinted in *The Philosophy of Sex*, 5th ed., edited by Alan Soble and Nicholas Power, 449–58. Lanham, Md.: Rowman & Littlefield, 2008.

Hampton, Jean. "Defining Wrong and Defining Rape." In *A Most Detestable Crime: New Philosophical Essays on Rape*, edited by Keith Burgess-Jackson, 118–56. New York: Oxford University Press, 1999.

Harrison, Ross. "Rape—A Case Study in Political Philosophy." In *Rape: An Historical and Social Enquiry*, edited by Sylvana Tomaselli and Roy Porter, 41–56. New York: Basil Blackwell, 1986.

Hasday, Jill. "Contest and Consent: A Legal History of Marital Rape." *California Law Review* 88 (October 2000), 1373–1505.

Heberle, Renée J., and Victoria Grace, eds. *Theorizing Sexual Violence*. New York: Routledge, 2009.

Hickman, Susan, and Charlene L. Muehlenhard. "By the Semi-Mystical Appearance of a Condom: How Young Women and Men Communicate Sexual Consent in Heterosexual Situations." *Journal of Sex Research* 36:3 (1999): 258–72.

Hurd, Heidi. "The Moral Magic of Consent." *Legal Theory* 2:2 (1996): 121–46.

Husak, Douglas. "The Complete Guide to Consent to Sex: Alan Wertheimer's *Consent to Sexual Relations*." *Law and Philosophy* 25:2 (March 2006): 267–87.

Husak, Douglas N., and George C. Thomas III. "Date Rape, Social Convention, and Reasonable Mistakes." *Law and Philosophy* 11:1 (1992): 95–126.

———. "Rapes without Rapists: Consent and Reasonable Mistake." In *Philosophical Issues* 11: *Social, Legal, and Political Philosophy*, edited by Ernest Sosa and Enrique Villanueva, 86–117. Oxford, U.K.: Blackwell, 2001.

Kennedy, Duncan. "Sexual Abuse, Sexy Dressing, and the Eroticization of Domination." In *Sexy Dressing Etc: Essays on the Power and Politics of Cultural Identity*. Cambridge, Mass.: Harvard University Press, 1993, pp. 126–213.

Kittay, Eva Feder. "Ah! My Foolish Heart: A Reply to Alan Soble's 'Antioch's "Sexual Offense Policy"': A Philosophical Exploration.'" *Journal of Social Philosophy* 28:2 (1997): 153–59. Reprinted in *The Philosophy of Sex*, 5th ed., edited by Alan Soble and Nicholas Power, 479–87. Lanham, Md.: Rowman & Littlefield, 2008.

Leone, Bruno, ed. *Rape on Campus*. San Diego: Greenhaven, 1995.

Marsh, Jeanne C., Alison Geist, and Nathan Caplan. *Rape and the Limits of Law Reform*. Boston: Auburn House, 1982.

May, Larry, and Robert Strikwerda. "Men in Groups: Collective Responsibility for Rape." *Hypatia* 9:2 (1994): 134–51. Reprinted in *Philosophy and Sex*, 3rd ed., edited by Robert B. Baker, Kathleen J. Wininger, and Frederick A. Elliston, 594–610. Amherst, N.Y.: Prometheus Books, 1998; and 4th ed., edited by Robert B. Baker and Kathleen J. Wininger, 447–94. Amherst, N.Y.: Prometheus Books, 2009.

McGlynn, Clare, and Vanessa E. Munroe, eds. *Rethinking Rape Law: International and Comparative Perspectives*. Abingdon, U.K.: Routledge, 2010.

McGowan, Mary Kate. "On Silencing and Sexual Refusal." *Journal of Political Philosophy* 17:4 (2009): 487–94.

McGregor, Joan. *Is It Rape? On Acquaintance Rape and Taking Women's Consent Seriously*. Aldershot, U.K.: Ashgate, 2005.

Muehlenhard, Charlene L., Sharon Danoff-Burg, and Irene G. Powch. "Is Rape Sex or Violence? Conceptual Issues and Implications." In *Sex, Power, Conflict: Evolutionary and Feminist Perspectives*, edited by David M. Buss and Neil M. Malamuth, 119–37. Oxford: Oxford University Press, 1996. Reprinted in *Philosophy and Sex*, 3rd ed., edited by Robert B. Baker, Kathleen J. Wininger, and Frederick A. Elliston, 621–39. Amherst, N.Y.: Prometheus Books, 1998.

Muehlenhard, Charlene L., and Lisa C. Hollabaugh. "Do Women Sometimes Say No When They Mean Yes? The Prevalence and Correlates of Women's Token Resistance to Sex." *Journal of Personality and Social Psychology* 54:5 (1988): 872–79.

Muehlenhard, Charlene L., Irene G. Powich, Joi L. Phelps, and Laura M. Givsi, "Definitions of Rape: Scientific and Political Implications." *Journal of Social Issues* 48:1 (1992): 23–44.

Muehlenhard, Charlene L., and Jennifer L. Schrag. "Nonviolent Sexual Coercion." In *Acquaintance Rape: The Hidden Crime*, edited by A. Parrot and L. Bechhofer, 115–28. New York: John Wiley, 1991.

Murphy, Jeffrie. "Some Ruminations on Women, Violence, and the Criminal Law." *In Harm's Way: Essays in Honor of Joel Feinberg*, edited by Jules Coleman and Allen Buchanan, 209–30. Cambridge: Cambridge University Press, 1994.

Paglia, Camille. *Sex, Art, and American Culture.* New York: Vintage, 1992.

Parrot, Andrea, and Laurie Bechhofer, eds. *Acquaintance Rape: The Hidden Crime.* New York: John Wiley, 1991.

Peterson, Susan Rae. "Coercion and Rape: The State as a Male Protection Racket." In *Feminism and Philosophy*, edited by Mary Vetterling-Braggin, Frederick Elliston, and Jane English, 360–71. Totowa, N.J.: Littlefield Adams, 1977.

Primoratz, Igor. "Sexual Morality: Is Consent Enough?" *Ethical Theory and Moral Practice* 4:3 (2001): 201–18.

Prins, Baukje. "Sympathetic Distrust: Liberalism and the Sexual Autonomy of Women." *Social Theory and Practice* 34:2 (2008): 243–70.

Reitan, Eric. "Date Rape and Seduction: Towards a Defense of Pineau's Definition of 'Date Rape.'" *Southwest Philosophy Review* 20:1 (2004): 99–106.

———. "Rape as an Essentially Contested Concept." *Hypatia* 16:2 (2001): 43–66.

Remick, Lani Anne. "Read Her Lips: An Argument for a Verbal Consent Standard in Rape." *University of Pennsylvania Law Review* 141:3 (1993): 1103–51.

Schulhofer, Stephen J. "The Gender Question in Criminal Law." *Punishment and Rehabilitation*, 3rd ed., edited by Jeffrie Murphy, 274–311. Belmont, Calif.: Wadsworth, 1995.

———. *Unwanted Sex: The Culture of Intimidation and the Failure of Law.* Cambridge, Mass.: Harvard University Press, 1998.

Shafer, Carolyn M. , and Marilyn Frye. "Rape and Respect." In *Feminism and Philosophy*, edited by Mary Vetterling-Braggin, Frederick Elliston, and Jane English, 333–46. Totowa, N.J.: Littlefield Adams, 1977.

Shields, William, and Lea Shields. "Forcible Rape: An Evolutionary Perspective." *Ethology and Sociobiology* 4:3 (1983): 115–36.

Silliman, Matthew C. "The Antioch Policy, a Community Experiment in Communicative Sexuality." In *Date Rape: Feminism, Philosophy, and the Law*, edited by Leslie Francis, 167–75. University Park, Pa.: Pennsylvania State University Press, 1996. Reprinted in *Philosophy and Sex*, 3rd ed., edited by Robert B. Baker, Kathleen J. Wininger, and Frederick A. Elliston, 661–67. Amherst, N.Y.: Prometheus Books, 1998.

Soble, Alan. "Antioch's 'Sexual Offense Policy': A Philosophical Exploration." *Journal of Social Philosophy* 28:1 (1997): 22–36. Reprinted, revised, in *The Philosophy of Sex*, 5th ed., edited by Alan Soble and Nicholas Power, 459–77. Lanham, Md.: Rowman & Littlefield, 2008.

———. "In Defense of Bacon." *Philosophy of the Social Sciences* 25:2 (1995): 192–215. Reprinted, revised, in *A House Built on Sand: Exposing Postmodernist Myths about Science*, edited by Noretta Koertge, 195–215. New York: Oxford University Press, 1998.

Sommers, Christina Hoff. *Who Stole Feminism? How Women Have Betrayed Women.* New York: Simon and Schuster, 1994.

Spivak, Andrew L. *Sexual Violence: Beyond the Feminist-Evolutionary Debate.* El Paso, Tex.: LFB Scholarly Publishing, 2011.

Stinchcombe, Arthur L., and Laura Beth Nielsen. "Consent to Sex: The Liberal Paradigm Reformulated." *Journal of Political Philosophy* 17:1 (2009): 66–89.

Taylor, Chloë. "Disciplinary Relations/Sexual Relations: Feminist and Foucauldian Reflections on Professor-Student Sex." *Hypatia* 26:1 (2011): 187–206.

————. "Foucault, Feminism, and Sex Crimes." *Hypatia* 24:4 (2009): 1–25.

Thornhill, Randy, and Craig Palmer. *A Natural History of Rape: Biological Bases of Sexual Coercion.* Cambridge, Mass.: MIT Press, 2000.

Tomaselli, Sylvana, and Roy Porter, eds. *Rape: An Historical and Cultural Inquiry.* New York: Blackwell, 1986.

Warshaw, Robin. *I Never Called It Rape: The Ms. Report on Recognizing, Fighting, and Surviving Date and Acquaintance Rape.* New York: Harper and Row, 1988.

Watkins, Christine, ed. *Date Rape.* Detroit, Mich.: Greenhaven Press, 2007.

Wertheimer, Alan. *Consent to Sexual Relations.* Cambridge: Cambridge University Press, 2003.

West, Robin. "Sex, Law, and Consent." In *The Ethics of Consent: Theory and Practice,* edited by Franklin G. Miller and Alan Wertheimer, 221–50. Oxford: Oxford University Press, 2010.

CHILDREN

Adler, Amy. "The Perverse Law of Child Pornography." *Columbia Law Review* 101 (March 2001): 209–73.

Alcoff, Linda Martín. "Dangerous Pleasures: Foucault and the Politics of Pedophilia." In *Feminist Interpretations of Michel Foucault,* edited by Susan J. Hekman, 99–135. University Park, Pa.: Pennsylvania State University Press, 1996. Reprinted in *Philosophy and Sex,* 3rd ed., edited by Robert B. Baker, Kathleen J. Wininger, and Frederick A. Elliston, 500–529. Amherst, N.Y.: Prometheus Books, 1998.

Benatar, David, and Michael Benatar. "Between Prophylaxis and Child Abuse: The Ethics of Neonatal Male Circumcision." In *Cutting to the Core: The Ethics of Contested Surgeries,* edited by David Benatar, 23–45. Lanham, Md.: Rowman & Littlefield, 2006.

Califia, Pat. "A Thorny Issue Splits a Movement." *Advocate* (October 30, 1980): 17–24, 45.

Cannold, Leslie. "The Ethics of Neonatal Male Circumcision: Helping Parents to Decide." In *Cutting to the Core: The Ethics of Contested Surgeries,* edited by David Benatar, 47–61. Lanham, Md.: Rowman & Littlefield, 2006.

David, Dena S. "Genital Alteration of Female Minors." In *Cutting to the Core: The Ethics of Contested Surgeries,* edited by David Benatar, 63–75. Lanham, Md.: Rowman & Littlefield, 2006.

Dreger, Alice Domurat. "'Ambiguous Sex'—or Ambivalent Medicine? Ethical Issues in the Treatment of Intersexuality." *Hastings Center Report* 28:3 (1998): 24–35.

————. "A History of Intersex: From the Age of Gonads to the Age of Consent." *Journal of Clinical Ethics* 9:4 (1998): 345–55. Reprinted in *Philosophy and Sex,* 4th ed., edited by Robert B. Baker and Kathleen J. Wininger, 372–86. Amherst, N.Y.: Prometheus Books, 2009.

Ehman, Robert. "Adult-Child Sex." In *Philosophy and Sex,* 2nd ed., edited by Robert Baker and Frederick Elliston, 431–46. Buffalo, N.Y.: Prometheus, 1984, pp. 431–46.

————. "What Really Is Wrong with Pedophilia?" *Public Affairs Quarterly* 14:2 (2000): 129–40.

Finkelhor, David. "What's Wrong with Sex between Adults and Children?" *American Journal of Orthopsychiatry* 49:4 (1979), 692–97.

Frye, Marilyn. "Critique [of Robert Ehman]." In *Philosophy and Sex,* 2nd ed., edited by Robert Baker and Frederick Elliston, 447–55. Buffalo, N.Y.: Prometheus, 1984. Reprinted, revised, as "Not-Knowing about Sex and Power," in *Willful Virgin.* Freedom, Calif.: Crossing Press, 1992, pp. 39–50.

Geraci, Joseph, ed. *Dares to Speak: Historical and Contemporary Perspectives on Boy-Love.* Swaffham, U.K.: Gay Men's Press, 1997.

Hiber, Amanda, ed. *Child Pornography.* Detroit, Mich.: Greenhaven Press, 2009.

Kershnar, Stephen. "The Moral Status of Harmless Adult-Child Sex." *Public Affairs Quarterly* 15:2 (2001): 111–32. Reprinted, revised, in *Sex, Discrimination, and Violence: Surprising and Unpopular Results in Applied Ethics.* Lanham, Md.: University Press of America, 2009, pp. 1–19.

Kipnis, Kenneth and Milton Diamond. "Pediatric Ethics and the Surgical Assignment of Sex." *Journal of Clinical Ethics* 9:4 (1998): 398–410. Reprinted in *Philosophy and Sex,* 4th ed., edited by Robert B. Baker and Kathleen J. Wininger, 387–405. Amherst, N.Y.: Prometheus Books, 2009.

Levy, Neil. "Virtual Child Pornography: The Eroticization of Inequality." *Ethics and Information Technology* 4:4 (2002): 319–23.

Ost, Suzanne. *Child Pornography and Sexual Grooming.* New York: Cambridge University Press, 2009.

Primoratz, Igor. "Pedophilia." *Public Affairs Quarterly* 13:1 (1999): 99–110.

Schinaia, Cosimo. *On Paedophilia.* Translated by Antonella Sansone. London: Karnac, 2010.

Spiecker, Ben, and Jan Steutel. "A Moral-Philosophical Perspective on Paedophilia and Incest." *Educational Philosophy and Theory* 32:3 (2000): 283–91.

———. "Paedophilia, Sexual Desire and Perversity." *Journal of Moral Education* 26:3 (1997): 331–42.

SEXUAL HARASSMENT

Altman, Andrew. "Making Sense of Sexual Harassment Law." *Philosophy and Public Affairs* 25:1 (1996): 36–64.

Christensen, Ferrel M. "'Sexual Harassment' Must Be Eliminated." *Public Affairs Quarterly* 8:1 (1994): 1–17.

Crosthwaite, Jan, and Graham Priest. "The Definition of Sexual Harassment." *Australasian Journal of Philosophy* 74:1 (1996): 66–82.

Crouch, Margaret A. "The 'Social Etymology' of 'Sexual Harassment.'" *Journal of Social Philosophy* 29:3 (1998): 19–40.

Dershowitz, Alan M. "The Talmud as Sexual Harassment." In *The Abuse Excuse and Other Cop-outs, Sob Stories, and Evasions of Responsibility,* 251–53. Boston: Little, Brown, 1994.

Dodds, Susan M., Lucy Frost, Robert Pargetter, and Elizabeth W. Prior. "Sexual Harassment." *Social Theory and Practice* 14:2 (1988): 111–30.

Francis, Leslie Pickering, ed. *Sexual Harassment as an Ethical Issue in Academic Life.* Lanham, Md.: Rowman & Littlefield, 2001.

Gallop, Jane. *Feminist Accused of Sexual Harassment.* Durham, N.C.: Duke University Press, 1997.

Hajdin, Mane. *The Law of Sexual Harassment: A Critique.* Selinsgrove, Penn.: Susquehanna University Press, 2002.

———. "Sexual Harassment and Negligence." *Journal of Social Philosophy* 28:1 (1997): 37–53.

———. "Sexual Harassment in the Law: The Demarcation Problem." *Journal of Social Philosophy* 25:3 (1994): 102–22.

Hughes, John C., and Larry May. "Sexual Harassment." *Social Theory and Practice* 6:3 (1980): 249–80.

Kenrick, Douglas T., Melanie R. Trost, and Virgil L. Sheets. "Power, Harassment, and Trophy Mates: The Feminist Advantages of an Evolutionary Perspective." In *Sex, Power, Conflict: Evolutionary and Feminist Perspectives,* edited by David M. Buss and Neil M. Malamuth, 29–53. New York: Oxford University Press, 1996.

Klatt, Heinz-Joachim. "Regulating 'Harassment' in Ontario." *Academic Questions* 8:3 (1995): 48–58.

Landau, Iddo. "Is Sexual Harassment Research Biased?" *Public Affairs Quarterly* 13:3 (1999): 241–54.

LeMoncheck, Linda, and Mane Hajdin. *Sexual Harassment: A Debate.* Lanham, Md.: Rowman & Littlefield, 1997.

LeMoncheck, Linda, and James P. Sterba, eds. *Sexual Harassment: Issues and Answers.* New York: Oxford University Press, 2001.

MacKinnon, Catharine A. *Sexual Harassment of Working Women.* New Haven, Conn.: Yale University Press, 1979.

McBride, William L. "Sexual Harassment, Seduction, and Mutual Respect: An Attempt at Sorting It Out." In *Feminist Phenomenology: Contributions to Phenomenology,* vol. 40, edited by Linda Fisher and Lester Embree, 249–66. Dordrecht, Netherlands: Kluwer, 2000.

Paludi, Michele A., ed. *Sexual Harassment on College Campuses: Abusing the Ivory Power,* revised ed. Albany, N.Y.: State University of New York Press, 1990.

Patai, Daphne. *Heterophobia: Sexual Harassment and the Future of Feminism.* Lanham, Md.: Rowman & Littlefield, 1998.

Paul, Ellen Frankel. "Sexual Harassment as Discrimination: A Defective Paradigm." *Yale Law and Policy Review* 8:2 (1990): 333–65.

Robinson, Paul. "'Dear Paul': An Exchange between Student and Teacher." In *Opera, Sex, and Other Vital Matters.* Chicago: University of Chicago Press, 2002, pp. 219–37.

Rocha, James. "The Sexual Harassment Coercive Offer." *Journal of Applied Philosophy* 28:2 (2011): 203–16.

Roiphe, Katie. *The Morning After: Sex, Fear, and Feminism on Campus.* New York: Little, Brown, 1993.

Sanday, Peggy Reeves. *A Woman Scorned: Acquaintance Rape on Trial.* New York: Doubleday, 1996.

Stan, Adele M., ed. *Debating Sexual Correctness.* New York: Delta, 1995.

Superson, Anita M. "A Feminist Definition of Sexual Harassment." *Journal of Social Philosophy* 24:1 (1993): 46–64.

Taylor, James Stacey. "Autonomy, Responsibility, and Women's Obligation to Resist Sexual Harassment." *International Journal of Applied Philosophy* 21:1 (2007): 55–63.

Tuana, Nancy. "Sexual Harassment: Offers and Coercion." *Journal of Social Philosophy* 19:2 (1988): 30–42.

Wall, Edmund, ed. *Sexual Harassment: Confrontations and Decisions.* Buffalo, N.Y.: Prometheus, 1992. Revised ed., 2000.

PROSTITUTION

Anderson, Clelia Smyth, and Yolanda Estes. "The Myth of the Happy Hooker: Kantian Moral Reflections on a Phenomenology of Prostitution." In *Violence against Women: Philosophical Perspectives,* edited by Stanley G. French, Wanda Teays, and Laura M. Purdy, 152–58, 231–33. Ithaca, N.Y.: Cornell University Press, 1998.

Anderson, Scott A. "Prostitution and Sexual Autonomy: Making Sense of the Prohibition of Prostitution." *Ethics* 112:4 (2002): 748–80.

Archard, David. "Criminalizing the Use of Trafficked Prostitutes: Some Philosophical Issues." In *Demanding Sex: Critical Reflections on the Regulation of Prostitution,* edited by Vanessa E. Munroe and Marina Della Giusta, 149–62. Aldershot, U.K.: Ashgate, 2008.

Christina, Greta, ed. *Paying for It: A Guide by Sex Workers for Their Clients.* Oakland, Calif.: Greenery Press, 2004.

"Code of Ethics for Prostitutes." *Coyote Howls* 5:1 (1978): 9.

Davidson, Julia O'Connell. "Prostitution and the Contours of Control." In *Sexual Cultures: Communities, Values and Intimacy,* edited by Jeffrey Weeks and Janet Holland, 180–98. New York: St. Martin's, 1996.

Delacoste, Frédérique, and Priscilla Alexander, eds. *Sex Work: Writings by Women in the Sex Industry*. Pittsburgh, Penna.: Cleis Press, 1987.

De Marneffe, Peter. *Liberalism and Prostitution*. Oxford: Oxford University Press, 2010.

Ditmore, Melissa Hope, Antonia Levy, and Alys Willman, eds. *Sex Work Matters: Exploring Money, Power, and Intimacy in the Sex Industry*. London: Zed Books, 2010.

Elias, James E., Vern L. Bullough, Veronica Elias, and Gwen Brewer, eds. *Prostitution: On Whores, Hustlers, and Johns*. Amherst, N.Y.: Prometheus, 1998.

Ericsson, Lars O. "Charges against Prostitution: An Attempt at a Philosophical Assessment." *Ethics* 90:3 (1980): 335–66.

Estes, Yolanda. "Moral Reflections on Prostitution," *Essays in Philosophy* 2:2 (2001), http://commons.pacificu.edu/eip/vol2/iss2/10. Revised, reprinted as "Prostitution: A Subjective Position," in *The Philosophy of Sex*, 5th ed., edited by Alan Soble and Nicholas Power, 353–65. Lanham, Md.: Rowman & Littlefield, 2008.

Garb, Sarah H. "Sex for Money Is Sex for Money: The Illegality of Pornographic Film as Prostitution." *Law and Inequality* 13:2 (1995): 281–301.

Gauthier, Jeffrey. "Prostitution, Sexual Autonomy, and Sex Discrimination." *Hypatia* 26:1 (2011): 166–86.

Green, Karen. "Prostitution, Exploitation and Taboo." *Philosophy* 64 (1989): 525–34.

Jaggar, Alison. "Prostitution." In *The Philosophy of Sex*, 2nd ed., edited by Alan Soble, 259–80. Savage, Md.: Rowman & Littlefield, 1991.

Kupfer, Joseph. "Prostitutes, Musicians and Self-Respect." In *Prostitutes, Musicians, and Self-Respect: Virtues and Vices of Personal Life*, 141–57. Lanham, Md.: Lexington Books, 2007.

Liberto, Hallie Rose. "Normalizing Prostitution versus Normalizing the Alienability of Sexual Rights: A Response to Scott A. Anderson." *Ethics* 120:1 (2009): 138–45.

Marshall, S. E. "Bodyshopping: The Case of Prostitution." *Journal of Applied Philosophy* 16:2 (1999): 139–50.

Miriam, Kathy. "Stopping the Traffic in Women: Power, Agency and Abolition in Feminist Debates over Sex-Trafficking." *Journal of Social Philosophy* 36:1 (2005): 1–17.

Nagle, Jill, ed. *Whores and Other Feminists*. New York: Routledge, 1997.

Overall, Christine. "What's Wrong with Prostitution? Evaluating Sex Work." *Signs* 17:4 (1992): 705–24.

Pateman, Carole. "Defending Prostitution: Charges against Ericsson." *Ethics* 93 (1983): 561–65.

———. "Sex and Power." *Ethics* 100:2 (1990): 398–407.

———. *The Sexual Contract*. Stanford, Calif.: Stanford University Press, 1988.

Primoratz, Igor. "What's Wrong with Prostitution?" *Philosophy* 68 (1993): 159–82.

Shrage, Laurie. "Is Sexual Desire Raced? The Social Meaning of Interracial Prostitution." *Journal of Social Philosophy* 23:1 (1992): 42–51.

———. *Moral Dilemmas of Feminism: Prostitution, Adultery, and Abortion*. New York: Routledge, 1994.

———. "Prostitution and the Case for Decriminalization." *Dissent* (Spring 1996): 41–45.

———. "Should Feminists Oppose Prostitution?" *Ethics* 99:2 (1989): 347–61.

Stewart, Robert M. "Moral Criticism and the Social Meaning of Prostitution." In *Philosophical Perspectives on Sex and Love*, edited by Robert Stewart, 81–83. New York: Oxford University Press, 1995.

Weitzer, Ronald, ed. *Sex for Sale: Prostitution, Pornography, and the Sex Industry*. New York: Routledge, 2010.

PORNOGRAPHY

Adler, Amy. "The Perverse Law of Child Pornography." *Columbia Law Review* 101 (March 2001): 209–73.

Allen, Amy. "Pornography and Power." *Journal of Social Philosophy* 32:4 (2001): 512–31.

Assiter, Alison, and Avedon Carol, eds. *Bad Girls and Dirty Pictures*. London: Pluto Press, 1993.

Attwood, Feona, ed. *Porn.com: Making Sense of Online Pornography*. New York: Peter Lang, 2010.

Baird, Robert M., and Stuart E. Rosenbaum, eds. *Pornography: Private Right or Public Menace?* Buffalo, N.Y.: Prometheus, 1991.

Baldwin, Margaret. "The Sexuality of Inequality: The Minneapolis Pornography Ordinance." *Law and Inequality: A Journal of Theory and Practice* 2:2 (1984): 629–53.

Beauvoir, Simone de. (1951-52) "Must We Burn Sade?" translated by Annette Michelson. In *The Marquis de Sade: The 120 Days of Sodom and Other Writings*, compiled by Austryn Wainhouse and Richard Seaver, 3–64. New York: Grove Press, 1966.

Berger, Fred R. "Pornography, Sex, and Censorship." *Social Theory and Practice* 4:2 (1977): 183–209. Reprinted in *The Philosophy of Sex*, 1st ed., edited by Alan Soble, 322–47. Totowa, N.J.: Rowman & Littlefield, 1980.

Berns, Walter. "Dirty Words." *The Public Interest* no. 114 (Winter 1994): 119–25.

Brod, Harry. "Pornography and the Alienation of Male Sexuality." *Social Theory and Practice* 14:3 (1988): 265–84. Reprinted in *The Philosophy of Sex*, 2nd ed., edited by Alan Soble, 281–99. Savage, Md.: Rowman & Littlefield, 1991.

Brown, Beverley. "Pornography and Feminism: Is Law the Answer?" *Critical Quarterly* 34:2 (1992): 72–82.

Burger, John R. *One-Handed Histories: The Eroto-Politics of Gay Male Video Pornography*. New York: Haworth Press, 1995.

Burstyn, Varda, ed. *Women against Censorship*. Vancouver, B.C.: Douglas and McIntyre, 1985.

Butler, Judith. *Excitable Speech: A Politics of the Performative*. New York: Routledge, 1997.

Butterworth, Dianne. "Wanking in Cyberspace: The Development of Computer Porn." In *Feminism and Sexuality: A Reader*, edited by Stevi Jackson and Sue Scott, 314–20. New York: Columbia University Press, 1996.

Carse, Alisa L. "Pornography: An Uncivil Liberty?" *Hypatia* 10:1 (1995): 156–82.

Caught Looking, Inc., eds. *Caught Looking: Feminism, Pornography, and Censorship*. East Haven, Conn.: Long River Books, 1992.

Chancer, Lynn S. "From Pornography to Sadomasochism: Reconciling Feminist Differences." *Annals of the American Academy of Political and Social Science* 571:1 (2000): 77–88.

Christensen, Ferrel M. "The Alleged Link between Pornography and Violence." In *The Handbook of Forensic Sexology: Biomedical and Criminological Perspectives*, edited by J. J. Krivacska and J. Money, 422–48. Amherst, N.Y.: Prometheus, 1994.

———. "Cultural and Ideological Bias in Pornography Research." *Philosophy of the Social Sciences* 20:3 (1990): 351–75.

———. *Pornography: The Other Side*. New York: Praeger, 1990.

Cohen, Joshua. "Freedom, Equality, Pornography." In *Justice and Injustice in Law and Legal Theory*, edited by Austin Sarat and Thomas R. Kearns, 99–137. Ann Arbor, Mich.: University of Michigan Press, 1996.

Cornell, Drucilla, ed. *Feminism and Pornography*. Oxford: Oxford University Press, 2000.

Dines, Gail. *Pornland: How Porn Has Hijacked Our Sexuality*. Boston: Beacon Press, 2010.

Dworkin, Andrea. *Life and Death*. New York: Free Press, 1997.

———. *Pornography: Men Possessing Women*. New York: Perigee, 1981.

Dworkin, Andrea, and Catharine A. MacKinnon. *Pornography and Civil Rights: A New Day for Women's Equality*. Minneapolis, Minn.: Organizing Against Pornography, 1988.

Dworkin, Ronald. "Women and Pornography." *New York Review of Books*, October 21, 1993, pp. 36–42. Reply to letter, *New York Review of Books*, March 3, 1994, pp. 48–49.

Dwyer, Susan, ed. *The Problem of Pornography*. Belmont, Calif.: Wadsworth, 1995.

Easton, Susan M. *The Problem of Pornography: Regulation and the Right to Free Speech.* London: Routledge, 1994.

Eaton, A. W. "A Sensible Anti-Porn Feminism." *Ethics* 117:4 (2007): 674–715.

Ferguson, Frances. *Pornography, the Theory: What Utilitarianism Did to Action.* Chicago: University of Chicago Press, 2004.

Garry, Ann. "Pornography and Respect for Women." In *Philosophy and Women,* edited by Sharon Bishop and Marjorie Weinzweig, 128–39. Belmont, Calif.: Wadsworth, 1979.

———. "Sex, Lies, and Pornography." In *Ethics in Practice: An Anthology,* 2nd ed., edited by Hugh LaFollette, 344–55. Malden, Mass.: Blackwell, 2002.

Gibson, Pamela Church, and Roma Gibson, eds. *Dirty Looks: Women, Pornography, Power.* London: BFI Publishing, 1993.

Grebowicz, Margret. "Democracy and Pornography: On Speech, Rights, Privacies, and Pleasures in Conflict." *Hypatia* 26:1 (2011): 150–65.

Gubar, Susan, and Joan Hoff, eds. *For Adult Users Only: The Dilemma of Violent Pornography.* Bloomington, Ind.: Indiana University Press, 1989.

Heyman, Steven J. "Pornography." In *Free Speech and Human Dignity.* Yale University Press, 2008, pp. 184–205.

Hiber, Amanda, ed. *Child Pornography.* Detroit, Mich.: Greenhaven Press, 2009.

Hill, Judith M. "Pornography and Degradation." *Hypatia* 2:2 (1987): 39–54.

Hoffman, Eric. "Feminism, Pornography, and Law." *University of Pennsylvania Law Review* 133:2 (1985): 497–534.

Hornsby, Jennifer. "Disempowered Speech." *Philosophical Topics* 23:2 (1995): 127–47.

———. "Speech Acts and Pornography." *Women's Philosophical Review* no. 10 (November 1993): 38–45.

Hunter, Nan D., and Sylvia A. Law. "Brief Amici Curiae of Feminist Anticensorship Task Force et al., in *American Booksellers Association v. Hudnut.*" In *Feminist Jurisprudence,* edited by Patricia Smith, 467–81. New York: Oxford University Press, 1993.

Itzin, Catherine, ed. *Pornography: Women, Violence and Civil Liberties.* Oxford: Oxford University Press, 1992.

Jacobson, Daniel. "Freedom of Speech Acts? A Response to Langton." *Philosophy and Public Affairs* 24:1 (1995): 64–79.

Jarvie, Ian C. "Pornography and/as Degradation." *International Journal of Law and Psychiatry* 14 (1991): 13–27.

———. *Thinking about Society: Theory and Practice.* Dordrecht, Netherlands: Reidel, 1986.

Jensen, Robert. *Getting Off: Pornography and the End of Masculinity.* Cambridge, Mass.: South End Press, 2007.

Kaite, Berkeley. *Pornography and Difference.* Bloomington, Ind.: Indiana University Press, 1995.

Kappeler, Susanne. *The Pornography of Representation.* Minneapolis, Minn.: University of Minnesota Press, 1986.

Kershnar, Stephen. "Is Violation Pornography Bad for Your Soul?" *Journal of Social Philosophy* 35 (2004): 349–66. Reprinted, revised, in *Sex, Discrimination, and Violence: Surprising and Unpopular Results in Applied Ethics.* Lanham, Md.: University Press of America, 2009, pp. 21–40.

Kimmel, Michael S., ed. *Men Confront Pornography.* New York: Crown, 1990.

Kipnis, Laura. *Bound and Gagged: Pornography and the Politics of Fantasy in America.* New York: Grove Press, 1996.

———. "(Male) Desire and (Female) Disgust: Reading *Hustler.*" In *Cultural Studies,* edited by Lawrence Grossberg, Cary Nelson, and Paula A. Treichler, 373–91. New York: Routledge, 1992.

Kittay, Eva Feder. "Pornography and the Erotics of Domination." In *Beyond Domination,* edited by Carol C. Gould, 145–74. Totowa, N.J.: Rowman & Allanheld, 1984.

Langton, Rae. *Sexual Solipsism: Philosophical Essays on Pornography and Objectification.* Oxford: Oxford University Press, 2009.

Levin, Abigail. *The Cost of Free Speech: Pornography, Hate Speech and Their Challenge to Liberalism.* Basingstoke, U.K.: Palgrave Macmillan, 2010.

———. "Pornography, Hate Speech, and Their Challenge to Dworkin's Egalitarian Liberalism." *Public Affairs Quarterly* 23:4 (2009): 357ff.

Lynn, Barry W. "'Civil Rights' Ordinances and the Attorney General's Commission: New Developments in Pornography Regulation." *Harvard Civil Rights-Civil Liberties Law Review* 21:1 (1986): 27–125.

MacKinnon, Catharine A. *Only Words.* Cambridge, Mass.: Harvard University Press, 1993.

———. "Pornography Left and Right." In *Sex, Preference, and Family: Essays on Law and Nature,* edited by David M. Estlund and Martha C. Nussbaum, 102–25. New York: Oxford University Press, 1997.

———. "Sexuality, Pornography, and Method: 'Pleasure Under Patriarchy.'" *Ethics* 99:2 (1989): 314–46.

———. "Vindication and Resistance: A Response to the Carnegie Mellon Study of Pornography in Cyberspace." *Georgetown Law Journal* 83 (1995): 1959–67.

MacKinnon, Catharine A., and Andrea Dworkin, eds. *In Harm's Way: The Pornography Civil Rights Hearings.* Cambridge, Mass.: Harvard University Press, 1997.

McCormack, Thelma. "If Pornography Is the Theory, Is Inequality the Practice?" *Philosophy of the Social Sciences* 23:3 (1993): 298–326.

McGowan, Mary Kate. "Conversational Exercitives and the Force of Pornography." *Philosophy and Public Affairs* 31:2 (2003): 155–89.

McGowan, Mary Kate, Alexandra Adelman, Sara Helmers, and Jacqueline Stolzenberg. "A Partial Defense of Illocutionary Silencing." *Hypatia* 26:1 (2011): 132–49.

Monroe, Dave, ed. *Porn-Philosophy for Everyone: How to Think with Kink.* Wichester, U.K.: Wiley-Blackwell, 2010.

Morgan, Robin. "Theory and Practice: Pornography and Rape." In *Going Too Far: The Personal Chronicle of a Feminist.* New York: Random House, 1977, pp. 163–69.

Nathan, Debbie. *Pornography.* Toronto: Groundwood Books, 2007.

Ost, Suzanne. *Child Pornography and Sexual Grooming.* New York: Cambridge University Press, 2009.

Parent, W. A. "A Second Look at Pornography and the Subordination of Women." *Journal of Philosophy* 87:4 (1990): 205–11.

Rea, Michael C. "What Is Pornography?" *Noûs* 35:1 (2001): 118–45.

Richlin, Amy, ed. *Pornography and Representation in Greece and Rome.* New York: Oxford University Press, 1992.

Rimm, Marty. "Marketing Pornography on the Information Superhighway: A Survey of 917,410 Images, Descriptions, Short Stories, and Animations Downloaded 8.5 Million Times by Consumers in over 2000 Cities in Forty Countries, Provinces, and Territories." *Georgetown Law Journal* 83 (1995): 1849–934.

Russell, Diana E. H, ed. *Making Violence Sexy: Feminist Views on Pornography.* New York: Teachers College Press, 1993.

———. "Pornography and Rape: A Causal Model." *Political Psychology* 9:1 (1988): 41–73. Reprinted, revised, in *Making Violence Sexy: Feminist Views on Pornography,* edited by D. E. H. Russell, 120–50. New York: Teachers College Press, 1993.

Saul, Jennifer. "On Treating Things as People: Objectification, Pornography, and the History of the Vibrator." *Hypatia* 21:2 (2006): 45–61.

———. "Pornography, Speech Acts, and Context." *Proceedings of the Aristotelian Society* (2005–2006): 229–48.

Saunders, Kevin W. *Degradation: What the History of Obscenity Tells Us about Hate Speech.* New York: New York University Press, 2011.

Segal, Lynne, and Mary McIntosh, eds. *Sex Exposed: Sexuality and the Pornography Debate.* New Brunswick, N.J.: Rutgers University Press, 1993.

Skipper, Robert. "Mill and Pornography." *Ethics* 103:4 (1993): 726–30.

Soble, Alan. "Bad Apples: Feminist Politics and Feminist Scholarship." *Philosophy of the Social Sciences* 29:3 (1999): 354–88.

———. "The Mainstream Has Always Been Pornographic." *Bridge* no. 12 (October-November 2004): 33–36.

———. "Pornography: Defamation and the Endorsement of Degradation." *Social Theory and Practice* 11:1 (1985): 61–87.

———. *Pornography: Marxism, Feminism, and the Future of Sexuality.* New Haven, Conn.: Yale University Press, 1986.

———. *Pornography, Sex, and Feminism.* Amherst, N.Y.: Prometheus, 2002.

———. "Pornography and the Social Sciences." *Social Epistemology* 2:2 (1988): 135–44. Reprinted in *The Philosophy of Sex*, 5th ed., edited by Alan Soble and Nicholas Power, 433–47. 5th ed. Lanham, Md.: Rowman & Littlefield, 2008.

Stark, Cynthia A. "Is Pornography an Action? The Causal vs. the Conceptual View of Pornography's Harm." *Social Theory and Practice* 23:2 (1997): 277–306.

Stoltenberg, John. *Refusing to Be a Man: Essays on Sex and Justice.* Portland, Ore.: Breitenbush, 1989.

Stoner, James R., and Donna M. Hughes, eds. *The Social Costs of Pornography: A Collection of Papers.* Princeton, N.J.: Witherspoon Institute, 2010.

Strossen, Nadine. *Defending Pornography: Free Speech, Sex, and the Fight for Women's Rights.* New York: Scribner, 1995.

Strub, Whitney. *Perversion for Profit: The Politics of Pornography and the Rise of the New Right.* New York: Columbia University Press, 2011.

Tisdale, Sallie. "Talk Dirty to Me." *Harper's Magazine* (February 1992): 37–46. Reprinted in *The Philosophy of Sex*, 5th ed., edited by Alan Soble and Nicholas Power, 419–31. Lanham, Md.: Rowman & Littlefield, 2008.

Tong, Rosemarie. "Feminism, Pornography, and Censorship." *Social Theory and Practice* 8 (1982): 1–17.

———. "Women, Pornography, and the Law." In *The Philosophy of Sex*, 2nd ed., edited by Alan Soble, 301–16. Savage, Md.: Rowman & Littlefield, 1991.

Tucker, Scott. "Gender, Fucking, and Utopia: An Essay in Response to John Stoltenberg's *Refusing to Be a Man.*" *Social Text* no. 27 (1990): 3–34.

Turley, Donna. "The Feminist Debate on Pornography: An Unorthodox Interpretation." *Socialist Review* 16:3–4 (1986): 81–96.

Vadas, Melinda. "A First Look at the Pornography/Civil Rights Ordinance: Could Pornography Be the Subordination of Women?" *Journal of Philosophy* 84:9 (1987): 487–511.

———. "The Manufacture-for-Use of Pornography and Women's Inequality." *Journal of Political Philosophy* 13:2 (2005): 174–93.

———. "The Pornography/Civil Rights Ordinance v. the BOG: And the Winner Is. . . ?" *Hypatia* 7:3 (1992): 94–109.

Valverde, Mariana. "Beyond Gender Dangers and Private Pleasures: Theory and Ethics in the Sex Debates." *Feminist Studies* 15:2 (1989): 237–54.

Ward, David. "Should Pornography Be Censored?" In *Classic Philosophical Questions*, edited by James A. Gould, 504–12. New York: Prentice Hall, 1995.

Watson, Lori. "Pornography and Public Reason." *Social Theory and Practice* 33:3 (2007): 467–88.

Weitzer, Ronald, ed. *Sex for Sale: Prostitution, Pornography, and the Sex Industry.* New York: Routledge, 2010.

Williams, Linda. *Hard Core: Power, Pleasure, and the "Frenzy of the Visible."* Berkeley, Calif.: University of California Press, 1989.

———. "Second Thoughts on Hard Core: American Obscenity Law and the Scapegoating of Deviance." In *Dirty Looks: Women, Pornography, Power*, edited by Pamela Church Gibson and Roma Gibson, 46–61. London: BFI Publishing, 1993.

SADOMASOCHISM

Airaksinen, Timo. *The Philosophy of the Marquis de Sade*. London: Routledge, 1995.

Bartky, Sandra Lee. "Feminine Masochism and the Politics of Personal Transformation," *Women's Studies International Forum* 7:5 (1984): 323–34.

Beckmann, Andrea. *The Social Construction of Sexuality and Perversion: Deconstructing Sadomasochism*. Basingstoke, U.K.: Palgrave Macmillan, 2009.

Burr, Viv, and Jeff Hearn, eds. *Sex, Violence and the Body: The Erotics of Wounding*. Basingstoke, U.K.: Palgrave Macmillan, 2008.

Califia, Pat. "Feminism and Sadomasochism." *Heresies* no. 12 ["Sex Issue"]: 3–4 (1981): 30–34. Reprinted in *Feminism and Sexuality: A Reader*, edited by Stevi Jackson and Sue Scott, 230–37. New York: Columbia University Press, 1996.

———. *Macho Sluts*. Los Angeles: Alyson Books, 1988.

———. *Public Sex: The Culture of Radical Sex*. Pittsburgh, Penn.: Cleis Press, 1994.

———, ed. *The Lesbian S/M Safety Manual*. Boston: Lace Publications, 1988.

Card, Claudia. "Review Essay: Sadomasochism and Sexual Preference." *Journal of Social Philosophy* 15:2 (1984): 42–52.

Chancer, Lynn S. "From Pornography to Sadomasochism: Reconciling Feminist Differences." *Annals of the American Academy of Political and Social Science* 571:1 (2000): 77–88.

———. *Sadomasochism in Everyday Life: The Dynamics of Power and Powerlessness*. New Brunswick, N.J.: Rutgers University Press, 1992.

Corvino, John. "Naughty Fantasies." *Southwest Philosophy Review* 18:1 (2002): 213–20.

Cross, Patricia A., and Kim Matheson. "Understanding Sadomasochism: An Empirical Examination of Four Perspectives." *Journal of Homosexuality* 50:2–3 (2006): 133–66.

Fitzpatrick-Hanly, Margaret Ann, ed. *Essential Papers on Masochism*. New York: New York University Press, 1995.

Gebhardt, Paul. "Fetishism and Sadomasochism." In *Sex Research: Studies from the Kinsey Institute*, edited by M. Weinberg, 156–66. New York: Oxford University Press, 1976.

Hopkins, Patrick D. "Rethinking Sadomasochism: Feminism, Interpretation, and Simulation." *Hypatia* 9:1 (1994): 116–41. Reprinted in *The Philosophy of Sex*, 3rd ed., edited by Alan Soble, 189–214. Lanham, Md.: Rowman & Littlefield, 1997.

———. "Simulation and the Reproduction of Injustice: A Reply." *Hypatia* 10:2 (1995): 162–70.

Kenney, Shawna. *I Was a Teenage Dominatrix: A Memoir*. New York: Retro Systems Press, 1999.

Kleinplatz, Peggy J., and Charles Moser, eds. *Sadomasochism: Powerful Pleasures*. New York: Harrington Park Press, 2006.

Langdridge, Darren, and Meg Baker, eds. *Safe, Sane, and Consensual: Contemporary Perspectives on Sadomasochism*. Basingstoke, U.K.: Palgrave Macmillan, 2007.

Linden, Robin Ruth, Darlene R. Pagano, Diana E. H. Russell, and Susan Leigh Star, eds. *Against Sadomasochism: A Radical Feminist Analysis*. East Palo Alto, Calif.: Frog in the Well, 1982.

Mann, Jay, and Natalie Shainess. "Sadistic Fantasies." *Medical Aspects of Human Sexuality* 8:2 (1974): 142–48.

Nielsen, Morten Ebbe Juul. "Safe, Sane, and Consensual—Consent and the Ethics of BDSM." *International Journal of Applied Philosophy* 24:2 (2010): 265–88.

Noyes, John K. *The Mastery of Submission: Inventions of Masochism*. Ithaca, N.Y.: Cornell University Press, 1997.

Reik, Theodor. *Masochism in Sex and Society*. Translated by M. H. Beigel and G. M. Kurth. New York: Grove Press, 1962.

Sade, The Marquis de. *Justine, Philosophy in the Bedroom, and Other Writings*, translated by Richard Seaver and Austryn Wainhouse. New York: Grove Press, 1965.

Samois, ed. *Coming to Power: Writings and Graphics on Lesbian S/M*, 1st ed. Palo Alto, Calif.: Up Press, 1981; 2nd ed., Boston: Alyson Publications, 1982.

Shattuck, Roger. *Forbidden Knowledge: From Prometheus to Pornography.* San Diego: Harcourt Brace, 1996.

Stear, Nils-Hennes. "Sadomasochism as *Make-Believe.*" *Hypatia* 24:2 (2009): 21–38.

Vadas, Melinda. "Reply to Patrick Hopkins." *Hypatia* 10:2 (1995): 159–61. Reprinted in *The Philosophy of Sex*, 3rd ed., edited by Alan Soble, 215–17. Lanham, Md.: Rowman & Littlefield, 1997.

Weinberg, Thomas S., ed. *S&M: Studies in Dominance & Submission.* Amherst, N.Y.: Prometheus, 1995.

Index

abortion, 14, 34, 189, 495, 552n10
abstinence, 79. *See also* celibacy
ACLU. *See* American Civil Liberties Union
acquaintance rape. *See* rape
Acquired Immune Deficiency Syndrome (AIDS), 18n9, 521; and prostitution, 423, 424, 431
Adams, Adi, 228
adultery, 1, 14, 18n14, 120n37, 124, 146, 305, 311, 457; definition of, 14, 130; and Internet "chatting," 123, 131, 132; and masturbation, 78, 81; moral condemnation of as culturally conditioned, 130–131; moral evaluation of, 6, 7, 8, 10, 14, 34, 125; and penal-vaginal penetration, 130, 132–133
aesthesis, 106
affection, 5, 293, 337, 388; and marriage, 63, 162, 172–173, 224; rape, absent from, 397; and sex, 59, 62, 84, 379, 381, 396–397, 398, 402, 404n12, 446, 469. *See also* love
AIDS. *See* Acquired Immune Deficiency Syndrome
akrasia, 303
alcohol and sex. *See* intoxication
Allen, Woody: on loss of autonomy in sex, 303; on masturbation, 73n6, 88
Alternatives to Marriage Project, 151
Altman, Irwin, 146
American Civil Liberties Union: on same-sex marriage, 145–146
American Law Institute's "Principles of the Law of Family Dissolution," 152–153
American Psychiatric Association: on homosexuality, 10, 513
American Psycho, 512

Amnesty International, 423
Anapol, Deborah (*Polyamory*), 147
Ancient Greece, 136, 412, 434n2, 552n10; *hetairai* and prostitution in, 415, 436n15, 438n41; sex and sexuality in, 95, 124, 128, 134, 438n41. *See also* Aristotle; Plato
Anderson, Elizabeth: on prostitution, 425–426, 429, 437n40, 438n42, 438n44
Anderson, Eric, 228
Anderson, Peter: on sexually aggressive women, 393
animality, 3, 67, 105, 546, 555n44
animals: as food, 7, 14, 35–36; and objectification, 338–339
animals, sex with. *See* bestiality
animal sexuality: compared with human sexuality, 11, 34, 58, 60, 85, 86–87, 111, 117n17–117n18, 336; epistemological use of, 12, 13, 19n15; human sexuality as only, for Immanuel Kant, 4, 19n19, 117n20, 297, 302–303, 322, 323, 330n7, 332n39
Annapurna Mahila Mandal (Bombay project), 435n9
Anscombe, G. E. M. (Elizabeth), 333n63
anticipation, sexual. *See* flirting; novelty and novel sexual encounters; seduction
Antioch University Sexual Offense Policy, 393, 461
Aquinas, Saint Thomas. *See* Thomas Aquinas, Saint
Archard, David: on Kantian sexual ethics, 330n15; on Martha Nussbaum on disgust, 555n43
Aristotle, 412, 425, 437n38, 511; on desire, 106, 108; on pleasure, 58,

597

masturbation and, 94, 96n6; permanency of, 129; and plain sex, 58, 62–63, 83, 114, 116n6; Susan Moller Okin on, 381; romantic, 63, 66, 146; Bertrand Russell on, 73n1; Jean-Paul Sartre on, 37; and self-love, 124; and sex together, 29, 112–113, 119n31; as union, 15, 323; uniqueness of its heterosexual form, 170–171; Russell Vannoy on, 18n6, 96n6

Lovelace, Linda (*Deep Throat*): and the marriage trap, 178

Lowell, Robert, 508

lust, 14, 52, 124–125, 131, 135; Augustine on, 4, 124–125; and chatting online, 124, 136–137; and control of that of females, 420–422; Immanuel Kant on, 303; and Thomas More on Martin Luther's, 137n3

Luther, Martin, 124, 137n3

Macedo, Stephen, 173n3

MacKinnon, Catharine: and a constructivist "general theory of sexuality," 536n23; *Only Words*, 535n2, 536n15, 539; on pornography and abuse of women, 541; on pornography and masturbation, 531, 541; pornography as a tool of genocide, 539, 551n1, 552n6; on pornography as constitutive of sexual violence, 528, 530; on pornography as merely speech, 523, 541, 543; on pornography as objectification, 337, 339, 355n4, 355n16; on pornography as subordination, 522, 526, 529–530, 541; and pornography defined in 1992 civil rights ordinance, 522, 540, 546, 552n5; on women's equality, 514, 527

Madonna's "Like a Prayer," 125

madonna/whore phenomenon, 133

magazines: *Harper's*, 554n30; *Hustler*, 524–525, 536n7, 550; *Loving More*, 147, 151; *Ms.*, 25, 31, 539; *Playboy*, 124, 544; *Village Voice*, 145, 158;

Weekly Standard, 143, 229n3

Mailer, Norman: on anal intercourse, 42

maisons de tolerance, 422, 427

Mappes, Thomas, ix, xi, 271–287n7; on consent, 16, 19n24; on deception, 273, 274–276; on exploitation, 286–287; on Kantian sexual ethics, 311–314, 323, 324, 328, 329, 331n26, 331n30, 445; Jeffrie Murphy on, 312; on prostitution, 331n30

Marciano, Linda. *See* Lovelace, Linda

marital rape. *See* rape

marriage, ix; abusive, 178, 181–182, 184–185, 187; auxiliary benefits of, 162, 178–179, 182, 191n1; and the "basic structure of society," 178, 183; coercing and pressuring into, 17, 231n19, 415, 428; and the companionate ideal, 146, 147, 148; and "conjugal debt," 323; contemporary ideals of, 224–225; death of sexual desire in ("bedroom death"), 8; as evil in its current legal form, 184; and gender roles, 165, 168, 173n5, 186, 228, 349, 431; interracial (miscegenation), 165, 187, 188–189, 222; as justifying sexual activity, 5, 15, 83, 91–93, 124, 137n3; in Immanuel Kant, 15, 292, 296, 320–323, 324, 326, 328–329, 332n45, 332n53, 333n59; love and, 62–63, 70; overcomes objectification, 442, 459n20, 459n28; polygamous, 143–158; as prepolitical institution, 169–173; and procreation, 92, 162, 387; sexual justice in, 380–381; and the welfare of children, 152, 157. *See also* adultery; divorce; friendship

marriage, gay. *See* homosexuality

marriage, same-sex. *See* homosexuality

Marx, Karl, 425, 434, 437n38, 438n45

Marxism, 391–392, 550

masochism. *See* sadomasochism

Mason-Grant, Joan, xi; on pornography, 521–536n25, 543–545, 553n18

masturbation, xiin1, 1, 51, 77–97n20; as adultery, 78; as black sheep of

About the Editors

Nicholas Power was introduced to the philosophy of sex after stumbling upon Alan Soble's *Pornography: Marxism, Feminism, and the Future of Sexuality* (1986) and was instantly infatuated by his analytical and rigorous treatment of topics typically left alone by Anglo-American philosophy. Having published in the philosophy of mind and philosophy of history prior to this exposure, his tentative first offerings in the area were two entries in Soble's encyclopedia, *Sex from Plato to Paglia* (2006), one of which was on the evolutionary psychology of human sexuality and the other on the Freudian left. He has given various presentations on these topics and on pornography at Florida's and Alabama's philosophical associations as well as at the Southern Society for Philosophy and Psychology and the North American Society for Utopian Studies. His next major step in the field was to coedit, under Soble's wing, the fifth edition (2008) of *The Philosophy of Sex*.

Raja Halwani does not quite remember how he stumbled upon the philosophy of sex, but he does remember that he has been interested in it for a long time. Being gay, his interest "naturally" started with some ethical questions having to do with homosexuality and some sexual practices often associated (correctly or incorrectly) with gay men—promiscuity, casual sex, and open relationships. Indeed, his first two publications, back in the days when he was a graduate student, were "Are One Night Stands Morally Problematic?" and "The Morality of Adultery." Convinced by the work of Alan Soble that thinking about sex is one of the most important philosophical endeavors, he has shed his guilt about publishing on sex and has even brazenly used the language of virtue to often do so. Being an Arab-American (originally from Lebanon), Halwani is also very much interested in issues of sex and the contemporary Middle East, often coming at them through the debate between essentialism and social constructionism. In addition, he publishes in the philosophy of art and in political philosophy and is an avid fan of *The Simpsons* and pop culture in general, simultaneously (or alternately?) loving it and scorning it. His next book will be (fingers crossed) about the evil that is romantic love.

Alan Soble began studying and writing about the philosophy of sex in the mid-1970s after reading Thomas Nagel's essay "Sexual Perversion" in the *Journal of Philosophy*. His first piece in this area of philosophy was "Sexual Desire and Sexual Objects," presented at the 1978 Pacific Division meetings of the American Philosophical Association, which were held in San Francisco (shortly after his thirty-first birthday). That public appearance was followed later that year by "What Philosophers Have Been Saying about Sex" and "Masturbation," Invited Visiting Scholar lectures delivered at California State University, Sacramento, November 21 and 22, 1978. His reference essays on the philosophy of sex include "La morale et la sexualité," in Monique Canto-Sperber, ed., *Dictionnaire d'éthique et de philosophie morale* (1996), pp. 1387–91; "Sexuality, Philosophy of," in Edward Craig, ed., *Routledge Encyclopedia of Philosophy* (1998), vol. 8, pp. 717–30; "Philosophy of Sexuality" (2000, 2004, 2009), in James Fieser, ed., *The Internet Encyclopedia of Philosophy* (http://www.iep.utm.edu/sexualit/); "Sexuality and Sexual Ethics," in Lawrence C. Becker and Charlotte B. Becker, eds., *Encyclopedia of Ethics*, 2nd edition (2001), vol. 3, pp. 1570–77; and "Philosophy of Sex," in Donald Borchert, ed., *Encyclopedia of Philosophy*, 2nd edition (2006), vol. 7, pp. 521–32. Among his essays published in nonphilosophy journals are "Correcting Some Misconceptions about St. Augustine's Sex Life," *Journal of the History of Sexuality* 11:4 (2002): 545–69, and "A History of Erotic Philosophy," in *Journal of Sex Research* 49:2–3 (2009): 104–20 (also *Annual Review of Sex Research*, Vol. XVII).